Linux Mint
21

Desktops
and
Administration

For Orrin, Harlow, and Cora

Linux Mint 21: Desktops and Administration

Richard Petersen

Surfing Turtle Press

Alameda, CA

www.surfingturtlepress.com

Please send inquires to: editor@surfingturtlepress.com

ISBN-13 9781949857313

Preface

This book covers the Linux Mint 21 release, focusing on desktops and administrative tools. The emphasis here is on what users will face when using Linux Mint, covering topics like installation, applications, software management, the Linux Mint desktops (Cinnamon, MATE, and Xfce), shell commands, network connections, and system administration tasks. Linux Mint 21 introduces several new features, as well as numerous smaller modifications. It is based on the Ubuntu 22.04 long-term support release. The Cinnamon and MATE desktops are examined in detail. Cinnamon and MATE have custom Linux Mint menus to manage access to applications and devices. Advanced components are also examined such as Samba server configuration, systemd service management, and Linux Mint software management applications (Software Manager and Update Manager).

The Linux Mint Cinnamon desktop is developed and maintained by Linux Mint, with several desktop configuration tools and a System Settings dialog. The MATE desktop is based on GNOME 2, with the traditional panel and applets implementation. Each desktop has its own file manager. The Cinnamon desktop uses the Nemo file manager. The MATE desktop uses the Caja file manager.

Part 1 focuses on getting started, covering Linux Mint information and resources, using the Linux Mint Live DVD/USB, installing and setting up Linux Mint, upgrading Linux Mint, basic use of the desktops (Cinnamon and MATE), configuring and using Warpinator file transfers, and connecting to wired and wireless networks. Repositories and their use are covered in detail. Software Manager and Synaptic Package manager, which provide easy and effective software management, are both discussed. The Linux Mint X-Apps are also reviewed, including Xed, Xviewer, and Timeshift. In addition, a listing of office, multimedia, mail, Internet, and social media applications is presented, including the Celluloid player.

Part 2 covers the Cinnamon and MATE (KDE is no longer supported by Linux Mint, though you can install the Ubuntu version, Kubuntu). The Cinnamon desktop retains popular GNOME 2 features, such as panels and applets. It also has the Cinnamon menu with a favorites sidebar similar to the Ubuntu launcher. The MATE desktop is derived from the GNOME 2 desktop, but with a more advanced applications menu.

Part 3 deals with administration topics, first discussing system tools like the GNOME system monitor, the Disk Usage Analyzer, Disk Utility, and Seahorse key management. Then a detailed chapter on Linux Mint system administration tools is presented, covering tasks such as managing users and file systems, Bluetooth setup, and network folder and file sharing. The network connections chapter covers a variety of network tasks, including manual configuration of wired and wireless connections, and firewalls.

Part 4 focuses on shared resources such as Samba, NFS, and CUPS, and covers how **systemd** manages services using unit and target files. Shared resources are also examined, including the CUPS printing server, the NFS Linux network file server, and Samba Windows file and printing server. Printer administration and installation are discussed, including configuration for local and remote printers.

Overview

Preface   5

Overview   7

Contents   9

Part 1: Getting Started

1. Linux Mint 21 Introduction   27

2. Installing Linux Mint   37

3. Usage Basics: Login, Desktop, Network, and Help   63

4. Installing and Updating Software   109

5. Applications   157

Part 2: Desktops

6. Cinnamon Desktop   187

7. MATE Desktop   261

Part 3: Administration

8. System Tools   309

9. System Administration   339

10. Network Connections   399

11. Shell Configuration   453

Part 4: Shared Resources

12. Managing Services   **477**

13. Print Services   **517**

14. Network File Systems and Network Information System: NFS and NIS   **549**

15. Samba   **567**

Table Listing   **591**

Figure Listing   **595**

Index   **611**

Contents

Preface 5

Overview.. 7

Contents 9

Part 1: Getting Started

1. Linux Mint 21 Introduction 27

Linux Mint 21 28
Linux Mint Editions... 28
Linux Mint Live DVD/USB.. 29
Linux Mint Software.. 31
Linux Mint Help and Documentation 32
Ubuntu... 33
Linux documentation.. 34
Open Source Software 34
Linux... 35

2. Installing Linux Mint 37

Upgrading directly from Linux Mint 20.3: Upgrade Tool.................. 38
Install Discs 42
Installing Multiple-Boot Systems 42
Installation Overview.. 43
Installation with the Linux Mint DVD/USB 44
Welcome and Language 45
Keyboard Layout... 45
Preparing to install (third party software) 46
Installation type.. 47
No detected operating systems 47
Advanced Features: LVM and Encryption.................................. 48

Encrypt the disk 49

Detected Linux Mint operating system 51

Detected Linux Mint operating system 51

Detected other operating systems with free space.............................. 52

Detected other operating system using entire disk (resize) 52

Something else... 52

Creating new partitions on a blank hard drive manually.................... 53

Reuse existing Linux partitions on a hard drive 56

Where Are You? 57

Who Are You?... 58

Install Progress 59

Recovery, rescue, and boot loader re-install 60

Recovery Mode 60

Re-Installing the Boot Loader: Boot Repair and grub-install 61

3. Usage Basics: Login, Desktop, Network, and Help 63

Accessing Your Linux Mint System 64

GRUB Boot Loader 64

The LightDM Display Manager... 66

Login Window Preferences 68

Lock Screen and Switch User.. 70

Shut down and Logging out 71

Accessing Linux from the Command Line Interface................................ 71

The Linux Mint Desktops 72

Cinnamon 73

MATE... 76

Xfce Desktop... 78

Linux Mint Debian Edition (LMDE) 80

First Steps 80

Accessing File Systems and Devices... 82

Accessing Archives from GNOME: Archive Manager.............................. 84

Mounting ISO Disk Image files: Disk Image Mounter............................. 84

File Manager CD/DVD Creator interface 84

ISO Image File Writing with Disk Utility and Brasero............................. 84

Laptop Power Management and Wireless Networks 85

Network Connections.. 86

Network Manager wired connections.. 86

Network Manager wireless connections 87
System Settings Network, Cinnamon (GNOME and proxies) 88
Warpinator: Local Network File Transfer 91
Printing 96
Display Configuration and Device Drivers.. 96
Device Drivers 97
Display (resolution and rotation) 98
Hi-DPI 99
Color Profiles... 99
Private Encrypted Folders (ecryptfs) 100
Online Accounts 101
System Reports.. 101
Help Resources 103
Application Documentation 103
The Man Pages 103
The Info Pages 104
Terminal Window.. 104
Command Line Interface.. 107

4. Installing and Updating Software...**109**

Installing Software Packages... 110
Linux Mint Package Management Software 111
Linux Mint Software Repositories... 111
Repository Components 112
Ubuntu Software Repositories 112
Repository Components 112
Repositories.. 112
Linux Mint Repository Configuration file: sources.list.d/ official-package-
repositories.list 113
Software Sources managed from Linux Mint 114
Codec packages on Linux Mint (mint-meta-codecs)............................... 117
Updating Linux Mint with Update Manager.. 117
Update Manager Preferences... 120
Update Manager Linux Kernels 121
Timeshift and Snapshots... 122
Managing Packages with Software Manager (mintinstall) 125
Flatpak 130
Synaptic Package Manager.. 132

Installing and removing packages..135

Search filters...136

Software Manager for separate DEB packages: GDebi.........136

Installing and Running Windows Software on Linux: Wine 137

Source code files 138

Software Package Types...139

DEB Software Packages...139

Managing software with apt and apt-get.....................................140

Updating packages (Upgrading) with apt and apt-get 142

Command Line Search and Information: dpkg-query and apt-cache tools 142

Managing non-repository packages with dpkg...........................143

Using packages with other software formats 144

Ubuntu Snap...144

Snaps Packages...145

Linux Mint restriction on installing Snap............................146

snap command 147

Snap Channels: tracks and risk levels 149

Snap Confinement..150

Snap Revisions: revert 151

Snap Package Configuration 152

Snap and Services 153

Snap Store..153

5. Applications **157**

X-Apps..159

Office Applications 159

LibreOffice..160

Calligra..161

GNOME Office Applications..161

Document Viewers..162

Ebook Readers: FBReader and Calibre................................163

Editors..163

Database Management Systems...164

SQL Databases (RDBMS)...165

LibreOffice Base 165

PostgreSQL...165

MySQL...165

MariaDB 166
Mail (email) and News 166
    Mail Clients 166
    Usenet News.. 167
Graphics Applications 168
Multimedia 170
    Multimedia support 170
    GStreamer 170
        GStreamer Plug-ins: the Good, the Bad, and the Ugly 171
    Music Applications.. 172
    Video Applications 172
        Video and DVD Players.. 173
        Videos Plugins (Totem) 174
        PiTiVi and Shotcut Video editors.. 174
        TV Players.. 174
        DVB and HDTV support 176
        Xvid (DivX) and Matroska (mkv) on Linux 176
    CD/DVD Burners 177
Internet Applications 177
    Web Browsers 177
    Web Apps 178
    Java for Linux 180
    BitTorrent Clients (transmission) 180
    FTP Clients 180
        Network File Transfer: FTP 181
        Web Browser–Based FTP 181
        GNOME Desktop FTP: Connect to Server 182
Social Networking 183

Part 2: Desktops

6. Cinnamon Desktop **187**

Cinnamon Desktop.. 188
    Desklets.. 190
    Hot Corners.. 192
    Keyboard and Mouse Shortcuts 193
    Menu 195

Windows 199
    Minimizing, Maximizing, and Closing Windows 201
    Grouped Windows List 202
    Resize and tiling Windows 204
    Switching Windows with the Windows QuickList 205
    Switching Windows with the Scale Screen and Alt-Tab 206
  Effects 208
  Workspace Selection with Hot Corners (expo) and expo applet 209
The Linux Mint Panel: modern layout 212
Linux Mint Applets 215
Linux Mint Traditional Layout 217
Nemo File Manager 219
  Home Folder Sub-folders and Bookmarks 219
  File Manager Windows 219
  File Manager Sidebar and Bookmarks 220
  Tabs 222
  Displaying Files and Folders 223
  File manager menus and tools 224
  Favorites Folder 225
  Navigating in the file manager 227
  Nemo File Manager Search 229
  Managing Files and Folders 230
    Using a file's pop-up menu 230
    Grouping Files 231
    Opening Applications and Files MIME Types 231
    Renaming Files 232
  File and Folder Properties 233
  Nemo Preferences 234
  Nemo Plugins and Extensions 236
System Settings 236
  Appearance 240
    Backgrounds 240
    Font Selection 242
  Themes 242
  Preferences 245
    Preferred Applications and Removable Media 245
    Time & Date Settings (Calendar applet) 247
    Screensaver and Lock Screen 249

Languages 250
Input Method 251
Accessibility 251
Startup Applications 252
Extensions 253
Notifications 254
Privacy 254
General 255
Hardware 255
System Info 255
Mouse and Touchpad 256
Power Management 256
Keyboard Settings 258

7. MATE Desktop **261**

The MATE Desktop 262
MATE Components 263
Drag-and-Drop Files to the Desktop 263
Desktop Settings 264
Applications on the Desktop 265
The Desktop Menu 265
Windows 266
Window List 267
Workspace Switcher 268
Linux Mint Menu for MATE 269
Linux Mint Menu Preferences dialog 271
MATE Panel 272
Panel Properties 273
Displaying Panels 274
Moving and Hiding Expanded Panels 274
Unexpanded Panels: Movable and Fixed 275
Panel Background 275
Panel Objects 275
Moving, Removing, and Locking Objects 276
Adding Objects 276
Application Launchers 276
Adding Drawers 277

Adding Menus...277

Adding Folders and Files...277

Adding Applets 277

Caja File Manager 278

Home Folder Sub-folders and Bookmarks 278

File Manager Windows..279

File Manager Side Pane 282

Tabs 283

Displaying Files and Folders..283

File manager tools and menus..284

Navigating in the file manager 285

Caja File Manager Search...288

Managing Files and Folders..288

Using a file's pop-up menu 288

Renaming Files 288

Grouping Files 288

Opening Applications and Files MIME Types 289

File and Folder Properties 290

Caja Preferences..291

Control Center 292

MATE Preferences..293

Mouse and Keyboard Preferences...295

About Me: photo, name, and password..296

Appearance...297

Desktop Themes...297

Desktop Background 298

Fonts 299

Configuring Fonts..300

Adding Fonts 300

MATE Power Management...300

Preferred Applications for Web, Mail, Accessibility, and terminal windows 301

Default Applications for Media 303

Screen Saver and Lock..303

Assistive Technologies 304

Popup Notifications...305

Part 3: Administration

8. System Tools **309**

GNOME System Monitor 310
Managing Processes 311
Glances..313
Scheduling Tasks 314
Logs 314
Disk Usage Analyzer..315
Virus Protection 316
Hardware Sensors 317
Disk Utility and Udisks..318
Plymouth 320
Sound 321
    Sound menu (volume control and player access) 322
    Sound 323
    PulseAudio applications..325
dconf editor 327
Managing keys with Seahorse..328
    Passwords and Keys 328
    Keyrings...329
    Creating a new GPG key 330
    Keyservers..332
    Importing Public Keys..333
    Sharing Keys 336

9. System Administration **339**

Administrative Tools...340
Controlled Administrative Access..341
    PolicyKit..341
    sudo 343
        sudo command 343
        sudo configuration 343
    Root User Access: root and su 345
    Nemo with elevated privileges on Cinnamon desktop...............................346
    pkexec 347
/etc/hostname and hostnamectl..349

18 *Contents*

Users and Groups (cinnamon-settings-users) 349
Users and Groups (MATE) 353
   New Users (Users and Groups) 355
   Groups (Users and Groups) 357
   Passwords 358
Managing Services 358
File System Access 358
   Access to Internal Linux File Systems 359
   Access to Windows NTFS File Systems on Local Drives 359
   Zero Configuration Networking: Avahi and Link Local Addressing 359
   Permissions for Shared Folders in User Home Folders 360
   Access to Linux Local Network Shared File Systems with mDNS (Avahi) 361
   Access to Windows Local Network Shared File Systems with Avahi 364
   Shared Folders for your network 366
   Accessing Linux Shared Folders from Windows 369
   File and Folder Permissions 370
   Automatic file system mounts with /etc/fstab 371
Bluetooth (Blueman) 372
DKMS 377
Editing Configuration Files Directly 378
GRUB 2 379
Backup Management 382
   Backup Tool (mintBackup) 383
   Deja Dup 384
   Individual Backups: archive and rsync 388
   BackupPC 389
   Amanda 389
Logical Volume Manager 389
   LVM Structure 390
   LVM Tools: using the LVM commands 390
      Displaying LVM Information 391
      Managing LVM Physical Volumes with the LVM commands 391
      Managing LVM Groups 391
      Activating Volume Groups 392
      Managing LVM Logical Volumes 392
   Steps to create a new LVM group and volume 393
   Steps to add a new drive to an LVM group and volume 394
   LVM Device Names: /dev/mapper 395

Using LVM to replace drives..395
LVM Snapshots..395
OpenZFS...396

10. Network Connections...**399**

Network Connections: Dynamic and Static...401
Network Manager 402
Network Manager menu 403
Network Manager manual configuration using GNOME Network (Network Settings)
....404
Network Manager Advanced Configuration using the nm-connection-editor (Network
Connections)...408
General tab 410
Wired Configuration 411
Wireless Configuration 413
DSL Configuration 414
Mobile Broadband 414
PPP Configuration 416
Network Manager VPN..416
Wireguard VPN 418
Managing Network Connections with nmcli 419
Dial-up PPP Modem Access: wvdial 423
Netplan 425
Netplan configuration file 425
Configuring a network with systemd-networkd 426
The systemd-networkd Netplan configuration file................................429
Netplan wireless configuration for systemd-networkd 431
Switching between systemd-networkd and network-manager................432
Firewalls 433
Important Firewall Ports...433
Setting up a firewall with ufw..434
Gufw 434
ufw commands 438
ufw rule files 439
FirewallD and firewall-config 440
firewall-config 441
firewall-cmd 445
GNOME Nettool...446

Predictable and unpredictable network device names.................................447
Network device path names 448
Renaming network device names with udev rules..............................450
Renaming network device names for systemd-networkd with systemd.link........451

11. Shell Configuration...**453**

Shell Initialization and Configuration Files 454
Configuration Directories and Files..455
Aliases..456
Aliasing Commands and Options 456
Aliasing Commands and Arguments...457
Aliasing Commands...457
Controlling Shell Operations 458
Environment Variables and Subshells: export...458
Configuring Your Shell with Shell Parameters 460
Shell Parameter Variables 460
Using Initialization Files..461
Your Home Directory: HOME 461
Command Locations: PATH 461
Specifying the BASH Environment: BASH_ENV...............................463
Configuring the Shell Prompt 464
Specifying Your News Server 465
Configuring Your Login Shell: .profile...465
Exporting Variables...466
Variable Assignments...466
Editing Your BASH Profile Script...467
Manually Re-executing the .profile script 468
System Shell Profile Script..468
Configuring the BASH Shell: .bashrc..469
The User .bashrc BASH Script..470
The System /etc/bash.bashrc BASH Script 471
The BASH Shell Logout File: .bash_logout 473

Part 4: Shared Resources

12. Managing Services **477**

systemd 478

systemd basic configuration files..479

units..479

unit file syntax..481

special targets..483

Modifying unit files: /etc/systemd/system...485

Execution Environment Options 486

service unit files 486

System V Scripts and generated systemd service files: /etc/init.d and
/run/systemd/generator.late...488

On Demand and Standalone Services (socket)..488

Path units 490

Template unit files 490

Runlevels and Special Targets 492

systemd and automatically mounting file systems: /etc/fstab...............493

systemd slice and scope units 495

System V: /etc/init.d..495

Shutdown and Poweroff...496

Managing Services...498

Enabling services: starting a service automatically at boot...................498

Managing services manually: systemctl...498

The service Command..498

Cockpit...499

/etc/default..499

Network Time Protocol: Chrony..500

The Chrony server 500

The chrony.conf configuration file...501

cronyc...503

AppArmor security 503

AppArmor utilities..504

AppArmor configuration..505

Remote Administration..506

Puppet 506

The Secure Shell: OpenSSH 507

Encryption 507

Authentication 508

SSH Packages, Tools, and Server 508

SSH Setup 510

Creating SSH Keys with ssh-keygen...510

Authorized Keys 511

Loading Keys 512

SSH Clients 512

Port Forwarding (Tunneling) 514

SSH Configuration 515

13. Print Services **517**

CUPS 518

Driverless Printing 520

Printer Devices and Configuration 520

Printer Device Files 520

Printer URI (Universal Resource Identifier) 521

Spool Directories 521

CUPS start and restart 521

Installing Printers 522

Configuring Printers on the Desktop with system-config-printer (System Settings
Printers) 522

system-config-printer 522

Editing Printer Configuration 525

Default System-wide and Personal Printers 526

Adding New Printers Manually 527

CUPS Web Browser-based configuration tool 530

Configuring Remote Printers on CUPS 533

Configuring Remote Printers with system-config-printer 533

Configuring Remote Printers with the CUPS Web-based Browser 536

Configuring remote printers manually 538

CUPS Printer Classes 538

CUPS Configuration files 539

cupsd.conf 539

Location Directives 541

Default Operation Policy: Limit Directives 542

cupsctl 543

printers.conf 543

subscriptions.conf 544

cups-files.conf 544

cups-browsed.conf 545

CUPS Command Line Print Clients 545

lpr 545

lpc 546

lpq and lpstat 546

lprm 546

CUPS Command Line Administrative Tools 546

lpadmin 547

lpoptions 548

cupsenable and cupsdisable 548

cupsaccept and cupsreject 548

lpinfo 548

14. Network File Systems and Network Information System: NFS and NIS 549

Network File Systems: NFS and /etc/exports 550

NFS Daemons 550

NFS Configuration: /etc/exports 554

NFS Host Entries 554

NFS Options 555

NFS User-Level Access 556

NFSv4 556

NFS File and Directory Security with NFS4 Access Lists 557

NFS /etc/exports Example 557

Applying Changes 558

Manually Exporting File Systems 558

Controlling Accessing to NFS Servers 559

/etc/hosts.allow and /etc/hosts.deny 559

rpcbind Service 559

Netfilter Rules 560

Mounting NFS File Systems: NFS Clients 560

Mounting NFS Automatically: /etc/fstab 560

Mounting NFS Manually: mount 561

Mounting NFS on Demand: autofs 562

Network Information Service: NIS 563

/etc/nsswitch.conf: Name Service Switch 563

15. Samba 567

Samba Applications 568

Starting up and accessing Samba 570

Firewall access..571

User-Level Security 573

Samba Passwords: smbpasswd..574

Managing Samba Users: smbpasswd and pdbedit.................574

The Samba smb.conf Configuration File.......................................575

Variable Substitutions...576

Global Settings...577

Browsing/Identification 577

Networking 578

Debugging/Accounting 578

Authentication 578

Domains..579

Misc...579

Share Definitions 580

Homes Section 580

The printers and print$ Sections 581

Shares..581

Printer shares...583

Testing the Samba Configuration 584

Samba Public Domain Controller: Samba PDC 584

Microsoft Domain Security 584

Essential Samba PDC configuration options 584

Basic configuration 585

Domain Logon configuration 585

Samba Active Directory Domain Controller................................586

Accessing Samba Services with Clients..588

Accessing Windows Samba Shares from the Desktop.........588

smbclient...588

mount.cifs: mount -t cifs 589

Table Listing **591**

Figure Listing **595**

Index **611**

Part 1: Getting Started

Introduction

Installation

Usage Basics

Managing Software

Applications

1. Linux Mint 21 Introduction

Linux Mint 21

Linux Mint Editions

Linux Mint Live DVD and USB

Linux Mint Software

Linux Mint Help and Documentation

Ubuntu Linux

Open Source Software

History of Linux and UNIX

Linux Mint aims to provide a user-oriented desktop system that is concise, elegant, and powerful. Linux Mint started in 2006 and is based on the Ubuntu distribution. Linux Mint has developed a desktop called Cinnamon, initially derived from GNOME 3. Though Cinnamon is developed and maintained by Linux Mint, it can also be installed on other Linux distributions.

You can think of Linux Mint as more like a portal to different underlying Linux implementations. Linux Mint directly supports desktops using Cinnamon and MATE. It also supports the Xfce desktop. The desktops are based on the Ubuntu Linux distribution with many of the packages taken directly from the Ubuntu software repositories.

Following the Ubuntu releases, Linux Mint provides both long-term and short-term support releases. Long-term support releases (LTS), are released every two years. Short-term releases are provided every six months between the LTS versions. They are designed to make available the latest applications and support for the newest hardware. The long-term support releases are supported for three years for desktops and five years for servers, whereas short-term support releases are supported for 18 months. Linux Mint numbers its releases sequentially.

Installing Linux Mint is easy to do. A core set of applications are installed, and you can add to them as you wish. Following installation, additional software can be downloaded from online repositories. There are only a few install screens, which move quickly through default partitioning, user setup, and time settings. Hardware components such as graphics cards and network connections are configured and detected automatically. With Software Manager (installed by default on all systems), you can find and install additional software with the click of a button. The Linux Mint distribution of Linux is available at **https://linuxmint.com.** You can download the current release of Linux Mint Linux from **https://linuxmint.com/download.php**.

Linux Mint 21

Linux Mint 21 introduces several new features, as well as numerous smaller modifications (see Figure 1-1). You can find out what is new at:

```
https://linuxmint.com/rel_vanessa_cinnamon_whatsnew.php
https://linuxmint.com/rel_vanessa_mate_whatsnew.php
https://linuxmint.com/rel_vanessa_xfce_whatsnew.php
```

Linux Mint Editions

Linux Mint is released in several editions, each designed for a distinct group of users or functions. Editions install different collections of software such as the Cinnamon desktop, the MATE desktop, and the Xfce desktop. Table 1-2 lists the editions. You can download these editions from mirrors that you can link to from the download page, which you can access from the Linux Mint site by clicking on the Download tab. The download page is:

```
https://linuxmint.com/download.php
```

The Linux Mint version of KDE has been discontinued. There will be no further releases for a Linux Mint KDE desktop. You can still install the Ubuntu version of KDE, Kubuntu, using the **kubuntu-desktop** meta package. The KDE desktop will be listed as Plasma on the LightDM list of desktop login options. However, you can still install and run any of the KDE applications on your Cinnamon or MATE desktops, such as Karbon (vector graphics), Clementine (music player),

Dragon player (media player), Ocular (PDF viewer), and the Calligra office suite. All can be directly installed from Software Manager (Linux Mint and Ubuntu repositories).

Only the 64-bit version is supported. The "no codecs" versions in previous releases have been replaced by a prompt on the second screen of the standard installation to install third-party codecs.

Figure 1-1: Linux Mint 21 Cinnamon Desktop

The Cinnamon and MATE releases allow you to install the full range of available codecs for Linux, including mp3, DVD, and video support. The second screen of the installation process will prompt you to choose whether to install these third party codecs. If you choose to do so, you do not have to bother about installing additional codecs to make multimedia applications work. This policy differs from Ubuntu, which does not install such codecs initially, and have to be installed manually later.

Linux Mint Live DVD/USB

All Linux Mint ISOs can be installed on either a DVD disk or a USB drive. They will operate as a Live DVD/USBs, so you can run Linux Mint from any DVD-ROM or USB drive. New users can also use the Live-DVD/USB to try out Linux Mint to see if they like it.

The Linux Mint Live ISO provided by Linux Mint includes a basic collection of software packages. You will have a fully operational Linux Mint system (see Figure 1-2). You have the full set of administrative tools, with which you can add users, change configuration settings, and even add software, while the Live DVD/USB is running. When you shut down, the configuration information is lost, including any software you have added. Files and data can be written to removable devices like USB drives and DVD write discs, letting you save your data during a Live DVD/USB session.

Linux Mint Editions	Description
Linux Mint Cinnamon	Live DVD/USB and Install with the Cinnamon interface, **https://linuxmint.com/download.php**. Add to other Linux Mint versions with the **mint-meta-cinnamon** metapackage.
Linux Mint MATE	Live DVD/USB and Install with the MATE interface, **https://linuxmint.com/download.php**. Add to other Linux Mint versions with the **mint-meta-mate** metapackage.
Linux Mint Xfce	Uses the Xfce desktop instead of GNOME, **https://linuxmint.com/download.php**. Useful for laptops. Add to other Linux Mint versions with the **mint-meta-xfce** metapackage.

Table 1-1: Linux Mint Editions

When you start up the Linux Mint Desktop DVD/USB, the Live desktop is then displayed (see Figure 1-2) and you are logged in as the **Linux Mint** user. On the left side, an install Linux Mint icon is displayed, along with the computer and home folder icons. Use the Cinnamon menu at the left side of the bottom panel to quit. Use the network manager menu on the right side of the bottom panel to configure network connections.

All the Live DVD/USBs also function as install discs for Linux Mint, providing an extensive collection of software, and installing a full-fledged Linux Mint operating system that can be expanded and updated from Linux Mint online repositories. An Install icon lets you install Linux Mint on your computer, performing a standard installation to your hard drive. From the Live DVD/USB desktop, double-click the "Install Linux Mint" icon on the desktop to start the installation.

Figure 1-2: Linux Mint 21 Cinnamon Live DVD

The Live USB drive is generated using the ISO image downloaded. You can install the Linux Mint Live ISO using either the USB Image Writer or the USB Startup Disk Creator. The

USB Image Writer is installed by default on Cinnamon, but you can download and install the Startup Disk Creator (**usb-creator-gtk**). The USB Image Writer will erase all data on the drive. The Startup Disk Creator will not erase data on your USB. You can still access it, even Windows data. The Linux Mint Live OS will coexist with your current data, occupying available free space. You also have the option to specify writable memory. This will allow you to save files to your USB drive as part of the Linux Mint Live operating system.

Alternatively, you could download and use the Fedora Media Writer to create the USB drive. The Fedora Media Writer can be installed on any operating system, including Windows and Mac.

To boot from the Live USB, be sure your computer (BIOS) is configured to boot from the USB drive. You may have to either temporarily select the boot disk (F12 at start up on many computers), or configure your BIOS to boot from the USB drive. The Live USB drive will then start up just like the Live DVD, displaying the install screen with options to try Linux Mint or directly install it.

Linux Mint Software

All Linux software for Linux Mint is currently available from online repositories. You can download applications for desktops, Internet servers, office suites, and programming packages, among others. Software packages are distributed through the Linux Mint and Ubuntu repositories, as well as Flatpak. Downloads and updates are handled automatically by your desktop software manager and updater.

The complete listing of Linux Mint software packages for a release can be found at:

`http://packages.linuxmint.com`

A more descriptive listing is kept at Linux Mint Community site at:

`https://community.linuxmint.com/software`

For the Ubuntu packages in the Linux Mint distribution, you can search the Ubuntu packages site at:

`http://packages.ubuntu.com`

Flatpak packages are downloaded from the Flathub repository.

`https://flathub.org/home`

All software packages in the Linux Mint and Ubuntu repositories are accessible directly with Software Manager and the Synaptic Package Manager, which provide easy software installation, removal, and searching. Flatpak support is integrated into Software Manager, letting you easily install Flatpak software directly from Flathub.

Due to licensing restrictions, multimedia support for popular operations like MP3, DVD, and DivX are installed separately by the **mint-meta-codecs** package. If not already installed, choose "Install Multimedia Codecs" from the Sound & Video menu, or, on the Welcome dialog's First Steps tab click the Launch button for Multimedia Codecs.

You can, if you want, install support for Snap and the Snap store. Snap is an Ubuntu service designed to replace APT, and is an alternative to Flathub. Keep in mind that most popular applications available on Snap are already available to you on Linux Mint from Flathub.

Linux Mint Help and Documentation

Help and documentation for Linux Mint are available on the Linux Mint site at **https://linuxmint.com/documentation.php** and at Linux Mint Community site at **https://community.linuxmint.com/** (see Table 1-2). The Linux Mint Community site provides extensive help resources. Here you will find detailed tutorials, package lists, hardware support information, and online chat for questions. You can also obtain help from the Linux Mint Forum at **https://forums.linuxmint.com**. The Linux Mint site (**https://linuxmint.com**) provides recent news and has tabs for Download, Project, About, and Link, as well as thumbnail links for the recent releases and the User guide. Passing your mouse over a tab displays a sub-tab such as FAQ and Documentation for the About tab, and Linux Mint 21 and Installation Guide for the Downloads tab. Click on a tab to open the page.

Site	Description
https://linuxmint.com	Linux Mint site
http://packages.linuxmint.com	Linux Mint software package list
https://community.linuxmint.com/software	Linux Mint software package list, organized by name and more descriptive
https://forums.linuxmint.com	Linux Mint forums
https://linuxmint.com/download.php	Download Linux Mint Editions
https://linuxmint.com/documentation.php	Linux Mint Documentation including User Guide, Installation Guide, Troubleshooting Guide, and Translation Guide.

Table 1-2: Linux Mint resources and help

Figure 1-3: Linux Mint Welcome dialog

After you install your system and start up your Linux Mint desktop, a welcome dialog is displayed with tabs for First Steps, Documentation, Help, and Contribute (see Figure 1-3). The Documentation tab has links to Linux Mint sites for documentation, new features, and the release notes (see Figure 1-4). The Documentation link displays the Linux Mint documentation site at **https://linuxmint.com/documentation.php**, which has the Installation Guide, User Guide, and Troubleshooting Guide, Translation Guide, and Developer Guide for download. The New Features link opens the New Features page for the desktop you are using such as **https://linuxmint.com/rel_vanessa_cinnamon_whatsnew.php** for the Cinnamon desktop. The Release Notes link opens the release notes page for the release you are using such as **https://linuxmint.com/rel_vanessa_cinnamon.php** for the Cinnamon release.

The Help tab has links to the Linux Mint Forums at **https://forums.linuxmint.com** and to the Linux Mint IRC chat room. The Contribute tab has a link to the Linux Mint Get Involved page at **https://linuxmint.com/getinvolved.php**, with links for donations, sponsorships, and the Linux Mint community forum.

Figure 1-4: Welcome dialog - Documentation

Ubuntu

Ubuntu Linux is currently one of the most popular end-user Linux distributions (**https://www.ubuntu.com**). Ubuntu Linux is managed by the Ubuntu foundation, which is sponsored by Canonical, Ltd (**https://www.canonical.com/**), a commercial organization that supports and promotes open source projects. Ubuntu is based on Debian Linux, one of the oldest Linux distributions, which is dedicated to incorporating cutting-edge developments and features (**http://www.debian.org**). Mark Shuttleworth, a South African and Debian Linux developer, initiated the Ubuntu project. Debian Linux is primarily a Linux development project, trying out new features. Ubuntu provides a Debian-based Linux distribution that is stable, reliable, and easy to use.

Ubuntu is designed as a Linux operating system that can be used easily by everyone. The name Ubuntu means "humanity to others." As the Ubuntu project describes it: "Ubuntu is an African word meaning 'Humanity to others", or "I am what I am because of who we all are." The

Ubuntu distribution brings the spirit of Ubuntu to the software world." Ubuntu aims to provide a fully supported and reliable, open source and free, easy to use and modify, Linux operating system.

Table 1-3 lists several Ubuntu help and resource sites. Ubuntu-specific documentation is available at **https://help.ubuntu.com**. Here, on listed links, you can find specific documentation for different releases. Always check the release help page first for documentation, though it may be sparse and cover mainly changed areas. The Ubuntu LTS release usually includes desktop, installation, and server guides. For Ubuntu 22.04 the Documentation section provides the Ubuntu Desktop Guide.

```
https://help.ubuntu.com/lts/ubuntu-help/index.html
```

Site	Description
https://help.ubuntu.com/	Help pages and documentation for Ubuntu
http://packages.ubuntu.com	Ubuntu software package list and search
https://ubuntuforums.org	Ubuntu forums
https://askubuntu.com	Ask Ubuntu Q&A site for users and developers (community based)
http://planet.ubuntu.com	Member and developer blogs
https://blog.canonical.com	Latest Canonical news
http://www.tldp.org	Linux Documentation Project website
https://www.ubuntu.com/community	Links to Documentation, Support, News, and Blogs

Table 1-3: Ubuntu help and documentation

One of the more helpful pages is the Community Contributed Documentation page, **https://help.ubuntu.com/community**. Here you will find detailed documentation on the installation of all Ubuntu releases, using the desktop, installing software, and configuring devices. Always check the page for your Ubuntu release first. Ubuntu forums provide detailed online support and discussion for users (**https://ubuntuforums.org**).

Linux documentation

The Linux Documentation Project (LDP) has developed a complete set of Linux manuals. The documentation is available at the LDP home site at **http://www.tldp.org**. The Linux documentation for your installed software will be available in your **/usr/share/doc** directory.

Open Source Software

Linux is developed as a cooperative Open Source effort over the Internet, so no company or institution controls Linux. Software developed for Linux reflects this background. Development often takes place when Linux users decide to work together on a project. Most Linux software is developed as Open Source software. The source code for an application is freely distributed along with the application. Programmers can make their own contributions to a software package's development, modifying and correcting the source code. As an open source operating system, the Linux source code is included in all its distributions and is freely available. Many major software development efforts are also open source projects, as are the KDE and GNOME desktops along with most of their applications. You can find more information about the Open Source movement at **https://opensource.org**.

Open source software is protected by public licenses that prevent commercial companies from taking control of open source software by adding modifications of their own, copyrighting those changes, and selling the software as their own product. The most popular public license is the GNU General Public License (GPL) provided by the Free Software Foundation. Linux is distributed under this license. The GNU General Public License retains the copyright, freely licensing the software with the requirement that the software and any modifications made to it are always freely available. Other public licenses have been created to support the demands of different kinds of open source projects. The GNU Lesser General Public License (LGPL) lets commercial applications use GNU licensed software libraries. The Qt Public License (QPL) lets open source developers use the Qt libraries essential to the KDE desktop. You can find a complete listing at **https://opensource.org**.

Linux is currently copyrighted under a GNU public license provided by the Free Software Foundation (see **http://www.gnu.org/**). GNU software is distributed free, provided it is freely distributed to others. GNU software has proved both reliable and effective. Many of the popular Linux utilities, such as C compilers, shells, and editors, are GNU software applications. In addition, many open source software projects are licensed under the GNU General Public License (GPL). Most of these applications are available on the Ubuntu software repositories. Chapter 4 describes in detail the process of accessing these repositories to download and install software applications from them on your system.

Under the terms of the GNU General Public License, the original author retains the copyright, although anyone can modify the software and redistribute it, provided the source code is included, made public, and provided free. In addition, no restriction exists on selling the software or giving it away free. One distributor could charge for the software, while another could provide it free of charge. Major software companies are also providing Linux versions of their most popular applications (you can use Wine, the Windows compatibility layer, to run many Microsoft applications on Linux, directly).

Linux

Linux is a fast, stable, and open source operating system for PCs and workstations that features professional-level Internet services, extensive development tools, fully functional graphical user interfaces (GUIs), and a massive number of applications ranging from office suites to multimedia applications. Linux was developed in the early 1990s by Linus Torvalds, along with other programmers around the world. As an operating system, Linux performs many of the same functions as UNIX, MAC OS-X, and Windows. However, Linux is distinguished by its power and flexibility, along with being freely available. Most PC operating systems, such as Windows, began their development within the confines of small, restricted personal computers, which have become more versatile and powerful machines. Such operating systems are constantly being upgraded to keep up with the ever-changing capabilities of PC hardware. Linux, on the other hand, was developed in a different context. Linux is a PC version of the UNIX operating system that has been used for decades on mainframes and is currently the system of choice for network servers and workstations.

Technically, Linux consists of the operating system program referred to as the kernel, which is the part originally developed by Linus Torvalds. However, it has always been distributed with a large number of open source software applications, ranging from network servers and security programs to office applications and development tools. Linux has evolved as part of the open source software movement, in which independent programmers joined to provide free quality software to any user. Linux has become the premier platform for open source software, much of it developed by the Free Software Foundation's GNU project. Most of these applications are also available on the Ubuntu repository, providing packages that are Debian compliant.

Linux operating system capabilities include powerful networking features, including support for Internet, intranets, and Windows networking. As a norm, Linux distributions include fast, efficient, and stable Internet servers, such as the Web, FTP, and DNS servers, along with proxy, news, and mail servers. In other words, Linux has everything you need to set up, support, and maintain a fully functional network.

Linux is distributed freely under a GNU General Public License (GPL) as specified by the Free Software Foundation, making it available to anyone who wants to use it. GNU (which stands for "GNU's Not Unix") is a project initiated and managed by the Free Software Foundation to provide free software to users, programmers, and developers. Linux is copyrighted, not public domain. The GNU General Public License is designed to ensure that Linux remains free and, at the same time, standardized. Linux is technically the operating system kernel, the core operations, and only one official Linux kernel exists. Its power and stability have made Linux an operating system of choice as a network server.

Originally designed specifically for Intel-based personal computers, Linux started out as a personal project of computer science student Linus Torvalds at the University of Helsinki. At that time, students were making use of a program called Minix, which highlighted different UNIX features. Minix was created by Professor Andrew Tanenbaum and widely distributed over the Internet to students around the world. Torvalds's intention was to create an effective PC version of UNIX for Minix users. It was named Linux, and in 1991, Torvalds released version 0.11. Linux was widely distributed over the Internet, and in the following years, other programmers refined and added to it, incorporating most of the applications and features now found in standard UNIX systems. All the major window managers have been ported to Linux. Linux has all the networking tools, such as FTP file transfer support, Web browsers, and the whole range of network services such as email, the domain name service, and dynamic host configuration, along with FTP, Web, and print servers. It also has a full set of program development utilities, such as C++ compilers and debuggers. Given all its features, the Linux operating system remains small, stable, and fast.

Linux development is overseen by The Linux Foundation (**https://www.linuxfoundation.org**), which is a merger of The Free Standards Group and Open Source Development Labs (OSDL). This is the group with which Linux Torvalds works to develop new Linux versions. Linux kernels are released at **https://www.kernel.org/**.

2. Installing Linux Mint

Install Discs

Installation Overview

Installation with the Linux Mint DVD/USB

Recovery

Re-Installing the Boot Loader

Installing Linux Mint Linux is a very simple procedure, using just a few screens with default entries for easy installation. A pre-selected collection of software is installed. Most of your devices, like your display and network connection, are detected automatically. The most difficult part would be a manual partitioning of the hard drive, but you can use automatic partitioning for fresh installs, as is usually the case. Installation is a straightforward process. The graphical installation is easy to use, providing full mouse support.

Check the Linux Mint Installation Guide for detailed instructions of how to install Linux Mint.

```
https://linuxmint-installation-guide.readthedocs.io/en/latest/index.html
https://linuxmint-installation-guide.readthedocs.io/en/latest/install.html
```

Upgrading directly from Linux Mint 20.3: Upgrade Tool

If you already have Linux Mint 20.3 64 bit versions, you can upgrade directly to 21. You cannot upgrade from 32 bit versions, unless you are using the 32 bit Debian version, LMDE. There are no 32 bit versions for Linux Mint 21 Cinnamon, MATE, and Xfce.

See the article "How to Upgrade to Linux Mint 21" on the Linux Mint blog for detailed instructions.

```
https://linuxmint-user-guide.readthedocs.io/en/latest/upgrade-to-mint-21.html
```

If you want to upgrade from an earlier version of Linux Mint, you first must upgrade sequentially to Linux Mint 20.3. For earlier versions it may be best to simply backup your data and perform a clean install.

You can perform a fresh upgrade or a package upgrade. The fresh upgrade is actually not an upgrade as such, but a completely new install performed after you make a backup of your data. It is the recommended form of upgrading. For a fresh upgrade, you first backup all your data to a separate drive, then install the new Linux Mint release, overwriting and erasing the old one. Then restore your backup to the new system. You do have to make sure that you backup all your data, including all configuration files, such as those for your Web browser.

A simple strategy for easily implementing a fresh upgrade is to set up a separate partition for your home directory (/**home**), which you then keep. Have the Linux Mint system installed on a separate partition (root partition, /), which you can overwrite to upgrade. Make sure to backup any configuration files, if any, that you may want from other partitions.

Before upgrading, be sure to update your system. In Update Manager, click the Refresh button and check for and install any updates. It would be advisable to also perform a Timeshift snapshot in case something goes wrong. You could then restore your old version. Also remove any third party repositories that could be incompatible.

Be sure you have the 64 bit version.

```
dpkg --print-architecture
```

Install the **mintupgrade** application.

```
sudo apt install mintupgrade
```

Then start the Upgrade Tool with the **mintupgrade** command (see Figure 2-1) .

```
sudo mintupgrade
```

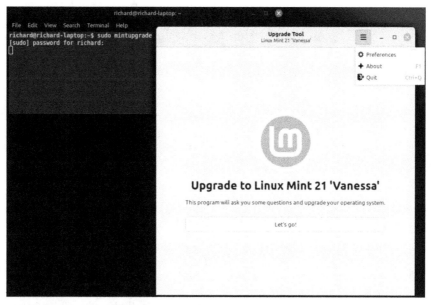

Figure 2-1: Upgrade Tool (mintupgrade)

Upgrade Tool preferences has two tabs: Requirements and Orphan packages. The Requirements tab has switches for tasks needed for a safe upgrade: a Timeshift snapshot, updated software, a supported Linux Mint version, and specified orphan packages.

Figure 2-2: Upgrade Tool Preferences Requirements

Orphan packages are those not in the Linux mint or Ubuntu repositories such as those that have been deprecated or separately installed third-party software. To keep an orphan package, list it on the Orphan Packages tab. Click the plus button to open a dialog where you can enter the name of a package to add.

Figure 2-3: Upgrade Tool Preferences Orphan Packages

When you perform the upgrade, tests are performed to check if you have updated your software, performed a recent Timeshift, and if there are orphaned packages (see Figure 2-4). You are then asked to perform the upgrade (see Figure 2-5). You can disable the tests in Preferences to save time. The packages are downloaded and your system is updated (see Figure 2-6. The actual commands performed are displayed in the terminal window you started **mintupgrade** from. On the panel, the Upgrade Tool icon show a progress bar as the upgrade progresses. When the upgrade is finishes, you are told to close the Upgrade Tool window and then restart your system, which completes the upgrade.

Figure 2-4: Upgrade Tool tests

Figure 2-5: Upgrade Tool upgrade

Figure 2-6: Upgrade Tool download and update

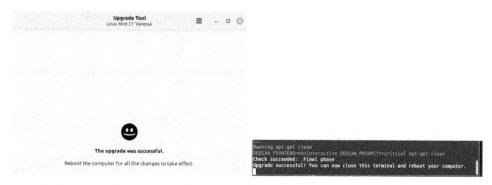

Figure 2-7: Upgrade Tool upgrade completion

The upgrade will overwrite your configuration files in the **/etc** directory. Should you want to restore some configuration files, use Timeshift to select the files you want from your last snapshot.

Should your system fail to boot due to a boot failure, you can start up your system using the Linux Mint 21 Live USB/DVD and then run the Boot Repair application to fix your boot files. It is also possible to run Timeshift from the Linux Mint USB/DVD and have it restore your old system from Timeshift snapshots on your hard drive.

Install Discs

Installation is performed using a Linux Mint DVD/USB that will install the Linux Mint, along with a pre-selected set of software packages for multimedia players, office applications, and games. The Linux Mint DVD/USB is also designed to run from the DVD disc or USB drive while providing the option to install Linux Mint on your hard drive. You create a Linux Mint DVD/USB using an ISO image that you will download from the Linux Mint download site. The Linux Mint 21 ISO has only a 64-bit version. The Linux Mint ISOs are available at:

```
https://linuxmint.com/download.php
```

You can download the ISO file directly from a mirror or by using a torrent file with a BitTorrent client like Transmission. Click on the Torrent link on the download page for the BitTorrent file.

The Linux Mint 21 64bit install ISO file with the Cinnamon desktop is:

```
linuxmint-21-cinnamon-64bit.iso
```

Installing Multiple-Boot Systems

The GRUB boot loader already supports multiple booting. Should you have both Linux Mint and Windows systems installed on your hard disks, GRUB will let you choose to boot either the Linux Mint system or a Windows system. During installation, GRUB will automatically detect any other operating systems installed on your computer and configure your boot loader menu to let you access them. You do not have to perform any configuration yourself.

If you want a Windows system installed on your computer, you should install it first. Windows would overwrite the boot loader installed by a previous Linux Mint system, cutting off access to the Linux system. If you installed Windows after having installed Linux Mint, you will need to re-install the Linux Mint GRUB boot loader. See the section at the end of this Chapter on re-installing the boot loader. There are several ways you can do it.

If you have already installed Windows on your hard drive and configured it to take up the entire hard drive, you can select the "Install alongside" option during installation to free up space and set up Linux Mint partitions.

If you do have an operating system installed, but the "Install alongside" message does not appear, then be sure to use the "Something else" option. Otherwise, you may overwrite and destroy your installed operating system. On some Windows installs with the EFI bios, the Windows install may not appear. Be sure to choose "Something else" and then manually configure your partitions for Linux Mint.

For EFI Bios systems with Windows installs, the GRUB 2 boot loader that is installed with Linux Mint, will detect the EFI bios partition and list Windows as a boot option when you start up your system.

Tip: You can also use the Linux Mint Live DVD/USB to start up Linux Mint and perform the necessary hard disk partitioning using GParted.

Installation Overview

Installing Linux Mint involves several processes, beginning with creating Linux partitions, then loading the Linux Mint software, selecting a time zone, and creating a new user. The installation program used for Linux Mint is a screen-based program that takes you through all these processes, step-by-step, as one continuous procedure. You can use either your mouse or the keyboard to make selections. When you finish with a screen, click the Continue button at the bottom to move to the next screen. If you need to move back to the previous screen, click Back. You can also press TAB, the arrow keys, SPACEBAR, and ENTER to make selections.

Most systems today already meet hardware requirements and have automatic connections to the Internet.

They also support booting a DVD-ROM disc and USB drives, though this support may have to be explicitly selected in the system BIOS.

If you are installing on a blank hard drive or on a drive with free space, or if you are performing a simple update that uses the same partitions, installing Linux Mint is a simple process. Linux Mint also features an automatic partitioning function that will perform the partitioning for you.

A preconfigured set of packages are installed, so you will not even have to select packages.

For a quick installation, you can simply start up the installation process by placing your DVD disc in the DVD drive or attaching your USB drive, and starting up your system. Graphical installation is a simple matter of following the instructions in each window as you progress. Installation follows a few easy stages:

1. **Welcome**   A default language is chosen for you, like English, so you can usually just click Continue.

2. **Keyboard Layout**   A default is chosen for you; you can usually just click Continue.

3. **Preparing to install**   On the "Preparing to install" screen your system is checked and you can opt to install third party software and multimedia codecs.

4. **Installation type**   For automatic partitioning you have different options, depending on what other operating systems may have been installed on your hard drive. For drives that have other operating systems installed, you can install alongside them or choose to erase the entire disk. In all cases, you can also choose to partition your disk manually instead.

5. **Installation type: partitioner**   Used for manual partitioning only, in which you set up partitions yourself. Otherwise, this is skipped.

6. **Where are you? Time Zone**   Use the map to choose your time zone or select your city from the drop-down menu.

7. **Who are you?**   Set up a username and hostname for your computer, as well as a password for that user. You can also choose to log in automatically, as well as encrypt your home folder.

After the installation, you will be asked to remove the DVD disc or USB drive and press ENTER. Then your system reboots.

Installation with the Linux Mint DVD/USB

The Linux Mint ISO can be installed either a DVD disk or USB drive. It is designed for running Linux Mint from the DVD/USB (Live DVD/USB) and installing Linux Mint. Most users will use the Linux Mint DVD/USB to install Linux Mint. You can first start up Linux Mint, and then initiate an installation. Place the DVD disc in the DVD-ROM drive or attach the USB drive, before you start your computer. Be sure that your computer is configured to boot from the USB drive or from the DVD drive. In most cases, to boot from the DVD or USB drive, you may have either temporarily select the boot disk by pressing a key such as F12 or ESC, or configure your BIOS to boot from the USB drive. After you start your computer, the installation program starts up. For most BIOS systems you will be told which key to press. For more details see:

```
https://linuxmint-installation-guide.readthedocs.io/en/latest/boot.html
```

Computers can boot using either the older Legacy BIOS mode or the newer EFI mode. Most newer computers use EFI. The options are much the same, though the Legacy BIOS mode has a few more.

In EFI mode, when the Linux Mint DVD/USB first boots, a text screen first appears with the following options:

```
Start Linux Mint 21 Cinnamon 64-bit
Start Linux Mint 21 Cinnamon 64-bit (compatibility mode)
OEM install (for manufacturers)
Check the integrity of the medium
```

This menu is displayed for each edition. The MATE and Xfce DVD/USBs will have those names instead of Cinnamon. Use the compatibility mode if you are not sure your video card will support the Live DVD/USB desktop. The OEM install starts up the install process in system manufacturer mode, letting you install the same configuration on several systems. There is no longer a separate OEM edition. The Check entry checks to see if your DVD or USB is usable.

You can press the **e** key on any entry to open a list of the boot options for that boot entry, which you can edit, changing the boot options. For example, if your video card has problems with the boot animation, you can edit the boot options (linux entry) to remove the **quiet splash** options and replace it with the **nomodeset** option. When finished press F10 or Ctrl-x to boot. ESC discards edits. For more information see:

```
https://linuxmint-installation-guide.readthedocs.io/en/latest/boot_options.html#
```

The Legacy BIOS mode has the same entries, but adds hardware detection, boot from local drive, and memory test. Selecting an entry and pressing tab opens an editable line listing the boot options for that option. You can modify the options.

```
Start Linux Mint
Start in compatibility mode
OEM install (for manufacturers)
Integrity check
Hardware Detection
Boot from local drive
Memory test
```

Welcome and Language

On the Linux Mint Live desktop, click the "Install Linux Mint" icon to start up the installation (see Figure 2-8). The Install window opens to the Welcome screen for choosing your language. Click the Continue button to start the installation.

On most screens, a Continue button is displayed on the lower-right corner of an installation dialog. Once finished with a screen, click Continue to move on. In some cases, you will be able to click a Back button to return to a previous screen. As each screen appears in the installation, default entries will be selected, usually by the auto-probing capability of the installation program. If these entries are correct, you can click Continue to accept them and go on to the next screen.

Figure 2-8: Live DVD/USB (Desktop) with Install icon.

Keyboard Layout

You are then asked to select a keyboard layout, "Choose your keyboard layout." Keyboard entries are selected first by location in the left scroll box, and then by type on the right scroll box. A default is already selected, such as English (US) (see Figure 2-9). If the selection is not correct, you can choose another keyboard, first by location in the left scroll box, and then by type on the right scroll box.

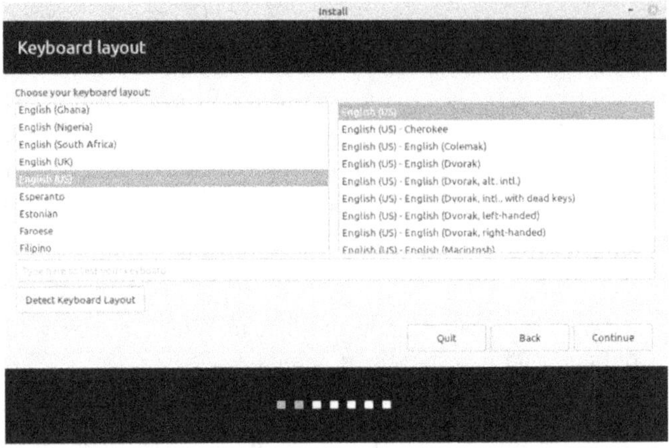

Figure 2-9: Keyboard Layout

To test your keyboard, click on the text box at the bottom of the screen and press keys, "Type here to test your keyboard."

The "Detect Keyboard Layout" button tries to detect the keyboard using your input. A series of dialogs opens, prompting you to press keys and asking you if certain keys are present on your keyboard. When the dialogs finish, the detected keyboard is then selected in the "Choose your keyboard layout" scroll boxes.

Click the Continue button to continue.

Preparing to install (third party software)

The "Preparing to install Linux Mint" dialog appears with an option to install third party software, such as multimedia codecs (see Figure 2-10). Leaving this option unchecked, installs the equivalent of the "no codecs" releases from earlier versions. Checking the option installs all available codecs. Click the Continue button to continue.

Figure 2-10: Install Third-Party Software

Click the Continue button to continue. Your system then detects your hardware, providing any configuration specifications that may be required.

Installation type

You are now asked to designate the Linux partitions and hard disk configurations you want to use on your hard drives. Linux Mint provides automatic partitioning that covers most situations, like using a blank or new hard drive and overwriting old partitions on a hard drive. Linux Mint can even repartition a system with an operating system that uses all of the hard drive, but with unused space within it. In this case, the install procedure reduces the space used by the original operating system and installs Linux Mint on the new free space. A default partition layout sets up a root partition of type **ext4** (Linux native) for the kernel and applications.

Alternatively, you can configure your hard disk manually (the "Something else" option). Linux Mint provides a simple partitioning tool you can use to set up Linux partitions.

For multiple boot systems using Windows, Linux Mint automatically detects a Windows system.

No partitions will be changed or formatted until you click the "Install Now" button. You can opt out of the installation until then, and your original partitions will remain untouched.

Warning: The "Erase disk and install Linux Mint" option will wipe out any existing partitions on the selected hard drive. If you want to preserve any partitions on that drive, like Windows or other Linux partitions, always choose a different option such as "Install Linux Mint alongside ..." or "Something else".

You are given choices, depending on the state of the hard disk you choose. A hard disk could be blank, have an older Linux Mint operating system on it, or have a different operating system, such as Windows, already installed. If an operating system is already installed, it may take up the entire disk or may only use part of the disk, with the remainder available for the Linux Mint installation.

Tip: Some existing Linux systems may use several Linux partitions. Some of these may be used for just the system software, such as the boot and root partitions. These can be formatted. Others may have extensive user files, such as a **/home** partition that normally holds user home directories and all the files they have created. You should not format such partitions.

No detected operating systems

If no operating systems are detected on the hard drive, which is the case with a drive with only data files or a blank hard drive, you are given two choices: to erase the entire disk, or to specify partitions manually (Something else) (see Figure 2-11). The Erase disk option has an Advanced Features button that lets you also choose LVM and Encryption. The message displayed on the Installation type dialog is:

"This computer currently has no detected operating systems. What would you like to do?"

You are given two choices.

```
Erase disk and install Linux Mint
Something else
```

If you choose to install "Erase disk and install Linux Mint", your hard drive is automatically partitioned creating a primary partition for your entire file system (a root file system).

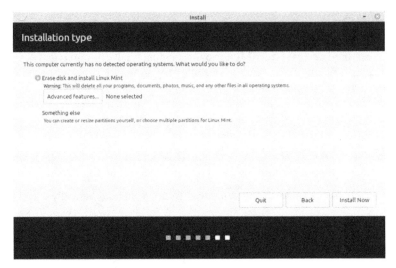

Figure 2-11: No detected operating systems

Advanced Features: LVM and Encryption

Should you want to use LVM and disk encryption for your partitions, click the "Erase disk and install Linux Mint" entry to activate the "Advanced features" button. Then click the "Advanced features" button to open a dialog showing options for LVM, with an additional option under LVM for disk encryption (see Figure 2-12).

Figure 2-12: LVM install option

There is also a None option in case you decided not use LVM. Once you have made your selection click the OK button. The Installation type screen will then show your selection, next to the "Advanced features" button. For LVM it will display "LVM selected" (see Figure 2-13). LVM is covered in more detail in Chapter 9.

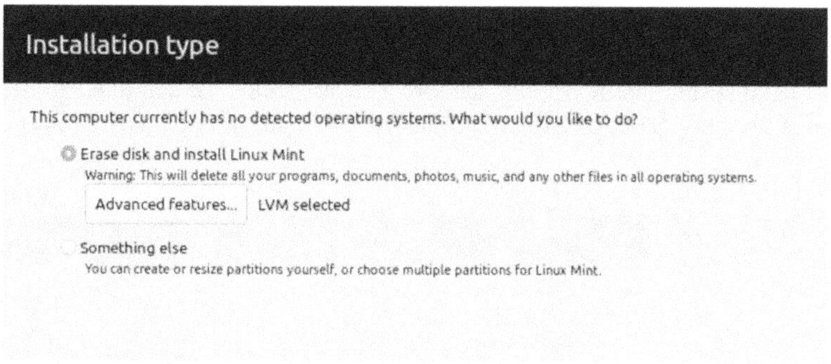

Figure 2-13: LVM selection

With the "Use LVM with the new Linux Mint installation" option, LVM partitions are set up using physical and logical volumes, which can be added to and replaced easily. An LVM physical volume is set up, which contains two LVM logical volumes, one for the swap space and one for the root (see Figure 2-13). After you have installed your system, you can manage your LVM partitions using the LVM commands (see Chapter 9). The default LVM partitions are shown here with **pvscan** (physical volumes), **vgscan** (volume group), and **lvscan** (logical volume) operations. There is one volume group, **vgmint**, with two logical volumes, **root** and **swap_1**. The physical LVM partition is named **lvm2**. Two physical partitions are created on your system, an EFI boot partition and the LVM physical partition.

```
$ sudo pvscan
  PV /dev/sda2   VG vgmint        lvm2 [<464.54 GiB / 0    free]
  Total: 1 [<464.54 GiB] / in use: 1 [<464.54 GiB] / in no VG: 0 [0    ]
$ sudo vgscan
  Found volume group "vgmint" using metadata type lvm2
$ sudo lvscan
  ACTIVE            '/dev/vgmint/root' [463.58 GiB] inherit
  ACTIVE            '/dev/vgmint/swap_1' [980.00 MiB] inherit
```

Encrypt the disk

The "Encrypt the new Linux Mint installation for security" option on the "Advanced Features" dialog lets you encrypt your entire system with a password (see Figure 2-14) .

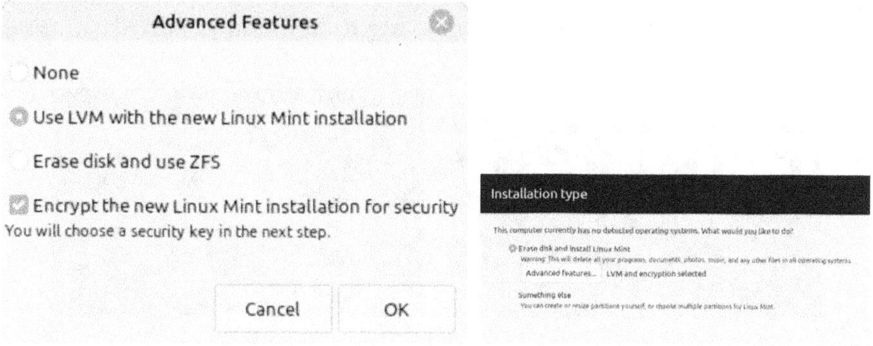

Figure 2-14: LVM with encryption

You cannot access your system without that password. The encryption option will destroy any existing partitions if there are any, creating new partitions. Your hard drive will then have only your new Linux Mint system on it. On the "Choose a security key" screen that follows you are prompted to enter a security key (password), along with the option to overwrite empty space (see Figure 2-15).

Figure 2-15: Security key for encrypted system

You also have the option to create a recovery key that you can use to unlock your disk, should you forget or lose your security key. The recovery key is saved on the USB/DVD installation session in memory at the **/home/mint** folder in a file named **recovery.key**. The key is a password consisting of 48 text numbers. Be sure to make a copy of the recovery key before you end the installation, saving it to a USB drive, to another system, or just open the **recovery.key** file and copy the key by hand. Otherwise you will lose it when you end the installation process. Should you want to save the **recovery.key** file, you have to have started the install process from a Live USB/DVD session. Choose "Try Linux Mint" instead of "Install Ubuntu" when you first start up the Live USB/DVD. Otherwise you will not be able to save the **recovery.key** file. If you have chosen "Install Linux Mint" the only way to save the recovery key it is open the **recovery.key** file and write down the numbers in it.

After installation, whenever you start up your system, you are prompted to enter that security key (see Figure 2-16).

Figure 2-16: Security key login

Detected Linux Mint operating system

If you have another Linux Mint operating system on your disk, you will have the option to erase the Linux Mint system and replace it with Linux Mint 21. If the installed Ubuntu system is version 21, then you are also given the option to upgrade your system, preserving your personal files and installed software. You are also given the option to erase the installed operating system, and install the new system.

If the current system has enough unused space, you are also given an install alongside option, resizing the disk to free up space, and installing Linux Mint 21 in added partitions on the free space. This will keep your original Linux system, as well as install the new one.

The message displayed on the Installation type dialog is something like this:

"This computer currently has Linux Mint 20 on it. What would you like to do?"

You are given three choices. The Upgrade Ubuntu option is selected by default.

If you choose to Erase Linux Mint and reinstall, you can also choose the options to encrypt the drive and to use LVM partitions.

On systems that also have Windows installed alongside Linux Mint, you are given the same options, but with an added option to erase everything including your Windows system. You are warned that both Windows and Linux Mint are installed on your system. Should you choose to erase Linux Mint and reinstall (the first entry), your Windows system will be preserved.

Detected Linux Mint operating system

If you have another Linux Mint operating system on your disk, you will have the option to erase the Linux Mint system and replace it with Linux Mint 21. If the installed Linux Mint system is version 21, then you are also given the option to upgrade your system, preserving your personal files and installed software. You are also given the option to erase the installed operating system, and install the new system.

If the current system has enough unused space, you are also given an install alongside option, resizing the disk to free up space, and installing Linux Mint 21 in added partitions on the free space. This will keep your original Linux system, as well as install the new one.

The message displayed on the Installation type dialog is something like this:

"This computer currently has Linux Mint 19 on it. What would you like to do?"

You are given three choices. The Upgrade Linux Mint option is selected by default.

If you choose to Erase Linux Mint and reinstall, you can also choose the options to encrypt the drive and to use LVM partitions.

On systems that also have Windows installed alongside Linux Mint, you are given the same options, but with an added option to erase everything including your Windows system. You are warned that both Windows and Linux Mint are installed on your system. Should you choose to erase Linux Mint 19 and reinstall (the first entry), your Windows system will be preserved.

Detected other operating systems with free space

If you have another operating system on your disk that has been allocated use of part of the disk, you will have an option beginning with "Install Linux Mint alongside" with the name of the installed operating system listed. For example, a system with Windows already installed will have the option "Install Linux Mint alongside Microsoft Windows ". This option is selected initially.

If you do have an operating system installed, but this message does not appear, then be sure to use the "Something else" option. Otherwise, you may overwrite and destroy your installed operating system. On some Windows installs with the EFI bios, the Windows install may not appear. Be sure to choose "Something else" and then manually configure your partitions for Linux Mint.

Detected other operating system using entire disk (resize)

If you have another operating system on your disk that has been allocated use of the entire disk, you will have an option beginning with "Install Linux Mint alongside" with the name of the installed operating system listed. A system with Windows already installed will have the option "Install Linux Mint alongside Microsoft Windows". This option is selected initially.

This option is designed for use on hard disks with no unallocated free space but with a large amount of unused space on an existing partition. This is the case for a system where a partition has already been allocated the entire disk. This option will perform a resize of the existing partition, reducing that partition, preserving the data on it, and then creating a Linux Mint partition on that free space. Be warned that this could be a very time-consuming operation. If the original operating system was used heavily, the disk could be fragmented, with files stored all over the hard disk. In this case, the files have to be moved to one area of the hard disk, freeing up continuous space on the remaining area. If the original operating system was used very lightly, then there may be unused continuous space already on the hard drive. In this case, re-partitioning would be quick.

On the "Install alongside" dialog two partitions are displayed, the original showing the new size it will have after the resize, and the new partition for Linux Mint 21 formed from the unused space. The size is automatically determined. You can adjust the size if you want by clicking on the space between the partitions to display a space icon, which you can drag left, or right to change the proportional sizes of the partitions.

Upon clicking the Install Now button, a dialog will prompt you with the warning that the resize cannot be undone, and that it may take a long time. Click Continue to perform the resize, or click Go Back to return to the "Installation type" screen. The time it will take depends on the amount of fragmentation on the disk.

Something else

All install situations will include a "Something else" option to let you partition the hard drive manually. The "Something else" option starts up the partitioner, which will let you create, edit, and delete partitions. You can set your own size and type for your partitions. Use this option to preserve or reuse any existing partitions. When you have finished making your changes, click the Install Now button to continue. At this point, your partitions are changed and software is installed, while you continue with the remaining install configuration for time zone and user login.

The partitioner screen displays the partitions on your current hard disk, and lists options for creating your Linux partitions. A graphical bar at the top shows the current state of your hard disk, showing any existing partitions, if any, along with their sizes and labels.

A Boot Loader section at the bottom of the screen provides a drop-down menu of hard drives where you can install the boot loader (see Figure 2-5). Your first hard drive is selected by default. If you have several hard drives on your system, you can choose the one on which to install the boot loader. Systems with only one hard drive, such as laptops, have only one hard drive entry.

The partitioner interface lists any existing partitions (see Figure 2-8). The graphical bar at the top will show the partitions on your selected hard drive. The depiction changes as you add, delete, or edit your partitions. Each partition device name and label will be displayed. Unused space will be labeled as free space.

Each hard disk is labeled by its device name, such as **sda** for the first Serial ATA device. Underneath the hard disk graphics bar are labels for the partitions and free space available, along with the partition type and size. The partitions are identified by their colors. At the bottom of the screen are actions you can perform on partitions and free space. To the right are the "New partition table" and Revert buttons for the entire disk. To the left are add, delete, and edit buttons for partitions (+, -, and Change). Your current hard disks and their partitions are listed in the main scrollable pane, with headings for Device, Type, Mount point, Format, Size, Used space, and System for each partition.

Creating new partitions on a blank hard drive manually

To create partitions on a blank hard drive manually, choose "Something else" (see Figure 2-17). The partitioner interface starts up with the "Installation type" screen, listing any existing partitions (see Figure 2-18). For a blank hard drive, the hard drive only is listed in the main pane.

Figure 2-17: Something Else (manual partitioning)

For a new blank hard drive, you first create the partition table by clicking the New Partition Table button (see Figure 2-18). This displays a warning that it will erase any data on the drive. Click Continue (see Figure 2-19). The warning dialog is there in case you accidentally click the New Partition Table button on a drive that has partitions you want to preserve. In this case, you can click Go Back and no new partition table is created.

Figure 2-18: Manually partitioning a new hard drive

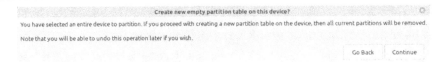

Figure 2-19: Create a new partition table on a blank hard drive

Once the new partition table is set up, the free space entry appears and a graphical bar at the top shows the free space (see Figure 2-20). If your system already has an operating system installed that takes up only part of the disk, you do not need to create a new partition table. Your free space is already listed.

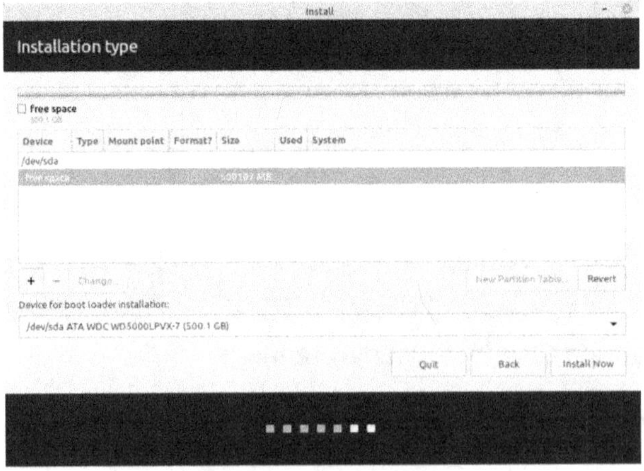

Figure 2-20: Select free space on a blank hard drive

For Linux Mint, you will have to create at least one partition, a Linux root partition, where your system will be installed. If your computer also supports EFI boot, as most do, you will also have to add a boot partition of type EFI System Partition. You can create other partitions if you wish. The swap partition is no longer needed. A swap file is used instead (**/swapfile**). You can, though, if you want, still set up and use a swap partition. To create a new partition, select the free space entry for the hard disk and click the + button. This opens a Create Partition dialog where you can choose the file system type (Use as) and the size of your partition (see Figure 2-21). Do this for each partition. The EFI and swap partitions have no mount point. You only set the size.

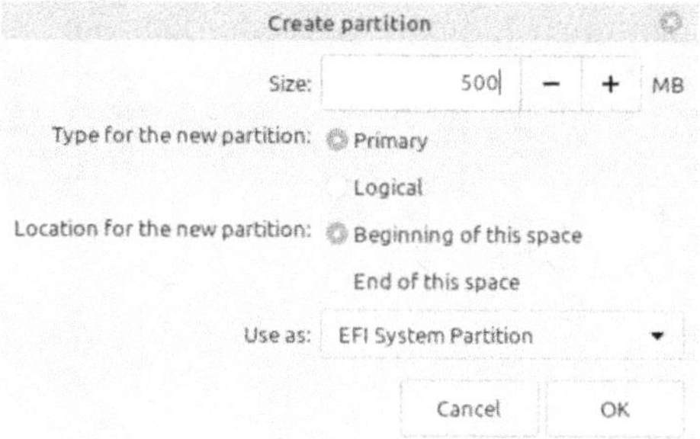

Figure 2-21: Create a new boot partition

The Create Partition dialog displays entries for the partition type (Primary or Logical), the size in megabytes, the location (beginning or end), the file system type (Use as), and the Mount point. For the partition type, the "Do not use" partition entry is initially selected. Choose a partition type from the drop-down menu. Select "Ext4 journaling file system" for the root partition and choose Boot for the boot partition.

For the root partition, from the Mount point drop down menu choose the mount point /, which is the root directory (see Figure 2-22). This is where your system will be installed. The size of the partition is specified in megabytes. It will be set to the remaining space. If you want to also set up additional partitions, such as a partition for the **/home** folder, reduce the size to allow space for those partitions.

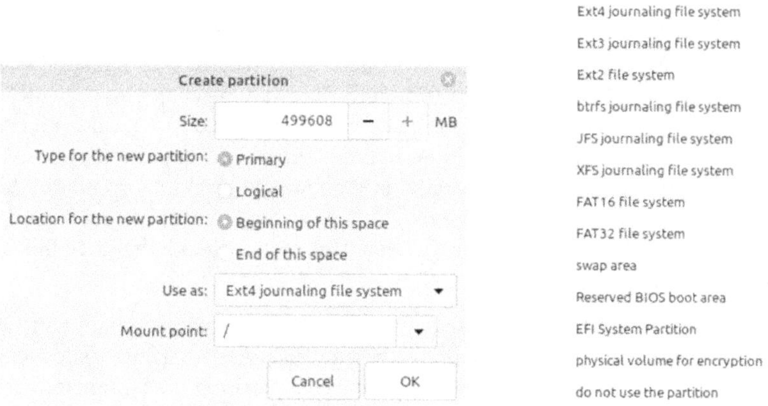

Figure 2-22: Create a new root partition

If you make a mistake, you can edit a partition by selecting it and clicking the Change button. This opens an Edit partitions window where you can make changes. You can also delete a partition, returning its space to free space, and then create a new one. Select the partition and click the - button (delete). The partition is not actually deleted at this point. No changes are made at all until you start installing Linux Mint. The "Revert" button is always available to undo all the possible changes you specified so far, and start over from the original state of the hard disk.

When you have finished setting up your partitions, you will see entries for them displayed. The graphical bar at the top will show their size and location (see Figure 2-23). Click the "Install Now" button to perform the partitioning, formatting, and installation.

Figure 2-23: Manual partitions

Reuse existing Linux partitions on a hard drive

If you already have a hard drive with Linux partitions that you want to reuse, you choose the "Something else" option on the "Installation type" screen. In this case, you have a hard disk you are using for Linux, with partitions already set up on the hard drive for your Linux Mint systems. However, you do not want to keep any of the data on those partitions. This situation occurs if you are using a previous Linux Mint version, but want a fresh install instead of an upgrade, and you do not want to perform any partitioning, keeping the current partition configuration. You can just overwrite the existing Linux Mint root partition. In effect, you just want to reuse those partitions for the new release, creating an entirely new install, but with the old partitions. With this action, all current data on those partitions will be destroyed. This procedure avoids having to change the partition table on the hard drive. You just keep the partitions you already have. In this case, you wish to overwrite existing partitions, erasing all the data on them.

This procedure is used often for users that have already backed up their data, and just want to create a fresh install on their hard disk with the new release. Also, a Linux system could be configured to save data on a partition separate from the root partition, like a separate partition for the /**home** directories. In this case, you would only need to overwrite the root partition, leaving the other Linux partitions alone.

Note: The New partition table becomes active whenever the top-level hard drive device name is selected instead of a particular partition. This will be initially selected when your Prepare partition screen is first displayed, activating the New partition table button. Do NOT click that button. It will wipe out any existing partitions.

To edit an existing partition, click on its entry and click the Change button. A dialog opens with entries for the partition type (Use as), a format checkbox, and the mount point.

To re-use partitions, all you have to do is edit your existing root partition. You will see your partitions listed.

You will have to know which partition is your root partition. It will have the type **ext4** and the mount point /. Once selected, the Change button will become active, which you click to open an Edit window. Select the type, which for Linux Mint 21 would be "Ext4 journaling file system", the **ext4** file system type. Then select the mount point, which, for the root partition, is /. The size remains the same. Once finished, you will see your Windows partition (**ntfs**) if there is one, as well as the swap and Linux root partition (**ext4**).

Once you have edited the root partition, you can click the "Install Now" button to continue on.

Where Are You?

On the "Where are you?" screen, you can set the time zone by using a map to specify your location (see Figure 2-24). The Time Zone tool uses a map feature that displays the entire earth, with sections for each time zone. Click on your general location, and the entire time zone for your part of the world will be highlighted. The major city closest to your location will be labeled with its current time. The selected city will appear in the text box located below the map. You can also select your time zone entering the city in the text box below. As you type in the city name, a pop-up menu appears showing progressively limited choices. The corresponding time zone will be highlighted on the map.

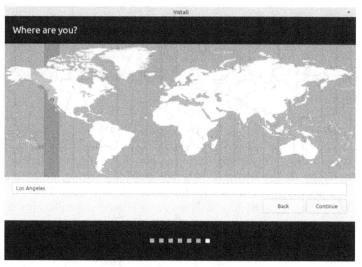

Figure 2-24: Where Are You, Time zone

Click the Continue button to continue.

At the same time as the "Where are you?" dialog appears, Linux Mint begins to format your partitions, copy files to your hard drive, and install the software. A progress bar at the bottom of the dialog shows the progression of the install process. You can click an expansion arrow next to the progress bar to open a small terminal section that displays the install operations as they occur.

Who Are You?

On the Who are you? screen you enter your name, your user login name, and password (see Figure 2-25). When you enter your name, a username will be generated for you using your first name, and a computer name will be entered using your first name and your computer's make and model name. You can change these names if you want. The name for the computer is the computer's network hostname. The user you are creating will have administrative access, allowing you to change your system configuration, add new users and printers, and install new software. When you enter your password a Strength notice is displayed indicating whether it is too short, weak, fair, or good. For a good password include numbers and uppercase characters.

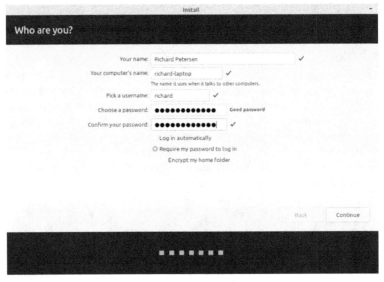

Figure 2-25: Who are you?

At the bottom of the screen, you have the options: "Log in automatically" and "Require my password to log in." The "Require my password to log in" option has an additional check box for "Encrypt my home folder." Choose the "Log in automatically" option to have your system login to your account when you start up, instead of stopping at the login screen. The "Require my password to log in" entry provides a standard login screen. If you choose "Encrypt my home folder" private directory encryption is set up for your home folder, encrypting all the home folder files and sub-folders.

If your computer supports a camera, the next screen will prompt you to choose an image to use for the user. You can choose an icon or snap a picture of yourself.

Install Progress

Your installation continues with a slide show of Linux Mint 21 features such as Web browsers, services, Software Manager, and photo editing. You can click on the arrow tabs at either end to move through the slide show manually (see Figure 2-26).

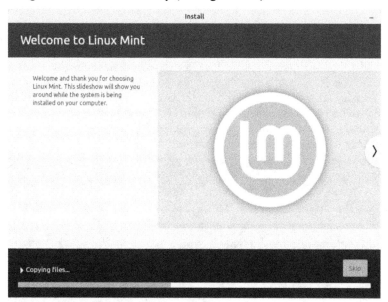

Figure 2-26: Install progress slide show

Note: Should the installation fail to install the boot loader, you can use Boot Repair to install it.

Once finished, the Installation Complete dialog appears (see Figure 2-27). Click the Restart Now button to restart and reboot to the new installation. A screen will appear prompting you to remove the disc, and then press ENTER. You are also given the option to return to the Live DVD/USB session.

Figure 2-27: Reboot or Continue Testing

Tip: Pressing ESC from the graphics menu places you at the boot prompt for text mode install.

Recovery, rescue, and boot loader re-install

Linux Mint provides the means to start up systems that have failed for some reason. A system that may boot but fails to start up, can be started in a recovery mode, already set up for you as an entry on your boot loader Advanced Options menu.

Recovery Mode

If for some reason your system is not able to start up, it may be due to conflicting configurations, libraries, or applications. On the GRUB menu first, choose the "Advanced options for Linux Mint" to open the advanced options menu (see Figure 2-28). Then select the recovery mode entry, the Linux Mint kernel entry with the (recovery mode) label attached to the end. This starts up a menu where you can use the arrow and ENTER keys to select from several recovery options (see Figure 2-29). These include resume, clean, dpkg, grub, network, and root. Short descriptions for each item are displayed on the menu.

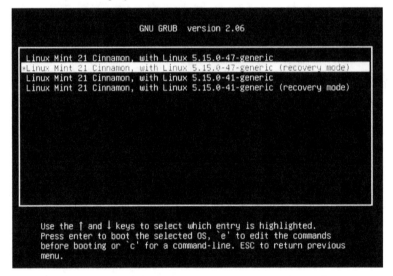

Figure 2-28: Grub advanced options menu with recovery kernels

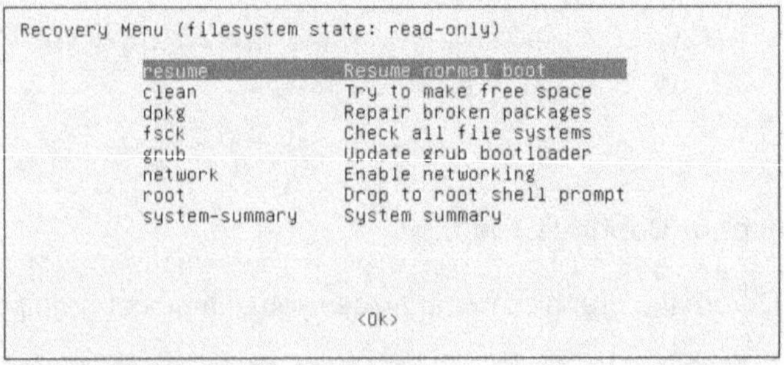

Figure 2-29: Recovery options

The root option starts up Linux Mint as the root user with a command line shell prompt. In this case, you can boot your Linux system in a recovery mode and then edit configuration files with a text editor such as Vi or nano, remove the suspect libraries, or reinstall damaged software with **apt**.

The resume entry will start up Linux Mint normally.

The **grub** entry will update the grub boot loader. With GRUB2 your hard drive is re-scanned, detecting your installed operating systems and Linux Mint kernels, and implementing any GRUB configuration changes you may have made without updating GRUB.

To rescue a broken system, choose the **root** entry. Your broken system will be mounted and made accessible with a command line interface. You can then use command line operations and editors to fix configuration files.

Re-Installing the Boot Loader: Boot Repair and grub-install

If you have a multiple-boot system, that runs both Windows and Linux on the same machine, you may run into a situation where you have to reinstall your GRUB boot loader. This problem occurs if your Windows system completely crashes beyond repair and you have to install a new version of Windows, if you added Windows to your machine after having installed Linux, or if you upgraded to a new version of Windows. A Windows installation will automatically overwrite your bootloader (alternatively, you could install your boot loader on your Linux partition instead of the master boot record, MBR). You will no longer be able to access your Linux system.

The Linux Mint ISO provides the Boot Repair tool, accessible from the Administration menu, which you can use to easily repair and reinstall the boot loader (see Figure 2-30). It provides a simple option (Recommended Repair) to automatically repair the boot loader. Should your install process fail to install the boot loader, you can use Boot Repair to install it. The Advanced Options opens tabs where you can back up the partition tables, rename Windows EFI files, specify the boot locations, Grub options such as secure boot, and add any other options you may need.

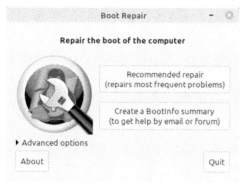

Figure 2-30: Boot Repair

You can reinstall your boot loader manually, using your Linux Mint USB/DVD live session. The procedure is more complicated, as you have to mount your Linux Mint system. On the Linux Mint USB/DVD Live session, you can use GParted to find out what partition your Linux Mint system uses. In a terminal window, create a directory on which to mount the system.

```
sudo mkdir mymint
```

Then mount it, making sure you have the correct file system type and partition name (usually **/dev/sda5** on dual boot systems).

```
sudo mount -t ext4 /dev/sda5  mymint
```

Then use **grub-install** and the device name of your first partition to install the boot loader, with the **--root-directory** option to specify the directory where you mounted your Linux Mint file system. The **--root-directory** option requires a full path name, which for the Linux Mint USB/DVD would be **/home/mint** for the home directory. Using the **mymint** directory for this example, the full path name of the Linux Mint file system would be **/home/mint/mymint**. You would then enter the following **grub-install** command.

```
sudo grub-install --root-directory=/home/mint/mymint /dev/sda
```

This will re-install your current GRUB boot loader. You can then reboot, and the GRUB boot loader will start up.

Tip: If the install fails with the failure to install the grub2 bootloader, try removing all network connections and disabling your network on the live disk desktop before installing.

3. Usage Basics: Login, Desktop, Network, and Help

Accessing your Linux Mint System

LightDM Display Manager

Linux Mint Desktops (Cinnamon, MATE, and Xfce)

First Steps

Network Connections: wired and wireless

Warpinator

Printing

Display configuration

Online Accounts

System Reports

Help Resources

Terminal Window

Command Line Interface

Using Linux Mint is an intuitive process, with easy-to-use interfaces, including graphical logins and desktops, including the Cinnamon, MATE, and Xfce Linux Mint desktops. Even the standard Linux command line interface is user-friendly with editable commands, history lists, and cursor-based tools. To start using Linux Mint, you have to know how to access your system and, once you are on the system, how to execute commands and run applications. Access is provided by a display manager that provides a graphical login.

Accessing Your Linux Mint System

You access your Linux Mint system using the GRUB bootloader to first start Linux Mint, and then use the display manager to log in to your account. Linux Mint, like Ubuntu, uses the systemd login manager, logind, to manage logins and sessions, replacing consolekit, which is no longer supported. You can configure login manager options with the **/etc/systemd/logind.conf** file. You can set options such as the number of terminals (default is 6), the idle action, and hardware key operations, such as the power key. Check the **logind.conf** man page for details.

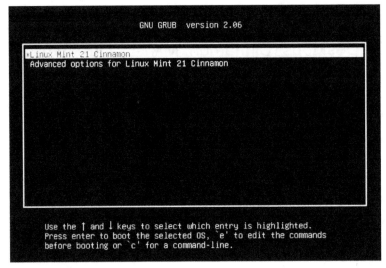

Figure 3-1: Linux Mint GRUB menu

GRUB Boot Loader

When your system starts, the GRUB boot loader will quickly select your default operating system and start up its login screen. If you have just installed Linux Mint, the default operating system will be Linux Mint.

If you have installed more than one operating system, you can select one using the GRUB menu. The GRUB menu is displayed for several seconds at startup, before loading the default operating system automatically. Press the ESC key to have GRUB wait until you have made a selection. Your GRUB menu is displayed as shown in Figure 3-1. The Advanced Options entry opens a menu of previously installed Linux Mint kernels you can start your system with, as well a recovery mode entry for each. A recovery mode entry allows you to start Linux Mint in recovery mode (See Chapter 2).

The GRUB menu lists Linux Mint and other operating systems installed on your hard drive, such as Windows. Use the arrow keys to move to the entry you want and press ENTER.

For graphical installations, some displays may have difficulty running the graphical startup display. If you have this problem, you can edit your Linux GRUB entry and remove the **splash** term at the end of the **linux** line. Press the **e** key to edit a GRUB entry (see Figure 3-2). To change a particular line, use the up/down arrow keys to move to the line. You can use the left/right arrow keys to move along the line. The Backspace key will delete characters and typing will insert characters. The editing changes are temporary. Permanent changes can only be made by directly editing the GRUB configuration **/etc/default/grub** file, and then running the following command:

```
sudo update-grub
```

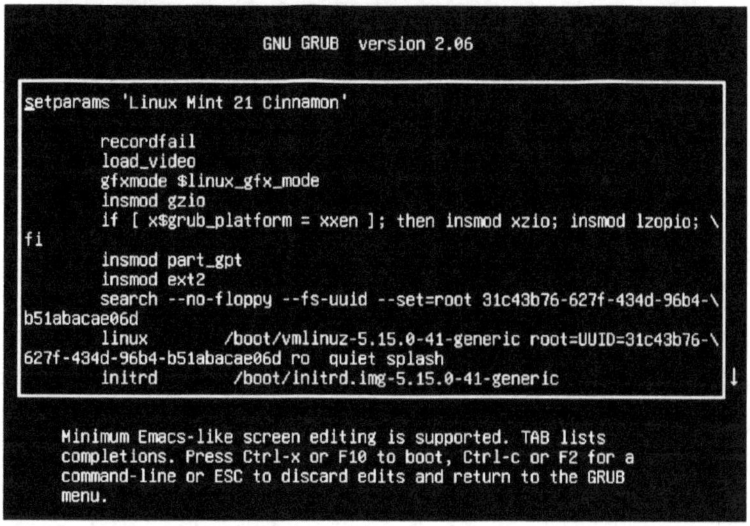

```
                    GNU GRUB  version 2.06

setparams 'Linux Mint 21 Cinnamon'

        recordfail
        load_video
        gfxmode $linux_gfx_mode
        insmod gzio
        if [ x$grub_platform = xxen ]; then insmod xzio; insmod lzopio; \
fi
        insmod part_gpt
        insmod ext2
        search --no-floppy --fs-uuid --set=root 31c43b76-627f-434d-96b4-\
b51abacae06d
        linux        /boot/vmlinuz-5.15.0-41-generic root=UUID=31c43b76-\
627f-434d-96b4-b51abacae06d ro  quiet splash
        initrd       /boot/initrd.img-5.15.0-41-generic              ↓


    Minimum Emacs-like screen editing is supported. TAB lists
    completions. Press Ctrl-x or F10 to boot, Ctrl-c or F2 for a
    command-line or ESC to discard edits and return to the GRUB
    menu.
```

Figure 3-2: Editing a GRUB menu item

When your Linux Mint operating system starts up, a Linux Mint logo appears during the startup. You can press the ESC key to see the startup messages instead. Linux Mint uses Plymouth with its kernel modesetting ability to display a startup animation. The Plymouth Linux Mint logo theme is used by default.

You can also install the new Linux Mint Grub theme for a more stylish Grub menu. Install the Grub2-theme-mint package (Grub2-theme-mint-2k for 2k displays) using Software Manager, the Synaptic Package Manager, or the **apt** command. Then run the **sudo update-grub** command in a terminal window.

```
sudo apt install grub2-theme-mint
sudo update-grub
```

When you start your system up again and display the Grub menu, you will see the new Linux Mint theme, with icons for different installed desktops (see Figure 3-3).

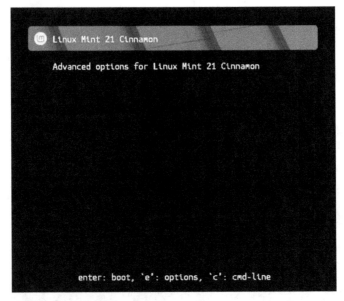

Figure 3-3: GRUB2 Linux Mint Theme

The LightDM Display Manager

The graphical login interface displays a login window listing a menu of usernames. The currently selected username displays a text box where you then enter your password. Upon pressing ENTER, you log in to the selected account and your desktop starts up. Graphical logins are handled by the LightDM display manager. LightDM manages the login interface along with authenticating a user password and username, and then starting up a selected desktop. LightDM replaces the older Mint Display Manager (MDM), though the Mint implementation of LightDM uses a customized greeter called Slick Greeter. LightDM and Slick Greeter can be configured with the System Settings Login Window dialog. You can also configure Slick Greeter with the dconf editor (**x.dm.slick-greeter**).

From the LightDM login screen, you can shift to the command line interface with the Ctrl-Alt-F1 keys, and then shift back to the LightDM with the Ctrl-Alt-F7 keys. The keys F1 through F6 provide different command line terminals, as in Ctrl-Alt-F3 for the third command line terminal.

When LightDM starts up, it shows a list of users, displaying a dialog that lets you enter a username at the login prompt. You can use your mouse or arrow keys to move through the list of users, displaying a login dialog for the currently selected user (see Figure 3-4). The login dialog displays the user's proper name. Below a selected username is a text box for entering a password. Once the password is entered, press ENTER. The desktop then starts up. If you log out from a user desktop, you will return to the LightDM login screen.

Figure 3-4: LightDM Login Screen with user list

To top right corner of the screen shows a power icon. When you click this icon, a menu appears with entries Suspend or Quit. Clicking the Quit entry displays a dialog with Shutdown and Restart buttons. Click the close box to cancel (see Figure 3-5). To shut down your Linux Mint system, click the Shut Down icon. The top right corner also shows current keyboard, time, and an assistive technology button. Click on the assistive technology button to display a menu for the onscreen keyboard, high contrast display, and the screen reader (voice). The top left corner shows your computer's hostname.

Figure 3-5: LightDM Login Screen with Shut Down options

To the right of each login name is a sessions button. The session button displays an emblem indicating the currently selected desktop. There are emblems for Cinnamon, MATE, and Xfce. If you have installed more than one desktop interface, such as Linux Mint MATE, you can use the session menu to choose one. Click on the session button to display the session menu (see Figure 3-6) from which you can select the desktop interface you want to start up. The menu shows all installed possible desktop interfaces. Here you can choose MATE to use the MATE Desktop, "Xfce Session" to use the Xfce desktop or Cinnamon for the Cinnamon desktop. Use the arrow keys or mouse to choose a selection. Once you have made the selection click the back arrow to return to the login entry. A desktop option is not shown unless you have already installed that desktop, such as MATE (use the **mint-meta** packages to install a desktop, such as **mint-meta-mate** for MATE). The default session is the last desktop you logged out of.

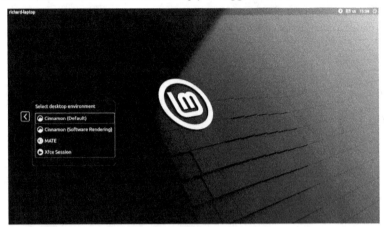

Figure 3-6: LightDM Login screen with desktop choices

Login Window Preferences

You can configure your login screen using Login Window dialog, accessible from System Settings Login Window and from the Administration menu as Login Window. The Login Window dialog shows three tabs: Appearance, Users, and Settings. The Appearance tab displays options such as the desktop (GTK) theme, icon theme, mouse cursor theme, background image, and background color (see Figure 3-7). The default theme is Mint-X. On the Users tab you can choose to allow manual logins and specify the automatic login user, as well as allow guest sessions or hide the user list. You can set a delay for the automatic login. On the Settings tab you can decide what panel indicators to display such as your hostname, battery status, clock, and quit menu. Turning off the show hostname and keyboard layout options removes them from the login screen (see Figure 3-8). Configuration files for LightDM are located in the **/etc/lightdm** folder.

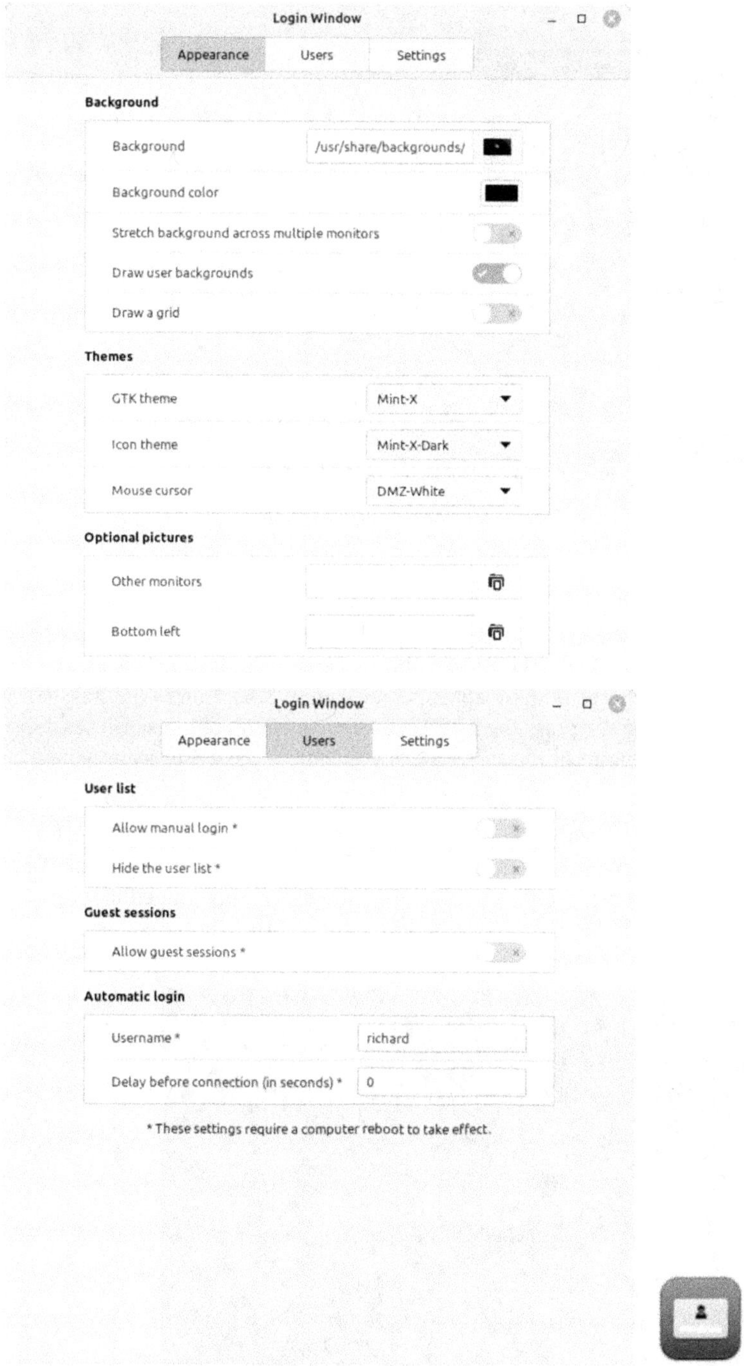

Figure 3-7: Login Window Preferences

Figure 3-8: Login Window with no hostname or keyboard layout

Lock Screen and Switch User

You can choose to lock your screen and suspend your system by choosing the Lock button in the desktop menu, or by pressing Ctrl-Alt-L. The Screen shows the time and date. To start up again, press the spacebar and the Lock Screen dialog appears (see Figure 3-9). Enter your password and click the unlock button (unlock icon) or press the ENTER key to start up your desktop session again. An onscreen keyboard (center bottom of the screen) lets you enter a password using your mouse.

You can switch to another user by clicking the Switch User button on the Logout dialog or, on the lock screen, the switch user button located next to the unlock button (people image). The LightDM login screen starts up and you can login as another user. Users already logged in will have an arrow emblem to the left of their names. When you log out, you are returned to the LightDM login screen.

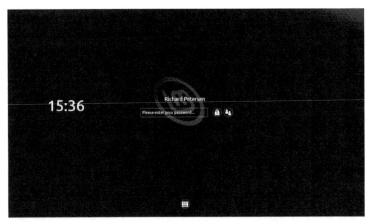

Figure 3-9: Lock Screen and Screensaver

Shut down and Logging out

To shut down from Linux Mint, click the power button on the desktop menu (Cinnamon or MATE). A dialog opens with the shutdown options: Suspend, Restart, and Shut Down (see Figure 3-10).

There are several ways to shut down your system:

Click the power button on the desktop menu to display the shutdown dialog.

Press the power button on your computer to open the shutdown dialog.

Open a terminal window and enter the **poweroff** command.

Should your display freeze or become corrupted, one safe way to shut down and restart is to press a command line interface key (like Ctrl-Alt-F1) to revert to the command line interface, and then press Ctrl-Alt-DEL to restart. You can also log in on the command line interface and then enter the **sudo poweroff** command.

Use Suspend to stop your system temporarily, using little or no power. Press the space key to redisplay the locked login screen where you can access your account again and continue your session from where you left off.

Figure 3-10: Shut Down and Restart dialog

To log out, you can use the Log Out button on the desktop menu (Cinnamon or MATE), which returns you to the log in screen where you log in again as a different user (see Figure 3-11). You also have the option to switch users.

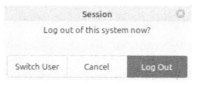

Figure 3-11: Log Out dialog

Accessing Linux from the Command Line Interface

You can access the command-line interface by pressing Ctrl-Alt-F1 at any time (Ctrl-Alt-F7 returns to the graphics interface). For the command line interface, you are initially given a login prompt. The login prompt is preceded by the hostname you gave your system. In this example, the hostname is **richard-laptop**. When you finish using Linux, you log out with the **logout** command. Linux then displays the same login prompt, waiting for you or another user to log in again. This is the equivalent of the login window provided by the LightDM. You can then log in to another account.

Once you log in as a user, you can enter and execute commands. To log in, enter your username and your password. If you make a mistake, you can erase characters with the BACKSPACE key. In the next example, the user enters the username **richard** and is then prompted to enter the password:

```
Linux Mint 21 Vanessa richard-laptop tty1

richard-laptop login: richard
Password:
```

When you type in your password, it does not appear on the screen. This is to protect your password from being seen by others. If you enter either the username or the password incorrectly, the system will respond with the error message "Login incorrect" and will ask for your username again, starting the login process over. You can then reenter your username and password.

Once you enter your username and password, you are logged in to the system and the command line prompt is displayed, waiting for you to enter a command. The command line prompt is a dollar sign (**$**). On Linux Mint, your prompt is preceded by the hostname and the directory you are in. The home directory is indicated by a tilde (~).

```
richard@richard-laptop:~$
richard@richard-laptop:~$ cd Pictures
richard@richard-laptop:~/Pictures$
```

To end your session, issue the **logout** or **exit** command. This returns you to the login prompt, and Linux waits for another user to log in.

```
richard@richard-laptop:~$ logout
```

To, instead, shut down your system from the command line, you enter the **poweroff** command. This command will log you out and shut down the system. If you are not a user with administrative access, you will have to add the **sudo** command.

```
richard@richard-laptop:~$ poweroff
```

The Linux Mint Desktops

Linux Mint 21 supports three different desktops: Cinnamon, MATE, and XFCE. Linux Mint is based on the Ubuntu Linux distribution. Many of its packages, especially in the case of servers, are taken directly from Ubuntu repositories. But its desktops are completely different. Cinnamon is a new desktop developed and maintained by Linux Mint. It is completely different than the Ubuntu desktop. MATE is derived directly from the older GNOME 2 desktop.

You can add a desktop to any Linux Mint version you installed, by using the Software Manager to install the **mint-meta** package for the desktop you want. There are mint-meta packages for Cinnamon, MATE, and XFCE.

```
mint-meta-cinnamon
mint-meta-mate
mint-meta-xfce
```

For the Linux Mint version of a desktop, be sure to install the **mint-meta** meta package for it, not the Ubuntu meta package.

Note: The Linux Mint version of KDE has been discontinued. You can still install the Ubuntu version of KDE, Kubuntu, using the kubuntu-desktop meta package. The KDE desktop will be listed as Plasma on the LightDM list of desktop login options.

Cinnamon

The Linux Mint Cinnamon desktop is a new desktop that retains some of the features found in GNOME 2, such as applets and panels (see Figure 3-12). Some of the configuration dialogs are similar to those used for GNOME 3. The Cinnamon bottom panel displays the system applets. The left side of the panel is the Cinnamon menu and the grouped window list applet, which shows buttons for the currently open windows. The Cinnamon ISO is available in 64-bit, **linuxmint-20-cinnamon-64bit.iso**.

Figure 3-12: Linux Mint Cinnamon desktop

The Cinnamon desktop prefers hardware acceleration support provided by the appropriate display driver. If your current graphics driver does not support hardware acceleration, you will be logged into Cinnamon using software rendering, which uses acceleration simulation with LLVMpipe on OpenGL running on the CPU. This can result in a slower system.

The right side of the panel holds system applets for the network manager, sound volume, updates, and date and time (calendar). When you open a window, a button for it is displayed on the bottom panel in the grouped window list applet. Unique to Cinnamon is the Cinnamon menu, which incorporates a favorites bar similar to the dock in Ubuntu (see Figure 3-13).

Figure 3-13: Linux Mint Cinnamon menu

Cinnamon places the window control buttons (close, maximize, and minimize buttons) on the right side of a window title bar, as shown here. There are three window buttons: an x for close, a dash (-) for minimize, and an expand icon for maximize.

window buttons

To move a window, click and drag its title bar. Double-clicking the title bar will maximize the window. Many keyboard operations are also similar as listed in Table 3-1.

Keypress	Action
SHIFT	Move a file or directory, default
Ctrl	Copy a file or directory
Ctrl-SHIFT	Create a link for a file or directory
F2	Rename selected file or directory
Ctrl-Alt-Arrow (right, left, up, down)	Move to a different desktop
Ctrl-w	Close current window
ALT-spacebar	Open window menu for window operations
ALT-F2	Open Run command box
ALT-F1	Open Applications menu
Ctrl-F	Find file

Table 3-1: Window and File Manager Keyboard shortcuts

Cinnamon uses the Nemo file manager. You can access your home folder by clicking the Home Folder icon on the desktop, or the home folder button on the panel. A file manager window opens showing your home directory. Your home directory will already have default directories created for commonly used files. These include Pictures, Documents, Music, Videos, and Downloads.

Your office applications automatically save files to the Documents directory by default. Image and photo applications place image files in the Pictures directory. The Desktop folder will hold all files and directories saved to your desktop. When you download a file, it is placed in the Downloads directory. The file manager window displays several components, including a browser toolbar, location bar, and a sidebar showing devices, file systems, and folders. When you open a new folder, the same window is used to display it, and you can use the forward and back arrows to move through previously opened folders. The location bar displays folder buttons showing your current folder and its parent folders. You can click on a parent folder to move to it. Figure 3-14 shows the file manager window.

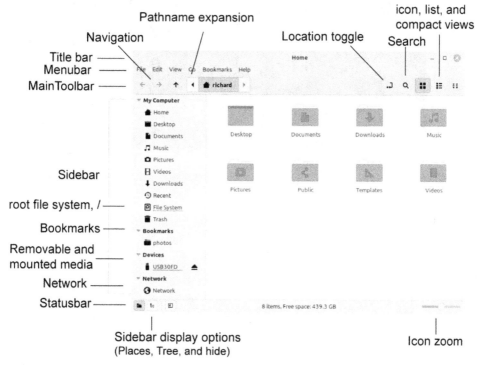

Figure 3-14: Nemo File manager

The file manager supports full drag-and-drop capabilities using combinations of key presses and mouse clicks. You can drag folders, icons, and applications to the desktop or other file manager windows open to other folders. The move operation is the default drag operation (you can also press the SHIFT key while dragging). To copy files, press the Ctrl key and then click-and-drag before releasing the mouse button. To create a link (shortcut), hold down both the Ctrl and SHIFT keys while dragging the icon to where you want the link to appear, such as the desktop.

MATE

The MATE desktop, though it appears similar to Cinnamon, is very much a GNOME 2 desktop (see Figure 3-15). The bottom panel displays applets. The left side of the panel is the Linux Mint menu for MATE. The right side of the panel holds system applets for the network manager, sound volume, updates, and the date and time. When you open a window, its button is displayed on the bottom panel in the window list applet. The MATE ISO is available in 64-bit, **linuxmint-20-mate-64bit.iso**.

Figure 3-15: Linux Mint MATE desktop

Unique to the Linux Mint version of MATE is the Linux Mint menu, which shows places and system sections, as well as a Favorites view for applications (see Figure 3-16).

Figure 3-16: Linux Mint Menu (MATE)

MATE places the window control buttons (close, maximize, and minimize buttons) on the right side of a window title bar, using the same buttons as Cinnamon: an x for close, a dash (-) for minimize, and an expand icon for maximize.

window buttons

To move a window, click and drag its title bar. Double-clicking the title bar will maximize the window. Many keyboard operations are also similar as listed in Table 3-1.

MATE uses the Caja file manager. You can access your home folder from its entry in the Places section of the Linux Mint menu, or by clicking the Home Folder icon on the desktop. A file manager window opens showing your home directory. Your home directory will already have default directories created for commonly used files. These include Pictures, Documents, Music, Videos, and Downloads.

Your office applications automatically save files to the Documents directory by default. Image and photo applications place image files in the Pictures directory. The Desktop folder will hold all files and directories saved to your desktop. When you download a file, it is placed in the Downloads directory.

The file manager window displays several components, including a browser toolbar, location bar, and a side pane with several views including places, tree, and information. When you open a new folder, the same window is used to display it, and you can use the forward and back arrows to move through previously opened directories. The location bar displays folder buttons showing your current folder and its parent folders. You can click on a parent folder button to move to it. Figure 3-17 shows the file manager window.

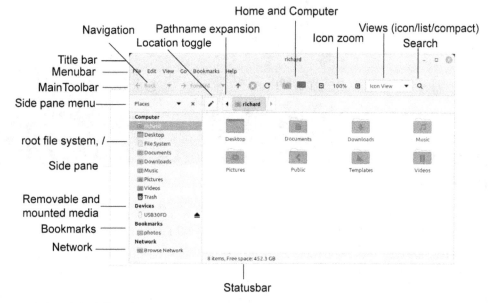

Figure 3-17: Caja File manager

The file manager supports full drag-and-drop capabilities using combinations of key presses and mouse clicks. You can drag folders, icons, and applications to the desktop or other file manager windows open to other folders. The move operation is the default drag operation (you can also press the SHIFT key while dragging). To copy files, press the Ctrl key and then click-and-drag before releasing the mouse button. To create a link (shortcut), hold down both the Ctrl and SHIFT keys while dragging the icon to where you want the link to appear, such as the desktop.

Xfce Desktop

The Xfce desktop is a lightweight desktop designed to run fast without the kind of overhead required for full-featured desktops like Cinnamon and MATE. You can think of it as a window manager with desktop functionality. It includes its own file manager and panel, but the emphasis is on modularity and simplicity. Like GNOME, Xfce is based on GTK+ GUI tools. The desktop consists of a collection of modules like the Thunar file manager, xfce4-panel panel, and the xfwm4 window manager. Keeping with its focus on simplicity, Xfce features only a few common applets on its panel. It small scale makes it appropriate for laptops or dedicated systems, that have no need for the complex overhead found in other desktops. Xfce is also useful for desktops designed for just a few tasks, like multimedia desktops.

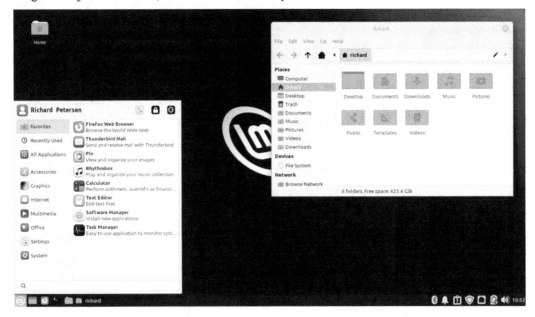

Figure 3-18: Xfce desktop

To install Xfce as an alternative desktop on a Linux Mint system, select the Xfce metapackage, **mint-meta-xfce**. This installs the Linux Mint Xfce desktop.

You can install the Linux Mint version of Xfce as the primary desktop using the Linux Mint Xfce ISO. The Xfce ISO is available as a 64-bit version, **linuxmint-20-xfce-64bit.iso**. You can then burn the ISO and run it as a USB/DVD. Double-click the Install icon to install Xfce on your computer. Follow the same basic steps for installing Linux Mint Xfce as for Linux Mint

Cinnamon or MATE. Like Cinnamon and MATE, Xfce also uses the LightDM Display Manager (LightDM) for logging in. Linux Mint 21 installs Xfce version 4.14.

Xfce desktop shows a single expanded panel at the bottom (see Figure 3-18). The desktop displays an icon for your Home directory (upper left). Xfce displays a bottom panel with a button for a Whisker applications menu at the left. From this menu, you can access any software applications, along with administration tools. You can configure the Whisker menu by right-clicking on its icon and choose Properties to open its configuration dialog. To the right of the menu are icons for Show Desktop, the Firefox Web browser, the terminal window, the file manager, and the taskbar, showing buttons for open windows. The right side of the panel shows the time and date, network connections (Network Manager), sound volume, and notifications. A helpful item to add to the panel is the Places menu, which shows entries for your home folder, recent documents, and bookmarked folders, such as Documents and Pictures, as well as for the File System, Desktop folder, and your attached storage devices.

You can add more items by clicking the panel and choosing the Panel menu, and then selecting the "Add New Items" entry. This opens a window with several applets, such as the clock, workspace switcher, applications menu, and launcher. The launcher applet lets you specify an application to start and choose an icon image for it. To move an applet, right-click it and choose Move from the pop-up menu. Then move the mouse to the new insertion location and click.

The top of the Whisker menu shows the username and a toolbar with buttons for Settings, Lock screen, and the shutdown dialog (see Figure 3-19). At the bottom of the menu is a search box for locating applications. The left side of the menu lists the application categories, including Favorites, Recently Used, and All Applications. The Settings entry lists your system administration tools.

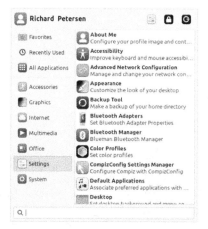

Figure 3-19: Xfce Whisker menu

Xfce file manager is called Thunar. The file manager will open a side pane in the shortcuts view that lists entries not only for the home directory but also for your file system, desktop, and trash contents. The File menu lets you perform folder operations, such as creating new directories. From the Edit menu, you can perform tasks on a selected file, such as renaming the file or creating a link for it. You can change the side pane view to a tree view of your file system by selecting from the menu bar View | Side Pane | Tree (Ctrl+e). The Shortcuts entry changes the view back (Ctrl+b).

To configure the Xfce interface, you use the Xfce Settings Manager, accessible by clicking the system settings icon in the top bar of the Whisker applications menu. This opens the Settings window, which shows icons for your desktop, display, panel, and appearance, among others (see Figure 3-20). Use the Appearance tool to select themes, icons, and toolbar styles (Settings). The Panel tool lets you add new panels and control features, such as fixed for freely movable and horizontally or vertically positioned. To configure the desktop, select the Desktop icon in the Settings window to open the Desktop window where you can select the background image (Background tab), control menu behavior (Menus tab), and set icon sizes (Icons tab).

Note: You can also access applications and Desktop Settings by right clicking on the desktop background to display the desktop menu.

Figure 3-20: Xfce Settings Manager

Linux Mint Debian Edition (LMDE)

The Linux Mint Debian Edition, LMDE, installs the original Debian Linux distribution, instead of the Ubuntu distribution. Debian upgrades packages as they are changed, instead of waiting for a release version as Ubuntu does. LMDE runs the latest version of Cinnamon and MATE. Major upgrades to both Debian packages and Cinnamon/MATE packages are installed as they become available. The install process is much the same as Linux Mint, with a few exceptions. You can choose the partition to install the GRUB bootloader on, and manual partitioning uses GParted and has an expert mode for complex installs.

First Steps

When you first start up your Linux Mint desktop, a welcome screen is displayed with tabs for First Steps, Documentation, Help, and Contribute. You can also display this screen by choosing Welcome Screen under Preferences in the Cinnamon menu. The First Steps tab lists applications you should run to set up your system as well as configuration options such as layout and colors (see Figure 3-21).

Figure 3-21: Welcome Screen - First Steps

Desktop Colors sets the colors used for icons, highlights, and buttons. Click on one of the colors displayed. For better contrast, especially at night, you can switch from a light theme to a dark theme for your windows, changing the background for titlebars, toolbars, sidebars, and the main window from light to dark, and changing the font color for text from black to white.

The Desktop Layout allows you to choose the Traditional layout used in previous releases or the Modern layout used since Linux Mint 19.1. The Modern layout makes changes to the panel, which features grouped windows and a larger panel. You can switch between the two by starting the Welcome Screen (Preferences menu) and selecting the one you want on the First Steps tab. The change will be made immediately. The Modern layout is used in the examples for this book. The Traditional Layout is discussed in Chapter 6.

The System Snapshot sets up a recovery point for restoring your system, should it fail (Timeshift, see Chapter 4). The Driver Manager lets you install any proprietary drivers you may need such as graphics drivers. The Update Manager installs the latest updates (see Chapter 4). You should always run this after installing a new system to make sure you have the latest updates.

System Settings lists numerous dialogs for configuring your system (desktop configuration is described in chapter 6). With the Software Manager you can install new applications, all free and available directly from the Linux Mint and Ubuntu repositories (see Chapter 4). Firewall lets you start and set up your firewall (Gufw) (see Chapter 10).

Accessing File Systems and Devices

From the file manager, desktop, and panel you can access removable media and all your mounted file systems, remote and local, including any Windows shared directories accessible from Samba.

On Cinnamon and MATE, you can access your file systems and removable media using any file manager window's sidebar or side pane, as shown here.

On Cinnamon and MATE, you can also access file systems and removable media by opening the Computer folder. To open the computer folder, double click on the Computer desktop icon or select Computer from a file manager Go menu. The Computer folder shows icons for all removable media (mounted CD/DVD-ROMs, USB drives, and so on), your local file system, additional partitions, and your network shared resources (see Figure 3-22). Double-click any icon to open a file manager window displaying its contents. The File System icon will open a window showing the top-level directory for your file system. Access will be restricted for system folders. On Cinnamon, you can use the "Open as Root" entry on the desktop menu (right-click on the desktop) to open a file manager window that can access system files with read/write access. Also, in a terminal window, you can use the **sudo** command to perform any operations on system files.

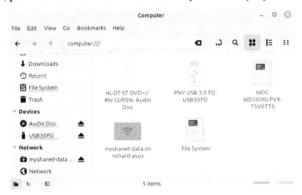

Figure 3-22: Computer folders

On Cinnamon and MATE, file systems on removable media and mounted file systems will also appear automatically as icons on the desktop. A DVD/CD-ROM is automatically mounted when you insert it into your DVD/CD-ROM drive, displaying an icon for it with its label (see Figure 3-23). The same kind of access is also provided for card readers, digital cameras, USB drives, and external hard drives. When you attach an external drive, it will be mounted automatically and opened in a file manager window. Be sure to unmount (Eject) the USB or external drives before removing them so that data will be written.

On Cinnamon and MATE, when removable drives are attached, a button for removable drives appears on the panel (the Removable drives applet). Clicking on the button opens a menu listing attached drives, with an eject button you can click to remove the drive (See Figure 3-22). On Cinnamon, you can also access removable drives from the Mint menu under the Places submenu.

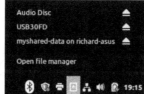

Figure 3-23: Accessing removeable drives on the desktop

If you have already configured associated applications for audio and video CD/DVD discs, or discs with images, sound, or video files, the disc will be opened with the appropriate application; like Pix for images, Rhythmbox for audio, and Celluloid for DVD/video.

You can access a DVD/CD-ROM disc or USB drive from the desktop by double-clicking its icon on the desktop, or from the Computer window by right clicking on the DVD/CD-ROM icon and selecting the Open entry, or from a file manager window's side pane. A file manager window opens to display the contents of the DVD/CD-ROM disc. To eject a DVD/CD-ROM, you right-click its icon and select Eject from the pop-up menu. The same procedure works for USB drives, using the USB drive icon.

To see network resources, click the Other Locations entry in the file manager sidebar. This network window will list your connected network Linux computers. Opening these networks displays the shares they provide, such as shared folders that you can have access to. Drag-and-drop operations are supported for all shared directories, letting you copy files and folders between a shared folder on another computer with a folder on your system. Opening a network resource may require you to login to access the resource. Currently, because of the transition from SMBv1 to

SMBv3, browsing for Windows shares (Samba) does not work. You have to access a specific Windows share directly using its host name and folder name (see Chapter 9).

Accessing Archives from GNOME: Archive Manager

Linux Mint supports the access of archives directly from GNOME using Archive Manager. You can select the archive file, then right-click and select Archive Mounter to open the archive. The archive contents are listed by Archive Manager. You can extract or display the contents.

You can also use Archive Manager to open CD/DVD disk ISO image files as archives. You can then browse and extract the contents of the CD/DVD. Right-click on a ISO disk image file (**.iso** extension) and select "Open with Other Application" and then choose "Archive Manager" on the Select Application dialog. The ISO image file is opened as an archive in Archive Manager.

Mounting ISO Disk Image files: Disk Image Mounter

You can use the GNOME Disk Utility's Disk Image Mounter to mount any ISO disk image file as a file system, accessible with the file manager. Right-click on the ISO image file (**.iso** extension) and select "Open with Other Application" and then choose "Disk Image Mounter" on the Select Application dialog. The ISO image is then mounted as a file system and a notification is displayed with an Open entry you can click to open the image file with a file manager window. An entry for it will also appear on the file manager sidebar, and in the Computer folder (Go | Computer). It will be read-only. To unmount the disk image, click the eject button on a file manager sidebar, or right-click on the sidebar entry or the image file's desktop icon, and then choose Unmount.

File Manager CD/DVD Creator interface

Using the GNOME file manager to burn data to a DVD or CD is a simple matter of dragging files to an open blank CD or DVD. When you insert a blank DVD/CD disc, a file manager window will open for it with "Blank DVD Disc" as its folder name. To burn files, just drag them to that window. The files are immediately written to the disc.

ISO Image File Writing with Disk Utility and Brasero

The GNOME Disk Utility supports burning ISO images to either a USB drive or a DVD drive. Right-click on the ISO image file and choose "Open with and select "Disk Image Writer". The GNOME Disks utility will then open and display a Restore Disk image dialog with the destination set to None. Use the Destination menu to carefully select the USB drive or DVD drive you want to write the image to (see Figure 3-24). Then click the Start Restoring button. You are then asked to confirm the write operation. Click Restore to have Disk Utility write the image to the drive.

Figure 3-24: Disk Writer, writing ISO image to USB drive.

You can also still use the older Brasero CD/DVD burner to write an ISO image file to a DVD disc (not a USB drive). Brasero is not installed by default and is no longer supported by Linux Mint or Ubuntu (Universe repository). Once installed you can select it as one of the options (right-click on the ISO file and choose Open with). This opens the Image Burning Setup dialog, which prompts you to burn the image. Be sure first to insert a blank CD or DVD into your CD/DVD burner.

Laptop Power Management and Wireless Networks

For working on a laptop, you will need two important operations: power management, and support for multiple network connection, including wireless and LAN. Both are configured automatically. For power management, Linux Mint uses the Power dialog accessible from System Settings dialog. On a Laptop, the battery icon displayed on the panel will show how much power you have left, as well as when the battery becomes critical. It will indicate an AC connection, as well as when the battery is recharging.

For network connections, Linux Mint uses Network Manager. Network Manager will detect available network connections automatically. Click on the Network Manager icon in the panel. This displays a pop-up menu showing all possible wireless networks, as well as any wired networks. You can then choose the one you want to use. The name and strength of each wireless connection will be listed. When you try to connect to an encrypted wireless network, you will be prompted for the password. Wireless networks that you successfully connect to will be added to your Network Manager configuration. You also have the option to connect to a hidden wireless network.

On the Cinnamon desktop, you can also use the Network tool, accessible from System Settings as Network and from the Network Manager applet's menu on the panel as Network Settings, to quickly configure your wireless connection.

Network Connections

Network connections will be set up for you by Network Manager, which will detect your network connections automatically, both wired and wireless. Network Manager provides status information for your connection and allows you to switch easily from one configured connection to another as needed. For initial configuration, it detects as much information as possible about the new connection.

Wired connections will be started automatically. For wireless connections, when a user logs in, Network Manager selects the connection preferred by that user. The user can choose the wireless connection to use from a menu of detected wireless networks.

The network menu is displayed from the Network Manager applet on the bottom panel to the right in the system tray (Figure 3-25). The Network Manager icon will vary according to the type of connection and your connection status. An Ethernet (wired) connection would display three connected squares. A wireless connection will display a staggered wave graph. If you have both a wired and wireless connection, and the wired connection is active, the wired connection image () will be used. If you have turned off your connections or cannot make one, two opposing arrows with and x are shown.

Figure 3-25: Network Manager panel system tray connections icons

Network Manager wired connections

For computers connected to a wired network, like an Ethernet connection, Network Manager will automatically detect the network connection and establish a connection. Most networks use DHCP to provide network information like an IP address and network DNS server automatically. With this kind of connection, Network Manager can connect automatically to your network whenever you start your system. The network connection would be labeled something like Wired connection 1. When you connect, a connection established message is displayed, as shown here. You do have the option to not display the connection message again.

The Network Manager menu displays your wired connection as Wired, with a switch to turn it on or off (see Figure 3-26). To disconnect your wired connection, you can click the switch, turning it to the off position. Your Network Manager icon on the panel becomes grayed out. To reconnect later, click the switch again.

Figure 3-26: Network Manager connections menu

Network Manager wireless connections

With multiple wireless access points for Internet connections, a system could have several different network connections to choose from, instead of a single-line connection like a wired connection. This is particularly true for notebook computers that could access different wireless connections at different locations. Instead of manually configuring a new connection each time one is encountered, the Network Manager tool can configure and select a connection to use automatically.

Network Manager will scan for wireless connections, checking for Extended Service Set Identifiers (ESSIDs). If an ESSID identifies a previously used connection, then it is selected by Network Manager. If several are found, then the recently used one is chosen. If only a new connection is available, then Network Manager waits for the user to choose one. A connection is selected only if the user is logged in.

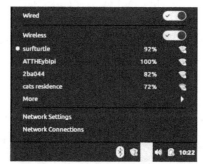

Figure 3-27: Network Manager connections menu: wired and wireless

Open the Network Manager menu to see a list of all possible network connections, including all available wireless connections (see Figure 3-27). Wireless entries display the name of the wireless network and a wave graph showing the strength of its signal. Computers with both wired and wireless devices show entries for both Wired Network and Wireless Networks. Computers with only a wireless device only show entries for Wireless Networks. You can disable the display of wireless networks by clicking the ON switch, turning it to OFF. To re-activate your wireless connections, click switch again.

To connect to a wireless network, find its network entry in the Network Manager menu and click on it. If this the first time you are trying to connect to that network, you will be prompted to enter the passphrase for that Wi-Fi connection. The type of wireless security used by the network will be automatically detected. Figure 3-28 shows the prompt for the passphrase to a wireless network. A checkbox lets you see the passphrase should you need to check that you are entering it correctly. Click Connect to activate the connection.

Figure 3-28: Network Manager wireless authentication

Once connected a message is displayed indicating that the connection has been established, as shown here. You have the option to not show the connection message again.

To disconnect from your wireless network, on the Network Manager menu click on the ON switch to turn it off.

When you connect to a wireless network for the first time, a configuration entry will be made for the wireless connection in the Wi-Fi tab of the Network Connections dialog.

System Settings Network, Cinnamon (GNOME and proxies)

GNOME 3 provides a network dialog for basic information and network connection management, including proxy settings. It is designed to work with Network Manager. The dialog has been incorporated into the Cinnamon Desktop as Network. To open the Networking dialog, choose Network Settings from the Network Manager applet menu, or click the Network icon in the System Settings dialog, or choose Network in the Preferences menu (see Figure 3-29).

Tabs for network connections are listed to the right. You should have entries for Wired, Wi-Fi, and Network proxy (Wireless is displayed on computers with wireless connections). The Wired tab lets you turn the wired connection on or off. The Wi-Fi tab lets you choose a wireless network and then prompts you to enter a passphrase. The connection and security type is automatically detected. Instead of using a wireless network, you can choose to connect to a local hidden network (Connect to a Hidden Network button). A switch at the top right lets you turn the wireless connection on or off. The status of the Wi-Fi connection is shown below the Wi-Fi label at the top (Connected, Unavailable, Authentication required).

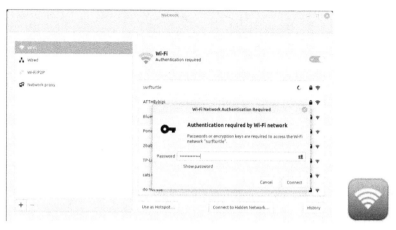

Figure 3-29: System Settings Networking wireless connections (Cinnamon)

Your current active connection will have a checkmark next to it, with a gear button to the right, as shown below. Click on the entry to deactivate the connection. The checkmark will disappear.

For quick access to networks you have already configured, you can click the History button to open the History dialog listing all your configured networks (see Figure 3-30). The configuration button opens that network's configuration dialog. To remove a network, click its checkbox, which activates the Forget button at the lower left, then click that button.

Figure 3-30: System Settings Networking wireless History (Cinnamon)

Click on the gear button to display a dialog with tabs for managing the connection. The Details tab provides information about the connection (see Figure 3-31). The Security, Identity, IPv4, and IPv6 tabs let you perform a detailed configuration of your connection, as described in Chapter 10. The settings are set to automatic by default. Should you make any changes, click on the Apply button to have them take effect. To remove a network's connection information, open the Reset tab and click the Forget button. The Reset button on the Reset tab lets you reset the settings. You can also remove a network using the History dialog (click the History button on the Networking dialog).

Figure 3-31: System Settings Networking wireless information (Cinnamon)

The Identity tab has options for connecting automatically and to make available to other users. These are set by default. Should you not want to connect to the wireless network automatically, be sure to un-check this option.

On the Networking dialog, the Wired tab shows basic information about the wired connection, including the IP addresses and DNS server. A switch at the top right corner allows you to disconnect the wired connection, letting you effectively work offline. The wrench/screwdriver button at the lower right opens a configuration dialog similar to the wireless configuration dialog, with tabs for Details, Security, Identity, IPv4, IPv6, and Reset. The Profile button to the left lets you add a different set of wired connection information (security, IPv protocols, and identity), should you connect to a different wired network.

The Proxy tab provides a Method menu with None, Manual, and Automatic options (see Figure 3-32). The Manual options let you enter address and port information. For the Automatic option, you enter a configuration address.

Figure 3-32: Proxy settings (System Settings Networking) (Cinnamon)

To add a new connection, such as a VPN connection, click the plus button (**+**) below the network devices listing. You are prompted to choose the interface types. The NetworkManager configuration dialogs will then start up to let you enter configuration information.

Figure 3-33: Connect to a Hidden Wireless Network

Wireless connections can also be hidden. These are wireless connections that do not broadcast an SSID, making them undetectable by an automatic scan. To connect to a hidden wireless network, you select "Connect to hidden network" on the Networking dialog Wi-Fi tab (see Figure 3-33). The Connection drop-down menu will select the New entry. If you have set up any hidden connections previously, they also are listed in the Connection drop-down menu. For a New connection, enter the wireless network name and select a security method. You are prompted in either case for your network keyring password.

Warpinator: Local Network File Transfer

With Linux Mint 21, the Warpinator file transfer tool can transfer files and folders between Linux computers on your local network that are also running Warpinator. Warpinator is installed during installation. You can access it from the Accessories menu. Warpinator allows you to transfer files and folders without having to set up a shared folder and to run a Samba or NFS server to make your files and folders available to other systems. With Warpinator you can transfer specific files and folders to one host directly. To install Warpinator on other Linux distributions such as Ubuntu, see:

```
https://github.com/linuxmint/warpinator
```

You will have to install the Samba server to allow Avahi multicast DNS discovery (browsing by remote Linux systems). Use Software Manager, the Synaptic Package Manager, or the **apt** command to install Samba.

```
sudo apt install samba
```

There are also Warpinator apps for Android, Apple IOS, and Windows, that lets you transfer files with another Linux Mint host.

If you are running a firewall, be sure that the firewall is configured for allowing access by Warpinator. You can do this easily for those systems running the UFW firewall used on Linux Mint and Ubuntu. To set firewall access, open Warpinator and select Preferences from its menu on the left side of the toolbar. On the Warpinator Preferences dialog click the "Update firewall rules" button in the Network section at the bottom of the screen (see Figure 3-34). Warpinator rules will be added to the firewall. There are rules for both the ports for incoming transfers (42000) and registration (42001), both IPv6 (v6) and IPv4 versions. This only works for the UFW firewall. All computers running Warpinator have to have their firewall configured. You only have to configure the firewall on each system once. Also, on Gufw (UFW firewall) (Preferences | Firewall Configuration), be sure that the rules are added for Samba and multicast DNS discovery (mdns).

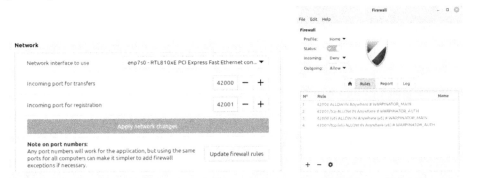

Figure 3-34: Warpinator UFW Firewall Automatic Configuration

Currently there is no easy configuration for the FirewallD. You can, however, manually add a Warpinator service to the FirewallD configuration using the **firewall-cmd** command.

```
sudo firewall-cmd --permanent --new-service=warpinator
sudo firewall-cmd --permanent --service=warpinator --set-description="Linux Mint
Warpinator Service"
sudo firewall-cmd --permanent --service=warpinator --set-short=warpinator
sudo firewall-cmd --permanent --service=warpinator --add-port=42000/tcp
sudo firewall-cmd --permanent --service=warpinator --add-port=42000/udp
sudo firewall-cmd --permanent --service=warpinator --add-port=42001/tcp
sudo firewall-cmd --info-service=warpinator
```

Once added, you can use firewall-config (Administration | Firewall), in the runtime and permanent configurations, to manage the warpinator service. On the Zones tab's Services tab you will find warpinator now listed. Select it to enable it. For its ports you will see entries for 42000 and 42001. You can now use Warpinator on systems using FirewallD. Also, for FirewallD, on firewall-config (Administration | Firewall), be sure that the **mdns**, **samba**, and **samba-client** services are enabled (Zones | Services tab) (see Figure 3-35).

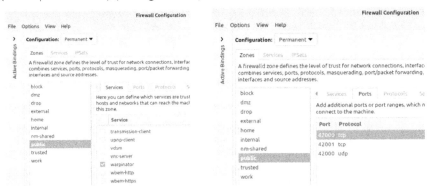

Figure 3-35: Warpinator FirewallD Configuration with warpinator service

When you start up Warpinator, it will automatically locate other Linux hosts that are also running Warpinator. These will be listed (see Figure 3-36). If you have many, you can use the search box to locate the one you want.

Figure 3-36: Warpinator Host List

Click on a host to open a dialog for transferring files and folders. The dialog will display the host name and its IP address. Below that, a File Transfers toolbar shows the status of the connection and a Send button for selecting and sending files. Click on the Send button to open a "Select File(s) to Send" dialog where you can locate and select the files and folders to send (see Figure 3-37). Once you have made the selection, click the Send button on this dialog.

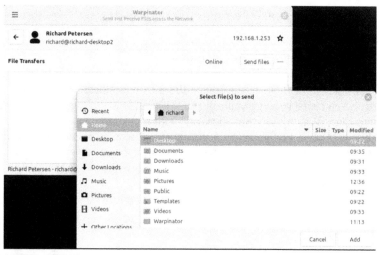

Figure 3-37: Warpinator - selecting files to send

The files and folders you are sending are then listed, preceded by a up arrow. There is a close button to the right you can use to cancel the transfer. The type of the file is indicated with its icon. The file name and size are displayed, along with the message "Waiting for approval" (see

Figure 3-38). On the host the file is being sent to, an approval request is displayed on that host's Warpinator application. Once the approval is given, the transfer begins, showing a progress bar and the remaining time for the transfer. When completed, the transfer is noted as Completed. The Close button becomes a remove button, which you can use to remove the transfer listing from the display (see Figure 3-39).

Figure 3-38: Warpinator - File Transfer

Figure 3-39: Warpinator - Completed Transfer

Should someone send you a file from a Warpinator application on another host, the transfer is listed and preceded by a down arrow, indicating that it is a files you are receiving. The listing has the message "Waiting for your approval" with check button to the right (see Figure 3-40). Click this button to accept the transfer. A notification is also displayed on your desktop with Accept and Decline buttons you can click to receive or reject the transfer.

Figure 3-40: Warpinator - Received Transfer Approval

The transfer then proceeds showing a progress bar (see Figure 3-41). A stop button is shown to the right which you can click to stop and cancel the transfer. Once completed, a folder button is displayed to the right, which you can click to open the folder the transferred file was saved to. By default, this is the Warpinator folder in your home folder.

Figure 3-41: Warpinator - Received Transfer

Note: Should you want to skip the approval request for received files and folders, you can turn off the "Require approval before accepting files" option in the File Transfers section of the Warpinator Preferences dialog.

You can configure Warpinator by selecting the Preferences entry from the Warpinator menu on the left side of the title bar, a shown here.

The Warpinator Preferences dialog has sections for Desktop, File Transfers, and Network (see Figure 3-42). On the Desktop section you can show a notification icon and choose to start Warpinator automatically when you log in. In the File Transfer section you can set the location for the received files. Click on this menu to choose from you home folders or choose Other to navigate to a folder. You can also require approval for accepting files or overwriting a file. The notification on the desktop for received files can be turned off. You can choose to use compression if supported. On the Network section you select the group code. Warpinator applications on different hosts have to have the same group code in order to transfer files. The default code is Warpinator. You can also specify the ports to use for transfers and registration. The default for transfers is 42000, and for registration it is 42001. As noted, you can click the Update Firewall button to automatically add a UFW firewall rule for Warpinator on your system.

Figure 3-42: Warpinator Preferences

Printing

When you first attach a new printer, it is automatically configured and its print driver installed. If the driver cannot be found for that printer, you will have to perform a manual configuration using the Linux Mint Printers configuration application, system-config-printer, accessible from the Administration menu as Printers, from System Settings, or from the Printer panel applet menu (see Chapter 13).

Figure 3-43: Desktop Printer applet menu with print jobs

On the desktop, when a printer is present, the printer icon will appear on the panel to the right, next to the NetworkManager icon. Clicking on the icon displays your installed printer and a Printers entry which opens the Printers (system-config-printer) configuration application. When you print a document, the print job is listed on the Printer panel applet's menu (see Figure 3-43) . As printing progresses, a red emblem appears on the Printer icon, and, when finished, a notification is displayed in the upper right corner of the desktop. If you right-click on the printer icon, you display a menu with a Configure entry you can use use to configure the Printer applet. You can choose to always show the icon, only if a printer is installed, or only when printing.

Display Configuration and Device Drivers

The graphics interface for your desktop display is implemented by the X Window System. The version used on Linux Mint is X.org (**x.org**). X.org provides its own drivers for various graphics cards and monitors. You can find out more about X.org at **https://www.x.org/wiki/**. X.org will automatically detect most hardware.

Device Drivers

Your display is detected automatically, configuring both your graphics card and monitor. Normally you should not need to perform any configuration yourself. However, if you have a graphics card that uses Graphics processors from a major Graphics vendor like Nvidia, you have the option of using their driver, instead of the open source X drivers installed with Linux Mint. Some graphics cards may work better with the vendor driver, and provide access to more of the card's features like 3D support. The open source AMD driver is **xserver-xorg-video-amdgpu** for newer cards and **xserver-xorg-video-radeon** for older ones. The open source NVidia driver is **xserver-xorg-video-nouveau**. When you install a new kernel, compatible kernel drivers for your proprietary graphics driver are generated automatically for you by the DKMS (Dynamic Kernel Module Support) utility.

If available, you can select proprietary drivers to use instead, such as the Nvidia driver. Open the Driver Manager application from System Setting (Administration | Driver Manager), from the Administration menu | Driver Manager, or from the First Steps tab on the Welcome Screen (see Figure 3-44). Select the driver entry you want and then click on the Apply Changes button to download and install the driver. The drivers are part of the restricted repository, supported by the vendor but not by Linux Mint. They are not open source, but proprietary.

Figure 3-44: Hardware Drivers: Driver Manager

Once installed, an examination of the Device Drivers application will show the selected driver in use. Should you want to use the original driver, click the Revert button. The open source Xorg driver will be automatically selected and used. For Nvidia cards, the Nouveau open source drivers are used, which provides some acceleration support. You can switch to another driver by selecting it and clicking the Apply Changes button.

The graphic vendors also have their own Linux-based configuration tools, which are installed with the driver. The Nvidia configuration tool is in the **nvidia-settings** package. This interface provides Nvidia vendor access to many of the features of Nvidia graphics cards like color corrections, video brightness and contrast, and thermal monitoring. You can also set the screen resolution and color depth.

For laptop computers with Nvidia graphic GPUs, for better performance, Nvidia Optimus software will switch between the integrated Intel GPU on the laptop CPU and the dedicated Nvidia

GPU. On Linux Mint, you can use the Nvidia Prime GPU Display applet on laptops that support Nvidia Optimus, to select different Nvidia GPU modes such as power saving, performance, on-demand. Support for Nvidia Optimus is also integrated into the menu (right-click), letting you run an application using the Nvidia GPU.

For AMD you would use the open source drivers, Xorg amdgpu, radeon, or ati. For AMD video cards with GCN 1.2 capability and above (series 300 and above), it is recommended that you use the amdgpu AMD open source driver, **xserver-xorg-video-amdgpu**.

If you have problems with the vendor driver, you can always switch back to the original (Revert button). Your original Xorg open source driver will be used instead. The changeover will be automatic.

If the problem is more severe, with the display not working, you can use the GRUB menu on startup to select the recovery kernel. Your system will be started without the vendor graphics driver. You can use the "drop to shell" option to enter the command line mode. From there you can use the **apt** command line APT tool to remove the graphics driver. The Nvidia drivers have the prefix **nvidia**. In the following example, the asterisk will match on all the **nvidia** packages.

```
sudo apt remove nvidia*
```

Display (resolution and rotation)

Any user can specify their own resolution or orientation without affecting the settings of other users. The System Settings Displays dialog (Hardware section) provides a simple interface for setting rotation, resolution, refresh rate, and selecting added monitors, allowing for cloned or extended displays across several connected monitors (see Figure 3-45).

Figure 3-45: Displays

From the drop-down menus, you can set the resolution, refresh rate, and rotation. After you select a resolution, click Apply. The new resolution is displayed with a dialog, with buttons that ask you whether to keep the new resolution or return to the previous one. You can use the Detect Displays button to detect any other monitors connected to your system. With multiple displays, you can turn a monitor off or mirror displays. Use the "Set as Primary" button to make one the primary display. The "User interface scale" menu lets you set the scale: automatic, normal, or double (Hi-DPI for high resolution monitors).

If available on your monitor, you can click the "Fractional scaling" button to enable fractional scaling and select a percentage from the menu.

On the Settings tab you can disable automatic screen rotation for monitors or devices that support that feature.

Hi-DPI

For smaller screens with very high resolutions (High Dots Per Inch), icons, windows, and fonts should be scaled to display them at a usable size. Cinnamon does this automatically in most cases. Should you need to manually configure Hi-DPI support, open the System Settings Monitor dialog, and set the "User interface scaling" option to Double (Hi-DPI).

On MATE, you open the Desktop Settings dialog to the Windows tab and set the "User interface scaling" option to Double (Hi-DPI).

Color Profiles

You can manage the color for different devices using color profiles specified with the Color dialog accessible from System Settings (Hardware section). The Color dialog lists devices for which you can set color profiles. Your monitor will have a profile set up automatically (see Figure 3-46). Click a device to display buttons at the bottom of the screen to Add profile and Calibrate. Click the Add Profile button to open a dialog with an Automatic Profiles menu from which you can choose a color profile to use. Click the Add button to add the Profile. Available profiles include Best RGB, D65, and Wide Gamut RGB. You can also import a profile from an ICC profile file of your own.

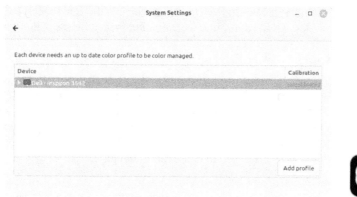

Figure 3-46: Color Management dialog

When you click on a profile entry, its Profiles are listed. Click on a profile to display buttons to Set for all users, Remove profile, and View details (see Figure 3-47). Click the View details button for the color profile information. You may have to install the **gnome-color-manager** package to see the Details information.

Figure 3-47: Color Management dialog

Private Encrypted Folders (ecryptfs)

Linux Mint provides each user with the capability of setting up a private encrypted folder. Encryption adds a further level of security. Should others gain access to your home folder, they still would not be able to read any information in your private encrypted folder.

Private folder encryption is implemented using the **ecryptfs** utilities, **ecryptfs-utils** on the Linux Mint main repository. You use the **ecryptfs-setup-private** command to set up an encrypted private folder. During setup, an **.ecryptfs** folder is created which holds your encryption keys and manages access.

```
ecrypts-setup-private
```

You are prompted to enter your user password, and then your mount password. The mount password is the password used to recover your private folder manually. Leave blank to have one generated automatically. A folder named **.Private** is set up which is the actual encrypted folder, holding the encrypted data files. This is a dot file, with a period preceding the name. Then a folder is set up named **Private**, which will serve as a mount point for the **.Private** folder. For security purposes, your encrypted private folder (**.Private**) remains unmounted until you decide to access it.

The **Private** folder is located in your home folder. You can open your file browser to the home folder where you will find an icon for the Private folder. When you start up your computer and first login, the Private folder will be unmounted (lock emblem). Open the folder to display a file named "Access Your Private Data." Click on it to mount the **.Private** folder. The contents of your Private folder are then displayed. You can double-click on this icon to mount and access your Private folder contents. You will be prompted to enter your login password.

The first time you try to run the "Access Your Private Data" file, you will receive a message saying that there is no application for it. The execute permission needs to be set to allow you to run it. Ownership is set originally to the root user. Use the following command in a terminal window to change ownership. For *user*, use your username.

```
sudo chown user Access-Your-Private-Data.desktop
```

You can then right click on the file, select Properties to open the Properties dialog, and on the Permissions tab, you can click the Execute checkbox.

If you are working from the command line interface, you can mount the **.Private** folder with the **ecryptfs-mount-private** command. Do not try to run this command from within the **Private** folder.

```
mount.ecryptfs_private
```

You can later unmount it with the **ecryptfs-umount-private** command.

To create a passphrase for your private directory, you use the **ecryptfs-manager** command. This displays a simple menu for creating passphrases.

Online Accounts

You can configure your online accounts using the Online Accounts dialog in Settings. Instead of separately configuring mail and chat clients, you can set up access once, using online accounts. Click on an entry to start the sign-in procedure. You are prompted to sign in using your e-mail and password. Access is provided to Google, Facebook, Flickr, Microsoft, Microsoft Exchange, Nextcloud, Foursquare, and Pocket. Once access is granted, you will see an entry for the service. Clicking on the service shows the different kinds of applications that it can be used for such as mail, calendar, contacts, chat, and documents (see Figure 3-48). Switches that you can use to turn access on and off are provided.

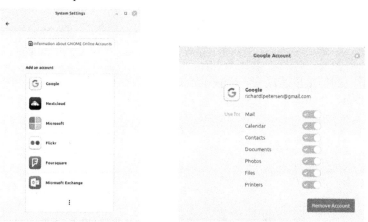

Figure 3-48: Online Accounts

System Reports

System Reports provides reports on disk crashes and tasks you may have to perform on your system (see Figure 3-49). The System Reports dialog is accessible from the Administration menu. The dialog displays three tabs, System Reports, System Information, and Disk Crashes.

The System Reports tab lists tasks you should perform such as setting up snapshots with Timeshift (system restore) or installing the mint-meta-codecs (Multimedia codecs) . Clicking on an entry displays information about it, which may include a button to launch the appropriate application to perform the task. The reports are designed to be tailored to your specific system, taking into consideration factors such as the desktop you have installed, your hardware components, and applications you have installed. Be sure to check this tab when first setting up your system.

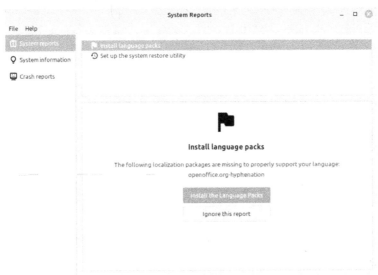

Figure 3-49: System Reports - System reports

Should your system crash, a crash report is generated, which is displayed on the System Reports Disk Crashes tab (see Figure 3-50). The crashes are listed by date. Selecting one displays a stack trace of the crash, indicating where the failure occurred. You can use the Pastebin and Local Files buttons to share the trace.

Figure 3-50: System Reports - Crash reports

The System Information tab shows all your system and device information. Headings include System, Machine, Battery, CPU, Network, and Graphics (see Figure 3-51). The System heading lists your information such as your host name, kernel version, desktop version, window manager, Linux Mint version, and Ubuntu version. The Machine, Battery, CPU, Graphics, Network, Drives, and Audio headings provided detailed device and driver information such as the specific name of your CPU and graphics card. The System Information tab also list all your active repositories, system temperature and fan speeds, your USB hubs, storage drives, and the partitions on your drives.

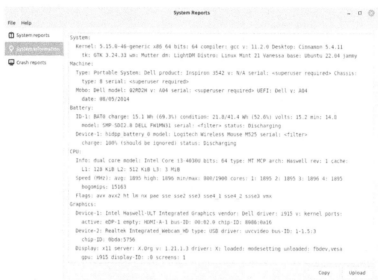

Figure 3-51: System Reports - System information

Help Resources

A great deal of support documentation is already installed on your system and is accessible from online sources. The Linux Mint User Guide is available as a PDF you can download from **https://linuxmint.com/documentation.php**. As Linux Mint is based on Ubuntu, the help sites listed in Table 1-3 may prove helpful.

Application Documentation

On your system, the **/usr/share/doc** directory contains documentation files installed by each application. Within each directory, you can usually find HOW-TO, README, and INSTALL documents for that application.

The Man Pages

You can access the Man pages, which are manuals for Linux commands available either from the command line interface, using the **man** command. In a terminal window, enter **man** along with the command on which you want information. The following example asks for information on the **ls** command:

```
$ man ls
```

Pressing the SPACEBAR key advances, you to the next page. Pressing the **b** key moves you back a page. When you finish, press the **q** key to quit the Man utility and return to the command line. You activate a search by pressing either the slash (/) or question mark (?) keys. The / key searches forward and the ? key searches backward. When you press the / key, a line opens at the bottom of your screen, where you can enter a text to search for. Press ENTER to activate the search. You can repeat the same search by pressing the **n** key. You need not re-enter the pattern.

The Info Pages

Documentation for GNU applications, such as the gcc compiler and the Emacs editor, also exist as info pages accessible from the GNOME Help Center. You can also access this documentation by entering the command **info** in a terminal window. This brings up a special screen listing different GNU applications. The info interface has its own set of commands. You can learn more about it by entering **info info** at the command prompt. Typing **m** opens a line at the bottom of the screen where you can enter the first few letters of the application. Pressing ENTER brings up the info file on that application.

Terminal Window

The Terminal window (GNOME Terminal) allows you to enter Linux commands on a command line, accessible as Terminal from the Administration menu, and from the Cinnamon and MATE panels (see Figure 3-38). It also provides you with a shell interface for using shell commands instead of your desktop. The command line is editable, allowing you to use the backspace key to erase characters on the line. Pressing a key will insert that character. You can use the left and right arrow keys to move anywhere on the line, and then press keys to insert characters, or use backspace to delete characters. Folders, files, and executable files are color-coded: white for files, blue for folders, green for executable files, and aqua for links. Shared folders are displayed with a green background. GNOME Terminal features dark mode support, displaying its window with dark backgrounds. You can turn off dark mode support by opening GNOME Terminal's Preferences dialog and selecing the General tab. On the "Theme variant" menu you can select from Dark, Light, and default options. Selecting the Light option disables the dark mode support.

The terminal window will remember the previous commands you entered. Use the up and down arrows to have those commands displayed in turn on the command line. Press the ENTER key to re-execute the currently displayed command. You can even edit a previous command before running it, allowing you to execute a modified version of a previous command. This can be helpful if you need to re-execute a complex command with a different argument, or if you mistyped a complex command and want to correct it without having to re-type the entire command. The terminal window will display all your previous interactions and commands for that session. Use the scrollbar to see any previous commands you ran and their displayed results.

The menubar provides a full set options for your terminal window including search, help, zoom, and edit operations (see Figure 3-52). The Terminal menu lets you lock the current window to a read only status, reset and clear the window, erasing previously displayed commands, and change the size of the terminal window from a set of listed sizes. You can also access several common terminal operations such as opening a tab and accessing Preferences from a pop-up menu accessible by right-clicking anywhere on the terminal window.

Figure 3-52: Terminal Window

You have the option to hide the menubar. Click the "Show Menubar" entry in the View menu. To re-display the menubar on the terminal window, choose the "Show Menubar" entry from the terminal pop-up menu. (see Figure 3-53).

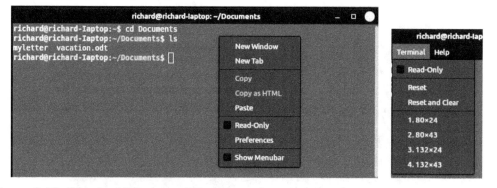

Figure 3-53: Terminal Window without menubar

To quickly locate either a previous command or message in the terminal window you can use the the Find dialog (see Figure 3-54). Select Find from the terminal window's Search menu. This open a search dialog with options for case, words, regular expressions, and wrap around.

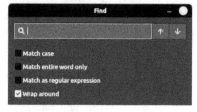

Figure 3-54: Terminal Window Find dialog

You can open as many terminal windows as you want, each working in its own shell. Instead of opening a separate window for each new shell, you can open several shells in the same window, using tabs. Use the keys **Shift-Ctrl-t** or click the Tab button on the left side of the terminal window's titlebar (plus symbol) to open a new tab. A tab toolbar opens at the top of the terminal window with the folder name and a close button for each added tab. Each tab runs a separate shell, letting you enter different commands in each (see Figure 3-55). You can right-click on the tab's folder name to display a pop-up menu with options to move to the next or previous tab, close the tab, or detach the tab to a new terminal window. You can move to any tab by clicking on a tab's folder name, selecting its name from the Tabs menu, or pressing the **Ctrl-PageUp** and **Ctrl-PageDown** keys to move through the tabs sequentially. The Tabs menu is the down arrow on the right side of the terminal window and to the right of the tab names. It is displayed if multiple tabs are open.

The terminal window also supports desktop cut/copy and paste operations. You can copy a line from a Web page and then paste it to the terminal window by pressing **Shift-Ctrl-v**. The command will appear and then you can press ENTER to execute the command. This is useful for command line operations displayed on an instructional Web page. Instead of typing in a complex command yourself, just select and copy from the Web page directly, and then paste to the Terminal window. You can also perform any edits on the command, if needed, before executing it. Also, should you want to copy a command on the terminal window, select the text with your mouse and then use **Shift-Ctrl-c** keys to copy the command. You can select part of a line or multiple lines, as long as they are shown on the terminal window.

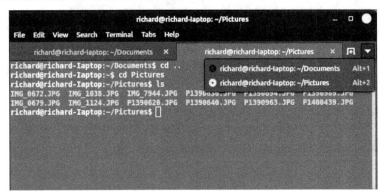

Figure 3-55: Terminal Window with tabs

You can customize terminal windows using profiles. A default profile is set up already. To customize your terminal window, select Preferences from the terminal window menu or the Terminal applications menu on the top bar. This opens a window for setting your default profile options with option categories on the sidebar for Global and Profiles. In the Profiles section there will be an "Unnamed" profile, the default. Click on the down menu button to the right to open a menu with the options to copy (clone) the profile or change the name. To add another profile, click on the plus button to the right of the "Profiles" heading to open a dialog to create a new profile. For profiles you create you have the added options to delete them and or to set one as the default. A selected profile displays tabs for Text, Colors, Scrolling, Command, and Compatibility (see Figure 3-56). On the Text tab, you can select the default size of a terminal window in text rows and columns, as well as the font, spacing, and cursor shape.

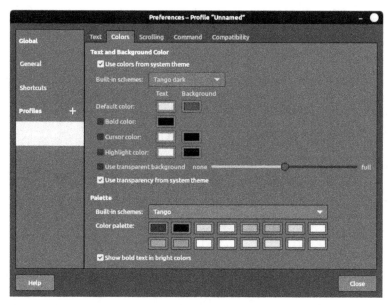

Figure 3-56: Terminal Window Profile configuration

Your terminal window will be set up to use a white background with dark text. To change this, you can edit the profile to change the background and text colors on the Colors tab. De-select the "Use colors from system theme" entry. This enables the "Built-in schemes" menu from which you can select a "Black on white" display. Other color combinations are also listed, such as "Black on light yellow" and "Green on black." The Custom option lets you choose your own text and background colors. The colors on your open terminal window will change according to your selection, allowing you to see how the color choices will look. For a transparent background, choose the "Use transparent background" entry and then set the amount of shading (none is completely transparent and full shows no transparency).

The Scrolling tab specifies the number of command lines your terminal history will keep, as well as other scroll options such as whether to display the scrollbar. These are the lines you can move back through and select to re-execute. You can de-select the Limit scrollback option to set this to unlimited to keep all the commands.

To later edit a particular profile, select Preferences from the terminal window menu to open the Preferences window, and then click on the one you want in the Profiles section.

Command Line Interface

When using the command line interface, you are given a simple prompt at which you type in a command. Even when you are using a desktop like GNOME, you sometimes need to execute commands on a command line. You can do so in a terminal window, which is accessed from the Administration menu as Terminal, and from the Cinnamon and MATE panel. You could also enter the command line interface with a Ctrl-Alt-F1 key (F1 through F6). Use the Ctrl-Alt-F7 keys to return to the graphic interface. Linux commands make extensive use of options and arguments. Be careful to place your arguments and options in their correct order on the command line. The format for a Linux command is the command name followed by options, and then by arguments, as shown here:

```
$ command-name options arguments
```

Linux commands make extensive use of options and arguments. Be careful to place your arguments and options in their correct order on the command line. The format for a Linux command is the command name followed by options, and then by arguments.

```
$ command-name options arguments
```

An option is a one-letter code preceded by one or two hyphens, which modifies the type of action the command takes. Options and arguments may or may not be optional, depending on the command. For example, the **ls** command can take an option, **-s**. The **ls** command displays a listing of files in your directory, and the **-s** option adds the size of each file in blocks. You enter the command and its option on the command line as follows.

```
$ ls -s
```

If you are uncertain what format and options a command uses, you can check the command syntax quickly by displaying its man page. Most commands have a man page. Just enter the **man** command with the command name as an argument.

An argument is data the command may need to execute its task. In many cases, this is a filename. An argument is entered as a word on the command line that appears after any options. For example, to display the contents of a file, you can use the **more** or **less** commands with the file's name as its argument. The **less** or **more** command used with the filename **mydata** would be entered on the command line as follows.

```
$ less mydata
```

The command line is actually a buffer of text you can edit. Before you press ENTER to execute the command, you can edit the command on the command line. The editing capabilities provide a way to correct mistakes you may make when typing a command and its options. The **Backspace** key lets you erase the character you just typed (the one to the left of the cursor) and the **Del** key lets you erase the character the cursor is on. With this character-erasing capability, you can backspace over the entire line if you want, erasing what you entered. **Ctrl-u** erases the whole command line and lets you start over again at the prompt.

You can use the **Up Arrow** key to redisplay your last executed command. You can then re-execute that command, or you can edit it and execute the modified command. This is helpful when you have to repeat certain operations, such as editing the same file. It is also helpful when you have already executed a command you entered incorrectly.

4. Installing and Updating Software

Installing Software Packages

Linux Mint Package Management Software

Linux Mint Software Repositories

Updating Linux Mint with Update Manager

Timeshift and Snapshots

Managing Packages with Software Manager

GDebi

Flatpak

Synaptic Package Manager

Managing software with apt and apt-get

Source code files

DEB Software Packages

Managing non-repository packages with dpkg

Using packages with other software formats

Ubuntu Snap and the snap command

GNOME Software and Snap

Linux Mint software distribution is implemented using the online software repositories, which contain an extensive collection of Linux Mint-compliant software. With the integration of repository access into your Linux system, you can think of that software as an easily installed extension of your current collection. You can add software to your system by accessing software repositories that support Debian packages (DEB) and the Advanced Package Tool (APT). Software is packaged into DEB software package files. These files are, in turn, installed and managed by APT. Software Manager provides an easy-to-use front end for installing software with just a click, accessible from the Administration menu and, on Cinnamon, from the Favorites icon bar on the Cinnamon menu.

The software repositories used by Linux Mint are based on the Ubuntu software repositories, which are organized into sections, depending on how the software is supported. Software supported directly is located in the main Linux Mint repository section. Other Linux software that is most likely compatible is placed in the Universe repository section. Many software applications, particularly multimedia applications, have potential licensing conflicts. Such applications are placed in the Multiverse repository section, which is not maintained directly by Ubuntu. Software from the Multiverse and Universe sections are integrated into Software Manager, and can be installed just as easily as Linux Mint main section software.

The Linux Mint is configured with support for Flatpak packages. These are applications designed to run on any Linux distribution. A Flatpak package installs its own set of supporting libraries that can be kept up to date without affecting those on your system. In effect, Flatpak packages run inside their own environment, separate from your system. Flatpak packages are downloaded from the Flathub repository. Flatpak support is integrated into Software Manager, letting you easily install Flatpak software.

You can also download source code versions of applications, then compile, and install them on your system. Where this process once was complex, it has been streamlined significantly with the use of configure scripts. Most current source code, including GNU software, is distributed with a configure script, which automatically detects your system configuration and creates a binary file that is compatible with your system.

You can download Linux software from many online sources directly, but it is always advised that you use the Linux Mint/Ubuntu prepared package versions. Most software for GNOME and KDE have corresponding Linux Mint and Ubuntu compliant packages in the Ubuntu Universe and Multiverse repository sections.

Installing Software Packages

Installing software is an administrative function performed by a user with administrative access. During the Linux Mint installation, only some of the many applications and utilities available for users on Linux were installed on your system. On Linux Mint, you can install or remove software from your system with the Linux Mint Software Manager, the Synaptic Package Manager, or the **apt** and **apt-get** commands. Alternatively, you could install software as separate DEB files, or by downloading and compiling its source code.

APT (Advanced Package Tool) is integrated as the primary tool for installing packages. When you install a package with the Software Manager or with the Synaptic Package Manager, APT will be invoked and will select and download the package automatically from the appropriate online repository. This will include the entire Linux Mint online repository.

A DEB software package includes all the files needed for a software application. A Linux software application often consists of several files that must be installed in different folders. The application program itself is placed in a system folder such as **/usr/bin**, online manual files go in another folder, and library files go in yet another folder. When you select an application for installation, APT will install any additional dependent (required) packages. APT also will install all recommended packages by default. Many software applications have additional features that rely on recommended packages.

Linux Mint Package Management Software

Although all Linux Mint software packages have the same DEB format, they can be managed and installed using different package management software tools. The underlying software management tool is APT.

Software Manager (mintinstall) is the primary interface for locating and installing Linux Mint software, repository files at **/var/apt**. Designed as a central software management application for handling all Linux Mint packages.

APT (Advanced Package Tool) performs the actual software management operations for all applications installed from a repository. Software Manager, the Synaptic Package Manager, update-manager, dpkg, and **apt** are all front-ends for APT, repository files at **/var/apt**.

Synaptic Package Manager is a Graphical front end for APT that manages packages; repository files are located at **/var/apt**.

Update Manager is the Linux Mint graphical front end for updating installed software using APT.

tasksel is a cursor-based screen for selecting package groups and particular servers (front-end for APT). You can run it in a terminal window on a desktop (**sudo tasksel**). Use arrow keys to move to an entry, the spacebar to select, and the tab key to move to the OK button. Press ENTER on the OK button to perform your installs.

dpkg is the older command line tool used to install, update, remove, and query software packages; uses its own database, **/var/lib/dpkg**; repository files are kept at **/var/cache/apt**, the same as APT.

apt and **apt-get** are the primary command line tools for APT to install, update, and remove software; uses its own database, **/var/lib/apt/**.

aptitude is a cursor based front end for **dpkg** and **apt-get**, which uses its own database, **/var/lib/aptitude**.

Linux Mint Software Repositories

Linux Mint is derived from the Ubuntu Linux distribution and is configured to directly access the Ubuntu software repository. Five main components or sections make up the Linux Mint repository: main, upstream, import, backports, and romeo.

To see a listing of all packages in the Linux Mint repository see:

```
http://packages.linuxmint.com
```

To see the packages in the Linux Mint repositories, click on the Linux Mint link for your release. Linux Mint supported packages are listed, separated into sections for their repositories.

Repository Components

The following repository components are included in the Linux Mint repository:

main: Officially supported Linux Mint software, includes Cinnamon, and MATE.

upstream: Linux Mint compliant software, such as Synaptic, Firefox, and Caja.

import: Includes third-party software such as Celluloid, Skype, and Dropbox.

backports: Software under development for the next Linux Mint release, but packaged for use in the current one. Not guaranteed or fully tested. Backports access is enabled by default.

Ubuntu Software Repositories

Linux Mint is derived from the Ubuntu Linux distribution and is configured to directly access the Ubuntu APT software repository. Four main components or sections make up the Ubuntu APT repository: main, restricted, universe, and multiverse. These components are described in detail at:

`https://help.ubuntu.com/community/Repositories`

To see a listing of all packages in the Ubuntu repository see:

`http://packages.ubuntu.com`

Repository Components

The following repository components are included in the Ubuntu APT repository:

main: Officially supported Ubuntu software (canonical), includes GStreamer Good plug-ins.

restricted: Software commonly used and required for many applications, but not open source or freely licensed, like the proprietary graphics card drivers from Nvidia needed for hardware support. Because they are not open source, they are not guaranteed to work.

universe: All open source Linux software not directly supported by Ubuntu includes GStreamer Bad plug-ins.

multiverse: Linux software that does not meet licensing requirements and is not considered essential. It is not guaranteed to work. For example, the GStreamer ugly package is in this repository. Check **https://www.ubuntu.com/about/about-ubuntu/licensing**.

Repositories

In addition to the Ubuntu APT repository, Ubuntu maintains several other APT repositories used primarily for maintenance and support for existing packages. The updates repository holds updated packages for a release. The security updates repository contains critical security package updates every system will need.

Ubuntu main repository: Collection of Ubuntu-compliant software packages for releases organized into main, universe, multiverse, and restricted sections.

Updates: Updates for packages in the main repository, both main and restricted sections.

Backports: Software under development for the next Ubuntu release, but packaged for use in the current one. Not guaranteed or fully tested. Backports access is now enabled by default.

Security updates: Critical security fixes for main repository software.

Partner: Third party proprietary software tested to work on Ubuntu. You need to authorize access manually.

The Backports repository provides un-finalized or development versions for new and current software. They are not guaranteed to work, but may provide needed features.

Note: Though it is possible to add the Debian Linux distribution repository, it is not advisable. Packages are designed for specific distributions. Combining them can lead to irresolvable conflicts.

Linux Mint Repository Configuration file: sources.list.d/ official-package-repositories.list

Repository configuration is managed by APT using configuration files in the **/etc/apt** folder. The **/etc/apt/sources.list** file traditionally holds repository entries. However, on Linux Mint, the main repository file is located in the in the **/etc/apt/sources.list.d** folder, and is named **official-package-repositories.list**. APT reads any text files in the **/etc/apt/sources.list.d** folder as part of the **sources.list** file.

```
/etc/apt/sources.list.d/official-package-repositories.list
```

A repository entry in the file consists of a single line with the following format:

```
format   URI   release   section
```

The format is normally **deb**, for Debian package format. The URI (universal resource identifier) provides the location of the repository, such as an FTP or Web URL. The release name is the official name of a particular Linux Mint distribution like tina or vanessa. Linux Mint 21 has the name **vanessa**. The section can be one or more terms that identify a section in that release's repository. There can be more than one section like **main** and **upstream**. For Linux Mint there is one entry for the Linux Mint set of packages. All packages from the main repository, as well as any updated and advanced packages from the upstream, import, and backport are accessed.

```
deb http://packages.linuxmint.com/ vanessa   main upstream import backport
```

In addition, all the Ubuntu repositories are activated, including the packages (jammy), package updates (jammy-updates, and security updates (jammy-security). The entry for the Ubuntu Jammy (Ubuntu 22.04) repositories is shown here.

```
deb http://archive.ubuntu.com/ubuntu/ jammy   main restricted universe multiverse
```

On Linux Mint, the Ubuntu restricted, universe, and multiverse repositories are added to the main repository, enabling all.

The update repository for a section is referenced by the **-updates** suffix, as in **jammy-updates**.

```
deb http://archive.ubuntu.com/ubuntu/ jammy-updates main restricted universe
multiverse
```

The security repository for a section is referenced with the suffix **-security**, as **jammy-security**.

```
deb http://archive.ubuntu.com/ubuntu/ jammy-security main restricted universe
multiverse
```

The Ubuntu Backports repository has the suffix **-backports**.

```
deb http://archive.ubuntu.com/ubuntu/ jammy-backports main restricted universe
multiverse
```

You could also add corresponding source code repositories, which use a **deb-src** format.

```
deb-src http://archive.ubuntu.com/ubuntu/ jammy main restricted universe
multiverse
```

Comments begin with a # mark. You can add comments of your own if you wish. Commenting an entry effectively disables that component of a repository. Placing a # mark before a repository entry will effectively disable it.

Most entries, including third-party entries for Linux Mint partners, can be managed using Software Sources. Entries can also be managed by editing the **official-package-repositories.list** file with the following command, though it is recommended that you use Software Sources instead.

```
sudo xed /etc/apt/sources.list.d/official-package-repositories.list
```

You could also open the file manager as root (Desktop menu) and navigate to the **/etc/apt/sources.list.d** folder and then double-click the **official-package-repositories.list** file.

You could add or remove the # at the beginning of the line to deactivate or activate a repository such as partners.

```
# deb http://archive.canonical.com/ubuntu/ jammy partner
```

Software Sources managed from Linux Mint

You can manage your repositories with the Software Sources dialog allowing you to enable or disable repository sections, as well as add new entries. This dialog edits the **official-package-repositories.list** file directly. You can access Software Sources from the System Settings dialog, or from the Administration menu. You can also access it on the Synaptic Package Manager from the Settings menu as the Repositories entry. The Software Sources dialog displays five tabs: Official Repositories, PPAs, Additional Repositories, Authentication Keys, and Maintenance (see Figure 4-1). The Official Repositories tab lists the Linux Mint and Ubuntu repository locations. There are options to include source code repositories and unstable (testing) software. On this tab, you could change to a different repository mirror, should you find that the current ones are slow.

Figure 4-1: Software Sources Linux Mint Official Repositories.

Repository locations are specified in the Mirrors section. The "Main (vanessa)" mirror is set to the main Linux Mint website. You can choose another mirror that may be closer and faster. Click on the "Main (vanessa)" button to open the "Select a mirror" dialog with a list of current mirrors, with flags denoting the country they are in (see Figure 4-2). You can do the same with the "Base (jammy)" mirror, the mirror for Ubuntu packages.

Figure 4-2: Software Sources Mirrors

On the "Additional repositories" tab, you can add repositories for third-party software (see Figure 4-3). The repository for "CD-ROM (Installation Disc)" will already be listed, but not checked. To add a repository, click the Add button to open a dialog where you enter the complete APT entry, starting with the **deb** keyword, followed by the URL, release, and sections or packages. This is the line as it will appear in the sources file. Once entered, click the OK button. Use the Edit button to change an entry, and the Remove button to remove one.

Figure 4-3: Software Sources Additional Repositories

The PPAs tab lets you add Personal Package Archive repositories (see Figure 4-4). These are often repositories for specialized drivers or custom software. Click the Add button to open a dialog where you can enter the PPA's URL and repository. Once installed, you can select the PPA and click the "Open PPA" button to open a dialog listing the PPA's packages. You can then choose the ones you want to install. The packages are installed directly from Software Sources.

Figure 4-4: Software Sources PPA

The Authentication tab shows additional repository software signature keys that are installed on your system (see Figure 4-5). Most other third party or customized repositories will provide a signature key file for you to download and import. You can add such keys manually from the Authentication tab. Click the Import Key File to open a file browser where you can select the downloaded key file. This procedure is the same as the **apt-key add** operation. Both add keys that APT then uses to verify DEB software packages downloaded from repositories before it installs them.

Figure 4-5: Software Sources Authentication Keys

The Maintenance tab lets you fix update issues such as mergelist problems and residual configuration (dependent files left over from removed applications), as well as adding any missing keys for your repositories and removing duplicate repository definitions.

If you have made changes, a dialog appears at the bottom of the screen with the message "Your configuration changed" and the instruction "Click OK to update your APT cache", as shown here. OK and Cancel buttons are displayed to the right. Click the OK button to make the changes such as new repositories or components available on your package managers like Software Manager and the Synaptic Package Manager. The "Updating Cache" dialog opens and downloads the latest software listings from your repositories.

Codec packages on Linux Mint (mint-meta-codecs)

Applications and codecs with licensing issues, like the DVD Video commercial decoder (**libdvdcss2**), are installed by the **mint-meta-codec** package. The **mint-meta-codecs** package also installs the Gstreamer bad, ugly, ffmpeg packages, Microsoft fonts, as well as the **unrar** archiver and the Linux Mint Flash plugin.

Updating Linux Mint with Update Manager

New updates are continually being prepared for particular software packages as well as system components. These are posted as updates you can download from software repositories and install on your system. These include new versions of applications, servers, and even the kernel. Such updates may range from single software packages to whole components. Updating your Linux Mint system is a simple procedure, using Update Manager, a graphical update interface for APT.

The first time you start the Update Manager, the Welcome page is displayed, which describes its use for security updates and software updates, and recommends that you set up system snapshots (Timeshift) (see Figure 4-6).

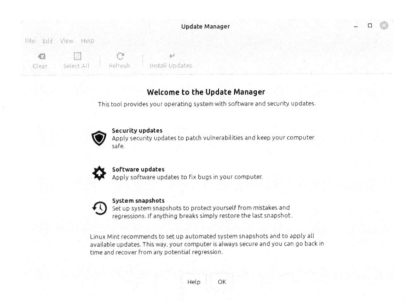

Figure 4-6: Update Welcome

When updates are available, the Update Manager icon on the panel displays a red dot and a split light and dark image (see Figure 4-7). You can start the Update Manager clicking the Update Manager icon, or by selecting it from the Administration menu. To ensure that the update is current, you can click the Refresh button to download an updated listing of your packages from all your active repositories, detecting the modified packages. As updates are performed, the Update Manager icon displays a gear image. Once updates are complete, it displays a solid image.

Figure 4-7: Update Manager update icon and package information dialog

The Update Manager dialog shows a listing of packages to be updated (see Figure 4-8). The checkboxes for each entry lets you de-select any packages you do not want to update. Four columns are displayed: Type, Upgrade, Name, and New version. The Type column indicates the update type, whether it is a normal update (up arrow icon), security update (shield icon), kernel (lightning icon), backports (new/unstable Ubuntu packages), and romeo (new/unstable Linux Mint packages). The Name column shows the package names. The "New version" column displays the version number of the package. There are three other columns you can choose to display: Old version, Size, and Origin. You can select these from the View | Visible Columns menu. The "Old version" column displays the version of the currently installed package.

All updates are selected automatically. You can use the checkboxes in the Upgrade column to select or de-select a package. On the toolbar, you can click the Clear button to deselect all selected updates, and the Select All button to select them all. The Refresh button downloads the latest listing of packages from your repositories.

Figure 4-8: Update Manager with selected packages

To see a detailed description of a particular update, select the update to display the description in the section at the bottom of the screen. Three tabs are displayed in this section: Description, Packages, and Changelog. The Changelog tab lists detailed update information, Packages lists dependent packages, and Description tab provides information about the software.

Click the Install Updates button on the toolbar to start updating. The packages will be downloaded from their appropriate repository. Once downloaded, the packages are updated. When downloading and installing, a dialog appears showing the download and install progress (see Figure 4-9). Click the Details arrow to see install messages for particular software packages. A window will open up that lists each file and its progress. During the update process, the update manager icon on the panel shows a progress bar indicating the overall progress. Once downloaded, the updates are installed. When the update completes, Update Manager will display a message saying that your system is up-to-date.

Figure 4-9: Update download and install

Update Manager notifies you of any issues with accessing your repositories. It warns you if the mirror you are using is not up to date, if it is corrupted, or if a faster one is available. When you first use Update Manager, you will likely be prompted to use a local mirror for faster access, as shown here. Clicking on the OK button opens the Software Sources dialog at the "Official repositories" tab, where you can change to a different mirror.

Update Manager Preferences

You can configure the Update Manager using the Update Manager's Preferences dialog accessible from the Update Manager's Edit menu from the Update Manager panel applet menu (see Figure 4-10). The Update Manager Preferences dialog has three tabs: Options, Blacklist, and Automation.

Figure 4-10: Update Manager Preferences - Options

The Options tab, has three sections: Interface, Auto-refresh, and Notifications. On the Interface section you can set options such as hiding the update manager after updating, and showing the update icon on the panel if updates are available. The Auto-Refresh section lets you specify how often updates are checked. The Notifications sections lets you schedule notifications for various updates such as security and kernel updates, unapplied updates, and older updates. You can choose to not show notifications for updates already applied. By default, only the security and kernel updates for noted. For all updates turn off the switch for "Only show notifications for security and kernel updates." On the Blacklist tab you can specify packages that you would not want to be updated. Packages can be specified by version, so that you could update to a later version, skipping the specified one. Specific kernel versions could be blocked in this way. The Automation tab lets you choose to automatically install all updates, as they become available, as well as remove obsolete kernels and their dependencies (Automatic Maintenance section). You can also automatically update just Cinnamon spices (Cinnamon applets, themes, extensions, and desklets) and Flatpak applications (Other Updates). It is advisable that you have your snapshots management configured before enabling automatic updates in case there are problems with the updates and you need to restore your system to a previous snapshot.

Update Manager Linux Kernels

The Linux Kernels dialog (View | Linux kernels) lists the available Linux kernels, showing what they fix and what changes they make. It shows which one is currently loaded and allows you to install new ones. It also shows how long a kernel is supported. The current kernel is labeled as Active, and previously installed kernel are labeled as Installed (see Figure 4-11). A Remove Kernel button lets you remove any obsolete installed kernels on your system. It opens a dialog listing your installed unused kernels with checkboxes you can use to select kernels for removal. Click Apply to perform the removal.

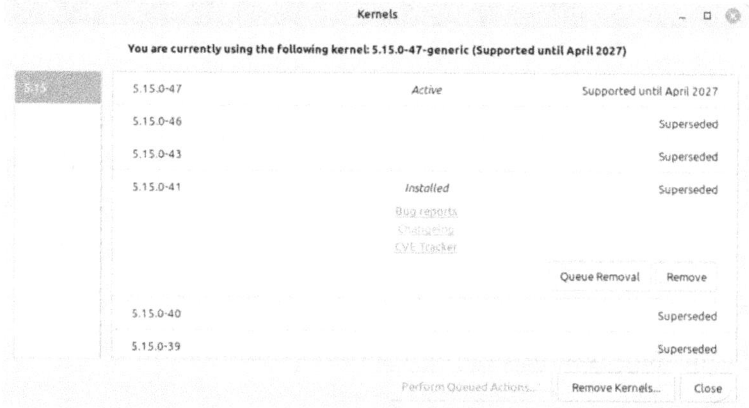

Figure 4-11: Update Manager - Linux Kernel dialog

The Linux Kernel dialog shows all available kernels, including newer ones, as well as generic kernels, kernel flavors such as server kernels, and custom kernels. To install a kernel, click its entry to display an Install button. Linux Mint will install the current stable kernel automatically. For Linux Mint 21 these are the 5.4 kernels. You could, if you wish, install one of the newer series kernels (should they be available), which may have better support for more recent hardware. Still, be sure to perform a snapshot before installing the kernel, and you can always load a previous kernel from the boot menu.

Clicking a kernel entry displays a Queued Removal and Remove button. You can use the Remove button to remove the kernel immediately. Queue removal lets you place the kernel on a list of kernels to be removed, which you then remove by clicking the Perform Queued Actions button.

A selected kernel will also display links for bug reports, changelog, and CVE tracker for that kernel. Be sure to always keep one older kernel installed, in case there are problems with the current one.

Timeshift and Snapshots

Linux Mint encourage users to create snapshots of you system with which you can restore your system should problems occur. A snapshot is a copy of the files on your system, including all your system files. You can create a series of snapshots over time. The first one you create is a full copy of your system, and later ones are incremental, copying only changed files and relying on the previous snapshot for the unchanged ones. Timeshift is maintained as an X-app.

Note: Should your system become corrupt to the point it cannot even boot, you can run Timeshift from the Linux Mint USB/DVD and have it restore your system from Timeshift snapshots on your hard drive.

Snapshots are created and managed using the Timeshift application (Administration | Timeshift) (see Figure 4-12). The Timeshift dialog lists your snapshots. It has an icon bar with buttons for Create, Restore, Delete, Browse, Settings, and Wizard.

Figure 4-12: Timeshift - snapshots

The easiest way to create a snapshot is to use the snapshot wizard. Click the Wizard button to open the Setup Wizard, showing the "Select Snapshot Type" where you can choose from either Rsync or BTRFS (see Figure 4-13). The Rsync operation saves the snapshot to an external drive, which you can then use to restore your system should it be damaged. The BTRFS option is available only to users that have installed their system on a BTRFS filesystem. Snapshots are saved to the same disk as your system and rely on the structure of the BTRFS filesystem to restore it.

Figure 4-13: Snapshot wizard

For the Rsync operation, a Select Snapshot Location dialog then lets you choose a device to save the snapshot to (see Figure 4-14). The device must have a Linux file system. On the "Select Snapshot Levels" dialog you can set up a basic schedule for snapshots and the number of snapshots to keep (see Figure 4-15). Older ones are removed. Not choosing any schedule will disable scheduled snapshots.

Figure 4-14: Snapshot wizard - Location

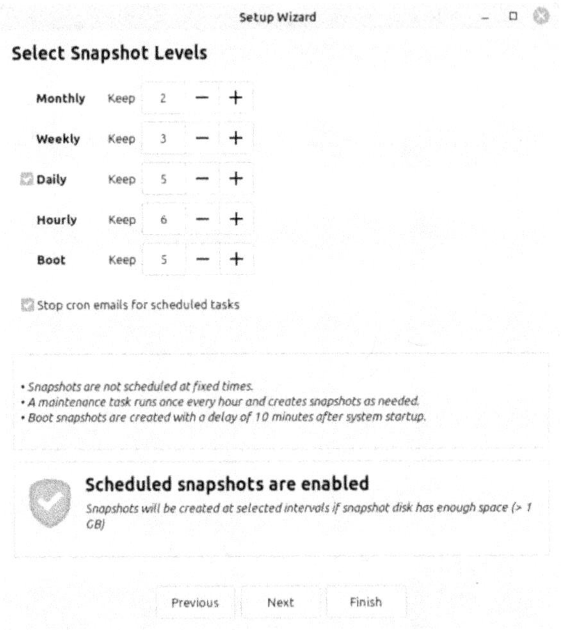

Figure 4-15: Snapshot wizard - Level

On the Timeshift dialog, you can click the Settings button to open the Settings dialog with the same setup tabs. Two additional tabs are listed: Users and Filters. On the Users tab you can specify what user home folders are excluded or included (See Figure 4-16). You can include just hidden files (the user configuration files) or all the user files and subfolders. Initially all are excluded.

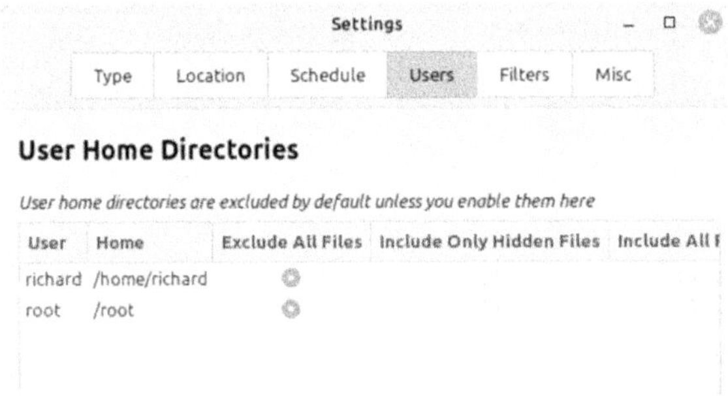

Figure 4-16: Timeshift Settings - Users tab

On the Filters tab you can choose what folders and files to include or exclude, using patterns to detect them (Include /Exclude Patterns) (see Figure 4-17). Basic patterns for your system are already listed. For each pattern there is an exclude and include option (the + and - columns). You can choose which to include or exclude. Buttons at the bottom let you add new patterns (Add), add files to the list, add folders, and to remove an entry. The Summary button opens a dialog listing all the folders that will be excluded according to the patterns and those individually added.

Figure 4-17: Timeshift Settings - Filters tab

Managing Packages with Software Manager (mintinstall)

To perform installation and removal of software, you can use Software Manager (mintinstall), which is the primary supported package manager for Linux Mint. Software Manager is designed to be the centralized utility for managing all your software. Software Manager is a front end for the APT package manager, as well as the Flatpak package manager (Flathub repository). When you install a package with Software Manager, APT is invoked and automatically selects and downloads the package from the appropriate online repository. Software Manager will display and manage any installed software, even the software was not installed by Software Manager. To manually update the package list, select the "Refresh the list of packages" entry from the menu, located on the right side of the toolbar. When removing applications, Software Manager accurately detects and removes any dependencies, taking care not to remove critical libraries and tools needed by other applications.

Software Manager displays a dialog with two sections: Editor's Picks and Categories (see Figure 4-18). Editor's picks list the popular and best applications. Click on an icon to open its application page. The Categories section shows category buttons you can click to list packages in that category such as Office, Sound and video, and Graphics, as well as Flatpak. You can return to the Categories dialog at any time by clicking the back button in the upper left corner. Many categories will have subcategories, such as Graphics, which has subcategories for Drawing,

Photography, and Publishing (see Figure 4-19). These are listed as tabs in a sidebar. Clicking on a tab displays the applications in that subcategory.

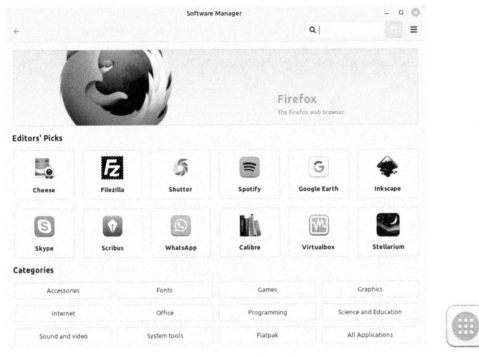

Figure 4-18: Software Manager

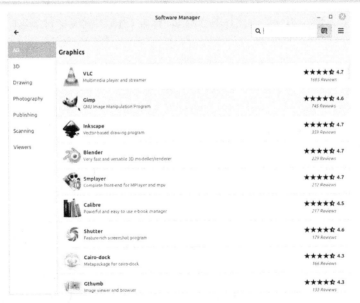

Figure 4-19: Software Manager sub-categories

Instead of scrolling through category listings, you can use the search box (upper right) to search directly for a package (see Figure 4-20). You can click on an entry to open an application page. Click the back button (left-arrow on the left side of the toolbar) to return to the list of applications. The menu to the right of the search box lets you search the package summary (default) and description.

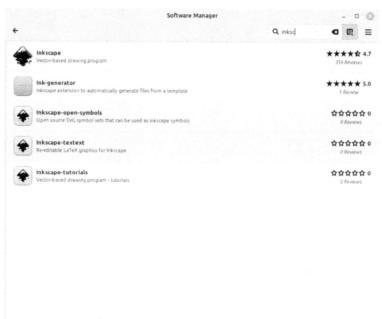

Figure 4-20: Software Manager search

Should you want to just see a list of application that you have installed with Software Manager, you choose the "Show installed applications" entry from the menu at the top right.

The Linux Mint Software Manager also supports Flatpak packages. These are applications designed to run on any Linux distribution. A Flatpak package installs its own set of supporting libraries that can be kept up to date without affecting those on your system. In effect, Flatpak packages run inside their own environment, separate from your system. Click the Flatpak category to see the list of Flatpak packages. These include popular applications such as VLC, Spotify, Bookworm, Krita, Steam, and Blender. These applications are downloaded from the Flathub repository.

Clicking on an entry opens its application page. The application page displays a detailed description of the application, install details, and reviews (see Figure 4-21). You can click the website link at the end of the description to access the application's website, which may provide detailed documentation. You can also write and submit a review. The software package's score and number of reviews are displayed in the upper left below the package name. The Details section shows the Version and size of the package.

To install a package, first, locate it. Then double-click it to open the application page (see Figure 4-21). The application page for an uninstalled package will have an Install button at the upper right. To install the application, click the Install button.

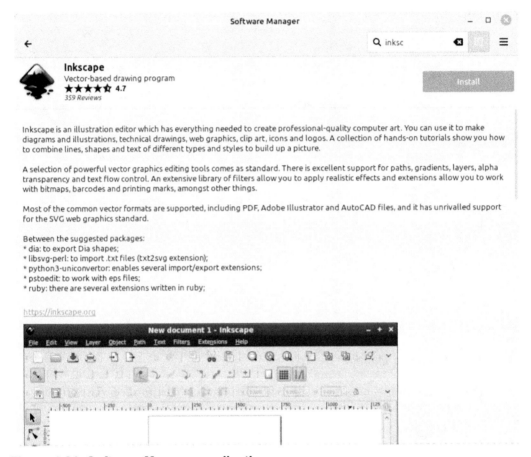

Figure 4-21: Software Manager application

During the install, a progress bar appears on the page and a circular animation appears at the top left by the back arrow that indicates the installation progress. When finished, the application page displays Launch and Remove buttons (see Figure 4-22). The entry for the application in the list of applications will have a green checkmark emblem next to its name or on its icon indicating that the application is installed. To remove a package, first, locate it in the applications lists, click on it to open its application page, and click the Remove button.

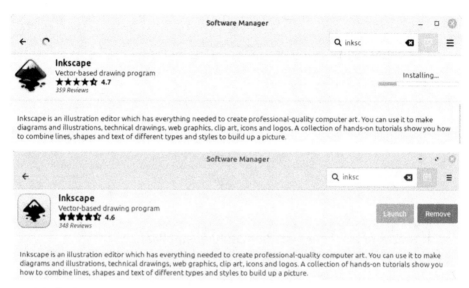

Figure 4-22: Software Manager Installing application

During installation or removal of an application, you are free to move to other pages, even installing or removing other applications. As the install progresses, the circular animation button remains in the top left corner no matter what page you are on. You can click it at any time to see the list of packages being installed or removed. They are labeled as "Currently working on the following packages" (see Figure 4-23).

Figure 4-23: Software Manager Currently working on packages

You can install multiple packages quickly, not waiting for the previous ones to install. Open their application pages and click their install buttons. The applications will install in the background. A circular arrow animated button appears at the top left by the back arrow that indicates the installation is in progress. You can click on this button to display the list of applications being installed (see Figure 4-24). The same procedure applies for removal of multiple packages.

Figure 4-24: Software Manager Installing multiple applications

Flatpak

A Flatpak package installs its own set of supporting libraries that can be kept up to date without affecting those on your system (**https://www.flatpak.org/**). In effect, Flatpak packages run inside their own environment, separate from your system. These applications are downloaded from a repository referred to as a remote. The remote that is enabled for Linux Mint is the main Flatpak remote, Flathub (**https://flathub.org/home**). A Flatpak package is designed to run in an isolated sandbox, using copies of any configuration files, libraries, system folders it has to use. These copies can be updated and modified without affecting the corresponding system folders and libraries on your system. In addition, a Flatpak application use a Flatpak installed and maintained runtime environment for any dependencies the application needs. These are referred to as runtimes, such as a GNOME runtime for the GNOME desktop and a KDE runtime for the KDE desktop (**https://docs.flatpak.org/en/latest/available-runtimes.html**). Normally you will have runtimes installed for Freedesktop, GNOME, and KDE. For more information see **https://docs.flatpak.org/en/latest/**.

Flatpak support it already integrated into Software Manager. Click the Flatpak category to see the list of Flatpak packages (see Figure 4-25). These include popular applications such as VLC, Spotify, Bookworm, Krita, Steam, and Blender. Some applications, such as Bookworm, are only available as Flatpak packages. For Flatpak packages, Software Manager will list the **Flathub** site as the Remote on the application description page (see Figure 4-26). To install a Flatpak package, just click the Install button.

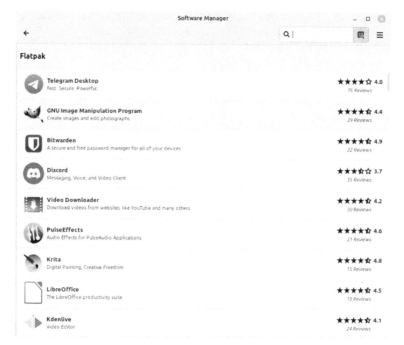

Figure 4-25: Software Manager - Flatpak Package List

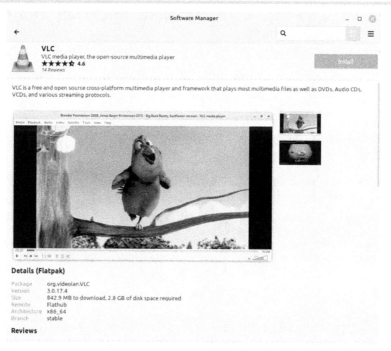

Figure 4-26: Software Manager - Flatpak Package

Flatpak packages are installed to the **/var/lib/flatpak/app** folder. For each application there are subfolders for the architecture (x86_64) and the release (stable). An active link, links to the activated version. Under the version are the system folders, libraries, and configuration files for the application such as **/bin**, **/lib**, **/sbin**, and **/share**.

You can also manage Flatpak applications using the **flatpak** command. Use the **--help** option to see a list of flatpak commands. The **list** command with the **--app** option displays your installed Flatpak applications.

```
flatpak list --app
```

The **list** command with no options will also list the runtime.

```
flatpak list
```

Use the search command for search for a Flatpak application.

```
flatpak search vlc
```

An application is identified by its application id. The application id for the VLC application is **org.videolan.VLC**.

To install an application use **install**, and to remove one use **uninstall**. You can either use its name or application id. The application, its dependencies, configuration files, and libraries will be installed in a folder by that application id, under the **/var/lib/flathub** folder. If you have more than one remote configured, you can specify which one you want to install from.

```
flatpak install vlc
```

Flatpak uses a search operation to locate the application to install. If it is unable to do this, use its application id instead of its name.

```
flatpak install org.videolan.VLC
```

The **info** command show information about an application. You have to reference the application using its application id.

```
flatpak info org.videolan.VLC
```

Use the **update** command to update your installed Flatpak applications.

```
flatpak update
```

To see the list of remotes (Flatpak repositories) you have access to, use the **remotes** command. You can add new remotes with the **remote-add** command.

```
flatpak remotes
```

Use the **--version** option to see the version of Flatpak you are using, and the **--installations** option to see where Flatpak and its applications are installed.

```
flatpak --version
flatpak --installations
```

Synaptic Package Manager

The Synaptic Package Manager has been replaced by Software Manager as the primary package manager, though it is installed by default. Packages are listed by name and include supporting packages like libraries and system critical packages. You can access the Synaptic Package Manager from the Administration menu. The Synaptic Package Manager is a front-end for the APT system and can only access APT repositories. It cannot manage Flatpak or Snap packages.

The Synaptic Package Manager displays three panes: a side pane for listing software categories and buttons, a top pane for listing software packages, and a bottom pane for displaying a selected package's description. When a package is selected, the description pane also displays a Get Screenshot button. Clicking this button will download and display an image of the application if there is one. Click the Get Changelog button to display a window listing the application changes.

Figure 4-27: Synaptic Package Manager: Quick search

Buttons at the lower left of the Synaptic Package Manager window provide options for organizing and refining the list of packages shown (see Figure 4-27). Five options are available: Sections, Status, Origin, Custom Filters, and Search results. The dialog pane above the buttons changes depending on which option you choose. Clicking the Sections button will list section categories for your software such as Graphics, Communications, and Development. The Status button will list options for installed and not installed software. The Origin button shows entries for different repositories and their sections, as well as those locally installed (manual or disc-based installations). Custom filters let you choose a filter to use for listing packages. You can create your own filter and use it to display selected packages. Search results will list your current and previous searches, letting you move from one to the other.

The Sections option is selected by default (see Figure 4-28). You can choose to list all packages, or refine your listing using categories provided in the pane. The All entry in this pane will list all available packages. Packages are organized into categories such as Cross Platform, Communications, and Editors. Each category is, in turn, subdivided by multiverse, universe, and restricted software.

Figure 4-28: Synaptic Package Manager: Sections

Status entries further refine installed software as manual or as upgradeable (see Figure 4-29). Local software consists of packages you download and install manually.

Figure 4-29: Synaptic Package Manager: Status

With the Origin options, Ubuntu and Linux Mint compliant repositories may further refine access according to mint, multiverse, universe, and restricted software. The main section selects Ubuntu and Linux Mint supported software. The Architecture options let you select software compatible with a specified architecture, such as 64-bit or 32-bit.

To perform a search, you use the Search tool. Click the Search button on the toolbar to open a Search dialog with a text box where you can enter search terms. A pop-up menu lets you specify what features of a package to search such as the "Description and Name" feature. You can search other package features like the Name, the maintainer name (Maintainer), the package version (Version), packages it may depend on (Dependencies), or associated packages (Provided Packages). A list of searches will be displayed in Search Results. You can move back and forth between search results by clicking on the search entries in this listing.

To find out information about a package, select the package and click the Properties button. This opens a window with Common, Dependencies, Installed Files, Versions, and Description tabs (see Figure 4-27). The Common tab provides section, versions, and maintainer information. The Installed Files tab show you exactly what files are installed, which is useful for finding the exact location, and names for configuration files, as well as commands. The Description tab displays detailed information about the software. The Dependencies tab shows all dependent software packages needed by this software, usually libraries.

Installing and removing packages

Before installing software, you should press the Reload button to load the most recent package lists from the active repositories

To install a package, single click on its empty checkbox or right-click on its name to display a pop-up menu and select the Mark for installation entry. Should any dependent packages exist, a dialog opens listing those packages. Click the Mark button in the dialog to mark those packages for installation. The package entry's checkbox will then be marked in the Synaptic Package Manager window.

Once you have selected the packages you want to install, click the Apply button on the toolbar to begin the installation process. A Summary dialog opens showing all the packages to be installed. You have the option to download the package files only. The number of packages to be installed is listed, along with the size of the download and the amount of disk space used. Click the Apply button on the Summary dialog to download and install the packages. A download window will then appear showing the progress of your package installations. You can choose to show the progress of individual packages, which opens a terminal window listing each package as it is downloaded and installed.

Once downloaded, the dialog name changes to Installing Software. You can choose to have the dialog close automatically when finished. Sometimes installation requires user input to configure the software. You will be prompted to enter the information if necessary.

When you right-click a package name, you also see options for Mark Suggested for Installation or Mark Recommended for Installation. These will mark applications that can enhance your selected software, though they are not essential. If there are no suggested or recommended packages for that application, then these entries will be grayed out.

Certain software, like desktops or office suites that require a significant number of packages, can be selected all at once using metapackages. A metapackage has configuration files that select, download, and configure the range of packages needed for such complex software. Linux Mint metapackages begin with the term mint-meta, such as those for Linux Mint desktops and codecs like **mint meta-xfce**, **mint-meta-mate**, and **mint-meta-codecs**.

To remove a package, first, locate it. Then right-click it and select the "Mark package for removal" entry. This will leave configuration files untouched. Alternatively, you can mark a package for complete removal, which will also remove any configuration files, "Mark for Complete Removal." Dependent packages will not be removed.

Once you have marked packages for removal, click the Apply button. A summary dialog displays the packages that will be removed. Click Apply to remove them.

The Synaptic Package Manager may not remove dependent packages, especially shared libraries that might be used by other applications. This means that your system could have installed packages that are never being used.

Search filters

You can further refine your search for packages by creating search filters. Select the Settings | Filters menu entry to open the Filters window. The Filters window shows two panes, a filter list on the left, and three tabs on the right: Status, Section, and Properties. To create a new filter, click the New button located just below the filter listing. Click the New Filter 1 entry in the filter list on the left pane. On the Status tab, you can refine your search criteria according to a package's status. You can search only uninstalled packages, include installed packages, include or exclude packages marked for removal, or search or those that are new in the repository. Initially, all criteria are selected. Uncheck those you do not want included in your search. The Section tab lets you include or exclude different repository sections like games, documentation, or administration. If you are looking for a game, you could choose to include just the game section, excluding everything else. On the Properties tab, you can specify patterns to search on package information such as package names, using Boolean operators to refine your search criteria. Package search criteria are entered using the two pop-up menus and the text box at the bottom of the tab, along with AND or OR Boolean operators.

Software Manager for separate DEB packages: GDebi

You can also use the GDebi Package Installer to perform an installation of a single DEB software package. Usually, these packages are downloaded directly from a website and have few or no dependent packages. When you use your browser to download a particular package, you will be prompted to open it with the GDebi package Installer. GDebi opens an install dialog for that software package, displaying information about the package and checking to see if it is compatible with your system (see Figure 4-30). The package name is shown in the title bar. A notification bar displays the number of additional packages that have to be installed (dependencies). Click the Details button to see what these additional packages are. The maintainer and size of the package is listed. Click the files button to display a list of all the files the package installs. Click the Install Package button to install the package.

Figure 4-30: GDebi Package Installer

You could also first download the package, and then later select it from your file manager window (usually the Downloads folder). Double clicking should open the package with GDebi. You can also right-click and choose to open it with the GDebi Package Installer. It is advisable to use GDebi to install a manually downloaded package.

Installing and Running Windows Software on Linux: Wine

Wine is a Windows compatibility layer that will allow you to run many Windows applications natively on Linux. The actual Windows operating system is not required. Windows applications will run as if they were Linux applications, able to access the entire Linux file system and use Linux-connected devices. Applications that are heavily driver-dependent, like graphic intensive games, may not run. Others that do not rely on any specialized drivers, may run very well, including Photoshop and Microsoft Office. For some applications, you may also need to copy over specific Windows dynamic link libraries (DLLs) from a working Windows system to your Wine Windows system32 or system folder.

You can install Wine on your system with Software Manager, the Synaptic Package Manager, or the **apt** command. Install the **wine-installer** package. The **ttf-mscorefonts-installer** for the Microsoft core fonts will also be installed. You will be prompted to accept the Microsoft end user agreement for using those fonts.

```
apt install wine-installer
```

Wine should work on both **.exe** and **.msi** files. You may have to make them executable by checking the file's Properties dialog Permissions tab's Execute checkbox. If an **.msi** file cannot be run, you may have to use the **msiexec** command with the **/a** option.

```
msiexec /a winprogram.msi
```

The Wine applications include Wine configuration (**winecfg**), the Wine software uninstaller, and Wine file browser, as well as Winetricks and notepad. The Winetricks application can be run directly on your Ubuntu desktop and provides an easy way to install compatible Windows applications.

For many windows applications, including **winecfg**, you will need to install the Wine Geckos package. You can download it directly from the WineHQ website at **https://wiki.winehq.org/Gecko**. Once installed you can use the **wine msiexec** command to install it.

```
wine msiexec wine-gecko-2.47.1-x86_64
```

To set up Wine, start the Wine Configuration tool (enter the **sudo winecfg** command in a terminal window) to open a window with tabs for Applications, Libraries (DLL selection), Audio (sound drivers), Drives, Desktop Integration, and Graphics. On the Applications tab, you can select the version of Windows an application is designed for. The Drives tab lists your detected partitions, as well as your Windows-emulated drives, such as drive C. The C: drive is actually just a folder, **.wine/drive_c**, not a partition of a fixed size. Your actual Linux file system will be listed as the Z drive.

```
sudo winecfg
```

Once configured, Wine will set up a **.wine** folder on the user's home folder (the folder is hidden, enable Show Hidden Files in the file manager View menu to display it). Within that folder will be the **drive_c** folder, which functions as the C: drive that holds your Windows system files and program files in the Windows and Program File subfolders. The System and System32 folders are located in the Windows folder. This is where you would place any needed DLL files. The Program Files folder holds your installed Windows programs, just as they would be installed on a Windows Program Files folder.

You can open a terminal window and run the `wine` command with a Windows application as an argument.

```
$ wine winprogram
```

The following starts the MS Paint application on your Ubuntu desktop using Wine.

```
wine mspaint
```

To run the Windows explorer file manager for your Wine Window files, enter the following.

```
wine explorer
```

The command for the Wine task manager is **taskmgr** and for the registry editor it is **regedit**. The Wine task manager lets you search for and run installed applications.

```
wine taskmgr
wine regedit
```

An easy way to install and manage Window applications on Wine is to use Winetricks. You can start Winetricks directly from the Ubuntu applications overview. A "What do you want to do" dialog lets you choose different task such as install an application or game. To install an application, click the "Install an application" entry and then click the OK button to display a list of possible compatible Windows applications. Some you can download and install directly. A few require an application DVD or CD. Some will require a manual download. Once installed you can then return to the wineprefix dialog. The "Select the default wineprefix" option lets you perform system tasks such as running **winecfg**, the explorer file manager, and install fonts. When Wine installs a Windows application, it may display several install messages. You can turn this off by choosing "Enable silent install" on the "What do you want to do" dialog. The term wineprefix in the Winetricks titebar refers to the folder Wine is installed on.

Alternatively, you can use the commercial Windows compatibility layer called Crossover Office. This is a commercial product tested to run certain applications like Microsoft Office. Check **https://www.codeweavers.com** for more details. Crossover Office is based on Wine, which CodeWeavers supports directly.

Source code files

You can install source code files using **apt-get**. Specify the **source** operation with the package name. Packages will be downloaded and extracted.

```
sudo apt-get source mplayer
```

The **--download** option lets you just download the source package without extracting it. The **--compile** option will download, extract, compile, and package the source code into a Debian binary package, ready for installation.

With the **source** operation, no dependent packages will be downloaded. If a software package requires any dependent packages to run, you would have to download and compile those. To obtain needed dependent files, you use the **build-dep** option. All your dependent files will be located and downloaded for you automatically.

```
sudo apt-get build-dep mplayer
```

Installing from source code requires that supporting development libraries and source code header files be installed. You can do this separately for each major development platform like GNOME or the kernel. Alternatively, you can run the APT meta-package **build-essential** for all the Linux Mint development packages. You will have to do this only once.

```
sudo apt-get install build-essential
```

Software Package Types

Linux Mint uses Debian-compliant software packages (DEB) whose filenames have a **.deb** extension. Other packages, such as those in the form of source code that you need to compile, may come in a variety of compressed archives. These commonly have the extension **.tar.gz**, **.tgz**, or **.tar.bz2**. Packages with the **.rpm** extension are Red Hat Package software packages used on Red Hat, Fedora, SuSE and other Linux distributions that use RPM packages. They are not compatible directly with Linux Mint. You can use the **alien** utility to convert most RPM packages to DEB packages that you can then install on Linux Mint. If you installed the Snap system, Snap packages will have the extension **.snap.** Table 4-1 lists several common file extensions that you will find for the great variety of Linux software packages available. You can download any Linux Mint-compliant deb package as well as the original source code package, as single files, directly from **http://packages.linuxmint.com**.

DEB Software Packages

A Debian package will automatically resolve dependencies, installing any other needed packages instead of simply reporting their absence. Packages are named with the software name, the version number, and the **.deb** extension. Check **https://www.debian.org/doc** for more information. The Debian package filename format is as follows:

the package name

version number

distribution label and build number. Packages created specifically for Linux Mint have the Linux Mint label here. Attached to it is the build number, the number of times the package was built for Linux Mint.

architecture   The type of system on which the package runs, like i386 for Intel 32-bit x86 systems, or amd64 for both Intel and AMD 64-bit systems, x86_64.

package format. This is always **deb**

For example, the package name for 3dchess is 3dchess, with a version and build number 0.8.1-20, and an architecture amd64 for a 64-bit system.

```
3dchess_0.8.1-20_amd64.deb
```

The following package has an Ubuntu label, a package specifically created for Ubuntu that is not the same as the original Debian version (**dfsg**). The version and build number is 4.11.6. The architecture is amd64 for a 64-bit system.

```
samba_4.11.6+dfsg-0ubuntu1.4_amd64.deb
```

Extension	File
.deb	A Debian/Linux Mint Linux package
.gz	A **gzip**-compressed file (use **gunzip** to decompress)
.bz2	A **bzip2**-compressed file (use **bunzip2** to decompress; also use the **j** option with **tar**, as in **xvjf**)
.tar	A tar archive file (use **tar** with **xvf** to extract)
.tar.gz	A **gzip**-compressed **tar** archive file (use **gunzip** to decompress and **tar** to extract; use the **z** option with **tar**, as in **xvzf**, to both decompress and extract in one step)
.tar.bz2	A **bzip2**-compressed **tar** archive file (extract with **tar -xvzj**)
.tz	A **tar** archive file compressed with the **compress** command
.Z	A file compressed with the **compress** command (use the **decompress** command to decompress)
.bin	A self-extracting software file
.rpm	A software package created with the Red Hat Software Package Manager used on Fedora, Red Hat, Centos, and SuSE distributions
.snap	A snap package, alternative to .deb

Table 4-1: Linux Software Package File Extensions

Managing software with apt and apt-get

APT is designed to work with repositories, and will handle any dependencies for you. It uses **dpkg** to install and remove individual packages, but can also determine what dependent packages need to be installed, as well as query and download packages from repositories. Several popular tools for APT let you manage your software easily, like the Synaptic Package Manager, Software Manager, and aptitude. Software Manager and the Synaptic Package Manager rely on a desktop interface like GNOME. If you are using the command line interface, you can use **apt** or **apt-get** to manage packages. Using the **apt** or **apt-get** commands on the command line you can install, update, and remove packages. Check the **apt** and **apt-get** man pages for a detailed listing of **apt-get** commands (see Table 4-2).

```
apt-get command package
```

The **apt** command is a new version of **apt-get** with fewer options. For example, the **apt-get** command has the **check** option to check for broken dependencies. Older systems may want to continue using **apt-get**, especially if the command is used in customized system scripts. For basic operations, such as upgrading, installing, or removing packages, you could use **apt** instead.

```
apt-get command package
```

```
apt command package
```

Command	Description
update	Download and resynchronize the package listing of available and updated packages for APT supported repositories. APT repositories updated for Linux Mint are those specified in **/etc/apt/sources.list.d/official-package-repositories.list**
upgrade	Update packages, install new versions of installed packages if available.
dist-upgrade	Update (upgrade) all your installed packages to a new release
install	Install a specific package, using its package name, not full package file name.
remove	Remove a software package from your system.
source	Download and extract a source code package
check	Check for broken dependencies
clean	Removes the downloaded packages held in the repository cache on your system. Used to free up disk space.

Table 4-2: apt and apt-get commands

The **apt** and **apt-get** commands usually take two arguments: the command to perform and the name of the package. Other APT package tools follow the same format. The command is a term such as **install** for installing packages or **remove** to uninstall a package. You only need to specify the software name, not the package's full filename. APT will determine that. To install the MPlayer package you would use:

```
sudo apt install mplayer
```

To make sure that **apt** or **apt-get** has current repository information, use the **update** command.

```
sudo apt update
```

To remove packages, you use the **remove** command.

```
sudo apt remove mplayer
```

You can use the **-s** option to check the remove or install first, especially to check whether any dependency problems exist. For remove operations, you can use **-s** to find out first what dependent packages will also be removed.

```
sudo apt-get remove -s mplayer
```

The **apt-get** and **apt** commands can be helpful if your X Windows System server ever fails (your display driver). For example, if you installed a restricted vendor display driver, and then your desktop fails to start, you can start up in the recovery mode, start the root shell, and use **apt** or **apt-get** to remove the restricted display driver. Your former X open source display drivers would be restored automatically. The following would remove the Nvidia restricted display driver.

```
sudo apt remove nvidia*
```

A complete log of all install, remove, and update operations are kept in the **/var/log/dpkg.log** file. You can consult this file to find out exactly what files were installed or removed.

Configuration for APT is held in the **/etc/apt** folder. Officially the **/etc/apt/sources.list** file is supposed to list the distribution repositories from where packages are installed. Source lists for additional third-party repositories are kept in the **/etc/apt/sources.list.d** folder. However, on Linux Mint, the list of distribution repositories is kept in the **/etc/apt/sources.list.d/official-package-repositories.list** fie. GPG (GNU Privacy Guard) database files hold validation keys for those repositories. Specific options for **apt-get** are can be found in an **/etc/apt/apt.conf** file or in various files located in the **/etc/apt/apt.conf.d** folder.

Updating packages (Upgrading) with apt and apt-get

The **apt** tool also lets you update your entire system at once. The terms **update** and **upgrade** are used differently from other software tools. In **apt**, the **update** command just updates your package listing, checking for packages that may need to install newer versions, but not installing those versions. Technically, it updates the package list that APT uses to determine what packages need to be updated. The term **upgrade** is used to denote the actual update of a software package. A new version is downloaded and installed. What is referred to as updating by **apt**, other package managers refer to as obtaining the list of software packages to be updated (the reload operation). In **apt**, upgrading is what other package managers refer to as performing updates.

Note: The terms **update** and **upgrade** can be confusing when used with **apt**. The update operation updates the Apt package list only, whereas an upgrade actually downloads and installs updated packages.

Upgrading is a simple matter of using the **upgrade** command. With no package specified, using **apt** or **apt-get** with the **upgrade** command will upgrade your entire system. Add the **-u** option to list packages as they are upgraded. First, make sure your repository information (package list) is up to date with the **update** command, then issue the **upgrade** command.

```
sudo apt update
sudo apt -u upgrade
```

Command Line Search and Information: dpkg-query and apt-cache tools

The **dpkg-query** command lets you list detailed information about your packages. It operates on the command line (terminal window). Use **dpkg-query** with the **-l** option to list all your packages.

```
dpkg-query -l
```

The **dpkg** command can operate as a front end for **dpkg-query**, detecting its options to perform the appropriate task. The preceding command could also be run as:

```
dpkg -l
```

Listing a particular package requires and exact match on the package name unless you use pattern matching operators. The following command lists the **samba** package.

```
dpkg-query -l samba
```

A pattern matching operator, such as *, placed after a pattern will display any packages beginning with the specified pattern. The pattern with its operators needs to be placed in single quotation marks to prevent an attempt by the shell to use the pattern to match on filenames in your current folder. The following example finds all packages beginning with the pattern "samba". This would include packages with names such as **samba-client** and **samba-common**.

```
dpkg-query -l 'samba*'
```

You can further refine the results by using **grep** to perform an additional search. The following operation first outputs all packages beginning with **samba**, and from those results, the **grep** operations lists only those with the pattern "common" in their name, such as **samba-common**.

```
dpkg -l 'samba*' | grep 'common'
```

Use the **-L** option to list the files that a package has installed.

```
dpkg-query -L samba
```

To see the status information about a package, including its dependencies and configuration files, use the **-s** option. Fields will include Status, Section, Architecture, Version, Depends (dependent packages), Suggests, Conflicts (conflicting packages), and Conffiles (configuration files).

```
dpkg-query -s samba
```

The status information will also provide suggested dependencies. These are packages not installed, but likely to be used. For the samba package, the **chrony** time server package is suggested.

```
dpkg-query -s  samba | grep Suggests
```

Use the **-S** option to determine to which package a particular file belongs to.

```
dpkg-query -S filename
```

You can also obtain information with the **apt-cache** tool. Use the search command with **apt-cache** to perform a search.

```
apt-cache search samba
```

To find dependencies for a particular package, use the **depends** command.

```
apt-cache depends samba
```

To display the package information, use the **show** command.

```
apt-cache show samba
```

Note: If you have installed Aptitude software manager, you can use the **aptitude** command with the **search** and **show** options to find and display information about packages.

Managing non-repository packages with dpkg

You can use **dpkg** to install a software package you have already downloaded directly, not with an APT enabled software tool such as **apt**, Software Manager, or the Synaptic Package Manager. In this case, you are not installing from a repository. Instead, you have manually downloaded the package file from a Web or FTP site to a folder on your system. Such a situation would be rare, reserved for software not available on the Linux Mint repository or any APT enabled repository. Keep in mind that most software is already on your Linux Mint or APT enabled repositories. Check there first for the software package before performing a direct download and installing with **dpkg**. The **dpkg** configuration files are located in the **/etc/dpkg** folder. Configuration is held in the **dpkg.cfg** file. See the **dpkg** man page for a detailed listing of options.

One situation, for which you would use **dpkg**, is for packages you have built yourself, like packages you created when converting a package in another format to a Debian package (DEB). This is the case when converting an RPM package (Red Hat Package Manager) to a Debian package format.

For **dpkg**, you use the **-i** option to install a package and **-r** to remove it.

```
sudo dpkg -i package.deb
```

The major failing for **dpkg** is that it provides no dependency support. It will inform you of needed dependencies, but you will have to install them separately. **dpkg** installs only the specified package. It is useful for packages that have no dependencies.

You use the **-I** option to obtain package information directly from the DEB package file.

```
sudo dpkg -I package.deb
```

To remove a package, you use the **-r** option with the package software name. You do not need version or extension information like **.386** or **.deb**. With **dpkg**, when removing a package with dependencies, you first have to remove all its dependencies manually. You will not be able to uninstall the package until you do this. Configuration files are not removed.

```
sudo dpkg -r packagename
```

If you install a package that requires dependencies, and then fail to install these dependencies, your install database will be marked as having broken packages. In this case, APT will not allow new packages to be installed until the broken packages are fixed. You can enter the **apt-get** command with the **-f** and **install** options to fix all broken packages at once.

```
sudo apt-get -f install
```

Using packages with other software formats

You can convert software packages in other software formats into DEB packages that can then be installed on Linux Mint. To do this you use the **alien** tool, which can convert several different kinds of formats such as RPM and even TGZ (**.tgz**). You use the **--to-deb** option to convert to a DEB package format that Linux Mint can then install. The **--scripts** option attempts also to convert any pre or post install configuration scripts. Once you have generated the **.deb** package, you can use **dpkg** or Software Manager to install it.

```
alien --scripts --to-deb package.rpm
```

Ubuntu Snap

Ubuntu supports two packages management systems, Snap and DEB (Debian package format). For the older DEB formatted packages, the underlying software management tool is APT. Snap packages (**snaps**) have a different format from DEB, and cannot be managed by APT. Instead they are managed by the Snap package manager, which uses the **snapd** daemon to install, update, and run snap applications. Snap is a completely different package management system, though

Snap packages can be installed alongside APT packages, and accessed seamlessly on both Linux Mint and the Ubuntu desktops.

APT (Advanced Package Tool) is the older tool for installing packages, and is still used for most applications. When you install a DEB package with Software Manager or with the Synaptic Package Manager, APT will be invoked and will select and download the package automatically from the appropriate online APT managed repository. This will include the entire Ubuntu online repository, including the main, universe, multiverse, and restricted sections.

A DEB software package includes all the files needed for a software application. A Linux software application often consists of several files that must be installed in different folders. The application program itself is placed in a system folder such as **/usr/bin**, online manual files go in another folder, and library files go in yet another folder. When you select an application for installation, APT will install any additional dependent (required) packages. APT also will install all recommended packages by default. Many software applications have additional features that rely on recommended packages.

Snap is the new package format that is intended to replace the DEB package management system on Ubuntu. As noted, the packages are called **snaps**. With the DEB format, as with other Linux pack formats like RPM, the component software files for a software application are installed directly to global system folders such as **/lib**, **/etc**, and **/usr/bin**. In effect, such a package has access to your entire system during installation, posing security risks. In addition, a DEB software package usually has several dependent packages, which also have to be installed. These can be extensive. Under this system, shared libraries, used by different applications can be a problem for developers, as changes in software may have to wait for supporting changes in the shared libraries.

With Snap, the software files for an application are no longer installed in global folders. They are installed in one separate folder, and any dependent software and shared libraries are included as part of the snap package. In effect, there are no longer any dependencies, and libraries are no longer shared. This makes for more secure and faster updates, though a larger set of installed files. The installation process no longer needs access to your entire system. The entire application is isolated in one location. The problem of a failed update due to broken dependencies is no longer an issue. Applications that used to make use of the same shared library, will now have their own copies of that library. Developers that used to have to wait for changes to be made to a shared library, can now directly just change their own copy.

Keep in mind that Flatpak, which is already enabled on Linux Mint, works much the same way as Snap (**https://www.flatpak.org/**). Many of the popular applications available as Snaps are already available on Linux Mint as Flatpaks.

Snaps Packages

Snaps are designed to provide a universal and independent software repository whose packages will run on any Linux distribution or, even, versions of a Linux distribution. A snap package can be downloaded and installed on any distribution, including Ubuntu, Fedora, Debian, Centos, Linux Mint, and openSUSE. A snap package can also run on any version of that distribution. The same snap package will also run on different Linux releases of a distribution, such as Ubuntu 18.04 and 20.04. Software developers can simply maintain the one snap package, instead of several for different distributions. This design make it much easier for commercial software companies to provide Linux clients of their proprietary applications. Currently these include Skype,

Zoom, and Slack. Such a structure makes updating a simple and fast procedure. Updates are performed automatically within six hours of a revision by the developer by the **snapd** server on your system. You can update manually if you wish or set a different update schedule.

The Snap system is maintained and supported by Ubuntu.

Check the Snapcraft documentation and tutorials at:

```
https://snapcraft.io/docs
https://snapcraft.io/tutorials
```

It is important to keep in mind the difference between a snap package and a snap application. Some snap packages install several applications. Most install only one. There are snap commands that work on packages, such as **install** and **disable**. But there are others that work only on snap applications, such as the **run** command. The Skype package installs only the Skype application, and the name for the package and application are the same. Whereas the Nextcloud service installs several applications, each with a different name such as **nextcloud.apache** for the web server. So for Skype, you can manage both the package and application with the just the name **skype**. But for nextcloud you use the name **nextcloud** to manage the package, but the name of particular nextcloud application to run the application.

```
snap enable nextcloud
snap run nextcloud.apache
```

Linux Mint restriction on installing Snap

Linux Mint 21 is configured to prevent the installation of Snap. The **snapd** package is listed, but it will not install. Linux Mint took this action because of the restrictions on the Snap Store. Snap packages can only be obtained from the Snap Store (repository), and there can be only one Snap Store, the one maintained by Ubuntu. By contrast, anyone can set up an APT repository or even a Flatpak store. For a detailed discussion of this policy see:

```
https://linuxmint-user-guide.readthedocs.io/en/latest/snap.html
```

It is possible to remove the restriction with a simple command and then install the **snapd** daemon and service, as noted in the Linux Mint 21 release notes. Even when enabled, Software Manager will not manage or detect applications in the snap store. You will have to install the Snap Store application or use the **snap** command to install software on the snap store.

As noted in the Linux Mint documentation, you run the following commands to enable the Snap, removing the **nosnap.pref** configuration file in the **/etc/apt/preferences.d** folder.

```
sudo rm /etc/apt/preferences.d/nosnap.pref
sudo apt update
sudo apt install snapd
```

Should you want to later remove Snap completely from your system, use the following command.

```
sudo apt autoremove --purge snapd
```

snap command

You can use the **snap** command in a terminal window to install and manage snap packages (see Table 4-3). To find a Snap package, use the **snap find** command with the search term (see Figure 4-31).

```
snap find chromium
```

You can also search on a search term. The following example searches for FTP clients and servers, and for Web servers.

```
snap find ftp
snap find "web server"
```

Without the search term, a list of popular snap packages is displayed.

```
snap find
```

Snaps are further organized into sections such as entertainment, games, and productivity. You can see the available sections with the **find --section** command.

```
snap find --section
```

To see available games you would enter the section name preceded by the = sign, as in **--section=games**.

```
snap find --section=games
```

To install a package, use the **snap** command with the **install** option. The following installs the Chromium snap package.

```
sudo snap install chromium
```

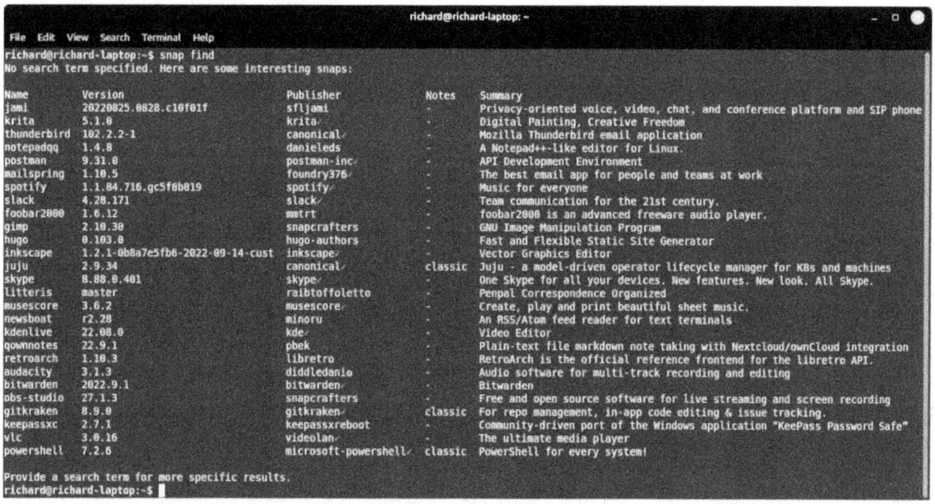

Figure 4-31: Listing of popular available snaps: find

Command	Description
find *pattern*	Search for available snap packages. Without a search term, a list of popular packages is displayed.
find --section	List the available snap package categories (sections)
find --section=section-name	List the snap packages in a section
refresh	Manually update packages, installing new revisions of installed packages if available. Snaps are automatically updated every six hours by default.
install *snap-package*	Install a snap package
remove	Remove a a snap package completely
revert [*revision-number*]	Revert to a previous installed revision of a snap. Without a revision number the previous installed revision is used.
disable *snap-package*	Disable a snap without uninstalling it. The installed snap remains on your system, but is unavailable to users. Will disable all snap applications installed by the package.
enable *snap-package*	Enable a disabled snap, making it available to users again. Will enable all snap applications installed by the package
list	List your installed snap packages
list --all	List all your snap packages along with the revisions for each package, which will also display the revision number of revision
list --all *snap-package*	List all the revisions for a snap package, which will also display the revision number for each
connections	List interfaces with their plugs and slots
interface	List available interfaces with a description of each
install channel=risk-level	Install a snap package revision from a specified risk-level (**stable**, **candidate**, **beta**, and **edge**)
info *snap-package*	Display detailed information for an installed snap package, including all revisions
connect *plug slot*	Manually connect a snap application (plug) to a system resource (slot)
get	List configuration options for a package you can set if there are any
set	Change configuration options for a package if there are any
unset	Set configuration options to nothing for a package if there are any
run *snap-application*	Run a snap application

Table 4-3: snap commands

Once installed, the snap applications installed by the package will appear on the Linux Mint menu, just as any other application.

Use the **remove** command to remove a package completely from your system.

```
sudo snap remove chromium
```

      With Snap, you have the option of simply disabling a package, instead of removing it completely. The Snap package remains installed, but is unavailable to any users. Use the **disable** command to disable a package. You can enable a disabled package with the **enable** command. Keep in mind that if the package installed several applications, all those applications are disabled by the **disable** command. The **enable** command will enable all of them.

```
sudo snap disable chromium
sudo snap enable chromium
```

      Use the **refresh** command to update your snap packages.

```
sudo snap refresh chromium
```

      To see a list of snap packages already installed, use the **list** command (see Figure 4-32).

```
snap list
```

      To display detailed information about a particular snap package, you use the **info** command.

```
snap info chromium
```

      Snap applications are stored as revisions in the **/snap** folder under the package name. Each revision has its own folder, which includes the application executables, as well as all configuration and system support files. In effect, each revision of a Snap application has its own **/etc**, **/usr**, **/bin**, **/lib**, and **/var** folder. A link to the application program currently enabled is held in the **/snap/bin** folder. User data for a Snap application is held in a **snap** folder in your home folder. Systemd support for Snap is provided by the systemd **snapd.service** and **snapd.socket** files.

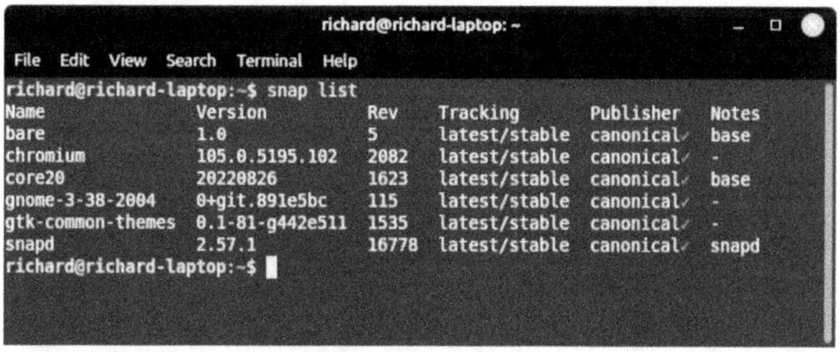

Figure 4-32: Listing of installed snaps: list

      Should you want to create a snap package, you can use **snapcraft**, which you can install the **snap install --classic** command or GNOME Software (Snap enabled).

Snap Channels: tracks and risk levels

      Snap packages are managed by channels which organize a package into tracks and risk levels. Developers may also add a branch category for short-term versions of an applications. You will see track and risk-levels listed as possible channel selections in GNOME Software for a Snap package.

`track/risk-level`

The track indicates the revision of a package installed. By default this is **latest**. The risk level indicates the reliability of the software. There are four risk levels: **stable**, **candidate**, **beta**, and **edge**. The **stable** risk level is for reliable software considered ready for mass distribution. The **candidate** risk level is for a version of the application being readied for release but still being tested. The **beta** risk level is for beta versions of applications that may incorporate new features but is considered unstable. The **edge** risk level is for versions that are still under development with ongoing changes that may not always run.

Packages are installed with the latest risk level by default.

`snap install`

Should you want to use a different risk level, you can specify it with the appropriate risk level track: **--stable**, **--candidate**, **--beta**, and **--edge**. You can also use the **--channel** option.

```
snap install --candidate
snap install --channel=candidate
```

You can later change the risk level tracked using the **switch** command. This only changes the tracking. It does not install the version for that track. To do that you would have to run the **refresh** command.

```
snap switch --candidate
```

To both perform a switch to a different track and install the version of the applications from that track, you can run the **refresh** command directly.

```
snap refresh --channel=candidate
```

Snap Confinement

Most snap packages are run using a strict confinement mode, running in isolation with only minimal access to system resources such as networks, system folders, and processes. Some snap packages are allowed to run in the classic mode, if officially approved, letting them access system resources just as a traditional DEB package can. These packages can only be installed with the **--classic** option. For a package to obtain classic status, it must be carefully examined by Snapcraft for security and stability issues. There is also a **devmode** reserved for developers. To see the confinement mode for a package use the **snap info** command with the **--verbose** option. The **snap list** command, which lists all your snap packages, will also display each package's confinement mode.

```
snap info --verbose chromium
```

Access to system resources by a package is setup up by interfaces, which are determined by the developer and implemented when the package is installed. Interfaces usually allow access to resources such as devices. This often includes your home folder, pulseaudio, network access, system files, and the display server (wayland or X11). A snap package can only access your system through these interfaces. Interfaces consist of plugs and slots. The plug is the package or process that needs the interface (the consumer), and the plug is the service that supports it (the provider). The **snap connections** command will list the interfaces for a package.

```
snap connections chromium
```

The **snap connections** command with no package as an argument, will list all the packages (plugs) along with the interfaces and slots they use.

```
snap connections
```

The **snap interface** command lists all your interfaces on your system with a description of each.

```
snap interface
```

To see the slots and plugs used for an interface, use the **snap interface** command with the name of that interface.

You can use the **connect** and **disconnect** commands to manually connect or disconnect an interface for a package. They take as their arguments the plug and slot, with the plug preceded by the package name and a colon. As noted, interfaces for packages are normally set up for you and activated when a package is installed. The following connects the Chromium browser to your home folder.

```
sudo snap connect chromium:home :home
```

Not all interfaces available to a package may be activated when you install it. You can also turn activated interfaces off, denying access for that package to the resource. You can also check the connections (permissions) allowed using the connections command with the package name, showing the slots and plugs for that package.

Snap Revisions: revert

Snaps are installed as revisions. For any given application, you may have several revisions of an application installed. Each revision is able to run as the application. Priority is given to the the current revision, the most recently installed. But you could easily decide to run a previous revision instead. This could happen if a new revision is installed that becomes unstable, or if the changes made to the software have deprecated capabilities you normally use. Major changes to an application are released as a version, which is also considered a revision. Though you could have several revisions for a given version, for most less complex applications you will usually have just the one revision per version.

Whereas a **list** command will display your installed snaps, adding the **--all** option will also display all the revisions of each snap. This operation will display the name, version, revision, tracking, publisher, and notes for each revision.

```
snap list --all
```

Instead of listing all the snaps, you could just list the revisions for a particular snap.

```
snap list --all chromium
```

The revision number is unique. You could have several revisions with the same version number, but the revision number is the unique identifier for that install. Previous revision can be run using their revision number.

Only one revision of an application can be enabled. This is the one that Snap will run. All other revision of that application are disabled, as shown in the Notes field of the **list --all** output.

You can enable a previous revision, disabling the current one, and thereby letting Snap run it. You do this with the **revert** command and the number of the revision you want to enable. The following example reverts Chromium to revision 1259.

```
sudo snap revert chromium 1259
```

If you just want to enable the previous revision, you can leave out the number.

```
sudo snap revert chromium
```

If you decide, after reverting to a previous revision, that you want to return to using the latest revision, run the **revert** command with the revision number of the latest revision.

```
sudo snap revert chromium 1260
```

You could also just run the **refresh** command on that snap. The latest revision is automatically enabled.

```
sudo snap refresh chromium
```

Keep in mind, that if a new update of a snap is later released, the automatic **refresh** operation, will update the snap to that new revision.

Snap Package Configuration

Some Snap package, such as those for services, may have configuration options you can manage using the **snap get**, **snap set**, and **snap unset** commands. The **snap get** command list configuration options for a snap and their current setting. The **snap set** command can change an option, and the **snap unset** command removes a value. Some Snap packages, such as servers, have options that can be set when the application is started. Each revision will have a configuration that will be applied when that revision is run. Using the **revert** command you could change from using one revision of a server to another, each running separate configurations.

In addition, all snap applications have supporting environment variables. Environment variables will show folders that the snap can access, as well as application information such as the revision and version number. You can see the environment variable for an application by first starting that application's shell with the **run --shell** command.

```
sudo snap run --shell chromium
```

Keep in mind that sometimes the package name may not be the same as the application name. A package could install several applications, as is the case with the nextcloud package. To access the Nextcloud web server you would use its application name, **nextcloud.apache**.

```
sudo snap run --shell nextcloud.apache
```

You can then use the shell **env** command to list your environment variables, filtering the output with **grep** and the SNAP pattern to show just the snap related ones.

```
env | grep SNAP
```

The environment variables for the current enabled revision is listed. The folder variables will show the folder of that revision. The SNAP_COMMON and SNAP_USER_DATA variables show the location of the folders that your application can write to.

To leave the shell enter the **exit** command.

Snap and Services

Services installed as snap packages can be managed by **systemctl** and **snap** commands such as **systemctl start** and **systemctl stop,** or **snap** start and stop, to start and stop a service. In addition, some snap packaged services will also provide configuration options you can manage using the snap **get**, **set**, and **unset** commands. There are few services currently available as snap packages. For most services like the FTP and Web servers, you would still use APT.

Services installed as snap packages have their systemd service files installed in the **/etc/systemd/system** folder, not in **/lib/systemd/system** as APT services are. All snap installed services are managed through the **snapd** server. The **snapd** server, in turn, has service files for **snapd** in the **/lib/system/system** folder. Furthermore, all the snap installed services have their service files begin with the term **snap**, as in **snap.nextcloud.apache.service** for the Nextcloud web server (part of the **nextcloud** snap package). You can then use **systemctl** and **snap** commands to manage the service.

```
systemctl status snap.nextcloud.apache
sudo system restart snap.nextcloud.apache
```

You can use the **snap** command directly to manage services for **start**, **stop**, and **restart** operations. For status, you would use the **services** option which simply lists is current status and the name of the service file.

```
sudo snap start nextcloud.apache
snap services nextcloud.apache
```

Snap Store

You can also install the Ubuntu Snap Store to manage snap applications. The Snap Store is a modified version of GNOME Software designed to access and manage Snap applications. It is referred to on Ubuntu as Ubuntu Software. The name of the Snap Store package is **snap-store**. It is a Snap application and is installed with the **snap** command.

```
sudo snap install snap-store
```

Should you want to later remove the Snap Store, use the remove command.

```
sudo snap remove snap-store
```

Once installed you can run it from the Administration menu (see Figure 4-33).

Figure 4-33: Snap Store on menu

A window opens with two tabs at the top for Explore and Installed. You can install applications from the Explore tab, which displays, a collection of category buttons, a list of editor picks, and recent releases (see Figure 4-34 and Figure 4-35).

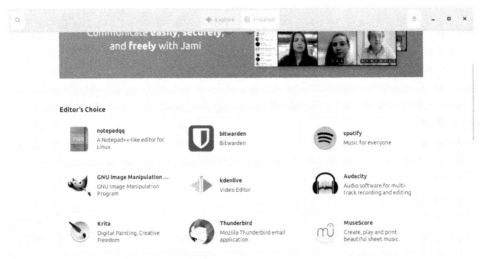

Figure 4-34: Snap Store on Linux Mint

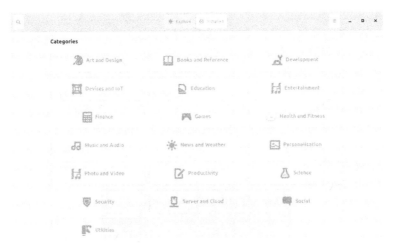

Figure 4-35: Snap Store categories

The software's description page provides a brief description of the software and a link to its related website (see Figure 4-36). Uninstalled software displays an Install button below the software's name, and installed software shows a Remove button. To the right of the name is a star rating with the number of reviews.

Figure 4-36: Snap Store software page

For packages installed from the Snap Store (**snapcraft.io**), you can choose from different channels including stable, candidate, beta, and edge. Channels are selected from the Channel menu on the right side of the titlebar (see Figure 4-17). Each version will list the URL, channel, and version. The URL is **snapcraft.io** for the Ubuntu Snap Store. The channel will list the track and risk level, usually **latest/stable** or **latest/beta**. The version shows the version of the software package. The **stable** and **candidate** risk levels usually have the same version, where the **beta** risk level will be different. Some applications will have tracks for special releases, such as the **esr/stable** channel for Firefox's Extended Support Release (**esr**).

Figure 4-37: Snap Store (snapcraft.io) snap package channels

For snapcraft packages, once installed, a Permissions button is displayed next to the Remove button (trash icon). Click this button to display permissions for the application such as access to the home folder and access to removable devices (see Figure 4-38). Snap packages are isolated from your system resources such as your home folder and the System Settings configuration dialogs. They must have permission to access them. Several basic permissions will be set by default when the package is installed. Others you will have to set.

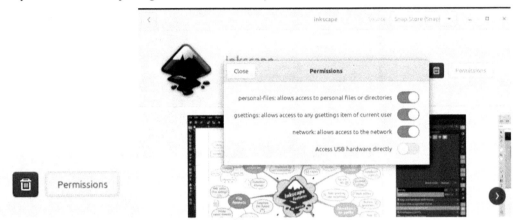

Figure 4-38: Snap Store package permissions

The Installed tab lists your installed software (see Figure 4-39). To remove an application, click its trash button to the right.

Figure 4-39: Snap Store installed packages

Note: It is possible to use the original GNOME Software (**gnome-software** package) to install Snap or Flatpak packages, but it is recommended that your use Linux Mint Software Manager for Flatpak packages and the Snap Store for Snap packages.

5. Applications

X-Apps

Office

Mail

Graphics

Multimedia

Internet

Social Networking

158 *Part 1: Getting Started*

All Linux software for Linux Mint is currently available from online repositories. You can download applications for desktops, Internet servers, office suites, and programming packages, among others. Software packages are distributed primarily through the official Linux Mint and Ubuntu repositories. Downloads and updates are handled automatically by your desktop software manager and updater. Many popular applications are included in separate sections of the repository. During installation, your system is configured to access Linux Mint repositories. You can update to the latest software from the Linux Mint repository using the Update Manager.

The listing of Linux Mint software packages for a release is provided for at:

`http://packages.linuxmint.com`

A more descriptive listing is kept at Linux Mint Community site at:

`https://community.linuxmint.com/software`

Linux Mint is based on Ubuntu. A listing of the software packages for the Ubuntu distribution is located at:

`http://packages.ubuntu.com`

All software packages in the Linux Mint and Ubuntu repositories are accessible directly with Software Manager and the Synaptic Package Manager, which provide easy software installation, removal, and searching.

Due to licensing restrictions, multimedia support for popular operations like MP3, DVD, and DivX are installed separately by the **mint-meta-codecs** package. If not already installed, choose "Install Multimedia Codecs" from the Sound & Video menu, or click the "Multimedia codecs" icon on the Welcome screen.

In addition, you could download from third-party sources software that is in the form of compressed archives or in DEB packages. DEB packages are archived using the Debian Package Manager and have the extension **.deb**. Compressed archives have an extension such as **.tar.gz**. You also can download the source version and compile it directly on your system. This has become a simple process, almost as simple as installing the compiled DEB versions.

You can also install and run any of the KDE applications on your Cinnamon or MATE desktops, such as Karbon (vector graphics), Clementine (music player), Dragon player (media player), Ocular (PDF viewer), and the Calligra office suite. All can be directly installed from Software Manager (Linux Mint and Ubuntu repositories).

Linux Mint also integrates Flatpak packages into Software Manager. You can easily download and install Flatpak packages from the FlatHub repository.

Should you wish, you could also install the Snap package management system developed by Ubuntu. You can then use the Snap Store package manager to access and install Snap packages from the Snap Store repository. Snap and APT are two different package management systems. Linux Mint, as originally installed, supports APT only. Keep in mind, that most popular package on the Snap Store may already be available on Linux Mint as Flatpak packages, which can be directly installed using the Linux Mint Software Manager.

X-Apps

The X-Apps project provides generic applications for traditional GTK (GNOME) desktops, such as MATE, Cinnamon, and Xfce. Improvements to an X-App would work automatically on all the desktops that X-Apps supports. X-Apps installed by Linux Mint desktops include Xed (text editor), Xviewer (image viewer), Pix (image editor and viewer), and Xreader (document viewer), as well as system tools such as Timeshift, slick-greeter (LightDM login screen), and lightdm-settings (login screen configuration). The Xplayer video player has been replaced by Celluloid as the default video player, which is much more capable and efficient. Though many GNOME applications may change with different releases, X-Apps remains the same, and will always work. You can still install and use the corresponding GNOME applications, such as Gedit and Eye of GNOME, but X-Apps will integrate more easily.

Linux Mint also provides X-App support tools such as the XApp Status Applet, which provides a desktop panel system tray holding XAppStatusicon icons, and XappIconChooser for changing application, folder, and file icons, as well as the menu icon. You can change an icon on the Properties dialog for any application, file, or folder. Timeshift is now maintained as an X-app.

Available X-Apps are listed in Table 5-1. Most options for an X-App can be set by the Preferences dialog. Options can also be set using the dconf editor (**org.x**), which can also set options such as the default display configuration.

Application	Description
Xed	Text Editor (based on Pluma)
Xviewer	Image viewer (based on Eye of GNOME)
Pix	Photo organizer (base on Gthumb)
Xreader	PDF reader (based on Atril)
XApp Status Applet	Desktop panel system tray with XAppStatusicon icons for system tools
XAppIconChooser	Change icons for files, folders, and applications.
Timeshift	System backup and snapshot
slick-greeter	LightDM login screen
lightdm-settings	LigthDM login screen configuration

Table 5-1: X-App Applications

Office Applications

Several office suites are now available for Linux. These include professional-level word processors, presentation managers, drawing tools, and spreadsheets. The freely available versions are described in this chapter. All the software are Ubuntu packages. LibreOffice is currently the primary office suite supported by Linux Mint. Calligra is an office suite designed for use with KDE, but will work on GNOME. can also purchase commercial office suites such as Oracle Open Office from Oracle.

Several database management systems are also available for Linux, which includes high-powered, commercial-level database management systems. Most of the database management systems available for Linux are designed to support large relational databases. Linux Mint includes both MySQL, MariaDB, and PostgreSQL open source databases in its distribution, which can support smaller databases.

Linux also provides several text editors that range from simple text editors for simple notes to editors with more complex features such as spell-checkers, buffers, or complex pattern matching. All generate character text files and can be used to edit any Linux text files. Text editors are often used in system administration tasks to change or add entries in Linux configuration files found in the **/etc** folder or a user's initialization or application configuration files located in a user's home folder (dot files). You can also use a text editor to work on source code files for any of the programming languages or shell program scripts.

Linux Mint also supports several Ebook readers. Some such as Calibre and FBReader run natively on Linux.

LibreOffice

LibreOffice is a fully integrated suite of office applications developed as an open source project and freely distributed to all. It is the primary office suite for Linux. LibreOffice applications are accessible from the Office menu. LibreOffice is the open source and freely available office suite derived originally from OpenOffice. LibreOffice is supported by the Document Foundation, which was established after Oracle's acquisition of Sun, the main developer for Open Office. LibreOffice is now the primary open source office software for Linux. Oracle retains control of all the original OpenOffice software and does not cooperate with any LibreOffice development. LibreOffice has replaced OpenOffice as the default Office software for most Linux distributions.

Application	Description
Calc (Spreadsheet)	LibreOffice spreadsheet
Draw (Drawing)	LibreOffice drawing application
Writer (Word Processing)	LibreOffice word processor
Math (Formula)	LibreOffice mathematical formula composer
Impress (Presentation)	LibreOffice presentation manager
Base (Database)	Database front end for accessing and managing a variety of different databases.

Table 5-2: LibreOffice Applications

LibreOffice includes word processing, spreadsheet, presentation, and drawing applications (see Table 5-2). Versions of LibreOffice exist for Linux, Windows, and Mac OS. You can obtain information such as online manuals and FAQs as well as current versions from the LibreOffice website at **https://www.libreoffice.org**. The LibreOffice suite of applications is installed as part of the Linux Mint installation.

Calligra

Calligra is an integrated office suite for the K Desktop Environment (KDE) consisting of several office applications, including a word processor, a spreadsheet, and graphics applications (see Table 5-3). You can download it from the Universe repository, using Software Manager or the Synaptic Package Manager. Calligra allows components from any one application to be used in another, letting you embed a spreadsheet from Calligra Sheets or diagrams from Karbon in a Calligra Words document. It also uses the open document format (ODF) for its files, providing cross-application standardization. There is also a Windows version available. You can obtain more information about Calligra from **https://www.calligra.org**.

Application	Description
Calligra Flow	Flow chart applications
Calligra Stage	Presentation application
Calligra Words	Word processor (desktop publisher)
Calligra Sheets	Spreadsheet
Karbon	Vector graphics program
Kexi	Database integration
Plan	Project management and planning
Krita	Paint and image manipulation program
Kontact (separate project)	Contact application including mail, address book, and organizer

Table 5-3: Calligra Applications

Application	Description
AbiWord	Cross-platform word processor
Gnumeric	Spreadsheet
Evince	Document Viewer
Evolution	Integrated email, calendar, and personal organizer
Dia	Diagram and flow chart editor
GnuCash	Personal finance manager
Glom	Database front end for PostgreSQL database
Planner	Project planner

Table 5-4: Office Applications for GNOME

GNOME Office Applications

There are several GNOME office applications available including AbiWord, Gnumeric, Evince, and Evolution. A current listing of common GNOME office applications is shown in Table 5-4. All implement the support for embedding components, ensuring drag-and-drop capability throughout the GNOME interface.

To manage your documents you can use the Thingy X-App document manager, accessible from the Office menu as Library (see Figure 5-1). Thingy lists recently opened documents as well as specified favorites. It works with any document accessible with the Xreader document viewer, as well as any LibreOffice document (Calc, Writer, Draw, Impress, or Base). To open a document, click on its icon or right click and select from the menu. Right-clicking on any icon displays a menu of options for that document. To make a document a favorite, choose the "Add to favorites" option. Should you want to open the folder that the document is located in, choose the "Open containing folder" entry. You can even delete a document directly from the document manager by choosing the "Move to trash" option.

Figure 5-1: Thingy X-App Document Manager (Library)

Document Viewers

Xreader is the default document viewer for Linux Mint. It is started automatically whenever you double-click a PDF file on the desktop (see Figure 5-2). Its menu entry is Document Viewer in the Accessories menu. Xreader is an X-App based on Atril, the MATE document viewer. Evince is the GNOME document viewer. Okular is the document viewer for KDE. The PDF viewers include many of the standard Adobe reader features such as zoom, two-page display, and full-screen mode. Evince and Okular can display both PostScript (**.ps**) and PDF (**.pdf**) files.

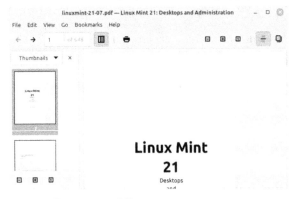

Figure 5-2: Xreader X-App Document Viewer

Viewer	Description
Xreader	X-App Document Viewer, the default (based on Atril)
Atril	MATE Document Viewer for PostScript, DVI, and PDF files
Evince	GNOME Document Viewer for PostScript, DVI, and PDF files
Okular	KDE tool for displaying PDF, DVI, and postscript files
Scribus	Desktop publisher for generating PDF documents
Simple Scan	GNOME Scanner interface for scanners
Thingy	Document manager for viewer and LibreOffice documents

Table 5-5: PostScript, PDF, and DVI viewers

Ebook Readers: FBReader and Calibre

To read E-books on Linux Mint, you can use Calibre, FBReader, and Foliate (see Table 5-6). FBReader is an open source reader that can read non-DRM ebooks, including mobipocket, html, palmdoc, chm, EPUB, text, and rtf. Calibre reads PDF, EPUB, Lit (Microsoft), and Mobipocket E-books. Calibre also can convert many document files and E-books to the EPUB format. Foliate is an easily configurable GNOME E-book reader.

Viewer	Description
Calibre	Ebook reader and library, also converts various inputs to EPUB ebooks.
E-book reader	FBReader Ebook reader
Foliate	GNOME E-book reader

Table 5-6: Ebook Readers

Editors

The Linux desktops support powerful text editors with full mouse support, scroll bars, and menus. These include basic text editors, such as Xed, Gedit, Pluma, and Kate, as well as word processors, such as LibreOffice Word, AbiWord, and Calligra Words. For simple desktop notes you can use Sticky, which replaces Gnote (Accessories menu | Notes). Sticky now has a search function and menu options for a note to control the size of the text (small, normal, large, and larger). It also allows you to duplicate notes. Xed is the default text editor (see Figure 5-3), an X-App designed to work on all Linux Mint desktops. It is accessible from the Accessories menu as Text Editor. Xed features a toolbar and search bar. Linux also provides the cursor-based editors Nano, Vim, and Emacs. Nano is the default cursor-based editor with an easy-to-use interface supporting menus and mouse selection (if run from a terminal window). Vim is an enhanced version of the Vi text editor used on the Unix system. These editors use simple, cursor-based operations to give you a full-screen format. Table 5-7 lists several desktop editors for Linux. Vi and Emacs have powerful editing features that have been refined over the years. Emacs, in particular, is extensible to a full-development environment for programming new applications. Later versions of Emacs and Vim, such as GNU Emacs, XEmacs, and Gvim provide support for mouse, menu, and window operations.

Note: Three helpful tools are the GNOME clocks, calendar, and weather applications. Clocks provided the time for global locations. Calendar provides an online calendar. Weather provides the weather, also for global locations.

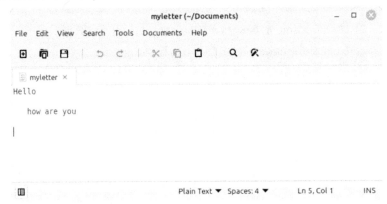

Figure 5-3: Xed X-App editor

Application	Description
Xed	X-App Text editor (based on Pluma)
Sticky	Desktop note taker
Kate	Text and program editor
Calligra Words	Desktop publisher, part of Calligra Suite
Gedit	GNOME Text editor
AbiWord	Word processor
OpenWriter	LibreOffice word processor that can edit text files
nano	Easy to use screen-based editor, installed by default
GNU Emacs	Emacs editor with X Window System support
XEmacs	X Window System version of Emacs editor
gvim	Vim version with X Window System support
Pluma	MATE text editor

Table 5-7: Desktop Editors

Database Management Systems

Several database systems are provided for Linux Mint and Ubuntu, including LibreOffice Base, MySQL, SQLite, and PostgreSQL. Ubuntu continues to provide the original MySQL database. In addition, commercial SQL database software is also compatible with Linux Mint and Ubuntu. SQLite is a simple and fast database server requiring no configuration and implementing the database on a single disk file. In addition, Linux Mint and Ubuntu also supports document-based non-SQL databases such as MongoDB. MongoDB is a document-based database that can be quickly searched. Table 5-8 lists database management systems currently available for Linux.

System	Site
LibreOffice	LibreOffice database: **http://www.libreoffice.org/discover/base/**
PostgreSQL	The PostgreSQL database: **http://www.postgresql.org**
MySQL	MySQL database: **http://www.mysql.com**
MariaDB	MariaDB database, based on MySQL: **https://mariadb.org/**
MongoDB	Document-based database: **http://www.mongodb.org**

Table 5-8: Database Management Systems for Linux

SQL Databases (RDBMS)

SQL databases are relational database management systems (RDBMSs) designed for extensive database management tasks. Many of the major SQL databases now have Linux versions, including Oracle and IBM. These are commercial and professional database management systems. Linux has proved itself capable of supporting complex and demanding database management tasks. In addition, many free SQL databases are available for Linux that offers much the same functionality. Most commercial databases also provide free personal versions.

LibreOffice Base

LibreOffice provides a basic database application, LibreOffice Base that can access many database files. You can set up and operate a simple database, as well as access and manage files from other database applications. When you start up LibreOffice Base, you will be prompted either to start a new database or connect to an existing one. File types supported include ODBC (Open Database Connectivity), JDBC (Java), MySQL, PostgreSQL, and MDB (Microsoft Access) database files (install the **unixodbc** and **java-libmysql** packages). You can also create your own simple databases. Check the LibreOffice Base page (**https://www.libreoffice.org/discover/base/**) for detailed information on drivers and supported databases.

PostgreSQL

PostgreSQL is based on the POSTURES database management system, though it uses SQL as its query language. POSTGRESQL is a next-generation research prototype developed at the University of California, Berkeley. Linux versions of PostgreSQL are included in most distributions, including Red Hat, Fedora, Debian, and Ubuntu. You can find more information on it from the PostgreSQL website at **https://www.postgresql.org**. PostgreSQL is an open source project, developed under the GPL license.

MySQL

MySQL is a true multi-user, multithreaded SQL database server, supported by MySQL AB. MySQL is an open source product available free under the GPL license. You can obtain current information on it from its website, **https://www.mysql.com**. The site includes detailed documentation, including manuals and FAQs.

MariaDB

MariaDB is a fully open source derivative of MySQL, developed after MySQL was acquired by Oracle. It is designed to be fully compatible with MySQL databases. Like MySQL, MariaDB is structured on a client/server model with a server daemon filling requests from client programs. MariaDB is designed for speed, reliability, and ease of use. It is meant to be a fast database management system for large databases and, at the same time, a reliable one, suitable for intensive use. To create databases, you use the standard SQL language. Packages to install are **mariadb-client** and **mariadb-server**.

Mail (email) and News

Linux supports a wide range of both electronic mail and news clients. Mail clients let you send and receive messages to and from other users on your system or users accessible from your network. News clients let you read articles and messages posted in newsgroups, which are open to access by all users.

Mail Client	Description
Kontact (KMail, KAddressbook, KOrganizer)	Includes the K Desktop mail client, KMail; integrated mail, address book, and scheduler
Evolution	Email client, **https://wiki.gnome.org/Apps/Evolution**
Thunderbird	Mozilla mail client and newsreader
Sylpheed	Gtk mail and news client
Claws-mail	Extended version of sylpheed Email client
Mutt	Screen-based mail client
bsd-mailx	Original Unix-based command line mail client
unity mail	GNOME email notification
gnubiff	Email checker and notification tool
Mail Notification	Email checker and notification that works with numerous mail clients, including MH, Sylpheed, Gmail, Evolution, and Mail

Table 5-9: Linux Mail Clients

Mail Clients

You can send and receive email messages in a variety of ways, depending on the type of mail client you use. Although all email utilities perform the same basic tasks of receiving and sending messages, they tend to use different interfaces. Some mail clients are designed to operate on a specific desktop interface such as GNOME. Several older mail clients use a screen-based interface and can be started only from the command line. For Web-based Internet mail services, such as Gmail and Yahoo, you use a Web browser instead of a mail client to access mail accounts provided by those services. Table 5-9 lists several popular Linux mail clients. Mail is transported to and from destinations using mail transport agents like Sendmail, Exim, and Postfix. To send mail over the Internet, the Simple Mail Transport Protocol (SMTP) is used.

Usenet News

Usenet is an open mail system on which users post messages that include news, discussions, and opinions. It operates like a mailbox to which any user on your Linux system can read or send messages. Users' messages are incorporated into Usenet files, which are distributed to any system signed up to receive them. Certain Usenet sites perform organizational and distribution operations for Usenet, receiving messages from other sites and organizing them into Usenet files, which are then broadcast to many other sites. Such sites are called backbone sites, and they operate like publishers, receiving articles and organizing them into different groups.

To access Usenet news, you need access to a news server, which receives the daily Usenet newsfeeds and makes them accessible to other systems. Your network may have a system that operates as a news server. If you are using an Internet service provider (ISP), a news server is probably maintained by your ISP for your use. To read Usenet articles, you use a newsreader, a client program that connects to a news server and accesses the articles. On the Internet and in TCP/IP networks, news servers communicate with newsreaders using the Network News Transfer Protocol (NNTP) and are often referred to as NNTP news servers. You can also create your own news server on your Linux system to run a local Usenet news service or to download and maintain the full set of Usenet articles. News transport agent applications can be set up to create such a server.

You read Usenet articles with a newsreader, such as Pan or tin, which enable you to select a specific newsgroup and then read the articles in it. A newsreader operates like a user interface, letting you browse through and select available articles for reading, saving, or printing. Most newsreaders employ a retrieval feature called threads that pulls together articles on the same discussion or topic. Several popular newsreaders are listed in Table 5-10.

Newsreader	Description
Pan	GNOME Desktop newsreader
Thunderbird	Mail client with newsreader capabilities (X based)
Sylpheed	GNOME Windows-like newsreader
Slrn	Newsreader (cursor based)
Emacs	Emacs editor, mail client, and newsreader (cursor based)
tin	Newsreader (command line interface)
trn4	Newsreader (command line interface)
Newsbin	Newsreader (Windows version works under Wine)
SABnzbd+	Binary only NZB based news grabber

Table 5-10: Linux Newsreaders

Most newsreaders can read Usenet news provided on remote news servers that use the NNTP. Desktop newsreaders have you specify the Internet address for the remote news server in their own configuration settings. Shell-based newsreaders such as **tin**, obtain the news server's Internet address from the NNTPSERVER shell variable, configured in the **.profile** file.

NNTPSERVER=*news.domain.com*
export NNTPSERVER

A binary newsreader can convert text messages to binary equivalents, like those found in **alt.binaries** newsgroups. There are some news grabbers, applications designed only to download binaries. The binaries are normally encoded with RAR compression, which has an **.rar** extension. To decode them you first have to install the **unrar-free** (free version) or **unrar** packages (proprietary version). The **mint-meta-codecs** package with install the **unrar** proprietary version for you. Binaries normally consist of several **rar** archive files, some of which may be incomplete. To repair them you can use Par2 recovery program. Install the **par2** or **parchive** package. A binary should have its own set of par2 files also listed on the news server that you can download and use to repair any incomplete **rar** files. The principle works much the same as RAID arrays using parity information to reconstruct damaged data.

Graphics Applications

The GNOME and KDE desktops support an impressive number of graphics applications, including image viewers, window grabbers, image editors, and paint tools (see Table 5-11). An extensive range of image formats are supported including the new Webp image format. These tools can be found on the Graphics menu. Xviewer is the default image viewer (an X-App) and is accessible as "Image Viewer" from the Graphics menu (see Figure 5-4). It is based on GNOME's Eye of GNOME image viewer, featuring a sidebar with image information and an thumbnail image gallery for easy access. Shotwell provides an easy and powerful way to manage, display, and import, and publish your photos and images. GNOME Photos is a simple image viewer and organizer for the images in your Pictures folder.

Figure 5-4: Xviewer X-App Image Viewer

The Eye of GNOME is the GNOME image viewer. Gthumb is an image viewer, organizer, and simple editor. Pix is the X-App version of Gthumb with many of the capabilities of Shotwell such as cropping and and image adjustments. It is installed by default (see Figure 5-5). Pix features dark mode support, displaying its window with dark backgrounds. You can turn off dark mode support by deselecting the "Prefer dark mode" option in the Pix Preferences dialog. GIMP is the

GNU Image Manipulation Program, a sophisticated image application much like Adobe Photoshop. Inkscape is a Gnome based vector graphics application for SVG (Scalable Vector Graphics) images. Drawing is a basic drawing application (Graphics menu . Xviewer, Pix and Drawing are installed by default. The others can be installed with the Linux Mint Software Manager. Older X Window System-based applications run directly on the underlying X Window System, such as Xpaint and Xfig (not to be confused with X-Apps).

Figure 5-5: Pix X-App Image Viewer, Organizer, and Editor

Tools	Description
Shotwell	GNOME digital camera application and image and video library manager (**https://wiki.gnome.org/Apps/Shotwell**)
Cheese	GNOME Webcam application for taking pictures and videos
Photos	GNOME photo viewer and organizer
Digikam	Digital photo management tool, works with both GNOME and KDE
KDE	
Gwenview	Image browser and viewer
ShowFoto	Simple image viewer, works with digiKam (**https://www.digikam.org**)
Spectacle	Screen grabber
KolourPaint	Paint program
Krita	Image editor (**https://www.calligra.org/krita/**)
GNOME	
Xviewer	X-App Image Viewer (based on Eye of GNOME)
Pix	X-App Image viewer, organizer, and editor (based on Gthumb)
Gthumb	GNOME image viewer, organizer, and editor
Eye of Gnome	GNOME Image Viewer

Drawing	GNOME basic drawing application
GIMP	GNU Image Manipulation Program (**https://www.gimp.org**)
Inkscape	GNOME Vector graphics application (**https://www.inkscape.org**)
gpaint	GNOME paint program
Blender	3d modeling, rendering, and animation
LibreOffice Draw	LibreOffice Draw program
X Window System	
Xpaint	Paint program
Xfig	Drawing program
ImageMagick	Image format conversion and editing tool

Table 5-11: Graphics Tools for Linux

Multimedia

Many applications are available for both video and sound, including sound editors, music players, and video players (see Tables 5-12 and 5-13).

Multimedia support

Linux Mint provides a codec wizard that automatically detects whenever you need to install additional multimedia codecs. If you try to run a media file for which you do not have the proper codec a warning that the codecs are missing is displayed.

Note: the Celluloid media player may not need additional codecs to play files.

To install support for most of the commonly used codecs, if not already installed, you can install the **mint-meta-codecs** package. There are several ways to do this. On the Welcome screen, you can simply click on the "Multimedia codecs" icon. On the Cinnamon menu, on the Sound & Video submenu, you can select the "Install Multimedia Codecs" item. You could also just use the Software Manager or the Synaptic Package Manager to install the **mint-meta-codecs** package.

The **mint-meta-codecs** package installs video plugins and the **mint-meta-codecs-core** package, which, in turn, installs the third-party codecs, including libdvdcss2, ffmpeg, vlc, Microsoft fonts, and unrar. The codecs provide support for DVD, MP3, MPEG4, DivX, and AC3, as well as Adobe Flash (see Figure 5-6). For GStreamer supported applications like the X-player movie player, the gstreamer-bad and gstreamer-ugly plugins are installed.

```
mint-meta-codecs
```

GStreamer

Many GNOME-based applications make use of GStreamer, a streaming media framework based on graphs and filters (**https://gstreamer.freedesktop.org**). Using a plug-in structure, GStreamer applications can accommodate a wide variety of media types:

The Videos (Totem) video player uses GStreamer to play DVDs, VCDs, and MPEG media.

Rhythmbox provides integrated music management.

Sound Juicer is an audio CD ripper.

GStreamer can be configured to use different input and output sound and video drivers and servers, using the GStreamer properties tool, the Multimedia System Selector.

Figure 5-6: Linux Mint mint-meta-codecs install

Application	Description
Rhythmbox	Music management (GStreamer), default Music player with iPod support
Sound Juicer	GNOME CD audio ripper (GStreamer)
Clementine	Multimedia audio player based on Amarok (KDE)
Audacious	Multimedia player
Goobox	CD player and ripper
JuK	KDE Music player (jukebox) for managing music collections
GNOME CD Player	CD player
GNOME Sound Recorder	Sound recorder
GNOME Music	GNOME Music player
XMMS2	CD player
ubuntustudio-audio	Ubuntu Studio metapackage (Meta Packages (universe)), includes a collection of audio applications. Use Synaptic Package Manager
QMidiRoute	MIDI event router and filter

Table 5-12: Music players, editors, and rippers

GStreamer Plug-ins: the Good, the Bad, and the Ugly

Many GNOME multimedia applications use GStreamer to provide multimedia support. To use such features as DVD Video and MP3, you have to install GStreamer extra plug-ins. You can

find more information about GStreamer and its supporting packages at
https://gstreamer.freedesktop.org.

GStreamer has four different support packages called the base, the good, the bad, and the ugly. The base package is a set of useful and reliable plug-ins. These are in the main repository. The good package is a set of supported and tested plug-ins that meets all licensing requirements. This is also part of the main repository. The bad package is a set of unsupported plug-ins whose performance is not guaranteed and may crash, but still meet licensing requirements. The ugly package contains plug-ins that work fine, but may not meet licensing requirements, like DVD support.

The base   Reliable commonly used plug-ins

The good   Reliable additional and useful plug-ins

The ugly   Reliable but not fully licensed plug-ins (DVD/MP3 support)

The bad   Possibly unreliable but useful plug-ins (possible crashes)

Another plug-in for GStreamer that you may want include is **ffmpeg** for Matroska (mkv) and OGG support (**gstreamer1.0-libav** package). The Gstreamer Video Acceleration API packages (**gstreamer1.0-vaapi**) provides hardware video acceleration for gstreamer applications, **https://01.org/linuxmedia/vaapi**.

Music Applications

Many music applications are currently available for GNOME, including sound editors, MP3 players, and audio players (see Table 5-12). You can use Rhythmbox, GNOME Music, and Sound Juicer to play music from different sources, and the GNOME Sound Recorder to record sound sources. Several KDE applications are also available for Cinnamon and MATE, including the media players Clementine and Juk, and a mixer (KMix).

Video Applications

Several projects provide TV, video, DivX, DVD, and DVB support for Linux (see Table 5-13). Aside from GStreamer applications, there are also several third-party multimedia applications you may want, including MPlayer and VideoLan.

The default video player is Celluloid. It is a GTK+ frontend for the MPV video player (**https://github.com/celluloid-player/celluloid**) (see Figure 5-7). It is accessible from the Sound & Video menu as Celluloid. It provides a basic interface with standard controls and playlist. From the menu, you can also select video, audio, and subtitle tracks, and toggle the playlist and control on or off. By default, Celluloid uses the dark mode for its window theme, providing better visual contrast. You can turn off dark mode support by deselecting the "Enable dark theme" option in the Celluloid Preferences dialog. Celluloid has video capabilities such as making use of your computer's graphic card or chip for video playback.

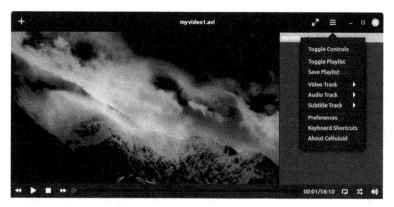

Figure 5-7: Celluloid Video Player

Video and DVD Players

Most current DVD and media players are provided on the Linux Mint/Ubuntu repositories.

Celluloid is a GTK+ frontend for the MPV video player (**https://github.com/celluloid-player/celluloid**) (see Figure 6-19). It is the default video player Linux Mint Cinnamon and MATE. It provides a basic interface with standard controls and playlist. You can also select video, audio, and subtitle tracks.

Totem is the GNOME movie player that uses GStreamer, labeled with the name Videos on the Sound & Videos menu. You can use the dconf editor to modify default settings (org.gnome.totem) (**totem** package).

The **VideoLAN** project (**http://www.videolan.org**) offers network streaming support for most media formats, including MPEG-4 and MPEG-2. It includes a multimedia player, VLC, which can work on any kind of system (**vlc** package, Universe repository). VLC supports high-def hardware decoding.

Dragon Player is a KDE multimedia player, installed with the KDE desktop but will play on the GNOME desktop.

mpv is an open source video player based on Mplayer and supports an extensive selection of codecs and formats. Run from the Sound & Video menu or from a terminal window with the **mpv** command. Install with Ubuntu Software or the Synaptic Package Manager.

Kaffeine is a KDE multimedia player (video and dvb) (**kaffeine** package).

MPlayer is one of the most popular and capable multimedia/DVD players in use. It is a cross-platform open source alternative to RealPlayer and Windows Media Player (**www.mplayerhq.hu**). MPlayer uses an extensive set of supporting libraries and applications like **lirc**, **lame**, **lzo**, and **aalib**. If you have trouble displaying video, be sure to check the preferences for different video devices and select one that works best (**mplayer** package).

Videos Plugins (Totem)

The Videos movie player (Totem) uses plugins to add capabilities like Internet video streaming. Select Edit | Preferences and click on the Plugins button to open the Configure Plugins window. Choose the plugins you want.

PiTiVi and Shotcut Video editors

The PiTiVi Video editor is an open source application that lets you edit your videos. Check the PiTiVi website for more details (**http://www.pitivi.org**). You can download a quick-start manual from the Documentation page. Pitivi is a GStreamer application and can work with any video file supported by an installed GStreamer plugin. Shotcut is a another open-source video editor that supports numerous video formats. Both feature dark mode support, which can turn off. In Shotcut, choose the theme entry in the Settings menu, and and in Pitivi switch off the dark theme in the Preferences dialog's Other tab.

Projects and Players	Sites
Celluloid	GTK+ frontend for the MPV video player (**https://github.com/celluloid-player/celluloid**). This is the default player for Linux Mint.
Totem (Videos)	Totem video and DVD player for GNOME using GStreamer, includes plugins for DVB, YouTube, and MythTV
Dragon Player	Dragon Player video and DVD player for KDE
VLC Media Player (vlc)	Network multimedia streaming. **www.videolan.org**
MPlayer	MPlayer DVD/multimedia player **www.mplayerhq.hu**
Hypnotix	IPTV Player for TV channels, movies, and TV series
tvtime	TV viewer, **http://tvtime.sourceforge.net**
XviD	Open Source DivX, **https://www.xvid.com/**
Kaffeine	KDE media player, including HDTV, DVB, DVD, CD, and network streams
PiTiVi	Video editor
Shotcut	Video editor

Table 5-13: Video and DVD Projects and Applications

TV Players

The IPTV player Hypnotix provides access to IPTV providers, letting you view TV channels as well as video-on-demand (VOD) movies and tv series (see Figure 5-8) . It is designed to play MPV files (Mpeg-2 video files). Along with Hypnotix, the Free-IPTV service is installed which provides you with access to free and publicly available TV channels, movies, and TV series. Should you have an IPTV service that you subscribe to, you could view it through Hypnotix. Both Hypnotix and Free-IPTV are installed by default.

The initial Hypnotix dialog displays icons for the TV, Movies, and TV series. Clicking one displays icons for what is available for that content. Hypnotix uses the dark mode for its window theme to provide better contrast. You can turn it off by switching off the "Prefer dark mode" option on the Hypnotix Preferences dialog's Preferences tab.

Buttons at the top right will open dialogs for your list of IPTV providers (TV button image) and Hypnotix preferences (gear button). Clicking on the IPTV providers button opens the Providers dialog, which will show the Free-TV providers listed. Click on the "Add a new provider" button at the bottom to add a new provider. You are prompted for a name, type such as M3U URL, the URL of the site, and the EPG for channel and show listing should you need one. On the Providers dialog, you can edit a provider's configuration by clicking on the pencil icon to the right.

The Preferences dialog lets you set MPV playback options and the network user agent, currently Mozilla.

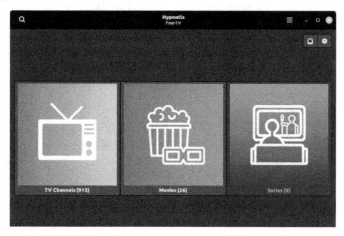

Figure 5-8: Hypnotix (IPTV Player)

The TV dialog show channel buttons to the left and displays the current show on the right. On right side of the header bar is a button to expand to full screen. Press the Esc key to leave full screen. You can also toggle to full screen and back with the F11 key. When you first click on the TV channels icon, the TV Channels dialog opens to display a list of countries, as well as button for movies and news. Choose your country to see and view the channels. Click on a channels button to the left to view it. Moving your mouse to the center bottom of a channel stream displays dialog for managing your stream with pause, forward, and reverse buttons, along with mute and subtitle buttons. For the US, Free-IPTV will provide news channels such as CNN, Reuters, ABC, and CBS. You can also view NASA tv, BBC food, and Bloomberg. From the menu on the right side of the header bar, you can use Keyboard Shortcuts to change the full screen toggle key. The Stream Information entry open a dialog with tabs for Video and Audio showing video information such as the aspect, codec, and bit rate.

When you select a TV channel, movie, or series it will continue to play should you return to the main dialog. The name of the currently running video is shown at the bottom of the window. Buttons to the right let you pause, stop, or view it, returning to the channel, movie, or series dialog.

On the movie and series dialogs there are icons for available movies and series. Free-IPTV does not provide any of these. TV player **tvtime** works with many common video capture cards, relying on drivers developed for TV tuner chips. It can only display a TV image. It has no recording or file playback capabilities. Check **http://tvtime.sourceforge.net** for more information.

MythTV is a popular video recording and playback application on Linux systems (multiverse repository).

Kaffeine is a popular KDE video recording and playback application on Linux systems. It can also play ATSC over the air digital broadcasts.

Note: To play DivX media on Linux Mint you use the Xvid OpenDivX codec, xvidcore.

DVB and HDTV support

For DVB and HDTV reception, you can use most DVB cards as well as many HDTV cards. The DVB kernel driver is loaded automatically. You can use the **lsmod** command to see if your DVB module is loaded. The VideoLan (VLC) player can run HD media (x264) using your display card's native high definition decoder (hardware decoding instead of software decoding), check Tools | Preferences | Codecs | Use GPU acceleration.

Kaffeine DVB and ATSC tuning

The Kaffeine KDE media player can scan for both DVB and ATSC channels. You will need to have a DVB or ATSC tuner installed on your system. On Kaffeine, from the Television menu choose Configure Television, and on the device tab choose the source such as ATSC. Then from the Television menu, select Channels to open a Channel dialog. Your tuner device is selected on the Search menu. Click on the Start scan button to begin scanning. Detected channels are listed on the "Scan results" scroll box. Select the ones you want and click Add Selected to place them in the Channels scroll box. Be sure to add the channel you want to watch on the Channel list.

Xvid (DivX) and Matroska (mkv) on Linux

MPEG-4 compressed files provide DVD-quality video with relatively small file sizes. They have become popular for distributing high-quality video files over the Internet. When you first try to play an MPEG-4, the codec wizard will prompt you to install the needed codec packages to play it. Many multimedia applications like VLC already support MPEG-4 files.

MPEG-4 files using the Matroska wrapper, also known by their file extension **mkv**, can be played on most video players including the VideoLan vlc player, Celluloid, Dragon Player, and Totem. You will need HDTV codecs, like MPEG4 AAC sound codec, installed to play the high definition **mkv** file files. If needed, the codec wizard will prompt you to install them. To manage and create MKV files you can use the **mkvtoolnix-gui** tools.

You use the open source version of DivX known as Xvid to play DivX video (**libxvidcore** package. Most DivX files can be run using XviD. XviD is an entirely independent open source project, but it is compatible with DivX files. You can also download the XviD source code from **https://www.xvid.com/**.

CD/DVD Burners

Several CD/DVD ripper and writer programs can be used for CD music and MP3 writing (burners and rippers). These include Sound Juicer, Brasero (see Chapter 3), and K3b (See Table 5-14). GNOME features the CD audio ripper Sound Juicer. For burning DVD/CD music and data discs, you can use Brasero CD/DVD burner.

Application	Description
Brasero	Full service CD/DVD burner, for music, video, and data discs (no longer installed by default)
Sound Juicer (Audio CD Extractor)	GNOME music player and CD burner and ripper
ogmrip	DVD ripping and encoding with DivX support
K3b	KDE CD writing interface

Table 5-14: CD/DVD Burners

Brasero, K3b, and dvdauthor can all be used to create DVD Video discs. All use mkisofs, cdrecord, and cdda2wav DVD/CD writing programs installed as part of your desktop. OGMrip can rip and encode DVD video. DVD-Video and CD music rippers may require additional codecs to be installed, for which the codec wizard will prompt you.

Internet Applications

Linux provides powerful Web and FTP clients for accessing the Internet. Some of these applications are installed automatically and are ready to use when you first start up your system. Linux also includes full Java development support, letting you run and construct Java applets. Web and FTP clients connect to sites that run servers, using Web pages and FTP files to provide services to users.

You can choose from several Web browsers, including Firefox, Epiphany, and Lynx. Firefox, and Epiphany are desktop browsers that provide full picture, sound, and video display capabilities. The Lynx browser is a line-mode browser that displays only lines of text.

Web browsers and FTP clients are commonly used to conduct secure transactions, such as logging into remote sites, ordering items, or transferring files. Such operations are currently secured by encryption methods provided by the Secure Sockets Layer (SSL). If you use a browser for secure transactions, it should be SSL enabled. Most browsers include SSL support. Linux distributions include SSL (OpenSSL) as part of a standard installation.

Web Browsers

Popular browsers for Linux Mint include Firefox (Mozilla), Web (Epiphany), and Lynx (see Table 5-15). Firefox is the default Web browser used on most Linux distributions. On Linux Mint, Firefox is installed directly by APT as a DEB package, whereas Ubuntu installs Firefox as a Snap package only. Web is the GNOME Web browser (formerly known as Epiphany). Lynx and ELinks are command line-based browsers with no graphics capabilities, but in every other respect, they are fully functional Web browsers.

Chromium, the open source version of the Google Web browser, is no longer available on Linux Mint 21. It is possible to download a version from an unofficial repository. You can also download it from the Snap store if you have enabled Snap. It is not on Flathub. For further details see:

`https://linuxmint-user-guide.readthedocs.io/en/latest/chromium.html`

Web Site	Description
Firefox	The Mozilla project Firefox Web browser, desktop default browser **https://www.mozilla.org**
Web	GNOME Web browser **https://wiki.gnome.org/Apps/Web**
lynx	Text-based command-line Web browser **http://lynx.browser.org/**
elinks	Text-based command-line Web browser **http://elinks.or.cz**

Table 5-15: Web browsers

Web Apps

Using Web Apps you can turn any Web site into an application that can be managed by the desktop just like any other application. You can place a Web App as an icon on the desktop or panel, and have an entry for it in the menu. Clicking on the Web App opens the Web site in a dedicated window, like other applications. This makes it easy to access a site that you frequently visit. A Web App entry lists the app's icon, the name you give to the app, and the browser used to access the site.

To create and manage Web Apps, open the Web Apps application from the Internet menu as Web Apps. This opens the Web Apps dialog, which lists your current Web Apps (see Figure 5-9). A toolbar at the bottom has buttons for adding (+), removing (-), changing (pencil icon), and launching a selected Web App (mouse and button icon).

Figure 5-9: Web Apps

Clicking on the plus button opens the "Add a new Web App" dialog with entries for a name you want to give it, the Web site address (URL), an icon to use for the Web App on the desktop, the menu category to place its entry in, and the browser to use (see Figure 5-10). Switches at the bottom lets you choose to include a browser navigation bar or to open the site in a private window. In the "Custom parameters" text box you can enter custom options for the browser. A button to the right of the Address text box opens a listing of icons online you could use for your Web App. Clicking on the Icon image opens a "Choose an icon" dialog where you can select an icon image on your system.

Figure 5-10: Web Apps, adding

Once created, you can access and run the Web Apps from the Mint menu as you would any application (see Figure 5-11). You can also add their icons to the desktop or panel.

Figure 5-11: Web Apps, on menu, desktop, and panel

Java for Linux

To develop Java applications, use Java tools, and run many Java products, you use the Java Software Development Kit (SDK) and the Java Runtime Environment (JRE). The SDK is a superset of the JRE, adding development tools like compilers and debuggers. Sun (now owned by Oracle) has open sourced Java as the OpenJDK project and supports and distributes Linux versions. The JRE subset can be installed as OpenJRE. The **openjdk-11-jre** package installs the Java runtime environment, and **openjdk-11-jdk** installs both the JRE and the Java development tools. Java packages and applications are listed in Table 5-16.

Application	Description
Java Development Kit, OpenJDK	An open source Java development environment with a compiler, interpreters, debugger, and more (include the JRE), **http://openjdk.java.net**, **openjdk-11-jdk**
Java Runtime Environment, OpenJRE	An open source Java runtime environment, including the Java virtual machine, **openjdk-11-jre**. **http://openjdk.java.net**
Java Platform Standard Edition (JSE)	Complete Java collection, including JRE, JDK, and API, **http://www.oracle.com/technetwork/java/javase/downloads/index.html**

Table 5-16: Java Packages and Java Web Applications

BitTorrent Clients (transmission)

GNOME provides effective BitTorrent clients. With BitTorrent, you can download very large files quickly in a shared distributed download operation where several users participate in downloading different parts of a file, sending their parts of the download to other participants, known as peers. Instead of everyone trying to access a few central servers, all peers participating in the BitTorrent operation become sources for the file being downloaded. Certain peers function as seeders, those who have already downloaded the file, but continue to send parts to those who need them.

Linux Mint will install and use the GNOME BitTorrent client, Transmission, accessible from the Internet menu. To perform a BitTorrent download you need the BitTorrent file for the file you want to download.

FTP Clients

With File Transfer Protocol (FTP) clients, you can connect to a corresponding FTP site and download files from it. These sites feature anonymous logins that let any user access their files. Basic FTP client capabilities are incorporated into the Nemo (Cinnamon) and Caja (MATE) file managers. You can use a file manager window to access an FTP site and drag files to local folders to download them. Effective FTP clients are also now incorporated into most Web browsers, making Web browsers the primary downloading tool. Firefox, in particular, has strong FTP download capabilities.

Although file managers and Web browsers provide effective access to public (anonymous login) sites, to access private sites, you may need a stand-alone FTP client like curl, wget, Filezilla, gFTP, lftp, or **ftp**. These clients let you enter usernames and passwords with which you can access a private FTP site. The stand-alone clients are also useful for large downloads from public FTP sites, especially those with little or no Web display support. Popular Linux FTP clients are listed in Table 5-17.

FTP Clients	Description
Nemo	GNOME file manager (Cinnamon)
Caja	GNOME file manager (MATE)
gFTP	GNOME FTP client, **gftp-gtk**
ftp	Command line FTP client
lftp	Command line FTP client capable of multiple connections
curl	Internet transfer client (FTP and HTTP)
Filezilla	Linux version of the open source Filezilla ftp client (Universe repository)

Table 5-17: Linux FTP Clients

Network File Transfer: FTP

With File Transfer Protocol (FTP) clients, you can transfer extremely large files directly from one site to another (see Table 5-4). FTP can handle both text and binary files. FTP performs a remote login to another account on another system connected to you on a network. Once logged into that other system, you can transfer files to and from it. To log in, you need to know the login name and password for the account on the remote system. Many sites on the Internet allow public access using FTP, however. Such sites serve as depositories for large files anyone can access and download. These sites are often referred to as FTP sites, and in many cases, their Internet addresses begin with the term ftp, such as **ftp.gnome.org**. These public sites allow anonymous FTP login from any user. For the login name, you use the word "anonymous," and for the password, you use your email address. You can then transfer files from that site to your own system.

Several FTP protocols are available for accessing sites that support them. The original FTP protocol is used for most anonymous sites. FTP transmissions can also be encrypted using SSH2, the SFTP protocol. More secure connections may use FTPS for TLS/SSL encryption. Some sites support a simplified version of FTP called File Service Protocol, FSP. FTP clients may support different protocols like gFTP for FSP and Filezilla for TLS/SSL. Most clients support both FTP and SSH2.

Web Browser–Based FTP

You can access an FTP site and download files from it with any Web browser. Browsers are useful for locating individual files, though not for downloading a large set of files. A Web browser is effective for checking out an FTP site to see what files are listed there. When you access an FTP site with a Web browser, the entire list of files in a folder is listed as a Web page. You can move to a subfolder by clicking its entry. You can easily browse through an FTP site to download files. To download a file, click the download link. This will start the transfer operation, opening a dialog for selecting your local folder and the name of the file. The default name is the same as on the remote system. On many browsers, you can manage your downloads with a download manager, which will let you cancel a download operation in progress or remove other downloads. The manager will show the time remaining, the speed, and the amount transferred for the current download.

GNOME Desktop FTP: Connect to Server

The easiest way to download files is to use the built-in FTP capabilities of the GNOME file managers, Nemo and Caja. On GNOME, the desktop file manager has a built-in FTP capability. The FTP operation has been seamlessly integrated into standard desktop file operations. Downloading files from an FTP site is as simple as dragging files from one folder window to another, where one of the folders happens to be located on a remote FTP site. Use the file manager to access a remote FTP site, listing files in the remote folder, just as local files are. In a file manager's Location bar (**Ctrl-l** or Location button), enter the FTP site's URL following the prefix **ftp://** and press ENTER. A dialog opens prompting you to specify how you want to connect. You can connect anonymously for a public FTP site, or connect as a user supplying your username and password (private site). You can also choose to remember the password.

For more access options such as a secure SSH connection, windows share, and Secure Web (HTTPS), you can use the Connect to Server dialog (see Figure 5-12). To open the Connect to Server dialog, choose File | Connect to Server menu item on any file manager window, or on the Desktop applications menu. From the Type menu, you can select the service type. Entry options change accordingly, with the "FTP (with login)" adding an entry for the username. Click the Connect button to access the site.

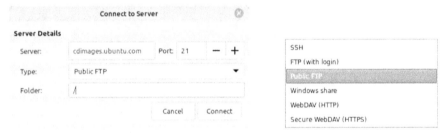

Figure 5-12: GNOME FTP access Connect to Server dialog

The top folder of the remote FTP site will be displayed in a file manager window (see Figure 5-13. Use the file manager to progress through the remote FTP site's folder tree until you find the file you want. Then, open another window for the local folder to which you want the remote files copied. In the window showing the FTP files, select those you want to download. Then click and drag those files to the window for the local folder. As files are downloaded, a dialog appears showing the progress.

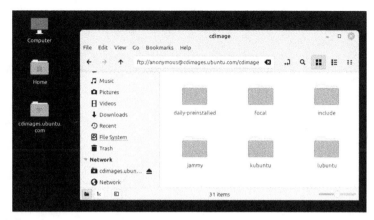

Figure 5-13: GNOME FTP access with Connect to Server and the file manager

The file manager window's sidebar (Network section) will list an entry for the FTP site accessed. An eject button is shown to the right of the FTP site's name. To disconnect from the site, click this button. The FTP entry will disappear along with the FTP sites icons and file listings.

Social Networking

Linux provides integrated social networking support for IM (Instant Messenger) and VoIP (Voice over Internet). Users can communicate directly with other users on your network (see Table 5-18). These applications are installed automatically and are ready to use when you first start up your system. Instant messenger (IM) clients allow users on the same IM system to communicate anywhere across the Internet. With Voice over the Internet Protocol applications, you can speak over Internet connections.

Skype can be installed with Software Manager. Once installed, you can access Skype from the Internet menu. When you first start Skype, you are asked to accept a user agreement. The interface is similar to the Windows version. A Skype panel icon will appear on the panel once you start Skype. You can use it to access Skype throughout your session. Click to open Skype and right-click to display a menu from which you can change your status, sign out, access options, list contact groups, and start a conference call. The panel icon changes according to your status.

Clients	Description
Skype	VoIP application (Partner repository)
empathy	GNOME instant messenger
Pidgin	Older instant messenger client
Jabber	Jabber IM service (gajim, psi, emacs, empathy)
Finch	Command line cursor-based IM client
Hexchat	IRC client

Table 5-18: Instant Messenger, Talk, and VoIP Clients

Part 2: Desktops

Cinnamon

MATE

6. Cinnamon Desktop

Cinnamon

Desklets

Windows

Cinnamon Menu

Panel

Applets

Workspaces

The Nemo File Manager

System Settings

Linux Mint features the Cinnamon desktop as its advanced desktop. Though Cinnamon was originally derived from GNOME 3, its interface is similar to GNOME 2, using a simple panel with applets. Linux Mint uses the Nemo file manager for Cinnamon, as well as some of GNOME 3 desktop configuration tools. Linux Mint 21 installs Cinnamon 5.4, which is based on a reworked version of the Muffin window manager, whose code is much closer to the Mutter window manager (Wayland, version 3.36) used on GNOME systems. Muffin is now very similar to the to the Mutter upstream code, making for a much more responsive, efficient, and visually streamlined interface. The older Metacity window manager is no longer used.

The Cinnamon desktop is designed to be easily extensible). You can add themes, applets, desklets and extensions from certified third-party developers and artists. These addons are called Spices and they are available from the Cinnamon Spices website at **https://cinnamon-spices.linuxmint.com/,** which is the official Cinnamon addons repository.

Cinnamon Desktop

The Cinnamon desktop is designed for ease of use on desktop systems, using a traditional panel with applets for most desktop tasks. Applets for Network Manager, sound volume, updates, and time and date are placed on the right side of the panel (see Figure 6-1). The left side of the panel is the Cinnamon menu, the panel launchers applet to quick start applications, and the Grouped Windows List applet for open windows. You can easily add and remove applets using the System Settings Applets dialog, accessible from the Panel applet. The Panel Edit mode (right-click on the panel) lets you reposition and remove applets. System supported folders, such as Computer and Home, are displayed on the desktop. You can restart the Cinnamon desktop without restarting the system, by pressing Ctrl-Alt-ESC.

Figure 6-1: Cinnamon desktop

You can search for desktop items quickly by clicking and holding down the meta key when entering the first character of a pattern. This opens a text box in which you enter a search pattern. It highlights the icon for the best first match.

The Cinnamon desktop features a Cinnamon menu for applications, places, and tasks, with a Favorites icon bar for the commonly used applications and tasks (see Figure 6-2). The Favorites icon bar shows icons for the Firefox browser, the Software Manager, System Settings, the terminal window, and the Nemo file manager. There are also icons for lock, logout, and shut down operations.

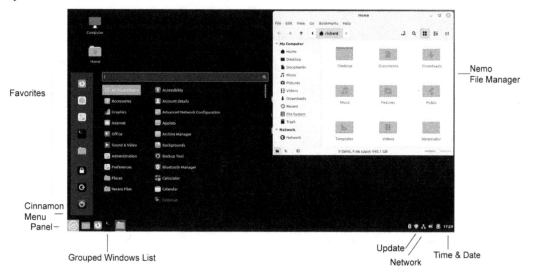

Figure 6-2: Cinnamon desktop with Cinnamon Menu and Nemo file manager

Right-clicking anywhere on the desktop displays the desktop menu, from which you can add new folders to the desktop, open the file manager with administrative (root) access, open a terminal window, change the background, and add desklets (see Figure 6-3). The Customize entry opens a "Current Monitor Layout" window that lets you control the display of your desktop icons. You can change the size (small, normal. and large), display them in a grid (Auto-arrange), display icons vertically (columns) or horizontally (lines), sort by name, size, date, and type, or turn off the Auto-arrange option to place icons anywhere. Scroll bars on the right side and the bottom let you adjust the spacing of the icons. A link at the bottom of the dialog opens the Desktop Settings dialog where you can determine what desktop icons to display.

Figure 6-3: Desktop menu and Current Monitor Layout window (Customize)

On the Desktop dialog, you can specify the icons to be displayed on the desktop (see Figure 6-4). By default, the computer and home icons are shown, along with icons for any file systems and devices that you mount, such as a USB drive or DVD disc. You can also choose to display the file manager's network folder (network servers) and the trash. The "Desktop layout" option lets you choose whether to show desktop icons, on all attached monitors, or just primary monitors. If an additional monitor is missing, you can choose to still display its icons.

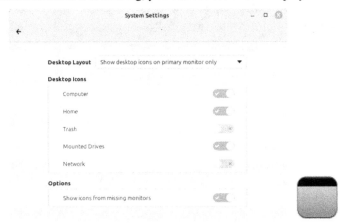

Figure 6-4: Desktop Settings

Desklets

A desklet works much like an applet, but for the desktop instead of the panel, as shown here. You can use the "Show desktop" icon on the panel to display only your desklets and desktop icons, hiding your open windows. You can also right-click on the "Show Desktop" icon to display a menu and select the "Show Desklets" entry to bring all desklets to the forefront, should your open windows be hiding them.

Three desklets are installed (but not activated) by default: clock, photo, and launcher. The Clock desklet displays a digital clock. The Digital photo frame desklet displays a small dialog that performs a slide show of the images in your Pictures folder. The Launcher desklet can be configured to launch an application. A listing of available applets can be found at **https://cinnamon-spices.linuxmint.com/desklets**.

You can add desklets to the desktop (activate) using the System Settings Desklets dialog or by right-clicking on the desktop background to display the desktop menu and clicking on the "Add Desklets" entry. Desklets has Manage, Download, and General Settings tabs (see Figure 6-5). The Manage tab lists desklets that have been installed on your computer. Desklet entries with a checkmark are those that are displayed on the desktop. You can search for desklets using the search box. If a desklet cannot be removed it has a lock icon. Desklets initially installed as part of the Cinnamon desktop are locked. At the bottom of the Manage tab is a toolbar with buttons to add (+) and remove (-) a desklet to and from the desktop, to delete the desklet from your system removing it from the list (x), a remove all button to delete all your installed desklets, and an About button to display information about a selected desklet, as shown here.

To activate a desklet, displaying it on the desktop, click on its entry and click the plus button (+) button on the toolbar. To remove a desklet from the desktop, click on the minus button (-).

Some desklets can be configured. These will have a gear icon displayed on their entries. Click on the icon to open a dialog with configuration settings. The Clock desklet configuration icon opens a dialog where you can set font size, text color, and specify a custom date format.

Figure 6-5: Desklets Manage tab

You can download and install additional desklets from the Linux Mint repository by clicking on the Download tab (see figure 6-6). The "Sort by" menu lets you sort by name, popularity, date (latest), and installed. To install a desklet, click on the desklet's download button (the down arrow) on the right side of its entry. After the download, the down arrow button disappears and a checkmark emblem then appears in the desklet entry. You will then see the desklet listed on the Manage tab. From there you can activate it to add it to the desktop.

A toolbar at the bottom of the Download tab has buttons for "More info" (lightbulb icon), Uninstall to remove desklets already installed, Updates to update your installed desklets, and Refresh to update the list of available desklets. To see more information about a selected desklet, click the "More info" button to open its Web page.

The "General Desklets Settings" tab lets you determine how desklets are displayed. You can show a border around them, no border, or both the border and desklet title (header). You can snap desklets to a grid, or allow a free placement.

Figure 6-6: Desklets Download and Settings tabs

Hot Corners

Hot Corners allows you to configure the corners of your screen to run the Expo workspace switcher, the Scale windows switcher, the show desktop function, or a program of your choosing (command). You can activate the operations by hovering the mouse in a corner. Moving the mouse to the corner and holding it there, runs the operation.

You configure Hot Corners using the System Settings Hot Corners dialog. A square image at the center shows the status of the corners. Active corners are green and inactive ones are gray. Each corner has a menu from which to choose an application: Show all workspaces (Expo), Show all windows (Scale), Show the desktop, and Run a command (custom). The "Show all workspaces" option runs the Expo workspace configuration and switcher, and the "Show all windows" option runs the Scale screen-based window switcher, which scales windows to a grid. The corners are disabled by default, showing a gray color for each corner. To turn a corner on, click the switch to the right of "Enable this corner" label. The corner then shows a solid green color. You move the mouse to the corner for a moment to activate the setting. The "Activation delay" entry lets you set the speed at which the corner is activated, letting you set a delay if you want. In Figure 6-7, as an example, the top left corner is configured to run the Expo workspace switcher with no delay. The right corner is configured to run the Scale window switcher with a short delay. Either will work.

The "Show desktop" option toggles the minimizing of your open windows on the desktop. If displayed, all windows are minimized to the window list applet on the panel. If all are minimized, they are then all displayed on the desktop. In Figure 6-7, the bottom left corner is configured to show the desktop.

The "Run a command" option opens a text box in which you can enter an application name. In Figure 6-7, the bottom right corner is configured to run the Nemo file manager. The **nemo** command is entered in the text box. With this setting, the Nemo file manager would open a window with your home folder each time you move the mouse to that corner.

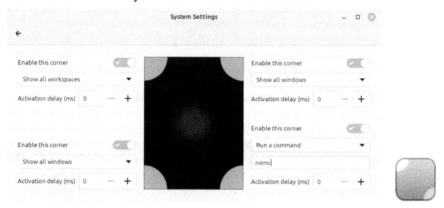

Figure 6-7: System Settings Hot Corners

Keyboard and Mouse Shortcuts

Keyboard shortcuts can be configured on the System Settings Keyboard dialog's Shortcuts tab (see Figure 6-8). There are shortcuts for the general, windows, workspaces, system, launchers, sound and media should your keyboard support those keys, and universal access. Categories are listed to the left, with additional expanded entries for specific operations, such a positioning of windows. Within a category, you can choose a shortcut task, for which the key is displayed in the Keyboard binding section below. To change or add a key click on its string in the Keyboard bindings section to open a window where you can type in the new key or key combinations. A listing of common shortcuts is provided in Table 6-1.

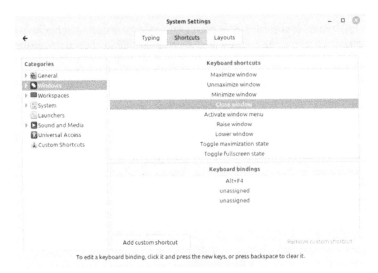

Figure 6-8: System Settings Keyboard, Keyboard Shortcuts

Keys	Description
Cinnamon	
Atl-F2	Run a command from a command line
Meta	Displays the Cinnamon menu (Windows key)
Meta with character	Opens a desktop search box for desktop icons
Ctrl-Alt-t	Opens a terminal window
Ctrl-Alt-Escape	Restart the Cinnamon desktop only
Workspaces	
Alt-F1	Toggle the Expo workspace switcher
Ctrl-Alt-*uparrow*	Toggle the Expo workspace switcher
Ctrl-Alt-*leftarrow*	Move to left workspace
Ctrl-Alt-*rightarrow*	Move to right workspace
Ctrl-Alt-Shift-*arrows*	Use left or right arrows to move a window to a new workspace
Panel	
Ctrl-Alt-L	Lock the screen
Ctrl-Alt-Delete	Log out
Windows	
Ctrl-Alt-*downarrow*	Toggle the scale window switcher
Alt-Tab	Switch between windows

Alt-Shift-Tab	Switch between windows, backwards
Alt-~	Switch between windows for the same application
Alt-F5	Unmaximize the current window
Alt-F4	Close the current window
Meta *-leftarrow*	Tile current window to left side of screen
Meta-*rightarrow*	Tile current window to right side of screen
Meta-*uparrow*	Tile current window to the top
Meta-*downarrow*	Tile current window to the bottom
Ctrl-Alt-Numpad 0	Maximize window
Ctrl-Alt-Numpad 5	Center/Maximize the window in the middle of the screen

Table 6-1: Cinnamon Keyboard Shortcuts

Menu

The Cinnamon menu consists of a Favorites icon bar for frequently used applications and operations, menus based on application categories, and a search box for locating applications (see Figure 6-9). In addition, the menu also displays folder bookmarks (Places) and recently accessed files. The Cinnamon menu is a panel applet located on the left side of the panel.

Figure 6-9: Cinnamon menu

On the Menu, favorites are displayed on the left. To the right is a category menu and a menu of items in a selected category. If all the items cannot be displayed, then the menu list becomes a scroll box, letting you scroll through items. The All Applications entry on the category list displays all applications. Items not assigned to a particular category can be located in this category. The Places category lists your folder bookmarks, and Recent Files lists recently accessed files. The search box at the top lets you search quickly for applications using patterns (see Figure 6-10). If two applications have the same label, such as the Gedit and Xed text editors, there will be a different entry for each on the menu with their application names listed in parenthesis, as in Text Editor (Gedit) and Text Editor (Xed). Also, if you install the same application from the Flatpak repository, the Flatpak version will have the term Flatpak in parenthesis, as in Calibre (Flatpak).

Figure 6-10: Cinnamon menu search

The favorites icon bar shows applications in the upper part, and system shutdown, logout, and lock tasks in the lower part (see Figure 6-11). The parts are separated by a blank space. When you move your mouse over an icon, its name and description appear in the lower right corner of the menu. Clicking on an application icon opens that application. Clicking on any of the shutdown, logout, and lock icons opens their respective dialogs and lets you perform the task.

Figure 6-11: Cinnamon menu favorites

Application favorites can be easily added or removed using an item's pop-up menu. Right-click on an item to display a menu with options to add the item to the panel, desktop, and favorites (see Figure 6-12). If you add an item to Favorites, then the item's pop-up menu will display a "Remove from favorites" entry, which you can use to remove it from the Favorites icon bar. As you add items to the Favorites bar, they become smaller and smaller to fit. To remove an item from Favorites, you can display its name in the lower right corner by passing the mouse over it and then use that name in the search box to locate the menu item. Right-click on the menu item and choose "Remove from favorites."

If the application also supports commands, those are listed in its the context menu. Click on the command to run it for that application. For example, LibreWriter will show a "New Document" to open LibreWriter for a new document. Rhythmbox will have several commands for playing music such as Play/Pause, Next, Previous, and Stop & Quit.

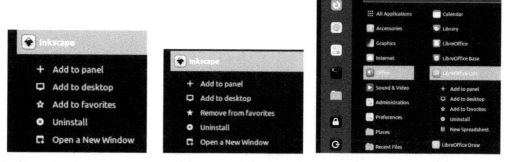

Figure 6-12: Cinnamon menu

Right clicking on the menu panel applet opens a menu with options to remove the menu or to configure the menu, as shown here. The "Remove this applet" entry removes the menu applet from the panel. Choosing the Configure option opens the System Settings Menu dialog.

The Menu configuration dialog's Panel tab lets you choose a panel icon and the text displayed for the Cinnamon menu (see Figure 6-13). Instead of clicking on the menu applet to open the menu, you can choose to simply move the mouse over it, along with specifying a hover delay. You can also force the panel to be visible when you open the menu. The keyboard shortcut keys to open and close the menu can also be set here. The Icon entry displays the icon used for the menu on the panel. Clicking it opens the XAppIconChooser at the Linux Mint tab, Choose an Icon dialog. You can choose a different Linux Mint logo to use or an icon from the other categories.

On the Menu tab, you can set display features such as to show bookmarks and places, application and category icons, and favorites and use a fixed menu hight, as well as set the icon sizes for applications and favorites, and set the minimum height of the favorites section (Layout and content section). You can also enable auto-scrolling in the application list, change categories on hover, and for searches, you can use full pathnames for applications (Behavior section).

Figure 6-13: Cinnamon Linux Mint menu menu configuration

The menu button (right-most button) lists a menu with options to reset defaults and to save or import your menu items.

Figure 6-14: Cinnamon Main Menu editor

To edit the items on the menu, click on the "Open the menu editor" button on the Menu tab of the Settings Menu dialog. This opens the Main Menu editor, where you can choose applications to be displayed on the menu (see Figure 6-14). Menu categories are listed in the left scroll box, and application items are shown in the right scroll box. To hide an item, deselect its checkbox. To remove an item permanently, select it and click the Delete button. To move an item to a different category, select it, click the Cut button, then click on the category you want it moved to, and then click the Paste button. Categories can be re-positioned, moving them up or down. To restore the original set of categories, applications, and their positions, you click the "Restore System Configuration" button.

The New Menu button lets you create new category menus. You enter a name and choose the icon to use. The New Item button lets you add a menu item, which can be an application, application in a terminal window (shell script), or location (folder). You will have to manually specify the name and the command.

Windows

Windows on Linux Mint operate much as they do on other Linux distributions, with similar maximizing, minimizing, and workspace operations. You use the window buttons on the right side of the window title bar to minimize (minus), maximize (square image), and close (x) a window.

Preferences for windows, such as the effect of double clicking the title bar, the title bar font, and the button order, can be set using the System Settings Windows dialog (see Figure 6-15). The dialog has three tabs: Titlebar, Behavior, and Alt-Tab. The Titlebar tab has a Buttons section where you can position window buttons and a Titlebar section for choosing actions that can be performed on the titlebar. In the Buttons section, the title bar buttons are already ordered for the right side. You could move them to the left side, by choosing the Left entry in the "Button layout" menu. This menu also has entries for Gnome, which has just a close button on the right side, and Classic Mac, with a close button on the left side and minimize and maximize buttons on the right.

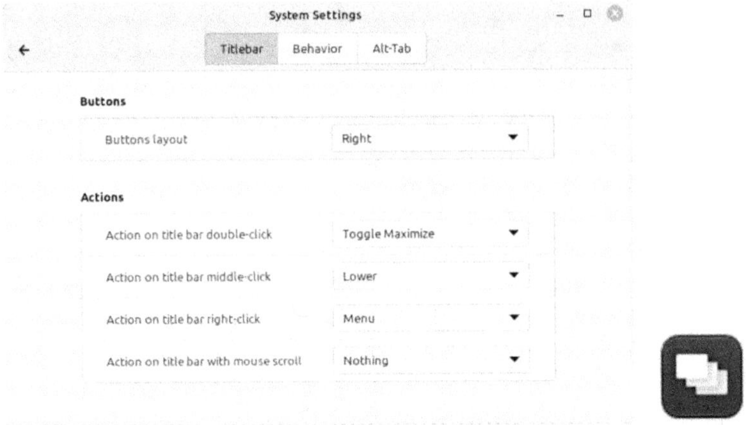

Figure 6-15: Windows Settings: Titlebar tab

In the Actions section, the action-double-click-titlebar key is set to toggle-maximize (maximize the window), but a menu lets you choose options such as toggle-shade, which rolls up the window instead of maximizing it. There are also menus for the middle-click and right-click operations (by default set to Menu - the window menu). The "Action on the title bar with mouse scroll" menu lets you change the opacity of a window by scrolling on the title bar, making it transparent so you can see windows or icons underneath it.

The Behavior tab lets you modify window movement and display (see Figure 6-16). It has two sections: "Windows Focus" and "Moving and Resizing Windows." In the Windows Focus section, you can set the focus mode (click, mouse, or sloppy). The "Focus mode for new windows" can be Smart or Strict. The "Attach dialog window to their parent window's titlebar" option will display a dialog opened by an application window as an overlay of the application window. In the "Moving and Resizing Windows" section you can determine the initial placement of new windows, choose a key to resize or move windows (Alt, Meta, Super, or Control). Alt is already selected.

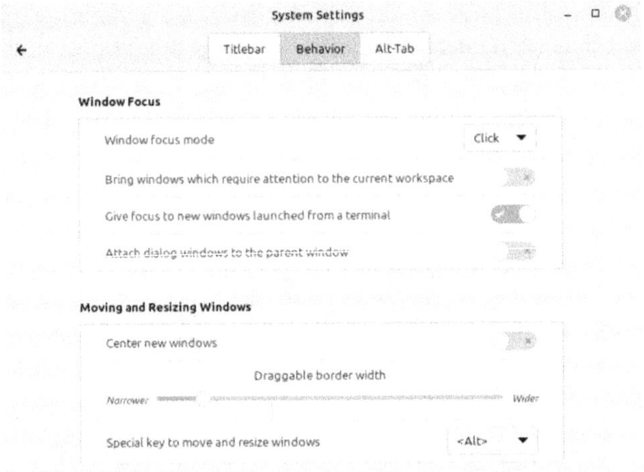

Figure 6-16: Windows Settings: Behavior tab

The Alt-Tab tab lets you configure the window switcher display (see Figure 6-17). You can choose a style for the menu such as icons only, thumbnails only, icons and window preview, and icons and thumbnails (the default). For accelerated supported graphics (3D), you can also choose coverflow and timeline. Most computers now support accelerated graphics. You can also choose to list windows in all your workspaces, not just your current one.

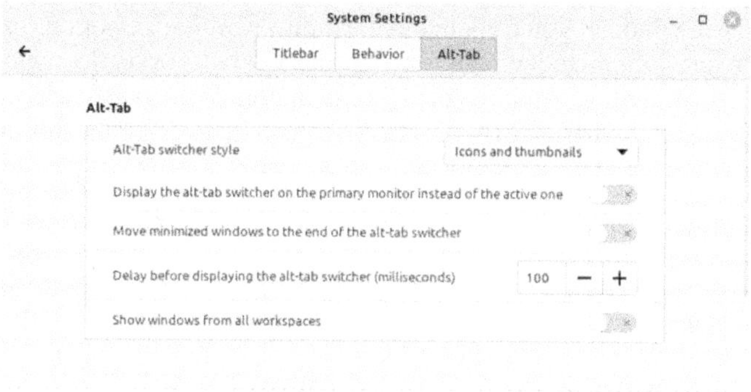

Figure 6-17: Windows Settings: Alt-tab tab

To manage window tiling and edge flipping you use the Window Tiling dialog on System Settings. The "Enable Window Tiling and Snapping" option enables window tiling and snapping when you move a window to the edge or corner of the screen (see Figure 6-18). It is turned on by default. When moving a window to the top edge of the screen it is set to tile, covering the top part of the screen. You can change this to maximize by turning on the "Maximize, instead of tile, when dragging a window to the top edge" option.

Figure 6-18: Window Tiling and Edge Flip

Minimizing, Maximizing, and Closing Windows

To maximize a window, you can double-click on the title bar or click on its maximize button (expand image) on the right side of the title bar. You can also right-click on the title bar and choose the Maximize entry from the pop-up menu or press the Ctrl-Alt-5 keys. As noted, if you want to be able to to maximize a window by moving it to the top edge of the screen, on the System Settings Windows Tiling dialog you have to turn on the "Maximize, instead of tile, when dragging a window to the top edge" option.

To unmaximize a window, drag its title bar down and away from the top of the screen, or click on it's maximize button on the left side of the title bar (expand image).

202 Part 2: Desktops

To move a window, click and drag on its title bar. As you move, your mouse pointer changes to a hand. You can also press the Alt key with a mouse click, and drag to move a window, or you can right-click on the title bar and choose the Move entry from the pop-up menu.

From the keyboard, you can press the Alt-space keys to display the window menu for that window, and use the arrow key to move to the Move entry. You can also press the Alt-F7 keys.

To minimize a window, you can click the window's minimize button (minus sign) on the right side of the title bar. Minimized windows are reduced to buttons on the window list applet on the panel. To restore a minimized window, click on its button. If the window is not maximized, you can also right-click on the title bar and choose the Minimize entry from the pop-up menu, or press the Ctrl-Alt-0 keys.

To close a window, click the window close button (the x character) on the right side of the title bar. You can also right-click on the title bar and choose the Close entry from the pop-up menu. From the keyboard, you can press Alt+F4, or press Alt+space to display the window menu and then press c to choose the Close entry.

Grouped Windows List

Each open window has a corresponding button on the window list applet on the bottom panel in the Grouped Window List. Clicking on it toggles the window between minimize and display. The button will show the number of windows open for that application in its upper left corner. You can right-click on a window list button to open a pop-up menu, which provides options to maximize, close, and move the window to another workspace (see Figure 6-19). A minimized window has the option to restore the window, instead of minimize. You can also close all windows, or just close all other windows. To move a window to another workspace, click on the "Move to another workspace" entry to expand the menu to a list of your workspaces. The Files button menu has added entries for Places (all your home folders) as well as Home, Computer, and Trash.

Figure 6-19: Window List button menus

To configure the window list, right click on a button on the panel and choose Preferences to expand the menu to show a Configure entry (see Figure 6-20).

Figure 6-20: Window List Preferences menu

This opens the Grouped Window List configuration dialog. From the menu in the upper right you can save and import window list configuration settings.

The Grouped Window List dialog is organized in to four tabs: General, Panel, Thumbnails, and Context Menu (see Figure 6-21). On the General tab you can control behavior and hot keys such as application grouping, mouse actions, and keys to cycle through applications. The Panel tab lets you add labels, configure animation, show count numbers, and allow button dragging (re-arranging buttons). The Thumbnails tab shows thumbnails for open windows and applications, configuring their size and display, as well as enabling mouse hovering for showing the thumbnails. The Context Menu tab adds entries to the context menu such as showing recent items and a new window option.

Figure 6-21: Grouped Window List configuration - General and Panel tabs

On the Panel tab's "Button Label" menu you can configure whether the button for an open window on the window list should have a label. You can choose from None (the default), Application name, Window title, and Window title for the focused window. Figure 6-22 shows these options.

Figure 6-22: Window List Button Labels - None, Application, Title

Moving your mouse over a Grouped Window List button displays thumbnails for any open windows for that application (see Figure 6-23). Moving the mouse over a thumbnail highlights it and displays a close button in the upper right corner as well as briefly showing what the opened window would be on the desktop. Clicking on the thumbnail restores the window if it is minimized or makes that window the active window on your desktop.

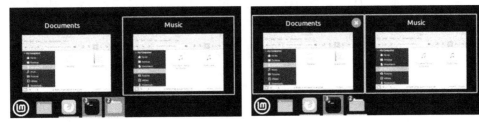

Figure 6-23: Window List Button Thumbnails

The Grouped window list Thumbnail tab lets you configure thumbnail behavior (see Figure 6-24). The Thumbnails section lets you turn off the thumbnail feature (Show thumbnails) as well as configure the display of thumbnails such as adjusting size and displaying them vertically instead of horizontally. The Hover Peak section lets you turn off and manage the display of a hovered thumbnail's window on the desktop.

Resize and tiling Windows

You can resize a window vertically, horizontally, or both at the same time. To resize in both directions at once, move the mouse to any corner of the window until it becomes a corner-pointer, an arrow with a right-angle pointer image. You can then click-and-drag to the size you want. For side changes, move the mouse to the left or right side edge of the window until it changes to a side-pointer, an arrow with a line image. The same operation works for changes at the top or bottom of the window.

Linux Mint supports window snapping (tiling). Moving the window to the right or left edge of the screen (when the mouse reaches the edge) expands the window to take up that side of the screen. Moving the window to the top of the screen maximizes the window to use the full screen, with the window menu bar and buttons across the top.

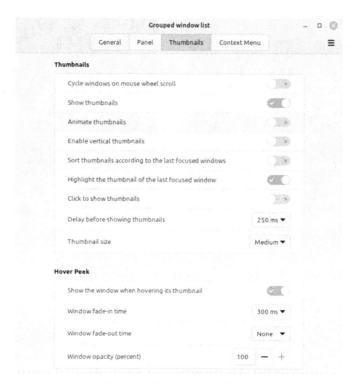

Figure 6-24: Grouped Window List Configuration - Thumbnails tab

You can also tile two windows so that one takes up one-half the screen, and the other uses the other half. Drag a window to left side (click and drag the title bar, or Alt-click on the window). When your mouse pointer meets the edge of your screen, the entire left side of the screen is highlighted. When you release your mouse, the window snaps to display on the entire left side of the screen. The same operation works for the right side. To restore the window to its previous size, simply drag it down and away from the edge.

Tiling also works for corners. Drag the window to a corner, and when your pointer reaches the corner, the window fills that corner. You could tile four open windows, each in a corner of the screen.

Tiling also works for the top and bottom edges. Drag the window to the top or bottom of the screen, and when your pointer reaches the top or bottom edge, the window fills that half of the screen. For the top edge, you can configure Window Tilting to maximize instead of tiling the window.

Switching Windows with the Windows QuickList

You can also switch windows using the Windows Quick List, which you can add to the panel. The windows quicklist lists all your open windows, organized by workspace (see Figure 6-25).

Figure 6-25: Windows QuickList menu

Switching Windows with the Scale Screen and Alt-Tab

You can switch between open windows using the Scale screen, which displays your open windows in a grid (see Figure 6-26). The window title and application icon is displayed below each window. Clicking on a window returns you to the desktop, with the selected window now the active window. You can also press the Esc key to return to the desktop. On the Scale screen, you can close windows. When you pass your mouse over a window, a close button appears in the upper right corner, which you can click to close the window.

Figure 6-26: Scale: zoomed windows to switch windows (Hot corners, Show all windows)

You can access the Scale screen by pressing the Ctrl-Alt-downarrow key. You can also use a hot corner configured for Scale, or by using the Scale applet (shown here). For hot corners, use the System Settings Hot Corners dialog to enable "Show all windows" at a corner and choose Hover enabled. The upper right corner already has "Show all windows" selected. When you move your mouse to that corner, the Scale screen is displayed. For the Scale applet, first, install it, then click the Scale applet button on the panel to display the Scale screen.

You can also switch between windows using the Alt-Tab keys to display the window switcher (see Figure 6-27). Open windows are displayed using their application icons in the center of the screen. Use the Alt-Tab key to select the one you want. As you move through the row of icons, a thumbnail of the currently selected window is displayed below the icon. The Alt-Shift-Tab keys move backward through the windows, and the Alt-~ keys move through windows of the same application.

Figure 6-27: Window switching with Alt-Tab (Icons and Thumbnails)

The window switcher can be configured on the System Settings Windows dialog, Alt-Tab tab. The "Alt-tab switcher style" menu lets you choose what the window switcher displays. The default is "Icons and thumbnails", but you can set it to just icons or use window previews instead of icons or thumbnails. The window preview blanks out the screen except for the selected window.

You can also use a 3D window switcher. The Coverflow (3D) option displays the non-selected windows on either side of the selected window (see Figure 6-28). Timeline 3D displays a single stack of non-selected windows to the side.

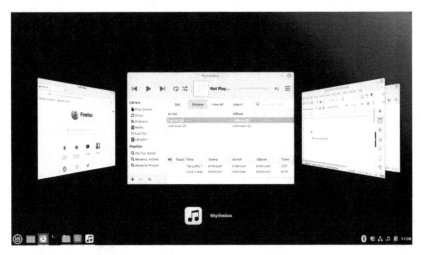

Figure 6-28: Window switching with Alt-Tab (Coverflow 3D)

Effects

The Effects dialog lets you enable desktop effects for windows, dialogs, and scroll boxes (see Figure 6-29). At the top of the dialog is a "Desktop and window effect" switch you can use to turn all effects on or off. You can turn window and menu effects on or off, enable effects for dialogs, and for resize and tiling operations, as well as the fade effect on Cinnamon scrollboxes. You can choose effects for specific window tasks, such as Traditional, Fly, Fade, or none for window minimize, unminimize, close operations, and for new windows For closing windows you can choose Traditional or Fly. Using the slider scale at the bottom you can set the Window animation speed.

Figure 6-29: System Settings Effects

Workspace Selection with Hot Corners (expo) and expo applet

Linux Mint supports workspaces, with two enabled by default. You can set up several workspaces, each with open windows. You can switch workspaces directly or through the Expo screen. To switch directly you have to add the workspace switcher applet to the panel or use the Ctrl-Alt-arrow keys to move to a workspace. Workspaces are arranged in a row. Initially, with four workspaces, you have a single row of four workspaces. Use the Ctrl-Alt-right-arrow to move to the next workspace, and Ctrl-Alt-left-arrow to move back. On the System Settings Workspaces dialog, you can enable the "Allow cycling through workspaces" option to cycle back to the first workspace by continually using the Ctrl-Alt-right-arrow key. Should you want to display the workspace name on your desktop briefly as you move to it, you can enable the "Enable workspace OSD" option on the System Settings Workspace dialog.

The Workspace switcher panel applet displays button for your workspaces on the panel, just as with the GNOME 2 desktop (see Figure 6-30). Click on the workspace button to switch to that workspace. The current workspace is highlighted. As you add workspaces, they are added to the row. Open the Configure option to display the Workspace switcher dialog where you can choose the type of display, either as simple numbered buttons or as visual representations (the default).

Figure 6-30: Workspace Switcher applet

Workspaces are managed using Expo. With Expo, you can add or remove workspaces, as well as change their names and move open windows directly from one workspace to another. You can access Expo in several ways. From the keyboard, you can press the Atl-F1 or the Ctrl-Alt-uparrow keys to toggle the Expo screen. You can also configure a hot corner to open the Expo screen, or install the Expo applet. The Expo applet (shown here) places an Expo button on the panel, which opens the Expo screen.

The hot corner Expo screen access is configured with the System Setting Hot Corners dialog (see Figure 6-31). Each corner of your screen can be enabled as a hot corner. Each corner has a menu with options for Show all workspaces (Expo), Show all windows (Scale), Show the desktop, and Run a command. The "Show all workspaces" option opens the Expo screen, whereas "Show all windows" opens a window switcher screen. A corner is not enabled until you click the "Enable this corner" switch. The corner in the center image then turns solid green. Un-enabled corners are gray. The defaults are shown in Figure 6-24, along with the upper left and right corners enabled. The upper left shows workspaces and the upper right shows windows.

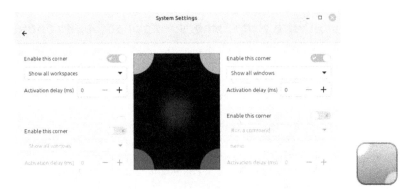

Figure 6-31: Hot Corner with Expo enabled

The Expo screen (Show all workspaces) displays your current workspaces, along with their names and plus button on the right side of the screen, which you use to add workspaces (see Figure 6-32). Moving your mouse over a workspace, highlights it and displays a close box in the upper right corner, which allows you to delete a workspace. It also scales your windows into a square grid. Clicking the plus buttons add a workspace. By default, these are added as part of a square grid. To leave the Expo screen, click on a particular workspace or press the Esc key.

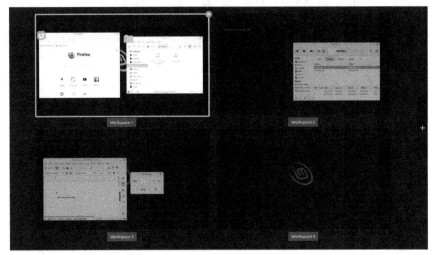

Figure 6-32: Expo workspace configuration (square grid)

You can use the System Setting Workspaces dialog to display the workspaces in the Expo screen as a row instead a grid (see Figure 6-33). Turn the "Display Expo view as a grid" switch to off. You can also change the workspace names. Each workspace has a textbox below it with its name. Click on it to edit the name.

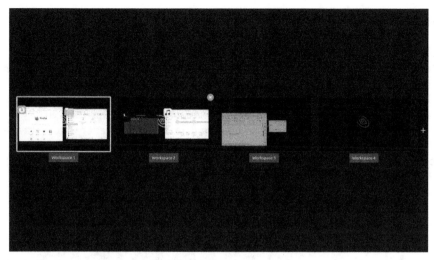

Figure 6-33: Expo workspace configuration (no grid)

Figure 6-34: System Settings Workspaces

To move a window to a different workspace, simply click and drag that window to a different workspace. When you pass your mouse over a window in a workspace, the windows are scaled to a grid, letting you easily select a window to move. You can also move windows to other workspaces directly from your desktop. To quickly move a window to another workspace, select the window, and then use **Ctrl+Alt+Shift**+arrow keys, with the left, right arrow keys moving the window to the next workspace. You can also right-click on the title bar and choose one of the Move to Workspace entries. The "Move to Another Workspace" entry displays a submenu listing all workspaces.

The System Setting Workspace dialog shows a few basic options for displaying your workspaces (see Figure 6-34).You can enable the workspace switching OSD, enable workspace cycling, display the Expo view as a grid, restrict workspace use to the primary monitor, and invert the arrow key directions for changing workspaces when window dragging.

The Linux Mint Panel: modern layout

With the panel, you can access menus, run applets, and start applications (see Figures 6-35). The panel is based on the GNOME 2 panel and provides a simple and effective use of applets for the desktop. With Linux Mint 19.1, Cinnamon implemented a new panel using a modern layout that is much more configurable with a grouped windows list, window previews, and zones for icon sizes. The left side of the panel features the Cinnamon menu, application buttons, and minimized windows. The right side features Xapp Status Applet system tray with standardized XAppStatusicon system applets, such as the time and date, Bluetooth, battery, Network Manager, and sound. You can customize a panel to fit your own needs, holding applets and menus of your own selection. You may add new panels, add applications to the panel, and add various applets.

Figure 6-35: The Linux Mint panel with menu, grouped window list, and applets, at the bottom of Linux Mint desktop

In the Xapp Status Applet system tray, the XAppStatusicon icons and menus have been standardized (see Figure 6-36) . They can also provide mouse wheel support, letting you change features using the mouse scroll wheel. Holding the mouse over the sound icon and scrolling the mouse wheel changes the volume. Doing the same on the power icon changes the brightness of your screen. On the sound icon, clicking the mouse wheel mutes the sound. The same XAppStatusicon system tray with the same icons is used Linux Mint MATE and Xfce. For automated processes such as Timeshift and software updates, a process monitor is shown on the system tray. Clicking on it shows the automated process running in the background.

Figure 6-36:XApp Status Applet system tray with mouse wheel support and XAppStatusicon icons

Panel configuration tasks such as adding applications, selecting applets, setting up menus, and creating new panels are handled from the Panel pop-up menu. Just right-click on the empty space on your panel (the middle) to display a menu with entries for Panel settings, Applets, Panel Edit mode, Move, Remove, Add a new panel, Troubleshoot, and System Settings (see Figure 6-37).

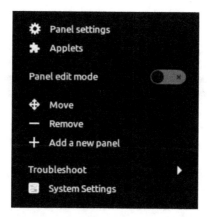

Figure 6-37: The panel pop-up menu (right-click on middle) and panel applet menu

The first two entries display the configuration dialogs for Applets and Panel, and the last entry displays System Settings. The Troubleshoot entry displays a submenu listing items to restart the desktop (Restart Cinnamon), restore desktop defaults (Restore all settings to default), and to start a scan for errors (Looking Glass) (see Figure 6-38).

There are also entries to remove or move the panel, and to add another panel. The move option displays the four edges of your screen an allows you to move the panel to any edge, including the sides. Click the edge you want to move the panel to.

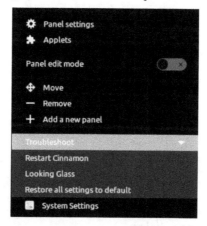

Figure 6-38: The panel menu Troubleshoot submenu

The "Panel Edit mode" switch allows you move or remove applets on the panel. The switch should remain off when the panel is in use. To edit the panel, click the switch to turn it on. The background for different sections will have colors, such as red for the application applets on the left side, green for empty parts of the panel (the middle), and blue for the applets on the right side (see Figure 6-39). To move an item, click and drag it. Your pointer image changes to a hand as you move the item. To remove an item, right-click on it to display a menu with a "Remove this applet" entry. When you are finished editing your menu, open the panel menu again and click on the "Panel Edit mode" switch to turn it off.

Figure 6-39: The Linux Mint panel in edit mode

The "Panel settings" entry opens the System Settings Panel dialog, letting you configure your panel (see Figure 6-40). You can add new panels, set the panel and icon sizes, and auto-hide panels. In the Panel Visibility section, if you choose auto hide from the Auto-hide panel menu, your panel is hidden until you move your mouse to the bottom of the screen.

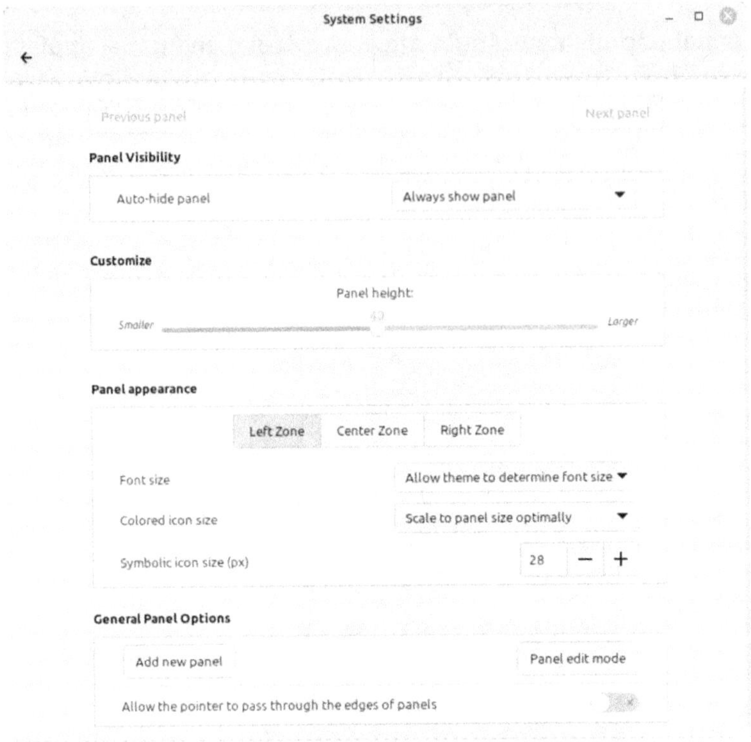

Figure 6-40: The panel settings dialog

In the Customize section, a scale is displayed where you can change the panel size. In the Panel Appearance section, you can also choose to adjust the icon sizes in the left, center, and right panel zones. Zones were implemented in the new Cinnamon panel introduced with Linux Mint 19.1. The panel is sectioned into three configurable zones: right, center, and left (top, center, and bottom for vertical zones). The sizes of icons in these zones can be configured separately. Icon sizes can be scaled to whatever the panel size is (the "Scale to panel size" options), or to one of several fixed "crisp" sizes. The fixed sizes are not dynamically scaled and so will appear clearer and sharper. There are two scale options: optimal and exact. The exact size scales the icons dynamically to the exact size of the panel and is not as sharp as the fixed sizes. The optimal size scales to the largest fixed size that will fit the panel. By default, the left and center zones are optimally scaled to the panel size, whereas the right zone, which has the system icons, is set to a fixed 24pt size.

In the General Panel Options section, you can add a new panel. The "Panel edit mode" button is an easy way to turn on the panel edit mode. You can also set the symbolic icon sizes.

Linux Mint Applets

Applets are small programs that perform tasks within the panel. A listing of available applets can be found at **https://cinnamon-spices.linuxmint.com/applets**. To add applets to the panel, open the System Settings Applets dialog, which you can open from System Settings or from the panel pop-up menu. On the Manage tab, the Applets dialog lists applets already available on your system. You can search for applets in the listing using the search box. Those that are active and on the panel have a checkmark to the left (see Figure 6-41). If an applet cannot be removed it has a lock icon. Applets initially installed as part of the Cinnamon desktop are locked. Some applets can be configured. These will have a gear icon displayed on their entries. The configuration button becomes active once you add the applet to the panel. Click on the icon to open a dialog with configuration settings.

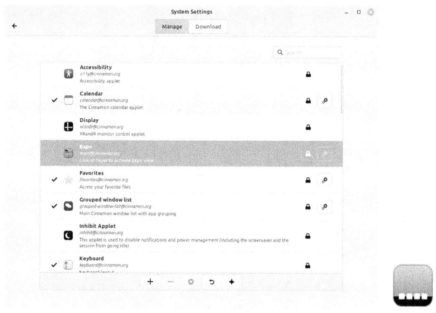

Figure 6-41: The Applets Dialog Manage tab

At the bottom of the Manage tab is a toolbar with buttons to add (+) and remove (-) an applet to and from the panel, to delete the applet from your system removing it from the list (x), a remove all button to delete all your installed applets, a "Reset all" button (curved arrow) to display only the applets originally enabled by the system (disables all the ones you added), and an About button to display information about a selected applet, as shown here.

To activate an applet, displaying it on the panel, click on its entry and click the plus button (+) button on the toolbar. To remove an applet from the panel, select it and click on the minus button (-).

A large number of additional applets can be added that are supported by third-party developers. These are listed on the Download tab (see Figure 6-42). The Sort by menu lets you sort the listing by name, score (popularity), and date.

To install an applet, click on the applet's download button (the down arrow) on the right side of its entry. After the applet is installed, the down button disappears and a check mark icon then appears in the applet entry. The applet also appears on the Manage tab. You can then select them and add them to the panel. Some third-party applets may require additional software installed. When you try to add them to the panel, you are notified of the packages that need to be installed.

A toolbar at the bottom of the Download tab has buttons for "More info" (lightbulb icon), Uninstall to remove applets already installed, Updates to update your installed applets, and Refresh to update the list of available applets. To see more information about a selected applet, click the "More info" button to open your Web browser to the Linux Mint page describing the applets and comments by users about it.

Figure 6-42: The Applets dialog "Available applets (online)" tab

Applets, along with other Cinnamon spices (desklets, extensions, and themes) can be updated directly using the **cinnamon-spice-updater**. Cinnamon spice updates are also supported by the Update Manger. To update spices manually, you can enter the **cinnamon-spice-updater** command in a terminal window. You can update either a specific spice type or all of them.

```
cinnamon-spice-updater --update-all
cinnamon-spice-updater --update applet
```

To see what spice updates are available, enter the **--list-simple** option and the spice type.

```
cinnamon-spice-updater --list-simple applet
```

Linux Mint Traditional Layout

The Traditional layout for Linux Mint, which you can select from the Welcome screen First Steps tab, uses many of the display features found in Linux Mint 19 and in earlier releases. Several of the prominent features are noted here.

The Panel uses Program Launchers instead of the grouped window list, with different menus (See Figure 6-43). The system tools on the right side uses the traditional icons and includes the user applets. The on and off switches used in applets are different.

The left side of the panel features the Cinnamon menu, application buttons, and minimized windows. The right side features applets, such as the date, battery, Network Manager, and sound.

Figure 6-43: Traditional Layout panel

The panel launcher applet lets you launch applications from the panel. A panel launcher applet is already installed at the left side of the Linux Mint panel and lists the Firefox Web browser, the terminal, and Files (Nemo file manager, home folder). Click on an application icon to start it. Moving your mouse over the icon displays its name. To display a menu of actions you can perform on an application icon, right click on any icon in the panel launcher applet (see Figure 6-44). The menu has entries for Launch, Add, Edit, and Remove. The Add and Edit entries open a dialog where you can manually enter or edit the application name and launch options. The Remove entry removes the application icon from the panel launcher applet. Additional entries are tailored to the application. The Firefox Web browser has entries to open in a new window or in a private window. The terminal has an entry to open a new terminal window. The file manager has entries for the home, computer, and trash folders, with the home folder as the default.

Figure 6-44: Traditional Layout Panel Launchers applets and menus

Though you can use the Cinnamon menu to log out, shutdown, and access System Settings, you could use the user applet instead (see Figure 6-45). The user applet has entries for Lock Screen, Switch User, Log Out, and Power Off. It is a very quick way to perform these tasks, without having to display the Cinnamon menu. Clicking on the user name displays the Account details dialog, where you can change the user icon, full name, and password. On the panel, the user applet displays a person icon. You can configure the applet (right-click on it and choose configure) to display the user's full name. You can also install the User applet on the Modern layout if you wish.

Figure 6-45: Traditional Layout User applet

The Traditional layout now use the same switches in its menus as show in Figure 6-46 for the Network Manager applet's menu.

Figure 6-46: Traditional Layout switches

Nemo File Manager

The Nemo file manager supports the standard features for copying, removing, and deleting items as well as setting permissions and displaying items. The name used for the file manager is Files, but the actual program name is still **nemo**.

Home Folder Sub-folders and Bookmarks

Like Ubuntu, Linux Mint uses the Common User Directory Structure (xdg-user-dirs at **https://freedesktop.org**) to set up sub-folders in the user home folder. Folders will include **Documents**, **Music**, **Pictures**, **Downloads**, and **Videos**. These localized user folders are used as defaults by many desktop applications. Users can change their folder names or place them within each other using the file browser. For example, Music can be moved into **Documents**, **Documents/Music**. Local configuration is held in the **.config/user-dirs.dirs** file. System-wide defaults are set up in the **/etc/xdg/user-dirs.defaults** file. The icons for these folders are displayed in Figure 6-47.

Figure 6-47: Nemo file manager home folders

The folders are also default bookmarks. You can access a bookmarked folder directly from the either the Nemo window sidebar or from the Bookmarks menu. You can also add your own bookmarks for folders by opening the folder and choosing "Add Bookmarks" from the Bookmarks menu. Your folder will appear in the Bookmarks section of the Nemo sidebar and on the Bookmarks menu. You can manage bookmarks using the file manager Bookmarks dialog, accessible from the Bookmarks menu as Edit Bookmarks. Here you can remove a bookmark or change is name and location.

You use Desktop dialog in System Settings to display basic folders such as the home, network, and trash folders on the desktop area.

File Manager Windows

When you click the Home folder icon on the desktop, the folder icon on the Panel Launcher applet, or the Home folder icon on the Cinnamon menu favorites icon bar, a file manager window opens showing your home folder. The file manager window displays several components, including a menubar, a main toolbar, and a sidebar (see Figure 6-48).

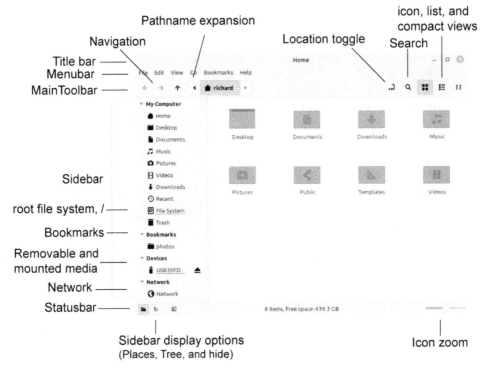

Figure 6-48: File manager with sidebar

The sidebar displays sections for My Computer, Bookmarks, Devices, and Network items showing your file systems and default home folder sub-folders. The Bookmarks and Devices items only appear if bookmarks exist or devices are attached. You can choose to display or hide the sidebar by selecting the "Sidebar" entry in the View menu's Sidebar submenu, or by clicking the hide button on the status bar below the sidebar. The main pane (to the right) displays the file and folder icons or listing of files and folders in the current working folder. When you select a file or folder, the status bar at the bottom of the window displays the name of the file or folder selected, and for files, the size, and for folders, the number of items contained. The status bar also displays the remaining free space on the selected file system.

Note: Nemo works as an operational FTP browser. You can use the Connect to Server entry on the Files top bar applications menu to open a "Connect to Server" dialog, where you can enter the URL for the FTP site.

The File menu has entries for opening a new tab (Ctrl-t), opening a new file manager window (Ctrl-n), creating a new folder (Shift-Ctrl-n), connecting to a remote FTP server, and displaying the properties of the current folder (Alt-Return). Most have corresponding keys.

File Manager Sidebar and Bookmarks

The file manager sidebar shows file system locations that you would normally access: computer folders (My Computer), devices (Devices), and network folders (Network) (see Figure 6-49). Selecting the File System entry places you at the top of the file system, letting you move to any accessible part of it. In the My Computer section, you can open your default folders, such as Documents and Pictures. The Recent folder entry lets you open a file manager window showing your recently accessed files. Should you bookmark a folder (Bookmarks menu, "Add Bookmark" entry (Ctrl-d)), the bookmark will appear on the sidebar in the Bookmarks section. To remove or rename a bookmark, right-click on its entry on the sidebar and choose Remove or Rename from the pop-up menu. The bookmark name changes, but not the original folder name.

Figure 6-49: File manager sidebar with bookmarks menu

The sidebar has two menu views: places and treeview. You can switch between the two using the buttons on the lower button bar, as shown here. The third button will hide the sidebar.

The places menu has expandable menus (see Figure 6-50). The My Computer menu expands to your home folder, default bookmarks, root folder (File System), and trash. When you create a bookmark, it is listed in the Bookmarks menu. When you attach a device, a Devices submenu appears which expands to show the attached devices. The devices have eject buttons, which you can use to remove the device. You can collapse all the menus to just the menu titles.

Figure 6-50: File manager sidebar Places menus, expanded and unexpanded

The treeview shows expandable menus for both the home folder and the file systems (see Figure 6-51). You can collapse them, showing just one or the other.

Figure 6-51: File manager sidebar Treeview menus, expanded and unexpanded

Tabs

The Nemo file manager supports tabs with which you can open up several folders in the same file manager window. To open a tab, select New Tab from the Files menu (see Figure 6-52) or press **Ctrl-t**. A tab bar appears with tab icons for each tab, displaying the name of the folder open, and an **x** close button. You can re-arrange tabs by clicking and dragging their tab icons to the right or left. You can also use the Ctrl-PageUp and Ctrl-PageDown keys to move from one tab to another. Use the Shift-Ctrl-PageUp and Shift-Ctrl-PageDown keys to rearrange the tabs. To close a tab, click its close **x** button on the right side of the tab. Tabs are detachable. You can drag a tab out to its own window, opening it in a new window.

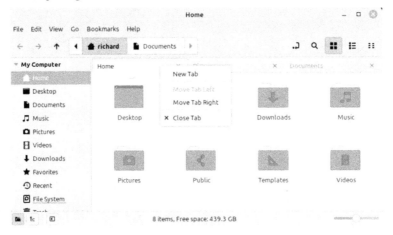

Figure 6-52: File manager window with tabs

Displaying Files and Folders

You can view a folder's contents as icons, a compact list, or as a detailed list, which you can choose from the View icons on the right side of the main toolbar: icon, list, and compact, as shown here.

Use the control keys to change views quickly: **Ctrl-1** for Icons, **Ctrl-2** for list, and **Ctrl-3** for the compact view. The List view provides the name, size, type, and date. Buttons are displayed for each field across the top of the main pane. You can use these buttons to sort the list according to that field. For example, to sort the files by date, click the Date Modified button. To sort by size, click Size button. Click again to alternate between ascending and descending order.

Certain types of file icons will display previews of their contents. For example, the icons for image files will display a thumbnail of the image. A text file will display in its icon the first few words of its text. You can turn off thumbnails by un-checking the Show Thumbnails entry in the file manager View menu. Thumbnails are supported by the **xapp-thumbnailers** application, which features thumbnail support for various file types such as images (including Webp images) videos, epub ebooks, album covers for music files, and applications.

The View menu has entries for managing and arranging your file manager icons (see Table 6-2) (see Figure 6-53). You can choose Icons, List, and Compact views. In the Icon view, the "Arrange items" submenu appears, which provides entries for sorting icons by name, size, type, and modification date. You can also reverse the order, or position icons manually.

Note: As you move our mouse over an item in the File, View, and Edit menus, a short description of the the item's function is displayed in the status bar at the bottom of the file manager window.

The Zoom In entry enlarges your view of the window, making icons bigger, and Zoom Out reduces your view, making them smaller. Normal Size restores them to the standard size. You can also use the **Ctrl-+** and **Ctrl--** keys to zoom in and out.

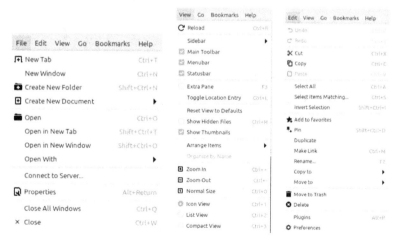

Figure 6-53: File manager File, View, and Edit menus

Menu Item	Description
Stop	Stop current task
Reload	Refresh file and folder list
Sidebar | Places, Tree	Displays sidebar in Places view or Tree view.
Sidebar | Show Sidebar	*Displays sidebar with Devices, Network, and Bookmark items.*
Main Toolbar	Displays main toolbar
Menubar	Displays menu bar
Status bar	Displays status bar at bottom of folder window
Extra Pane	Open dual panes in the file manager window, with different folders in each.
Location	Open the location box for folder path names
Reset View to Defaults	Default view and sorting
Show Hidden Files	Show administrative dot files.
Show Thumbnails	Show thumbnails of files in icon view for this folder. De-selecting this item will not show thumbnails.
Arrange Items: By Name, Size, Type, and Modification Date	Arrange files and folder by specified criteria
Organize by Name	In Icon View, order icons by name
Reversed Order	In List view, reverse order of file list
Zoom In	Provides a close-up view of icons, making them appear larger.
Zoom Out	Provides a distant view of icons, making them appear smaller.
Normal Size	Restores view of icons to standard size.
Icons	Displays icons
List	Displays file list with name, size, type, and date. Folders are expandable.
Compact	Displays compact file list using only the name and small icons

Table 6-2: File Manager View Menu

File manager menus and tools

From the File menu, you can perform key file manager tasks, such as creating a new folder, displaying a new tab, opening the file manager in a new window, connecting to a remote server (FTP), and opening the file manager properties dialog (see Table 6-3 and Figure 6-53).

Menu Item	Description
New Tab	Creates a new tab.
New Window	Open a new file manager window
Create New Folder	Creates a new subfolder in the folder.
Create New Document	Creates a text document.
Connect to server	Connect to an FTP server using the file manager
Properties	Properties for the currently open folder
Close All Windows	Close all file manage windows
Close	Close the file manager window.

Table 6-3: File Manager File Menu

From the Edit menu, you can paste files you have cut or copied to move or copy them between folders, or make duplicates (see Table 6-4 and see Figure 6-53). The selection menu items let you select all files and folders, those matching a simple regular expression, and to invert a selection, choosing all those not selected. You can also bookmark the folder, add a link in the Favorites folder, restore missing files, and close the file manager window. Properties opens the folder properties dialog with Basic and Permissions tabs. If a folder is selected, you can also change the folder icon's color. You can pin a selected file or folder so that it will be displayed at the beginning or top of the list of files and folders in that file manager window.

In the icon view, you can click anywhere on the empty space on the main pane of a file manager window to display a pop-up menu with entries to create a new folder, arrange icons, zoom icons, show hidden files, and open the folder properties dialog (see Table 6-5).

Favorites Folder

You can add links for folders and files to the Favorite folder by selecting the folder or file and choosing "Add to Favorites" from the Edit menu. The first time you add a favorite folder or file, the Favorites bookmark appears in the file manager sidebar (see Figure 6-54). Click on the Favorites bookmark to open the Favorites folder or file, showing links to your favorite folders and files. To remove a folder or file's link from the Favorite folder, right-click on it in the Favorite folder and choose "Remove from favorites". If you remove all the favorites from the Favorite folder, the Favorites bookmark on the sidebar is removed automatically. Folders and files designated as favorites will show a yellow star on the lower right corner of their icons.

When you choose a file or folder as a favorite, its display in a folder will be reordered to the top of the list, showing the Favorites in that folder first. Should you not want the favorites sorted to the beginning, open the file manager Preferences dialog (Edit | Preferences) and uncheck the "Sort Favorites before other files" option in the "Default View" section.

Menu Item	Description
Undo, Redo	Undo or Redo a paste operation
Cut, Copy	Move or copy a file or folder
Paste	Paste files that you have copied or cut, letting you move or copy files between folders, or make duplicates.
Select All	Select all files and folders in this folder
Select Items Matching	Quick search for files using basic pattern matching.
Invert Selection	Select all other files and folders not selected, deselecting the current selection.
Add to Favorites	Add a folder or file link to the Favorites folder
Pin	Pin folder or file so that it appears at the beginning or top of the displayed files and folders in a file manager window
Duplicate	Make a copy of a selected file
Make Links	Make a link to a file or folder
Rename	Rename a selected file or folder
Copy to	Copy a file or folder to one of the default bookmarks
Move to	Move a file or folder to one of the default bookmarks
Move To Trash	Move a file for folder to the trash folder for later deletion
Delete	Delete a file or folder immediately.
Use Full Context Menu	Add copy to, move to, and link entries to context menu.
Compress	Compress selected files and folders to a compressed archive file such as a tar, cpio, lmza, or zip file. The archive file can be password protected
Sharing Options	Active when a folder is selected. You can choose to share the folder on your network.
Preferences	The Nemo File Manager preferences for your account.

Table 6-4: File Manager Edit Menu

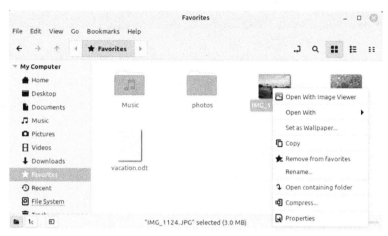

Figure 6-54: Favorites

Menu Item	Description
Create New Folder	Creates a new subfolder in the folder.
Create New Document	Creates a text document.
Create New Launcher	Create launcher icon for an application
Open in Terminal	Open the current folder in a terminal window
Show Hidden Files	Show administrative dot files.
Paste	Paste files that you have copied or cut.
Zoom In	Provides a close-up view of icons, making them appear larger.
Zoom Out	Provides a distant view of icons, making them appear smaller.
Properties	Opens the Properties dialog for the folder
Normal Size	Restores view of icons to standard size.

Table 6-5: File Manager Pop-up Menu

Navigating in the file manager

The file manager operates similarly to a Web browser, using the same window to display open folders. It maintains a list of previously viewed folders, and you can move back and forth through that list using the toolbar navigation buttons (left side) (see Figure 6-55). The left arrow button moves you to the previously displayed folder, the right arrow button moves you to the next displayed folder, and the up arrow moves to the parent folder. From the Go menu, you can perform the same navigation operation, as well as access the Home, Computer, Network and Trash folders (see Table 6-6).

Menu Item	Description
Open Parent	Move to the parent folder
Back	Move to the previous folder viewed in the file manager window
Forward	Move to the next folder viewed in the file manager window
Paste	Paste files that you have copied or cut, letting you move or copy files between folders, or make duplicates.
Same Location as Other Pane	If you have two panes open on the window, you can make both panes view the same folder
Home	Move to the Home folder
Computer	Move to the Computer folder, showing icons for your devices
Templates	Move to the Templates folder
Trash	Open the trash folder to see deleted files and folders, which can be restored.
Network	Move to the network folder showing connected systems on your network and open remote folders.
Search for Files	Search for files and folders using the file manager window

Table 6-6: File Manager Go Menu

When you open a new folder, the same window is used to display it, and you can use the Forward and Back arrows to move through previously opened folders (top left on the main toolbar). As you open sub-folders, the main toolbar displays buttons for your current folder and its parent folders (see Figure 6-56). You can click on a folder button to move to it directly. Clicking on the arrow to the left of the home folder button expands the list to the root folder, shown as a button with a hard drive icon.

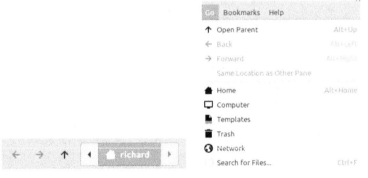

Figure 6-55: File manager navigation

You can also display a location URL text box instead of buttons, where you can enter the location of a folder, either on your system or on a remote system (see Figure 6-56). To display the location text box, press **Ctrl-l** or click the Location toggle button (curved arrow) on the right side of the location path on the main toolbar. You can also press F9 or choose Location on the View menu (View | Location). These access methods operate as toggles that move you a back and forth from the location text box to the button path.

Figure 6-56: Expanded and unexpanded paths and location

Use the sidebar's Places view to access your bookmarked folders, storage devices (USB, CD/DVD disc, and attached hard drives), and mounted network folders. On the "My Computer" section of the sidebar, you can access your home folders, trash, the file system (root folder), and additional bookmarks you created.

To open a subfolder, you can double-click its icon or right-click the icon and select Open from the menu. To open the folder in a new tab, select "Open in New Tab." You can also click on the folder to select it, and then choose the Open entry from the File menu (File | Open).

You can open any folder or file system listed in the sidebar by clicking on its bookmark. You can also right-click on a bookmark to display a menu with entries to Open, "Open in a New Tab", and "Open in a New Window" (see Table 6-7). The "Open in a New Window" item is an easy way to access devices from the file manager. The menu for the Trash bookmark lets you empty the trash. For any folder bookmark, you can also remove and rename the entry. Entries for removable devices in the sidebar such as USB drives also have menu items for Eject and Format. Internal hard drives have an Unmount entry instead.

Menu Item	Description
Open	Opens the file with its associated application. Folders are opened in the file manager. Associated applications are listed.
Open In A New Tab	Opens a folder in a new tab in the same window.
Open In A New Window	Opens a folder in a separate window, accessible from the toolbar, right-click.
Remove	Remove bookmark from the sidebar.
Rename	Rename a bookmark.

Table 6-7: The File Manager Sidebar Pop-Up Menu

Nemo File Manager Search

The Nemo file manager provides a search tool, which you can access either from the desktop menu or from any file manager window. From a file manager window, click the Search button on the toolbar (Looking glass at right), or select Go | Search for Files, to open a Search box below the toolbar. Enter the pattern to search and press ENTER. The results are displayed (see Figure 6-57). Buttons to the right let you choose whether the pattern searched is case sensitive (Aa button) and whether to search recursively through all subfolders or to just search the current one (the bent right arrow button). Click on a button to activate the option. There is also a content search entry to search the contents of text files for which you have a case sensitive button (Aa) and a regular expressions button (.*). The regular expressions button lets you search for partial patterns, such as those used for the **find** and **grep** commands. To remember the search, click the star button at the right side of the search box. To see previous searches, right-click on this button.

Figure 6-57: Nemo File Manager Search

Managing Files and Folders

As a GNOME-compliant file manager, Nemo supports desktop drag-and-drop operations for copying and moving files. To move a file or folder, drag-and-drop from one folder to another. The move operation is the default drag-and-drop operation in GNOME. To copy a file to a new location, press the Ctrl key as you drag-and-drop.

Using a file's pop-up menu

You can also perform remove, rename, and link creation operations on a file by right-clicking its icon and selecting the action you want from the pop-up menu that appears (see Table 6-8). For example, to remove an item, right-click it and select the Move To Trash entry from the pop-up menu. This places it in the Trash folder, where you can later delete it. Certain entries only appear in the Edit menu. These include Move to, Copy to, and Make link. To create a link, select the file and select Make Link from the Edit menu or press **Ctrl-m**. This creates a new link file that begins with the term "Link."

To rename a file, you can either right-click the file's icon and select the Rename entry from the pop-up menu or click its icon and press the F2 function key. The name of the icon will be bordered, encased in a small text box. You can overwrite the old one, or edit the current name by clicking a position in the name to insert text, as well as use the backspace key to delete characters. You can also rename a file by entering a new name in its Properties dialog box (Basic tab). Cinnamon also supports Quick-Rename, though this feature is not enabled by default. With Quick-Rename you can click the filename below the icon twice with an intervening pause to activate the renaming process (not a double-click). To turn on this feature, open the file manager Preferences dialog (Edit | Preferences) and select the Behavior tab. In the Behavior section, click on the checkbox for the entry "Click on a file's name twice to rename it."

Cinnamon provides a bulk renaming option using Bulky. You can access Bulky automatically by selecting a group of files, right-clicking to display the menu and choosing the Rename option. You can also choose the "File renamer" entry in the Accessories menu. This will display the Rename dialog listing your selected files (see Figure 6-58). You can choose to replace, remove, insert text, or change the case of a file name (left menu). You can also choose to change the name only, the extension of the files only, or both the name and extension (right menu). In the Find and Replace text boxes enter the pattern you want to change and the replacement patter. Checkboxes to the right let you specify whether the pattern is case sensitive or if you want to use regular expressions in your pattern (*, ?, or []). As you enter the new pattern in the Find box, the New Name list displays what the new file names will look like. To perform the renaming, click the Rename button (lower right).

Figure 6-58: Bulky bulk rename.

Grouping Files

You can select a group of files and folders by clicking the first item and then hold down the SHIFT key while clicking the last item, or by clicking and dragging the mouse across items you want to select. To select separated items, hold the Ctrl key down as you click the individual icons. If you want to select all the items in the folder, choose the Select All entry in the Edit menu (Edit | Select All) (**Ctrl-a**). You can then copy, move, or even delete several files at once. To select items that have a certain pattern in their name, choose Select Items Matching from the tools menu to open a search box where you can enter the pattern (**Ctrl-s**). Use the * character to match partial patterns, as in ***let*** to match on all filenames with the pattern "let" in them. The pattern **my*** would match on filenames beginning with the "my" pattern, and ***.png** would match on all PNG image files (the period indicates a filename extension).

Opening Applications and Files MIME Types

You can start any application in the file manager by double-clicking either the application itself or a data file used for that application. If you want to open the file with a specific application, you can right-click the file and select one of the Open With entries. One or more Open with entries will be displayed for default and possible applications, like "Open with Text Editor" for a text file. If the application you want is not listed, you can select Open with | Other Application to open a dialog listing available applications. Drag-and-drop operations are also supported for applications. You can drag a data file to its associated application icon (say, on the desktop). The application then starts up using that data file.

Menu Item	Description
Open	Opens the file with its associated application. Folders are opened in the file manager. Associated applications are listed.
Open In A New Tab	Opens a folder in a new tab in the same window.
Open In A New Window	Opens a folder in a new window
Open With	Selects an application with which to open this file. An Open With dialog opens listing possible applications.
Cut Copy	Entries to cut and copy the selected file.
Pin	Pin file or folder.
Rename (F2)	Renames the file.
Make Link	Creates a link to that file in the same folder (Full menu option).
Copy To	Copy a file to the Home Folder, Desktop, or to a folder displayed in another pane in the file manager window (Full menu option).
Move To	Move a file to the Home Folder, Desktop, or to a folder displayed in another pane in the file manager window (Full menu option).
Move To Trash	Moves a file to the Trash folder, where you can later delete it.
Delete	Delete the file or folder permanently
Send	Email the file using default mail application
Compress	Archives file using File Roller.
Sharing Options	Displays the Folder Sharing dialog (Samba and NFS).
Properties	Displays the Properties dialog.
Open in Terminal	Open the current folder in a terminal window
Open as Root	Open a terminal window as the administrative user

Table 6-8: The File and Folder Pop-Up Menu

Renaming Files

To change or set the default application to use for a certain type of file, you open a file's Properties dialog and select the Open With tab. Here you can choose the default application to use for that kind of file. Possible applications will be listed, organized as the default, recommended, related, and other categories. Click on the one you want to change to the default and click the "Set as default" button. Once you choose the default, it will appear in the Open With list for this file.

If you want to add an application to the Open With menu, click the "Show other applications" button to list possible applications. Select the one you want and click the Add button. If there is an application on the Open With tab you do not want listed in the Open With menu items, right-click on it, and choose **Forget association**.

File and Folder Properties

In a file's Properties dialog, you can view detailed information on a file and set options and permissions (see Figure 6-59). A file's Properties dialog has three tabs: Basic, Permissions, and Open With. Folders will have an additional share tab. The Basic tab shows detailed information such as type, size, location, and date modified. The type is a MIME type, indicating the type of application associated with it. The file's icon is displayed at the top with a text box showing the file's name. You can edit the filename in the Name text box, changing that name.

Figure 6-59: File properties on Nemo

If you want to change the icon image used for the file or folder, click the icon image (next to the name) to open a XAppIconChooser dialog (Choose an Icon dialog) to browse for the one you want. There are several tabs holding different collections such as Applications, Devices, Places, and Status (see Figure 6-60). Either browse the categories or use the Search box to locate icons. The icons currently used for your home folders can be found in the Places category. You can also click the Browse button on the toolbar to open a "Select image file" dialog where you can select an image file on your system. The **/usr/share/pixmaps** folder holds the set of possible images, though you can select your own images (click **pixmaps** entry in the Places sidebar). Double-click the image to add it to the "Choose an Icon" dialog. Then select the image and click the Select button to change the icon image.

The Permissions tab for files shows the read, write, and execute permissions for owner, group, and others, as set for this file. You can change any of the permissions here, provided the file belongs to you. You configure access for the owner, the group, and others, using drop-down menus. You can set owner permissions as Read Only or Read And Write. For group and others, you can also set the None option, denying access. Clicking on the group name displays a menu listing different groups, allowing you to select one to change the file's group. If you want to execute this as an application, you check the "Allow executing file as program" entry. This has the effect of setting the execute permission.

The Open With tab for files lists all the applications associated with this kind of file. You can select the one you want to use as the default. This can be particularly useful for media files, where you may prefer a specific player for a certain file or a particular image viewer for pictures.

Certain kinds of files will have additional tabs, providing information about the file. For example, an audio file will have an Audio tab listing the type of audio file and any other information like a song title or compression method used. An image file will have an Image tab listing the resolution and type of image.

Figure 6-60: Choose an Icon for a file, folder, or application

The Permissions tab for folders operates much the same way, but it includes two access entries: Folder Access and File Access. The Folder Access entry controls access to the folder with options for None, List Files Only, Access Files, and Create And Delete Files. These correspond to read, write, and execute permissions given to folders. The File Access entry lets you set permissions for all those files in the folder. They are the same as for files: for the owner, Read or Read and Write; for the group and others, the entry adds a None option to deny access. To set the permissions for all the files in the folder accordingly (not just the folder), you click the "Apply Permissions To Enclosed Files" button.

The Share tab for folders allows you to share folders as network shares. If you have Samba or NFS, these will allow your folders and files to be shared with users on other systems. You have the option to specify whether the shared folder or file will be read-only or allow write access. To allow write access check the "Allow other to create and delete files in this folder" entry. To open access to all users, check the Guest access entry.

Nemo Preferences

You can set preferences for your Nemo file manager in the Preferences dialog, accessible by selecting the Preferences item in any Nemo file manager window's Edit menu (Edit | Preferences) (see Figure 6-61).

The Views tab allows you to select how files are displayed by default, such as the list, icon, or compact view. You also can set default zoom levels for icon, compact, and list views.

Behavior lets you choose how to select files, manage the trash, and handle executable files.

Display lets you choose what added information you want displayed in an icon caption, like the size or date.

The List Columns tab lets you choose both the features to display in the detailed list and the order in which to display them. In addition to the already-selected Name, Size, Date, and Type, you can add permissions, group, MIME type, and owner.

The Preview tab lets you choose whether you want small preview content displayed in the icons, like beginning text for text files. You can also choose to show tooltips.

The Toolbar tab lets you choose some of the icons to display on the toolbar, such as search, refresh, computer, and home.

The Context Menus tab lets you choose what entries are to be shown on context menu for the selection of the item, the context menu for the file manager window background, additional entries for background context menu when in icon view, and additional entries for the Desktop context menus (right-click).

The Plugins tab lets you add new features to Nemo such as mounting archives and setting an image file as wallpaper.

Figure 6-61: Nemo File Manager Preferences

Nemo Plugins and Extensions

You can enhance Nemo using plugins and extensions such as NemoShare for folder sharing options, and "Nemo Fileroller" that allows you to create (compress) and extract archives. Several plugins and extensions are already installed are enabled by default, and will display entries in appropriate menus. To add more extension, use the Software Manager to install the nemo extension and plugin packages. Extension and plugin packages have the prefix **nemo-**, such as **nemo-share** and **nemo-fileroller**.

Plugins and Extensions are enabled on the the Nemo Preferences Plugins tab, accessible from the Edit menu (Edit | Plugins), also with the Alt+p key (see Figure 6-62). Actions are tasks that can be taken from the desktop menu (right-click on any empty area on the desktop) and from other pop-up file and folder menus. Enabling an action lists it in the menu. Disabling it will remove it from that menu. For example, enabling the "Set as Wallpaper" action places a "Set as Wallpaper" entry in the pop-up menu for an image file (right-click on an image file). Enabling the "Add Desklets" action adds an "Add Desklets" entry in the desktop pop-up menu. The Extensions section list the installed extensions, such as NemoShare and Nemo Fileroller. Those that are enabled have their checkbox checked. Click on a checkbox to toggle enabling and disabling an extension. If you disable or enable an extension, you have to restart Nemo to have the changes take effect. When you make a change, a button appears "Extension changed. Restart required." Click the button to restart Nemo. There are also buttons that allow you to disable or enable actions and extensions all at once.

Figure 6-62: Nemo Plugins and Extensions

You can also add your own action and script files to the actions and scripts folders in your **.local/share/nemo/** folder. Click on the folder icons in the actions and scripts sections to open these folders. Scripts allow you to add executable files of your own.

System Settings

You can configure desktop settings and perform most administrative tasks using the administration tools listed in the System Settings dialog, accessible from the Preferences menu and from the menu Favorites icon bar. System Settings organizes tools into Appearance, Preferences, Hardware, and Administration categories (see Figure 6-63 and see Figure 6-64). Some invoke the Ubuntu supported system tools available from previous releases such as Sound (PulseAudio) and Printers (system-config-printer). Others use the GNOME 3 configuration and administrative tools such as Network and Power Management.

Settings that deal with major administrative tasks (Administration section) such as Users and Groups, software sources, and firewalls, are discussed in the chapters dealing with those topics.

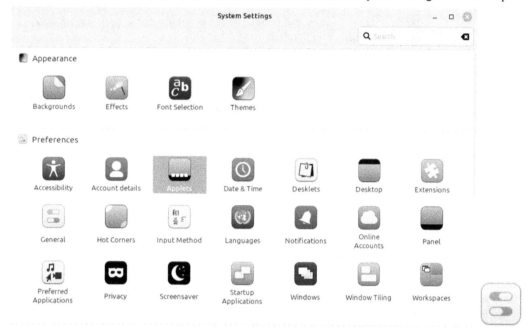

Figure 6-63: System Settings dialog (Appearance and Preferences)

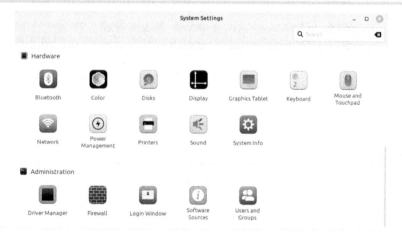

Figure 6-64: System Settings dialog (Hardware and Administration)

System Settings tools will open with a back arrow button at the top, which you can click to return to the System Settings dialog. Table 6-9 lists the System Settings tools.

Setting	Icon	Description
Appearance section		
Backgrounds		Selects Backgrounds with options for aspect, gradient, and colors.
Themes		Install themes and choose select styles for icons, controls, window borders, and pointers.
Fonts		Select default, window title, and document fonts with options for scaling, anti-aliasing, and hinting.
Effects		Fade and Scale effects for closing, opening, and maximize/minimizing windows and dialogs.
Preferences section		
Accessibility		Enables features like accessible login and keyboard screen
Account Details		Set your password, picture, and full name.
Applets		Add applets to the panel
Date & Time		Set the time and date manually or with network time, with options that let you set the time format.
Desklets		Add desklets to the desktop
Desktop		Choose icons to display on the desktop for the home folder, computer, and trash, as well as mounted volumes and network servers. The default is computer, home, and mounted volumes.
Extensions		Add desktop extensions, such as desktop cube, scroller, and dock.
General		Set desktop scaling and miscellaneous options
Hot Corners		Corner that when clicked can display the workspace selection screen (Show all workspaces option), scaled open windows (Show all windows option), show the desktop, or run a selected application.
Input Method		Configure and install instructions for supported languages.

Languages		Language selection
Notifications		Configure display of desktop notification
Online Accounts		Configure online account access
Panel		Set panel default and features such as panel size. Panel layout can be traditional (one bottom panel, default), flipped (panel at the top), and classic (two panels, one on the top and one on the bottom).
Preferred Applications		Set default applications and defaults for removable media.
Privacy		Enable remembering of recently accessed files
Screensaver		Screensaver and screen lock options, set the inactivity time to dim or lock the screen.
Startup Applications		Open the Startup Applications Preferences dialog to choose applications to start on startup.
Windows		Set window display options such as click actions on the title bar, focus mode, the title bar buttons to be displayed. You can also configure the open window switcher (Alt-tab).
Window Tiling		Set window display options for window tiling, snapping, and edge flipping.
Workspaces		Configure workspace display

Hardware section

Bluetooth		Bluetooth detection and configuration
Color		Set the color profile for a device.
Display		Change your screen resolution, refresh rate, and screen orientation.
Graphics Tablet		Configure a graphics tablet
Keyboard		Configure repeat key sensitivity and keys for special tasks.

Mouse and Touchpad		Mouse and touchpad configuration: select hand orientation, speed, and accessibility
Network		Lets you turn wired and wireless networks on and off. You can access an available wireless network and proxy configuration.
Power Management		Set the power options for laptop inactivity
Printers		Printer configuration with system-config-printer
Sound		Configure sound effects, output volume, sound device options, input volume, and sound application settings
System Info		System and hardware information
Administration section		
Device Drivers		Select device drivers for cards such as graphics cards.
Firewall		Open the Gufw dialog for managing the ufw firewall. Gufw needs to be installed.
Login Screen		Open the Login Window Preferences dialog for configuring the Linux LightDM display manager (LightDM).
Software Sources		Open the Linux Mint Software Sources selection dialog to activate and deactivate software repositories.
Users and Groups		Manage users

Table 6-9: Desktop System Settings

Appearance

The Appearance section on System Settings provides four dialogs to configure backgrounds, themes, fonts, and desktop effects.

Backgrounds

The Backgrounds dialog lists backgrounds you can choose from (see Figure 6-65). On the Images tab, a scrollbox to the left lists installed background collections. You can choose a custom image from a local folder by clicking on the plus button in the lower left corner of the scrollbox. This opens an "Add folder" dialog, allowing you to choose a folder of images. You can remove the folder using the minus button at the bottom left of the scrollbox.

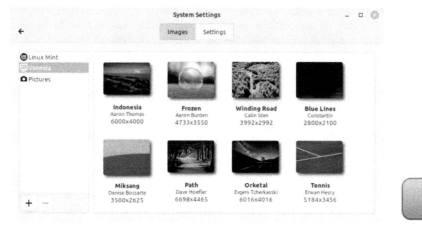

Figure 6-65: Backgrounds: Images tab

On the Settings, you can choose to run a slideshow from the selected folder, with options for random order and the time interval (see Figure 6-66). From the Picture aspect menu, you can choose display options such as Zoom, Centered, Scaled, Mosaic, Stretched, Spanned or No picture. A centered or scaled image will preserve the image proportions. Stretched and Spanned may distort it. Any space not filled, such as with a centered or scaled images, will be filled in with the desktop color.

Figure 6-66: Backgrounds: Settings tab

The Centered, Scaled, and Spanned options also show gradient options. For gradients, use the Gradient color buttons for selecting a color at each end of the gradient. From the Background gradient menu, you can choose a vertical or horizontal gradient. Click on the color button to open a "Pick a Color" dialog where you can select a color. Click the plus button on this dialog to open a color selector where you can enter a color hex number or choose one from a sliding scale, and then adjust its shade.

Initially, only the Linux Mint backgrounds are listed, including backgrounds from previous Linux Mint releases). Install the **gnome-backgrounds** package to add a collection of GNOME backgrounds. You can also add backgrounds from previous Linux Mint releases, such as **mint-backgrounds-nadia**. You can download more GNOME backgrounds from **https://www.gnome-look.org/**.

Font Selection

The Font Selection dialog lets you set the default font for the desktop, documents, and the window title on window title bars, as well as anti-aliasing, hinting, and text scaling features. It also sets the monospace font (see Figure 6-67).

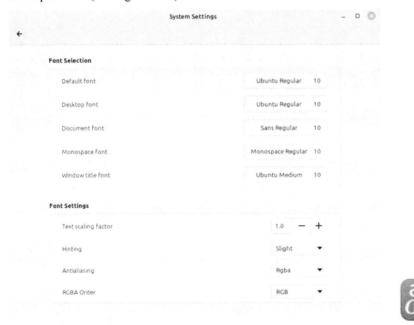

Figure 6-67: Font Selection

Themes

The Themes dialog has three tabs: Themes, Add/Remove, and Settings. The Themes tab shows the components of the currently selected theme (see Figure 6-68). You can customize your desktop by choosing different icon sets, different controls, window border, mouse styles, and desktop themes(see Figure 6-69). Clicking on the icon for an item opens an icon menu from which to can choose other sets. Clicking on the Desktop icon opens an icon menu that lets you choose another installed theme. Each theme may have window, icon, and control sets you can choose. Linux Mint uses the Mint Y for the window, icon, and control sets.

Themes can be either light or dark. Themes that have the term Dark in their name, such as Mint-Y-Dark, have dark icons, window buttons, desktop components. Those without the Dark term are light themes, such as Mint Y. You can mix different light and dark themes for icons, applications, and desktops. The default Linux Mint 21 theme for the desktop is Mint-Y-Dark, but for applications and icons it is Mint-Y, the Mint Y light theme.

In addition, individual applications can have either a dark mode or light mode. With dark mode support, even if the application theme used is light, that application will display its window and icons in dark mode. Certain applications have dark mode support. These are mostly multimedia and image applications that enable dark mode to enhance viewing. These include Hypnotic, Xviewer, Celluloid, Pix, and GNOME terminal. You can disable the dark mode support by de-selecting the dark mode option in the application's preferences.

Themes also feature color accents; were you can choose a variation on a theme tinted to different colors. The Mint Y theme for Icons and Applications has Mint-Y-Red, Mint-Y-Aqua, and Mint-Y-Dark-Pink accent themes. The Desktop themes include Mint-Y-Blue, Mint-Y-Purple, and Mint-Y-Dark-Brown accent themes.

Mint Y themes now use GNOME GTK4. Windows and icons appear similar to the current GNOME interface. Previous versions of Mint Y were based on the older Metacity window manager themes. Should you wish, you can still install the Mint Y Legacy theme, which has much the same appearance as the older Mint Y themes used in previous releases.

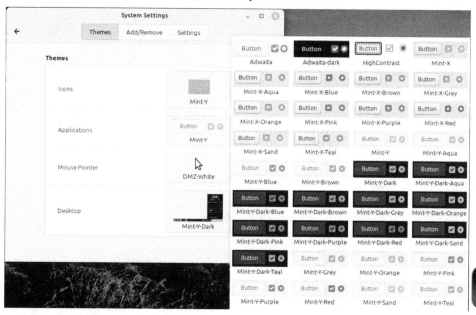

Figure 6-68: Themes - Applications

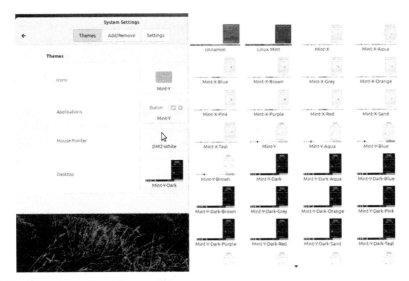

Figure 6-69: Themes - Desktops

On the Add/Remove tab you can download available themes (see Figure 6-70). The "Sort by" menu lets you sort them by popularity, name, or date. To install a theme, click on the theme's download button (the down arrow) on the right side of its entry. After the download, the down arrow button disappears and a checkmark icon then appears in the theme entry. You will then see it listed on the Desktop icon menu on the Themes tab.

A toolbar at the bottom of the Add/Remove tab has buttons for "More info" (lightbulb icon), Uninstall to remove themes already installed, Updates to update your installed themes, and Refresh to update the list of available themes. To see more information about a selected theme, click the "More info" button to open its Web page. A list of available themes can be found at **https://cinnamon-spices.linuxmint.com/themes**.

Figure 6-70: Themes (Online Themes)

On the Settings tab, you can set options for showing icons in menus and buttons, as well as setting scrollbar behavior options such as allowing overlay scrollbars (see Figure 6-71).

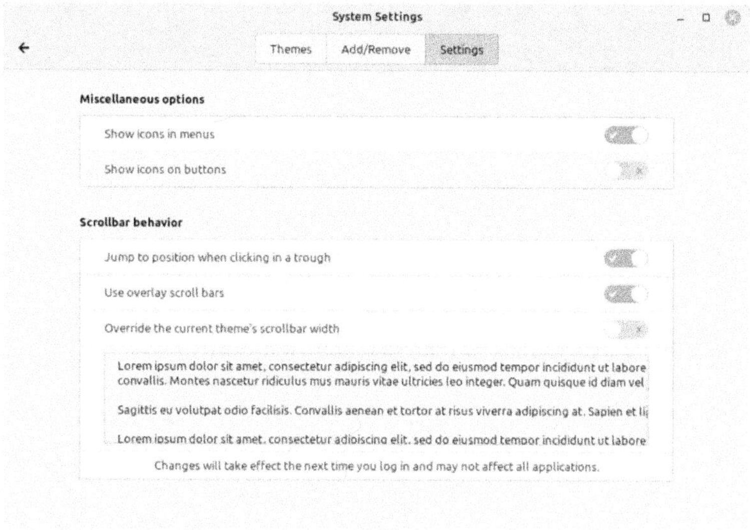

Figure 6-71: Themes (Settings tab)

Preferences

In the System Settings Preferences section, dialogs, such as Applets and Menu, let you configure your desktop. Preferences for Cinnamon, such as the time settings (calendar) and application defaults (Applications & Removable media), are discussed here.

Preferred Applications and Removable Media

The Preferred Applications dialog lets you set default applications for tasks and media. On the "Preferred applications" tab you set default applications for basic types of files: Web, Mail, Documents, Text editor, Music, Video, Photos, Source Code, and Terminal (see Figure 6-72). Use the menus to choose installed alternatives, such as Thunderbird instead of Evolution for Mail, or Image Viewer instead of Shotwell for Photos.

Figure 6-72: Preferred Applications

On the "Removable media" tab you can specify default actions for different kinds of media: CD Audio, DVD Video, Music Player, Photos, and Software media. You can turn off this function by switching off the "Prompt or start programs on media insertion" option. You can select the application to use for the different media from the menus (see Figure 6-73). These menus also include options for Ask What To Do, Do Nothing, and Open Folder. The Open Folder option will open a window displaying the files on the disc. A button labeled "Other Media" opens a dialog that lets you set up an association for less used media like Blu-Ray discs and Audio DVD. Initially, the "Ask what to do" option is set for all entries. Possible options are listed for the appropriate media, like Rhythmbox Media Player for CD Audio discs and Celluloid for video DVDs.

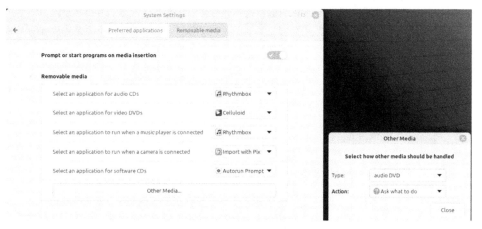

Figure 6-73: Preferred Applications: Removable media

When you insert removable media, such as a CD audio disc, its associated application is automatically started, unless you change that preference. If you want to turn off this feature for a particular kind of media, you can select the Do Nothing entry from its application menu. If you want to be prompted for options, use the "Ask what to do" entry. Then, when you insert a disc, a dialog with a drop-down menu for possible actions is displayed. From this menu, you can select another application or select the Do Nothing or Open Folder options.

Time & Date Settings (Calendar applet)

The Calendar applet is located on the bottom panel to the right (see Figure 6-742). The calendar shows the current date, but you can move to different months and years using the month and year scroll arrows at the top of the calendar. The Calendar applet also syncs with the evolution-data-server to display events listed in Evolution, GNOME Calendar, Google Calendar, and Thunderbird.

Figure 6-74: Calendar applet

Date & Time options are set using the System Settings Date & Time dialog, which opens by choosing "Date and Time Settings" in the Calendar menu, or by clicking the Date & Time icon in the System Settings Preferences section (see Figure 6-75).

Figure 6-75: Date & Time settings, network time

You set the time zone using the map to the left or by selection a region or city from the Region or City menus. You can also specify the time format, using a 24-hour clock, displaying the date, and also the seconds. The time and date can be set manually or automatically from a timeserver (the Network Time switch). For manual changes, you can set the time and date directly by turning off the Network Time switch.

Configuring the Calendar applet from the Applet dialog (or right-click on the date applet on the panel and choose Configure), displays options for specifying the date display format for the panel and the applet (see Figure 6-76). The format uses format specifiers for different date elements, such as **%a** for the day of the week, **%I** for the hour, and **%y** for the year. You can click on the "Show information on date format syntax" button to open a website where you can learn about formats.

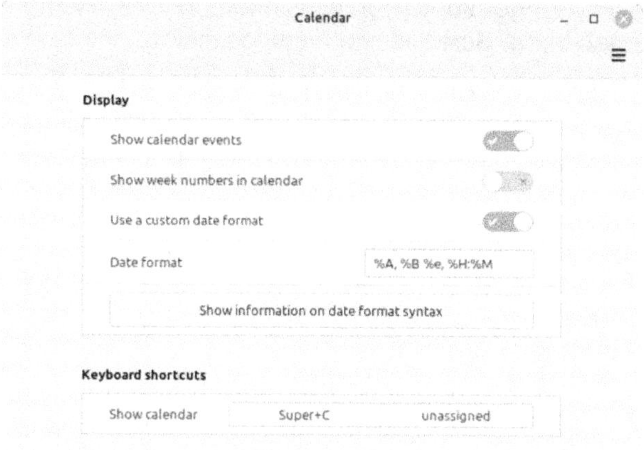

Figure 6-76: Calendar applet

Alternatively, you can manage the system time and date using the **timedatectl** command. The date and time on Linux Mint are implemented using the timedated daemon, a systemd daemon. The **timedatectl** command takes several options: **set-time** to set the time, **set-timezone** for the time zone, and **set-ntp** turns on NTP network time. The **status** option displays the current settings. See the **timedatectl** man page for a detailed listing of options and examples. Use dashes for the date and colons for the time. If you set both the date and time at the same time, enclose them in quotes. The following sets the date and time June 21, 2016 at 3:40 PM, ten seconds.

```
sudo timedatectl set-time "2016-6-21 15:40:10"
timedatectl status
```

Screensaver and Lock Screen

The System Settings Screensaver dialog incorporates the screen lock options from previous releases and lets you customize the lock screen display. On the Screensaver Settings tab, you can specify the idle time for the screen, having it turn off when not in use. You can also control whether to lock the screen or not. You can set the lock to a specific time, or to when the screen turns off (see Figure 6-77).

Figure 6-77: Screensaver Settings tab

Note: Xscreensaver is no longer supported by Cinnamon, There is no longer a
Screensaver tab in the Screensaver Settings dialog.

On the Customize tab, you can set up an away message to be displayed when you lock the
screen, customize the size and font of the time displayed, and enable additional options such as
allowing keyboard shortcuts, a floating clock, and displaying album art (see Figure 6-78).

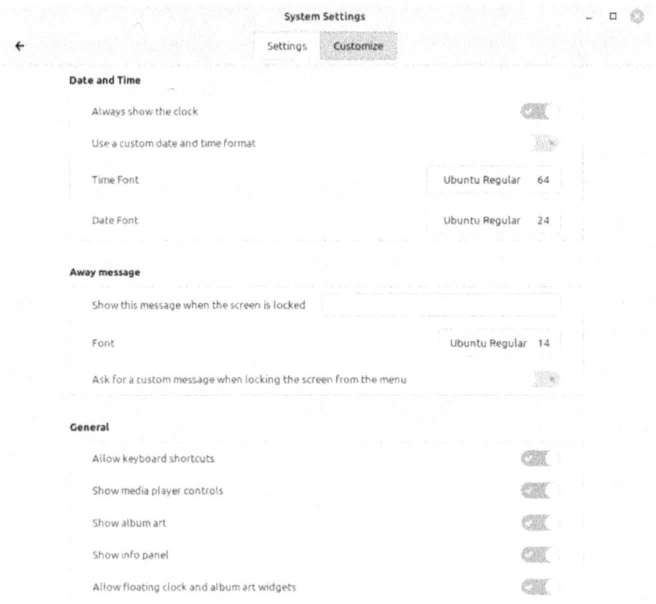

Figure 6-78: Screensaver - Customize tab

Languages

On the Language Settings, dialog you can choose the language for your menus and
windows (see Figure 6-79). The currently selected language is displayed. Click on the icon for the
language and region to display an icon menu for language variations, such as "English, Ireland" or
"English, India." The Region option adjusts for features such as currency, numbering, and
measurement, for example, "English, United Kingdom or "English Hong Kong." Click the "Apply
System-Wide" button to apply the language for your entire system. Use the "Install/Remove
Languages" button to open the "Install/Remove Languages" dialog, where you can add a new
language or remove installed ones. Click the Add button on this dialog to add a new language.

Figure 6-79: Languages

Input Method

The Input Method application provides install and configuration instructions for various languages such as Japanese, Korean, and Chinese). There are tabs for the supported languages (see Figure 6-80). A menu at the top lets you specify the XIM framework.

Figure 6-80: Input Method

Accessibility

The Accessibility dialog in System Settings lets you configure alternative access to your interface for your keyboard and mouse actions. Four tabs set the display, keyboard properties, typing, and mouse features. Visual lets you adjust the contrast and text size, and whether to allow use of screen reader (see Figure 6-81). Keyboard displays a screen keyboard and uses visual cues for alert sounds. "Typing assistance" adjusts key presses. Mouse lets you use the keyboard for mouse operations.

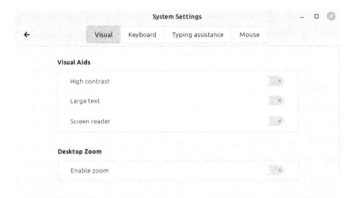

Figure 6-81: Accessibility

Startup Applications

On the Startup Applications dialog, you can select additional programs you want to be started automatically. Some are already turned on automatically (see Figure 6-82). Turn off an entry if you no longer want it to start up automatically. To add an application not listed, click the add button (+) on the button bar at the bottom of the dialog and choose either "Custom command" or "Choose application." The "Choose application" entry open an Applications dialog listing possible application. The "Custom command" entry opens a dialog where you can type in the application name and program (use Browse to select a program, usually in **/usr/bin**). To remove an entry from the list, select it and click the remove button (-) on the button bar.

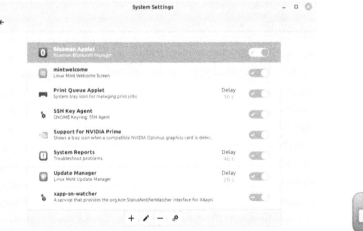

Figure 6-82: Startup Applications Preferences

You can select any entry and edit its name and application, as well as its startup delay time by selecting the entry and clicking the edit button (pencil icon) on the button bar. This opens the Edit Startup Program dialog with entries for Name, Command, Comment, and Startup delay. Any startup delay will be displayed on its entry.

Should you want to run the application immediately, you can select it and then click the "Run now" button (gears icon) on the button bar.

Extensions

Extensions add third-party enhancements of your desktop interface, such as transparent panels, watermarks on the desktop, and wobbly windows. Not all may be compatible, and you will be warned if they are not. Extensions displays two tabs: Manage and Download (see Figure 6-83). The Manage tab lists installed extensions. Use the button bar at the bottom to manage them. You can enable or disable an extension (+ and -), or delete it entirely (x). The curved arrow button will disable all extensions. A checkmark appears next to an enabled extension. If it can be configured, a gear button also appears, which you can click to open a configuration dialog.

Figure 6-83: Extension Manage tab

The Download tab lists available extensions (see Figure 6-84). Click on an extensions download button (down arrow) to download and install it. A checkmark then appears in place of the down arrow. A Sort by menu lets you sort by name, popularity, date, and installed. You can also search for an extension using the search box to the left. The button bar at the bottom lets you obtain more information about an extension (lightbulb), delete an installed extension (x), obtain updates (gear), and refresh the list (arrows circle).

Figure 6-84: Extensions Download tab

Notifications

The System Settings Notifications dialog lets you configure your desktop notifications (see Figure 6-85). There are switches to enable notifications, remove them after a timeout, and show them at the bottom side of the screen. The "Display a test notification" will show a sample of a notification, using your current settings. On this dialog, you can also set the size of the OSD media keys.

Figure 6-85: Notifications

Privacy

The System Settings Privacy dialog lets you decide if you want to remember recent files (see Figure 6-86). If you choose to remember recent files, you have the options to never forget them. You can also check for internet connectivity, checking to see if your network connections can reach the Internet.

Figure 6-86: Privacy

General

On the General dialog you can set scaling, miscellaneous, and memory limit options such as disabling automatic screen rotation, setting a time delay for logging out or shutting down, and restarting Cinnamon if it uses too much memory. (see Figure 6-87).

Figure 6-87: General

Hardware

Several hardware-based tasks such as configuring your mouse, keyboard, and power management are discussed here.

System Info

The System Info dialog shows system information, such as your hardware specifications (memory, processor, graphics card, and disk size), the distribution (64 or 32-bit system), and the Cinnamon version (see Figure 6-88).

Figure 6-88: System Info

Mouse and Touchpad

The System Settings Mouse and Touchpad dialog is the primary tool for configuring your mouse and touchpad (see Figure 6-89). On the Mouse tab, you can choose the mouse speed and size, scrolling direction, hand orientation, double-click times, and "Drag and drop" thresholds, as well as the double-click times. For laptops, you can configure your touchpad on the Touchpad tab, enabling touchpad clicks and edge scrolling (left side).

Figure 6-89: System Settings, Mouse and Touchpad

Power Management

For power management, Linux Mint uses the GNOME Power Manager, which makes use of Advanced Configuration and Power Interface (ACPI) support provided by a computer to manage power use. The GNOME Power Manager displays an icon on the panel showing the current power source, a battery (laptop) or lightning (desktop). Clicking on the battery icon displays a menu showing the power charge of your wireless devices, including your laptop and any other wireless devices like a wireless mouse (see Figure 6-90). The device entries include the device product and model names. You can right-click on the power manager panel icon to display a menu with a Configure entry. Click on it to display the Power Manager applet configuration dialog, which lists display options for the applet (see Figure 6-90). Should you want the percentage of battery power left displayed on the panel with the battery icon, you can select the "Show percentage" option.

You can also quickly turn off power management from the panel with the Inhibit applet (add it to the panel with Applets).

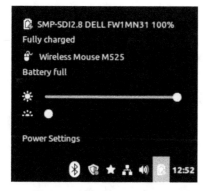

Figure 6-90: GNOME Power Manager menu and applet configuration

The GNOME Power manager is configured with the Power dialog, accessible as Power from System Settings. On the Power tab, you have the options to set the suspension time out, and what action to take when the lid is closed or the power is low (see Figure 6-91). If present, battery levels for your laptop and wireless mouse are displayed on the Batteries tab.

Figure 6-91: GNOME Power Manager

On the Brightness tab, you can set the screen brightness, as well as dimming options for when the system is inactive (see Figure 6-92).

To see how your laptop or desktop is performing with power, you can use Power statistics, accessible from the System Tools menu. The Power Statistics window displays a sidebar listing your different power devices. A right pane will show tabs with power use information for a selected device. The Laptop battery device will display three tabs: Details, History, and Statistics. The History tab will show your recent use, with graph options for Time to empty (time left), Time to full (recharging), Charge, and Rate. The Statistics tab can show charge and discharge graphs.

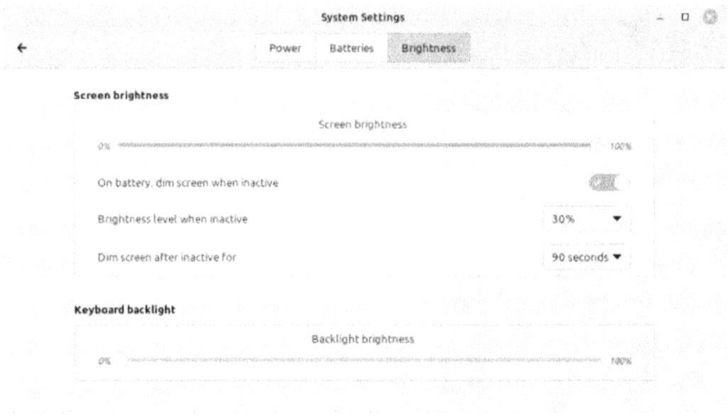

Figure 6-92: GNOME Power Manager: Brightness tab

Keyboard Settings

The System Settings Keyboard dialog shows tabs for typing, shortcuts, and layouts. The Typing tab adjusts repeat keys and cursor blinking (see Figure 6-93). The Shortcuts tab lets you assign keys to perform tasks such as starting the Web browser or mapping multimedia keys on a keyboard to media tasks, like play and pause. Just select the task and then press the key. There are tasks for the desktop (Cinnamon), multimedia (Sound and Media), window management, and workspace management. With workspace management, you can also map keys to perform workspace switching. Keys that are already assigned will be shown.

Figure 6-93: Keyboard Typing

The Layouts tab lets you choose a language (see Figure 6-94). The current input language source is listed and selected. Click the plus button to open a dialog listing other language sources, which you can add. Click the keyboard button to see the keyboard layout of your currently selected input source. You can also allow different language layouts for different windows.

Figure 6-94: Keyboard: Layouts tab

For specialized keyboard options, click the Options button to list options such as enabling the key sequence to kill the X server (see Figure 6-95).

The system location and keyboard layout settings can also be set using the **localectl** command in a terminal window. Check the **localectl** man page for a detailed listing of options. The **status** option displays the current locale and keyboard layout. The **set-locale** option changes the location and **list-locale** lists available locations. The **set-keymap** option sets the keyboard layout and the **list-keymaps** option lists possible layouts.

```
localectl status
```

Figure 6-95: Keyboard Layout Options

7. MATE Desktop

MATE Desktop

Windows

Workspaces

Linux Mint Menu (MATE)

MATE Panel

Applets

The Caja File Manager

Preferences (desktop configuration)

The MATE desktop is a simplified and easy-to-use desktop derived from the GNOME 2 desktop. MATE's official file manager is Caja. Those familiar with GNOME 2 will find similar features. MATE has only one panel, though you can add more. The workspace switcher is not installed by default but works that same way as in GNOME 2. The menu used for the Linux Mint version of MATE is the Linux Mint menu. Linux Mint 21 installs MATE version 1.24.

The GNU Network Object Model Environment, also known as GNOME, is a powerful and easy-to-use environment consisting primarily of a panel, a desktop, and a set of desktop tools with which program interfaces can be constructed. GNOME is designed to provide a flexible platform for the development of powerful applications.

The MATE Desktop

The MATE desktop is designed to be simple, with a single panel and desktop icons (see Figure 7-1). The panel appears as a long bar across the bottom of the screen. It holds menus, program launchers, and applet icons (an applet is a small program designed to be run within the panel). You can display the panel horizontally or vertically, and have it automatically hide to show you a full screen.

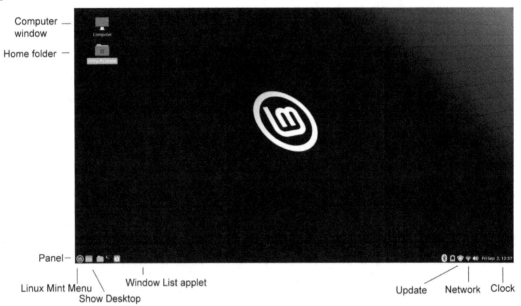

Figure 7-1: MATE desktop and panel

On the left side of the panel is the button for the Linux Mint menu. With this menu, you can access places and applications. Next to the menu are application buttons, followed by the Window List applet, which shows buttons for open windows. To the right of the panel are system tools such as icons for the Network Manager, Update Manager, Power, sound volume, and the clock.

The remainder of the screen is the desktop, where you can place folders, files, and application launchers. You can use a click-and-drag operation to move a file from one window to another or to the desktop. A drag-and-drop with the Ctrl key held down will copy a file. A drag-and-drop operation with both the Ctrl and SHIFT keys held down (Ctrl-Shift) creates a link on the desktop to that folder or file. Your home folder is accessed from the Home Folder icon on the desktop. Double clicking it opens a file manager window for your home folder. A right-click anywhere on the desktop displays a desktop menu with which you can align your desktop icons and create new folders.

To quit the desktop, you use the Quit entry in the menu. Clicking on it opens a dialog with options to Suspend, Hibernate, Restart, and Shut Down.

MATE Components

From a user's point of view, the desktop interface has four components: the desktop, the panels, the main menu, and the file manager (see Figure 7-2). You have a single panel displayed, used for menus, application icons, and managing your windows. When you open a window, a corresponding button for it will be displayed in the lower panel, which you can use to minimize and restore the window.

To start a program, you can select its entry from the Linux Mint menu. You can also click its application icon in the panel (if one appears) or drag-and-drop data files to its icon. To add an icon for an application to the desktop, right-click on its entry in the Linux Mint menu and select "Add to desktop."

Figure 7-2: MATE with Linux Mint menu and Caja file manager

Drag-and-Drop Files to the Desktop

Any icon for an item that you drag-and-drop from a file manager window to the desktop also appears on the desktop. The default drag-and-drop operation is a move operation. If you select a file in your file manager window and drag it to the desktop, you are actually moving the file from its current folder to the desktop folder, which is located in your home folder and holds all items on the desktop. The desktop folder is **Desktop**. In the case of dragging folders to the desktop, the entire folder and its subfolders will be moved to the desktop folder.

To remove an icon from the desktop, you right-click and choose "Move to Trash." If you choose to display the trash icon on the desktop, you can simply drag-and-drop it in the trash.

You can copy a file to your desktop by pressing the CTRL key and then clicking and dragging it from a file manager window to your desktop. You will see the mouse icon change to hand with a small + symbol, indicating that you are creating a copy, instead of moving the original.

You can also create a link on the desktop to any file. This is useful if you want to keep a single version in a folder and just be able to access it from the desktop. You could also use links for customized programs that you may not want to appear on the menu or panel. There are two ways to create a link. While holding down the Ctrl and Shift keys, Ctrl-SHIFT, drag the file to where you want the link created. A copy of the icon then appears with a small arrow in the right corner indicating it is a link. You can click this link to start the program, open the file, or open the folder, depending on the type of file to which you linked. Alternatively, first click and drag the file out of the window, and after moving the file but before releasing the mouse button, press the ALT key. This will display a pop-up menu with selections for Move Here, Copy Here, and Link Here. Select the Link Here option to create a link.

The drag-and-drop file operation works on virtual desktops provided by the Workspace Switcher. The Workspace Switcher creates icons for each virtual desktop in the panel, along with buttons for any window open on them. The Workspace Switcher is not added by default. You will have to add it to the panel.

Desktop Settings

You can configure desktop and window display settings using the Desktop Settings dialog, which you can access from the Preferences menu, or from the Control Center (see Figure 7-3). The Desktop Settings dialog has three tabs: Desktop, Windows, and Interface. The Desktop tab lets you choose which system icons to display on the desktop. The Computer and Home folder icons are initially selected, along with Mounted volumes for external file systems such as USB drives and DVDs that you insert. You can also choose to display the Network and Trash icons.

Figure 7-3: MATE Desktop Settings

On Windows tab, you can choose what window manager to use, Marco or the older Metacity. For each, you can further choose whether to support compositing, or to use the window manager without compositing. Marco+Compositing is the default. You can also set the "User Interface Scaling" option to support HiDPi, if needed. The settings for the chosen window manager appears in a following section on the tab. For Marco you can choose a button layout, whether to show content when moving windows, and to use the system font in the titlebar. For Metacity you can also choose the button layout and to use the system font in the the titlebar.

The Interface tab lets you choose whether to show icons on menus, buttons, and toolbars, as well as set the icon size for those in toolbars.

Applications on the Desktop

In some cases, you will want to create another way on the desktop to access a file without moving it from its original folder. You can do this either by using an application launcher icon or by creating a link to the original program. Application launcher icons are the components used in menus and panels to display and access applications. To place an application icon on your desktop for an entry in the menus, you can simply drag-and-drop the application entry from the menu to the desktop, or right-click and select "Add to desktop."

For applications that are not on a menu, you can either create an application launcher button or create a direct link for it. To create an application launcher, right-click the desktop background to display the desktop menu, and then select the "Create Launcher" entry. To create a simple link, click-and-drag a program's icon while holding the Ctrl-Shift keys down to the desktop.

The Desktop Menu

You can right-click anywhere on the empty desktop to display the desktop menu that includes entries for common tasks, such as creating an application launcher, creating a new folder, or organizing the icon display. Keep in mind that the New Folder entry creates a new folder on your desktop, specifically in your desktop folder (**DESKTOP**), not your home folder. The entries for this menu are listed in Table 7-1.

Menu Item	Description
Create Folder	Creates a new folder on your desktop, within your DESKTOP folder.
Create Launcher	Creates a new desktop icon for an application.
Create Document	Creates files using installed templates
Organize Desktop by Name	Arranges your desktop icons.
Keep Aligned	Aligns your desktop icons.
Cut, Copy, Paste	Cuts, copies, or pastes files, letting you move or copy files between folders.
Change Desktop Background	Opens a Background Preferences dialog to let you select a new background for your desktop.

Table 7-1: The Desktop Menu

Windows

You can resize a window by clicking any of its sides or corners and dragging. You can move the window with a click-and-drag operation on its title bar. You can also ALT-click and drag anywhere on the window. The upper-right corner of a window shows the Minimize, Maximize, and Close buttons (minus, expand, and x buttons) (see Figure 7-4). Clicking the Minimize button no longer displays the window on the desktop. A button for it remains on the bottom panel (the Window list applet) that you can click to restore it. The panel button for a window works like a display toggle. If the window is displayed when you click the panel button, it will no longer be shown. If not displayed, it will then be shown. Right-clicking anywhere on the title bar (or pressing Alt-space) displays the window menu with entries for window operations (see Figure 7-4). The options include workspace entries to move the window to another workspace (virtual desktop) or make visible on all workspaces, which displays the window no matter to what workspace you move.

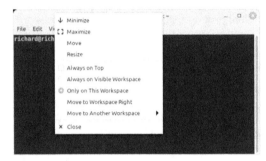

Figure 7-4: MATE window

You can quickly move between windows by pressing the Alt-Tab keys. A window switcher bar opens displaying thumbnails of open windows (see Figure 7-5). Continue pressing the Alt-Tab keys to move through them. You can use the Windows Preferences dialog's General tab (Control Center) to enable or disable thumbnails. The Compositing Window Manager enables them. If you disable thumbnails for the switcher, only small icons are displayed for the open windows.

Figure 7-5: Switching Windows with thumbnails

You can configure window behavior using the Window Preferences dialog's Behavior tab accessible as Windows from the Preferences menu and the Control Center. You choose features such as compositing, select windows by moving the mouse over them and use the meta key instead of the Alt key to move a window. From a menu, you can choose the action to perform when the title bar is double-clicked. The default is maximize, but other options include to roll up the window and minimize it.

Window List

The Window List applet shows currently opened windows (see Figure 7-6). The Window List arranges opened windows in a series of buttons, one for each window. A window can include applications such as a Web browser or a file manager window displaying a folder. You can move from one window to another by clicking its button. When you minimize a window, you can later restore it by clicking its entry in the Window List.

Right clicking a window's Window List button opens a menu that lets you Minimize or Unminimize, Move, Resize, Maximize, or Close the window, always display the window on top of other windows, show it only on its workspace or on the visible workspace, and move the window to another workspace. The Minimize operation will reduce the window to its Window List entry. Right clicking the entry will display the menu with an Unminimize option instead of a Minimize one, which you can then use to redisplay the window. The Close entry will close the window, ending its application. The Always On Top option will always show the window on top of any other open windows. The Always on on Visible Workspace will always show the window on whatever workspace you switch to. The Always on This Workspace (the default) will only display the window on this workspace. There are also entries for moving the window to an adjacent workspace, or to a specific one.

Figure 7-6: Window List applet

The Window List applet is represented by a small bar at the beginning of the window list applet (see Figure 7-6). To configure the Window List applet, right-click on this bar and select the Preferences entry to open the Window List Preferences dialog (see Figure 7-7). Here, you can set features such as whether to group windows on the panel, whether to display thumbnails along with the thumbnail size, whether to show all open windows or those from just the current workspace, or which workspace to restore windows to.

Figure 7-7: Window List Preferences

If you choose to group windows, then common windows are grouped under a button that will expand like a menu, listing each window in that group. For example, all open terminal windows would be grouped under a single button, which when clicked would pop up a list of their buttons. The button shows the number of open windows. You can also choose to group only if there is not enough space on the Window List applet to display a separate button for each window,

Workspace Switcher

The Workspace Switcher applet lets you switch to different virtual desktops (see Figure 7-8). You can add the Workspace Switcher to any panel by selecting it from that panel's "Add to Panel" box. It is not added by default. The Workspace Switcher shows your entire virtual desktop as separate rectangles listed next to each other. Open windows show up as small colored rectangles in these squares. You can move any window from one virtual desktop to another by clicking and dragging its image in the Workspace Switcher from one workspace to another.

Figure 7-8: Workspace switcher, one row and two rows

In addition to the Workspace Switcher, you can use the Ctrl-Alt-arrow keys to move from one workspace to another. When you use the Ctrl-Alt-arrow keys, the right and left arrows move you through a row, and the up and down keys move you from one row to another. A small workspace bar appears at the center of the screen, highlighting the current workspace and displaying its name (see Figure 7-9).

Figure 7-9: Switching workspaces, Ctrl-Alt-*arrow*

To configure the Workspace Switcher, right-click on the applet to display a menu, and then select Preferences to display the Workspace Switcher Preferences dialog box (see Figure 7-10). Here, you can select the number of workspaces and name them. The default is four. You can also choose the number of rows for the workspace. There are also options to show the names of the workspaces, allow workspaces to wrap around, and to show only the current workspace.

Figure 7-10: Workspace Switcher Preferences

Linux Mint Menu for MATE

Linux Mint provides its own menu for the MATE interface called the Linux Mint Menu. It is derived from the SUSE Slab menu. The Linux Mint Menu is located on the left side of the panel. You can also open it with the Ctrl-meta keys.

The Linux Mint Menu has three sections: Places, System, and Favorites/Applications (see Figure 7-11). The Places section displays buttons for accessing commonly used locations: the computer window for your devices and mounted folder, your home folder, the network window for shared devices and folders, your trash folder, and the Desktop folder that holds any files, folders, and launcher you have placed on your desktop screen.

The System section has buttons for software management, the Control Center, a terminal window, and for the lock, logout, and shut down operation. Software Manager opens the Linux Mint Software Manager, letting you install software from Linux Mint and Ubuntu repositories. The Package Manager button opens the older Synaptic Package Manager, with the same repository access.

Control Center opens a dialog similar to System Settings in the Cinnamon desktop, which shows icons for system and desktop configuration, and for administration. The Logout button logs you out to the login screen. The Quit button opens the shutdown dialog with options to suspend, hibernate, restart, and shut down.

The Applications/Favorites section is a toggle showing either your favorite applications or all installed applications. You can toggle between the two using the button on the upper right side of the menu. The Applications view is organized into two scroll boxes, one for software categories and the other for applications in those categories. You can use the scroll wheel on your mouse to scroll through the larger listings. In Figure 7-11, the applications in the Graphics category are listed. In the category list, the Preferences, Administration, and System Tools menus list the administration and configuration applications, such as Software Manager in System Tools.

Figure 7-11: Linux Mint Menu for MATE

The Linux Mint Menu supports a search operation, using the Search text box in the bottom right corner. The search is performed on installed software (see Figure 7-12). Clicking on the search button to the right displays a menu with other search options, such as DuckDuckGo (Web search), Wikipedia, your dictionary, and your computer, along with searching for users, finding tutorials, and information about devices and software. The Find entries for Software, Tutorials, Hardware, Ideas, and Users all open the Linux Community search site that performs the searches (**https://community.linuxmint.com**).

Figure 7-12: Linux Mint Menu search

Several actions can be performed on a menu application item using its pop-up menu. Right-click on the item to display the menu (see Figure 7-13).

Figure 7-13: Linux Mint Menu Applications pop-up menu.

You can add an application launcher to the panel or the desktop by dragging its icon from the menu to the desktop or panel. You can also right-click on the application icon and choose "Add to desktop" or "Add to panel" (see Figure 7-13).

Should you want an application to start up when you log in, you right-click on it on the menu and choose "Launch when I log in." From the pop-up menu, you can also directly uninstall an application, and open the application's properties dialog.

The Favorites section lists default favorites you may want. Click on the Favorites button in the top right corner to display your favorites. You can add any application to the favorites list by right-clicking on its entry and choosing "Show in my favorites" (see Figure 7-14). You can reorder favorites on the menu by simply clicking and dragging them to new locations. To remove a favorite, right-click and choose Remove.

Figure 7-14: Linux Mint Menu Favorites

Linux Mint Menu Preferences dialog

You can configure the menu using the Menu preferences dialog, which you can access by right-clicking on the Menu button on the panel and choosing "Preferences" from the pop-up menu. Menu Preferences has seven tabs: General, Appearance, Applications, Favorites, System, and Places (see Figure 7-15).

On the "General" tab you can specify the Linux Mint Menu applet's name (text) and whether to show an icon. You can choose a different icon, and specify the keyboard command to use to display the menu. You can also choose whether to show the system and places sections on the menu, as well as recently used documents and applications and tooltips (see Figure 7-16).

Figure 7-15: Linux Mint Menu Preferences dialog

Figure 7-16: Linux Mint Menu with Recent Documents option - General tab

The Appearance tab lets you choose theme for headings, borders, and background. You can also choose icon sizes for your Favorites, Applications, System, and Places menus.

On the Favorites tab you can set the layout and options for the Favorites menu including the number of columns and to show the Favorites menu when the Linux Mint menu is opened.

On the Applications tab, you can configure the Applications menu, choosing to display category icons, show application comments in pop-up notes, and to let mouse hovering select an entry. You can also configure the search function to search for uninstalled packages, and to remember the last search.

On the System tab, you can set the height and choose the default items to display.

For Places, you can choose which default items to display and whether to display your bookmarks. You can also add custom places (folders) for the menu. Click the New button to open a dialog where you can enter the place's name and the path name of the folder.

Note: You can replace the Linux Mint Menu with the MATE Menu by removing the Linux Mint Menu from the panel, and then adding the "Main Menu" applet to the panel. The name of the Linux Mint Menu is mintMenu, should you want to add it again later.

MATE Panel

The panel is the main component of the MATE interface. Through it, you can start your applications, run applets, and access desktop areas. You can think of the MATE panel as a type of tool you can use on your desktop. You can have several MATE panels displayed on your desktop, each with applets and menus you have placed in them. In this respect, MATE is flexible, enabling you to configure your panels any way you want. The MATE panel works much the same as the GNOME 2 panel. You can easily add applets to the panel, along with application launchers. A default panel is set up for you at the bottom of the screen, with applets for the menu, Show Desktop, application launchers, the window list, and several system applets (see Figure 7-17).

These include buttons for the Update Manager, volume control, Network Manager, the power manager, and the clock.

Figure 7-17: MATE Panel

Panel configuration tasks such as adding applications, selecting applets, setting up menus, and creating new panels are handled from the Panel pop-up menu (see Figure 7-18). Just right-click anywhere on the empty space in a panel to display a menu with entries for Properties, New Panel, Add To Panel, Reset Panel, and Delete This Panel, along with Help and About entries. New Panel lets you create other panels; Add To Panel lets you add items to the panel such as application launchers, applets for simple tasks like the Workspace Switcher, and menus like the Linux Mint menu. The Reset Panel entry restores the panel to its desktop default state, removing any changes you made to it such as added applets, applications, or folders. The Properties entry will display a dialog for configuring the features for that panel, like the position of the panel and its hiding capabilities.

To add a new panel, select the New Panel entry in the Panel pop-up menu (see Figure 7-18). A new expanded panel is automatically created and displayed at the top of your screen. You can then use the panel's Properties dialog to set different display and background features, as described in the following sections.

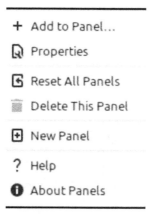

Figure 7-18: MATE Panel pop-up menu

Panel Properties

To configure individual panels, you use the Panel Properties dialog (see Figure 7-19). To display this dialog, you right-click a particular panel and select the Properties entry in the pop-up menu. For individual panels, you can set general configuration features and the background. The Panel Properties dialog displays two tabs, General and Background.

Displaying Panels

On the General tab of a Panel's Properties dialog, you determine how you want the panel displayed. Here you have options for orientation, size, and whether to expand, auto-hide, or display hide buttons. The Orientation entry lets you select which side of the screen you want the panel placed on. You can then choose whether you want a panel expanded or not. An expanded panel will fill the edges of the screen, whereas a non-expanded panel is sized to the number of items in the panel and shows handles at each end. Expanded panels will remain fixed to the edge of the screen, whereas unexpanded panels can be moved.

Figure 7-19: MATE Panel Properties

Moving and Hiding Expanded Panels

Expanded panels can be positioned at any edge of your screen. You can move expanded panels from one edge of a screen by selecting its orientation (side) on the Panel Properties General tab. If a panel is already there, the new one will stack on top of the current one. You cannot move unexpanded panels in this way. Bear in mind that if you place an expanded panel on the side edge, any menus titles will be displayed vertically. You can hide expanded panels either automatically or manually. These are features specified in the Panel Properties dialog General tab as Autohide and "Show hide buttons." To automatically hide panels, select the Autohide feature. To redisplay the panel, move your mouse to the edge where the panel is located. You can enable or disable the Autohide features in the panel's properties window.

If you want to be able to hide a panel manually, select the "Show hide buttons." Two hide buttons showing arrows are displayed at either end of the panel. You can further choose whether to have these buttons display arrows or not (displaying arrows is the default). You can then hide the panel at any time by clicking either of the hide buttons located on each end of the panel. The arrows show the direction in which the panel will hide.

Unexpanded Panels: Movable and Fixed

Whereas an expanded panel is always located at the edge of the screen, an unexpanded panel is movable. It can be located at the edge of a screen, working like a shrunken version of an expanded panel, or you can move it to any place on your desktop, just as you would an icon.

An unexpanded panel will shrink to the number of its components, showing handles at either end. You can then move the panel by dragging its handles. To access the panel menu with its Properties entry, right-click either of its handles.

To fix an unexpanded panel at its current position, select the "Show hide buttons" feature on the General tab of the Panel Properties dialog. This will replace the handles with Hide buttons and make the panel fixed. Clicking a Hide button will hide the panel to the edge of the screen, just as with expanded panels. If an expanded panel is already located on that edge, the button for a hidden unexpanded panel will be on top of it, just as with a hidden expanded panel. The Autohide feature will work for unexpanded panels placed at the edge of a screen.

If you want to fix an unexpanded panel to the edge of a screen, make sure it is placed at the edge you want, and then set its "Show hide buttons" feature.

Panel Background

With a panel's Background tab on its Panel Properties dialog, you can change the panel's background color or image. For a color background, you click the Color button to display a color selection window where you can choose a color from a color wheel or a list of color boxes, or you can enter its number. Once your color is selected, you can use the Style slide bar to make it more transparent or opaque. To use an image instead of a color, select the image entry and use the Browse button to locate the image file you want. For an image, you can also drag and drop an image file from the file manager to the panel. That image then becomes the background image for the panel.

Panel Objects

A panel can contain several different types of objects. These include menus, launchers, applets, drawers, and special objects.

Menus   A panel menu has launchers that are buttons used to start an application or execute a command.

Launchers   You can select any application entry in the Applications menu and create a launcher for it on the panel.

Applets   An applet is a small application designed to run within the panel. The Workspace Switcher showing the different desktops is an example of a GNOME applet.

Drawers   A drawer is an extension of the panel that can be opened or closed. You can think of a drawer as a shrinkable part of the panel. You can add anything to it that you can to a regular panel, including applets, menus, and even other drawers.

Special objects   These are used for special tasks not supported by other panel objects. For example, the Logout and Lock buttons are special objects.

Moving, Removing, and Locking Objects

To move any object within the panel, right-click it and choose the Move entry. You can move it either to a different place on the same panel or to a different panel. For launchers, you can just drag the object directly where you want it to be. To remove an object from the panel, right-click it to display a pop-up menu for it, and then choose the Remove From Panel entry. To prevent an object from being moved or removed, you set its lock feature (right-click the object and select the Lock To Panel entry). To later allow it to be moved, you first have to unlock the object (right-click it and select Unlock).

Adding Objects

To add an object to a panel, select the object from the panel's "Add to Panel" dialog (see Figure 7-20). To display the "Add to Panel" dialog, right-click on the panel and select the "Add to Panel' entry. This "Add to Panel" dialog displays a lengthy list of common objects, such as the mintMenu menu (Linux Mint Menu), Log Out, and Clock. For Application applets, you can click on the Applications Launcher entry and click the Forward button to list all your installed applications. Launchers can also be added to a panel by just dragging them directly. Launchers include applications, windows, and files. The Custom Application Launcher lets you create a custom launcher.

Application Launchers

To add an application that already has an application launcher to a panel is easy. You just have to drag the application launcher to the panel. This will automatically create a copy of the launcher for use on that panel. Launchers can be menu items or desktop icons. All the entries in the Linux Mint menu are application launchers. To add an application from the menu, just select it and drag it to the panel. For example, should you use the Pluma text editor frequently and want to add its icon to the panel, click and drag the Pluma menu entry in the Accessories menu to the panel. The Pluma text editor icon will appear in your panel. You can also drag any desktop application icon to a panel to add a copy of it to that panel.

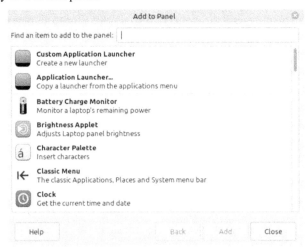

Figure 7-20: MATE Panel "Add to Panel" dialog for panel applets

For any menu item, you can also go to its entry and right-click it, and then select the "Add to panel" entry. An application launcher for that application is then added to the panel. To add the Pluma text editor to the panel, right-click the Text Editor menu entry in the Accessories menu, and select the "Add to panel" entry. The Pluma text editor icon now appears in your panel.

Also, as previously noted, you can open the Add to Panel dialog, and then choose the Application Launcher entry and click the Forward button. This will display a dialog with a listing of all the Application menu entries along with Preferences and Administration menus, expandable to their items. Just find the application you want added, select it, and click the Add button.

Adding Drawers

You can also group applications under a Drawer icon. Clicking the Drawer icon displays a list of the different application icons you can then select. To add a drawer to your panel, right-click the panel and select the "Add to panel" entry to display the "Add to Panel" dialog. From that list select the Drawer entry. This will create a drawer on your panel. You can then drag any items from desktop, menus, or windows (folders or launchers) to the drawer icon on the panel to have them listed in the drawer.

You can also add applets and applications to a drawer using the Add to Drawer dialog. Right-click on the drawer and choose the Add to Drawer entry to open the dialog. Then click the applet you want added to the drawer. To add applications, select the Applications Launcher entry and click for Forward to list your application menu categories, which are expandable to list applications. You can add a menu to the drawer by choosing the application category and clicking the Add button.

Adding Menus

A menu differs from a drawer in that a drawer holds application icons instead of menu entries. You can add application menus to your panel, much as you add drawers. To add an application menu to your panel, open the Add to Panel dialog and select the Application Launcher entry, clicking Forward to open the list of Application categories. Select the category you want, and click the Add button. That menu category with all its application items is added to your panel as a menu.

Adding Folders and Files

You can also add files and folders to a panel. For folders, click and drag the folder icon from the file manager window to your panel. Whenever you click this folder button, a file manager window opens, displaying that folder. You can also add folders to any drawer on your panel. To add a file, also drag it directly to the panel. To add a file (except for images, which, instead, change the background of the panel to that image), click and drag the file to the panel or drawer. When you click on the file icon, the file opens with its application.

Adding Applets

Applets are small programs that perform tasks within the panel. To add an applet, right-click the panel and select Add To Panel from the pop-up menu. This displays the Add To box listing common applets along with other types of objects, such as launchers. Select the one you want. For example, to add the clock to your panel, select Clock from the panel's Add To box. Once added, the applet will show up in the panel. If you want to remove an applet, right-click it and select the Remove From Panel entry.

MATE features a number of helpful applets. Some applets monitor your system, such as the Battery Charge Monitor, which checks the battery in laptops, and System Monitor, which shows a graph indicating your current CPU and memory use.

MATE features a number of helpful applets. Some applets monitor your system, such as the Battery Charge Monitor, which checks the battery in laptops, and System Monitor, which shows a graph indicating your current CPU and memory use.

Caja File Manager

The Caja file manager supports the standard features for copying, removing, and deleting items as well as setting permissions and displaying items. The program name for the file manager is **caja**. You can enhance Caja using extensions such as "Open terminal" to open the current folder in a new terminal window, and Engrampa that allows you to create (compress) and extract archives. Several extensions are already installed and enabled by default. They will display entries in appropriate menus. Extensions are enabled on the Extension tab of the File Management Preferences dialog (Edit | Preferences). To add more extension, use the Software Manager to install the caja extension packages. Extension packages have the prefix **caja-**, such as **caja-share**, **caja-dropbox**, and **caja-wallpaper**.

Home Folder Sub-folders and Bookmarks

Like Ubuntu, Linux Mint uses the Common User Directory Structure (xdg-user-dirs at **https://freedesktop.org**) to set up sub-folders in the user home folder. Folders will include **Documents**, **Music**, **Pictures**, **Downloads**, and **Videos**. These localized user folders are used as defaults by many desktop applications. Users can change their folder names or place them within each other using the file browser. For example, Music can be moved into **Documents**, **Documents/Music**. Local configuration is held in the **.config/user-dirs.dirs** file. System-wide defaults are set up in the **/etc/xdg/user-dirs.defaults** file. The icons for these folders are displayed in Figure 7-21.

Figure 7-21: Caja file manager home folders

The folders are also default bookmarks. You can access a bookmarked folder directly from the Caja window sidebar. You can also add your own bookmarks for folders by opening the folder and choosing "Add Bookmark" from the Bookmarks menu. Your folder will appear in the Bookmarks section of the Caja side pane Places menu and on the Bookmarks menu. Use the Edit Bookmarks dialog to remove bookmarks. Here you can remove a bookmark or change is name and location.

You use Desktop Settings to display basic folders such as the home, network, and trash folders on the desktop area.

File Manager Windows

When you click Home folder icon on the desktop or the Home folder entry on the MATE menu Places section, a file manager window opens showing your home folder. The file manager window displays several components, including a menubar, a main toolbar, and a side pane (see Figure 7-22).

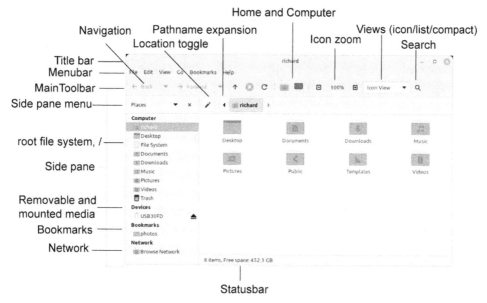

Figure 7-22: Caja file manager with sidebar

The side pane works like the sidebar in the Nemo and Nautilus file managers, but with a menu, like the file manager in GNOME 2. The file manager window's main pane (to the right) displays the icons or listing of files and sub-folders in the current working folder. When you select a file and folder, the status bar at the bottom of the window displays the name of the file or folder selected and for files the size, and for folders, the number of items contained. The status bar also displays the remaining free space on the current file system.

When you open a new folder, the same window is used to display it, and you can use the Forward and Back buttons to move through previously opened folders (top left on the main toolbar) (see Figure 7-23). Down triangles to the right of the Back and Forward buttons display menus of previously accessed folders, which you can use to access a previous folder directly. There is also an up arrow to move to the parent folder, and a Home folder button to move directly to your home folder. The Computer button displays the computer window showing your file systems and attached devices. You can also access these operations from the file manager's Go menu (see Table 7-2). In addition there are reload and stop reload buttons to refresh the folder listing, should the list of files or folders change.

Figure 7-23: Caja navigation buttons: back, forward, parent, home, computer

Menu Item	Description
Open Parent	Move to the parent folder
Back	Move to the previous folder viewed in the file manager window
Forward	Move to the next folder viewed in the file manager window
Paste	Paste files that you have copied or cut, letting you move or copy files between folders, or make duplicates.
Same Location as Other Pane	If you have two panes open on the window, you can make both panes view the same folder
Home Folder	Move to the Home folder
Computer	Move to the Computer folder, showing icons for your devices
Templates	Move to the Templates folder
Trash	Open the trash folder to see deleted files and folders, which can be restored.
Network	Move to the network folder showing connected systems on your network and open remote folders.
Location	Open the location navigation box for entering the path name of a file or folder
Search for Files	Search for files and folders using the file manager window

Table 7-2: File Manager Go Menu

As you open sub-folders, the main toolbar displays buttons for your current folder and its parent folders (see Figure 7-24). You can click on a folder button to move to it directly. Initially, the button shows a path of sub-folders from your home folder. Clicking on the small triangle arrow to the left expands the path to the top level, from the root folder (the hard disk icon).

You can also display a location URL text box instead of buttons, where you can enter the location of a folder, either on your system or on a remote system. To display the location text box, press **Ctrl-l**, or from the Go menu select Location, or click the Location toggle (pencil icon) at the beginning of the location path on the main toolbar (see Figure 7-24). These access methods operate as toggles that move you a back and forth from the location text box to the button path.

Figure 7-24: Caja locations: unexpanded, expanded, and location path

The File menu has entries for opening a new tab (Ctrl-t), opening a new file manager window (Ctrl-n), creating a new folder (Shift-Ctrl-n), connecting to a remote FTP server, and displaying the properties of the current folder (Alt-Return). Most have corresponding keys (see Table 7-3) (see Figure 7-28).

Menu Item	Description
New Tab	Creates a new tab.
New Window	Open a new file manager window
Create Folder	Creates a new subfolder in the folder.
Create Document	Creates a text document.
Connect to server	Connect to an FTP server using the file manager
Open in Terminal	Open the current folder in a new terminal window (Open Terminal extension)
Properties	Properties for the current open folder
Empty Trash	Empty the trash folder
Close All Windows	Close all file manage windows
Close	Close the file manager window.
Open With	When a file is selected the Open With item is displayed showing possible applications to open the file with
Open	When a folder is selected the Open item is displayed showing also the "Open in New Tab" and "Open in New Window" items, along with the Open With submenu.

Table 7-3: File Manager File Menu

Figure 7-25: File manager side pane menu and views

File Manager Side Pane

The file manager side pane has a menu from which you can choose to display places (Places), the tree view of the file system (Tree), information on the current or selected folder or file (Information), the history of previously opened folders for that login session (History), notes (Notes), and emblems you can place on a file or folder (Emblems).

Use the side pane's Places view to access your bookmarked folders, storage devices (USB, CD/DVD disc, and attached hard drives), and mounted network folders. On the Computer section of the side pane, you can access your home folders, trash, and the file system (root folder). On the Bookmarks section, you can access any additional bookmarks you created.

The default for the side pane is the Places view, which displays sections for Computer, Devices, Bookmarks, and Network items showing your file systems and default home folder subfolders (see Figure 7-25). You can choose to display or hide the side pane by selecting the "Side Pane" entry in the View menu, or by clicking the close button on the right side of the side pane menu. You can also use F9 to toggle the side pane on and off.

Selecting the File System entry in the side pane places you at the top of the file system, letting you move to any accessible part of it. In the Computer section, you can search your default folders, such as Documents and Pictures. Should you bookmark a folder (Bookmarks menu, "Add Bookmark" entry (Ctrl-d)), a Bookmark section appears on the side pane with the bookmark. To remove or rename a bookmark, right-click on its entry in the side pane and choose Remove or Rename from the pop-up menu (see Figure 7-26). The bookmark name changes, but not the original folder name.

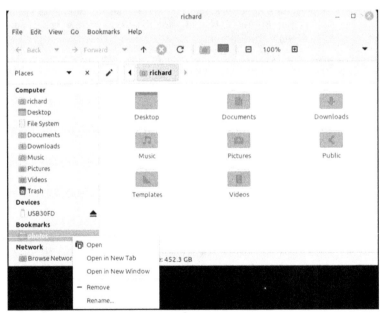

Figure 7-26: File manager side pane with bookmarks menu

Tabs

The Caja file manager supports tabs with which you can open up several folders in the same file manager window. To open a tab, select New Tab from the File menu or press **Ctrl-t**. A tab bar appears with tab icons for each tab, displaying the name of the folder open, and an **x** close button (see Figure 7-27). You can re-arrange tabs by clicking and dragging their tab icons to the right or left. You can also use the Ctrl-PageUp and Ctrl-PageDown keys to move from one tab to another. Use the Shift-Ctrl-PageUp and Shift-Ctrl-PageDown keys to rearrange the tabs. To close a tab, click its close **x** button on the right side of the tab.

Note: Caja works as an operational FTP browser. You can use the Connect to Server entry on the Files menu to open a "Connect to Server" dialog, where you can enter the address for the FTP site.

Figure 7-27: File manager window with tabs

Displaying Files and Folders

You can view a folder's contents as icons, a compact list, or as a detailed list, which you can choose from the menu on the right side of the main toolbar: icon, list, and compact views, as shown here.

Use the control keys to change views quickly: **Ctrl-1** for Icons, **Ctrl-2** for list, and **Ctrl-3** for the compact view. The List view provides the name, size, type, and date. Buttons are displayed for each field across the top of the main pane. You can use these buttons to sort the list according to that field. For example, to sort the files by date, click the Date Modified button; to sort by size, click Size button. Click again to alternate between ascending and descending order.

Certain types of file icons will display previews of their contents. For example, the icons for image files will display a thumbnail of the image. A text file will display in its icon the first few words of its text.

The View menu has entries for managing and arranging your file manager icons (see Table 7-4) (see Figure 7-28). You can choose Icons, List, and Compact views. In the Icon view, the "Arrange items" submenu appears, which provides entries for sorting icons by name, size, type, emblem, and modification date. You can also reverse the order, or position icons manually.

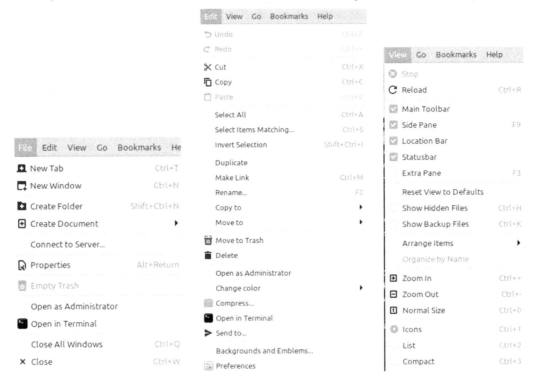

Figure 7-28: File manager File, Edit, and View menus

The View | Zoom In entry enlarges your view of the window, making icons bigger, and Zoom Out reduces your view, making them smaller. Normal Size restores icons to the standard size. You can also use the **Ctrl-+** and **Ctrl--** keys to zoom in and out.

File manager tools and menus

From the Edit menu, you can paste files you have cut or copied to move or copy them between folders, or make duplicates (see Table 7-5 and see Figure 7-28). The selection menu items let you select all files and folders, those matching a simple regular expression, and to invert a selection, choosing all those not selected. On the Files menu, the Properties entry opens the folder properties dialog with Basic and Permissions tabs.

In the icon view, you can click anywhere on the empty space on the main pane of a file manager window to display a pop-up menu with entries to create a new folder, arrange icons, zoom icons, and open the folder properties dialog (see Table 7-6).

Menu Item	Description
Stop	Stop current task
Reload	Refresh file and folder list
Main Toolbar	Displays main toolbar
Side Pane	Displays side pane
Location Bar	Displays location bar
Statusbar	Displays status bar at bottom of folder window
Extra Pane	Display dual panes for file manager window, with separate folders open in each
Reset View to Defaults	Displays files and folders in default view
Show Hidden Files	Show administrative dot files.
Arrange Items: By Name, Size, Type, Modification Date, and Emblems	Arrange files and folder by specified criteria
Organize by Name	Sort icons in Icon view by name
Zoom In	Provides a close-up view of icons, making them appear larger.
Zoom Out	Provides a distant view of icons, making them appear smaller.
Normal Size	Restores view of icons to standard size.
Icons	Displays icons
List	Displays file list with name, size, type, and date. Folders are expandable.
Compact	Displays compact file list using only the name and small icons

Table 7-4: File Manager View Menu

Navigating in the file manager

The file manager operates similarly to a web browser, using the same window to display opened folders. It maintains a list of previously viewed folders, and you can move back and forth through that list using the toolbar navigation buttons (left side). The Back button with the left arrow moves you to the previously displayed folder, the Forward button with the right arrow moves you to the next previously displayed folder, and the up arrow moves to the parent folder. The home folder icon opens your home folder, and the computer icon (monitor) opens the Computer window, which lists icons for your file system and removable devices.

Use the side pane's Places view to access your bookmarked folders, storage devices (USB, CD/DVD disc, and attached hard drives), and mounted network folders. On the Computer section of the side pane, you can access your home folders, trash, the file system (root folder). On the Bookmarks section, you can access any additional bookmarks you created. Attached devices are listed in the Devices section, and mounted network folders are listed in the Network section.

Menu Item	Description
Cut, Copy	Move or copy a file or folder
Paste	Paste files that you have copied or cut, letting you move or copy files between folders, or make duplicates.
Undo, Redo	Undo or Redo a paste operation
Select All	Select all files and folders in this folder
Select Items Matching	Quick search for files using basic pattern matching.
Invert Selection	Select all other files and folders not selected, deselecting the current selection.
Duplicate	Make a copy of a selected file
Make Link	Make a link to a file or folder
Rename	Rename a selected file or folder
Copy to	Copy a file or folder to one of the default bookmarks
Move to	Move a file or folder to one of the default bookmarks
Move To Trash	Move a file for folder to the trash folder for later deletion
Delete	Delete a file or folder immediately.
Compress	Compress selected files and folders to a compressed archive file such as a tar, cpio, or zip file (Engrampa extension).
Backgrounds and Emblems	Choose a background for the file manager windows. Add emblems to any folder or file in the file manager window.
Preferences	The Caja File Manager preferences for your account.

Table 7-5: File Manager Edit Menu

Menu Item	Description
Create Folder	Creates a new subfolder in the folder.
Create Document	Creates a text document.
Arrange Items:	Arrange files and folder by specified criteria
Organize by Name	Sort icons in Icon view by name
Open in Terminal	Open a terminal window at that folder (Open terminal extension)
Zoom In	Provides a close-up view of icons, making them appear larger.
Zoom Out	Provides a distant view of icons, making them appear smaller.
Normal Size	Restores view of icons to standard size.
Properties	Opens the Properties dialog for the folder

Table 7-6: File Manager Pop-up Menu

To open a subfolder, you can double-click its icon or right-click the icon and select Open from the menu. You can also open the folder in a new tab or a new window. The Open With submenu lists other possible file managers and applications to open the folder with such as Files (Caja). You can also click on the folder to select it, and then choose Open from the File menu (File | Open). The tab, new window, and open with items are also listed when a folder is selected. Figure 7-29 shows the File menu with the different Open items for a folder and the Open With submenu for a file. Table 7-3 lists the File menu options.

Figure 7-29: File manager File | Open with submenu for folders and files

You can open any folder or file system listed in the side pane Places view by clicking on its folder or bookmark. You can also right-click on a bookmark or folder to display a menu with entries to Open, "Open in a New Tab", and "Open in a New Window" (see Table 7-7). The "Open in a New Window" item is an easy way to access devices from the file manager. The menu for the Trash entry lets you empty the trash. For any bookmark, you can also remove and rename the entry. Entries for removable devices in the side pane such as USB drives also have a menu item for Eject. Internal hard drives have an Unmount entry instead.

Menu Item	Description
Open	Opens the file with its associated application. Folders are opened in the file manager. Associated applications are listed.
Open In A New Tab	Opens a folder in a new tab in the same window.
Open In A New Window	Opens a folder in a separate window, accessible from the toolbar, right-click.
Remove	Remove bookmark from the sidebar.
Rename	Rename a bookmark.

Table 7-7: The File Manager Side Pane Pop-Up Menu

Caja File Manager Search

The Caja file manager provides a search tool that operates the same as the Nemo file manager search. From a file manager window, click the Search button on the toolbar (Looking glass at right), or select Go | Search for Files, to open a Search box below the toolbar. Enter the pattern to search and press ENTER or click the looking glass button on the right side of the text box. The results are displayed.

Menus for location and file type will appear in the folder window, with + and - buttons for adding or removing search parameters, including location, file type, tags, modification time, size, and text in the content of the file. Click the plus + button to add more search parameters. The search begins from the folder opened, as specified by the first location parameter. But you can specify another folder to search, using the Location parameter's folder menu listing possible folders. To search multiple folders at once, click the + button to add a Location parameter, and specify the folder to be searched on that Location parameter's folder menu. You can do the same for multiple file types, specifying only files with certain types, as well as for modification times, file sizes, tags, and searched content.

Managing Files and Folders

As a GNOME-compliant file manager, Caja supports desktop drag-and-drop operations for copying and moving files. To move a file or folder, drag-and-drop from one folder to another. The move operation is the default drag-and-drop operation in GNOME. To copy a file to a new location, press the Ctrl key as you drag.

Using a file's pop-up menu

You can also perform remove, rename, and link creation operations on a file by right-clicking its icon and selecting the action you want from the pop-up menu that appears (see Table 7-8). For example, to remove an item, right-click it and select the Move To Trash entry from the menu. This places it in the Trash folder, where you can later delete it. To create a link, right-click the file and select Make Link from the pop-up menu. This creates a new link file that begins with the term "Link." If you select an archive file, the pop-up menu also displays entries to "Extract Here" and "Extract to".

Renaming Files

To rename a file, you can either right-click the file's icon and select the Rename entry from the pop-up menu or click its icon and press the F2 function key. The name of the icon will be bordered, encased in a small text box. You can overwrite the old one, or edit the current name by clicking a position in the name to insert text, as well as use the backspace key to delete characters. You can also rename a file by entering a new name in its Properties dialog box (Basic tab).

Grouping Files

You can select a group of files and folders by clicking the first item and then hold down the SHIFT key while clicking the last item, or by clicking and dragging the mouse across items you want to select. To select separated items, hold the CTRL key down as you click the individual icons. If you want to select all the items in the folder, choose the Select All entry in the Edit menu (Edit | Select All) (**Ctrl-a**). You can then copy, move, or even delete several files at once. To select items that have a certain pattern in their name, choose Select Items Matching from the Edit menu to open a search box where you can enter the pattern (**Ctrl-s**). Use the * character to match partial patterns, as in ***let*** to match on all filenames with the pattern "let" in them. The pattern **my*** would match on filenames beginning with the "my" pattern, and ***png** would match on all PNG image files.

Menu Item	Description
Open	Opens the file with its associated application. Folders are opened in the file manager. Associated applications are listed.
Open In A New Tab	Opens a folder in a new tab in the same window.
Open In A New Window	Opens a folder in a new window
Open With	Selects an application with which to open the file, or a file manager to use to open a folder.
Cut Copy	Entries to cut and copy the selected file.
Paste into Folder	Paste the selected folder
Make Link	Creates a link to that file in the same folder.
Rename (F2)	Renames the file.
Copy To	Copy a file to the Home Folder, Desktop, or to a folder displayed in another pane in the file manager window.
Move To	Move a file to the Home Folder, Desktop, or to a folder displayed in another pane in the file manager window.
Move To Trash	Moves a file to the Trash folder, where you can later delete it.
Delete	Delete the file or folder permanently
Compress	Archives files (Engrampa extension).
Extract Here Extract To	When an archive is selected, these entries appear (Engrampa extension).
Open in Terminal	Open the folder in a terminal window
Send to	Archive and compress folder to email or copy to removeable drive or shared folder
Sharing Options	Active when a folder is selected. You can choose to share the folder on your network. Install caja-share.
Open as Administrator	Open folder with administrative permissions.
Change color	Change folder icon's color
Properties	Displays the Properties dialog.

Table 7-8: The File and Folder Pop-Up Menu

Opening Applications and Files MIME Types

You can start any application in the file manager by double-clicking either the application itself or a data file used for that application. If you want to open the file with a specific application, you can right-click the file and select one of the "Open With" entries. One or more "Open With" entries will be displayed for default and possible application, like "Open with Text Editor" for a text file. If the application you want is not listed, you can select Open with | Other Application to open a dialog listing available applications. Drag-and-drop operations are also supported for applications. You can drag a data file to its associated application icon (say, on the desktop); the application then starts up using that data file.

Folders also have an Open With submenu, listing alternative file managers you can use to open the folder, such as Files (Caja). Applications that work on folders are also listed such as the Shotwell image manager and the Disk Usage Analyzer.

To change or set the default application to use for a certain type of file, you open a file's Properties dialog and select the Open With tab. Here you can choose the default application to use for that kind of file. Possible applications will be listed with a button next to each entry. The default has its button turned on. Click the button of the one you want to change to the default. Once you choose the default, it will appear in the Open With item for this type of file. If there is an application on the Open With tab you do not want listed in the Open With menu, select it and click the Remove button.

If you want to add an application to the Open With menu, click the "Add" button to open the Add Application dialog, which lists possible applications. Select the one you want and click the Add button. You can use the "Use a custom command" text box to enter a command. The Browse button lets you locate a command.

File and Folder Properties

In a file's Properties dialog, you can view detailed information on a file and set options and permissions (see Figure 7-30). A file's Properties dialog has five tabs: Basic, Emblems, Permissions, Open With, and Notes. Folders do not have an Open With tab. Certain kinds of files will have additional tabs, providing information about the file. For example, an audio file will have an Audio tab listing the type of audio file and any other information like a song title or compression method used. An image file will have an Image tab listing the resolution and type of image. Folders also have an "Access Control List" and "Extended user attributes" tabs that you can use to control user access to a folder.

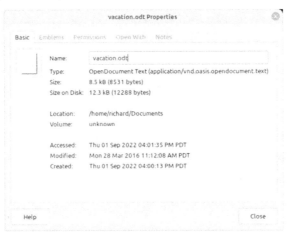

Figure 7-30: File properties on Caja

The Basic tab shows detailed information such as type, size, location, and date modified. The type is a MIME type, indicating the type of application associated with it. The file's icon is displayed at the top with a text box showing the file's name. You can edit the filename in the Name text box, changing that name.

If you want to change the icon image used for the file or folder, click the icon image (next to the name) to open a Select Custom Icon dialog to browse for the one you want. The **/usr/share/pixmaps** folder holds the set of current default images, though you can select your own images (click **pixmaps** entry in the Places side pane). Click an image file to see its icon displayed in the right pane. Double-click to change the icon image.

The Permissions tab for files shows the read, write, and execute permissions for owner, group, and others, as set for this file. You can change any of the permissions here, provided the file belongs to you. You configure access for the owner, the group, and others, using menus. You can set owner permissions as Read Only or Read And Write. For group and others, you can also set the None option, denying access. Clicking on the group name displays a menu listing different groups, allowing you to select one to change the file's group. If you want to execute the file as an application, you check the "Allow executing file as program" entry. This has the effect of setting the execute permission.

The Permissions tab for folders operates much the same way, but it includes two access entries: Folder Access and File Access. The Folder Access entry controls access to the folder with options for None, List Files Only, Access Files, and Create And Delete Files. These correspond to read, write, and execute permissions given to folders. The File Access entry lets you set permissions for all those files in the folder. They are the same as for files: for the owner, Read or Read and Write; for the group and others, the entry adds a None option to deny access. To set the permissions for all the files in the folder accordingly (not just the folder), you click the "Apply Permissions To Enclosed Files" button.

The Open With tab for files lists all the applications associated with this kind of file. You can select the one you want to use as the default. This can be particularly useful for media files, where you may prefer a specific player for a certain file or a particular image viewer for pictures. To add an applications that is not listed, click the Add button to open an "Add Application" dialog listing installed applications you can choose from.

The Notes tab lets you add notes about the file. A note emblem will then appear on the right top corner of the file's icon.

The Share tab for folders allows you to share folders as network shares. If you have Samba or NFS, these will allow your folders and files to be shared with users on other systems. You have the option to specify whether the shared folder or file will be read-only or allow write access. To allow write access check the "Allow other to create and delete files in this folder" entry. To open access to all users, check the Guest access entry.

Caja Preferences

You can set preferences for your Caja file manager in the Preferences dialog, accessible by selecting the Preferences item in any Caja file manager window's Edit menu (Edit | Preferences).

The Views tab allows you to select how files are displayed by default, such as the list, icon, or compact view. You can set default zoom levels for icon, compact, and list views.

Behavior lets you choose how to select files, manage the trash, and handle scripts.

Display lets you choose what added information you want displayed in an icon caption, like the size or date. You can also specify the format of the date.

The List Columns tab lets you choose both the features to display in the list view and the order in which to display them. In addition to the already-selected Name, Size, Date, and Type, you can add features such as permissions, group, MIME type, and owner. For folders you can also display a count the number of items.

The Preview tab lets you choose whether you want small preview content displayed in the icons, like beginning text for text files.

The Media tab lets you choose what applications to run for certain media, such as run the Celluloid media player for DVD videos, or Rhythmbox for audio files.

Extensions lists extensions installed for Caja such as "Open Terminal" which lets you open a folder in a terminal window ("Open in Terminal' menu item) (**caja-open-terminal** package), Engrampa which allows you to create and extract archives directly from the file manager window (Compress menu item), and **caja-seahorse** that allows you to encrypt files and folders (Encrypt menu item).

Control Center

Both Preference and Administration tools can be accessed either from the Linux Mint menu or from the Control Center (see Figure 7-31). You can access the Control Center from the System section on the Linux Mint menu. The Control Center opens a window listing the different applications by section: Administration, Hardware, Internet and Network, Look and Feel, and Personal. Icons for the tools are displayed. Single-click on an icon to open it. The Control Center also has a dynamic search capability. A side pane holds a filter search box and links for the groups. As you enter a pattern in the Filter search box, matching applications appear at the right. Commonly used applications can be listed under Common Tasks. If you want an application to be started when your system starts, you can right-click on its icon and choose "Add to Startup Programs" to add it directly to the Startup Applications dialog. Several of the tools are administration applications such as Software Manager, Backup Tool, Users and Groups, and Printers. Others are GNOME preferences used for MATE, such as Appearance, About Me, Screensaver, and Keyboard.

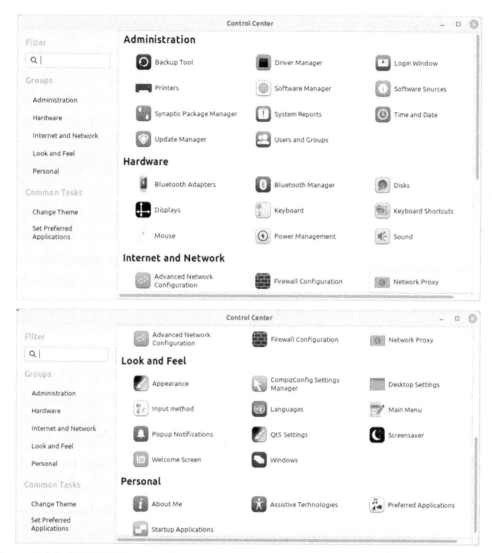

Figure 7-31: GNOME Control Center

MATE Preferences

You can configure different parts of your MATE interface using tools listed in the Preferences menu on the Linux Mint menu, and from the Control Center. Linux Mint provides several tools for configuring your MATE desktop. The MATE preferences are listed in Table 7-9. On some preferences tools, a Help button displays detailed descriptions and examples. Some of the more important tools are discussed here.

The keyboard shortcuts configuration (Keyboard Shortcuts) lets you map keys to certain tasks, like mapping multimedia keys on a keyboard to media tasks like play and pause. There are tasks for the desktop, window management, and sound. With window management, you can also map keys to perform workspace switching. The tasks and keys that are already assigned are listed. To change the keys used for a task, double click its shortcut entry and type the new keys. A task that has no assigned keys is disabled. Click the shortcut entry enter a key sequence for it. To add a new task, click add to choose the application and a name for it. These are added under the Custom Shortcuts section. Click the new task's shortcut to add a key for it. To disable a shortcut, click the shortcut entry and press the backspace key.

The Windows configuration (Windows) is where you can enable features like window roll-up (Titlebar Action), window movement key, and mouse window selection.

Preferences	Description
About Me	Personal information like image, addresses, and password.
Assistive Technologies	Enables features like accessible login and keyboard screen.
Appearance	Desktop Appearance configuration: Themes, Fonts, Backgrounds, and Visual Effects.
CompizConfig Settings Manager	Advanced configuration dialog for the GNOME enhanced graphics features, such as 3D windows, animations, and desktop cube workspace switching.
Desktop Settings	Basic settings such as the display of home and computer icons on the desktop, button layout on windows, and showing icons in menus.
Desktop Sharing	Configure access by others to your desktop.
Disk	Opens the GNOME Disks utility.
Displays	Opens the GNOME Monitor Preferences dialog for detecting monitors and setting resolution.
Domain Blocker	Blocks specified domains.
File Management	File Manager options including media handling applications, icon captions, and the default view (also accessible from file manager window, Edit | Preferences).
Keyboard	Configure your keyboard: selecting options, models, and typing breaks, as well as accessibility features like slow, bounce, and sticky keys.
Keyboard Shortcuts	Configure keys for special tasks, like multimedia operations.
Languages	Specify a language, same as Cinnamon.
Login Window	Configure the Login Window for the LightDM display manager, same as Cinnamon.
Main Menu	Add or remove categories and menu items for the Applications, Preferences, and System menus.
Displays	Change your screen resolution, refresh rate, and screen orientation.
Mouse	Mouse and touchpad configuration: select hand orientation, speed, and accessibility.

Network Proxy	Specify proxy configuration if needed: manual or automatic
Monitors	Change your screen resolution, refresh rate, and screen orientation.
Popup Notifications	Placement and display theme for notifications.
Power Management	The GNOME power manager for configuring display, suspend, and shutdown options.
Preferred Applications	Set default Web browser, mail application, music player, and terminal window.
Remote Desktop	Allow remote users to view or control your desktop. Can control access with a password.
Screensaver	Select and manage your screen saver, including the activation time.
Startup Applications	Manage your session with startup programs and save options.
Sound	Configure sound effects, output volume, sound device options, input volume, and sound application settings (Pulseaudio).
Time and Date	Set the time, date, and time zone.
Welcome Screen	Displays the Linux Mint welcome screen with links to the user guide, tutorial, and software manager.
Windows	Enable window abilities like roll up on the title bar, movement key, window selection.

Table 7-9: The MATE Preferences

Mouse and Keyboard Preferences

The Mouse and Keyboard preferences are the primary tools for configuring your mouse and keyboard. Mouse preferences lets you choose its speed, hand orientation, and double-click times. For laptops, you can configure your touchpad, enabling touchpad clicks and edge scrolling (left side). Keyboard preferences shows several tabs for selecting your keyboard model (Layouts), configuring keys (Layouts tab, Options button), repeat delay (General tab), and enforcing breaks from power typing as a health precaution (Typing Break) (see Figure 7-32).

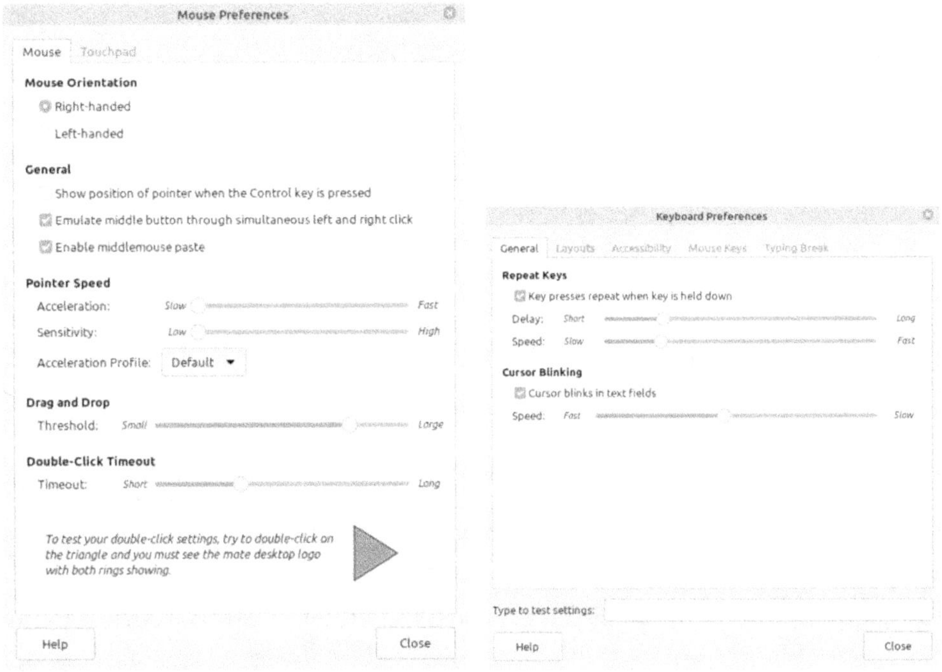

Figure 7-32: Mouse and Keyboard Preferences

To configure your sound devices you use the Sound Preferences tool (Sound), see Chapter 9. MATE uses sound themes to specify an entire set of sounds for different effects and alerts.

About Me: photo, name, and password

To set up personal information, including the icon to be used for your graphical login, you use the About Me preferences tool. You can access it from the Linux Mint menu Preferences menu (Preferences | About Me) and from the GNOME Control Center. The About Me preferences dialog lets you change your password (see Figure 7-33) and the icon or image used to represent the user. Should you want to change your password, you can click on the Change Password button to open a change password dialog.

Clicking on the image icon opens a browser window where you can select a personal image. The **/usr/share/pixmaps/faces** folder is selected by default, which displays several images. The selected image displays at the right on the browser window. For a personal photograph, you can select the Picture folder. This is the Pictures folder on your home folder. Should you place a photograph or image there, you could then select if for your personal image. The image will be used in the login screen when showing your user entry.

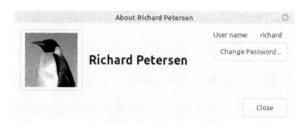

Figure 7-33: About Me: Preferences | About Me

Appearance

Several appearance-related configuration tasks are combined into the Appearance Preferences dialog (the Appearance entry in the Preferences menu or Appearance icon on the Control Center's Personal section). You can change your theme, background image, or configure your fonts. The Appearance dialog shows four tabs: Theme, Background, Fonts, and Interface (see Figure 7-11). On the Interface tab, you can choose to show icons in menus and on buttons.

Desktop Themes

You use the Themes tab on the Appearance Preferences dialog to select or customize a theme. Themes control your desktop appearance. The Themes tab will list icons for currently installed themes (see Figure 7-34). The icons show key aspects or each theme such as window, folder, and button images, in effect previewing the theme for you.

The Linux Mint custom theme is initially selected. You can move through the icons to select a different theme if you wish. If you have downloaded additional themes from **https://www.gnome-look.org/**, you can click the install button to locate and install them. Once installed, the additional themes will also be displayed in the Theme tab. If you download and install a theme or icon set from the Linux Mint repository, it will be automatically installed for you.

Figure 7-34: Selecting GNOME themes

The true power of Themes is shown its ability to let users customize any given theme. Themes are organized into five components: controls, colors, window border, icons, and pointer. Controls covers the appearance of window and dialog controls like buttons and slider bars. Window border lets you choose title bars, borders, and window buttons sets. Icons lets you choose different icon sets. Pointers provides different pointer sets to use. Colors lets you choose the backgrounds and text colors for windows, input boxes, selections, and tool tips. You can even download and install separate components like specific icon sets, which you can then use in a customized theme.

Clicking the Customize button opens a Customize Theme dialog with tabs for different theme components. The components used for the current theme are selected by default. In the Controls, Window Border, Icons, and Pointer tabs you will see listings of the different themes. You can then mix and match different components from those themes, creating your own customized theme, using window borders from one theme and icons from another. Upon selecting a component, your desktop changes automatically showing you how it looks. If you have added a component, like a new icon set, it also is shown.

Once you have created a new customized theme, a Custom Theme icon appears in the list on the Theme tab. To save the customized theme, click the Save As button. This opens a dialog where you can enter the theme name, any notes, and specify whether you also want to keep the theme background.

Customized themes and themes installed directly by a user are placed in the **.themes** folder in the user's home folder. Should you want these themes made available for all users, you can move them from the **.themes** folder to the **/usr/share/themes** folder. In a terminal window run a **cp** command as shown here for the **mytheme** theme. The operation requires administrative access (**sudo**).

```
sudo cp -r .themes/mytheme  /usr/share/themes
```

You can do the same for icon sets you have downloaded. Such sets will be installed in the user's **.icons** folder. You can then copy them to the **/usr/share/icons** folder to make them available to all users.

Desktop Background

You use the Background tab on the Appearance Preferences tool to select or customize your desktop background image (see Figure 7-35). You can also access the Background tab by clicking the desktop background and select Change Desktop Background from the desktop menu. Installed backgrounds are listed, with the current background selected. To add your own image, either drag-and-drop the image file to the Background tab or click on the Add button to locate and select the image file. To remove an image, select it and click the Remove button.

From the Style menu, you can choose display options such as Zoom, Centered, Scaled, Tiled, or Fill Screen. A centered or scaled image will preserve the image proportions. Fill screen may distort it. Any space not filled, such as with a centered or scaled images, will be filled in with the desktop color. From the Colors menu, you can set the desktop color to a solid color, horizontal gradient, or vertical gradient. Click on the color button next to the Colors menu to open a "Pick a Color" dialog where you can select a color from a color wheel. For gradients, two color buttons are displayed for selecting a color at each end of the gradient.

Initially, the Linux Mint/Ubuntu backgrounds are listed. Install the **gnome-background** package to add a collection of GNOME backgrounds. To download more backgrounds, click the "Get more backgrounds online" link.

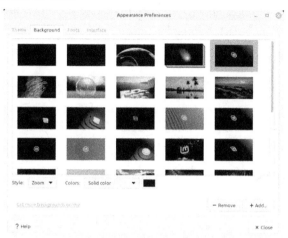

Figure 7-35: Choosing a desktop background, System | Preferences | Appearance

Fonts

On the Font tab, you can change font sizes, select fonts, and configure rendering options (see Figure 7-36). Fonts are listed for Applications, Documents, Desktop, Window title, and Fixed width. Click on a font button to open a "Pick a Font" dialog where you can select a font, choose its style (regular, italic, or bold), and change its size. You can further refine your font display by clicking the Details button to open a window where you can set features like the dots-per-inch, hinting, and smoothing.

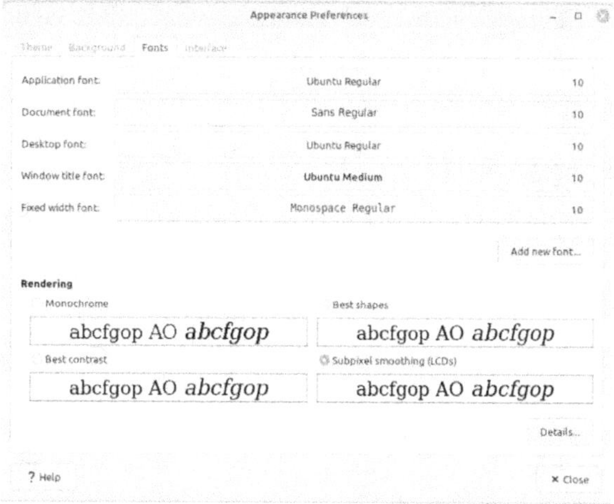

Figure 7-36: Fonts

With very large monitors and their high resolutions becoming more common, one feature users find helpful is the ability to increase the desktop font sizes. On a large widescreen monitor, resolutions less than the native one tend not to scale well. A monitor always looks best in its native resolution. With a large native resolution text sizes become so small they are hard to read. You can overcome this issue by increasing the font size. The default size is 10; increasing it to 12 makes text in all desktop features like windows and menus much more readable.

Configuring Fonts

To refine your font display, you can use the font rendering features. Open the Fonts tab on the Appearance tool. In the Font Rendering section are basic font rendering features like Monochrome, Best contrast, Best shapes, and Subpixel smoothing. Choose the one that works best. For LCD monitors choose subpixel smoothing. For detailed configuration, click the Details button. Here you can set Smoothing, Hinting (anti-aliasing), and Subpixel color order features. The Subpixel color order is hardware dependent.

On MATE, clicking on a font button in the Fonts Preferences tool will open a "Pick a Font" dialog that lists all available fonts. You can also generate a listing by using the **fc-list** command. The list will be unsorted, so you should pipe it first to the sort command. You can use **fc-list** with any font name or name pattern to search for fonts, with options to search by language, family, or styles.

```
fc-list | sort
```

Adding Fonts

Numerous font packages are available on the Linux repositories. When you install the font packages, the fonts are installed automatically on your system and ready for use. True type font packages begin with **ttf-** prefix. Microsoft true type fonts are available from the **ttf-mscorefonts-installer** package. Fonts are installed in the **/usr/share/fonts** folder. This folder will have subfolders for different font collections like **truetype** and **X11**. You can install fonts manually yourself by copying fonts to the **/user/share/fonts** folder (use the **sudo** command). For dual-boot systems, where Windows is installed as one of the operating systems, you can copy fonts directly from the Windows font folder on the Windows partition (which is mounted in **/media**) to **/usr/share/fonts**.

MATE Power Management

For power management, MATE uses the MATE Power Manager, **mate-power-manager**, which makes use of Advanced Configuration and Power Interface (ACPI) support provided by a computer to manage power use. The MATE Power Manager can display an icon on the panel showing the current power source, a battery or plugin (lightning). Clicking on the battery icon displays a menu showing the power charge of your wireless devices, both your laptop and any other wireless devices like a wireless mouse.

The MATE Power manager is configured with Power Management Preferences (**mate-power-preferences**), accessible from Preferences | Power Management, and by right clicking on the MATE Power Management panel icon and selecting Preferences from the pop-up menu (also on the GNOME Control Center | Hardware section). Power Manager preferences can be used to configure both a desktop and a laptop.

For a desktop, two tabs appear on the Power Management Preferences window, On AC Power and General. The AC Power tab offers two sleep options, one for the computer and one for the display screen. You can put each to sleep after a specified interval of inactivity. On the General tab, you set desktop features like actions to take when you press the power button or whether to display the power icon.

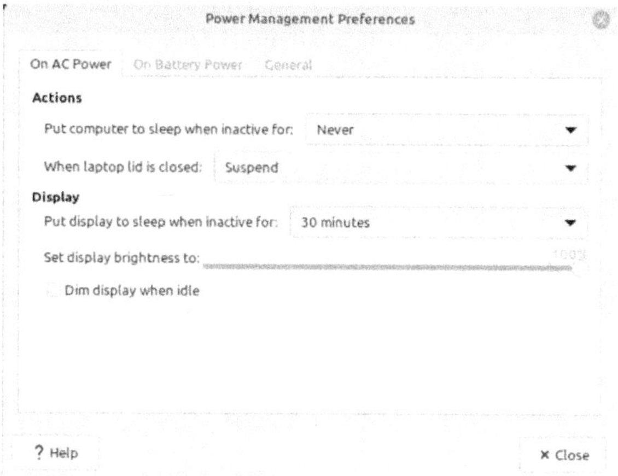

Figure 7-37: MATE Power Manager

Display of the Power Management icon on the panel is configured on the General tab. In the Notification Area section, you can set options to never display, always display the icon, displaying the icon when the battery is low, or when it is charging or discharging, or only if there is a battery. The default is to display the icon only when a battery is present.

Note: The MATE Power Manager will not only check the power level of a laptop battery, but also the power level of other battery wireless devices, like the battery of a wireless mouse or keyboard.

A laptop will also have an On Battery Power tab where you can set additional options for the battery and display, such as shutting down if the battery is too low, or dimming the display when the system is idle (see Figure7-37). The laptop On AC Power tab will also have an Actions option for actions to take when the laptop lid is closed, like suspend, blank screen, and shutdown.

To see how your laptop or desktop is performing with power, you can use Power statistics. This is accessible from the System Tool menus as Power Statistics. The Power Statistics window will display a sidebar listing your different power devices. A right pane will show tabs with power use information for a selected device. The Laptop battery device will display three tabs: Details, History, and Statistics. The History tab will show your recent use, with graph options for Time to empty (time left), Time to full (recharging), Charge, and Rate. The Statistics tab can show charge and discharge graphs.

Preferred Applications for Web, Mail, Accessibility, and terminal windows

Certain types of files will have default applications already associated with them. For example, double-clicking a Web page file will open the file in the Firefox Web browser. If you prefer to set a different default application, you can use the Preferred Applications tool (see Figure 7-38). You access the Preferred Applications tool from the Preferences menu (Preferences | Preferred Applications), and from the GNOME Control Center (Personal section). This tool will let you set default applications for Web pages, mail readers, accessibility tools, multimedia and office applications, and the system-level tools. Available applications are listed in popup menus. In Figure 7-38 the default mail reader is Thunderbird, and the default Web browser is Firefox. To make another application the default, click on the menu button to display a list of other possible installed applications. The Preferred applications tool has tabs for Internet, Multimedia, System, Office, and Accessibility. On the Multimedia tab, you can select default image viewer, video player, and multimedia player. On the Office tab, you can specify the default document viewer, word processor, and spreadsheet applications. On the System tab, you can choose the default text editor, terminal window application, and file manager. The Accessibility panel has options for selecting a magnifier.

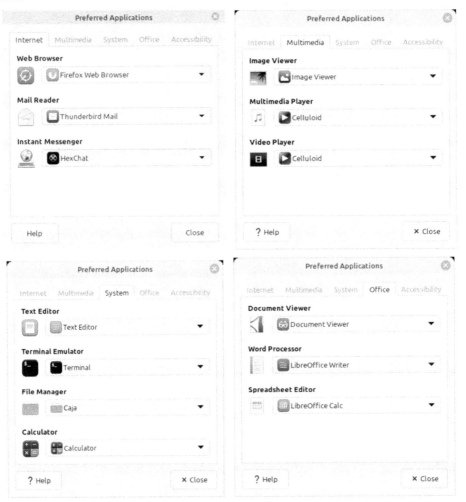

Figure 7-38: Preferred Applications tool

Default Applications for Media

Caja directly handles preferences for media operations. You set the preferences using the File Management Preferences dialog. It is accessible from the Edit | Preferences menu item on any Caja file manager window.

The Media tab of the File Management Preferences dialog lists entries for Cd Audio, DVD Video, Music Player, Photos, and Software. Pop-up menus let you select the application to use for the different media (see Figure 7-39). You also have options for Ask what to do, Do Nothing, and Open folder. The Open Folder options will just open a window displaying the files on the disc. A segment labeled "Other media" lets you set up an association for less used media like Blu-Ray discs. Initially, the "Ask what to do" option will be set for all entries. Possible options are listed for each menu, like Rhythmbox Music Player for Cd Audio discs and Celluloid for DVD Video. Photos can be opened with the Pix Photo-manager. Once you select an option, when you insert removable media, like an audio disc, its associated application is automatically started.

If you just want to turn off the startup for a particular kind of media, you can select the Do Nothing entry from its application pop-up menu. If you want to be prompted for options, then set the "Ask what to do" entry in the Media tab's pop-up menu. When you insert a disc, a dialog with a pop-up menu for possible actions is displayed. The default application is already selected. You can select another application or select the Do Nothing or Open Folder options.

You can turn the automatic startup off for all media by checking the box for "Never prompt or start programs on media insertion" at the bottom of the Media panel. You can also enable the option "browse media when inserted" to just open a folder showing its files.

Figure 7-39: File Management Preferences for Media

Screen Saver and Lock

With the Screensaver Preferences, you can control when the computer is considered idle and what screen saver to use if any (see Figure 7-40). You can access the Screensaver Preferences dialog from the Linux Mint menu Preferences menu as Screensaver, or from the Control Center in the Personal section. You can choose from various screen savers, using the scroll box to the left, with a preview displayed at the right. You can also control whether to lock the screen or not, when idle and for how long. You can turn off the Screensaver by unchecking the "Activate screensaver when computer is idle" box.

Figure 7-40: Screensaver Preferences

Assistive Technologies

On MATE, the Assistive Technologies dialog is a simple set of buttons for accessing accessibility tabs for other tools (see Figure 7-41). In the Assistive Technologies section, use the "Enable assistive technologies" checkbox to turn assistive technologies on and off. The Preferred Applications button opens the Accessibility tab on the Preferred Applications dialog.

Figure 7-41: Assistive Technologies Preferences and Accessibility Preferred Applications

In the Preferences section, there are buttons to open the accessibility tabs for the keyboard and mouse preferences dialogs. On the keyboard accessibility tab, you can configure features such as sticky, slow, and bound keys. The mouse button opens the mouse preferences dialog.

Popup Notifications

The Popup Notifications entry and icon (Preferences menu and Control Center) opens the Notification Settings dialog that allows you to select a position on your screen for popup notifications as well as choose a theme for the notification dialog (see Figure 7-42). You can choose to use the active monitor only as well as turn off popup notifications by selecting the "Enable Do Not Disturb" option. Themes include Coco (the default), Slider, Nodoka, and the Standard theme. Click to the Preview button to see what they would look like. Should you be using more than one monitor, you can choose which monitor to configure.

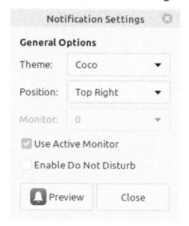

Figure 7-42: Popup Notifications

Part 3: Administration

System Tools
System Administration
Network Connections
Shell Configuration

8. System Tools

GNOME System Monitor

Scheduling Tasks

System Log

Disk Usage Analyzer

Virus Protection

Hardware Sensors

Disk Utility

Sound (PulseAudio)

dconf Editor

Managing Keys with Seahorse

Useful system tools, as well as user specific configuration tools, can be found in the Accessories, Preferences, and Administration menus (see Table 8-1). The Administration menu includes tools like the System Monitor and the Disk Usage Analyzer. The Accessories menu holds Disk Utility and the ClamTK Virus Scanner (Virus Scanner). Desktop configuration, such as mouse, keyboard, displays, and sound configuration, are handled by Cinnamon and MATE directly (System Settings) and can be accessed from the Preferences menu.

Linux Mint System Tools	Name	Description
gnome-system-monitor	System Monitor	GNOME System Monitor
gnome-logs	Logs	GNOME Logs
gnome-terminal	Terminal	GNOME Terminal Window
baobab	Disk Usage Analyzer	Disk usage analyzer with graphic representation
gnome-nettool	Network Tools	Network analysis
ClamTK	Virus Scanner	Clam Virus scanner
Disk Utility	Disk Utility	Udisks utility for managing hard disks and removable drives
PulseAudio	Sound	Sound drivers and server

Table 8-1: Linux Mint System Tools

GNOME System Monitor

Linux Mint provides the GNOME System Monitor for displaying system information and monitoring system processes, accessible from the Administration menu as System Monitor. There are three tabs: Processes, Resources, and File Systems (see Figure 8-1). The Resources tab displays graphs for CPU History, Memory and Swap History, and Network History. If your system has a multi-core CPU, the CPU History graph shows the usage for each CPU. The Memory and Swap Memory graph shows the amount of memory in use. The Network History graph displays both the amount of sent and received data, along with totals for the current session. The File Systems tab lists your file systems, where they are mounted, and their type, as well as the amount of disk space used and how much is free. Double clicking on a file system entry will open that file system in a file manager window.

The Processes tab lists your processes, letting you sort and search processes. You can use field buttons to sort by name (Process Name), process ID (ID), the percentage of use (%CPU), and memory used (Memory), among others. The menu (right-side of the menu bar) lets you select all processes, just your own (My Processes), or active processes. You can stop any process by selecting it and then clicking the End Process button (lower-right corner) or by right-clicking on it and choosing End. You can right-click a process entry to display a menu with actions you can take on the selected process, such as stopping (Stop), ending (End), killing (Kill), and continuing a process (Continue), as well as changing the priority of the process (Change Priority). The Open Files entry opens a dialog listing all the files, sockets, and pipes the process is using. The Properties entry displays a dialog showing all the details for a process, such as the name, user, status, memory use, CPU use, and priority. The Memory Maps display, selected from the Memory Maps entry, shows information on virtual memory, inodes, and flags for a selected process.

Display features such as the colors used for CPU graphs can be set using the dconf editor's gnome-system-monitor keys at org.gnome.gnome-system-monitor.

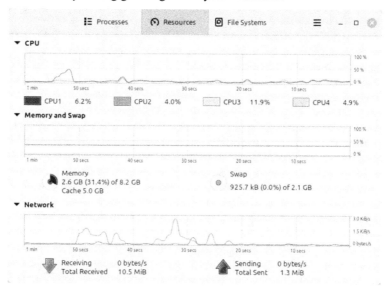

Figure 8-1: GNOME System Monitor: Resources

Managing Processes

Should you have to force a process or application to quit, you can use the Gnome System Monitor Processes tab to find, select, and stop the process. You should be sure of the process you want to stop. Ending a critical process could cripple your system. Application processes will bear the name of the application, and you can use those to force an application to quit. Ending processes manually is usually performed for open-ended operations that you are unable to stop normally. In Figure 8-2, the Firefox application has been selected. Clicking the End Process button on the lower left will then force the Firefox Web browser to end.

The pop-up menu for a process (right-click) provides several other options for managing a selected process: stop, continue, end, kill, and change priority. There are corresponding keyboard keys for most options. The stop and continue operations work together. You can stop (Stop) a process, and then later start it again with the Continue option. The End option stops a process safely, whereas a Kill option forces an immediate end to the process. The End option is preferred, but if it does not work, you can use the Kill option. Change Priority can give a process a lower or higher priority, letting it run faster or slower. The Properties option opens a dialog listing process details such as the name, user, status, different types of memory used, CPU usage, start time, process id, and priority. The Open Files option lists all the files, sockets, and pipes the process is using.

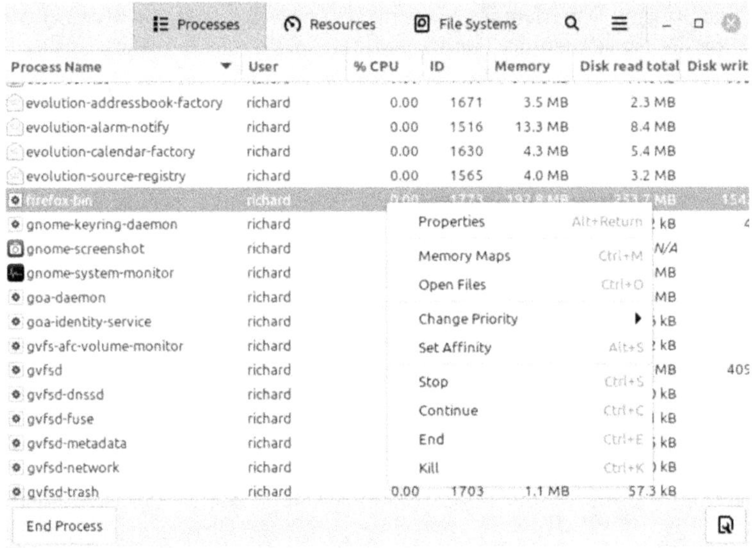

Figure 8-2: GNOME System Monitor: Processes

You can also use the **pkill** command with a process name or a process ID to end a process. To use a process name, enter the process name with the **-n** option for the most recent process for that name.

```
pkill -n firefox
```

You can use the **kill** command in a terminal window to end a process. The **kill** command takes as its argument a process number. Be sure you obtain the correct one. Use the **ps** command to display a process id. Entering in the incorrect process number could cripple your system. The **ps** command with the **-C** option searches for a particular application name. The **-o pid=** option will display only the process id, instead of the process id, time, application name, and tty. Once you have the process id, you can use the **kill** command with the process id as its argument to end the process.

```
$ ps -C firefox -o pid=
5555
$ kill 5555
```

One way to ensure the correct number is to use the **ps** command to return the process number directly as an argument to a **kill** command. In the following example, an open-ended process was started with the **mycmd** command. An open-ended process is one that will continue until you stop it manually.

```
mycmd > my.ts
```

The process is then ended by first executing the **ps** command to obtain the process id for the **mycmd** process (back quotes), and then using that process id in the **kill** command to end the process. The **-o pid=** option displays only the process id.

```
kill `ps -C mycmd -o pid=`
```

To search for a process using a pattern, you can use a **ps** command with the **-aux** option to list all processes and pipe the output to a **grep** command with a specified pattern. The following command lists all X Window System processes.

```
ps -aux | grep 'firefox'
```

You can obtain just the process IDs with the **pidof** command.

```
pidof firefox
```

Glances

Glances is a comprehensive system monitoring tool run from the command line in a terminal window with the **glances** command. It shows detailed resource use for the system, network, disk, file system, sensors, and processes. (see Figure 8-3). It also warns you of any critical alerts. The system section covers detailed memory, CPU, swap and load usage. The network section shows the activity on each network device. The Disk I/O section lists your storage devices and their read/write usage. The File Sys section shows all your partitions and how much memory is used. The Sensors section shows the temperature detected by your sensors such as those for CPU, GPU, and the ambient temperature. The Tasks section lists your active processes by CPU usage, showing memory used, pid, user and the command. Press **q** to end your glances session.

Glances is organized into modules which you can disable to show only a limited set of reports. For example, if you are not interested in the disk I/O reports, you can disable the diskio module with the **--disable-diskio** option. See the **glances** man page for a complete list of module options you can use.

```
glances -- disable-diskio.
```

There are also several runtime commands you can use to show and hide modules, such as **f** to toggle the file system reports on an off, **d** to toggle disk I/O, **n** for network stats, **s** for showing sensors, and **p** to sort processes by name.

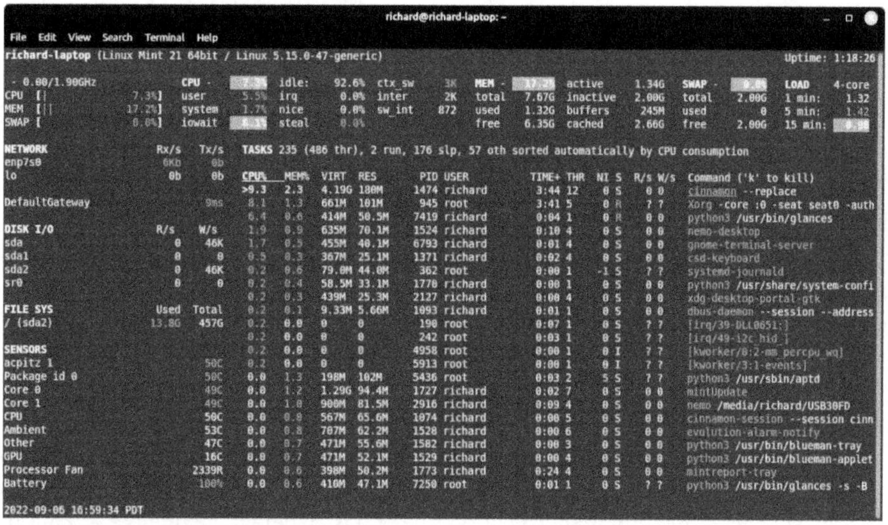

Figure 8-3: Glances System Monitor

Scheduling Tasks

Scheduling regular maintenance tasks, such as backups, can be managed either by using the systemd timers or by the cron service. The systemd timers are systemd files that run service files. Check the man page for **systemd.timers** for a detailed description of timers. They have the extension **.timer**. A timer file will automatically run a corresponding service file that has the same name. For example, the **dnf-automatic.timer** will run the **dnf-automatic.service** file. The timer file only contains scheduling information. Its filename determines which service file to run. It is possible to designate a different service file with the Unit directive in the timer file. If you want to run a command line operation for which there is no service file, you can create your own with an ExecStart entry for that command.

The timer files have a timer section in which you define when the service file is run. There are options that are relative to certain starting points like when system booted up, and the **OnCalendar** option that that reference calendar dates. The **OnCalendar** option uses calendar event expressions as defined on the **systemd.time** man page. A calendar event expression consists of a weekday, year, month, and time. The time is specified in hour, minute, and second, separated by colons. A range of weekdays is separated by two periods, and specific weekdays by commas. Leaving out the year or month selects any year or month. The following references weekdays in May at 2 pm.

```
OnCalendar=Mon..Fri 05 14:00
```

You can create timer files and place them in the **/etc/systemd/system** folder. If you also have to set up a service file for it, you can place it in the same folder. To activate a timer be sure to enable it with **systemctl**. If you created a service file, be sure to enable that also.

You can still use the older cron service to schedule tasks. The cron service is implemented by the cron daemon that constantly checks for certain actions to take. These tasks are listed in the **crontab** file. The **cron** daemon constantly checks the user's **crontab** file to see if it is time to take these actions. Any user can set up a **crontab** file. An administrative user can set up a **crontab** file to take system administrative actions, such as backing up files at a certain time each week or month.

Creating cron entries can be a complicated task, using the **crontab** command to make changes to crontab files in the **/etc/crontab** folder. Instead, you can use desktop cron scheduler tools to set up cron actions.

Logs

Various system logs for tasks performed on your system are stored in the **/var/log** folder. Here you can find logs for mail, news, and all other system operations, such as Web server logs (see Figure 8-4). This usually includes startup tasks, such as loading drivers and mounting file systems. If a driver for a device failed to load at startup, you will find an error message for it here. Logins are also recorded in this file, showing you who attempted to log into what account. The **/var/log/mail.log** file logs mail message transmissions and news transfers.

To view logs, you can use Gnome Logs accessible as Logs on the Administration menu. A side panel lists different log categories. Selecting one displays the log messages to the right. Critical messages are listed under the Important category. The "Logs" label on the title bar is a button you can click to display a list of recent boot sessions. You can select one to refine the messages displayed. By default, the most recent one is chosen. A search button on the top right opens a search box where you can search for messages in the selected log. Search has options (menu to the right) for refining the search by fields and by time.

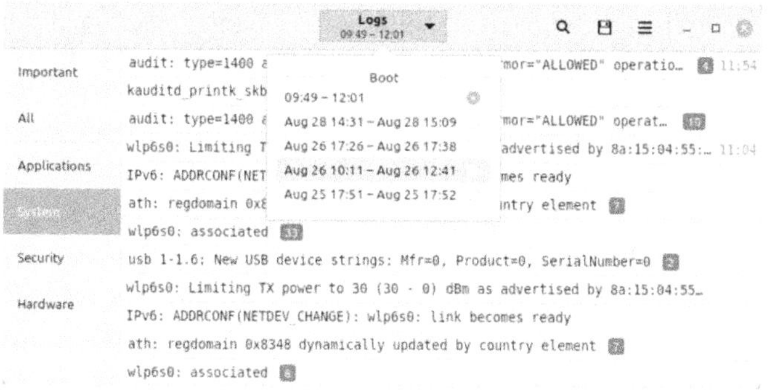

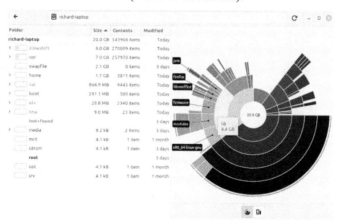

Figure 8-4: Logs

Disk Usage Analyzer

The disk usage analyzer lets you see how much disk space is used and available on all your mounted hard disk partitions (see Figure 8-5). You can access it from the Administration menu as Disk Usage Analyzer. It will also check all LVM and RAID arrays. Usage is shown in a simple graph, letting you see how much overall space is available and where it is. On the scan dialog you can choose to scan a hard disk (disk drive icon), your home folder, or an attached device like a floppy or USB drive (see Figure 8-6). Clicking on the menu button to the right lets you choose a particular folder to scan, either local for remote. When you scan a folder or a file system, disk usage for your folder is analyzed and displayed. Each file system is shown with a graph for its usage, as well as its size and the number of top-level directories and files. Then the directories are shown, along with their size and contents (files and directories).

Figure 8-5: Disk Usage Analyzer

A representational graph for disk usage is displayed on the right pane. The graph can be either a Ring Chart or a Treemap. The Ring Chart is the default. Choose the one you want from the buttons on the lower right. For the Ring Chart, directories are shown, starting with the top-level directories at the center and moving out to the subdirectories. Passing your mouse over a section in the graph displays its folder name and disk usage, as well as all its subdirectories. The Treemap chart shows a box representation, with greater disk usage in larger boxes, and subdirectories encased within folder boxes.

Figure 8-6: Disk Usage Analyzer: Scan dialog

Virus Protection

For virus protection, you can use the Linux version of ClamAV, which uses a GNOME front-end called ClamTk, **https://www.clamav.net**. This Virus scanner is included on the Ubuntu main repository. You can install ClamTk from Software Manager. The supporting ClamAV packages will also be selected and installed for you (clamav-base and clamav-freshclam). You can also install ClamAV using the Synaptic Package Manager, choose the clamav, clamav-base, clamav-freshclam (online virus definitions), and ClamTK packages. Selecting just ClamTk will automatically select the other clamav packages for installation. The **clamav-freshclam** package retrieves current virus definitions from the ClamAV servers. For ClamAV to check your mail messages automatically, you need to install the ClamAV scanner daemon (**clamav-daemon** and **clamdscan** packages).

Figure 8-7: The ClamTK tool for ClamAV virus protection.

You can access ClamTk from the Accessories menu as ClamTk. With ClamTk, you can scan specific files and directories, as well as your home folder (see Figure 8-7). Searches can be recursive, including subdirectories (Settings). You have the option to check configuration files (scan files with a dot). You can also perform quick or recursive scans of your home folder. Infected files are quarantined.

Your virus definitions will be updated automatically. If you want to check manually for virus definitions, you need to click Update Assistant and choose to update the signatures yourself. Then click Updates and click the OK button next to "Check for updates."

Sensor application	Description
lm-sensors	Detects and accesses computer (motherboard) sensors like CPU and fan speed. Run **sensors-detect** once to configure.
hddtemp	Detects hard drive temperatures (also detected by Disk Utility)
Disk Utility	Disk Utility provides SMART information for hard disks showing current hard disk temperatures as well as detailed disk health information and checks.
Psensor	Application to detect and display system and hard drive temperatures.
Xsensors	Application to detect and display system temperatures and fans.
indicator-cpufreq	CPU Frequency Scaling Indicator for monitoring and changing CPU frequency.
CPU Frequency Applet	CPU frequency scaling (Cinnamon applet).
CPU Temperature Indicator	Display CPU temperature (Cinnamon applet)
Simple CPU Monitor	Display CPU usage (Cinnamon applet)
GPU Temperature	Display GPU temperature (Cinnamon applet)
Graphical Hardware Monitor	Display information on all your devices and components (Cinnamon applet)

Table 8-2: Sensor packages and applications

Hardware Sensors

A concern for many users is the temperatures and usage of computer components. You can install different software packages to enable certain sensors (see Table 8-2). You can add the applet "CPU Temperature Indicator" to display your CPU temperatures. If your system supports CPU Scaling you can add the CPU Frequency Selector. For CPU, system, fan speeds, and any other motherboard supported sensors, you can use Psensor, Xsensors, or the **lm-sensors** service. Psensors installs the hddtemp hard drive temperature server and displays your CPU, graphics card, and hard drive temperatures. You can set temperature thresholds for alerts. Xsensors displays your CPU temperature. There are also several Cinnamon applets you can install for your panel, including the CPU Temperature Indicator, GPU Temperature, and the Graphical Hardware Monitor.

If not already installed, install the **lm-sensors** package. Then you have to configure your sensor detection. In a terminal window enter the following command and press ENTER to answer yes to the prompts.

```
sudo sensors-detect
```

Disk Utility (Disks on the Preferences and Accessories menus) lets you know your hard disk temperature. Disk Utility uses Udisks to access SMART information about the disk drive, including the temperature and overall health. Open Disk Utility, select the hard disk. On the right pane, the Assessments entry lists the disk temperature.

Disk Utility and Udisks

Disk Utility is a Udisks supported user configuration interface for your storage media, such as hard disks, USB drives, and DVD/CD drives (**gnome-disk-utility** package, installed by default) . Tasks supported include disk labeling, mounting disks, disk checks, and encryption. You can also perform more advanced tasks, like managing RAID and LVM storage devices, as well as partitions. Disk Utility is accessible from the Accessories and Preferences menus as Disks. Users can use Disk Utility to format removable media like USB drives. Disk Utility is also integrated into Nemo and Caja, letting you format removable media directly.

The Disk Utility window shows a sidebar with entries for your storage media (see Figure 8-8). Clicking on an entry displays information for the media on the right pane. Removable devices such as USB drives display power and eject buttons on the title bar, along with a task menu with an entry to format the disk. If you are formatting a partition, like that on removable media, you can specify the file system type to use.

Figure 8-8: Disk Utility

If you select a hard disk device, information about the hard disk is displayed on the right pane at the top, such as the model name, serial number, size, partition table type, and SMART status (Assessment) (see Figure 8-9). Click the menu button to display a menu on the upper right with tasks you can perform on the hard drive: Format, Benchmark, and SMART Data.

Figure 8-9: Disk Utility, hard drive

The Volumes section on the hard disk pane shows the partitions set up on the hard drive (see Figure 8-10). Partitions are displayed in a graphical icon bar, which displays each partition's size and location on the drive. Clicking on a partition entry on the graphical icon bar displays information about that partition such as the file system type, device name, partition label, and partition size. The "Contents" entry tells if a partition is mounted. If in use, it displays a "Mounted at:" entry with a link consisting of the path name where the file system is mounted. You can click on this path name to open a folder with which you can access the file system. The button bar below the Volumes images provides additional tasks you can perform, such as unmounting a file system (square button) and deleting a partition (minus button). From the more tasks menu (gear button), you can choose entries to check and repair the file system, resize or format it, and change the partition label (Edit Filesystem), partition type (Edit partition), and mount options (Edit Mount Options). Certain partitions, like extended partitions, display limited information and have few allowable tasks.

Figure 8-10: Disk Utility, Volumes

For more detailed hardware information about a hard drive, you can click on the "SMART Data and Tests" entry from the task menu in the upper right. This opens a SMART data dialog with hardware information about the hard disk (see Figure 8-11) including temperature, power cycles, bad sectors, and the overall health of the disk. The Attributes section lists SMART details such as the Read Error Rate, Spinup time, temperature, and write error rate. Click the switch to on to enable the tests, and off to disable testing. Click the "Refresh" button to manually run the tests. Click the "Start Self-test" button to open a menu with options for short, extended, and conveyance tests.

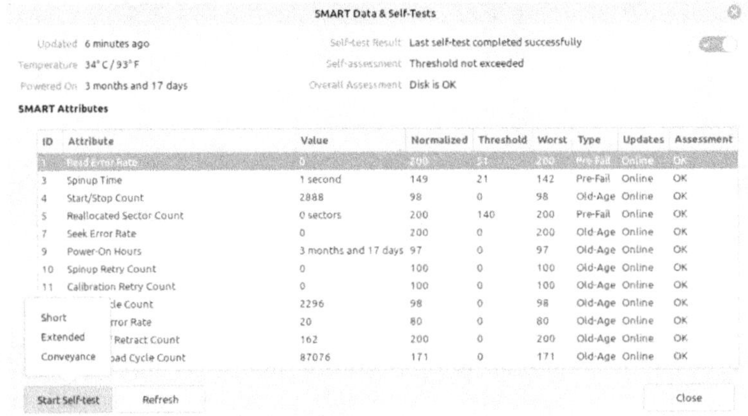

SMART Data & Self-Tests						
Updated 6 minutes ago		Self-test Result Last self-test completed successfully				
Temperature 34°C / 93°F		Self-assessment Threshold not exceeded				
Powered On 3 months and 17 days		Overall Assessment Disk is OK				

SMART Attributes

ID	Attribute	Value	Normalized	Threshold	Worst	Type	Updates	Assessment
1	Read Error Rate	0	200	51	200	Pre-Fail	Online	OK
3	Spinup Time	1 second	149	21	142	Pre-Fail	Online	OK
4	Start/Stop Count	2888	98	0	98	Old-Age	Online	OK
5	Reallocated Sector Count	0 sectors	200	140	200	Pre-Fail	Online	OK
7	Seek Error Rate	0	200	0	200	Old-Age	Online	OK
9	Power-On Hours	3 months and 17 days	97	0	97	Old-Age	Online	OK
10	Spinup Retry Count	0	100	0	100	Old-Age	Online	OK
11	Calibration Retry Count	0	100	0	100	Old-Age	Online	OK
	cle Count	2296	98	0	98	Old-Age	Online	OK
Short	rror Rate	20	80	0	80	Old-Age	Online	OK
Extended	Retract Count	162	200	0	200	Old-Age	Online	OK
Conveyance	bad Cycle Count	87076	171	0	171	Old-Age	Online	OK

Start Self-test   Refresh   Close

Figure 8-11: Disk Utility: Hard Disk hardware SMART data

Plymouth

Plymouth provides a streamlined, efficient, and faster graphical boot that does not require X server support. It relies on the kernel's Kernel Modesettings (KMS) feature that provides direct support for basic graphics. With the Direct Rendering Manager driver, Plymouth can make use of different graphical plugins. KMS support is currently provided for AMD, Nvidia, and Intel graphics cards. The Plymouth Linux Mint logo theme is installed by default. You can install others like solar and glow. The theme packages begin with the prefix **plymouth-theme**. You can search for them on the Synaptic Package Manager. You can also install them from Software Manager (search on Plymouth).

Choosing to use a Plymouth theme involves using the Debian alternatives system, which is designed to designate an application to use when there are several alternative versions to select. A link is set up for the application to use in the **/etc/alternatives** folder. For Plymouth, this link is named **default.plymouth**. You can choose a Plymouth theme by entering the **update-alternatives** command with the **--config** option, the **default.plymouth** link, and the **sudo** command in a terminal window as shown here.

```
sudo update-alternatives --config default.plymouth
```

This displays a numbered menu listing your installed themes. An asterisk indicates the current theme. Enter the number of the theme you want to use. The **default.plymouth** link is then set to the theme you choose. When your system starts up again, it will use that Plymouth theme.

Some of the non-Linux Mint themes may hang on start up. In that case, you can edit the boot kernel line to remove the **splash** option and then boot to your system (see Chapter 3). Then use **update-alternatives** to change your Plymouth theme.

Sound

Your sound cards are detected automatically for you when you start up your system, by ALSA, which is invoked by udev when your system starts up. Removable devices, like USB sound devices, are also detected. See Table 8-3 for a listing of sound device and interface tools.

In addition to hardware drivers, sound systems also use sound interfaces to direct encoded sound streams from an application to the hardware drivers and devices. Linux Mint uses the PulseAudio server for its sound interface. PulseAudio aims to combine and consolidate all sound interfaces into a simple, flexible, and powerful server. The ALSA hardware drivers are still used, but the application interface is handled by PulseAudio. PulseAudio is installed as the default for Linux Mint and Ubuntu.

Note: Sound devices on Linux are supported by hardware sound drivers. With the Linux kernel, hardware support is implemented by the Advanced Linux Sound Architecture (ALSA) system. You can find more about ALSA at http://alsa-project.org.

PulseAudio is a cross-platform sound server, allowing you to modify the sound level for different audio streams separately. See **https://www.freedesktop.org/wiki/Software/PulseAudio/** for documentation and help. PulseAudio offers complete control over all your sound streams, letting you combine sound devices and direct the stream anywhere on your network. PulseAudio is not confined to a single system. It is network capable, letting you direct sound from one PC to another.

Sound tool	Description
alsamixer	ALSA sound connection configuration and volume tool
amixer	ALSA command for sound connection configuration
Sound Preferences	GNOME Sound Preferences, used to select and configure your sound interface (Sound)
PulseAudio	PulseAudio sound interface, the default sound interface for Linux Mint. **www.pulseaudio.org**
PulseAudio Volume Control	PulseAudio Volume Control, controls stream input, output, and playback, **pavucontrol** package
PulseAudio Volume Meter	Volume Meter, displays active sound levels
PulseAudio Manager	Manager for information and managing PulseAudio, **pman** package
PulseAudio Preferences	Options for network access and virtual output

Table 8-3: Sound device and interface tools

As an alternative, you can use the command-line ALSA control tool, **alsamixer**. This will display all connections and allow you to use keyboard commands to select (arrow keys), mute (m key), or set sound levels (Page Up and Down). Press the ESC key to exit. The **amixer** command lets you perform the same tasks for different sound connections from the command line. To actually play and record from the command-line, you can use the **play** and **rec** commands.

Sound menu (volume control and player access)

The sound menu (speaker icon, sound applet) displays volume control, media player access, sound settings access, and sound device selection entries (see Figure 8-12).

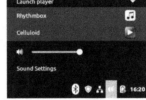

Figure 8-12: Sound Menu

You can change your application's sound volume using a sliding bar. When you click on the sound volume slider, you can use your mouse scroll button to adjust the sound volume. To perform volume control for specific devices like a microphone, you use the Sound dialog, which you can access from the System Settings, or from the sound menu's Sound Settings entry.

The sound menu provides basic access to the media players, such as Rhythmbox, showing the title of the current track and displaying controls to play, pause, and move to the previous and next tracks. Click the "Launch player" entry to open a listing of your installed players. As you play an audio source, a description of the audio track and basic control buttons are displayed on the sound menu. When you are playing, the sound icon on the panel changes to a music note.

If you wish to mute the sound, you can right-click on the sound icon to display switches for muting the output and input (see Figure 8-13). Click the switch to mute the sound.

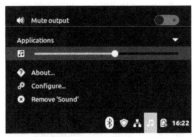

Figure 8-13: Sound Menu, right click, mute options

Sound

You configure sound devices and set the volume for sound effects, input and output, and applications using the GNOME sound tool. Choose Sound on the System Settings dialog, select Sound on the Preferences menu, or select Sound Settings from the panel sound applet menu. This opens the Sound dialog, which has four tabs: Output, Input, Sounds, Applications, and Settings (see Figure 8-14).

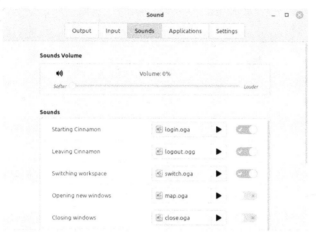

Figure 8-14: Sound: Sounds

The Sounds tab lets you choose sounds for different operations such as switching workspaces or closing a window. A play button to the right of each effect lets you play the sound, and a button with the filename of the sound can be clicked to open the **/usr/share/mint-artwork-cinnamon/sounds** folder where you can choose a different sound file to use. You can turn a sound off by clicking the switch to the right of the play button. A sliding bar at the top in the Sounds Volume section lets you set the volume for your sound effects.

On the Input tab, you choose the input device and set the input volume. Input devices are listed in the Device section at the top. In the "Device settings" section you can set the volume for a selected device. When speaking or recording, the input level is displayed (see Figure 8-15).

Figure 8-15: Sound: Input

On the Output tab, you can configure settings for a selected device: Digital, Headphones, and Speakers. The available settings will become active according to the device and profile selected. From the "Output profile " menu you can choose from available outputs, if supported, such as analog speakers or surround sound. For a simple Analog Stereo Output, only the Volume and Balance settings are active (see Figure 8-16).

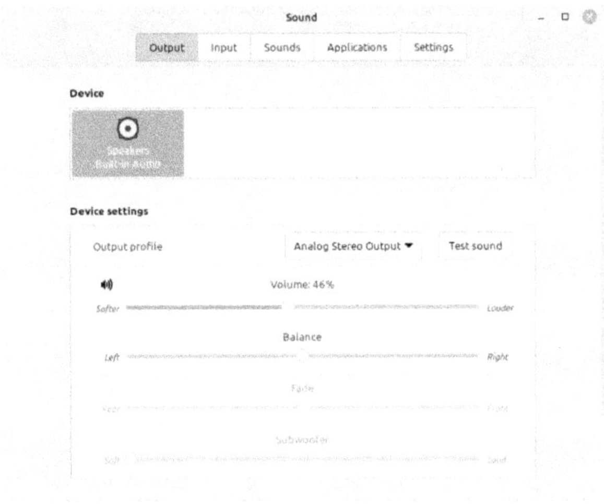

Figure 8-16: Sound: Output

Sound devices that support multiple interfaces like analog surround sound 7.1 or digital SPDIF output, will display a list of interface combinations in the "Output profile" menu. Settings for Fade and Subwoofer are activated. From the menu, you can choose the type of output you want. Configuring digital output for Digital Output (S/PDIF) connectors is a simple matter of selecting the digital output and input entries on the Output and Input tabs. Only the Balance entry will be active.

A laptop may support only a simple internal audio device with left and right balance. Computers with more powerful sound devices have many more options. To test your speakers, click the 'Test sound" button to open the Speakers Testing dialog with test buttons for each speaker.

The Applications tab will show applications currently using sound devices. You can set the sound volume for each (see Figure 8-17).

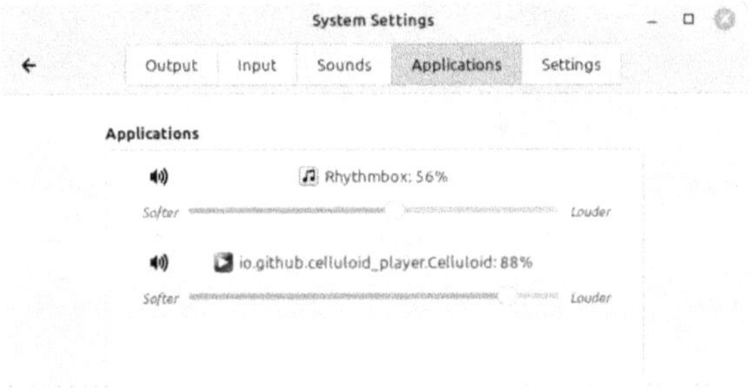

Figure 8-17: Sound: Applications

The Settings tab sets the maximum sound level for the sound controls for all applications (see Figure 8-18). Those controls will adjust according to the maximum volume setting in the Settings tab. Ranges will extend only to the maximum limit. The highest you can set the maximum is at 150%.

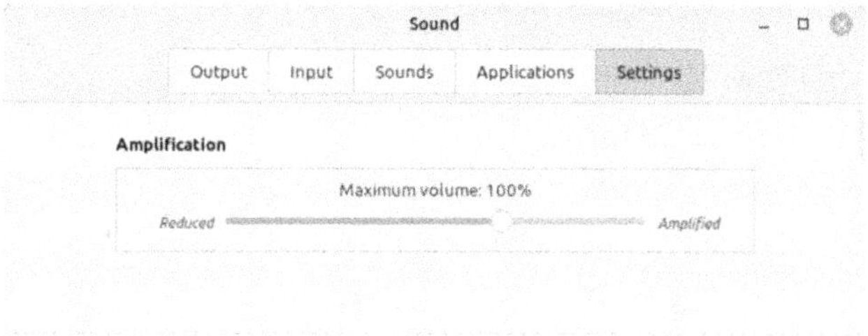

Figure 8-18: Sound: Settings

Installed with Pulse Audio are the Pulse Audio utilities (**pulseaudio-utils** package). These are command line utilities for managing Pulse Audio and playing sound files (see Table 8-4). The **paplay** and **pacat** will play sound files, **pactl** will let you control the sound server and **pacmd** lets you reconfigure it. Check the Man pages for each for more details. If you change your sound preferences frequently, you could use these commands in a shell script to make the changes, instead of having to use the preferences dialog each time. Some of these commands such as **parec** and **paplay** are links to the **pacat** command, which performs the actual tasks.

Sound tool	Description
pa-info	Detailed information about PulseAudio on your system
pacat	Play, record, and configure a raw audio stream
pacmd	Generates a shell for entering configuration commands
pactl	Control a PulseAudio server, changing input and output sources and providing information about the server
padsp	PulseAudio wrapper for OSS sound applications
pamon	Link to pacat
paplay	Playback audio. The -d option specifies the output device, the -s option specifies the server, and the --volume option sets the volume (link to pacat)
parec	Record and audio stream (link to pacat)
parecord	Record and audio stream (link to pacat)
pasuspender	Suspend a PulseAudio server
pax11publish	Access PulseAudio server credentials

Table 8-4: PulseAudio commands (command-line)

PulseAudio applications

For additional configuration abilities, you can also install the Pulse Audio applications. Most begin with the prefix **pa** in the package name. You can install them from the Software

Manager by searching for pulseaudio. Most PulseAudio tools are accessible from the Sound & Video menu. The PulseAudio tools and their command names are shown here.

PulseAudio Volume Control, **pavucontrol**

PulseAudio Volume Meter, **pavumeter**

PulseAudio Manager, **paman**

PulseAudio Preferences, **paprefs**

You can use the PulseAudio Volume Control tool to set the sound levels for different playback applications and sound devices (choose PulseAudio Volume Control in the Sound & Video menu).

The PulseAudio Volume Control applications will show five tabs: Playback, Recording, Output Devices, Input Devices, and Configuration (see Figure 8-19). The Playback tab shows all the applications currently using PulseAudio. You can adjust the volume for each application separately.

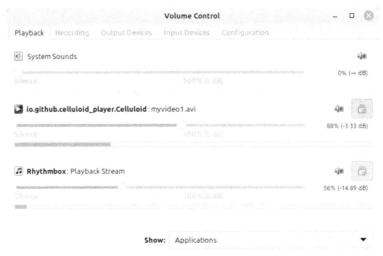

Figure 8-19: PulseAudio Volume Control, Playback

You can use the Output Devices tab panel to set the volume control at the source, and to select different output devices like Headphones (see Figure 8-20). The volume for input and recording devices are set on the Recording and Input Devices tabs. The configuration tab lets you choose different device profiles, like selecting Digital output or Surround Sound 5.1. To find the actual name of the SPDIF output is not always obvious. You may need to run **aplay -L** in a terminal window to see what the name of the digital output device is on your system. It will be the entry with Digital in it.

You can also use the PulseAudio Volume control to direct different applications (streams) to different outputs (devices). For example, you could have two sound sources running, one for video and another for music. The video could be directed through one device to headphones and the music through another device to speakers, or even to another PC. To redirect an application to a different device, right-click its name in the Playback tab. A pop-up menu will list the available devices and let you select the one you want to use.

The PulseAudio Volume Meter tool will show the actual volume of your devices.

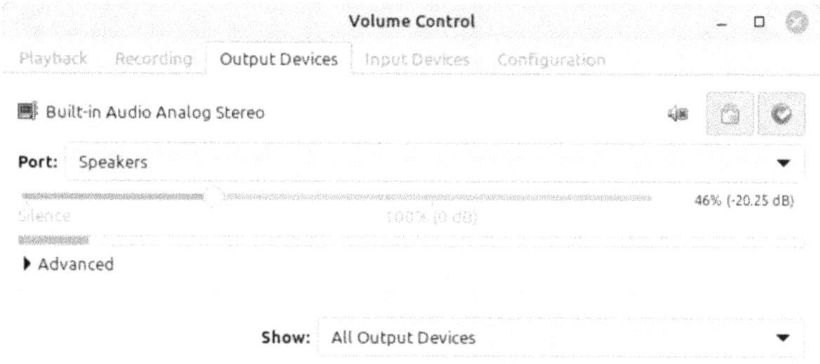

Figure 8-20: PulseAudio Volume Control, Output Devices

To configure network access, you use the PulseAudio Configuration tool. Here you can permit network access, configure the PulseAudio network server, and enable multicast and simultaneous output. If you are connected to a network with Linux systems also running PulseAudio that have allowed network access to their sound devices, their shared sound devices will be listed in the Sound Preferences Hardware tab, allowing you to access them.

Simultaneous output creates a virtual output device to the same hardware device. This lets you channel two sources onto the same output. With PulseAudio Volume Control, you could then channel playback streams to the same output device, but using a virtual device as the output for one. This lets you change the output volume for each stream independently. You could have music and voice directed to the same hardware device, using a virtual device for music and the standard device for voice. You can then reduce the music stream, or raise the voice stream.

dconf editor

The dconf editor provides key base configuration options for your GNOME-based desktops (Cinnamon and MATE), GNOME applications, and for X-Apps applications (see Figure 8-21). You can configure both your desktop and GNOME applications, such as the Cinnamon and MATE file managers (nemo and caja), the GNOME system monitor, and X-Apps. Most options deal with display features, such as the default size for dialogs, or whether to display an application's toolbar.

Configuration with dconf is performed on keys, which can be numbers, checkboxes, text, and menus listing possible options. Text editing supports click-and-drag with the mouse to select text, along with Ctrl-c, Ctrl-x, and Ctrl-v to copy, cut, and paste. Type to insert, use backspace to delete. For very long text entries, a scrollbar appears to let you scroll through the line. Changes take effect immediately. Should you make mistakes you can reset to the default settings by selecting the "Reset visible keys" entry from the menu in the titlebar.

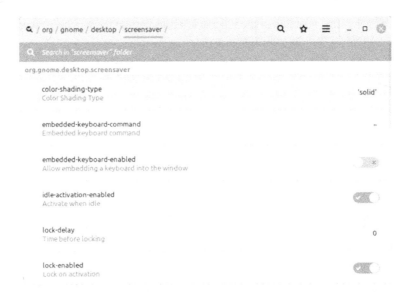

Figure 8-21: dconf editor

The dconf editor organizes keys into schemas, accessible as an expandable tree on the sidebar. The main schemas are apps, ca, com, desktop, io, org, and system. The org schema is where you will find the Cinnamon configuration keys, with subschemas for desklets, the desktop, background, and the muffin window manager. Here also are the MATE keys (**org.mate**) and the gnome applications keys (**org.gnome**). Under the com schema, you will find linuxmint subschema with a mintmenu subschema for Mint menu keys (**com.linuxmint.mintmenu**). Keep expanding subschemas until you find the key you want, in this case, com.linuxmint.mintmenu.

The keys for GNOME applications are located at **org.gnome**. Most deal with default display options.

The x schema lists the X-Apps application keys. Some let you set application specific options. The editor (Xed) lets you set margin, save, indent, and font options (**org.x.editor**).

The keys for the Celluloid player (the default video player for Linux Mint) is located under the **io.github** schema, **io.github.celluloid-player**, along with the MPV player it is based on, **io.github.gnome-mpv**.

Managing keys with Seahorse

For GPG and SSH encryption, signing, and decryption of files and text, GNOME provides Seahorse. With Seahorse you can manage your encryption keys stored in keyrings as well as SSH keys and passphrases. You can import keys, sign keys, search for remote keys, and create your own keyrings, as well as specify keyservers to search and publish to. All these operations can also be performed using the **gpg** command. Seahorse is installed by default.

Passwords and Keys

To import, sign, and locate keys you use the Password and Keys application, accessible from the Utilities application folder on the applications overview (Utilities | Passwords and Keys).

The Passwords and Keys window displays a sidebar with three sections: Passwords, Keys, and Certificates (see Figure 8-22). The Seahorse menu on the right side of the Seahorse header bar shows options for viewing keys (personal, trusted, and any) and the "Password and Keys" folder menu (left side) shows options for finding remote keys, syncing and publishing keys, preferences, and help.

Figure 8-22: Seahorse Passwords and Keys (version 3.3)

Keyrings

The Passwords section lists your keyrings. Keyrings store network and application passwords. A login keyring is set up for you. You can create new keyrings by clicking the plus button on the left of the "Passwords and Keys" title bar and select Password keyring. An "Add password keyring" dialog prompts you for the name of the keyring, and then a "New keyring password" dialog prompts you to enter the keyring password. The strength of the password is indicated. The new keyring is listed in the Passwords section.

To manage keys in your keyring, right-click on the key entry and choose Properties from the menu (see Figure 8-23). Here you can change the description, password for accessing the key, and delete the key. Information about the key's use, type, login, and additional details. A key used to access a network would have the server accessed, protocol used, domain, and the user needed.

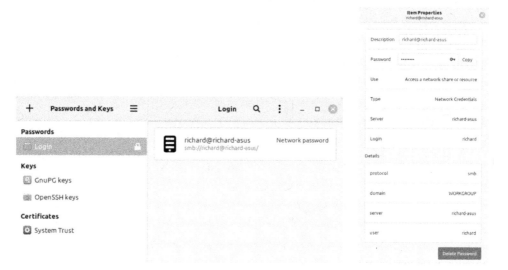

Figure 8-23: Seahorse Keyring key Properties dialog

Creating a new GPG key

Your personal encryption keys are displayed on the PGP Keys section. The entry "GnuPG keys" in the sidebar displays your GPG keys. To create your own private/public click the plus button (+) on the left side of the title bar. You can choose whether to set up a GPG, Private, or Secure Shell key. Choose the "GPG key" entry and click Continue (see Figure 8-24). Keep in mind that before you can perform any encryption, you first have to set up your own GPG key pair, private and public.

Figure 8-24: Choose Encryption key type

This opens a New PGP Key window where you enter your name and email address. In the "Advanced key options" section you can set Encryption type (DSA, RSA, or the signature only for each), Key strength, and Expiration Date (see Figure 8-25). You can also choose to never have it expire. Then click the Create button.

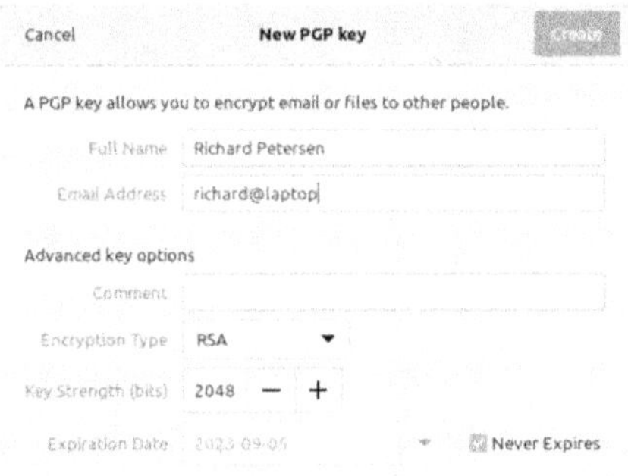

Figure 8-25: Create Encryption key

You are then asked to enter a passphrase (password) for the encryption key (see Figure 8-26). This passphrase will allow you to decrypt any data encrypted by your key.

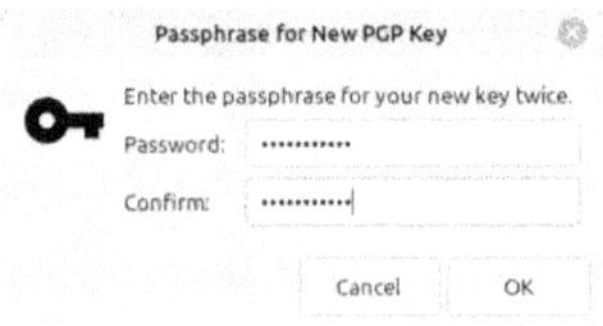

Figure 8-26: Passphrase for encryption key

The key is then generated. This can take a few moments.

Once you key is created, it will appear in the "GnuPG keys" tab of the Passwords and Keys dialog (see Figure 8-27).

Figure 8-27: My Personal Keys

Right-clicking on the key and selecting Properties, displays a dialog titled with the name of the key and showing three sections: User IDs, Subkeys, and Trust. The Owner section shows the key type and ID, as well as a photo for the key and a button to allow you to change the passphrasse for the key (see Figure 8-28). Click the plus button to select a new image file for the photo. Clicking on the calendar button on the Expires entry opens a calendar where you can set an expiration date. The menu on the top left side of the titlebar lists entries for changing the passphrase for the key and exporting the key to a file as a public or secret key.

Any subkeys are also listed, which you can expire, revoke, or delete. You can add new subkeys, specifying a key type, length, and expiration date. Expanding a subkey shows the key's fingerprint, type, and creation date. Buttons allow you to change the expiration date, revoke the key, and delete it..

Figure 8-28: GnuPGP key dialog: Owner tab

In the User IDs section, you can expand the key to show its signatures. The entry for the key shows a menu to the right with entries for "Make primary", Sign, and Delete. Selecting the Sign entry opens the Sign Key dialog where you can sign the key (see Figure 8-29), choose how much you trust the key, and whether others can see it and if you want to be able to revoke it. Then click the Sign button to sign the key.

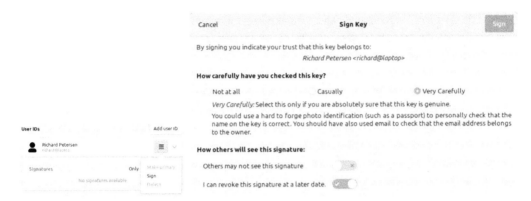

Figure 8-29: GnuPGP key dialog: Details tab

Keyservers

When you created your own private key, you also generated a corresponding public key that others can use to encrypt data they send to you and decrypt signatures of messages you send to them. Many applications will publish public keys that you can download and import to your system with Seahorse. The keys are available on keyservers. To manage your keyservers, choose Preferences from the Seahorse folder menu to open the Preferences dialog (see Figure 8-30). Here you can specify the keyservers to access. Two default servers are listed: **hkp://keyserver.ubuntu.com:11371** and **ldap://keyserver.pgp.com**. To add a keyserver, click the Add button to open a dialog where you enter the keyserver address and port. You will see the keyserver added to the list.

Figure 8-30: Seahorse Preferences - Keyservers

The list of keyservers in the Linux Mint installation of Seahorse does not have the Ubuntu keyserver. You may want to add it to your list of keyservers. Click the "Add keyserver" button to open an "Add Key Server" dialog (see Figure 8-31). For the "Key server type" choose the HTTP Key Server". This will have a protocol **hkp://** (for HTTPS Key Servers the protocol is **hkps://**). Enter just the key server name and domain, as in:

```
keyserver.ubuntu.com
```

Be sure to also add the port number, 11371. The address generated would be:

```
hkp://keyserver.ubuntu.com:11371
```

Cancel	**Add Key Server**	Save
Key Server Type:	HTTP Key Server	▼
Host:	keyserver.ubuntu.com : 11371	

Figure 8-31: Seahorse Add Key Server

Click the Save button to save the keyserver address and add the keyserver to the list of Seahorse keyservers. The new keyserver will appear in the list of keyservers. Figure 8-32 shows the Ubuntu keyserver added to the list.

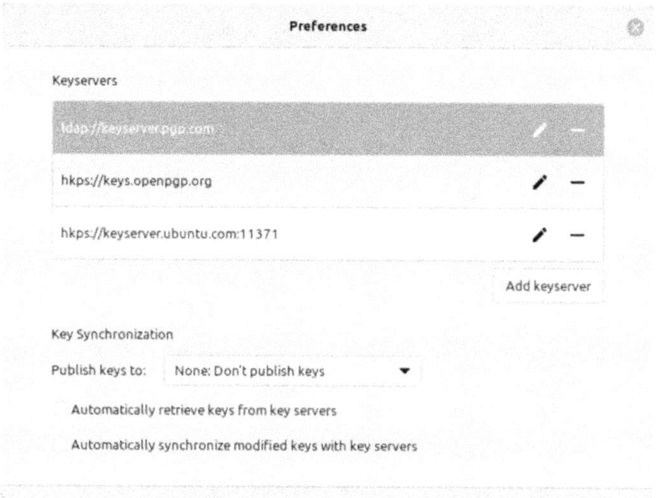

Preferences

Keyservers

ldap://keyserver.pgp.com

hkps://keys.openpgp.org

hkps://keyserver.ubuntu.com:11371

Add keyserver

Key Synchronization

Publish keys to: None: Don't publish keys ▼

Automatically retrieve keys from key servers

Automatically synchronize modified keys with key servers

Figure 8-32: Seahorse Preferences with added Ubuntu key server

Importing Public Keys

In the "Passwords and Keys" dialog, press **Ctrl-i** to import a public key from a file you have already downloaded to your system. Alternatively, if you know the name of the key, you can try searching the keyservers for it. Choose "Find remote keys" from the "Passwords and Keys" folder menu on the left side of the title bar to open the Find Remote Keys dialog where you can enter a search string for the key (see Figure 8-33). The search term is treated as a prefix, matching on all possible completions. The keyservers to search are listed in the "Where to search" section, with checkboxes to choose those you want searched.

Results are listed in a new window labeled "Remote keys containing" (see Figure 8-34). Select the one you want, and then click the download/import button to the right of the key entry to import the key. To see information about a key, double click the entry (see Figure 8-35).

Information about the owner (Owner tab), the trust level (Trust tab), and details about the key such as type and strength are displayed (Details tab).

Figure 8-33: Searching for keys

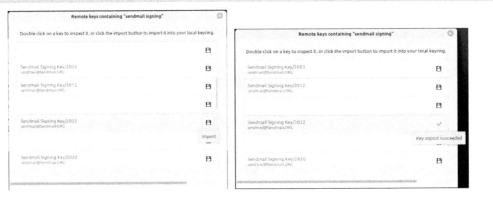

Figure 8-34: Importing keys

Figure 8-35: Key information

Once you have imported the key, it will appear in the "GnuPG keys" tab in the Passwords And Keys window (see Figure 8-36). The Seahorse menu on the right side of the title bar lists the types of keys to display: Show personal, Show trusted, and Show any. For newly imported keys, be sure to choose the "Show any" option otherwise the new entry will not be displayed.

Figure 8-36: Imported keys

If you know that you can trust the key, you can sign it, making it a valid key. Double click on its entry, or right-click and select Properties, to open its Properties dialog, and in the Trust section (see Figure 8-37), click the "Signature trust" switch. Then click the "Sign Key" button to open the Sign key dialog (see Figure 8-38). You are asked how carefully you have checked the key: Not at all, Casually, or Very Carefully. You also choose whether others can see your signature and if you can revoke it later. Then click the Sign button. A dialog appears prompting you to enter your GPG passphrase. On the Properties dialog, the Sign entry is replaced by a "Revoke key signature" entry, and the User ID section lists the key signatures (see Figure 8-39). The key is then listed as a trusted key when you choose the "Show trusted" option in the Seahorse menu (see Figure 8-40).

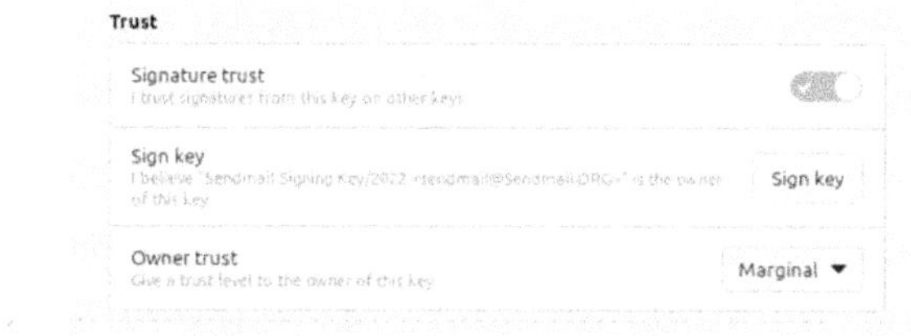

Trust

Signature trust
I trust signatures from this key on other keys

Sign key
I believe "Sendmail Signing Key/2022 <sendmail@Sendmail.ORG>" is the owner
of this key   Sign key

Owner trust
Give a trust level to the owner of this key   Marginal ▼

Figure 8-37: Imported key Trust tab for an unsigned key

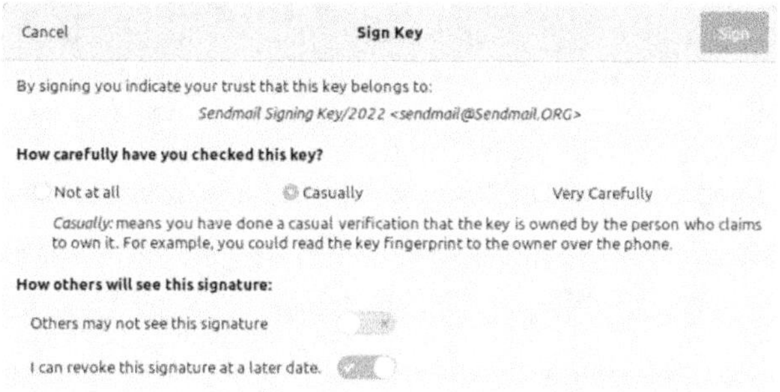

Cancel   **Sign Key**   Sign

By signing you indicate your trust that this key belongs to:
Sendmail Signing Key/2022 <sendmail@Sendmail.ORG>

How carefully have you checked this key?

Not at all   ○ Casually   Very Carefully

Casually: means you have done a casual verification that the key is owned by the person who claims
to own it. For example, you could read the key fingerprint to the owner over the phone.

How others will see this signature:

Others may not see this signature   ⬜

I can revoke this signature at a later date.   ⬜

Figure 8-38: Signing a key

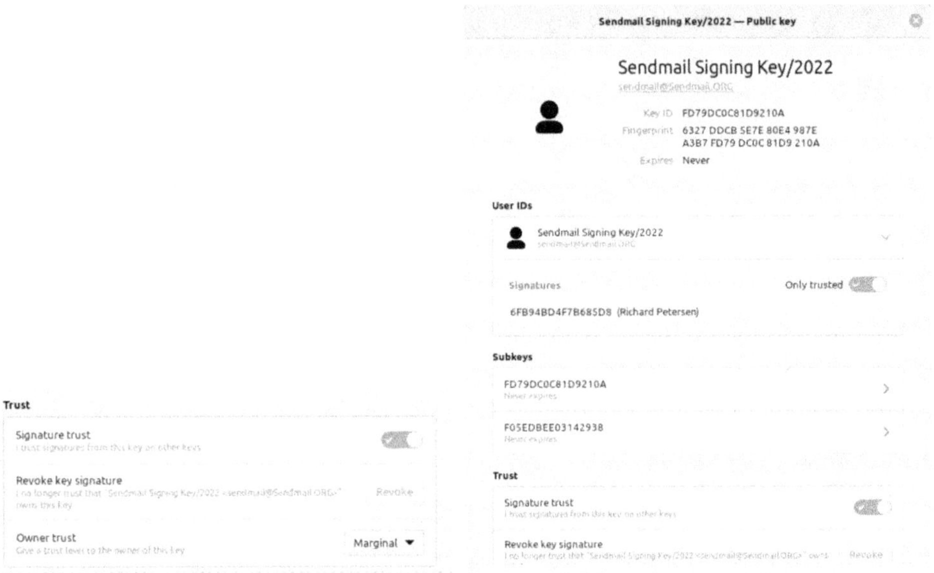

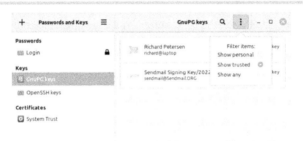

Figure 8-39: Signed key

Figure 8-40: Trusted keys

Sharing Keys

To make your public key available to others, you can export it to a file to send directly to other users, automatically share it with other users on your system, or publish on a keyserver. You export your public key to a **.pgp** binary file by right-clicking on it and choosing Export from the pop-up menu. Alternatively, you can export the public key to an ASCII-armored coded **.asc** text file by opening the key's Properties dialog, selecting the Details tab, and then clicking the "Export" button and selecting "Export public key." You can do this for your private (secret) key also.

You can also share your key by publishing it on a public keyserver for anyone to download and import. On the Seahorse Preferences dialog (folder menu), from the "Publish Keys to:" menu you can choose the keyserver to publish to or choose not to publish (the default) (see Figure 8-41). You also have the options to automatically retrieve keys and synchronize modified keys. To then publish a key choose "Sync and publish keys" from the Seahorse folder menu to open the Sync Keys dialog and click the Sync button. The Key Servers button opens the Preferences dialog showing the keyservers, letting you choose the one you want to publish to ("Publish keys to" menu).

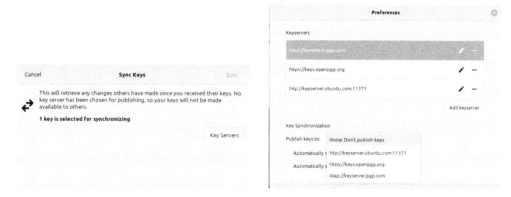

Figure 8-41: Seahorse Preferences

Seahorse integrates support for GPG. Should you import a key with the **gpg** command, it will appear in the GnuPG keys tab. Also, you can sign a key using the **gpg** command with the **--sign-key** option and the key is validated.

9. System Administration

Linux Mint Administrative Tools

Controlled Administrative Access

Users and Groups (Cinnamon and MATE)

Bluetooth

File System Access

Shared Folders

GRUB Bootloader

Editing Configuration Files Directly

Backup Management

Logical Volume Management

Most administrative configurations tasks are performed for you automatically. Devices like printers, hard drive partitions, and graphics cards are detected and set up for you. There are cases where you may need to perform tasks, manually like adding new users and installing software. Such administrative operations can be performed with user-friendly system tools. Most administration tools are listed in the Administration and Preferences menus.

Linux Mint Administration Tools	Description
Software Manager	Software management using online repositories
Update Manager	Update tool using Linux Mint repositories
Synaptic Package Manager	Software management using online repositories (no longer supported by Linux Mint, available on the Universe repository)
apt	Command line tool to install software
Network Manager	Detects, connects, and configures your network interfaces
Users and Groups	User configuration tool
system-config-printer	Printer configuration tool
gnome-language-selector	Selects a language to use
Gufw	Configures your network firewall
FirewallD	FirewallD firewall daemon
Deja-dup	Backup tool using rsync
Backup Tool	Linux Mint backup tool

Table 9-1: Linux Mint Administration Tools

Administrative Tools

Administration is handled by a set of specialized administrative tools, such as those for user management and printer configuration (see Table 9-1). To access the desktop-based administrative tools, you need to log in as a user who has administrative access. You created this user when you first installed Linux Mint. System administrative tools are accessed from the Administration, Preferences, and Accessories menus. On the Cinnamon desktop, you can also access tools from the System Settings dialog. There are tools to set the time and date, manage users, configure printers, and install software. Users and Groups lets you create and modify users. Printers lets you install and reconfigure printers. All tools provide easy-to-use and intuitive desktop interfaces. Tools are identified by simple descriptive terms.

Linux Mint uses the GNOME administrative tools, administrative tools adapted from the Fedora distribution supported by Red Hat Linux, and independent tools developed by open source projects. PolicyKit is used for device authorizations, and Linux Mint's Software Manager and the **apt** command, provide software management. The Synaptic Package Manager is available, but no longer supported.

Virus protection is handled by a third party application, ClamAV.

Many configuration tasks can also be handled on the command line, invoking programs directly. To use the command line, select the Terminal entry in the Administration menu to open a terminal window with a command line prompt. You will need administrative authorization, so precede the application name with the **sudo** command.

Controlled Administrative Access

To access administrative tools, you have to log in as a user who has administrative permissions. The user that you created during installation is given administrative permissions automatically. Log in as that user. When you attempt to use an administrative tool, a dialog opens prompting you to enter your user password. This is the password for the user you logged in as. Some tools will open without authorization but remain locked, preventing any modifications. These tools may have an Unlock button you can press to gain access. You can use the user management tool, Users and Groups, to grant or deny particular users administrative access.

To perform system administration operations, you must first have to have access rights enabling you to perform administrative tasks. There are several ways to gain such access: login as a sudo supported user, unlocking an administrative tool for access (PolicyKit authorization), and logging in as the **root** user. PolicyKit is the preferred access method and is used on many administrative tools. The **sudo** granted access method was used in previous Linux Mint releases and is still used for many tasks including software upgrade and installation. The **root** user access is still discouraged but provides complete control over the entire system.

PolicyKit: Provides access only to specific applications and only to users with administrative access for that application. Requires that the specific application be configured for use by PolicyKit. Linux Mint 21 uses the policykit-1version of PolicyKit. The original version, which is named simply policykit, is no longer available.

sudo and **pkexec**: Provides access to any application will full administrative authorization. It imposes a time limit to reduce risk. The **pkexec** command is used for graphical administrative tools like the Synaptic Package Manager. You will still need to use **sudo** to perform any command-line Linux commands at the administrative level, like moving files to an administrative directory or running the **systemctl** command to start or stop servers.

root user access, **su**: Provides complete direct control over the entire system. This is the traditional method for accessing administrative tools. It is disabled by default on Linux Mint, but can be enabled. The **su** command will allow any user to log in as the **root** user if they know the **root** user password.

nemo with administrative access: From the desktop Cinnamon menu (right-click on the desktop), you can choose the "Open as Root" option to open the Nemo file manager with administrative access. The file manager window displays a red bar below the toolbar showing "Elevated Privileges" title. You can then remove and modify any system files. This remains the most dangerous method of access, as you could easily remove or change critical system files and folders. Deletes are permanent and cannot be undone.

PolicyKit

PolicyKit controls access to certain applications and devices. It is one of the safest ways to grant a user direct access. PolicyKit configuration and support is already set up for you. A new version of PolicyKit, PolicyKit-1, is now used for PolicyKit operations. Configuration files for these operations are held in **/usr/share/polkit-1**. There is, as yet, no desktop tool you can use to configure these settings.

Note: External hard drives, such as USB connected hard drives, are mounted automatically

Difficulties occur if you want to change the authorization setting for certain actions, like mounting internal hard drives. Currently, you can change the settings by manually editing the configuration files in the **/usr/share/polkit-1/actions** directory. To make changes, you first have to know the action to change and the permission to set. The man page for **polkit** lists possible authorizations. The default authorizations are **allow_any** for anyone, **allow_inactive** for a console, and **allow_active** for an active console only (user logged in). These authorizations can be set to the following specific values.

auth_admin	Administrative user only, authorization required always
auth_admin_keep	Administrative user only, authorization kept for a brief period
auth_self	User authorization required
auth_self_keep	User authorization required authorization kept for a brief period
yes	Always allow access
no	Never allow access

You will need to know the PolicyKit action to modify and the file to edit. The action is listed in the PolicyKit dialog that prompts you to enter the password (expand the Details arrow) when you try to use an application. The filename will be the first segments of the action name with the suffix "policy" attached. For example, the action for mounting internal drives is:

```
org.freedesktop.udisks2.filesystem-mount-system
```

Its file is:

```
org.freedesktop.udisks2.policy
```

The file is located in the **/usr/share/polkit-1/actions** directory. It's full path name is:

```
/usr/share/polkit-1/actions/org.freedesktop.UDisks2.policy
```

Users with administrative access, like your primary user, can mount partitions on your hard drives automatically. However, users without administrative access require authorization using an administrative password before they can mount a partition (see Figure 9-13). Should you want to allow non-administrative users to mount partitions without an authorization request, the **org.freedesktop.UDisks2.policy** file in the **/usr/share/polkit-1** directory has to be modified to change the **allow_active** default for **filesystem-mount-system** action from **auth_admin_keep** to **yes**. The **auth_admin_keep** option requires administrative authorization.

Enter the following to edit the **org.freedesktop.UDisks2.policy** file in the **/usr/share/polkit-1/actions** directory.

```
sudo xed /usr/share/polkit-1/actions/org.freedesktop.UDisks2.policy
```

Locate the **action id** labeled as:

```
<action id ="org.feedesktop.udisks2.filesystem-mount-system">
  <description>Mount a filesystem on a system device</description>
```

This is usually the second action id. At the end of that action section, you will find the following entry. It will be located within a defaults subsection, <defaults>.

```
<allow_active>auth_admin_keep</allow_active>
```

Replace **auth_admin_keep** with **yes**.

```
<allow_active>yes</allow_active>
```

Save the file. Non-administrative users will no longer have to enter a password to mount partitions.

sudo

The sudo service provides administrative access to specific users. You have to be a user on the system with a valid username and password that has been authorized by the sudo service for administrative access. This allows other users to perform specific super user operations without having full administrative level control. You can find more about sudo at **https://www.sudo.ws**.

TIP: If you have difficulties with your system configuration, check the Linux Mint forum and community sites for possible solutions, https://forums.linuxmint.com and https://community.linuxmint.com.

sudo command

Some administrative operations require access from the command line in the terminal window. For such operations, you would use the **sudo** command. You can open a terminal window from Accessories menu. On the Cinnamon desktop, you click the terminal icon on the panel or on the favorites bar in the Cinnamon menu.

To use **sudo** to run an administrative command, you would precede the command with the **sudo** command. You are then prompted to enter your password. You will be issued a time-restricted ticket to allow access. The following example sets the system date using the **date** command.

```
sudo date 0406165908
password:
```

You can also use the **sudo** command to run an application with administrative access. From the terminal window, you would enter the **sudo** command with the application name as an argument. For example, to use the **nano** editor to edit a system configuration file, you would start **nano** using the **sudo** command in a terminal window, with the **nano** command and the filename as its argument. This starts up the **nano** editor with administrator privileges. The following example will allow you to edit the **/etc/fstab** file to add or edit file system entries. You will be prompted for your user password.

```
sudo nano /etc/fstab
```

sudo configuration

Access for **sudo** is controlled by the **/etc/sudoers** file. This file lists users and the commands they can run, along with the password for access. If the NOPASSWD option is set, then users will not need a password. The ALL option, depending on the context, can refer to all hosts on your network, all root-level commands, or all users. See the Man page for **sudoers** for detailed information on all options.

```
man sudoers
```

To make changes or add entries, you have to edit the file with the special sudo editing command **visudo**. This invokes the **nano** editor (see Chapter 5) to edit the **/etc/sudoers** file. Unlike a standard editor, **visudo** will lock the **/etc/sudoers** file and check the syntax of your entries. You are not allowed to save changes unless the syntax is correct. If you want to use a different editor, you can assign it to the EDITOR shell variable. Use Ctrl-x to exit and Ctrl-o to save. Be sure to invoke **visudo** with the **sudo** command to gain authorized access.

```
sudo visudo
```

A **sudoers** entry has the following syntax:

```
user    host=command
```

The *host* is a host on your network. You can specify all hosts with the ALL term. The *command* can be a list of commands, some or all qualified by options such as whether a password is required. To specify all commands, you can also use the ALL term. The following gives the user **george** full root-level access to all commands on all hosts.

```
george  ALL = ALL
```

In addition, you can let a user run as another user on a given host. Such alternate users are placed within parentheses before the commands. For example, if you want to give **george** access to the **beach** host as the user **mydns**, you use the following.

```
george beach = (mydns) ALL
```

To specify a group name, you prefix the group with a **%** sign, as in **%mygroup**. This way, you can give the same access to a group of users. By default, **sudo** will grant access to all users in the **admin** group. These are user granted administrative access. The ALL=(ALL) ALL entry allows access by the administrative group users to all hosts as all users to all commands.

```
%admin  ALL=(ALL)    ALL
```

With the NOPASSWD option, you can allow members of a certain group access without a password. A commented **sudo** group is provided in the **/etc/sudoers** file.

```
%sudo   ALL=NOPASSWD:   ALL
```

Though on Linux Mint, **sudo** is configured to allow **root** user access, Linux Mint does not create a **root** user password. This prevents you from logging in as the **root** user, rendering the **sudo** root permission useless. The default **/etc/sudoers** file does configure full access for the **root** user to all commands. The ALL=(ALL) ALL entry allows access by the **root** user to all hosts as all users to all commands. If you were to set up a password for the **root** user, the **root** user could then log in and have full administrative access.

```
root    ALL=(ALL)    ALL
```

If you want to see what commands you can run, you use the **sudo** command with the -**l** option. The -**U** option specifies a particular user. In the following example, the user richard has full administrative access.

```
$ sudo -U richard -l
User richard may run the following commands on this host:
    (ALL) All
```

Root User Access: root and su

You can access the root user from any normal terminal window using the **sudo** command on the **su** command. The **su** command is the superuser command. Superuser is another name for the **root** user. A user granted administrative access by **sudo** could then become the **root** user. The following logs into the root user.

```
sudo su
```

Like Ubuntu, Linux Mint is designed never to let anyone directly log in as the root user. The **root** user would have total control over the entire system. Instead, certain users are given administrative access with which they can separately access administrative tools, performing specific tasks. Even though a **root** user exists, a password for the root user is not defined, never allowing access to it.

It is possible activate the root user by using the **passwd** command to create a **root** user password. Enter the **passwd** command with the **root** username in a **sudo** operation.

```
sudo passwd root
```

You are prompted for your administrative password and then prompted by the **passwd** command to enter a password for the **root** user. You are then prompted to repeat the password.

```
Enter new UNIX password:
Retype new UNIX password:
passwd: password updated successfully
```

You can then log in with the **su** command as the root user, making you the superuser (you still cannot login as the root user from the display manager login window). Because a superuser has the power to change almost anything on the system, such a password is usually a carefully guarded secret, changed very frequently, and given only to those whose job it is to manage the system. With the correct password, you can log into the system as a system administrator and configure the system any way you want.

```
su root
```

The **su** command alone will assume the root username.

```
su
```

The **su** command can also be used to login to any user, provided you have that user's password.

```
su richard
```

To exit from a **su** login operation, just enter **exit**.

```
exit
```

Nemo with elevated privileges on Cinnamon desktop

The easiest way to edit system files on the Cinnamon desktop is to open the Nemo file manager with elevated privileges, essentially opening a file manager window that has root (administrative) access. To edit a configuration file in the /**etc** directory, you could then use the file manager to access the /**etc** directory, and then double-click on the file to open it with the Xed editor. This opens the file in Xed with administrative access, letting you change it easily. A red bar below the navigation bar displays an "Elevated Privileges" notice so that you know you are running the file manager with administrative access. To open the file manager with elevated privileges, open the desktop menu (right-click on the desktop) and choose the "Open as Root" entry (see Figure 9-1).

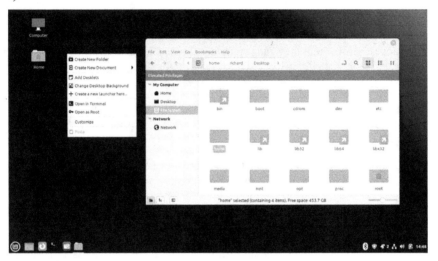

Figure 9-1: Nemo File Manager with Elevated Privileges (as root)

To do this you have to be a user with administrative access (not a standard user). You are first prompted to enter your password (see Figure 9-2). Clicking on the File System entry in the sidebar places you at the root directory where you can access the system folders and files (see Figure 9-1).

Figure 9-2: Prompt to open file manager as root (administrative access)

You can add or remove system folders and files. Be careful of what actions you take. It is easy to use file manager operations to delete critical system folders and files, which would have catastrophic consequences for your system. Deletes are permanent and cannot be undone. At the same time, if you are careful and know what you want to do, this an easy way to edit system configuration files. In Figure 9-3, the user has opened the **grub** configuration file in the **/etc/default** folder, which can then be edited directly. When invoked from the file manager with elevated privileges, the Xed editor has administrative access letting it change system files. A red bar below the toolbar displays an "Elevated Messages" notice so that you know you are running the Xed editor with administrative access.

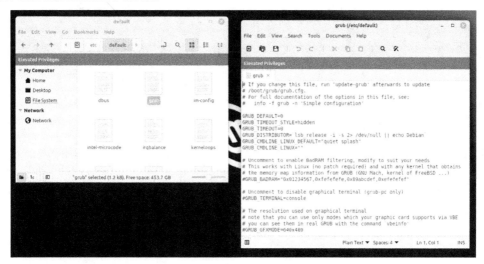

Figure 9-3: Editing System Files from the file manager opened as root

pkexec

You can use the **pkexec** command in place of **sudo** to run graphical applications with administrative access. The **pkexec** tool is a policykit alternative to **sudo**, and requires that your application has a corresponding policykit action file. Applications like Users and Groups, Udisks, and NetworkManager already have action files. Others, like Xed, do not. To use **pkexec** with Xed, you have to create a policykit action file for it. This is a simple process, copying most of the entries from the example in the **pkexec** man page. The askubuntu site (**https://askubuntu.com**) also has a detailed explanation on how to do this (search on "pkexec" and open the "How to configure pkexec" entry). Whenever you use the **pkexec** tool, it will prompt you to enter your password (See Figure 9-4).

Figure 9-4: pkexec prompt for secure access

You can enter the **pkexec** command in a terminal window with the application as an argument, or set up an application launcher with **pkexec** as the command. The following example will start up the Xed editor with administrative access, allowing you to edit system configuration files directly (see Figure 9-5). A red bar below the toolbar displays an "Elevated Messages" notice so that you know you are running the Xed editor with administrative access.

```
pkexec xed
```

One way to set up a policy file for an application such as Xed is to copy the example in the **pkexec** man page. Change the example entries to xed. For the message entry, you only need a simple message. Be sure to add an annotate line at the end for desktop access, setting the **exec.allow_gui** option to true.

```
<annotate key="org.freedesktop.policykit.exec.allow_gui">true</annotate>
```

Alternatively, you could simply copy a simple policy file, change the name, and edit it to replace the program names and the message (for example, making a copy of **com.ubuntu.pkexec.synaptic.policy** located in the **/usr/share/polkit-1/actions** folder).

You could open the file manager with elevated privileges (see following sectin) and then navigate to the /usr/share/polkit-1/actions folder. Then copy the **com.ubuntu.pkexec.synaptic.policy** file, change the name **synaptic** to **xed**, and double click on the that file to edit it. Alternatively you can use the **sudo** command. Use the **sudo** command with **cp** command in a terminal window to perform the copy.

sudo cp com.ubuntu.pkexec.synaptic.policy org.freedesktop.policykit.pkexec.xed.policy

Edit the file and replace **synaptic** with **xed**, and change the message.

A sample policy file for Xed is follows.

org.freedesktop.policykit.pkexec.xed.policy

```
<?xml version="1.0" encoding="UTF-8"?>
   <!DOCTYPE policyconfig PUBLIC
     "-//freedesktop//DTD PolicyKit Policy Configuration 1.0//EN"
     "http://www.freedesktop.org/standards/PolicyKit/1/policyconfig.dtd">
 <policyconfig>

  <action id="org.freedesktop.policykit.pkexec.xed">
    <description>Run the Xed program</description>
    <message>Authentication is required to run Xed to edit system files</message>
    <icon_name>xed</icon_name>
    <defaults>
       <allow_any>auth_admin</allow_any>
       <allow_inactive>auth_admin</allow_inactive>
       <allow_active>auth_admin</allow_active>
    </defaults>
    <annotate key="org.freedesktop.policykit.exec.path">/usr/bin/xed</annotate>
    <annotate key="org.freedesktop.policykit.exec.allow_gui">true</annotate>
  </action>

</policyconfig>
```

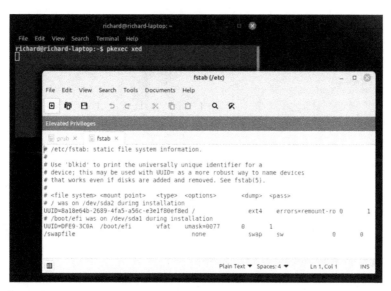

Figure 9-5: Invoking Xed with the pkexec command

/etc/hostname and hostnamectl

The **/etc/hostname** file contains your hostname. You can use the **hostnamectl** command in a terminal window to display your current hostname and all information pertaining to it such as the machine ID, the kernel used, the architecture, chassis (type of computer), and the operating system (you can add the **status** option if you want). Three different kinds of hostnames are supported: static, pretty, and transient. You can set each with the **hostnamectl**'s **set-hostname** command with the corresponding type. The static hostname is used to identify your computer on the network (usually a fully qualified hostname). You can use the **--static** option to set it. The pretty hostname is a descriptive hostname made available to users on the computer. This can be set by **set-hostname** with the **--pretty** option. The transient hostname is one allocated by a network service such as DHCP, and can be managed with the **--transient** option. Without options, the **set-hostname** command will apply the name to all the hostname types.

```
hostnamectl set-hostname --pretty "my computer"
```

The **set-chassis** command sets the computer type, which can be desktop, laptop, server, tablet, handset, and vm (virtual system). Without a type specified it reverts to the default for the system. The **set-icon-name** command sets the name used by the graphical applications for the host.

Users and Groups (cinnamon-settings-users)

On the Cinnamon desktop, you can configure and create users and groups using the Users and Groups tool accessible from the Administration menu, and also from the System Settings dialog. Users and Groups is the cinnamon-settings-users tool available on the Cinnamon desktop. Users and Groups provides control for both users and groups.

Figure 9-6: Users and Groups (Cinnamon)

The Users and Groups dialog displays two tabs: Users and Groups. The Users tab displays two panes, a left scrollable pane for a list of users, showing their icon and login name and a right pane showing information about a selected user (see Figure 9-6). Below the left pane are buttons for adding and deleting users.

PolicyKit controls administrative access. When you first start up Users and Groups, a dialog appears that asks you to enter your password. Access is granted only to users that are administrators (administrator account type). Once the Users and Groups dialog appears you can then add or delete users, and change the password, name, group, account type, and a picture of any existing user.

When you add a new account, a dialog opens letting you set the account type (standard or administrator), the full name of the user, and the username (see Figure 9-7). Click Add to create the user. The new account appears on the right pane showing the name, icon, account type, password, and groups.

Figure 9-7: Users and Groups: new users

The account remains inactive until you specify a password (see Figure 9-8). The password entry displays the text "No password set." Click on the password entry to open the "Change Password" dialog open where you can enter the new password (see Figure 9-9). The "Show password" checkbox lets you see what the password is. Once the password is selected, the account becomes enabled.

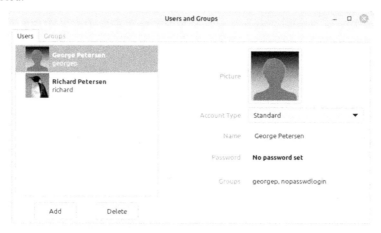

Figure 9-8: Users and Groups: inactive user

To choose an icon, click on the icon image to open an icon selection menu. Choose the one you want, or click on the "Browse for more pictures" entry at the bottom of the menu to open an image selection dialog to locate an image of your own.

You can change the icon, account type, name, password, and group selection by clicking on their entries.

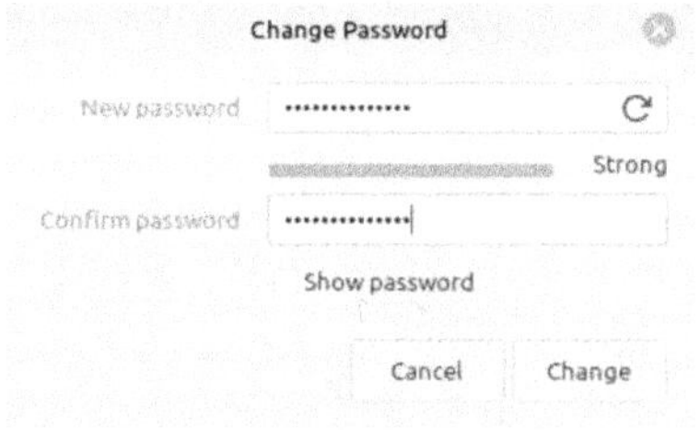

Figure 9-9: Users and Groups: password dialog

To manage groups, click the Groups tab on the Users and Groups window. This displays a list of all groups (see Figure 9-10). To add a new group, click the Add button to open a dialog, where you can specify the group name (see Figure 9-11). If you want to remove a group, just select its entry in the Groups tab window and click the Delete button.

You use the Users tab on the Users and Groups window to add or remove users to or from a group. To add or remove a group for a user, select that user, and then click on the user's group entries (Groups). This opens a dialog listing all available groups (see Figure 9-12). Those that the user already belongs to are checked. You can add the users to a group by simply clicking the checkbox for that group. Uncheck groups you want to remove the user from.

Figure 9-10: Users and Groups: Groups tab

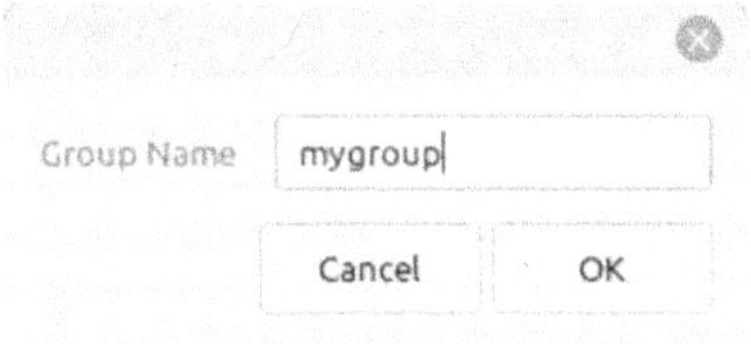

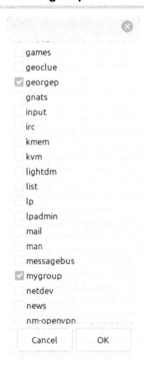

Figure 9-11: Users and Groups: add a group

Figure 9-12: Users and Groups: Users group dialog

Users and Groups (MATE)

The MATE desktop uses the older "Users and Groups" application (users-admin), accessible from "User and Groups" on the Administration menu. You can also install it on the Cinnamon desktop by installing the **gnome-system-tools** package. The "Users and Groups" application opens a User Settings window, which displays two panes, a left scrollable pane for a list of users, showing their icon and login name, and a right pane showing information about a selected user. Below the left pane are buttons for adding and deleting users, and for managing groups. At the bottom of the right pane is a button for a selected user's Advanced Settings.

When you start up the users-admin application, only read access is allowed, letting you scroll through the list of users, but not make any changes or add new ones (see Figure 9-13). Read-only access is provided to all users. Users will be able to see the list of users on your system, but they cannot modify their entries, add new ones, or delete current users. Administrative access is required to perform these operations.

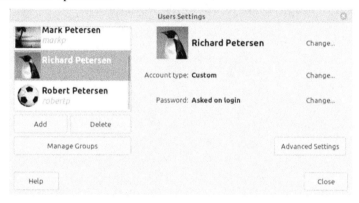

Figure 9-13: Users and Groups (MATE)

PolicyKit controls administrative access for the users-admin tool. When you first click a task button, such as Add, Delete, or Advanced Settings, an Authenticate dialog will open and prompt you to enter your user password. You will also be prompted to authenticate if you click a Change link to change a user password, account type, or name.

To change settings for a user, select the user in the User Settings window. On the right pane the username, account type and password access are listed with a Change link to the right of each. Clicking on a Change link lets you change that property. When you click a Change link, an authentication dialog will prompt you to enter an administrative user password. To change a username, click the Change link to the right of the username to open the "Change Username and Login" dialog with a text box for entering the new name.

To change a user password, you would click the Change link to the right of the Password entry to open the "Change User Password" dialog with entries for the current password and the new password (see Figure 9-14). You can also choose to generate a random password.

Figure 9-14: User Settings: Change User Password dialog

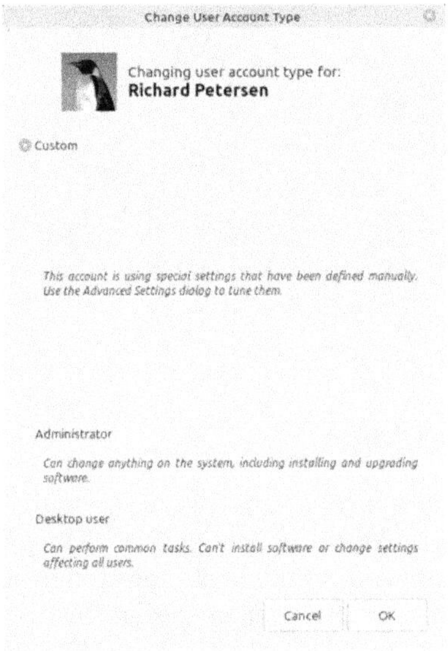

Figure 9-15: User Settings: Change User Account Type

An account type can be Administrator, Desktop User, or Custom. When you click the Change link for the Account type, the "Change User Account Type" dialog opens with options for each (see Figure 9-15).

For more detailed configuration, you click the Advanced Settings button to open the "Change Advanced User Settings" dialog, which has tabs for Contact Information, User Privileges, and Advanced (see Figure 9-16. On the Contact tab, you can add basic contact information if you wish, for an office address, as well as work and home phones.

On the User Privileges tab, you can control device access and administrative access (see Figure 9-13). You can restrict or allow access to CD-ROMs, scanners, and external storage like USB drives. You can also determine whether the user can perform administrative tasks. For a user to create a share, they have to have permission to do so. Desktop users are not given this permission, whereas administrative users are. To allow desktop users to share files check the "Share files with the local network" option.

The Advanced tab lets you select a home directory, the shell to use, a main group, and a user ID. Defaults are already chosen for you. A home directory in the name of the new user is specified and the shell used is the BASH shell. Normally you would not want to change these settings, though you might prefer to use a different shell, like the C-Shell. For the group, the user has a group with its own username (same as the short name).

Figure 9-16: Users and Groups: Change User Privileges

Should to you decide to delete a user, you are prompted to keep or delete the user's home directory along with the user's files.

New Users (Users and Groups)

To create a new user, click the Add button in the Users Settings window to open a "Create New User" dialog, where you can enter the username. A short name is automatically entered for you, using the user's first name and the first letter of the last name. You can change the short name if you wish, but it must be in lowercase. The short name is also the name of the new user main group (see Figure 9-17). The new user is then added to the User Settings window.

The "Change User Password" dialog is then displayed, with entries for the new password and confirmation. You can also choose to use a randomly generated password instead (see Figure 9-18). Click the Generate button generate a password.

If you decide not to enter a password (click Cancel), the account will remain disabled. To enable it later, click on the Enable Account button to open the "Change User Password" dialog where you can add the password.

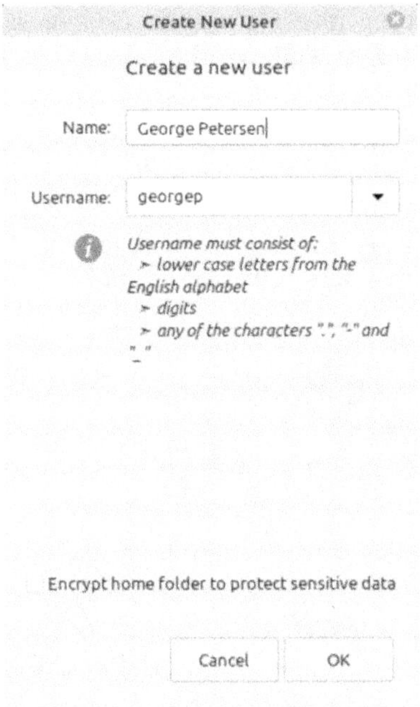

Figure 9-17: Users and Groups: Create New User

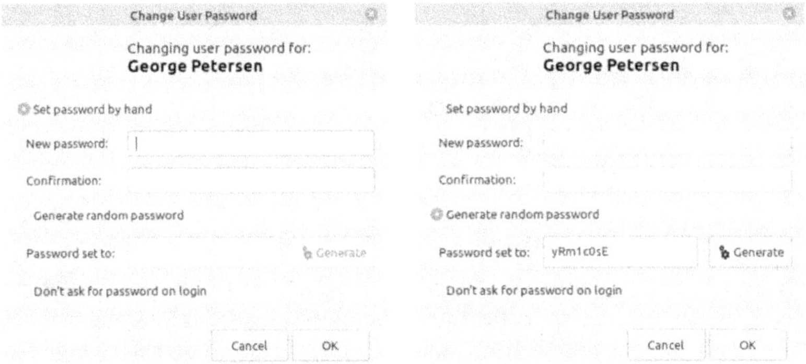

Figure 9-18: Users and Groups: new user password

The Account type is set initially to Desktop user, restricting access by the new user. Should you want to enable administrative access for this user, click the Change link to the right of the Account type entry to open the "Change User Account Type" dialog, where you can change the account type to Administrator (see Figure 9-15). To set more specific privileges and for key user configuration settings such as the home directory and user id, click the Advanced Settings button to open the "Change Advanced User Settings" dialog with Contact Information, User Privileges, and Advanced tabs (see Figure 9-16).

Alternatively, you can use the **useradd** command in a terminal window or command line to add Users and Groups and the **userdel** command to remove them. The following example adds the user **dylan** to the system:

```
$ useradd dylan
```

Groups (Users and Groups)

To manage groups, click the Manage Groups button in the Users Settings window. This opens a Group Settings dialog that lists all groups (see Figure 9-19). To add or remove users to or from a group, click the group name in the Group Settings dialog and click Properties. You can then check or uncheck users from the Group Members listing.

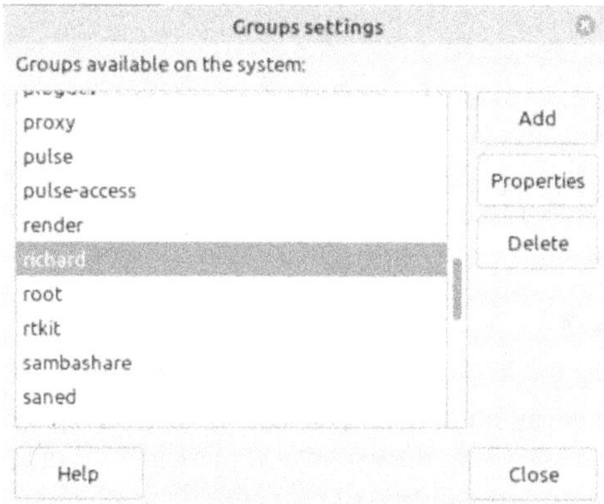

Figure 9-19: Users and Groups: Groups settings

To add a new group, click the Add Group button in the Group Settings dialog to open a New Group dialog, where you can specify the group name, its id, and select the users to add to the group (see Figure 9-20). If you want to remove a group, just select its entry in the Groups Settings window and click the Delete button.

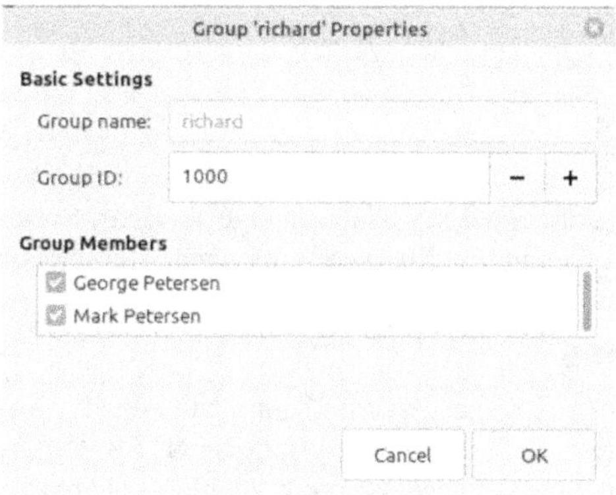

Figure 9-20: Group Properties: Group Users panel

Passwords

The easiest way to change your password is to use the Users and Groups dialog available from System Settings as Users and Groups, and from the Administration menu. Select your username, then click the link to the right of the Password label to open the Change Password dialog (see Figure 9-7).

Alternatively, you can use the **passwd** command. In a terminal window enter the **passwd** command. The command prompts you for your current password. After entering your current password and pressing ENTER, you are then prompted for your new password. After entering the new password, you are asked to re-enter it. This makes sure you have actually entered the password you intended to enter.

```
$ passwd
Changing password for richard.
(current) UNIX password:
Enter new UNIX password:
Retype new UNIX password:
passwd: password updated successfully
$
```

Managing Services

Many administrative functions operate as services that need to be turned on (see Chapter 12). They are daemons, constantly running and checking for requests for their services. When you install a service, its daemon is normally turned on automatically. You can start, stop, and restart a service from a terminal window using the **systemctl** command with the service name and the commands: **start**, **stop**, **restart**, and **status**. The status command tells you if a service is already running. To restart the Samba file sharing server (**smdb**) you would use the following command.

```
sudo systemctl restart smbd
```

To disable a service so that it is not turned on automatically, you would use the **disable** command. To have it turned on you use the **enable** command. The **enable** command starts up the service when you system starts. If you enable before a restart and want to run the service, you would use the **start** command.

```
sudo systemctl disable smbd
sudo systemctl enable smbd
sudo systemctl start smbd
```

Linux Mint and Ubuntu use systemd to manage services. Systemd services are managed using **.service** configuration files in the **/lib/systemd/system** and **/etc/systemd/system** directories.

File System Access

Various file systems can be accessed on Linux Mint easily. Any additional internal hard drive partitions on your system, both Linux and Windows NTFS, will be detected automatically, but not mounted. In addition, you can access remote Windows shared folders and make your shared folders accessible.

Access to Internal Linux File Systems

Linux Mint will automatically detect other Linux file systems (partitions) on all your internal hard drives. Entries for these partitions are displayed on a file manager sidebar's Computer section. Initially, they are not mounted. Administrative users can mount internal partitions by clicking on its entry or icon, which mounts the file system and displays its icon on the desktop. A file manager window opens displaying the top-level contents of the file system. The file system is mounted under the **/media** directory in a folder named with the file system (partition) label, or, if unlabeled, with the device UUID name.

Non-administrative users (users you create with a standard account type), cannot mount internal partitions unless the task is authenticated using an administrative user's password. An authorization window will appear. You will be asked to choose a user who has administrative access from a menu, and then enter that user's password. If there is only one administrative user, that user is selected automatically and you are prompted to enter that user's password. Whenever a standard user logs in again, that user will still have to mount the file system, again providing authorization.

Access to Windows NTFS File Systems on Local Drives

If you have installed Linux Mint on a dual-boot system with Windows, Linux NTFS file system support is installed automatically. Your NTFS partitions are mounted using Filesystem in Userspace (FUSE). The same authentication control used for Linux file systems applies to NTFS file systems. Entries for the NTFS partitions are placed on the file manager sidebar's Devices section with an eject button to mount and unmount the file system. If you are a user with administrative access, the file system is mounted (Eject button on file manager sidebar). If you are a user without administrative access, you will be asked to choose a user that has administrative access from a menu, and then enter that user's password, providing authorization. The NTFS file system is then mounted with icons displayed on the Launcher. You can access the file system by clicking on its desktop icon or its entry in a file manager sidebar Devices section. The partitions will be mounted under the **/media** directory with their UUID numbers or labels used as folder names. The NTFS partitions are mounted using **ntfs-3g** drivers.

Zero Configuration Networking: Avahi and Link Local Addressing

Zero Configuration Networking (Zeroconf) allows the setup of non-routable private networks without the need of a DHCP server or static IP addresses. A Zeroconf configuration lets users automatically connect to a network and access all network resources, such as printers, without having to perform any configuration. On Linux, Zeroconf networking is implemented by Avahi (**http://avahi.org**), which includes multicast DNS (mDNS) and DNS service discovery (DNS-SD) support that automatically detects services on a network. IP addresses are determined using either IPv6 or IPv4 Link Local (IPv4LL) addressing. IPv4 Link Local addresses are assigned from the 168.254.0.0 network pool. Derived from Apple's Bonjour Zeroconf implementation, it is a free and open source version currently used by desktop tools, such as the GNOME virtual file system. Ubuntu implements full Zeroconf network support with the Avahi daemon that implements multicast DNS discover, and **avahi-autoipd** that provides dynamic configuration of local IPv4 addresses. Both are installed as part of the desktop configuration. Avahi support tools like **avahi-browse** and **avahi-publish** are located in the **avahi-utils** package.

Permissions for Shared Folders in User Home Folders

New and fresh installations of either Linux Mint 21 or Ubuntu 22.04 implements an added security measure for protecting users home folders. In previous releases the permissions for user home folders was set to allow any user read access to anyone's home folder. This has been changed to restrict access to the user only. The permissions for user home folders in prior releases in octal format was 755, with the last 5 allowing read and execute permission to anyone (other). This has been changed to 750, removing any permissions for other users. In symbolic format the permissions would be **u+rwx** and **g+rx**, with no entries for **o**, the other users.

```
$ ls -ld /home/richard
drwxr-x---  16 richard richard 4096 Sep 25 10:23  /home/richard
```

This restriction means that you can no longer share folders in your home folder. The mDNS (Avahi) operation is denied access and will not work on any shared folder in a user's home folder.

One way around this restriction is to the change the permission of the user's home folder. For users that want to share a folder in their home folder, you can simply change their home folder permission to 755, allowing access (read and execute) to any users. These are the less secure permissions used in previous releases. You can use the **chmod** command in a terminal window to change the permission.

```
sudo chmod 755 /home/richard
```

or

```
sudo chmod o+rx /home/richard
```

You could also open the file manager as the root user from the desktop menu, navigate to the **/home** folder, and then right-click on the user folder you want to change permissions for, and select Properties. On the Permissions tab change the Folder access permission (the last permission) to the kind of access you want to allow, "List Files only" for read access only, and "Create and delete files" for read and write permission (see Figure 9-21).

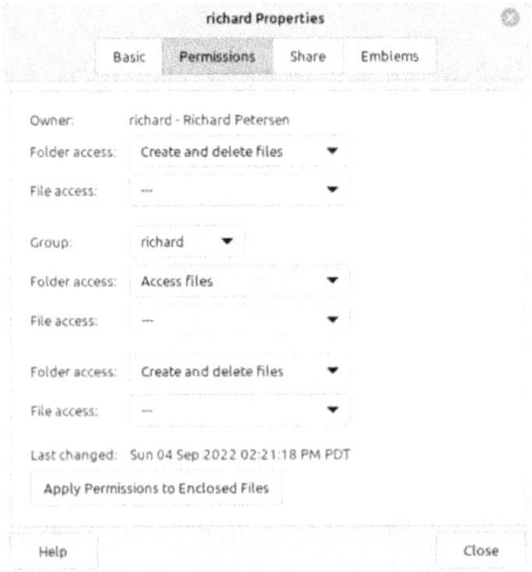

Figure 9-21: Access permission on user's home folder

Reverting back to the original permissions loses the protections for user folders provided with the new permissions (750). There is a way to keep these protections and still allow shared folders in a user's home folder. You can set up a share definition for the shared folder in the Samba **/etc/smb.conf** file. You will have to add **force** commands to the configuration to allow other user to access the shared folder, as if they were you. You will need a **force** command for the create, directory, and user options, setting the mode to 0666 (read and write for all users) for the create, and 0777 (read, write, and execute for all users) for the shared folder (directory). For the user, specify the user's user name.

```
force create mode = 0666
force directory mode = 0777
force user = richard
```

The following example sets up the Documents folder in the user richard's home folder as a shared folder open to other users. The configuration allows read and write access (writable = yes).

```
[Documents]
path = /home/richard/Documents
guest ok = yes
browsable = yes
writable = yes
read only = no
force create mode = 0666
force directory mode = 0777
force user richard
```

Be sure that Samba is installed. You can use the "Open as root" entry in the desktop menu to open the file manager as an administrator and then navigate to the the the **/etc/samba/** folder. Double click on the file **smb.conf** file to edit it and add the share entry at the end. Then save the file. In a terminal window you can then use **systemctl** command to restart the samba server, **smbd**.

```
sudo systemctl restart smbd
```

Other users can now use mDNS (Avahi) and Samba to access the shared folder in that user's home folder. Other local Linux users can use nDNS Avahi to access the share folder, and Windows systems can use Samba to access it.

Access to Linux Local Network Shared File Systems with mDNS (Avahi)

Once configured, shared Windows folders and printers on any of the computers connected to your local network are accessible from any file manager window sidebar. The multicast DNS discovery service, mDNS (called Avahi in Linux), automatically detects hosts on your home or local network. Supporting Samba libraries are already installed and will let you directly access any shared folders. Shared folders in user home folders can also be accessed with the correct configuration as noted in the previous section.

You can use the multicast DNS discovery service (Avahi) to access any shared Linux folders on Linux systems that are running a Samba server. For such Linux system network browsing is enabled. You can open the Network folder on the file manager to see the other Linux systems on your network. Double click on the one you want to access to open a listing of the shared folders on that system. The shared folders are then displayed (see Figure 9-22). Double click on the folder you want to open it. You are first asked to login using the remote systems user name and password (see Figure 9-23). It is mounted on your system, with and entry for it on the file manager sidebar and an icon for it on the desktop. When finished, you can eject the folder using either the sidebar entry or the icon's menu (right-click) (see Figure 9-24).

Figure 9-22: Accessing shared folders using multicast DNS discovery (Avahi)

Figure 9-23: Permission to access a remote shared Linux folder

Figure 9-24: Accessing and mounting a shared Linux folders using Avahi

If you are using a firewall, be sure that it is configured for access to allow multicast DNS discovery. For the UFW firewall installed with Linux Mint, access for multicast DNS discovery service is already configured (UDP port 5353). For FirewallD, on firewall-config (Administration | Firewall), be sure that the **mdns** service is enabled, both runtime and permanent (Zones | Services tab) (see Figure 9-25) .

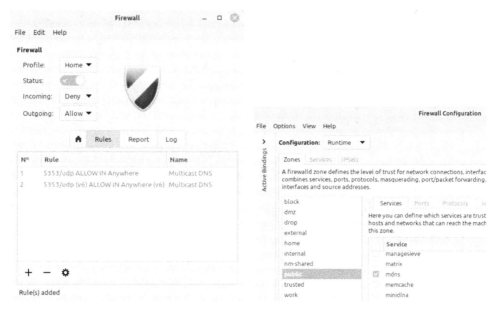

Figure 9-25: Gufw and FirewallD configuration for multicast DNS discovery (Avahi), mdns service

Problems can occur if the discovery process is not able to resolve the names of the hosts on your network. The multicast DNS discovery (mdns) service will append a **.local** to your host name for use by mdns, such as **richard-laptop.local**. If your host has the **.local** extension added irregularly or if it is missing, you will not be detected on your network. The way to ensure that your host is referenced is to create a **/etc/mdns.allow** file with entries for the **.local** and **.local.** which will remove the strict mdns requirement for the **.local** part of the host name. In the **/mdns.allow** file place the two lines as shown here.

/etc/mdns.allow
```
.local
.local.
```

In addition, you have to use **mdns4** instead of **mdns4_minimal** in the **/etc/nsswitch.conf** file. **mdns4_minimal** does not check the **/etc/mdns.allow** file, whereas **mdns4** does check it. In the **/etc/nsswitch.conf** file, modify the current hosts line:

```
hosts    files mdns4_minimal [NOTFOUND=return] dns myhostname
```

to the following:

```
hosts    files mdns4 [NOTFOUND=return] dns myhostname
```

Discovery is handled by the **nss-mdns** tool. For more information check:

```
https://github.com/lathiat/nss-mdns
```

Access to Windows Local Network Shared File Systems with Avahi

Currently, both Linux and Windows are in the process of transitioning from the older SMBv1 protocol (Secure Message Block) to the more secure SMBv3 protocol. As a result, network browsing through the Linux file manager does not work currently. You can access Windows shares directly either by entering the shared folder's address directly in the location box of any file manager window, or by using the Connect to Server dialog, accessible from the file manager's File menu.

To access Windows shares directly from the location box, enter in the **smb://** protocol (Avahi), the host name of the Windows system, and the name of the shared folder. You will be asked to provide authorization, as in Figure 9-26, specifying the host name and password. Then press ENTER. A file manage window will open to the shared folder (see Figure 9-27).

On the Connect to Server dialog (File menu) first be sure to select the "Windows share" entry in the Type menu. Then enter the host name of the Windows system (Server) and the name of the shared folder (Share) (see Figure 9-27). Add the user name and password if needed. Then click Connect. A file manage window will open to the shared folder (see Figure 9-28).

The Network section of the file manager sidebar will show an entry for the folder with an Eject button for un-mounting it, as well as an icon for the folder on the desktop. Figure 9-28 shows the **myshared-data** shared folder on a Windows system mounted on the Network window and on the desktop.

You can also use these methods to browse all the shared folders on a specific Windows system. Instead of including a shared folder, you simply specify the host preceded by the **smb://** protocol (see Figure 9-29). You can then double-click on a shared folder to mount it.

If you are using a firewall, be sure that it is configured for access by Samba. For Gufw (Preferences | Firewall Configuration), be sure that the rules are added for Samba. For FirewallD, on firewall-config (Administration | Firewall), be sure that samba and samba-client services are enabled (Zones | Services tab).

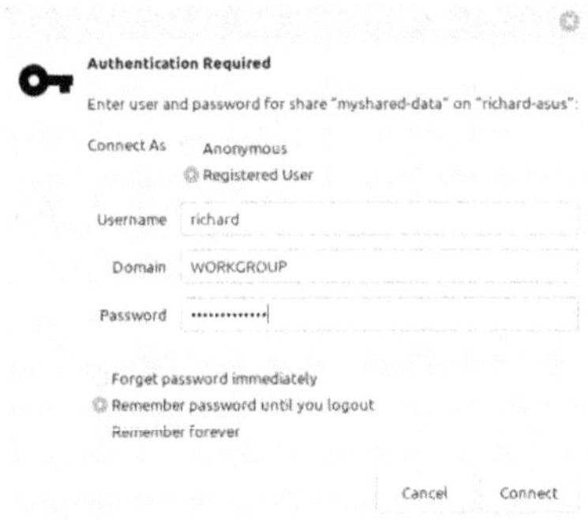

Figure 9-26: Network authorization

Figure 9-27: Connect to Server

Note: If you are running a firewall, be sure to configure access for the NFS and Samba services. Otherwise, access to your shared folders by other computers may be blocked (see Firewalls in Chapter 10).

Figure 9-28: Mount remote Windows shares

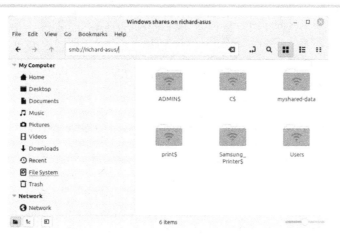

Figure 9-29: Window remote host

Shared Folders for your network

To share a folder on your Linux Mint system, right-click on it and select Sharing Options. This opens a window where you can allow sharing and choose whether to permit modifying, adding, or deleting files in the folder. If you have not already installed the Samba server, you will be notified to do so, and then reboot your system.

As initially set up, you can access any Windows shared folders from your Linux system, but you cannot access shared Linux folders from your Windows systems, or share your Linux folders with other Windows systems. For this you need to install and configure the Samba server on your Linux system as described in chapter 15. Should you attempt to share a folder, a notice is displayed notifying you to install the Samba sharing service (see Figure 9-30). You cannot create a shared folder until the sharing service is installed.

Figure 9-30: Folder Sharing prompt to install Samba

The folder is shared with read access. The "allow others to create and delete files in this folder" option can also be checked, allowing other users to create and remove file in the folder (see Figure 9-31). You can also allow access to anyone who does not also have an account on your system (guest). This option is initially unchecked. You can check it to allow guest access. Once you have made your selections, click the Create Share button. Sharing is implemented on the Nemo and Caja file manager with the **nemo-share** and **caja-share** packages. For MATE, be sure to install the **caja-share** package.

Note: On MATE, for a user to create a share, they have to have permission to do so. New users are not given this permission by default. On the Users and Groups's Advanced dialog's Privileges tab set the "Share files with the local network" option.

You can later change the sharing options, if you want, on the Share tab on the file's properties dialog (see Figure 9-32). You can set the permissions for create and delete access to the files and sub-folders in that folder, as well as allow guest access access.

Permissions on the user home folder no longer allow folders in their home folder to be shared. If you try to do so, a warning message is displayed telling you that access is prevented (see Figure 9-32).

```
The permissions for /home/richard
prevent other users from accessing this share
```

To allow access, you can either change the permission of the user home folder to allow access by other users to the entire user home folder (755), or add a Samba share definition for the share folder in the **/etc/samba/smb.conf** file using the **force** commands with **create**, **directory**, and **user** options. The Samba share definition method preserves the permissions of the user home folder, making it more secure. See the previous section "Permissions for Share Folders in User Home Folders" for more details.

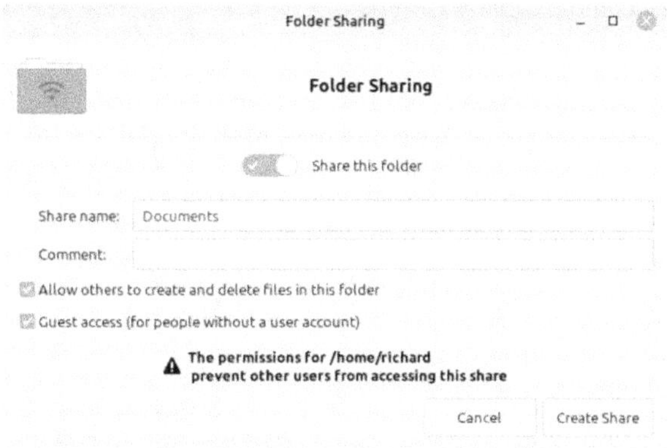

Figure 9-31: Folder Sharing Options

Folders that are shared display a sharing emblem next to their icon on a file manager window, as shown here.

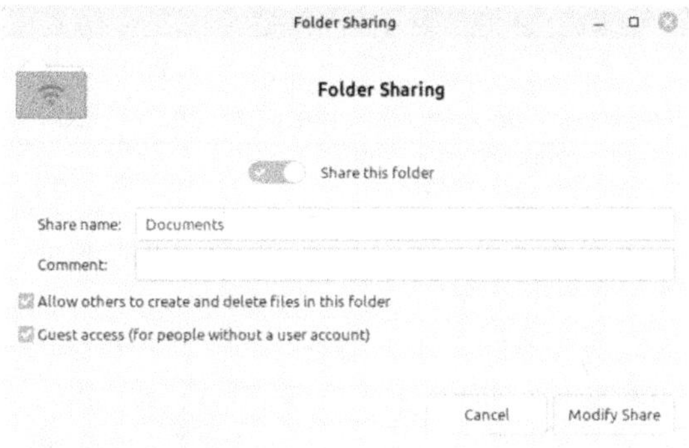

Figure 9-32: Folder Share panel

To allow access by other users, permissions on the folder will have to be changed. You will be prompted to allow Nemo or Caja to make these changes for you. Just click the "Add the permissions automatically" button (see Figure 9-33).

Figure 9-33: Folder Sharing permissions prompt

To allow other computers to access your folders be sure the sharing servers are installed, Samba for Windows systems and NFS (**nfs-kernelserver**) for Linux/Unix systems. Once installed, the servers are configured automatically for you and run. You will not be able to share folders until these servers are installed.

You can install the Samba server (**samba** package) with Software Manager, the Synaptic Package Manager, and the **apt** command. Two servers are installed and run using the **smbd** and **nmbd** service scripts. The **smbd** server is the Samba server, and the **nmbd** server is the network discovery server.

Should the Samba server fail to start, you can start it manually in a terminal window with the commands:

```
sudo systemctl start nmbd
sudo systemctl start smbd
```

You can check the current status with the **status** option and restart with the **restart** option:

```
systemctl status nmbd
systemctl status smbd
```

When first installed, Samba imports the Users and Groups already configured on your Linux Mint system. Corresponding Windows users with the same username and password as a Linux Mint account on your Linux Mint system are connected automatically to the Linux Mint shared folders. Should the Windows user have a different password, that user is prompted on Windows to enter a username and password. This is a Linux Mint username and password. In the case of a Windows user with the same username but different password, the user would enter the same username with a Linux Mint user password, not the Windows password.

Access is granted to all shares by any user. Should you want to implement restricted access by specific users and passwords, you have to configure user level access, as discussed in Chapter 15.

To change the sharing permissions for a folder later, open the folder's Properties window and then select the Share tab. When you make a change, a Modify Share button is displayed. Click it to make the changes. In Figure 9-34 Guest access is added to the Pictures folder.

If you are using a firewall, be sure that it is configured for access by Samba to allow multicast DNS discovery. For Gufw (Preferences | Firewall Configuration), be sure that the rules are added for Samba. For FirewallD, on firewall-config (Administration | Firewall), be sure that the mdns, samba, and samba-client services are enabled (Zones | Services tab) (see Figure 9-33) .

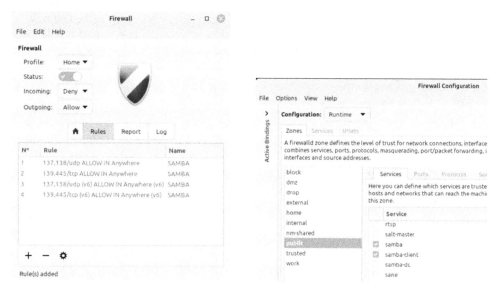

Figure 9-34: Samba Firewall Configuration, Gufw (UFW) and firewall-config (FirewallD)

Accessing Linux Shared Folders from Windows

It is easy to access your Linux shared folders from Windows 10. The Windows Network folder in the Windows file manager may display the Linux systems on your local network. Click on one to see the shared Linux folders for that system (see Figure 9-35). Keep in mind, that for Windows to access a Linux system, it has to be running a Samba server.

If you want to access shared folders in a Linux user's home folder, be sure that the folder is configured for access either by changing the permissions on the user's home folder or by adding a share definition for it in the **/etc/samba/smb.conf** file. See the previous section "Permissions for Shared Folders in User Home Folders" for more details.

Figure 9-35: Accessing Linux Shared Folders from Windows

Should the Linux hosts not be displayed, you can still access their shares by adding a new network location for a shared Linux folder, that will be accessible from a shortcut you can set up for it on your Windows file manager "This PC" folder. To set up the shortcut, open the Windows file manager to any folder and right-click on the "This PC" entry in the sidebar to display a menu. Click on the "Add a network location" entry to open the "Add Network Location Wizard" and click

Next. Click on the "Choose a custom network location" entry and click Next. In the text box labelled "Internet or network address:" enter the host name of your Linux system that holds the shares you want to access, beginning with the two backward slashes and followed by a backward slash (you may have to also enter the name of one of the shared folders on that system).

```
\\richard-laptop\
```

You can then click the Browse button to open a dialog showing a tree of all the shared folders on that host. You can choose a share, or any of a share's subfolders. Their file pathname is automatically added to the address textbox. Alternatively, you could enter the folder path name in the text box directly with the subfolders separated by single backward slashes. If you are sharing your Linux home directories, then the shared folder is the name of the user's Home folder, the user name. Samples are shown here.

```
\\richard-laptop\richard
```

```
\\richard-laptop\richard\Pictures
```

```
\\richard-laptop\mydocs
```

Once the locations for your shared folders are set up in Windows, you can access them again quickly from their shortcuts in the "This PC" folder.

File and Folder Permissions

On the desktop, you can set a folder or file permission using the Permissions tab in its Properties window (see Figure 9-36). For Files, right-click the icon or entry for the file or folder in the file manager window and select Properties. Then select the Permissions tab. Here you will find menus for read and write permissions, along with rows for Owner, Group, and Other. You can set owner permissions as Read Only or Read And Write. For the group and others, you can also set the None option, denying access. The group name expands to a menu listing different groups. Select one to change the file's group. If you want to execute this file as an application (say, a shell script) check the "Allow executing file as program" entry. This has the effect of setting the execute permission

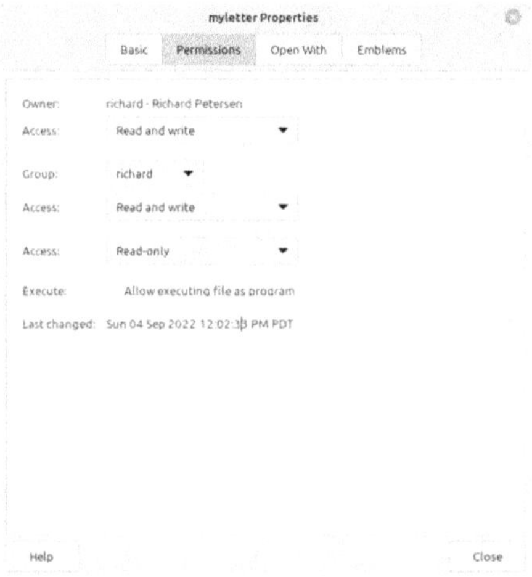

Figure 9-36: File Permissions

The Permissions tab for folders operates much the same way, but it displays two access entries, Folder Access and File Access (see Figure 9-37). The Folder Access entry controls access to the folder with options for List Files Only, Access Files, and Create And Delete Files. These correspond to the read, read and execute, and read/write/execute permissions given to folders. The File Access entry lets you set permissions for all those files in the folder. They are the same as for files: for the owner, there are Read or Read and Write permissions. For the group and others, there is a None option to deny access. To set the permissions for all the files in the folder accordingly (not just the folder), click the "Apply Permissions To Enclosed Files" button.

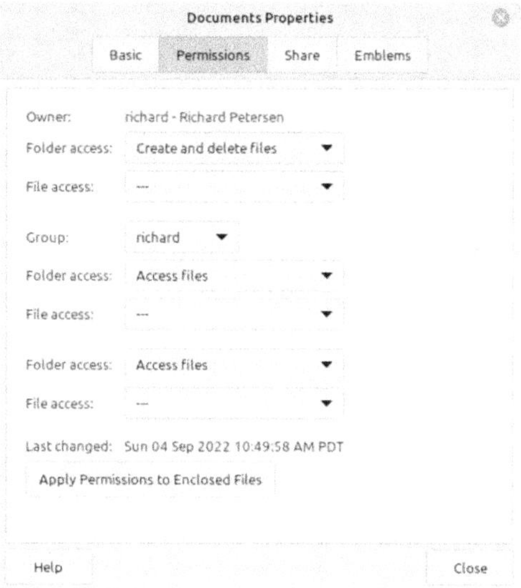

Figure 9-37: Folder Permissions

Automatic file system mounts with /etc/fstab

Though most file systems are automatically mounted for you, there may be instances where you need to have a file system mounted manually. Using the **mount** command you can do this directly, or you can specify the mount operation in the **/etc/fstab** file to have it mounted automatically. Linux Mint file systems are uniquely identified with their UUID (Universally Unique IDentifier). These are listed in the **/dev/disk/by-uuid** directory (or with the **sudo blkid** command). In the **/etc/fstab** file, the file system disk partitions are listed as a comment and then followed by the actual file system mount operation using the UUID. The following example mounts the file system on partition **/dev/sda3** to the **/media/sda3** directory as an **ext4** file system with default options (**defaults**). The UUID for device **/dev/sda3** is b8c526db-cb60-43f6-b0a3-5c0054f6a64a.

```
# /dev/sda3
UUID=b8c526db-cb60-43f6-b0a3-5c0054f6a64a /media/sda3 ext4 defaults 0 2
```

You can also identify your file system by giving it a label. You can use the **ext2label** command to label a file system. In the following **/etc/fstab** file example, the Linux file system labeled **mydata1** is mounted to the **/mydata1** directory as an **ext4** file system type.

Should you have to edit your **/etc/fstab** file, you can use the **sudo** command with the **xed** editor on your desktop. In a terminal window enter the following command. You will first be prompted to enter your password.

```
sudo xed /etc/fstab
```

/etc/fstab

```
# /etc/fstab: static file system information.
#
# <file system>                       <mount point>  <type>  <options>      <dump>  <pass>
# / was on /dev/sda2 during installation
UUID=a179d6e6-b90c-4cc4-982d-a4cfcedea7df /           ext4 errors=remount-ro 0      1
# /boot/efi was on /dev/sda1 during installation
UUID=7982-2520                           /boot/efi   vfat umask=0077        0      1
# /dev/sda3
UUID=b8c526db-cb60-43f6-b0a3-5c0054f6a64a /media/sda3 ext4 defaults         0      2
/swapfile                                none        swap sw                0      0
LABEL=mydata1                            /mydata1    ext4 defaults          1      1
```

To mount a partition manually, use the **mount** command and specify the type with the **-t** option. Use the **-L** option to mount by label. List the file system first, and then the directory name to which it will be mounted. For an NTFS partition, you would use the type **ntfs**. For partitions with the Ext4 file system you would use **ext4**, and for older Linux partitions you would use **ext3**. The mount option has the format:

```
mount -t type  file-system  directory
```

The following example mounts the **mydata1** file system to the **/mydata1** directory

```
mount -t ext4  -L mydata1  /mydata1
```

If you used LVM, only the LVM logical volumes are listed, along with the boot partition.

/etc/fstab (LVM)

```
# /etc/fstab: static file system information.
#
# <file system> <mount point>   <type>   <options>         <dump>   <pass>
/dev/mapper/vgmint-root /           ext4    errors=remount-ro 0         1
# /boot/efi was on /dev/sda1 during installation
UUID=5AF4-3E52 /boot/efi        vfat     umask=0077        0         1
/dev/mapper/vgmint-swap_1 none  swap     sw                0         0
```

Bluetooth (Blueman)

Linux Mint Linux provides Bluetooth support for both serial connections and BlueZ protocol supported devices. Bluetooth is a wireless connection method for locally connected devices such as keyboards, mice, printers, and cell phones. BlueZ is the official Linux Bluetooth protocol and is integrated into the Linux kernel. The BlueZ protocol was developed originally by Qualcomm and is now an open source project, located at **http://bluez.sourceforge.net**. It is included with Linux Mint in the **bluez-utils** and **bluez-libs** packages, among others. Check the BlueZ site for a complete list of supported hardware.

The Bluetooth applet, blueman-applet, is displayed on your panel to the right. Click it to display the Bluetooth Blueman device manager dialog, labeled Bluetooth Devices (see Figure 9-

38). You can also access Blueman dialog from the Preferences menu or from System Settings as Bluetooth Manager.

Note: Should you prefer to use the GNOME Bluetooth application (Blueberry), you can install it from the Software Manager as **GNOME-bluetooth**.

Figure 9-38: Bluetooth Settings (System Settings)

On the menubar there are menus for adapters, devices, views, and help. The Adapter menu lists your adapters. You can choose the Search entry to find all the Bluetooth adapters on your system. You usually just have one. The Preferences menu opens a Bluetooth Adapters dialog where you can choose the visibility for the adapter: Hidden, Always visible, and Temporarily visible (see Figure 9-39). For the "Temporarily visible" option there is a slider to let you easily choose the number for minutes the adapter is visible. You can also change the name you want to use for the adapter.

Figure 9-39: Bluetooth Adapters

The View menu has options for showing the toolbar and the statusbar. The statusbar is displayed at the bottom of the Bluetooth Manager dialog. You can also hide any unnamed devices.

On the toolbar there are buttons for search (looking glass), pairing (a key), marking a device as trusted (checkmark), removing a device (minus symbol), and sending a file to a device. A

Sort By submenu lets you sort by name, in descending or ascending order, or by when a device is added. The Plugins entry opens a Plugins dialog listing plugins to the left and information about a selected plugin to the right (see Figure 9-40). If the plugin can be configured, it will show an active Configuration button. Clicking the button displays the configurable options.

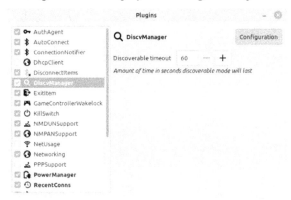

Figure 9-40: Bluetooth Plugins

The Local Services entry opens the Local Service dialog with tabs for Network and Transfer (see Figure 9-41). The Network tab lists your network settings. You can choose an access point, Pan support, and Dun support. By default these are provided by Network Manager. On the Transfer tab you can select the folder for incoming transfers and whether to receive files only from trusted devices.

Figure 9-41: Bluetooth Local Services

When you select a device, the Devices menu becomes active (see Figure 42). There are entries to connect the device, display information about it, send a note to it, and send a file to it if possible, You can also pair the device should you need to, mark it as trusted or untrusted, block the device, rename it and remove it.

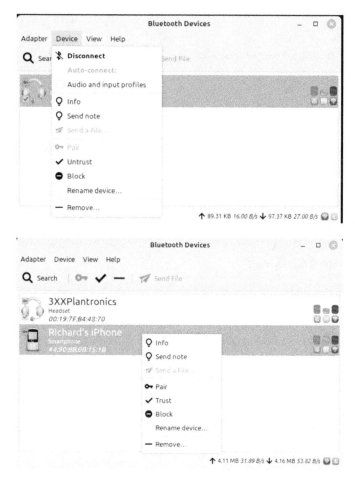

Figure 9-42: Bluetooth Device menu

To find your Bluetooth devices, click on the Search button. Your active devices will be listed (see Figure 9-43). Clicking on a newly discovered device will start the pairing process. A dialog will be displayed to confirm the pairing code. Should you need to pair it manually, select the device and click on the key button on the toolbar. Once paired you can click on the checkmark button to mark it as trusted. Should you want to remove the device, click on the minus button. You can use to Devices menu to manage your device, or right-click on the device to display a Devices menu with the same entries.

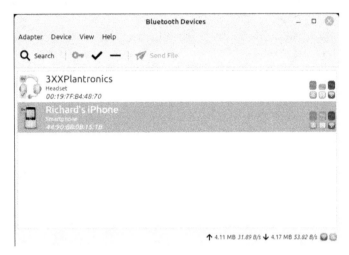

Figure 9-43: Bluetooth Devices

A device entry shows the name of the device, its type, and the address. An icon for the device shows indicates its type. For connected device a blue arrow emblem is shown on the icon. For paired devices a green checkmark emblem is also shown. To the right of the device are emblems indicating the to and from connections.

The statusbar shows the amount of data transferred to and from devices with emblems for active network connections.

If the device supports sound, you can open the PulseAudio Sound Settings dialog and select the device to configure its sound settings (see Figure 9-44).

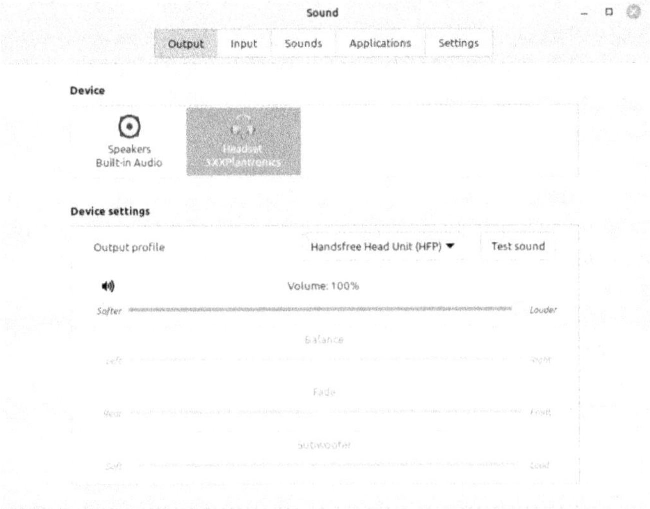

Figure 9-44: Bluetooth Sound

When connecting to a phone, a pin number is detected and displayed. If you enable a phone to operate as a mobile phone network device (PAN/NAP), then a Mobile Broadband entry is shown on the Network Manager applet's menu (see Figure 9-45).

Figure 9-45: Bluetooth Setup Device Wizard: phone

Right-clicking on the Bluetooth applet on the panel displays a menu with an entry to turn Bluetooth off (see Figure 9-46). It acts as a toggle, showing a "Turn Bluetooth On" entry if Bluetooth is off. When Bluetooth is off, the Bluetooth applet is grayed. There are also entries to send files to a device and to open various Blueman Manager dialogs. Adapters opens the Bluetooth Adapters dialog. Local Services opens the Local Services dialog. Plugins opens the Bluetooth Plugins dialog, Devices open the Bluetooth Devices application (Bluetooth Manager). There are also Help and Exit entries. The Recent Connections entry opens a submenu showing your recent Bluetooth connections.

Figure 9-46: Bluetooth applet menu

DKMS

DKMS is the Dynamic Kernel Module Support originally developed by DELL. DKMS enabled device drivers can be generated automatically whenever your kernel is updated. This is helpful for proprietary drivers like the Nvidia and AMD proprietary graphics drivers (the X11 open source drivers, Xorg, are automatically included with the kernel package). In the past, whenever you updated your kernel, you also had to download and install a separate proprietary kernel module compiled just for that new kernel. If the module was not ready, then you could not use a proprietary driver. To avoid this problem, DKMS was developed, which uses the original proprietary source code to create new kernel modules as they are needed. When you install a new kernel, DKMS detects the new configuration and compiles a compatible proprietary kernel module for your new kernel. This action is fully automatic and entirely hidden from the user.

On Linux Mint and Ubuntu both the Nvidia and AMD proprietary graphics drivers are DKMS enabled packages that are managed and generated by the DKMS service. The generated kernel modules are placed in the **/lib/modules/***kernel-version***/kernel/updates** directory. When you install either graphics proprietary package, their source code is downloaded and used to create a graphics driver for use by your kernel. The source code is placed in the **/usr/src** directory. The DKMS configuration files and build locations for different DKMS-enabled software are located in subdirectories in the **/var/lib/dkms** directory.

DKMS configuration files are located in the **/etc/dkms** directory. The **/etc/dkms/framework.conf** file holds DKMS variable definitions for directories that DKMS uses, like the source code and kernel module directories. The **/etc/init.d/dkms_autoinstaller** is a script the runs the DKMS operations to generate and install a kernel module. DKMS removal and install directives for kernel updates are maintained in the **/etc/kernel** directory.

Should DKMS fail to install and update automatically, you can perform the update manually using the **dkms** command. The **dkms** command with the **build** action creates the kernel module, and then the **dkms** command with the **install** action installs the module to the appropriate kernel module directory. The **-m** option specifies the module you want to build and the **-k** option is the kernel version (use **uname -r** to display your current kernel version). Drivers like Nvidia and AMD release new versions regularly. You use the **-v** option to specify the driver version you want. See the man page for **dkms** for full details.

Editing Configuration Files Directly

Though the administrative tools will handle all configuration settings for you, there may be times when you will need to make changes by editing configuration files directly. Most system configuration files are text files located in the **/etc** directory. To change any of these files, you will need administrative access, requiring you use the **pkexec** or **sudo** commands, or to open the file manager with root access (the "Open as root" entry on the desktop menu).

You can use any standard editor, such as nano or Vi, to edit these files, though one of the easiest ways to edit them is to use the Xed editor on the GNOME desktop. In a terminal window, enter the **sudo** command with the **xed** command. You will be prompted for the root user password. The Gedit window then opens (see Figures 9-2 and 9-3 near the beginning of this chapter). Click Open to open a file browser where you can move through the file system to locate the file you want to edit.

```
sudo xed
```

Caution: Be careful when editing your configuration files. Editing mistakes can corrupt your configurations. It is advisable to make a backup of any configuration files you are working on first, before making major changes to the original.

On the Linux Mint Cinnamon desktop, the easiest way to edit an administrative file with the Xed editor is to right-click on the desktop and select the "Open as root" entry to open the file manager with administrative access (Elevated Privileges). Find the file you want to edit and double-click it to open it in the Xed editor. Alternatively, to edit the file with the Xed editor (Pluma on MATE) with elevated privileges, open a terminal window and enter the following command.

```
sudo xed
```

Xed (and Pluma) will let you edit several files at once, opening a tab for each. You can use Xed to edit any text file, including ones you create yourself. Two commonly edited configuration files are **/etc/default/grub** and **/etc/fstab**. The **/etc/fstab** file lists all your file systems and how they are mounted, and **/etc/default/grub** file is the configuration file for your Grub 2 boot loader.

You also can specify the file to edit when you first start up the Xed editor (Pluma on MATE).

```
sudo xed /etc/default/grub
```

User configuration files, dot files, can be changed by individual users directly without administrative access. An example of a user configuration file is the **.profile** file, which configures your login shell. Dot files like **.profile** have to be chosen from the file manager window, not from the Xed open operation. First configure the file manager to display dot files by opening the Preferences dialog (select Preferences in the Edit menu of any file manager window), then check the Show Hidden Files entry, and close the dialog. This displays the dot files in your file manager window. Double-click the file to open it in Xed.

GRUB 2

The Grand Unified Bootloader (GRUB) is a multiboot boot loader used for most Linux distributions. Linux and Unix operating systems are known as multiboot operating systems and take arguments passed to them at boot time. With GRUB, users can select operating systems to run from a menu interface displayed when a system boots up. Use arrow keys to move to an entry and press ENTER. If instead, you need to edit an entry, press **e**, letting you change kernel arguments or specify a different kernel. The **c** command places you in a command line interface. Provided your system BIOS supports very large drives, GRUB can boot from anywhere on them. For detailed information on Grub2, check the Grub2 Wiki at:

```
https://wiki.ubuntu.com/Grub2
```

Check the GRUB Man page for GRUB options. GRUB is a GNU project with its home page at **https://www.gnu.org/software/grub**, the manual at **https://www.gnu.org/software/grub/index.html**. The Ubuntu forums and Ubuntu help site have several helpful threads on using Grub2 on Ubuntu, **https://ubuntuforums.org** and **https://help.ubuntu.com**. Search on Grub2.

Grub2 detects and generates a menu for you automatically. You do not have to worry about keeping a menu file updated. All your operating systems and Linux Mint kernels are detected when the system starts up, and a menu to display them as boot options is generated at that time.

With Grub2, configuration is placed in user-modifiable configuration files held in the **/etc/default/grub** file and in the **/etc/grub.d** directory. There is a Grub2 configuration file called **/boot/grub/grub.cfg**, but this file is generated by Grub each time the system starts up, and should never be edited by a user. Instead, you would edit the **/etc/default/grub** file to set parameters like the default operating system to boot. To create your own menu entries, you create entries for them in the **/etc/grub.d/40_custom** file.

Grub options are set by assigning values to Grub options in the **/etc/default/grub** file. You can edit the file directly to change these options. The easiest way to edit the file with the Xed editor in Cinnamon is to right-click on the desktop and select the "Open as root" entry to open the file manager with administrative access (Elevated Privileges). Then navigate to the **/etc/default** folder, locate the **grub** file, and double-click it to open it in the Xed editor (see Figure 9-1). Alternatively, to edit the file with the Xed editor (Pluma on MATE) with elevated privileges, open a terminal window and enter the following command (see Figure 9-47). You will be prompted to enter your password. Alternatively, you can configure Xed to use policykit and run it with **pkexec**.

```
sudo xed /etc/default/grub

pkexec xed /etc/default/grub
```

You can then edit the file carefully. A red bar below the toolbar displays an "Elevated Messages" notice so that you know you are running the Xed editor with administrative access. The **grub** file used on Linux Mint 21 is shown here:

/etc/default/grub

```
# If you change this file, run 'update-grub' afterwards to update
# /boot/grub/grub.cfg.

GRUB_DEFAULT=0
GRUB_TIMEOUT_STYLE=hidden
GRUB_TIMEOUT="0"
GRUB_DISTRIBUTOR=`lsb_release -i -s 2> /dev/null || echo Debian`
GRUB_CMDLINE_LINUX_DEFAULT="quiet splash"
GRUB_CMDLINE_LINUX=""

# Uncomment to enable BadRAM filtering, modify to suit your needs
# This works with Linux (no patch required) and with any kernel that obtains
# the memory map information from GRUB (GNU Mach, kernel of FreeBSD ...)
#GRUB_BADRAM="0x01234567,0xfefefefe,0x89abcdef,0xefefefef"

# Uncomment to disable graphical terminal (grub-pc only)
#GRUB_TERMINAL=console

# The resolution used on graphical terminal
# note that you can use only modes which your graphic card supports via VBE
# you can see them in real GRUB with the command `vbeinfo'
#GRUB_GFXMODE=640x480

# Uncomment if you don't want GRUB to pass "root=UUID=xxx" parameter to Linux
#GRUB_DISABLE_LINUX_UUID=true

# Uncomment to disable generation of recovery mode menu entrys
#GRUB_DISABLE_RECOVERY="true"

# Uncomment to get a beep at grub start
#GRUB_INIT_TUNE="480 440 1"
```

For dual boot systems (those with both Linux Mint and Windows or Mac), the option that users are likely to change is GRUB_DEFAULT, which sets the operating system or kernel to boot automatically if one is not chosen. The option uses a line number to indicate an entry in the Grub boot menu, with numbering starting from 0 (not 1). First, check your Grub menu when you boot up (press the ESC key on boot to display the Grub menu), and then count to where the entry of the operating system you want to make the default is listed. If the Windows entry is at 4th, which would be line 3 (counting from 0), to make it the default you would set the GRUB_DEAULT option to 3.

```
GRUB_DEFAULT=3
```

With Grub 2.06, the OS Prober application that detects other operating systems on your computer, has been disabled for security reasons. Other operating systems may not be detected. You can re-enable OS_Prober by editing the **/etc/default/grub** file and adding the GRUB_DISABLE_OS_PROBER option and setting it to false.

```
GRUB_DISABLE_OS_PROBER=false
```

Should the listing of operating systems and kernels change (adding or removing kernels), you would have to edit the **/etc/default/grub** file again and each time a change occurs. A safer way to set the default is to configure GRUB to use the **grub-set-default** command. First, edit the **/etc/default/grub** file and change the option for GRUB_DEFAULT to **saved**.

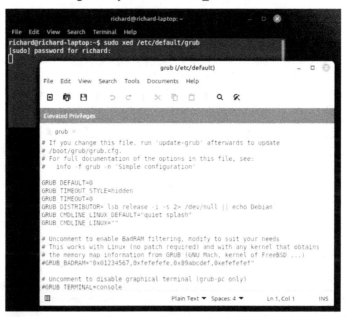

Figure 9-47: Editing the /etc/default/grub file

```
GRUB_DEFAULT=saved
```

Then update GRUB.

```
sudo update-grub
```

The **grub-set-default** command takes as its option the number of the default you want to set (numbering from 0), or the name of the kernel or operating system. The following sets the default to 0, the first kernel entry.

```
sudo grub-set-default 0
```

For a kernel name or operating system, you can use the name as it appears on the GRUB menu (enclosing the name in quotes), such as:

```
sudo grub-set-default 'Windows XP (loader) (on /dev/sda1)'
```

The GRUB_TIMEOUT option sets the number of seconds Grub will wait to allow a user to access the menu, before booting the default operating system. The default options used for Linux Mint kernels are listed by the GRUB_CMDLINE_LINUX_DEFAULT option. Currently, these include the **splash** and **quiet** options to display the Linux Mint emblem on startup (**splash**), but not the list of startup tasks being performed (**quiet**).

The GRUB_TIMEOUT_STYLE option sets whether the menu is displayed or not during the timeout period. Options can be **menu**, which displays the Grub menu, **countdown**, which only displays a countdown timer for the timeout period, and **hidden**, which does not display the menu unless the user presses the ESC key. On Linux Mint this option is set to **hidden** by default.

```
GRUB_TIMEOUT_STYLE=hidden
```

The following would always display the Grub menu.

```
GRUB_TIMEOUT_STYLE=menu
```

Once you have made your changes, you have to run the **update-grub** command with **sudo**, as noted in the first line of the **/etc/default/grub** file. Otherwise, your changes will not take effect. This command will generate a new **/etc/grub/grub.cfg** file, which determines the actual Grub 2 configuration.

```
sudo update-grub
```

You can add your own Grub2 boot entries by placing them in the **/etc/grub.d/40_custom** file. The file is nearly empty except for an initial **exec tail** command that you must take care not to change. After you make your additions to the **40_custom** file, you have to run **sudo update-grub** to have the changes take effect.

When the GRUB package is updated by Linux Mint, you will be given the choice to keep your current local version or use the maintainer's version. Keeping the local version is selected by default. However, unless you have extensively customized your configuration, it is always advisable to select the maintainer's version. The maintainer's version is the most up-to-date. If you had made any changes previously to the **/etc/default/grub** file, you will have to edit that file and make the same changes again, such as setting the default operating system to load. Be sure to run **sudo update-grub** to make the changes take effect.

Backup Management

Backup operations have become an important part of administrative duties. Several backup tools are provided on Linux systems, including Amanda and the traditional dump/restore tools, as well as the **rsync** command used for making individual copies. Linux Mint provides the Backup Tool (mintBackup) for basic backup operations. Deja Dup is a front end for the duplicity backup tool, which uses **rsync** to generate backup archives. Deja Dup is the recommended default backup tool, available from the System Settings dialog as Backup. Amanda provides server-based backups, letting different systems on a network backup to a central server. BackupPC provides network and local backup using configured **rsync** and **tar** tools. The dump tools let you refine your backup process, detecting data changed since the last backup. Table 9-2 lists websites for Linux backup tools.

Backup Tool (mintBackup)

The Backup Tool (mintBackup) provides basic backup of files, folders, and file systems, as well as a backup of your currently installed software. Backup Tool is available on both the Cinnamon and MATE desktops (Administration | Backup Tool. The initial dialog displays buttons for the backup options (see Figure 9-48).

Website	Tools
`https://linuxmint.com`	mintBackup (Backup Tool)
`https://rsync.samba.org`	rsync remote copy backup
`https://launchpad.net/deja-dup` `http://www.nongnu.org/duplicity`	Deja Dup frontend for duplicity which uses rsync to perform basic backups
`http://www.amanda.org`	Amanda network backup
`http://dump.sourceforge.net`	dump and restore tools
`https://backuppc.github.io/backuppc/`	BackupPC network or local backup using configured rsync and tar tools.

Table 9-2: Backup Resources

Figure 9-48: Backup Tool

When performing a backup, you choose the source, destination, and set advanced options such as preserving permissions (see Figure 9-49). Backups are made to folders or archives.

Figure 9-49: Backup Tool backup

Deja Dup

Deja Dup is a front end for the duplicity backup tool, which uses **rsync** to generate backup archives (**http://www.nongnu.org/duplicity/**). Once installed, you can access Deja Dup as "Backups" on both the Cinnamon and MATE desktops from the Preferences and Accessories menus. On the MATE desktop you can also access it as Backups on the Control Center, Other section).

The default backup setting for Deja Dup is to store your backups on Google Drive. However, you can change this setting to a local folder or a network share (Storage location tab). Should you want to use Google Drive, you will also have to install the **python3-pydrive** package, which will manage access to your Google drive account.

The deja-dup dialog shows buttons for backing up and restoring backups (see Figure 9-50). A menu on the upper right of the titlebar has entries for Preferences, Help, and Keyboard shortcuts. Select the Help entry on the titlebar menu to display the Deja Dup manual.

Figure 9-50: Deja Dup settings - overview

The deja-dup Preferences dialog shows tabs for General and Folders (see Figure 9-51). A switch in the Schedule section of the dialog allows you to turn automatic backups on and off. The General tab provides storage and scheduling settings with buttons to automatically perform a backup and a menu for selecting the the time interval for your backups.

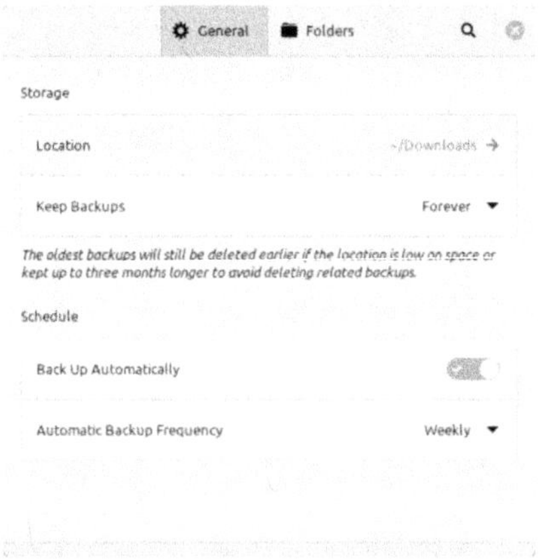

Figure 9-51: Deja Dup Preferences

The Storage section lets you specify the location and how long you want to keep backups (see Figure 9-52). You can choose different locations, such as an FTP account, a cloud account, SSH server, Samba (Windows) share, or a local folder. Choose the one you want from the "Storage Location" menu. With each choice, you are prompted for the appropriate configuration information.

Figure 9-52; Deja Dup settings - storage for Windows share and Local folder

In the Storage section, the Keep Backups menu lets you specify the frequency of your backups and how long to keep them (see Figure 9-53). First turn on Automatic backup. Backups can be performed daily, weekly, every two weeks, or monthly. They can be kept for a week, month, several months, a year, or forever.

Figure 9-53: Deja Dup settings - backup times

The Folders tab has sections for "Folders to Back Up" and "Folders to Ignore" (see Figure 9-54). Click the plus button (+) at the bottom of the folders list to add a new folder for backup. Do the same to specify folders to ignore. The minus button at the right of each entry removes selected folders from the list. Your home folder has been added already. The "Folders to ignore" section specifies folders you do not want to back up. The Downloads and Trash folders are already specified.

Figure 9-54: Deja Dup settings - Folders to save and ignore

When you perform a backup, you first choose the folders to backup and to ignore. Click the Forward button to continue. Next you choose a storage location. You are then are prompted to backup with or without encryption. For encrypted backups, you are prompted to enter a password, which you will need to restore the files (see Figure 9-55). You are then asked to select the date of the backup to use, the most recent being the default.

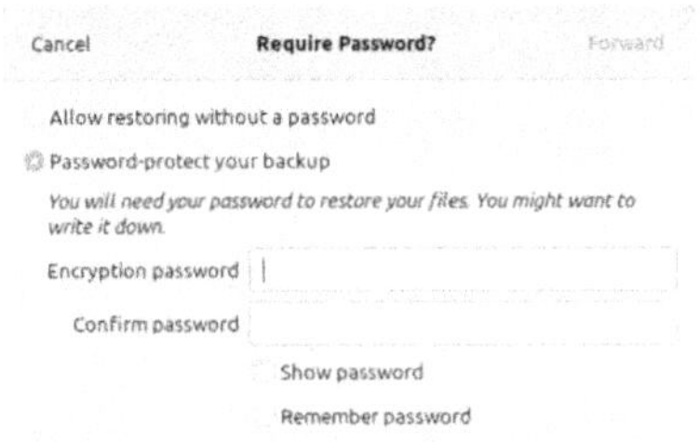

Figure 9-55: Deja Dup backup: encryption

To restore a backup, click on the Restore tab on the Deja-dup window. This displays all the folders in your current backup (see Figure 9-56). Click on the ones you want to restore. The Restore button on the lower left becomes active. Click it to the start the restore process. You can choose what backup to use from the Date menu on the lower right. To automatically choose all the folders and files either press Ctrl-a or click on the check-mark button on the right side of the Deja-dup window header bar. Click on the "Click on items to select them" button on the center of the header to display a menu with "Select All" and "Select None" options (see Figure 9-57). You can also search for files and folders by clicking the Search button (looking glass) on the right side of the Deja-dup header bar.

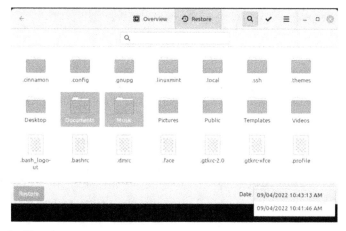

Figure 9-56: Deja Dup backup: encryption

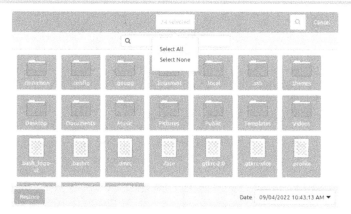

Figure 9-57: Deja Dup Restore

Once you have selected the files to restore and have clicked the Restore button, you can choose whether to restore to the original location or a specific folder (see Figure 9-58). The backup restore operation is then performed.

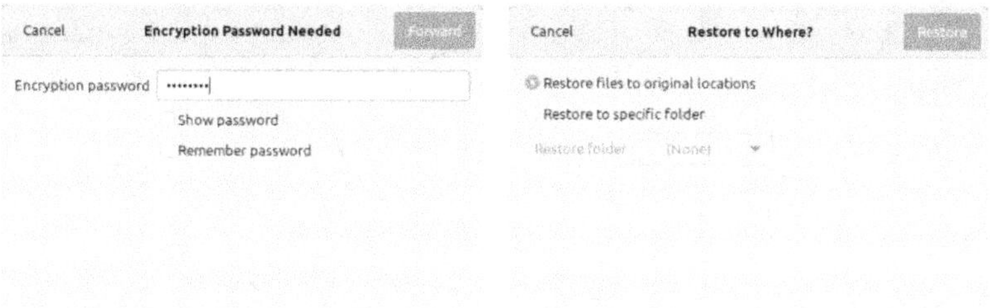

Figure 9-58: Deja Dup restore locations

Individual Backups: archive and rsync

You can backup and restore particular files and directories with archive tools like **tar**, restoring the archives later. For backups, **tar** is used usually with a tape device. To schedule automatic backups, you can schedule appropriate **tar** commands with the **cron** utility. The archives can be also compressed for storage savings. You can then copy the compressed archives to any medium, such as a DVD disc, a USB drive, external disk, or tape. On GNOME you can use File Roller (Archive Manager) to create archives easily (Accessories menu), or Engrampa, the MATE archive manager.

File Roller and Engrampa also support LZMA compression, a more efficient and faster compression method. On Archive Manager, when creating a new archive, select "Tar compressed with lzma (.tar.lzma)" for the Archive type. When choosing Create Archive from GNOME Files file manager window on selected files, on the Create Archive dialog, choose the **.lzma** file type for just compression, and the **.tar.lzma** type for a compressed archive.

If you want to remote-copy a directory or files from one host to another, making a particular backup, you can use **rsync**, which is designed for network backups of particular directories or files, intelligently copying only those files that have been changed, rather than the contents of an entire directory. In archive mode, it can preserve the original ownership and permissions, providing corresponding users exist on the host system. The following example copies the **/home/george/myproject** directory to the **/backup** directory on the host **rabbit**, creating a corresponding **myproject** subdirectory. The -t specifies that this is a transfer. The remote host is referenced with an attached colon, **rabbit:**

```
rsync -t /home/george/myproject   rabbit:/backup
```

If instead, you wanted to preserve the ownership and permissions of the files, you would use the **-a** (archive) option. Adding a **-z** option will compress the file. The **-v** option provides a verbose mode.

```
rsync -avz  /home/george/myproject   rabbit:/backup
```

A trailing slash on the source will copy the contents of the directory, rather than generating a subdirectory of that name. Here the contents of the **myproject** directory are copied to the **george-project** directory.

```
rsync -avz  /home/george/myproject/   rabbit:/backup/george-project
```

The **rsync** command is configured to use Secure Shell (SSH) remote shell by default. You can specify it or an alternate remote shell to use with the **-e** option. For secure transmission, you can encrypt the copy operation with SSH. Either use the **-e ssh** option or set the **RSYNC_RSH** variable to ssh.

```
rsync -avz -e ssh  /home/george/myproject   rabbit:/backup/myproject
```

You can copy from a remote host to the host you are on.

```
rsync -avz  lizard:/home/mark/mypics/  /pic-archive/markpics
```

You can also run **rsync** as a server daemon. This will allow remote users to synchronize copies of files on your system with versions on their own, transferring only changed files rather than entire directories. Many mirror and software FTP sites operate as rsync servers, letting you update files without have to download the full versions again. Configuration information for **rsync** as a server is kept in the **/etc/rsyncd.conf** file.

Tip: Though it is designed for copying between hosts, you can also use **rsync** to make copies within your own system, usually to a directory in another partition or hard drive. Check the **rsync** Man page for detailed descriptions of each.

BackupPC

BackupPC provides an easily managed local or network backup of your system or hosts, on a system using configured rsync or tar tools. There is no client application to install, just configuration files. BackupPC can backup hosts on a network, including servers, or just a single system. Data can be backed up to local hard disks or to network storage such as shared partitions or storage servers. You can configure BackupPC using your Web page configuration interface. This is the host name of your computer with the **/backuppc** name attached, like **http://richard1/backuppc**. Detailed documentation is installed at **/usr/share/doc/BackupPC**. You can find out more about BackupPC at **https://backuppc.github.io/backuppc/**. You can install BackupPC using the Synaptic Package Manager and with the **apt** command. Canonical provides critical updates. Configuration files are located at **/etc/BackupPC**. The **config.pl** file holds BackupPC configuration options and the **hosts** file lists hosts to be backed up.

BackupPC uses both compression and detection of identical files to reduce the size of the backup, allowing several hosts to be backed up in limited space. Once an initial backup is performed, BackupPC will only backup changed files, reducing the time of the backup significantly.

Amanda

To back up hosts connected to a network, you can use the Advanced Maryland Automatic Network Disk Archiver (Amanda) to archive hosts. Amanda uses **tar** tools to back up all hosts to a single host operating as a backup server. Backup data is sent by each host to the host operating as the Amanda server, where they are written out to a backup medium such as tape. With an Amanda server, the backup operations for all hosts become centralized in one server, instead of each host having to perform its backup. Any host that needs to restore data simply requests it from the Amanda server, specifying the file system, date, and filenames. Backup data is copied to the server's holding disk and from there, to tapes. Detailed documentation and updates are provided at **http://www.amanda.org**. For the server, be sure to install the amanda-server package, and for clients you use the amanda-clients package. You can install Amanda using the Synaptic Package Manager and from Software Manager. Canonical does not provide critical updates.

Logical Volume Manager

For easier hard disk storage management, you can set up your system to use the Logical Volume Manager (LVM), creating LVM partitions that are organized into logical volumes, to which free space is automatically allocated. Logical volumes provide a more flexible and powerful way of dealing with disk storage, organizing physical partitions into logical volumes in which you can easily manage disk space. Disk storage for a logical volume is treated as one pool of memory, though the volume may, in fact, contain several hard disk partitions spread across different hard disks. Adding a new LVM partition merely increases the pool of storage accessible to the entire system. Check the LVM HOWTO at **www.tldp.org** for detailed examples.

LVM Structure

In an LVM structure, LVM physical partitions, also known as extents, are organized into logical groups, which are, in turn, used by logical volumes. In effect, you are dealing with three different levels of organization. At the lowest level, you have physical volumes. These are physical hard disk partitions that you create with partition creation tools such as **Gparted** or **fdisk**. The partition type will be a Linux LVM partition, **fdisk** code **8e**. These physical volumes are organized into logical groups, known as volume groups, that operate much like logical hard disks. You assign collections of physical volumes to different logical groups.

Once you have your logical groups, you can then create logical volumes. Logical volumes function much like hard disk partitions on a standard setup. For example, on the **turtle** group volume, you could create a **/var** logical volume, and on the **rabbit** logical group, you could create **/home** and **/projects** logical volumes. You can have several logical volumes on one logical group, just as you can have several partitions on one hard disk.

You treat the logical volumes as you would any ordinary hard disk partition. Create a file system on it with the **mkfs** command, and then you can mount the file system to use it with the **mount** command. For Linux Mint, the file system type would be **ext4**.

Storage on logical volumes is managed using what are known as extents. A logical group defines a standard size for an extent, say 4MB, and then divides each physical volume in its group into extents of that size. Logical volumes are, in turn, divided into extents of the same size, which are then mapped to those on the physical volumes.

Logical volumes can be linear, striped, or mirrored. The mirror option will create a mirror copy of a logical volume, providing a restore capability. The striped option lets you automatically distribute your Logical volume across several partitions, as you would a RAID device. This adds better efficiency for very large files but is complicated to implement. Like a RAID device, stripe sizes have to be consistent across partitions. As LVM partitions can be of any size, the stripes sizes have to be carefully calculated. The simplest approach is just to use a linear implementation, much like a RAID 0 device, just treating the storage as one large ordinary drive, with storage accessed sequentially.

There is one restriction and recommendation for logical volumes. The boot partition cannot be part of a logical volume. You still have to create a separate hard disk partition as your boot partition with the **/boot** mountpoint in which your kernel and all needed boot files are installed. This is why a default partition configuration set up during Linux Mint installation for LVM will include a separate **/boot** partition of type **ext4**, whereas the root partition will be installed on Logical volumes. There will be two partitions, one for the logical group (LVM physical volume, **pv**) holding the root volume, and another for the boot partition (**ext4**). The logical volumes will in turn both be **ext4** file systems.

LVM Tools: using the LVM commands

To use LVM be sure that the **lmv2** package is installed. Use the Synaptic Package Manager or the **apt** command. You can then use a collection of LVM tools to manage your LVM volumes, adding new LVM physical partitions and removing current ones. For the LVM tools, you can either use LVM tools directly or use the **lvm** command to generate an interactive shell from which you can run LVM commands. There are Man pages for all the LVM commands. LVM maintains configuration information in the **/etc/lvm/lvm.conf** file, where you can configure LVM options such as the log file, the configuration backup directory, or the directory for LVM devices (see the **lvm.conf** Man page for more details).

Displaying LVM Information

You can use the **pvdisplay**, **vgdisplay**, and **lvdisplay** commands to show detailed information about a physical partition, volume groups, and logical volumes. The **pvscan**, **vgscan**, and **lvscan** commands list your physical, group, and logical volumes.

Managing LVM Physical Volumes with the LVM commands

A physical volume can be any hard disk partition or RAID device. A RAID device is seen as a single physical volume. You can create physical volumes either from a single hard disk or from partitions on a hard disk. On very large systems with many hard disks, you would more likely use an entire hard disk for each physical volume.

You would first use a partition utility like **fdisk**, **parted**, or **gparted** to create a partition of the LVM partition type (**8e**). Then, you can initialize the partition as a physical volume using the **pvcreate** command.

To initialize a physical volume on an entire hard disk, you use the hard disk device name, as shown here:

```
pvcreate /dev/sdc
```

This will initialize one physical partition, **pv**, called **sdc1** on the **sdc** hard drive (the third Serial ATA drive, c).

If you are using a particular partition on a drive, you create a new physical volume using the partition's device name, as shown here:

```
pvcreate /dev/sda3
```

To initialize several drives, just list them. The following create two physical partitions, sdc1 and sdd1.

```
pvcreate /dev/sdc /dev/sdd
```

You could also use several partitions on different hard drives. This is a situation in which your hard drives each hold several partitions. This condition occurs often when you are using some partitions on your hard drive for different purposes like different operating systems, or if you want to distribute your Logical group across several hard drives. To initialize these partitions at once, you simply list them.

```
pvcreate /dev/sda3 /dev/sdb1 /dev/sdb2
```

Once you have initialized your partitions, you have to create LVM groups on them.

Managing LVM Groups

Physical LVM **partitions** are used to make up a volume group. You can manually create a volume group using the **vgcreate** command and the name of the group along with a list of physical partitions you want in the group.

If you are then creating a new volume group to place these in, you can include them in the group when you create the volume group with the **vgcreate** command. The volume group can use one or more physical partitions. The configuration described in the following example used only one physical partition for the **VolGroup00**. In the following example, a volume group called **mymedia** that is made up two physical volumes, **sdc** and **sdd**.

```
vgcreate mymedia  /dev/sdc /dev/sdd
```

The previous example sets up a logical group on two serial ATA hard drives, each with its own single partition. Alternatively, you can set up a volume group to span partitions on several hard drives. If you are using partitions for different functions, this approach gives you the flexibility for using all the space available across multiple hard drives. The following example creates a group called **mygroup** consisting of three physical partitions, **/dev/sda3**, **/dev/sdb4**, and **/dev/sdb4**:

```
vgcreate mygroup  /dev/sda3 /dev/sdb2 /dev/sdb4
```

If you later want to add a physical volume to a volume group you would use the **vgextend** command. The **vgextend** command adds a new partition to a logical group. In the following example, the partition **/dev/sda4** is added to the volume group **mygroup**. In effect, you are extending the size of the logical group by adding a new physical partition.

```
vgextend mygroup  /dev/sda4
```

To add an entire new drive to a volume group, you would follow a similar procedure. The following example adds a fifth serial ATA hard drive, **sde**, first creating a physical volume on it and then adding that volume, sde, to the **mymedia** volume group.

```
pvcreate /dev/sde
vgextend mymedia /dev/sde
```

To remove a physical partition, first, remove it from its logical group. You may have to use the **pmove** command to move any data off the physical partition. Then use the **vgreduce** command to remove it from its logical group.

You can remove an entire volume group by first deactivating it with **vgchange -a n** and then using the **vgremove** command.

Activating Volume Groups

Whereas in a standard file system structure you mount and unmount hard disk partitions, with an LVM structure, you activate and deactivate entire volume groups. The group volumes are accessible until you activate them with the **vgchange** command with the **-a** option. To activate a group, first, reboot your system, and then enter the **vgchange** command with the **-a** option and the **y** argument to activate the logical group (an **n** argument will deactivate the group).

```
vgchange -a  y  mygroup
```

Managing LVM Logical Volumes

To create logical volumes, you use the **lvcreate** command and then format your logical volume using the standard formatting command like **mkfs.ext4**. With the **-n** option you specify the volume's name, which functions like a hard disk partition's label. You use the **-L** or **--size** options to specify the size of the volume. Use a size suffix for the measure, **G** for Gigabyte, **M** for megabyte, and **K** for kilobytes. There are other options for implementing features like whether to implement a linear, striped, or mirrored volume, or to specify the size of the extents to use. Usually, the defaults work well. The following example creates a logical volume named **projects** on the **mygroup** logical group with a size of 20GB.

```
lvcreate -n projects  -L 20GB mygroup
```

The following example sets up a logical volume on the **mymedia** volume group that is 540GB in size. The mymedia volume group is made up of two physical volumes, each on 320GB hard drives. In effect, the two hard drives are logically seen as one.

```
lvcreate -n myvideos  -L 540GB mymedia
```

Once you have created your logical volume, you then need to create a file system to use on it. The following creates an **ext4** file system on the **myvideos** logical volume.

```
mkfs.ext4 myvideos
```

You could also use:

```
mkfs -t ext4 myvideos
```

With **lvextend**, you can increase the size of the logical volume if there is unallocated space available in the volume group.

Should you want to reduce the size of a logical volume, you use the **lvreduce** command, indicating the new size. Be sure to reduce the size of any file systems (**ext4**) on the logical volume, using the **resize2fs** command.

To rename a logical volume use the **lvrename** command. If you want to completely remove a logical volume, you can use the **lvremove** command.

Steps to create a new LVM group and volume

Physical Partition   First create a physical partition on your hard drive. You can use GParted, QTparted, or fdisk with the disk device name to create the partition. For example, to use fdisk to create a new partition on a new hard drive, whose device name is **/etc/sde**, you would enter:

```
fdisk /etc/sde
```

Then, in the fdisk shell, use the fdisk **n** command to create a new partition, set it as a primary partition (**p**), and make it the first partition. If you plan to use the entire hard drive for your LVM, you would need only one partition that would cover the entire drive.

Then use the **t** command to set the partition type to 8E. The 8E type is the LVM partition type. To make your changes, enter **w** to write changes to the disk.

Physical Volume   Next create a physical volume (pv) on the new and empty LVM partition, using the **pvcreate** command and the device name.

```
pvcreate /dev/sde
```

Volume Group   Then, create your volume group with **vgcreate** command, with the volume group name and the hard disk device name.

```
vgcreate mynewgroup  /dev/sde
```

Be sure the volume group is activated. Use the **vgs** command to list it. If not listed, use the following command to activate it.

```
vgchange -a  y  mynewgroup
```

Logical Volume   Then, create a logical volume, or volumes, for the volume group, using the **lvcreate** command. The **--size** or **-L** options determines the size and the **--name** option specifies the name. To find out the available free space, use the **vgs** command. You can have more than one logical volume in a volume group, or just one if you prefer. A logical volume is conceptually similar to logical volumes in an extended partition on Windows systems.

```
lvcreate --size --name mynewvol1
```

Format the Logical volume. You then use the **mkfs** command with the **-t** option to format the logical volume. The logical volume will be listed in a directory for the LVM group, within the **/dev** directory, **/dev/mynewgroup/mynewvol1**.

```
mkfs -t ext4 /dev/mynewgroup/mynewgroup-mynewvol1
```

Steps to add a new drive to an LVM group and volume

Physical Partition   First create a physical partition on your hard drive. You can use GParted or **fdisk** with the disk device name to create the partition. For the type specify LVM (**8E**).

Physical Volume   Next, create a physical volume (pv) on the new and empty LVM partition, using the **pvcreate** command and the device name.

```
pvcreate /dev/sdf
```

Add to Logical Group   Use the **vgextend** command to add the new physical volume to your existing logical group (LG).

```
vgextend mynewgroup /dev/sdf
```

Add to Logical Volume   Then, you can create new logical volumes in the new space, or expand the size of a current logical volume. To expand the size of a logical volume to the new space, first, unmount the logical volume. Then use the **lvextend** command to expand to the space on the new hard drive that is now part the same logical group. With no size specified, the entire space on the new hard drive will be added.

```
umount /dev/mynewgroup/mynewvol1
lvextend /dev/mynewgroup/mynewvol  /dev/sdf
```

Use the **-L** option to specify a particular size, **-L +250G** . Be sure to add the + sign to have the size added to the current logical volume size. To find out the available free space, use the **vgs** command.

Add to file system   Use the **resize2fs** command to extend the Linux file system (ext4) on to logical volume to include the new space, formatting it. Unless you specify a size (second parameter), all the available unformatted space is used.

```
resize2fs /dev/mynewgroup/mynewvol1
```

Note: You can back up volume group metadata (configuration) using the **vgcfgbackup** command. This does not backup your logical volumes (no content). Metadata backups are stored in **/etc/lvm/backup**, and can be restored using **vgcfgrestore**.

LVM Device Names: /dev/mapper

The **device-mapper** driver is used by LVM to set up tables for mapping logical devices to hard disk. The device name for a logical volume is kept in the **/dev/mapper** directory and has the format *logical group –logical volume*. The default LVM setup for Linux Mint has the name **vgmint-root**. The **mypics** logical volume in the **mymedia** logical group would have the device name, **/dev/mapper/mymedia-mypics**. In addition, there will be a corresponding device folder for the logical group, which will contain logical volume names. For the **vgmint** logical group, there is a device folder called **/dev/vgmint**.

Using LVM to replace drives

LVM can be very useful when you need to replace an older hard drive with a new one. Hard drives are expected to last about six years on the average. You could want to replace the older drive with a larger one (hard drive storage sizes double every year or so). Replacing additional hard drives is easy. To replace a boot drive is much more complicated.

To replace the drive, simply incorporate the new drive to your logical volume (see Steps to add a new drive to an LVM group and volume). The size of your logical volume will increase accordingly. You can use the **pmove** command to move data from the old drive to the new one. Then, issue commands to remove the old drive (**vgreduce**) from the volume group. From the user and system point of view, no changes are made. Files from your old drive will still be stored in the same directories, though the actual storage will be implemented on the new drive.

Replacement with LVM become more complicated if you want to replace your boot drive, the hard drive from which your system starts up and which holds your linux kernel. The boot drive contains a special boot partition and the master boot record. The boot partition cannot be part of any LVM volume. You would first have to create a boot partition on the new drive using a partition tool such as Parted or fdisk, labeling it as boot (the boot drive is usually very small, about 200 MB). Then mount the partition on your system, and copy the contents of your /**boot** directory to it. Then add the remainder of the disk to your logical volume and logically remove the old disk, copying the contents of the old disk to the new one. You would still have to boot with the Linux DVD/USB, and issue the **grub-install** command to install the master boot record on your new drive. You can then boot from the new drive.

LVM Snapshots

A snapshot records and defines the state of the logical volume at a designated time. It does not create a full copy of data on the volume, but only just changes since the last snapshot. A snapshot defines the state of the data at a given time. This allows you to back up the data in a consistent way. Should you need to restore a file to its previous version, you can use the snapshot of it. Snapshots are treated as logical volumes and can be mounted, copied, or deleted.

To create a snapshot, use the **lvcreate** command with the **-s** option. In this example, the snapshot is given the name mypics-snap1 (**-n** option). You need to specify the full device name for the logical group you want to create the snapshot for. Be sure there is enough free space available in the logical group for the snapshot. In this example, the snapshot logical volume is created in the **/dev/mymedia** logical group. It could just as easily be created in any other logical group. Though a snapshot normally uses very little space, you have to guard against overflows. If the snapshot is allocated the same size as the original, it will never overflow. For systems where little of the original data changes, the snapshot can be very small. The following example allocates one-third the size of the original (60GB).

```
sudo lvcreate -s -n mypics-snap1 -l 20GB /dev/mymedia
```

You can then mount the snapshot as you would any other file system.

```
sudo mount /dev/mymedia/mypic-snap1 /mysnaps
```

To delete a snapshot you use the **lvremove** command, removing it like you would any logical volume.

```
sudo lvremove -f /dev/mymedia/mypics-nap1
```

Snapshots are very useful for making backups while a system is still active. You can use tar or dump to back up the mounted snapshot to a disk or tape. All the data from the original logical volume will be included, along with the changes noted by the snapshot.

Snapshots also allow you to perform effective undo operations. You can create a snapshot of a logical volume, then unmount the original and mount the snapshot in its place. Any changes you make will be performed on the snapshot, not the original. Should problems occur, unmount the snapshot and then mount the original. This restores the original state of your data. You could also do this using several snapshots, restoring to a previous snapshot. With this procedure, you could test new software on a snapshot, without endangering your original data. The software would be operating on the snapshot, not the original logical volume.

You can also use them as alternative versions of a logical volume. You can read and write to a snapshot. A write will change only the snapshot volume, not the original, creating, in effect, an alternate version.

OpenZFS

The ZFS file system incorporates the features of a logical volume manager (LVM), RAID systems, and file systems. It is now a filesystem type option for manual partition formatting (Something Else). ZFS abstracts a file system, much like LVM, setting up a pool of storage from which a file system can be generated. Checksums for data blocks are saved outside the data blocks and are checked for any corruption within the blocks. This makes ZFS effective in protecting against silent data corruption from problems such as write interrupts, driver bugs, and access failures. If RAID-Z support has been set up, corrupted blocks can be recovered. RAID-Z implements a data-oriented RAID-like support with automatic mirroring of your data within the file system. In addition, the LVM-like abstraction of ZFS allows for large files. Writes are performed with a copy-on-write transaction method, where data is not overwritten directly, but added.

ZFS was developed by SUN, which is now controlled by Oracle. Since 2010, OpenZFS provides an open source version of ZFS for Linux systems. Linux Mint and Ubuntu support the ZFS file system, using the OpenZFS kernel module. Tools to manage ZFS file systems can be installed with the **zfsutils-linux** package (Synaptic Package Manager or **apt** command). See the following for more information:

```
https://wiki.ubuntu.com/Kernel/Reference/ZFS
```

Much like an LVM system, you have the physical devices (called virtual devices, VDEVs) that are combined and striped into a data pool (**zpool** command), which can then be used to create the ZFS file system. At the pool level, you can implement RAIDZ options. With the **zfs** command, you can then create file systems in your pool, as well as create snapshots (read-only copy) of a ZFS file system, or a clone (writeable copy). To perform an integrity check of the pool, use the **zpool** command's **scrub** option.

ZFS will automatically generate snapshots as you update your system. To restore your system to one of these snapshots, you would access the History entry in the Grub boot menu when you start your system. This opens a list of previous snapshots. Choose the one you want to open options for restoring the system with or without user data, or to a recovery state.

Linux Mint also provides the ZSys system tool (**zsys** package) for easily managing your ZFS file systems. It is still under development. ZSys implements the **zsysctl** command that interfaces with ZFS through the **zsysd** daemon. You can use the **zsysctl** command to perform operations on your ZFS file systems. The **list** command lists your file systems and the **show** command shows their status.

```
zsysctl list

zsysctl show
```

If you choose the ZFS install option during installation, both the **zfsutils-linux** and **zsys** packages are installed for you. You can find out more about ZSys at:

```
https://github.com/ubuntu/zsys
```

10. Network Connections

Network Connections: Dynamic and Static

GNOME Network (Network Settings)

Network Manager

nm-connection-editor (Network Connections)

nmcli

Dial-up PPP Access: wvdial

Netplan

Network Configuration with systemd-networkd

Setting up a firewall with Gufw and ufw

Setting up a firewall with FirewallD

Network Information

You configure your network connections using network managers. Linux Mint 21 uses the same network managers as Ubuntu 22.04. You have two network managers to choose from: NetworkManager and systemd-networkd. On Linux Mint 21, as well as on Ubuntu 22.04 desktop, NetworkManager is the default and is installed and activated at installation. It can be managed using System Settings Network or Network Connections. The alternative network manager, systemd-networkd, is also installed, but not configured.

Both network managers use Netplan to configure and manage network devices. Netplan is a network abstract configuration renderer, which generates network device configuration files using simple user-defined configuration files. The older ifupdown package along with its collection of network device management tools, such as **ifup** and **ifdown**, have been deprecated, but is still available and supported. Netplan provides a level of abstraction for network device configuration, making the process much more flexible. Netplan creates network device configuration files in the **/etc/netplan** directory, which users can edit. It then uses these files to generate the network device configuration files at startup.

Network devices now use a predictable naming method that differs from the older naming method. Names are generated based on the specific device referencing the network device type, its hardware connection and slot, and even its function. You can use the **ifconfig** command in a terminal window to find the names of your network devices.

Network Configuration Tool	Description
Network Manager	Automates Wi-Fi and wired network connections, selection, and notification. Used for all network connections including wired, wireless, mobile broadband, VPN, and DSL.
GNOME Network (Network Settings)	GNOME Network connection preferences, allowing connection and configuration of wired, Wi-Fi, and VPN connections. Used to set up proxy configuration.
nm-connection-editor (Network Connections)	The Network Manager connection editor for configuring all types of connections, including DSL, PPP, and Mobile Broadband.
nmcli	**nmcli** is the command line interface version of Network Manager.
ufw	Sets up a network firewall.
Gufw	GNOME interface for UFW firewall
Firewalld	Sets up a network firewall using firewalld.
wvdial	PPP dial-up modem connection
systemd-networkd	systemd-based network configuration

Table 10-1: Linux Mint Network Configuration Tools

Linux Mint will automatically detect and configure your network connections with Network Manager. Should the automatic configuration either fail or be incomplete for some reason, you can use Network Manager to perform a manual configuration. If you want to make a simple dial-up modem connection, you can use WvDial. Your network will also need a firewall. UFW (with the Gufw interface) or FirewallD is recommended. Table 10-1 lists several network configuration tools.

Linux Mint provides two tools for configuring your NetworkManager connections: GNOME Network and the nm-connection-editor. Gnome Network provides basic configuration, including Wi-Fi, wired, and VPN connections, as well as proxy configuration. It is accessed as Network on the Preferences menu and in System Settings. On the NetworkManager applet it is listed as Network Settings. The nm-connection-editor provides additional configuration such as DSL, PPP, and Mobile Broadband. It is referred to as Advanced Network Configuration in the Preferences menu and as Network Connections on the NetworkManager applet.

Network Connections: Dynamic and Static

If you are on a network, you may need to obtain certain information to configure your connection interface. Most networks now support dynamic configuration using either the older Dynamic Host Configuration Protocol (DHCP) or the IPv6 Protocol and its automatic address configuration. In this case, you need only check the DHCP entry in most network configuration tools. If your network does not support DHCP or IPv6 automatic addressing, or you are using a static connection (DCHP and IPv6 connections are dynamic), you will have to provide detailed information about your connection. For a static connection, you would enter your connection information manually such as your IP address and DNS servers, whereas in a dynamic connection this information is provided automatically to your system by a DHCP server or generated by IPv6 when you connect to the network. For DHCP, a DHCP client on each host will obtain the information from a DHCP server serving that network. IPv6 generates its addresses directly from the device and router information such as the device hardware MAC address.

In addition, if you are using a dynamic DSL, ISDN, or a modem connection, you will also have to supply provider, login, and password information, and specify whether your system is dynamic or static. You may also need to supply specialized information such as DSL or modem compression methods or dialup number.

You can obtain most of your static network information from your network administrator, or from your ISP (Internet Service Provider). You would need the following information:

The device name for your network interface   For LAN and wireless connections, this is network device name, which you can find using the **ifconfig** or **ip l** commands. For a modem, DSL, or ISDN connection, this is a PPP device named **ppp0** (**ippp0** for ISDN). Virtual private network (VPN) connections are also supported.

Hostname   Your computer will be identified by this name on the Internet. Do not use localhost. That name is reserved for special use by your system. The name of the host should be a simple word, which can include numbers, but not punctuation such as periods and backslashes. On a small network, the hostname is often a single name. On a large network that could have several domains, the hostname includes both the name of the host and its domain.

Domain name   This is the name of your network.

The Internet Protocol (IP) address assigned to your machine   This is needed only for static Internet connections. Dynamic connections use the DHCP protocol to assign an IP address for you automatically. Every host on the Internet is assigned an IP address. Small and older network addresses might still use the older IPv4 format consisting of a set of four numbers, separated by periods. The IP protocol version 6, IPv6, uses a new format with a complex numbering sequence that is much more automatic.

Your network IP address   Static connections only. This address is similar to the IP address but lacks any reference to a particular host.

The netmask   IPv4 Static connections only. This is usually 255.255.255.0 for most networks. If, however, you are part of a large network, check with your network administrator or ISP.

The broadcast address for your network, if available (optional)   IPv4 Static connections only. Usually, your broadcast address is the same as your IP address with the number 255 added at the end.

The IP address of your network's gateway computer   Static connections only. This is the computer that connects your local network to a larger one like the Internet.

Name servers   The IP address of the name servers your network uses. These enable the use of URLs.

NIS domain and IP address for an NIS server   Necessary if your network uses an NIS server (optional).

User login and password information   Needed for dynamic DSL, ISDN, and modem connections.

Network Manager

Network Manager detects your network connections automatically, both wired and wireless. It uses the automatic device detection capabilities of udev to configure your connections. Should you instead need to configure your network connections manually, you can also use GNOME network (Network Settings) or the older nm-connections editor (Network Connections) to enter the required network connection information. Network Manager operates as a daemon with the name Network Manager. It will automatically scan for both wired and wireless connections. Information provided by Network Manager is made available to other applications. The Network Manager monitors your network connection, indicating its status on the Network Manager panel applet.

Network Manager is designed to work in the background, providing status information for your connection and switching from one configured connection to another as needed. For an initial configuration, it detects as much information as possible about a new connection.

Network Manager operates as a daemon with the name NetworkManager. If no Ethernet connection is available, Network Manager will scan for wireless connections, checking for Extended Service Set Identifiers (ESSIDs). If an ESSID identifies a previously used connection, then it is automatically selected. If several are found, then the most recently used one is chosen. If only a new connection is available, then Network Manager waits for the user to choose one. A connection is selected only if the user is logged in. If an Ethernet connection is later made, then Network Manager will switch to it from wireless.

The Network Manager daemon can be turned on or off using the **systemctl** command with the **sudo** command.

```
sudo systemctl start NetworkManager
sudo systemctl stop NetworkManager
```

Network Manager is also user specific. When a user logs in, wireless connections the user prefers will start up (wired connections are started automatically). By default, an Ethernet connection will be preferred if available. For wireless connections, you will need to choose the one you want.

Network Manager menu

Network Manager displays a network applet on the right side of the Linux Mint panel. The Network Manager icon will vary according to the type of connection. An Ethernet (wired) connection displays two connected plugs. A wireless connection displays a staggered wave graph (see Figure 10-1). If the connection is not active, an empty wave graph is shown. If you have both a wired and wireless connection, and the wired connection is active, the wired connection icon is used.

Figure 10-1: Network Manager wired, wireless, and disconnect icons.

The Network Manager applet menu displays your wired connection as Wired, with a switch to turn it on or off (see Figure10-2). To disconnect your wired connection, you can click the switch, turning it to the off position. Your Network Manager icon on the panel becomes grayed out. To reconnect later, click the switch again.

Figure 10-2: Network Manager applet menu

Network Manager will scan for wireless connections, checking for Extended Service Set Identifiers (ESSIDs). If an ESSID identifies a previously used connection, then it is selected by Network Manager. If several are found, then the recently used one is chosen. If only a new connection is available, then Network Manager waits for the user to choose one. A connection is selected only if the user is logged in.

Network Manager manual configuration using GNOME Network (Network Settings)

The GNOME Network tool, available from System Settings as Network, from the Preferences menu as Network, and from the Network Manager applet's menu as Network Settings, can be used to configure your network connections. Automatic wireless and wired connections were covered in Chapter 3. For detailed manual configuration, Network features similar dialogs to those used in Network Connections. When you access GNOME Network, it displays a Network dialog that shows three tabs: Wi-Fi, Wired, Wi-Fi P2P, and Network Proxy (see Figure 10-3).

The History button opens the History dialog listing all your configured Wi-Fi networks (see Figure 10-3). The configuration button opens that network's configuration dialog. To remove a Wi-Fi configuration, click its checkbox, which activates the Forget button at the lower left, then click that button.

Figure 10-3: Network (System Settings) Wi-Fi Tab and History

On the Wi-Fi tab, available wireless connections are listed to the right. Selecting an entry will create a gear button for it, which you can click to open the network configuration dialog with tabs for Details, Security, Identity, Ipv4, Ipv6, and Reset. The Details tab show strength, speed, security methods, IP and hardware addresses, routes, and the DNS server IP address. To edit the connection manually you use the Security, Identity, and IP tabs. The Security tab displays a menu from which you can choose a security method and a password (see Figure 10-4).

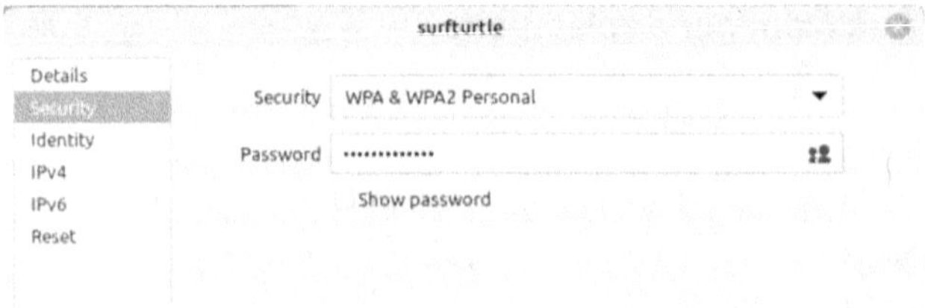

Figure 10-4: Network wireless configuration: Security tab

On the Identity tab you can specify the SSID name, choose a firewall zone, choose to connect automatically when you log in, and whether to make the connection system wide (available to other users (see Figure 10-5).

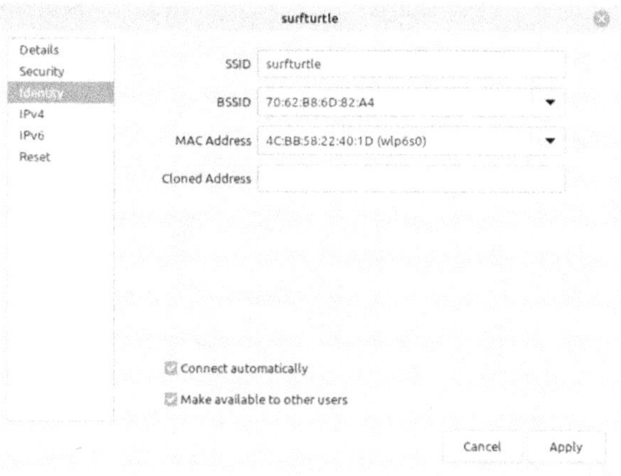

Figure 10-5: Network wireless configuration: Identity tab

On the IPv4 Settings tabs a switch allows you to turn the IP connection on or off. There are sections for Addresses, the DNS servers, and Routes (see Figure 10-6). An Addresses menu lets you choose the type connection you want. By default, it is set to Automatic. If you change it to Manual, new entries appear for the address, netmask, and gateway. On the IPv6 tab, the netmask is replaced by the prefix. You can turn off Automatic switches for the DNS and Routes sections to make them manual. The DNS section has a plus button to let you add more DNS servers.

Figure 10-6: Network wireless configuration: IP tabs, manual

The Networking dialog's Wired tab displays information about the wired connection such as the IP, hardware, and DNS server addresses. A gear button is displayed on the lower right. A switch lets you turn the connection on or off (see Figure 10-7). Clicking on the gear button opens a configuration dialog with tabs for Details, Security, Identity, IPv4, IPv6, and Reset (see Figure 10-8).

Figure 10-7: Network wired tab

Figure 10-8: Network wired configuration dialog

You can use the Security, Identity, and IP tabs to manually configure the connection. The Security tab lets you turn on 802.1 security and choose an authentication method as well as provide a username and password (see Figure 10-9).

Figure 10-9: Network wired configuration, Security

On the Identity tab you can choose the firewall zone, set the name, choose the hardware address, set the MTU blocks, choose to connect automatically, and whether to make the connection system wide (see Figure 10-10).

Figure 10-10: Network wired configuration, Identity

On the IPv tabs, a switch allows you to turn the connection on or off. The tab has sections for Addresses, DNS servers, and Routes. DNS and Routs have a switch for automatic. Turing the switch off allows you to manually enter a DNS server address or routing information. From the Addresses menu, you can also choose to make the connection automatic or manual. When manual, new entries appear that let you enter the address, netmask, and gateway (see Figure 10-11). On the IPv6 tab, the Netmask entry is replaced by a Prefix entry.

Figure 10-11: Network wired configuration, IPv4

On the Network dialog, you can add a new connection by clicking the plus button on the lower left corner. An "Add VPN" dialog opens to let you add a VPN connection. Select the kind of VPN connection you want to use (see Figure 10-12). The OpenVPN entry displays an Add VPN dialog with Identity, IPv4, and IPv6 tabs. On the Identity tab, click the Advanced button to open the Advanced Properties dialog with tabs for General, Security, TLS Authentication, Proxies, and Misc (see Figure 10-13). Click the Apply button for changes on the Advanced Properties dialog. Click the Add button when you are finished with your VPN configuration.

Figure 10-12: VPN Selection

Figure 10-13: VPN configuration

Network Manager Advanced Configuration using the nm-connection-editor (Network Connections)

You can also use the older **nm-connection-editor** (Network Connections) to edit any network connection, accessible from the Network Manager applet's menu as Network Connections, and from the Preferences menu as Advanced Network Configuration. This opens Network Manager's Network Connections window as shown in Figure 10-14.

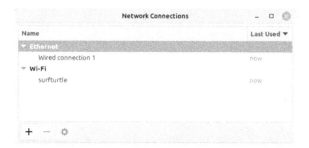

Figure 10-14: Network Connections

Established connections are listed, with Add, Edit, and Delete buttons for adding, editing, and removing network connections. Your current network connections should be listed, having been detected automatically. In Figure 10-14 a wired Ethernet connection referred to as **Wired connection 1** is listed, the first Ethernet connection. This is an automatic configuration set up by Network Manager when it automatically connected to the wired network.

When you add a connection, you can choose the type of connection from a drop-down menu (see Figure 10-15). The menu organizes connection types into three categories: Hardware, Virtual, and VPN (Virtual Private Network) (see Figure 10-16). Hardware connections cover both wired (Ethernet, DSL, and Infiniband) and wireless connections (Wi-Fi, WiMax, and Mobile Broadband). VPN lists the supported VPN types such as OpenVPN, PPTP, and Cisco (install support for additional ones). You can also import a previously configured connection. Virtual supports VLAN, Bridge, and Bond virtual connections.

Figure 10-15: Choosing a connection type for a new network connection

Hardware

Bluetooth

DSL/PPPoE

Ethernet

InfiniBand

Mobile Broadband

Wi-Fi

Virtual

Bond

Bridge

IP tunnel

MACsec

Team

VLAN

WireGuard

VPN

OpenVPN

Point-to-Point Tunneling Protocol (PPTP)

Import a saved VPN configuration...

Figure 10-16: New connection types

General tab

Configuration editing dialogs display a General tab where you can make your configuration available to all users, and automatically connect when the network connection is available. You can also choose to use a VPN connection and specify a firewall zone. Figure 10-17 shows the General tab with a wired connection.

Figure 10-17: General tab

Wired Configuration

To edit a wired connection, select the connection and click the Edit button on the Ethernet tab. This opens an Editing window as shown in Figure 10-18. The Add button is used to add a new connection and opens a similar window, with no settings. There are six tabs: General, Ethernet, 8.02.1x Security, DCB, IPv4 Settings, and IPv6 Settings. The Ethernet tab lists the MAC hardware address and the MTU. The MTU is usually set to automatic. Figure 10-16 shows the standard default configuration for a wired Ethernet connection using DHCP.

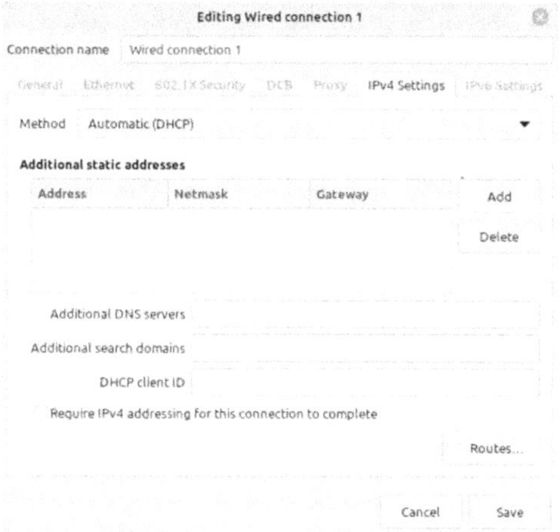

Figure 10-18: DHCP Wired Configuration

The IPv4 and IPv6 Settings tabs let you select the kind of protocol your wired connection uses. A check box at the bottom of the dialog lets you require the given protocol to complete the connection. The IPv4 and IPv6 have different entries. The IPv4 options are:

Automatic (DHCP): DHCP connection, address information is blocked out.

Automatic (DHCP) addresses only: DHCP connection that lets you specify your DNS server addresses.

Manual: Enter your IP, network, and gateway addresses along with your DNS server addresses and your network domain name.

Link-local only: IPv6 private local network. All address entries are blocked out.

Shared to other computers: All address entries are blocked out.

The IPv6 options are:

Ignore: Do not use IPv6.

Automatic: IPv6 automatic address detection (similar to DHCP).

Automatic, addresses only: Use IPv6 to determine network addresses, but not DNS (domain) information. You can enter the DNS server addresses and search domains manually.

Manual: Enter your IP, network, and gateway addresses along with your DNS server addresses and your network domain name. IPv6 addresses use an address and a prefix.

Link-local only: IPv6 private local network. All address entries are blocked out.

Figure 10-19 shows the manual configuration entries for an IPv4 wired Ethernet connection. Click the Add button to enter the IP address, network mask, and gateway address. Then enter the address for the DNS servers and your network search domains. The Routes button will open a window where you can manually enter any network routes. Figure 10-20 shows the manual configuration for an IPv6 connection, with address and prefix entries for the address.

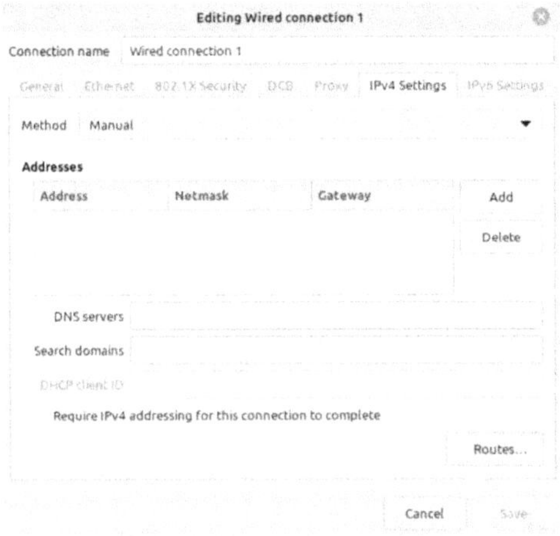

Figure 10-19: Manual IPv4 Wired Configuration

Figure 10-20: Manual IPv6 Wired Configuration

The 802.1 tab allows you to configure 802.1 security if your network supports it (see Figure 10-21). It supports MD5, TLS, PWD, FAST, Tunneled TLS, and Protected EAP methods.

Figure 10-21: 802.1 Security Configuration

The DCB tab allows you to configure Data Center Bridging connections, should your network support them. DCB provides extensions to the Internet protocol to manage high-speed connections better, such as storage area network (SAN) connections and data center fiber channels. Connections supported include Fiber Channel over the Ethernet (FCoE and FIP (Fiber Channel Initialization Protocol)) and iSCSI. For each, you can set the flow control priorities (Priority Pause Transmission) and priority groups priorities.

Wireless Configuration

Wireless connections are listed on the Network Connections window's Wi-Fi listing. To add or edit a wireless connection, use the Add or Edit buttons. When you click the Edit button, the Editing window opens with tabs for your wireless information, security, IPv4, and IPv6 settings (See Figure 10-22). On the Wi-Fi tab, you specify your SSID, along with your Mode and device.

Figure 10-22: Wi-Fi configuration

On the Wi-Fi Security tab, you enter your wireless connection security method (see Figure 10-23). The commonly used method, WEP, is supported, along with WPA personal. The WPA personal method only requires a password. More secure connections like Dynamic WEP and

Enterprise WPA are also supported. These will require more configuration information such as authentication methods, certificates, and keys.

On the IPv4 Settings tab, you enter your wireless connection's network address settings. This tab is the same as the IPv4 Setting on the Wired connection (see Figure 10-19). You have the same options: DHCP, DHCP with DNS addresses, Manual, Link-local only, and Shared. If your wireless connection uses the IPv6 protocol, you would use the IPv6 Settings tab, also the same as IPv6 Settings on a wired connection (see Figure 10-20).

Figure 10-23: Wi-Fi Security: WEP and WPA

DSL Configuration

To add or edit a direct DSL connection, you click the Add or Edit buttons on the Network Connections window's DSL tab. The DSL connection window opens, showing tabs for DSL configuration and for wired, PPP, and IPv4 network connections. On the DSL tab you enter your DSL username, service provider, and password (see Figure 10-24). The PPP tab is the same as that used for Mobile Broadband, and IPv4 is the same as the IPv4 Settings tab used for Wired, Wireless, and Mobile Broadband connections (see Figure 10-19).

Figure 10-24: DSL manual configuration

Mobile Broadband

Mobile Broadband connections are listed in the Mobile Broadband tab. For a new broadband connection, click the Add button. A wizard starts up to help you set up the appropriate configuration for your particular broadband service (see Figure 10-25). Configuration steps are listed on the left pane. If your device is connected, you can select it from the drop-down menu on the right pane. On the next step, you choose your country. The wizard then displays a service provider window listing mobile broadband service providers (see Figure 10-26). You then select the billing plan. For the last step, you are asked to confirm your selections.

Figure 10-25: Mobile Broadband Wizard

Once a service is selected, you can further edit the configuration by clicking its entry in the Mobile Broadband tab and clicking the Edit button. The Editing window opens with tabs for Mobile Broadband, PPP, IPv4 settings. On the Mobile Broadband tab, you can enter your number, username, and password. Advanced options include the APN, Network, and PIN (see Figure 10-27). The APN should already be entered.

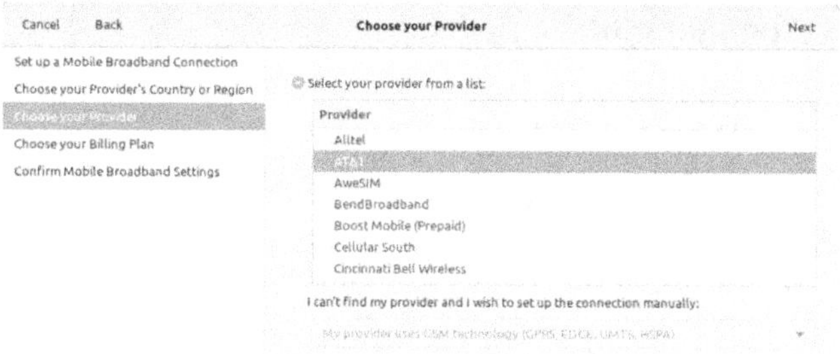

Figure 10-26: Mobile Broadband Provider Listings

Figure 10-27: Mobile Broadband configuration

PPP Configuration

For either Wireless Broadband or DSL connections, you also can specify PPP information. The PPP tab is the same for both (see Figure 10-28). There are Authentication, Compression, and the Echo sections. Check the features that are supported by your particular PPP connection. For Authentication, click the Configure Methods button to open a dialog listing possible authentication methods. Check the ones your connection supports.

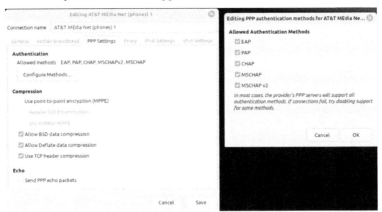

Figure 10-28: PPP Configuration

Network Manager VPN

On the Network Manager menu, the VPN Connection entry submenu will list configured VPN connections for easy access. The Configure VPN entry will open the Network Connections window to the VPN tab where you can then add, edit, or delete VPN connections. The Disconnect VPN entry will end the current active VPN connection.

Several VPN services are available from the Universe repository (not Snap). You can install them with either the Synaptic Package Manager (search on network-manager) or the **apt** command. The PPTP service for Microsoft VPN connections and OpenVPN are installed by default. Other popular VPN services include Fortinet (SSL), OpenConnect (SSL), Layer 2 Tunneling Protocol (IPSec encryption), Cisco Concentrator, Iodine (DNS tunneling), and Openswan (IPSec). Network Manager support is installed using the corresponding Network Manager plugin for these services. The plugin packages begin with the name **network-manager**. OpenVPN, which uses the **openvpn** software along with the **network-manager-openvpn** plugin, is install be default. For the Layer 2 Tunneling Protocol VPN install the **network-manager-l2tp** plugin. For the Fortinet SSL VPN install the **network-manager-fortisslvpn** plugin. For the OpenConnect VPN (Juniper SSL client) install the **network-manager-openconnect** plugin. For Cisco Concentrator based VPN, install the **network-manager-vpnc** plugin. Strongswan uses the **network-manager-strongswan** plugin. For the Iodine VPN (DNS tunneling) install the **network-manager-iodine** plugin.

To add a VPN connection, choose a VPN Connection type from the connection type menu. (see Figure 10-29).

VPN

Fortinet SSLVPN

Layer 2 Tunneling Protocol (L2TP)

Cisco AnyConnect or openconnect (OpenConnect)

Juniper Network Connect (OpenConnect)

Palo Alto Networks GlobalProtect (OpenConnect)

Pulse Connect Secure (OpenConnect)

F5 BIG-IP SSL VPN (OpenConnect)

Fortinet SSL VPN (OpenConnect)

Array SSL VPN (OpenConnect)

OpenVPN

Point-to-Point Tunneling Protocol (PPTP)

IPsec/IKEv2 (strongswan)

Cisco Compatible VPN (vpnc)

Import a saved VPN configuration...

Figure 10-29: VPN connection types

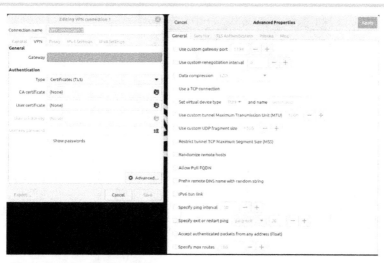

Figure 10-30: VPN configuration (openvpn)

The "Editing VPN connection" dialog then opens with three tabs: General, VPN, and IPv4 Settings. On the VPN tab, you enter VPN connection information such as the gateway address and any additional VPN information that may be required. For an OpenVPN connection, you will need to provide the authentication type, certificates, and keys (see Figure 10-30). Clicking on the Advanced button opens the Advanced Options dialog. An OpenVPN connection will have tabs for General, Security, and TLS Authentication. On the Security tab, you can specify the cipher to use.

Options will differ depending on the type of VPN connection you choose. The PPTP connection used on Microsoft networks requires only a gateway address on the VPN tab. Advanced options let you specify the authentication method and security options (see Figure 10-31). Like OpenVPN, a Strongswan IPSec connection also requires certificates and keys. It does not have an Advanced Options dialog. The IPv4 tab lets you specify your DNS servers if you want. The Cisco Connector connection only requires a group name and password. You also can specify the encryption method, domain, and username.

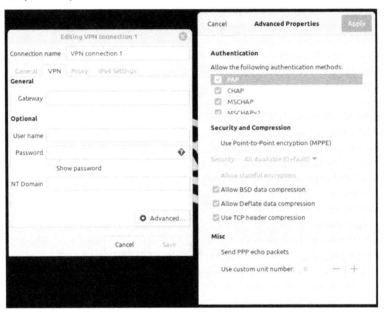

Figure 10-31: VPN configuration (pptp)

Wireguard VPN

Linux Mint and Ubuntu support the Wireguard virtual network manager, which provides better encryption and efficiency than the older IPsec and OpenVPN tools . Wireguard works by setting up dedicated network interfaces (**wg**), which are then uses for the VPN connections. Check the Wireguard Web site for instructions on how to configure and manage a Wireguard connection (**https://www.wireguard.com**). You can install Wireguard with Software Manager, the **apt** command (Universe repository), or with the Synaptic Package Manager (Universe repository).

```
sudo apt install wireguard
```

You can use Network Connections to configure a Wireguard connection. Choose Wireguard in the Virtual section to set up a Wireguard connection (see Figure 10-32). This opens the "Editing WireGuard connection" dialog at the WireGuard tab where you can specify the interface name, the private key to use, the port to use, fwmark, and MTU. You can then list the public keys allowed in the Peer section. Click the Add button to open a "Edit WireGuard peer" dialog to enter the key and its allowed addresses.

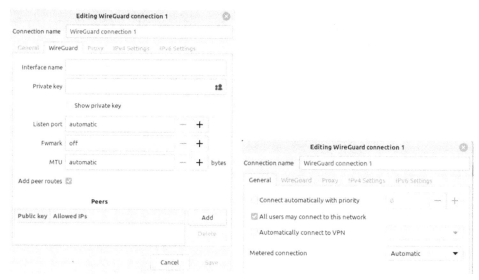

Figure 10-32: WireGuard configuration

Managing Network Connections with nmcli

The **nmcli** command is NetworkManager Command Line Interface command. Most network configuration tasks can be performed by **nmcli**. The **nmcli** command manages NetworkManager through a set of objects: general (**g**), networking (**n**), radio (**r**), connection (**c**), device (**d**), and agent (**a**). Each can be referenced using the full name or a unique prefix, such as **con** for connection or **dev** for device. The unique prefix can be as short as a single character, such as **g** for general, **c** for connections, or **d** for device. See Table 10-2 for a list of the objects and commonly used options. The **nmcli** man page provides a complete listing with examples.

The general object shows the current status of NetworkManager and what kind of devices are enabled. You can limit the information displayed using the **-t** (terse) and **-f** (field) options. The STATE field show the connection status, and the CONNECTIVITY field the connection.

```
$ nmcli general
STATE        CONNECTIVITY  WIFI-HW  WIFI     WWAN-HW  WWAN
connected    full          enabled  enabled  enabled  enabled

$ nmcli -t -f STATE general
connected
```

The **connection** object references the network connection and the **show** option displays that information. The following example displays your current connection.

nmcli connection showYou can use **c** instead of **connection** and **s** instead of show.

```
$ nmcli c s
NAME        UUID                                   TYPE           DEVICE
enp7s0      f7202f6d-fc66-4b81-8962-69b71202efc0   802-3-ethernet enp7s0
AT&T LTE 1  65913b39-789a-488c-9559-28ea6341d9e1   gsm            --
```

Object	Description
`general`	NetworkManager status and enabled devices. Use the terse (**-t**) and field (**-f**) option to limit the information displayed.
`networking`	Manage networking, use `on` and `off` to turn networking on or off, and `connectivity` for the connection state.
`radio`	Turns on or off the wireless networking (on or off). Can turn on or off specific kinds of wireless: `wifi`, `wwan` (mobile broadband), and `wimax`. The `all` option turns on or off all wireless.
`connection`	Manage network connections.
	`show` List connection profiles. With `--active` show only active connections.
	`up` Activate a connection
	`down` Deactivate a connection
	`add` Add a new connection, specifying `type`, `ifname`, `con-name` (profile).
	`modify` Edit an existing connection, use + and – to add new values to properties
	`edit` Add a new connection or edit an existing one using the interactive editor
	`delete` Delete a configured connection (profile)
	`reload` Reload all connection profiles
	`load` Reload or load a specific
`device`	Manage network interfaces (devices).
	`status` Display device status
	`show` Display device information
	`connect` Connect the device
	`disconnect` Disconnect the device
	`delete` Delete a software device, such as a bridge.
	`wifi` Display a list of available wifi access points
	`wifi rescan` Rescan for and display access points
	`wifi connect` Connect to a wifi network; specify `password`, `wep-key-type`, `ifname`, `bssid`, and `name` (profile name)
	`wimax` List available WiMAX networks
`agent`	Run as a Network Manager secret agent or polkit agent.
	`secret` As a secret agent, nmcli listens for secret requests.
	`polkit` As a polkit agent it listens for all authorization requests.

Table 10-2: The nmcli objects

As with the general object, you can limit the fields displayed using the **-f** option. The following only list the name and type fields.

```
$ nmcli -f name,type c s
NAME         TYPE
enp7s0       802-3-ethernet
AT&T LTE 1  gsm
```

Adding the **--active** option will only show active connections.

```
nmcli c s --active
```

To start and stop a connection (like **ifconfig** does), use the **up** and **down** options.

```
nmcli con up enp7s0.
```

Use the **device** object to manage your network devices. The **show** and **status** options provide information about your devices. To check the status of all your network devices use the **device** object and **status** options:

```
nmcli device status
DEVICE  TYPE      STATE         CONNECTION
enp7s0  ethernet  connected     enp7s0
wlp6s0  wifi      disconnected  --
lo      loopback  unmanaged     --
```

You can abbreviate **device** and **status** to **d** and **s**.

```
nmcli d s
```

You also use the **device** object to connect and disconnect devices. Use the **connect** or **disconnect** options with the interface name (ifname) of the device, in this example, **enp7s0**. With the **delete** option, you can remove a device.

```
nmcli device disconnect enp7s0
nmcli device connect enp7s0
```

To turn networking on or off you use the **networking** object and the **on** and **off** options. Use the **connectivity** option to check network connectivity. The networking object alone tells you if it is enabled or not.

```
$ nmcli networking
enabled

$ nmcli networking on

$ nmcli networking connectivity
full
```

Should you want to just turn on or off the Wifi connection, you would use the **radio** object. Use **wifi**, **wwan**, and **wimax** for a specific type of wifi connection and the **all** option for all of them. The radio object alone shows wifi status of all your wifi connection types.

```
$ nmcli radio
WIFI-HW   WIFI  WWAN-HW   WWAN
enabled   enabled  enabled   enabled

$ nmcli radio wifi on
```

```
$ nmcli radio all off
```

nmcli Wired Connections

You can use **nmcli** to add connections, just as you can with the desktop NetworkManager tool. To add a new static connection use the connection object with the **add** option. Specify the connection's profile name with the **con-name** option, the interface name with the **ifname** option, the **type**, such as ethernet. For a static connection you would add the IP address (**ipv4** or **ipv6**), and the gateway address (**gw4** or **gw6**). For a DHCP connection simply do not list the IP address and gateway options. The profile name can be any name. You could have several profile names for the same network device. For example, for your wireless device, you could have several wireless connection profiles, depending on the different networks you want to connect to. Should you connect your Ethernet device to a different network, you would simply use a different connection profile that you have already set up, instead of manually reconfiguring the connection. If you do not specify a connection name, one is generated and assigned for you. The connection name can be the same as the device name as shown here, but keep in mind that the connection name refers to the profile and the device name refers to the actual device.

```
$ nmcli c s
NAME     UUID                                   TYPE            DEVICE
enp7s0   f7202f6d-fc66-4b81-8962-69b71202efc0   802-3-ethernet  enp7s0
```

For a DHCP connection, specify the profile name, connection type, and ifname. The following example creates an Ethernet connection with the profile name "my-wired."

```
nmcli con add con-name my-wired type ethernet ifname enp7s0
```

For a static connection add the IP (**ip4** or **ip6**) and gateway (**gw4** or **gw6**) options with their addresses.

```
nmcli con add con-name my-wired-static ifname enp7s0 type ethernet ip4
192.168.1.0/24 gw4 192.168.1.1
```

In most cases, the type is Ethernet (wired) or wifi (wireless). Check the **nmcli** man page for a list of other types, such as gsm, infiniband, vpn, vlan, wimax, and bridge.

You can also add a connection using the interactive editor. Use the **edit** instead of the **add** option, and specify the **con-name** (profile) and connection type.

```
nmcli con edit type ethernet con-name my-wired
```

To modify an existing connection, use the **modify** option. For an IP connection, the property that is changed is referenced as part of the IP settings, in this example, **ip4**. The IP properties include addresses, gateway, and method (ip4.addresses, ip4.gateway, and ip4.method).

```
nmcli con mod my-wired ip4.gateway 192.168.1.2
```

To add or remove a value for a property use the + and - signs as a prefix. To add a DNS server address you would use **+ip4.dns**. To remove one use **-ip4.dns**.

```
nmcli con mod my-wired +ip4.dns 192.168.1.5
```

You can also modify a connection using the interactive editor. Use the edit instead of the modify option with the connection name.

```
nmcli con edit enp7s0
```

You are then placed in the interactive editor with an **nmcli>** prompt and the settings you can change are listed. The **help** command lists available commands. Use the **describe** command to show property descriptions.

Use **print** to show the current value of a property and **set** to change its value. To see all the properties for a setting, use the **print** command and the setting name. Once you have made changes, use the **save** command to effect the changes.

```
print ipv4
print ipv4.dns
print connection
set ipv4.address 192.168.0.1
```

The connection edit command can also reference a profile using the **id** option. The Name field in the connection profile information is the same as the ID. Also, each profile is given a unique system UUID, which can also be used to reference the profile.

Once you are finished editing the connection, enter the **quit** command to leave the editor.

nmcli Wireless Connections

To see a list of all the available wifi connections in your area, you use the **wifi** option with the **device** object. You can further qualify it by interface (if you have more than one) by adding the **ifname** option, and by BSSID adding the **bssid** option.

```
nmcli device wifi
```

To connect to a new Wifi network, use the **wifi connect** option and the SSID. You can further specify a password, wep-key-type, key, ifname, bssid, name (profile name), and if it is private. If you do not provide a name (profile name), nmcli will generate one for you.

```
nmcli dev wifi connect surfturtle password mypass wep-key-type wpa ifname wlp6s0
name my-wireless1
```

To reconnect to a Wifi network for which you have previously set up a connection, use the **connection** object with the **up** command and the **id** option to specify the profile name.

```
nmcli connection up id my-wireless1
```

You can also add a new wireless connection using the **connection** object and the **wifi** type with the **ssid** option.

```
nmcli con add con-name my-wireless2 ifname wlp6s0 type wifi ssid ssidname
```

Then, to set the encryption type use the **modify** command to set the **sec.key-mgmt** property, and for the passphrase set the **wifi-sec.psk** property.

```
nmcli con mod my-wirless2 wifi-sec.key-mgmt wpa-psk
nmcli con modify my-wireless2 wifi-sec.psk mypassword
```

Dial-up PPP Modem Access: wvdial

For direct dial-up PPP modem connections, you can use the wvdial dialer, an intelligent dialer that, not only dials up an ISP service, but also performs login operations, supplying your username and password. The wvdial tool runs on the command line using the wvdial command,

and on the desktop with the GNOME PPP application (**gnome-ppp**). The wvdial program first loads its configuration from the **/etc/wvdial.conf** file. In this file, you can place modem and account information, including modem speed, ISP phone number, username, and password.

The **wvdial.conf** file is organized into sections, beginning with a section label enclosed in brackets. A section holds variables for different parameters that are assigned values, such as **username = chris**. The default section holds default values inherited by other sections, so you need not repeat them. Table 10-3 lists the wvdial variables.

Variable	Description
Inherits	Explicitly inherits from the specified section. By default, sections inherit from the [Dialer Defaults] section.
Modem	The device wvdial should use as your modem. The default is **/dev/modem**.
Baud	The speed at which wvdial communicates with your modem. The default is 57,600 baud.
Init1...Init9	Specifies the initialization strings to be used by your modem; wvdial can use up to 9. The default is "ATZ" for Init1.
Phone	The phone number you want wvdial to dial.
Area Code	Specifies the area code, if any.
Dial Prefix	Specifies any needed dialing prefix—for example, 70 to disable call waiting or 9 for an outside line.
Dial Command	Specifies the dial operation. The default is "ATDT".
Login	Specifies the username you use at your ISP.
Login Prompt	If your ISP has an unusual login prompt, you can specify it here.
Password	Specifies the password you use at your ISP.
Password Prompt	If your ISP has an unusual password prompt, you can specify it here.
Force Address	Specifies a static IP address to use (for ISPs that provide static IP addresses to users).
Auto Reconnect	If enabled, wvdial attempts to reestablish a connection automatically if you are randomly disconnected by the other side. This option is on by default.

Table 10-3: Variables for wvdial

You can use the **wvdialconf** utility to create a default **wvdial.conf** file, detecting your modem and setting default values for basic features automatically. You can then edit the **wvdial.conf** file and modify the Phone, Username, and Password entries entering your dial-up information. Remove the preceding semicolon (**;**) to unquote the entry. Any line beginning with a semicolon is ignored as a comment.

```
wvdialconf
```

You can also create a named dialer. This is helpful if you have different location or services you log in to.

To start wvdial, enter the command **wvdial** in a terminal window, which then reads the connection configuration information from the **/etc/wvdial.conf** file. wvdial dials the location and initiates the PPP connection, providing your username and password when requested.

You can set up connection configurations for any number of connections in the **/etc/wvdial.conf** file. To select one, enter its label as an argument to the `wvdial` command, as shown here:

```
wvdial mylocation
```

Netplan

Netplan is used to configure and set up your network connections. The **/etc/netplan** directory holds network service and interface information for configuring your network device. The actual configuration file is generated when the system starts up and, for NetworkManager, is placed in the **/run/NetworkManager/system-connections** directory (for systemd-networkd it is placed in the **/var/run/systemd/network** directory). There is no fixed configuration file in the **/etc** directory. Instead a simple Netplan configuration file in the **/etc/netplan** directory is used to generate the network configuration file. The **/etc/netplan** files are written using YAML (YAML Ain't Markup Language) and have the extension **.yaml**. This method provides a level of abstraction that make configuration of different available network devices much more flexible. The default network service for the Linux Mint desktop is NetworkManager. You can use networkd on the Linux Mint desktop, instead of NetworkManager if you want. You can find out more about Netplan at:

```
https://netplan.io
```

Use the **networkctl status** command to check on the status of your network connections.

```
networkctl status
```

For information about a specific device add the device name to the status command.

```
networkctl status enp7s0
```

Detailed examples of Netplan configurations files can be found at:

```
/usr/share/doc/netplan/examples
```

These include examples for static, wireless, NetworkManager, dhcp, bridge, bonding, and vlans.

Netplan configuration file

The Netplan configuration files are located in the **/etc/netplan** directory. The Linux Mint Cinnamon distribution generates a Netplan configuration file for NetworkManager, **1-network-manager-all.yaml**. NetworkManager is the default for Linux Mint Cinnamon. You can edit this file to add configuration for more devices, or you can add more configuration files, each of which will be read by Netplan and a corresponding runtime configuration file generated in the **/run/NetworkManager/system-connections** directory. As NetworkManager is designed to configure multiple devices, you only need the one Netplan configuration file. But for other network managers such as **systemd-network**, you could have files for different types of network devices such as ethernet and Wi-Fi, or a different file for each device. Configuration file names usually begin with a number, starting with **1-** for the default, though they can be any name. An easy way to create a new file is to copy the default or an example file from **/usr/share/doc/netplan/examples** and then edit it.

A Netplan configuration file is organized into keys consisting of upper level configuration definitions that apply to different types of devices such as ethernets, and lower level IDs that are used to configure devices. The file begins with the top-level **network:** key followed by the Netplan version, in this case, version 2. The **renderer:** ID specifies the network service to use. For the Linux Mint this is **NetworkManager**. Linux Mint uses NetworkManager by default instead of systemd-networkd, which simplifies the default Netplan configuration file. The file holds only the renderer information, as NetworkManager handles all the details. You would use the System Settings Network or Network Connections to configure your network.

/etc/netplan/1-network-manager-all.yaml

```
# Let NetworkManager manage all devices on this system
network:
  version: 2
  renderer: NetworkManager
```

For other types of connections such as systemd-networkd, there are additional keys you can use. For a wired connection, the configuration type is **ethernets:** Under **ethernets:** the keys for the available network devices are listed. Under each device are the IDs used to configure it. In the case of a DHCP connection you usually only need one, **dhcp:** Other IDs such as **address:** for a static connection or **gateway:** for a gateway address could also be listed. An sample configuration is shown here.

The run time configuration files for NetworkManager are in the **/run/NetworkManager/system-connections** directory and have the NetworkManager name of the connection, such as **'Wired connection-1'.nmconnections**.

Configuring a network with systemd-networkd

The systemd based network manager called **systemd-networkd** can currently be used for basic operations. You would use it as a small, fast, and simple alternative to a larger manager such as NetworkManager. systemd is described in detail in Chapter 12. The service, target, and socket files for systemd-networkd are located in the **/lib/systemd/system**: **systemd-networkd.service**, **systemd-networkd-wait-online.service**, and **systemd-networkd.socket.** Network resolvconf operations are handled with **systemd-resolved.service**. User configuration files for systemd-networkd are located in **/etc/systemd/network**.

In the **systemd-networkd.service** file several security features are enabled. A capability bounding set (CapabilityBoundingSet) lets you limit kernel capabilities to those specified. The man page for **capabilities** list the available capabilities. The CAP_NET capabilities limit the networkd service to network operations such as interface configuration, firewall administration, multicasting, sockets, broadcasting, and proxies. The CAP_SET capabilities allow for file and process GID and UIDs. The CAP_CHOWN, CAP_DAC_OVERRIDE, and CAP_FOWNER capabilities deal with bypassing permission checks for files. The CAP_SYS capabilities that provide system administrative capabilities are not included. In addition, the ProtectSystem option (**systemd.exec**) prevents the service from making any changes to the system (**/usr**, **/boot**, and **/etc** directories are read only for this service). The ProtectHome option makes the **/home**, **/root**, and **/run/user** directories inaccessible. WatchdogSec sets the watchdog timeout for the service. Check the **systemd.directives** man page for a list of all systemd directives.

systemd-networkd.service

```
[Unit]
Description=Network Service
Documentation=man:systemd-networkd.service(8)
ConditionCapability=CAP_NET_ADMIN
DefaultDependencies=no
# systemd-udevd.service can be dropped once tuntap is moved to netlink
After=systemd-networkd.socket systemd-udevd.service network-pre.target systemd-
sysusers.service systemd-sysctl.service
Before=network.target multi-user.target shutdown.target
Conflicts=shutdown.target
Wants=systemd-networkd.socket network.target

[Service]
AmbientCapabilities=CAP_NET_ADMIN CAP_NET_BIND_SERVICE CAP_NET_BROADCAST
CAP_NET_RAW
CapabilityBoundingSet=CAP_NET_ADMIN CAP_NET_BIND_SERVICE CAP_NET_BROADCAST
CAP_NET_RAW
ExecStart=!!/lib/systemd/systemd-networkd
ExecReload=networkctl reload
LockPersonality=yes
MemoryDenyWriteExecute=yes
NoNewPrivileges=yes
ProtectClock=yes
ProtectControlGroups=yes
ProtectHome=yes
ProtectKernelModules=yes
ProtectKernelLogs=yes
ProtectSystem=strict
Restart=on-failure
RestartSec=0
RestrictAddressFamilies=AF_UNIX AF_NETLINK AF_INET AF_INET6 AF_PACKET AF_ALG
RestrictNamespaces=yes
RestrictRealtime=yes
RestrictSUIDSGID=yes
RuntimeDirectory=systemd/netif
RuntimeDirectoryPreserve=yes
SystemCallArchitectures=native
SystemCallErrorNumber=EPERM
SystemCallFilter=@system-service
Type=notify

User=systemd-network
WatchdogSec=3min

[Install]
WantedBy=multi-user.target
Also=systemd-networkd.socket
Alias=dbus-org.freedesktop.network1.service
```

```
Also=systemd-network-generator.service

# We want to enable systemd-networkd-wait-online.service whenever this service
# is enabled. systemd-networkd-wait-online.service has
# WantedBy=network-online.target, so enabling it only has an effect if
# network-online.target itself is enabled or pulled in by some other unit.
Also=systemd-networkd-wait-online.service
```

The **systemd-networkd.socket** file sets **systemd.socket** options for buffer size (ReceiveBuffer), network link (ListenNetlink), passing credentials (PassCredentials). As a condition for starting the service, the CAP_NET_ADMIN capability needs to be set in the capability bounding set (ConditionCapability).

systemd-networkd.socket

```
[Unit]
Description=Network Service Netlink Socket
Documentation=man:systemd-networkd.service(8) man:rtnetlink(7)
ConditionCapability=CAP_NET_ADMIN
DefaultDependencies=no
Before=sockets.target shutdown.target
Conflicts=shutdown.target

[Socket]
ReceiveBuffer=128M
ListenNetlink=route 1361
PassCredentials=yes

[Install]
WantedBy=sockets.target
```

The **systemd-resolved.service** provides for the resolvconf operations (DNS server information). It has the same capabilities as **systemd-networkd.service**, except for the network capabilities.

systemd-resolved.service

```
[Unit]
Description=Network Name Resolution
Documentation=man:systemd-resolved.service(8)
Documentation=man:org.freedesktop.resolve1(5)
Documentation=https://www.freedesktop.org/wiki/Software/systemd/writing-network-
configuration-managers
Documentation=https://www.freedesktop.org/wiki/Software/systemd/writing-resolver-
clients

DefaultDependencies=no
After=systemd-sysusers.service systemd-networkd.service
Before=network.target nss-lookup.target shutdown.target
Conflicts=shutdown.target
Wants=nss-lookup.target

[Service]
AmbientCapabilities=CAP_SETPCAP CAP_NET_RAW CAP_NET_BIND_SERVICE
BusName=org.freedesktop.resolve1
```

```
CapabilityBoundingSet=CAP_SETPCAP CAP_NET_RAW CAP_NET_BIND_SERVICE
ExecStart=!!/lib/systemd/systemd-resolved
LockPersonality=yes
MemoryDenyWriteExecute=yes
NoNewPrivileges=yes
PrivateDevices=yes
PrivateTmp=yes
ProtectProc=invisible
ProtectClock=yes
ProtectControlGroups=yes
ProtectHome=yes
ProtectKernelLogs=yes
ProtectKernelModules=yes
ProtectKernelTunables=yes
ProtectSystem=strict
Restart=always
RestartSec=0
RestrictAddressFamilies=AF_UNIX AF_NETLINK AF_INET AF_INET6
RestrictNamespaces=yes
RestrictRealtime=yes
RestrictSUIDSGID=yes
RuntimeDirectory=systemd/resolve
RuntimeDirectoryPreserve=yes
SystemCallArchitectures=native
SystemCallErrorNumber=EPERM
SystemCallFilter=@system-service
Type=notify
User=systemd-resolve
WatchdogSec=3min

[Install]
WantedBy=multi-user.target
Alias=dbus-org.freedesktop.resolve1.service
```

In addition, the **systemd-networkd-wait-online.service** delays activation of other services until **systemd-networkd** service comes online.

The systemd-networkd Netplan configuration file

You have to create a Netplan configuration file for the systemd-networkd service. You could have files for different types of network devices such as ethernet and Wi-Fi, or a different file for each device. Configuration file names usually begin with number, starting with **1-** for the default, though they can be any name.

You would then have to know how networking on your system is configured. For many systems, especially those using DHCP, this is a simple configuration, but for others, such as a static connection, it can be complex. For a system using a standard DHCP connection, as shown in this chapter, you can simply copy the **dhcp.yaml** file from the **/usr/share/doc/netplan/examples** directory to the **/etc/netplan** directory. Prefix the file name with a number, such as 2-. You can leave the **1-network-manager-all.yaml** file in **/etc/netplan** in case you should want to switch back to using NetworkManager

```
cd /usr/share/doc/netplan/examples
sudo cp dhcp.yaml /etc/netplan/2-dhcp.yaml
```

If you do not know it already, find out the name of your Ethernet device with **ip link** command. Then use a text editor like **nano** to edit the **2-dhcp.yaml** and replace the name of ethernet device, **enp3s0**, with the name of the one on your system. You can use the **ifconfig** command to find the name or your device. Be sure to use the **sudo** command to start the editor.

```
cd /etc/netplan
sudo nano 2-dhcp.yaml
```

A Netplan configuration file is organized into keys consisting of upper level configuration definitions that apply to different types of devices such as ethernets, and lower level IDs that are used to configure devices. The file begins with the top-level **network:** key followed by the Netplan version, in this case, version 2. The **renderer:** ID specifies the network service to use. **networkd**. For a wired connection, the configuration type is **ethernets:**, as shown in this example. Under **ethernets:** the keys for the available network devices are listed. Under each device are the IDs used to configure it. In the case of a DHCP connection you usually only need one, **dhcp:** Other IDs such as **address:** for a static connection or **gateway:** for a gateway address could also be listed. The final would look something like the following.

/etc/netplan/2-dhcp.yaml

```
network:
  version: 2
  renderer: networkd
  ethernets:
    enp7s0:
        dhcp4: true
```

The runtime file generated by Netplan for network configuration will be located in **/var/run/systemd/network** and will have a name that includes "netplan" and the network device name, such as **10-netplan-enp7s0.network**. This file is generated automatically at startup. If you have edited the Netplan configuration file or added a new one, and do not wish to restart your system, you can use the Netplan **generate** command to create the run time configuration file directly, and then use the **apply** command to have Netplan apply that configuration to your network connections.

```
sudo netplan generate
sudo netplan apply
```

You then have to shut down and disable NetworkManager. The service script for managing NetworkManager is **network-manager**.

```
sudo systemctl stop network-manager
sudo systemctl disable network-manager
```

Then enable and start systemd-networkd.

```
sudo systemctl enable systemd-networkd
sudo systemctl start systemd-networkd
```

You can check the status of your network device configuration and activation with the **networkctl** command.

```
networkctl
```

Netplan wireless configuration for systemd-networkd

For systemd-networkd wireless devices you have to edit your Netplan configuration file to add your wireless device name, the wireless network you want to access, and the password for that network. Instead of editing the default file directly, you can copy the **2-dhcp.yaml** file with the 2 changed to 3 and give it a name such as **3-wireless.yaml**. Netplan will read any **yaml** file in the **/etc/netplan** directory. You can find an example of a wireless configuration file at **/usr/share/doc/netplan/examples**, but it is for the network that does not support dhcp and is more complicated.

```
cd /etc/netplan
sudo cp 2-dhcp.yaml 3-wireless.yaml
```

Then edit the file to add keys for Wi-Fi, accesspoints, the SSID, and the password.

```
sudo nano 3-wireless.yaml
```

An example of a wireless Netplan configuration is shown below. Instead of the **ethernets:** definition you use the **wifis:** definition. This is followed by a key consisting of the wireless device name, such as **wlp6s0:**. Below that key is the **dhcp4:** ID and the **accesspoints:** ID, used to configure the Wi-Fi device. Under the accesspoints: ID you add an ID consisting of the SSID of the wireless network you want to connect to (the wireless network's name). The SSID must be within quotes. Under this ID you add the **password:** ID and the password for accessing that wireless network. The password must be within quotes.

/etc/netplan/3-wireless.yaml

```
network:
  version: 2
  renderer: networkd
  wifis:
    wlp6s0:
      dhcp4: true
        accesspoints:
          "SSID":
              password: "password"
```

Netplan generates a wireless configuration file at startup in **/run/netplan**. A wireless file will have the name of the device added along with the name of wireless network (SSID), such as **netplan-wlp6s0-surfturtle**.

This file is then use the by **netplan-wpa@service** to submit the SSID and password to **wpa_supplicant**, which then accesses the wireless network. The **netplan-wpa@.service** file is shown here.

netplan-wpa@.service

```
[Unit]
Description=WPA supplicant for netplan %I
Requires=sys-subsystem-net-devices-%i.device
After=sys-subsystem-net-devices-%i.device
Before=network.target
Wants=network.target
```

```
[Service]
Type=simple
ExecStart=/sbin/wpa_supplicant -c /run/netplan/wpa-%I.conf -i%I
```

If you reboot, the wireless netplan file will be read and your wireless device configured. To configure your device without rebooting, you can use the Netplan **generate** command to create the run time configuration file directly (**/var/run/systemd/network**), and then use the **apply** command to have Netplan apply that configuration to your network connection.

```
sudo netplan generate
sudo netplan apply
```

Then restart systemd-networkd.

```
sudo systemctl restart systemd-networkd
```

You can use the **networkctl** command to see if your wireless device has been properly configured and is connected. The **networkctl** command works only for systemd-networkd..

```
$ networkctl
IDX LINK          TYPE           OPERATIONAL SETUP
  1 lo            loopback       carrier     unmanaged
  2 enp7s0        ether          routable    configured
  3 wlp6s0        wlan           routable    configured

3 links listed.
```

Switching between systemd-networkd and network-manager

Your original Netplan configuration file for NetworkManager, **1-network-manager-all.yaml**, should still be in your **/etc/netplan** directory.

To change from systemd-networkd back to NetworkManager, first stop and disable systemd-networkd with the **systemctl** command.

```
sudo systemctl stop systemd-networkd
sudo systemctl disable systemd-networkd
```

Then enable and start NetworkManager. Use the service name for NetworkManager, **network-manager**. Also, remove or move the systemd-networkd netplan file in the **/etc/netplan** directory so that it is not read. You could also just rename the extension.

```
sudo systemctl enable network-manager
sudo systemctl start network-manager
sudo mv /etc/netplan/netplan/2-dhcp.yaml /home
```

You can use the **status** command for **systemctl** to see if your network device is active or inactive.

```
systemctl status systemd-networkd
systemctl status network-manager
```

To change back to systemd-networkd, disable NetworkManager and enable systemd-networkd. Also add your systemd-networkd netplan file back to the **/etc/netplan** directory.

```
sudo systemctl stop network-manager
sudo systemctl disable network-manager
```

```
sudo systemctl enable systemd-networkd
sudo systemctl start systemd-networkd
```

If your NetworkManager file is, for some reason, missing from the **/etc/netplan** directory, you can just copy the **network_manager.yaml** file from the **netplan.io** doc directory, **/usr/share/doc/netplan/examples**.

```
cd /usr/share/doc/netplan/examples
sudo cp network_manager.yaml  /etc/netplan/1-network-manager-all.yaml
```

Then use the **netplan** command with the apply option to generate a new network configuration file.

```
sudo netplan generate
sudo netplan apply
```

Firewalls

You can choose from several different popular firewall management tools. Linux Mint provides a firewall management tool called the Uncomplicated Firewall (ufw), which is a frontend for IPtables. You can also choose to use other popular management tools like Firewalld and Fwbuilder. Both ufw and FirewallD are covered in this chapter. Search Software Manager or the Synaptic Package Manager for "firewall" to see a complete listing.

IPtables has been replaced by nftables. Whereas IPtables works like an interpreter, processing each individual rule one at a time, nftables operates more like a programming language, able to handle many rules at once on incoming packets. On Linux Mint 21 and on Ubuntu 22.04, the **/sbin/iptables** command is a link to the **/etc/alternatives/iptables** command, which, in turn, is a link to the **/usr/sbin/iptables-nft-multi**, which is one of the **iptables-nft** commands such as **iptables-nft-save** and **iptables-nft-restore**. The **iptables-nft** commands read IPtables rules and convert them to nftables format using the **nft_compat** module. Though the ufw frontend manages IPtables rules, these rules are converted and used by nftables. FirewallD, on the other hand, operates as a frontend for nftables directly. Also, if you have to add rules directly to your firewall and need to covert from IPtables to nftables, you can use the **iptables-translate** command. The **iptables-translate** command takes as its argument an IPtables rule and generates the nftables equivalent. You can find out more about nftables at: **https://wiki.nftables.org/**.

Important Firewall Ports

Commonly used services like Linux and Windows file sharing, FTP servers, BitTorrent, and Secure SHell remote access, use certain network connection ports on your system (see Table 10-4). A default firewall configuration will block these ports. You have to configure your firewall to allow access to the ports these services use before the services will work.

For example, to access a Windows share, you not only have to have the Samba service running, but also have to configure your firewall to allow access on ports 135, 137, 138, and 445 (the ports Samba services use to connect to Windows systems), and port 5353 used for multicast DNS discovery (Avahi). Most can be selected easily as preconfigured items in firewall configuration tools, like Gufw and FirewallD. Some, though, may not be listed.

Port number	Service
135,137,138,and 445	Samba ports: 135 and 445 use the TCP Protocol, and 137 and 138 use the UDP protocol.
139	Netbios-ssn
22	Secure SHell, ssh
2049	NFS, Linux and Unix shares
631	IPP, Internet Printing Protocol, access to remote Linux/Unix printers
21	FTP
25	SMTP, forward mail
110	POP3, receive mail
143	IMAP, receive mail
5353	multicast DNS discovery service (mdns), Zeroconf

Table 10-4: Service ports

Setting up a firewall with ufw

The Uncomplicated Firewall, ufw, is the supported firewall application for Linux Mint. It provides a simple firewall that can be managed with the Gufw desktop interface or with **ufw** commands. ufw uses the IPtables format to define rules and run the firewall. The ufw application is just a management interface for IPtables rules. The IPtables rule files are held in the **/etc/ufw** directory. Default IPtables rules are kept in **before** and **after** files, with added rules in user files. Firewall configuration for certain packages will be placed in the **/usr/share/ufw.d** directory. Keep in mind, that these IPtable rules are automatically converted for use by nftables. nftables is the actual firewall backend for Linux Mint 21. You can find out more about ufw at the Ubuntu Firewall site at **https://wiki.ubuntu.com/UncomplicatedFirewall** and at the Ubuntu firewall section in the Ubuntu Server Guide at **https://ubuntu.com/server/docs**. The Server Guide also shows information on how to implement IP Masquerading on ufw.

Gufw

Gufw provides an easy to use GNOME interface for managing your ufw firewall. A simple interface lets you add rules, both custom and standard. Gufw is installed by default, and can be accessed from the Preferences menu as Firewall Configuration.

Gufw will initially open with the firewall disabled, with no ports configured. The Status button is set to off, and the shield image will be gray. To enable the firewall, just click the left side of the Status button, setting the status to on. The shield image will be colored and the firewall rules will be listed. Figure 10-33 shows the firewall enabled and several rules listed Samba ports. Rules for both IPv4 and IPv6 (**v6**) network protocols are listed.

The Gufw dialog has a Firewall section and three tabs: Rules, Report, and Log. The Firewall section has a Status button for turning the firewall on or off. There is a Profile menu for Home, Office, and Public configurations. The Incoming and Outgoing drop down menus for setting the default firewall rules. Options are Deny, Reject, or Allow, and are applied to incoming and outgoing traffic respectively. By default, incoming traffic is denied (Deny), and outgoing traffic is allowed (Allow). Rules you specified in the Rules tab will make exceptions, allowing only certain traffic in or out. Should you select the Allow option, the firewall accepts all incoming traffic. In this case you should set up rules to deny access to some traffic, otherwise, the firewall becomes ineffective, allowing access to all traffic. The Report tab lists active services and ports such as the Samba server (smbd) on port 139. The Log tab list firewall notices. You can copy notices, as well as delete a log. The Home tab provides basic help on how to use Gufw.

Figure 10-33: Gufw

Figure 10-34: Gufw Preconfigured rules

To add a rule, click the Rules tab and then click the plus button (+) on the lower left corner of the Rules tab to open the "Add rule" dialog, which has three tabs for managing rules: Preconfigured, Simple, and Advanced (see Figure 10-34). The Preconfigured tab provides five menus: the first for the policy (Allow, Deny, Reject, and Limit), the second for the traffic direction (In or Out), the third for the category of the application and the fourth for a subcategory, and the fifth for the particular application or service for the rule. The main categories are Audio video, Games, Network, Office, and System. The Network category lists most network services like SSH, Samba, and FTP. Should there be a security issue with the rule, a warning is displayed. Alternatively, if you know the name of the service you want to make a rule for, you can simply enter the name or search pattern in the Application filter, which will find it for you.

Should you need to modify the default rule for an application, you can click on the arrow button to the right of the search box to open the Advanced tab for that rule.

Click the Add button to add the rule. Once added a port entry for the rule appears in the Rules section. In Figure 10-32, the Samba service has been selected and then added, showing up in the Rules section as "137,138/udp ALLOW IN Anywhere." If you need to add several rules at once, you can keep the Add dialog open to select, configure, and add them.

Applications and services can also be blocked. To prevent access by the FTP service, you would first select Deny, then Service, and then the FTP entry.

Besides Allow and Deny, you can also choose a Limit option. The Limit option will enable connection rate limiting, restricting connections to no more than 6 every 30 seconds for a given port. This is meant to protect against brute force attacks.

Should there be no preconfigured entry, you can use the Simple tab to allow access to a port (see Figure 10-35). The first menu is for the rule (Allow, Deny, Reject, and Limit), and the second for the protocol (TCP, UDP, or both). In the Port text box, you enter the port number.

Figure 10-35: Gufw Simple rules

On the Advanced tab, you can enter more complex rules. You can set up allow or deny rules for tcp or udp protocols, and specify the incoming and outgoing host (ip) and port (see Figure 10-36).

Figure 10-36: Gufw Advanced rules

If you decide to remove a rule, select it in the Rules section and then click the minus button on the lower left corner (–). To remove several rules, click and press Shift-click or use Ctrl-click to select a collection of rules, and then click the minus button.

You can edit any rule by selecting it and clicking the edit button (gear image) to open an "Update a Firewall Rule" dialog (see Figure 10-37). For a default or simple rule, you can only change a few options, but you can turn on logging.

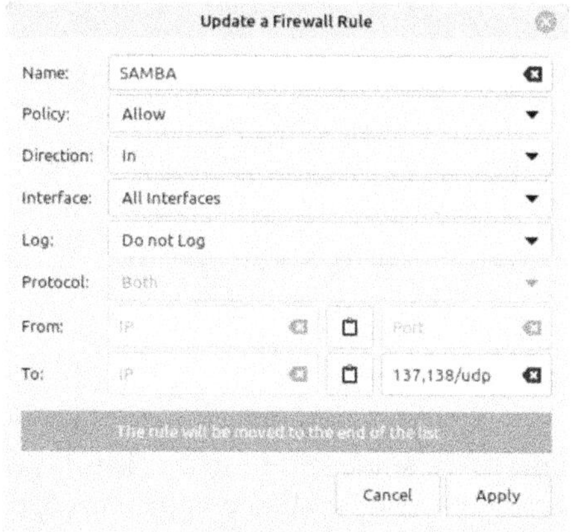

Figure 10-37: Gufw edit a rule

You can also create rules for detected active ports. Click the Report tab and then select a port and click on the plus button at the bottom of the tab. An "Add a Firewall Rule" dialog opens to the Advanced tab with the name of the service active on that port and the port number (see Figure 10-38). You can change any of the options. The port number is already entered.

Should you want to you can pause any activity on a port by selecting it and clicking the pause button at the bottom of the tab. The button will change to a play button. Select the port and click the play button to activate the port.

Figure 10-38: Gufw create a rule for an active port

ufw commands

You can also manage your ufw firewall using **ufw** commands entered on a command line in a Terminal window. A **ufw** command requires administrative access and must be run with the **sudo** command. To check the current firewall status, listing those services allowed or blocked, use the **status** command.

```
sudo ufw status
```

If the firewall is not enabled, you first will have to enable it with the **enable** command.

```
sudo ufw enable
```

You can restart the firewall, reloading your rules, using the **systemctl** command with the **restart** option.

```
sudo systemctl restart ufw
```

You can add rules using allow and deny rules and their options as listed in Table 10-5. To allow a service, specify the allow rule and the service name. This is the name for the service listed in the **/etc/services** file. For connection rate limiting, use the **limit** option in place of **allow**. The following allows the ftp service.

```
sudo ufw allow ftp
```

If the service you want is not listed in **/etc/services**, and you know the port and protocol it uses, you can specify the port and protocol directly. For example, the Samba service uses port 139 and 445 and protocol tcp (among others, see Table 10-4).

```
sudo ufw allow 445/tcp
```

Commands	Description
enable | disable	Turn the firewall on or off
status	Display status along with services allowed or denied.
logging on | off	Turn logging on or off
default allow | deny	Set the default policy, allow is open, whereas deny is restrictive
allow *service*	Allow access by a service. Services are defined in **/etc/services**, which specify the ports for that service.
allow *port /protocol*	Allow access on a particular port using specified protocol.
deny *service*	Deny access by a service
delete *rule*	Delete an installed rule, use allow, deny, or limit and include rule specifics.
proto *protocol*	Specify protocol in allow, deny, or limit rule
from *address*	Specify source address in allow, deny, or limit rule
to *address*	Specify destination address in allow, deny, or limit rule
port *port*	Specify port in allow, deny, or limit rule for from and to address

Table 10-5: UFW firewall operations

The status operation shows what services the firewall rules allow.

```
sudo ufw status
To                      Action         From
21:tcp                  ALLOW          Anywhere
21:udp                  ALLOW          Anywhere
139,445:tcp             ALLOW          Anywhere
```

To remove a rule, prefix it with the **delete** command.

```
sudo ufw delete allow 445/tcp
```

More detailed rules can be specified using address, port, and protocol commands. These are very similar to the actual IPtables rules. Packets to and from particular networks, hosts, and ports can be controlled. The following denies ssh access (port 22) from host 192.168.03.

```
sudo ufw deny proto tcp from 192.168.03 to any port 22
```

ufw rule files

The rules you add are placed in the **/etc/ufw/user.rules** file as IPtables rules. The ufw program is just a front end for **iptables-restore**, which will read this file and set up the firewall using **iptables** commands. **ufw** will also have **iptables-restore** read the **before.rules** and **after.rules** files in the **/etc/ufw** directory. These files are considered administrative files that include needed supporting rules for your IPtables firewall. Administrators can add their own IPtables rules to these files for system specific features like IP Masquerading. The **before.rules** file will specify a table with the * symbol, as in ***filter** for the netfilter table. For the NAT table, you would use ***nat**. At the end of each table segment, a COMMIT command is needed to instruct ufw to apply the rules. Rules use **-A** for allow and **-D** for deny, assuming the **iptables** command.

Default settings for ufw are placed in **/etc/default/ufw**. Here you will find the default INPUT, OUTPUT, and FORWARD policies specified by setting associated variables, like DEFAULT_INPUT_POLICY for INPUT and DEFAULT_OUTPUT_POLICY for OUTPUT. The DEFAULT_INPUT_POLICY variable is set to DROP, making DROP the default policy for the INPUT rule. The DEFAULT_OUTPUT_POLICY variable is set to ACCEPT, and the DEFAULT_FORWARD_POLICY variable is set to DROP. To allow IP Masquerading, DEFAULT_FORWARD_POLICY would have to be set to ACCEPT. These entries set default policies only. Any user rules you have set up would take precedence.

FirewallD and firewall-config

FirewallD runs as a daemon implementing a dynamic firewall. Instead of loading rules offline from a file, you add them directly to the FirewallD daemon. FirewallD operates as a frontend for nftables, directly. FirewallD is not supported by Ubuntu and Linux Mint but is available on the Ubuntu/Linux Mint repository. It is the default firewall for Fedora and Suse Linux. For documentation see:

```
https://fedoraproject.org/wiki/FirewallD
```

FirewallD sets up network zones to define the level of trust for different kinds of network connections. Each zone can have several connections, but a connection can belong only to one zone. FirewallD defines several zones, most of which you can change (mutable). The drop and block zones are immutable and designed to stop all incoming packets. The public, external, and dmz zones are designed for untrusted networks, exposing only part of your system. The work, home, and internal zone are used for trusted networks. The trusted zone (also immutable) allows all network connections.

Zone configurations are located in **/etc/firewalld/zones**. You can use **firewall-config** or **firewall-cmd** to manage your zones and add new ones. The default zone is set in the **/etc/firewalld/firewalld.conf** configuration files by the DefaultZone variable. Initially, it is set to public. The default and fallback zones are saved in **/lib/firewalld/zones**.

Zone files are saved as XML files which list the zone name and the services and ports allowed, along with any masquerade, ICMP, and port forwarding options.

Traditionally firewalls were static. You modified firewall rules and then restarted your firewall to load the rules. A dynamic firewall, such as FirewallD, can apply modified rules without restarting the firewall. Rules, however, have to be managed directly by the FirewallD daemon. You use to **firewall-config** and **firewall-cmd** tools to directly configure your firewall.

Though not supported by Linux Mint directly, you can use the new Firewalld dynamic firewall daemon to set up a firewall. To configure Firewalld you use the **firewalld-config** graphical interface. You can also use **firewalld-cmd** command from the command line. To set up your firewall, run **firewall-config**, accessible as the Firewall entry on the Preferences menu (see Figure 10-39). Install both the **firewalld** and **firewall-applet** packages. The **firewall-applet** package includes **firewalld-config** and displays a firewall applet on the panel. A right-click on the applet displays a menu with options to edit and configure the firewall. You can start FirewallD from the menu as Administration menu as Firewall.

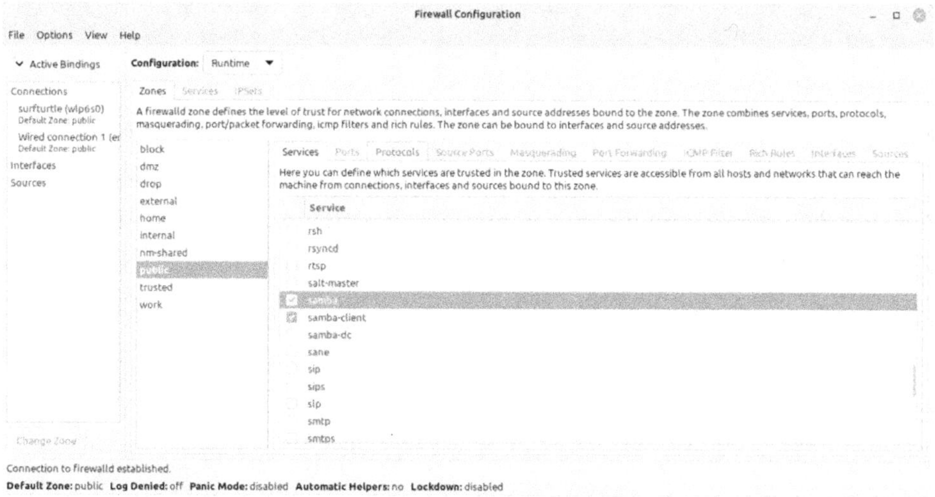

Figure 10-39: firewall-config: Runtime Configuration

You can disable and enable FirewallD manually using the **systemctl** command.

```
sudo systemctl enable firewalld
sudo systemctl disable firewalld
```

On Linux Mint, FirewallD is managed by the **firewalld** service script. You can start and stop it using the **systemctl** command. You will have to start the FirewallD daemon in a terminal window with the following command.

```
sudo systemctl start firewalld
```

You can stop it with a stop command.

```
sudo systemctl stop firewalld
```

firewall-config

With **firewall-config** you can configure either a Runtime or Permanent Configuration. Select one from the Configuration menu. The Runtime Configuration shows your current runtime set up, whereas a Permanent configuration does not take effect until you reload or restart. If you wish to edit your zones and services you need to choose the Permanent Configuration (see Figure 10-40). This view displays a zone toolbar for editing zone at the bottom of the zone scroll box, and an Edit button on the Services tab for editing service protocols, ports, and destination addresses.

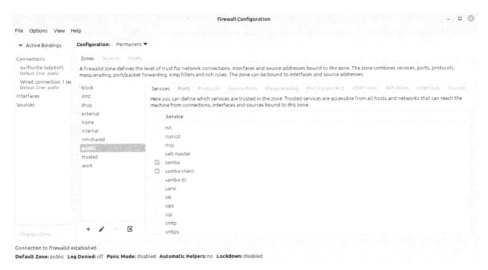

Figure 10-40: firewall-config: Permanent Configuration

Additional tabs can be displayed from the View menu for configuring ICMP types, and for adding firewall rules directly (Direct Configuration).

From the Options menu, you can reload your saved firewall.

A firewall configuration is set up for a given zone, such as a home, work, internal, external, or public zone. Zones provide an added level of protection by the firewall. They divide the network protected by the Firewall into separate segments, which can only communicate as permitted by the firewall. In effect, zones separate one part of your network from another. Each zone has its own configuration. Zones are listed in the Zone scroll box on the left side of the firewall-config window (see Figure 10-40). Select the one you want to configure. The firewall-config window opens to the default, Public. You can choose the default zone from the System Default Zone dialog (see Figure 10-41), which you open from the Options menu as "Change Default Zone."

Figure 10-41: Default Zone

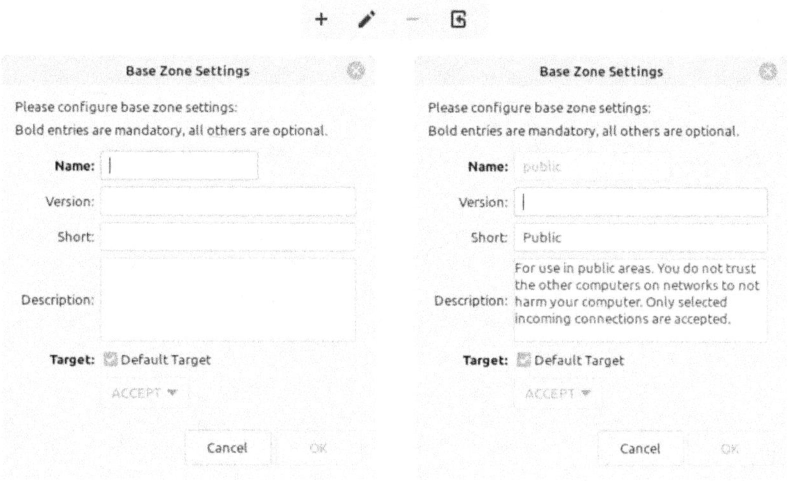

Figure 10-42: Base Zone Settings

To the left of the Zones tab is the Active Bindings section, which list the network connections, interfaces, and sources on your system. For each active connection, the zone bound to it is listed, such as the public zone bound to the wired connection in Figure 10-42. To change the zone bound to a connection you select the entry and click the Change Zone button at the bottom of the Active Binding section. This open a Select zone dialog where you can choose a different zone to be bound to a connection. You can choose from any of the zones in the zones tab. You can also change a connection binding from the Options menu by choosing Change Zones of Connections.

Figure 10-43: Service Settings

If you choose Permanent Configuration from the Current View Menu, a toolbar for zones is displayed below the Zone scroll box. The plus button lets you add a zone and the minus button removes a zone. The pencil button lets you edit a zone. The add and edit buttons open the Base

Zone Settings dialog, where you enter or edit the zone name, version, description, and the target (see Figure 10-42). The default target is ACCEPT. Other options are REJECT and DROP. The Load Zone Defaults button (yellow arrow) loads default settings, removing any you have made.

Each zone, in turn, can have one or more network connections. From the Options menu choose "Change Zones of Connections" to open the Network Connections dialog where you can add a network connection.

For a selected service, you can specify service settings such as ports and protocols it uses, any modules, and specific network addresses. Default settings are already set up for you such as port 139 for Samba, using the TCP protocol. To modify the settings for a service, click the Services tab on the Firewall Configuration window to list your services (see Figure 10-43). Choose the service you want to edit from the Service scroll box at the left. For a given service you can then use the Ports, Protocols, Modules, and Destination tabs to specify ports, protocols, modules, and addresses. On the Ports tab, click the Add button to open the Port and Protocol dialog where you can add a port or port range, and choose a protocol from the Protocol menu (see Figure 10-44). On the Destination tab, you can enter an IPv4 or IPv6 destination address for the service.

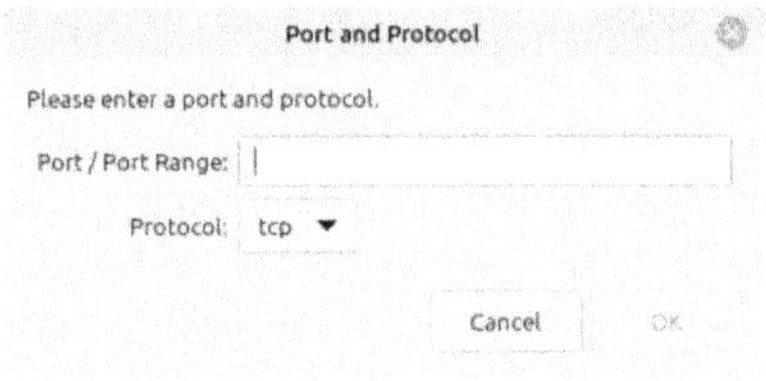

Figure 10-44: Service Protocols and Ports

On the Zones tab, the Ports tab lets you specify ports that you may want opened for certain services, like BitTorrent. Click the Add button to open a dialog where you can select the port number along with the protocol to control (tcp or udp), or enter a specific port number or range.

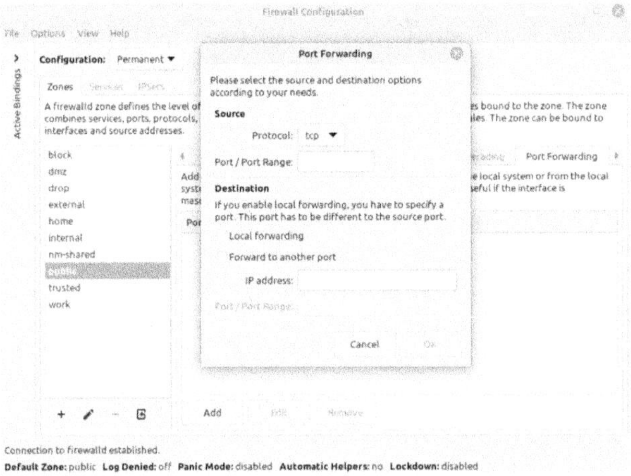

Figure 10-45: Port Forwarding

If your system is being used as a gateway to the Internet for your local network, you can implement masquerading to hide your local hosts from outside access from the Internet. This also requires IP forwarding which is automatically enabled when you choose masquerading. Local hosts will still be able to access the Internet, but they will masquerade as your gateway system. You would select for masquerading the interface that is connected to the Internet. Masquerading is available only for IPv4 networks, not IPv6 networks.

The Port Forwarding tab lets you set up port forwarding, channeling transmissions from one port to another, or to a different port on another system. Click the Add button to add a port, specifying its protocol and destination (see Figure 10-45).

The ICMP Filters tab allows you to block ICMP messages. By default, all ICMP messages are allowed. Blocking ICMP messages makes for a more secure system. Certain types of ICMP messages are often blocked as they can be used to infiltrate or overload a system, such as the ping and pong ICMP messages (see Figure 10-46).

If you have specific firewall rules to add, use the Direct Configuration tab (displayed from the View | Direct Configuration menu).

Figure 10-46: ICMP Filters

firewall-cmd

The **firewall-cmd** command works on a command line interface, using options to set features for different zones. Zone modification options such as **--add-service**, can be either runtime or permanent. Runtime changes expire after a restart or reload. To make the changes permanent you add the **--permanent** option, making changes for a persistent configuration, instead of a runtime one.

Use the **get** options to display information about the firewall. The **--get-zones** option lists your zones, the **--get-services** option list services supported by the current zone, and the **--get-icmptypes** lists the ICMP types.

```
firewall-cmd --get-zones
firewall-cmd --get-services
firewall-cmd --get-icmptypes
```

The **--get-default-zone** option lists the default zone, and **--set-default-zone** sets up a new default zone.

```
firewall-cmd --set-default-zone  home
```

To find out what features have been enabled for a zone, use the **--list-all** option with a **--zone=** option to specify the zone.

```
firewall-cmd home --zone=home  --list-all
```

Zone are assigned network interfaces. There are interface options to add, remove, or change an interface. Use the query option to check if an interface belongs to a zone.

```
firewall-cmd --zone=home  --query-interface=enp7s0
```

The service, port, masquerade, icmp, and forwarding options can be either runtime or persistent (permanent). The **--service** options can add and remove services to a zone.

```
firewall-cmd -add-service=vsftp
```

To make the change permanent (persistent mode), add the **--permanent** option.

```
firewall-cmd --permanent -add-service=vsftp
```

The **--query-service** option checks to see if a service is enabled for a zone.

```
firewall-cmd --zone=home -query-service=http
```

The **--port** options are used to add, remove, or query ports.

```
firewall-cmd --zone=home --add-port=22
```

Add the **--permanent** option to make it permanent.

```
firewall-cmd --permanent --zone=home --add-port=22
```

The **masquerade** options add, removes, and queries zones for masquerading.

```
firewall-cmd --zone=work --add-masquerade
```

The **icmp-block** options add, remove, and query ICMP types.

```
firewall-cmd --zone=work --add-icmp-block=echo-reply
```

Should your firewall have to use custom firewall rules, you can add, remove, and list them using the **--direct** option. These are rules written in the IPtables syntax. You have to specify the protocol, table, chain, and arguments. The following lists the rules you added to the netfilter table. The rules are not saved and have to be added again each time you restart or reload. You could have a script of **firewall-cmd** rules to do this.

```
firewall-cmd --direct --get-rules ipv4 netfilter
```

The following adds a simple netfilter rule.

```
Firewall-cmd --direct -add-rule ipv4 netfilter INPUT  Deny
```

GNOME Nettool

The GNOME Nettool utility (**gnome-nettool**) provides a GNOME interface for network information tools like the ping and traceroute operations as well as Finger, Whois, and Lookup for querying users and hosts on the network (see Figure 10-47). Once installed, Nettool is accessible from the Administration menu as Network Tools. The first tab, Devices, describes your connected network devices, including configuration and transmission information about each device, such as the hardware address and bytes transmitted. Both IPv4 and IPv6 host IP addresses are listed.

Figure 10-47: Gnome network tool

You can use the ping, finger, lookup, whois, and traceroute operations to find out status information about systems and users on your network. The ping operation is used to check if a remote system is up and running. You use finger to find out information about other users on your network, seeing if they are logged in or if they have received mail. The traceroute tool can be used to track the sequence of computer networks and systems your message passed through on its way to you. Whois will provide domain name information about a particular domain, and Lookup will provide both domain name and IP addresses. Netstat shows your network routing (addresses used) and active service (open ports and the protocols they use). Port Scan lists the ports and services they use on a given connection (address); use 12.0.0.1 for your local computer.

Predictable and unpredictable network device names

Network devices now use a predictable naming method that differs from the older naming method. Names are generated based on the specific device referencing the network device type, its hardware connection and slot, and even its function. The traditional network device names used the **eth** prefix with the number of the device for an Ethernet network device. The name **eth0** referred to the first Ethernet connection on your computer. This naming method was considered unpredictable as it did not accurately reference the actual Ethernet device. The old system relied on probing the network driver at boot, and if you're your system had several Ethernet connections, the names could end up being switched, depending you how the startup proceeded. With systemd udev version 197, the naming changed to a predictable method that specifies a particular device. The predictable method references the actual hardware connection on your system.

The name used to reference predictable device names connection has a prefix for the type of device followed by several qualifiers such as the type of hardware, the slot used, and the function number. Instead of the older unpredictable name like **eth0**, the first Ethernet device is referenced by a name like **enp7s0**. The interface name **enp7s0** references an Ethernet (en) connection, at pci slot 7 (p7) with the hotplug slot index number 0 (s0). **wlp6s0** is a wireless (wl) connection, at pci slot 6 (p6) with the hotplug slot index number 0 (s0). **virvb0** is a virtual (vir) bridge (vb) network interface. Table 10-6 lists predictable naming prefixes.

Name	Description
sen	Ethernet
sl	serial line IP (slip)
wl	wlan, wireless local area network
ww	wwan, wireless wide area network (mobile broadband)
p	pci geographical location (pci-e slot)
s	hotplug slot index number
o	onboard cards
f	function (used for cards with more than one port)
u	USB port
i	USB port interface

Table 10-6: Network Interface Device Naming

Unlike the older unpredictable name, the predictable name will most likely be different for each computer. Predictable network names, along with alternatives, are discussed at:

```
https://www.freedesktop.org/wiki/Software/systemd/PredictableNetworkInterfaceName
s/
```

The naming is carried out by the kernel and is describe in the comment section of the kernel source's **systemd/src/udev/udev-bultin-net_id.c** file.

Network device path names

The directory **/sys/devices** lists all your devices in subdirectories, including your network devices. The path to the devices progresses through subdirectories named for the busses connecting the device. To quickly find the full path name, you can us the **/sys/class** directory instead. For network devices use **/sys/class/net**. Then use the **ls -l** command to list the network devices with their links to the full pathname in the **/sys/devices** directory (the **../..** path references a cd change up two directories (**class/net**) to the **/sys** directory).

```
$ cd /sys/class/net
$ ls
enp7s0  lo  wlp6s0
$ ls -l
```

```
total 0
lrwxrwxrwx 1 root root 0 Feb 19 12:27 enp7s0 ->
../../devices/pci0000:00/0000:00:1c.3/0000:07:00.0/net/enp7s0
lrwxrwxrwx 1 root root 0 Feb 19 12:27 lo -> ../../devices/virtual/net/lo
lrwxrwxrwx 1 root root 0 Feb 19 12:28 wlp6s0 ->
../../devices/pci0000:00/0000:00:1c.2/0000:06:00.0/net/wlp6s0
```

So the full path name in the **/sys/devices** directory for enp7s0 is:

```
/sys/devices/pci0000:00/0000:00:1c.3/0000:07:00.0/net/enp7s0
```

You can find the pci bus slot used with the **lspci** command. This command lists all your pci connected devices. In this example, the pci bus slot used 7, which is why the pci part of the name enp7s0 is p7. The s part refers to a hotplug slot, in this example s0.

```
$ lspci
06:00.0 Network controller: Qualcomm Atheros QCA9565 / AR9565 Wireless Network
Adapter (rev 01)
07:00.0 Ethernet controller: Realtek Semiconductor Co., Ltd. RTL8101/2/6E PCI
Express Fast/Gigabit Ethernet controller (rev 07)
```

Devices have certain properties defined by udev, which manages all devices. Some operations, such as systemd link files, make use these properties. The ID_PATH, ID_NET_NAME_MAC, and INTERFACE properties can be used to identify a device to udev. To display these properties, you use the **udevadm** command to query the udev database. With the **info** and **-e** options, properties of all active devices are displayed. You can pipe (|) this output to a **grep** command to display only those properties for a given device. In the following example, the properties for the **enp7s0** device are listed. Preceding the properties for a given device is a line, beginning (^) with a "P" and ending with the device name. The .* matching characters match all other intervening characters on that line, **^P.*enp7s0**. The -A option displays the specified number of additional lines after that match, **-A 22**.

```
$ udevadm info -e | grep -A 22 ^P.*enp7s0
P: /devices/pci0000:00/0000:00:1c.3/0000:07:00.0/net/enp7s0
E: DEVPATH=/devices/pci0000:00/0000:00:1c.3/0000:07:00.0/net/enp7s0
E: ID_BUS=pci
E: ID_MM_CANDIDATE=1
E: ID_MODEL_FROM_DATABASE=RTL8101/2/6E PCI Express Fast/Gigabit Ethernet
controller
E: ID_MODEL_ID=0x8136
E: ID_NET_DRIVER=r8169
E: ID_NET_LINK_FILE=/lib/systemd/network/99-default.link
E: ID_NET_NAME_MAC=enx74e6e20ec729
E: ID_NET_NAME_PATH=enp7s0
E: ID_OUI_FROM_DATABASE=Dell Inc.
E: ID_PATH=pci-0000:07:00.0
E: ID_PATH_TAG=pci-0000_07_00_0
E: ID_PCI_CLASS_FROM_DATABASE=Network controller
E: ID_PCI_SUBCLASS_FROM_DATABASE=Ethernet controller
E: ID_VENDOR_FROM_DATABASE=Realtek Semiconductor Co., Ltd.
E: ID_VENDOR_ID=0x10ec
E: IFINDEX=2
E: INTERFACE=enp7s0
E: SUBSYSTEM=net
```

```
E: SYSTEMD_ALIAS=/sys/subsystem/net/devices/enp7s0
E: TAGS=:systemd:
E: USEC_INITIALIZED=1080179
```

For certain tasks, such as renaming, you many need to know the MAC address. You can find this with the **ip link** command, which you can abbreviate to **ip l**. The MAC address is before the brd string. In this example, the MAC address for enp7s0 is 74:e6:e2:0e:c7:29. The ip link command also provides the MTU (Maximum Transmission Unit) and the current state of the connection.

```
$ ip link
1: lo: <LOOPBACK,UP,LOWER_UP> mtu 65536 qdisc noqueue state UNKNOWN mode DEFAULT
group default qlen 1 link/loopback 00:00:00:00:00:00 brd 00:00:00:00:00:00
2: enp7s0: <BROADCAST,MULTICAST,UP,LOWER_UP> mtu 1500 qdisc fq_codel state UP
mode DEFAULT group default qlen 1000 link/ether 74:e6:e2:0e:c7:29 brd
ff:ff:ff:ff:ff:ff
3: wlp6s0: <BROADCAST,MULTICAST> mtu 1500 qdisc noop state DOWN mode DEFAULT
group default qlen 1000 link/ether 4c:bb:58:22:40:1d brd ff:ff:ff:ff:ff:ff
```

Renaming network device names with udev rules

If you should change your hardware, like your motherboard with its Ethernet connection, or, if you use an Ethernet card and simply change the slot it is connected to, then the name will change. For firewall rules referencing a particular Ethernet connection, this could be a problem. You can, if you wish, change the name to one of your own choosing, even using the older unpredictable names. This way you would only have to update the name change, rather than all your rules and any other code that references the network device by name.

You can change a device name by adding a user udev rule for network device names. Changes made with udev rules work for both NetworkManager and systemd-networkd. In the **/etc/udev/rules.d** directory, create a file with the **.rules** extension and prefixed by a number less than 80, such as **70-my-net-names.rules**.The .rules files in **/etc/udev/rules.d** take precedence over those in the udev system directory, **/lib/udev/rules.d**.

In the udev rule, identify the subsystem as net (SUBSYSTEM=="net"), the action to take as add (ACTION=="add")), then the MAC address (ATTR[address}, the address attribute). Use **ip link** to obtain the mac address. The MAC address is also listed as the ID_NET_NAME_MAC entry in the **udevadm info** output (be sure to remove the prefix and add intervening colons). Use the NAME field to specify the new name for the device. Use the single = operator to make the name assignment.

/etc/udev/rules.d/70-my-net-names.rules

```
SUBSYSTEM=="net", ACTION=="add", ATTR{address}=="74:e6:e2:0e:c7:29", NAME="eth0"
```

To further specify the device you can add the kernel name (KERNEL) of the device. The kernel name is the INTERFACE entry.

```
SUBSYSTEM=="net", ACTION=="add", ATTR{address}=="74:e6:e2:0e:c7:29",
KERNEL=="enp7s0", NAME="eth0"
```

Renaming network device names for systemd-networkd with systemd.link

The systemd-networkd manager provides an alternate way to change network device names (keep in mind that an udev rule will also work for systemd-networkd). To change the name you would set up a systemd link file in the **/etc/systemd/network** directory. The **systemd.link** man page shows how to do this. A systemd link file consists of Match and Link sections. In the Match section you specify the network device, and in the Link section specify the name you want to give it. The network device can be referenced by its predictable name (Path) or MAC address (MACAddress).

The default systemd link file is **/lib/systemd/network/99-default.link**. The file had only a Link section which lists policies to use in determining the name. The NamePolicy key lists the policies to be checked, starting with the kernel, then the udev database, udev firmware onboard information, udev hot-plug slot information, and the device path. In most cases, the slot policy is used. The MACAddressPolicy is set to persistent, for devices that have or need fixed MAC addresses.

99-default.link

```
[Link]
NamePolicy=kernel database onboard slot path
MACAddressPolicy=persistent
```

To rename a device, you would set up a systemd link file in the **/etc/systemd/network** directory. The **/etc/systemd** directory takes precedence over the **/lib/systemd** directory. A link file consists of a priority number, any name, and the **.link** extension. Lower numbers have a higher priority. In this example, the network device enp7s0 has its named changed to eth0. The Match section uses the Path key to match on the device path, using the ID_PATH property for the device provided by udev.

You can query the udev database for information on your network device using the **udevadm info** command and match on the device. An added **grep** operation for ID_PATH= will display only the ID_PATH property.

```
$ udevadm info -e | grep -A 22 ^P.*enp7s0 | grep ID_PATH=
E: ID_PATH=pci-0000:07:00.0
```

For the Path key, use the udev ID_PATH value and a * glob matching character for the rest of the path. The Link section uses the Name key to specify the new name. The MacAddressPolicy should be set to persistent, indicating a fixed connection. Start the name of the link file with a number less than 99, so as to take precedence over the 99-default.link file.

10-my-netname.link

```
[Match]
Path=pci-0000:07:00.0-*

[Link]
Name=eth0
MacAddressPolicy=persistent
```

Instead of the Path key, you could use the MACAddress key to match on the hardware address of the network device. The MAC address is udev ID_NET_NAME_MAC property without

the prefix and with colons separation. The MAC address in this example is 74:e6:e2:0e:c7:29.
You can also use **ip link** to find the MAC address (the numbers before **brd**).

10-my-netname.link

```
[Match]
MACAddress=74:e6:e2:0e:c7:29

[Link]
Name=eth0
MacAddressPolicy=persistent
```

Alternatively, you could use the OriginalName key in the Match section instead of the
Path. The original name is the udev INTERFACE property, which also the name of the device as
displayed by **ifconfig**.

10-my-netname.link

```
[Match]
OriginalName=enp7s0*

[Link]
Name=eth0
MacAddressPolicy=persistent
```

11. Shell Configuration

Shell Configuration Files

Configuration Directories and Files

Aliases

Controlling Shell Operations

Environment Variables and Subshells: export

Configuring Your Login Shell

Four different major shells are commonly used on Linux systems: the Bourne Again shell (BASH), the AT&T Korn shell, the TCSH shell, and the Z shell. The BASH shell is an advanced version of the Bourne shell, which includes most of the advanced features developed for the Korn shell and the C shell. TCSH is an enhanced version of the C shell, originally developed for BSD versions of UNIX. The Z shell is an enhanced version of the AT&T UNIX Korn shell. Although their UNIX counterparts differ greatly, the Linux shells share many of the same features. In Linux, the BASH shell incorporates all the advanced features of the Korn shell and C shell, as well as the TCSH shell. All four shells are available for your use.

Command	Description
bash	BASH shell, **/bin/bash**
bsh	BASH shell, **/bin/bsh** (link to **/bin/bash**)
sh	BASH shell, **/bin/sh** (link to **/bin/bash**)
tcsh	TCSH shell, **/usr/tcsh**
csh	TCSH shell , **/bin/csh** (link to **/bin/tcsh**)
ksh	Korn shell, **/bin/ksh** (also added link **/usr/bin/ksh**)
zsh	Z shell, **/bin/zsh**

Table 11-1: Shell Invocation Command Names

The BASH shell is the default shell for most Linux distributions. If you are logging in to a command line interface, you will be placed in the default shell automatically and given a shell prompt at which to enter your commands. The shell prompt for the BASH shell is a dollar sign (**$**). In the desktop interface, such as GNOME, you can open a terminal window that will display a command line interface with the prompt for the default shell (BASH). Though you log in to your default shell or display it automatically in a terminal window, you can change to another shell by entering its name. Entering **tcsh** invokes the TCSH shell, **bash** the BASH shell, **ksh** the Korn shell, and **zsh** the Z shell. You can leave a shell by pressing CTRL-D or using the **exit** command. You only need one type of shell to do your work. Table 11-1 shows the different commands you can use to invoke different shells. Some shells have added links you can use to invoke the same shell, like **sh** and **bsh**, which link to and invoke the **bash** command for the BASH shell.

This chapter describes common features of the BASH shell, such as aliases, as well as how to configure the shell to your own needs using shell variables and initialization files. The other shells share many of the same features and use similar variables and configuration files.

Though the basic shell features and configurations are shown here, you should consult the respective online manuals and FAQs for each shell for more detailed examples and explanations.

Shell Initialization and Configuration Files

Each type of shell has its own set of initialization and configuration files. The TCSH shell uses **.login**, **.tcshrc**, and **.logout** files in place of **.profile**, **.bashrc**, and **.bash_logout**. The Z shell has several initialization files: **.zshenv**, **.zlogin**, **.zprofile**, **.zschrc**, and **.zlogout**. See Table 11-2 for a listing. Check the Man pages for each shell to see how they are usually configured. When you install a shell, default versions of these files are automatically placed in user home directories.

Except for the TCSH shell, all shells use much the same syntax for variable definitions and assigning values (TCSH uses a slightly different syntax, described in its Man pages).

Filename	Function
BASH Shell	
.profile	Login initialization file
.bashrc	BASH shell configuration file
.bash_logout	Logout name
.bash_history	History file
/etc/profile	System login initialization file
/etc/bash.bashrc	System BASH shell configuration file
/etc/profile.d	Directory for specialized BASH shell configuration files
/etc/bash_completion	Completion options for applications
TCSH Shell	
.login	Login initialization file
.tcshrc	TCSH shell configuration file
.logout	Logout file
Z Shell	
.zshenv	Shell login file (first read)
.zprofile	Login initialization file
.zlogin	Shell login file
.zshrc	Z shell configuration file
.zlogout	Logout file
Korn Shell	
.profile	Login initialization file
.kshrc	KORN shell configuration file

Table 11-2: Shell Configuration Files

Configuration Directories and Files

Applications often install configuration files in a user's home directory that contain specific configuration information, which tailors the application to the needs of that particular user. This may take the form of a single configuration file that begins with a period, or a directory that contains several configuration files. The directory name will also begin with a period. For example, Mozilla installs a directory called **.mozilla** in the user's home directory that contains configuration files. On the other hand, many mail applications use a single file called **.mailrc** to hold alias and feature settings set up by the user, though others like Evolution also have their own, **.evolution**. Most single configuration files end in the letters **rc**. **FTP** uses a file called **.netrc**. Most newsreaders use a file called **.newsrc**. Entries in configuration files are usually set by the application, though you can usually make entries directly by editing the file. Applications have their own set of special variables to which you can define and assign values. You can list the configuration files in your home directory with the **ls -a** command.

Aliases

You can use the **alias** command to create another name for a command. The alias command operates like a macro that expands to the command it represents. The alias does not literally replace the name of the command. It simply gives another name to that command. An alias command begins with the keyword **alias** and the new name for the command, followed by an equal sign and the command the alias will reference.

Note: No spaces should be placed around the equal sign used in the `alias` command.

In the next example, **list** becomes another name for the **ls** command:

```
$ alias list=ls
$ ls
mydata today
$ list
mydata today
$
```

If you want an alias to be automatically defined, you have to enter the alias operation in a shell configuration file. On Linux Mint, aliases are defined in either the user's **.bashrc** file or in a **.bash_aliases** file. To use a **.bash_aliases** file, you have to first uncomment the commands in the .bashrc file that will read the **.bash_aliases** file. Just edit the **.bashrc** file and remove the preceding # so it appears like the following.

```
if [ -f ~/.bash_aliases ]; then
    . ~/.bash_aliases
fi
```

You can also place aliases in the **.bashrc** file directly. Some are already defined, though commented out. You can edit the **.bashrc** file and remove the # comment symbols from those lines to activate the aliases.

```
# some more ls aliases
alias ll='ls -l'
alias la='ls -A'
alias l='ls -CF'
```

Aliasing Commands and Options

You can also use an alias to substitute for a command and its option, but you need to enclose both the command and the option within single quotes. Any command you alias that contains spaces must be enclosed in single quotes as well. In the next example, the alias **lss** references the **ls** command with its **-s** option, and the alias **lsa** references the **ls** command with the **-F** option. The **ls** command with the **-s** option lists files and their sizes in blocks, and **ls** with the **-F** option places a slash after directory names. Notice how single quotes enclose the command and its option.

```
$ alias lss='ls -s'
$ lss
mydata 14    today  6    reports  1
$ alias lsa='ls -F'
$ lsa
mydata today reports/
$
```

Aliases are helpful for simplifying complex operations. In the next example, **listlong** becomes another name for the **ls** command with the -l option (the long format that lists all file information), as well as the -**h** option for using a human-readable format for file sizes. Be sure to encase the command and its arguments within single quotes so that they are taken as one argument and not parsed by the shell.

```
$ alias listlong='ls -lh'
$ listlong
-rw-r--r--   1 root    root    51K  Sep  18  2008 mydata
-rw-r--r--   1 root    root    16K  Sep  27  2008 today
```

Aliasing Commands and Arguments

You may often use an alias to include a command name with an argument. If you execute a command that has an argument with a complex combination of special characters on a regular basis, you may want to alias it. For example, suppose you often list just your source code and object code files, those files ending in either a **.c** or **.o**. You would need to use as an argument for **ls** a combination of special characters such as *.[co]. Instead, you can alias **ls** with the .[co] argument, giving it a simple name. In the next example, the user creates an alias called **lsc** for the command **ls.[co]**.

```
$ alias lsc='ls *.[co]'
$ lsc
main.c main.o lib.c lib.o
```

Aliasing Commands

You can also use the name of a command as an alias. This can be helpful in cases where you should use a command only with a specific option. In the case of the **rm**, **cp**, and **mv** commands, the -**i** option should always be used to ensure an existing file is not overwritten. Instead of always being careful to use the -**i** option each time you use one of these commands, you can alias the command name to include the option. In the next example, the **rm**, **cp**, and **mv** commands have been aliased to include the -**i** option.

```
$ alias rm='rm -i'
$ alias mv='mv -i'
$ alias cp='cp -i'
```

The **alias** command by itself provides a list of all aliases that have been defined, showing the commands they represent. You can remove an alias by using the **unalias** command. In the next example, the user lists the current aliases and then removes the lsa alias.

```
$ alias
lsa=ls -F
list=ls
rm=rm -i
$ unalias lsa
```

Controlling Shell Operations

The BASH shell has several features that enable you to control the way different shell operations work. For example, setting the **noclobber** feature prevents redirection from overwriting files. You can turn these features on and off like a toggle, using the **set** command. The **set** command takes two arguments: an option specifying on or off and the name of the feature. To set a feature on, you use the **-o** option, and to set it off, you use the **+o** option. Here is the basic form.

```
$ set -o feature        turn the feature on
$ set +o feature        turn the feature off
```

Features	Description
`$ set -+o` *feature*	BASH shell features are turned on and off with the `set` command; `-o` sets a feature on and `+o` turns it off: `$ set -o noclobber` *set noclobber on* `$ set +o noclobber` *set noclobber off*
`ignoreeof`	Disables CTRL-D logout
`noclobber`	Does not overwrite files through redirection
`noglob`	Disables special characters used for filename expansion: `*`, `?`, `~`, and `[]`

Table 11-3: BASH Shell Special Features

Three of the most common features are **ignoreeof**, **noclobber**, and **noglob**. Table 11-3 lists these different features, as well as the **set** command. Setting **ignoreeof** enables a feature that prevents you from logging out of the user shell with CTRL-D. CTRL-D is not only used to log out of the user shell, but also to end user input entered directly into the standard input. CTRL-D is used often for the Mail program or for utilities such as **cat**. You can easily enter an extra CTRL-D in such circumstances and accidentally log yourself out. The **ignoreeof** feature prevents such accidental logouts. In the next example, the **ignoreeof** feature is turned on using the **set** command with the **-o** option. The user can then log out only by entering the **logout** command.

```
$ set -o ignoreeof
$ CTRL-D
Use exit to logout
$
```

Environment Variables and Subshells: export

When you log in to your account, Linux generates your user shell. Within this shell, you can issue commands and declare variables. You can also create and execute shell scripts. When you execute a shell script, however, the system generates a subshell. You then have two shells: the one you logged in to and the one generated for the script. Within the script shell, you can execute another shell script, which then has its own shell. When a script has finished execution, its shell terminates and you return to the shell from which it was executed. In this sense, you can have many shells, each nested within the other. Variables you define within a shell are local to it. If you define a variable in a shell script, then, when the script is run, the variable is defined with that script's shell and is local to it. No other shell can reference that variable. In a sense, the variable is hidden within its shell.

Shell Variables	Description
BASH	Holds full pathname of BASH command
BASH_VERSION	Displays the current BASH version number
GROUPS	Groups that the user belongs to
HISTCMD	Number of the current command in the history list
HOME	Pathname for user's home directory
HOSTNAME	The hostname
HOSTTYPE	Displays the type of machine the host runs on
OLDPWD	Previous working directory
OSTYPE	Operating system in use
PATH	List of pathnames for directories searched for executable commands
PPID	Process ID for shell's parent shell
PWD	User's working directory
RANDOM	Generates random number when referenced
SHLVL	Current shell level, number of shells invoked
UID	User ID of the current user

Table 11-4: Shell Variables, Set by the Shell

You can define environment variables in all types of shells, including the BASH shell, the Z shell, and the TCSH shell. The strategy used to implement environment variables in the BASH shell, however, is different from that of the TCSH shell. In the BASH shell, environment variables are exported. That is to say, a copy of an environment variable is made in each subshell. For example, if the EDITOR variable is exported, a copy is automatically defined in each subshell for you. In the TCSH shell, on the other hand, an environment variable is defined only once and can be directly referenced by any subshell.

In the BASH shell, an environment variable can be thought of as a regular variable with added capabilities. To make an environment variable, you apply the **export** command to a variable you have already defined. The **export** command instructs the system to define a copy of that variable for each new shell generated. Each new shell will have its own copy of the environment variable. This process is called exporting variables. To think of exported environment variables as global variables is a mistake. A new shell can never reference a variable outside of itself. Instead, a copy of the variable with its value is generated for the new shell.

Configuring Your Shell with Shell Parameters

When you log in, Linux will set certain parameters for your login shell. These parameters can take the form of variables or features. See the previous section "Controlling Shell Operations" for a description of how to set features. Linux reserves a predefined set of variables for shell and system use. These are assigned system values, in effect, setting parameters. Linux sets up parameter shell variables you can use to configure your user shell. Many of these parameter shell variables are defined by the system when you log in. Some parameter shell variables are set by the shell automatically, and others are set by initialization scripts, described later. Certain shell variables are set directly by the shell, and others are simply used by it. Many of these other variables are application specific, used for such tasks as mail, history, or editing. Functionally, it may be better to think of these as system-level variables, as they are used to configure your entire system, setting values such as the location of executable commands on your system, or the number of history commands allowable. See Table 11-4 for a list of those shell variables set by the shell for shell-specific tasks. Table 11-5 lists those used by the shell for supporting other applications.

A reserved set of keywords is used for the names of these system variables. You should not use these keywords as the names of any of your own variable names. The system shell variables are all specified in uppercase letters, making them easy to identify. Shell feature variables are in lowercase letters. For example, the keyword HOME is used by the system to define the HOME variable. HOME is a special environment variable that holds the pathname of the user's home directory. On the other hand, the keyword noclobber is used to set the noclobber feature on or off.

Shell Parameter Variables

Many of the shell parameter variables automatically defined and assigned initial values by the system when you log in can be changed if you wish. However, some parameter variables exist whose values should not be changed. For example, the HOME variable holds the pathname for your home directory. Commands such as **cd** reference the pathname in the HOME shell variable to locate your home directory. Some of the more common of these parameter variables are described in this section.

Other parameter variables are defined by the system and given an initial value that you are free to change. To do this, you redefine them and assign a new value. For example, the PATH variable is defined by the system and given an initial value; it contains the pathnames of directories where commands are located. Whenever you execute a command, the shell searches for it in these directories. You can add a new directory to be searched by redefining the PATH variable yourself so that it will include the new directory's pathname.

Still, other parameter variables exist that the system does not define. These are usually optional features, such as the EXINIT variable that enables you to set options for the Vi editor. Each time you log in, you must define and assign a value to such variables. Some of the more common parameter variables are SHELL, PATH, PS1, PS2, and MAIL. The SHELL variable holds the pathname of the program for the type of shell you log in to. The PATH variable lists the different directories to be searched for a Linux command. The PS1 and PS2 variables hold the prompt symbols. The MAIL variable holds the pathname of your mailbox file. You can modify the values for any of these to customize your shell.

Note: You can obtain a listing of the currently defined shell variables using the **env** command. The **env** command operates like the **set** command, but it lists only parameter variables.

Using Initialization Files

You can automatically define parameter variables using special shell scripts called initialization files. An *initialization file* is a specially named shell script executed whenever you enter a certain shell. You can edit the initialization file and place in it definitions and assignments for parameter variables. When you enter the shell, the initialization file will execute these definitions and assignments, effectively initializing parameter variables with your own values. For example, the BASH shell's **.profile** file is an initialization file executed every time you log in. It contains definitions and assignments of parameter variables. However, the **.profile** file is basically only a shell script, which you can edit with any text editor such as the Vi editor; changing, if you wish, the values assigned to parameter variables.

In the BASH shell, all the parameter variables are designed to be environment variables. When you define or redefine a parameter variable, you also need to export it to make it an environment variable. This means any change you make to a parameter variable must be accompanied by an export command. You will see that at the end of the login initialization file, **.profile**, there is usually an export command for all the parameter variables defined in it.

Your Home Directory: HOME

The HOME variable contains the pathname of your home directory. Your home directory is determined by the administrator when your account is created. The pathname for your home directory is automatically read into your HOME variable when you log in. In the next example, the **echo** command displays the contents of the HOME variable:

```
$ echo $HOME
/home/chris
```

The HOME variable is often used when you need to specify the absolute pathname of your home directory. In the next example, the absolute pathname of **reports** is specified using HOME for the home directory's path.

```
$ ls $HOME/reports
```

Command Locations: PATH

The PATH variable contains a series of directory paths separated by colons. Each time a command is executed, the paths listed in the PATH variable are searched, one by one, for that command. For example, the **cp** command resides on the system in the directory **/bin**. This directory path is one of the directories listed in the PATH variable. Each time you execute the **cp** command, this path is searched and the **cp** command located. The system defines and assigns PATH an initial set of pathnames. In Linux, the initial pathnames are **/bin** and **/usr/bin**.

Shell Variables	Description
BASH_VERSION	Displays the current BASH version number
CDPATH	Search path for the cd command
EXINIT	Initialization commands for Ex/Vi editor
FCEDIT	Editor used by the history fc command.
GROUPS	Groups that the user belongs to
HISTFILE	The pathname of the history file
HISTSIZE	Number of commands allowed for history
HISTFILESIZE	Size of the history file in lines
HOME	Pathname for user's home directory
IFS	Interfield delimiter symbol
IGNOREEOF	If not set, EOF character will close the shell. Can be set to the number of EOF characters to ignore before accepting one to close the shell (default is 10)
INPUTRC	Set the **inputrc** configuration file for Readline (command line). Default is current directory, **.inputrc**. Most Linux distributions set this to **/etc/inputrc**
LOGNAME	Login name
MAIL	Name of specific mail file checked by Mail utility for received messages, if MAILPATH is not set
MAILCHECK	Interval for checking for received mail
MAILPATH	List of mail files to be checked by Mail for received messages
HOSTTYPE	Linux platforms, such as i686, x86_64, or ppc
PROMPT_COMMAND	Command to be executed before each prompt, integrating the result as part of the prompt
HISTFILE	The pathname of the history file
PS1	Primary shell prompt
PS2	Secondary shell prompt
SHELL	Pathname of program for type of shell you are using
TERM	Terminal type
TMOUT	Time that the shell remains active awaiting input
USER	Username
UID	Real user ID (numeric)

Table 11-5: System Environment Variables Used by the Shell

The shell can execute any executable file, including programs and scripts you have created. For this reason, the PATH variable can also reference your working directory; so, if you want to execute one of your own scripts or programs in your working directory, the shell can locate it. No spaces are allowed between the pathnames in the string. A colon with no pathname specified references your working directory. Usually, a single colon is placed at the end of the pathnames as an empty entry specifying your working directory. For example, the pathname **//bin:/usr/bin:** references three directories: **/bin**, **/usr/bin**, and your current working directory.

```
$ echo $PATH
/bin:/usr/sbin:
```

You can add any new directory path you want to the PATH variable. This can be useful if you have created several of your own Linux commands using shell scripts. You can place these new shell script commands in a directory you create, and then add that directory to the PATH list. Then, no matter what directory you are in, you can execute one of your shell scripts. The PATH variable will contain the directory for that script so that directory will be searched each time you issue a command.

You add a directory to the PATH variable with a variable assignment. You can execute this assignment directly in your shell. In the next example, the user **chris** adds a new directory, called **bin,** to the PATH. Although you could carefully type in the complete pathnames listed in PATH for the assignment, you can also use an evaluation of PATH, **$PATH**, in its place. In this example, an evaluation of HOME is also used to designate the user's home directory in the new directory's pathname. Notice the last colon, which specifies the working directory.

```
$ PATH=$PATH:$HOME/mybin:
$ export PATH
$ echo $PATH
/bin:/usr/bin::/home/chris/mybin
```

If you add a directory to PATH while you are logged in, the directory will be added only for the duration of your login session. When you log back in, the login initialization file, **.profile**, will again initialize your PATH with its original set of directories. The **.profile** file is described in detail later in this chapter. To add a new directory to your PATH permanently, you need to edit your **.profile** file and find the assignment for the PATH variable. Then, you insert the directory, preceded by a colon, into the set of pathnames assigned to PATH.

Specifying the BASH Environment: BASH_ENV

The BASH_ENV variable holds the name of the BASH shell initialization file to be executed whenever a BASH shell is generated. For example, when a BASH shell script is executed, the BASH_ENV variable is checked, and the name of the script that it holds is executed before the shell script. The BASH_ENV variable usually holds **$HOME/.bashrc**. This is the **.bashrc** file in the user's home directory. (The **.bashrc** file is discussed later in this chapter.) You can specify a different file if you wish, using that instead of the **.bashrc** file for BASH shell scripts.

Configuring the Shell Prompt

The PS1 and PS2 variables contain the primary and secondary prompt symbols, respectively. The primary prompt symbol for the BASH shell is a dollar sign ($). You can change the prompt symbol by assigning a new set of characters to the PS1 variable. In the next example, the shell prompt is changed to the -> symbol.

```
$ PS1='->'
-> export PS1
->
```

The following table lists the codes for configuring your prompt:

Prompt Codes	Description
\!	Current history number
\$	Use $ as prompt for all users except the root user, which has the # as its prompt
\d	Current date
\#	History command number for just the current shell
\h	Hostname
\s	Shell type currently active
\t	Time of day in hours, minutes, and seconds.
\u	Username
\v	Shell version
\w	Full pathname of the current working directory
\W	Name of the current working directory
\\	Displays a backslash character
\n	Inserts a newline
\[\]	Allows entry of terminal specific display characters for features like color or bold font
\nnn	Character specified in octal format

You can change the prompt to be any set of characters, including a string, as shown in the next example:

```
$ PS1="Please enter a command: "
Please enter a command: export PS1
Please enter a command: ls
mydata /reports
Please enter a command:
```

The PS2 variable holds the secondary prompt symbol, which is used for commands that take several lines to complete. The default secondary prompt is >. The added command lines begin with the secondary prompt instead of the primary prompt. You can change the secondary prompt just as easily as the primary prompt, as shown here:

```
$ PS2="@"
```

Like the TCSH shell, the BASH shell provides you with a predefined set of codes you can use to configure your prompt. With them, you can make the time, your username, or your directory pathname a part of your prompt. You can even have your prompt display the history event number of the current command you are about to enter. Each code is preceded by a \ symbol: \w represents the current working directory, \t the time, and \u your username; \! will display the next history event number. In the next example, the user adds the current working directory to the prompt:

```
$ PS1="\w $"
/home/dylan $
```

The codes must be included within a quoted string. If no quotes exist, the code characters are not evaluated and are themselves used as the prompt. PS1=\w sets the prompt to the characters \w, not the working directory. The next example incorporates both the time and the history event number with a new prompt:

```
$ PS1="\t \! ->"
```

The default BASH prompt is \s-\v\$ to display the type of shell, the shell version, and the $ symbol as the prompt. Some distributions have changed this to a more complex command consisting of the username, the hostname, and the name of the current working directory. A sample configuration is shown here. A simple equivalent is shown here with @ sign in the hostname and a $ for the final prompt symbol. The home directory is represented with a tilde (~).

```
$ PS1="\u@\h:\w$"
richard@turtle.com:~$
```

Linux Mint also includes some complex prompt definitions in the **.bashrc** file to support color prompts and detect any remote user logins.

Specifying Your News Server

Several shell parameter variables are used to set values used by network applications, such as web browsers or newsreaders. NNTPSERVER is used to set the value of a remote news server accessible on your network. If you are using an ISP, the ISP usually provides a Usenet news server you can access with your newsreader applications. However, you first have to provide your newsreaders with the Internet address of the news server. This is the role of the NNTPSERVER variable. News servers on the Internet usually use the NNTP protocol. NNTPSERVER should hold the address of such a news server. For many ISPs, the news server address is a domain name that begins with **nntp**. The following example assigns the news server address **nntp.myservice.com** to the NNTPSERVER shell variable. Newsreader applications automatically obtain the news server address from NNTPSERVER. Usually, this assignment is placed in the shell initialization file, **.profile**, so that it is automatically set each time a user logs in.

```
NNTPSERVER=news.myservice.com
export NNTPSERVER
```

Configuring Your Login Shell: .profile

The **.profile** file is the BASH shell's login initialization file. It is a script file that is automatically executed whenever a user logs in. The file contains shell commands that define system environment variables used to manage your shell. They may be either redefinitions of system-defined variables, or definitions of user-defined variables. For example, when you log in, your user shell needs to know what directories hold Linux commands. It will reference the **PATH** variable to find the pathnames for these directories. First, the **PATH** variable must be assigned those pathnames. In the **.profile** file, an assignment operation does just this. Because it is in the **.profile** file, the assignment is executed automatically when the user logs in.

.profile

```
# ~/.profile: executed by the command interpreter for login shells.
# This file is not read by bash(1), if ~/.bash_profile or ~/.bash_login
# exists.
# see /usr/share/doc/bash/examples/startup-files for examples.
# the files are located in the bash-doc package.

# the default umask is set in /etc/profile; for setting the umask
# for ssh logins, install and configure the libpam-umask package.
#umask 022

# if running bash
if [ -n "$BASH_VERSION" ]; then
    # include .bashrc if it exists
    if [ -f "$HOME/.bashrc" ]; then
        . "$HOME/.bashrc"
    fi
fi

# set PATH so it includes user's private bin if it exists
if [ -d "$HOME/bin" ] ; then
    PATH="$HOME/bin:$PATH"
fi

# set PATH so it includes user's private bin if it exists
if [ -d "$HOME/.local/bin" ] ; then
    PATH="$HOME/.local/bin:$PATH"
fi
```

Exporting Variables

Any new parameter variables you may add to the **.profile** file will also need to be exported, using the export command. This makes them accessible to any subshells you may enter. You can export several variables in one export command by listing them as arguments. The **.profile** file contains no variable definitions, though you can add ones of your own. In this case, the **.profile** file would have an export command with a list of all the variables defined in the file. If a variable is missing from this list, you may be unable to access it. The **.bashrc** file contains a definition of the **HISTCONTROL** variable, which is then exported. You can also combine the assignment and export command into one operation as shown here for NNTPSERVER:

```
export NNTPSERVER=news.myservice.com
```

Variable Assignments

A copy of the standard **.profile** file, provided for you when your account is created, is listed in the next example. Notice how PATH is assigned. PATH is a parameter variable the system has already defined. PATH holds the pathnames of directories searched for any command you enter. The assignment PATH="$PATH:$HOME/bin" has the effect of redefining PATH to include your **bin** directory within your home directory so that your **bin** directory will also be searched for any commands, including ones you create yourself, such as scripts or programs.

Should you want to have your current working directory searched also, you can use any text editor to add another PATH line in your **.profile** file PATH="$PATH:". You would insert a colon : after PATH. You can change this entry to add as many directories as you want to search. Making commands automatically executable in your current working directory could be a security risk, allowing files in any directory to be executed, instead of in certain specified directories. An example of how to modify your **.profile** file is shown in the following section.

```
PATH="$PATH:"
```

Editing Your BASH Profile Script

Your **.profile** initialization file is a text file that can be edited by a text editor, like any other text file. You can easily add new directories to your PATH by editing **.profile** and using editing commands to insert a new directory pathname in the list of directory pathnames assigned to the PATH variable. You can also add new variable definitions. If you do so, be sure to include the new variable's name in the export command's argument list. For example, if your **.profile** file does not have any definition of the EXINIT variable, you can edit the file and add a new line that assigns a value to EXINIT. The definition EXINIT='set nu ai' will configure the Vi editor with line numbering and indentation. You then need to add EXINIT to the export command's argument list. When the **.profile** file executes again, the EXINIT variable will be set to the command set nu ai. When the Vi editor is invoked, the command in the EXINIT variable will be executed, setting the line number and auto-indent options automatically.

In the following example, the user's **.profile** has been modified to include definitions of EXINIT and redefinitions of PATH, PS1, and HISTSIZE. The PATH variable has the ending colon added to it that specifies the current working directory, enabling you to execute commands that may be located in either the home directory or the working directory. The redefinition of HISTSIZE reduces the number of history events saved, from 1,000 defined in the system's **.profile** file, to 30. The redefinition of the PS1 parameter variable changes the prompt to just show the pathname of the current working directory. Any changes you make to parameter variables within your **.profile** file override those made earlier by the system's **.profile** file. All these parameter variables are then exported with the export command.

.profile

```
# ~/.profile: executed by the command interpreter for login shells.
# This file is not read by bash(1), if ~/.bash_profile or ~/.bash_login
# exists.
# see /usr/share/doc/bash/examples/startup-files for examples.
# the files are located in the bash-doc package.

# the default umask is set in /etc/profile
#umask 022

# if running bash
if [ -n "$BASH_VERSION" ]; then
    # include .bashrc if it exists
```

```
    if [ -f "$HOME/.bashrc" ]; then
      . "$HOME/.bashrc"
    fi
fi

# set PATH so it includes user's private bin if it exists
if [ -d "$HOME/bin" ] ; then
    PATH="$HOME/bin:$PATH"
fi


# set PATH so it includes user's private bin if it exists
if [ -d "$HOME/.local/bin" ] ; then
    PATH="$HOME/.local/bin:$PATH"
fi


HISTSIZE=30
NNTPSERVER=news.myserver.com
EXINIT='set nu ai'
PS1="\w \$"
export PATH HISTSIZE EXINIT PS1 NNTPSERVER
```

Manually Re-executing the .profile script

Although the **.profile** script is executed each time you log in, it is not automatically re-executed after you make changes to it. The **.profile** script is an initialization file that is executed *only* whenever you log in. If you want to take advantage of any changes you make to it without having to log out and log in again, you can re-execute the **.profile** script with the dot (.) command. The **.profile** script is a shell script and, like any shell script, can be executed with the . command.

```
$ . .profile
```

Alternatively, you can use the source command to execute the **.profile** initialization file or any initialization file such as **.login** used in the TCSH shell or **.bashrc**.

```
$ source .profile
```

System Shell Profile Script

Your Linux system also has its own profile file that it executes whenever any user logs in. This system initialization file is simply called **profile** and is found in the /etc directory, **/etc/profile**. This file contains parameter variable definitions the system needs to provide for each user. On Linux Mint, the **/etc/profile** script checks the **/etc/profile.d** directory for any shell configuration scripts to run, and then runs the **/etc/bash.bashrc** script, which performs most of the configuration tasks.

The number of configuration settings needed for different applications would make the **/etc/profile** file much too large to manage. Instead, application task-specific aliases and variables are placed in separate configuration files located in the **/etc/profile.d** directory. There are corresponding scripts for both the BASH and C shells. The BASH shell scripts are run from **/etc/profile** with the following commands. A **for** loop sequentially accesses each script and executes it with the dot (.) operator.

```
for i in /etc/profile.d/*.sh; do
  if [ -r $i ]; then
    . $i
  fi
done
```

For a basic install, you will have only the **gvfs-bash-completion.sh** script. As you install other shells and application there may be more. The **/etc/profile.d** scripts are named for the kinds of tasks and applications they configure. Files run by the BASH shell end in the extension **.sh**, and those run by the C shell have the extension **.csh**. The **/etc/profile** script will also check first if the **PS1** variable is defined before running any **/etc/profile.d** scripts.

A copy of the system's **profile** file follows

/etc/profile

```
# /etc/profile: system-wide .profile file for the Bourne shell (sh(1))
# and Bourne compatible shells (bash(1), ksh(1), ash(1), ...).

if [ "$PS1" ]; then
  if [ "$BASH" ] && [ "$BASH" != "/bin/sh" ]; then
    # The file bash.bashrc already sets the default PS1.
    # PS1='\h:\w\$ '
    if [ -f /etc/bash.bashrc ]; then
      . /etc/bash.bashrc
    fi
  else
    if [ "`id -u`" -eq 0 ]; then
      PS1='# '
    else
      PS1='$ '
    fi
  fi
fi

if [ -d /etc/profile.d ]; then
  for i in /etc/profile.d/*.sh; do
    if [ -r $i ]; then
      . $i
    fi
  done
  unset i
fi
```

Configuring the BASH Shell: .bashrc

The **.bashrc** script is a configuration file executed each time you enter the BASH shell or generate any subshells. If the BASH shell is your login shell, **.bashrc** is executed along with your **.profile** script when you log in. If you enter the BASH shell from another shell, the **.bashrc** script is automatically executed, and the variable and alias definitions it contains will be defined. If you enter a different type of shell, the configuration file for that shell will be executed instead. For example, if you were to enter the TCSH shell with the tcsh command, the **.tcshrc** configuration file would be executed instead of **.bashrc**.

The User .bashrc BASH Script

The **.bashrc** shell configuration file is actually executed each time you generate a BASH shell, such as when you run a shell script. In other words, each time a subshell is created, the **.bashrc** file is executed. This has the effect of exporting any local variables or aliases you have defined in the **.bashrc** shell initialization file. The **.bashrc** file usually contains the definition of aliases and any feature variables used to turn on shell features. Aliases and feature variables are locally defined within the shell. But the **.bashrc** file defines them in every shell. For this reason, the **.bashrc** file usually holds aliases and options you want defined for each shell. As an example of how you can add your own aliases and options, aliases for the **rm**, **cp**, and **mv** commands and the shell **noclobber** and **ignoreeof** options have been added to the example shown here. For the root user **.bashrc**, the **rm**, **cp**, and **mv** aliases have already been included in the root's **.bashrc** file.

The **.bashrc** file will check for aliases in a **.bash_aliases** file and run **/etc/bash_completion** for command completion directives.

The **.bashrc** file will set several features including history, prompt, alias, and command completion settings. The **HISTCONTROL** directive is defined to ignore duplicate commands and lines beginning with a space (**ignoreboth**). The history file is appended to, and the history size and history file sizes are set to 1000 and 2000.

```
# don't put duplicate lines or lines starting with space in the history
# See bash(1) for more options
HISTCONTROL=ignoreboth

# append to the history file, don't overwrite it
shopt -s histappend

# for setting history length see HISTSIZE and HISTFILESIZE in bash(1
HISTSIZE=1000
HISTFILESIZE=2000
```

Several commands then define terminal display features and command operations, including the shell prompt, beginning with **PS1=.**

The code for reading the user's **.bash_aliases** script is included. Possible aliases are also provided, some of which are commented. You can remove the comment symbols, #, to activate them. Aliases that provide color support for the **ls**, **grep**, **fgrep**, and **egrep** commands are listed. An alert alias is also provided which notifies you of long running commands.

```
# enable color support of ls and also add handy aliases
if [ -x /usr/bin/dircolors ]; then
    test -r ~/.dircolors && eval "$(dircolors -b ~/.dircolors)" || eval
"$(dircolors -b)"
    alias ls='ls --color=auto'
    #alias dir='dir --color=auto'
    #alias vdir='vdir --color=auto'
```

```
    alias grep='grep --color=auto'
    alias fgrep='fgrep --color=auto'
    alias egrep='egrep --color=auto'
fi

# some more ls aliases
#alias ll='ls -alF'
#alias la='ls -A'
#alias l='ls -CF'

# Add an "alert" alias for long running commands. Use like so:
# sleep 10; alert
alias alert='notify-send --urgency=low -i "$([ $? = 0 && echo terminal || echo
error)" "$(history | tial -n1 | sed -e '\''s/^\s*[0-
9]\+\s*//;s/[;&|]\s*alert$//'\'')"'

# Alias definitions.
# You may want to put all your additions into a separate file like
# ~/.bash_aliases, instead of adding them here directly.
# See /usr/share/doc/bash-doc/examples in the bash-doc package.

#if [ -f ~/.bash_aliases ]; then
#    . ~/.bash_aliases
#fi
```

The **bash_completion** file is then read to set up command completion options.

```
# enable programmable completion features (you don't need to enable
# this, if it's already enabled in /etc/bash.bashrc and /etc/profile
# sources /etc/bash.bashrc).

if ! shopt -oq posix; then
  if [ -f /usr/share/bash-conpletion/bash_completion ]; then
    . /usr/share/bash-completion/bash_completion

  elif [ -f /etc/bash_completion ]; then
    . /etc/bash_completion
  fi
fi
```

You can add any commands or definitions of your own to your **.bashrc** file. If you have made changes to **.bashrc** and you want them to take effect during your current login session, you need to re-execute the file with either the . or the **source** command.

```
$ . .bashrc
```

The System /etc/bash.bashrc BASH Script

Linux Mint has a system **bashrc** file executed for all users, called **bash.bashrc**. Currently the **/etc/bash.bashrc** file sets the default shell prompt, updates the window size, identifies the root directory, and checks whether a user is authorized to use a command. The **bash.bashrc** file is shown here:

```
# System-wide .bashrc file for interactive bash(1) shells.

# To enable the settings / commands in this file for login shells as well,
# this file has to be sourced in /etc/profile.

# If not running interactively, don't do anything
[ -z "$PS1" ] && return

# check the window size after each command and, if necessary,
# update the values of LINES and COLUMNS.
shopt -s checkwinsize

# set variable identifying the chroot you work in (used in the prompt below)
if [ -z "$debian_chroot" ] && [ -r /etc/debian_chroot ]; then
    debian_chroot=$(cat /etc/debian_chroot)
fi
# set a fancy prompt (non-color, overwrite the one in /etc/profile)
# but only if not SUDOing and have SUDO-PS1 set; then assume smart user.
if ! [ -n "${SUDO_USER}" -a -n "${SUDO_PS1}" ]; then
    PS1='${debian_chroot:+($debian_chroot)}\u@\h:\w\$ '
fi

# sudo hint
if [ ! -e $HOME/.sudo_as_admin_successful ] && [ ! -e "$HOME/.hushlogin" ]; then
    case " $(groups) " in *\ admin\ *|*\ sudo\ *)
    if [ -x /usr/bin/sudo ]; then
        cat <<-EOF
        To run a command as administrator (user "root"), use "sudo <command>".
        See "man sudo_root" for details.

        EOF
    fi
    esac
fi

# if the command-not-found package is installed, use it
if [ -x /usr/lib/command-not-found -o -x /usr/share/command-not-found/command-
not-found ]; then
        function command_not_found_handle {
                # check because c-n-f could've been removed in the meantime
                if [ -x /usr/lib/command-not-found ]; then
                   /usr/bin/python /usr/lib/command-not-found -- "$1"
                     return $?
                elif [ -x /usr/share/command-not-found/command-not-found ]; then
                   /usr/bin/python /usr/share/command-not-found/command-not-found
-- "$1"
                     return $?
                else
                   printf "%s: command not found\n" "$1" >&2
                   return 127
                fi
        }
fi
```

Though commented out, the file also includes statements to set the title of a terminal window to the user, hostname, and directory. Several commands define terminal display features and command operations, including the shell prompt, beginning with **PS1=.**

Though not enabled, you can enable the bash completion feature in the **/etc/bash.bashrc** file by removing the comment characters (#). This runs the **/usr/share/bash-completion/bash_completion** script, which makes use of configuration files in its **completions** subdirectory. The **bash.bashrc** file ends with the command-not-found exception handling.

```
# enable bash completion in interactive shells
#if ! shopt -oq posix; then
#  if [ -f /usr/share/bash-completion/bash_completion ]; then
#    . /usr/share/bash-completion/bash_completion
#  elif [ -f /etc/bash_completion ]; then
#    . /etc/bash_completion
#  fi
#fi
```

The BASH Shell Logout File: .bash_logout

The **.bash_logout** file is also a configuration file, but it is executed when the user logs out. It is designed to perform any operations you want to occur whenever you log out. Instead of variable definitions, the **.bash_logout** file usually contains shell commands that form a kind of shutdown procedure, actions you always want taken before you log out. One common logout command is to clear the screen and then issue a farewell message. As with **.profile**, you can add your own shell commands to **.bash_logout**. You edit the file to add a farewell message or other operations. The default **.bash_logout** file includes instructions to invoke the **clear_console** command to clear the screen.

.bash_logout

```
# ~/.bash_logout: executed by bash(1) when login shell exits.
# when leaving the console clear the screen to increase privacy
    if [ "$SHLVL" = 1 ]; then
        [ -x /usr/bin/clear_console ] && /usr/bin/clear_console -q
    fi
```

Part 4: Shared Resources

Managing Services

Print Services: CUPS

Network File System (NFS), Network Information System (NIS)

Samba (Windows)

12. Managing Services

systemd

systemd unit files: /lib/systemd/system

special targets (runlevels)

managing services

Network Time Protocol, Chrony

AppArmor security

OpenSSH

A single Linux system can provide several different kinds of services, ranging from security to administration, and including more obvious Internet services like Web and FTP sites, e-mail, and printing. Security tools, such as the Secure Shell (SSH) run as services, along with administrative network tools, such as Dynamic Host Control Protocol (DHCP) and the BIND Domain Name Server. The network connection interface is itself, a service that you can restart at will. Each service operates as a continually running daemon looking for requests for its particular services. In the case of a web service, the requests come from remote users. You can turn services on or off by starting or shutting down their daemons. System startup is managed by the **systemd** service. The original System V init system for starting individual services has been phased out.

systemd

Linux systems traditionally used the Unix System V init daemon to manage services by setting up runlevels at which they could be started or shutdown. Linux has since replaced the System V init daemon with the **systemd** init daemon. Whereas the System V init daemon would start certain services when the entire system started up or shut down using shell scripts run in sequence, **systemd** uses sockets for all system tasks and services. **systemd** sets up sockets for daemons and coordinates between them as they start up. This allows **systemd** to start daemons at the same time (in parallel). Should one daemon require support from another, **systemd** coordinates the data from their sockets (buffering), so that one daemon receives the information from another daemon that it needs to continue. This parallel startup compatibility allows for very fast boot times.

In effect, you can think of **systemd** as a combination of System V init scripts and the inetd daemon (xinetd), using socket activation applied to all system startup tasks and to network servers. The socket activation design was originally inspired by the inetd service that used sockets (AT_INET) to start internet daemons when requested. The socket activation design was used by in Apple's OS X system to apply to all sockets (AF_UNIX). This allowed all start up processes to start at the same time in parallel, making for fast boot times. Such sockets are set up and managed by **systemd**. When D-BUS needs to write to journald (logging), it writes to the systemd-journald socket managed by **systemd**. It does not have to communicate directly with journald. This means that services no longer have to be started and shutdown in a particular sequence as they were under System V. They can all start and stop at the same time. Also, as **systemd** controls the socket, if a service fails, its socket remains in place. The service can be restarted using the same socket with no loss of information. **systemd** manages all types of sockets including UNIX (system), INET (network), NETLINK (devices), FIFO (pipes), and POSIX (messages). See the following for more details.

https://docs.fedoraproject.org/en-US/quick-docs/understanding-and-administering-systemd/index.html
https://www.freedesktop.org/wiki/Software/systemd/

systemd sets up sockets for all system tasks and services. Configuration for systemd tasks is defined in unit files in **/lib/systemd/system** directory. In this respect, **systemd** files replace the entries that used to be in the Sys V init's **/etc/inittab** file. **systemd** also has its own versions of **shutdown, reboot, halt, init**, and **telinit**, each with their own man page.

systemd is entirely compatible with both System V scripts in the **/etc/init.d** directory and the **/etc/fstab** file. The SystemV scripts and **/etc/fstab** are treated as additional configuration files for **systemd** to work with. If System V scripts are present in the **/etc/init.d** directory, it will use them to generate a corresponding unit configuration file, if there are no corresponding **systemd** unit configuration files already. **systemd** configuration always takes precedence. **systemd** will also, if needed, use the start and stop priority files in the System V init **/etc/init.d** directories to determine dependencies. Entries in **/etc/fstab** are used to generate corresponding **systemd** unit files that are then used to manage file systems. **systemd** also supports snapshots that allow restoring services to a previous state.

The systemd configuration (**.service**) files are located in the **/lib/systemd/system** directory and are considered system files that you should not modify. It is possible to copy them to the **/etc/systemd/system** directory and make changes to the copies. Files in the **/etc/systemd/system** file take precedence. The configuration file for the logind daemon, **logind.conf**, is located in the **/etc/systemd** directory. A few applications, like the NIS server, do not yet have systemd service files. **systemd** automatically generates service files for then in the **/var/run/systemd/generator.late** directory.

Linux Mint also uses systemd services for time (**timedated**), location (**localed**), login (**logind**), and hostname (**hostnamed**) (**systemd-services** package). They can be managed with corresponding systemd control applications: **timedatectl**, **localectl**, and **hostnamectl**.

systemd basic configuration files

You can configure **systemd** for system, login manager, users, and journal service using the configuration files located in the **/etc/systemd** directory. When run for a system service, systemd uses the **system.conf** file, otherwise it uses the **user.conf** file. You can set options such as the log level (LogLevel) and resource size limits. See the man page for **systemd.conf** (**system.conf** and **user.conf**), **logind.conf**, and **journald.conf** for details on the options available.

units

systemd organizes tasks into units, each with a unit configuration file. There are several types of units (see Table 12-1). A unit file will have an extension to its name that specifies the type of unit it is. Service types have the extension **.service**, and mount types have the extension **.mount**. The service type performs much the same function as System V init scripts. Services can be stopped, started and restarted. The **systemctl** command will list all units, including the ones that **systemd** generates.

Units can also be used for socket, device, and mount tasks. The socket type implements the kind of connection used for inetd and xinetd, allowing you to start a service on demand. The device type references devices as detected by udev. The mount type manages a file system's mount point, and automount activates that mount point should it be automounted. An automount unit file has a corresponding mount unit file, which it uses to mount a file system. Similarly, a socket type usually has a corresponding service type file used to perform a task for that socket.

Within each unit are directives that control a service, socket, device, or mount point. Some directives are unique to the type of unit. These are listed in the man page for that service, such as **systemd.service** for the service unit, or **systemd.mount** for a mount unit (see Table 12-1).

```
man systemd.service
```

Options common to units are listed in the **systemd.exec** and **systemd.unit** pages. The **systemd.unit** page lists directives common to all units such as Wants, Conflicts, Before, SourcePath, and Also. The **systemd.exec** pages list options for the execution of a program for a unit, such as the starting of a server daemon. These include options such as User, Group, WorkingDirectory, Nice, Umask, and Environment. The **systemd.exec** page covers options for service, socket, mount, and swap units. The **systemd.directives** man page provides a listing of all systemd unit options and the man page for each option.

Unit Type	Unit Man page	Description
service	systemd.service	Services such as servers, which can be started and stopped
socket	systemd.socket	Socket for services (allows for inetd like services, AF_INET)
device	systemd.device	Devices
mount	systemd.mount	File system mount points
automount	systemd.automount	Automount point for a file system. Use with mount units.
target	systemd.target	Group units
path	systemd.path	Manage directories
snapshot	systemd.snapshot	Created by systemd using the **systemctl snapshot** command to save runtime states of systemd. Use **systemctl isolate** to restore a state.
swap	systemd.swap	Swap unit file generated by systemd for the swap file system.
timer	systemd.timer	Time-based activation of a unit. Corresponds to a service file. Time formats are specified on the **systemd.time** man page.
	systemd.unit	Man page with configuration options common to all units
	systemd.exec	Man page for execution environment options for service, socket, mount, and swap units
	systemd.special	Man page for systemd special targets such as multi-user.target and printer.target.
	systemd.time	Time and date formats for **systemd**
	systemd.directives	Listing of all systemd options and the man page they are described on.

Table 12-1: systemd unit types and man pages

The target unit is used to group units. For example, targets are used to emulate runlevels. A multi-user target groups units (services) together that, in System V, would run on runlevel 3. In effect, targets group those services that run on a certain runlevel for a certain task. The printer target activates the CUPS service, and the graphical target emulates runlevel 5. A target can also be used to reference other targets. A default target designates the default runlevel. Some unit files are automatically generated by **systemd**. For example, operations specified in the **/etc/fstab** are performed by mount units, which are automatically generated from the **fstab** entries.

Units can be dependent on one another, where one unit may require the activation of other units. This dependency is specified using directories with the **.wants** extension. For example, the **poweroff.target** is dependent on the **plymouth-poweroff** service. The directory

poweroff.target.wants has a symbolic link to this service. Should you want a service dependent on your graphical desktop, you can add symbolic links to it in the **graphical.target.wants** directory.

It is important to distinguish between the wants directories in the **/etc/systemd/system** directory and those in the **/lib/systemd/system** directory. Those in the **/lib/systemd** directory are set up by your system and should be left alone. To manage your own dependencies, you can set up corresponding wants directories in the **/etc/systemd/system** directory. The **/etc/systemd** directory always takes priority. For example, in the **/etc/systemd/system/multi-user.target.wants** directory you can place links to services that you want started up for the multi-user.target (runlevel 3). Your system automatically installs links for services you enable, such as **ufw.service** and **vsftpd.service**. These are all links to the actual service files in the **/lib/systemd/system** directory. The **multi-user.target.wants** directory holds a link to **ufw.sevice**, starting up the firewall. The **printer.target.wants** directory has a link to the cups service.

Disabling a service removes its link from its wants directory in **/etc/systemd/system**. For example, disabling the vsftpd service removes its link from the **/etc/systemd/system/multi-user.target.wants** directory. The original service file, in this case, **vsftpd.service**, remains in the **/lib/systemd/system** directory. If you enable the service again, a link for it is added to the **/etc/systemd/system/multi-user.target.wants** directory.

The **/etc/systemd/system** directory also hold links to services. The **/etc/systemd/system/syslog.service** file is a link to **/lib/systemd/system/rsyslog.service**. The **/etc/systemd/system/dbus-org.freedesktop.Avahi.service** link references **/lib/systemd/system/avahi-daemon.service**.

To manage **systemd** you can use **systemctl**. The older service management tool, **service**, has been modified to use **systemctl** to perform actions on services such as starting and stopping.

unit file syntax

A unit file is organized into sections designated by keywords enclosed in brackets. All units have a unit section, **[Unit]**, and an install section, **[Install]**. The options for these sections are described in the **systemd.unit** Man page. Comments can be written by beginning a line with the # or ; characters. See Table 12-2 for a listing of commonly used Unit and Install section options.

The Unit section of a unit file holds generic information about a unit. The Description option provides information about the task the unit manages, such as the Vsftpd server as shown here.

```
Description=vsftpd FTP server
```

The Documentation option lists URIs for the application's documentation.

```
Documentation=man:dhcpd(8)
```

Note: The syntax for unit file is based on .desktop files, which in turn are inspired by Windows ini files. The .desktop type of file conforms to the XDB Desktop Entry Specification.

Types of dependencies can be specified using the Before, After, Requires, Wants, and Conflicts options in the unit section. After and Before configure the ordering of a unit. In the following After option in the **vsftpd.service** file, the vsftpd service is started after networking.

```
After=network.target
```

Unit options	Description
[Unit]	
Description	Description of the unit.
Documentation	URIs referencing documentation.
Requires	Units required by the service. This is a strict requirement. If the required units fail, so will the unit.
PartOf	Dependent units started and stopped by the service. This is not a strict requirement. If the dependent units fail, the unit will still start up.
Wants	Units wanted by the service. This is not a strict requirement. If the required units fail, the unit will still start up. Same functionality as the wants directories.
Conflicts	Negative unit dependency. Starting the unit stops the listed units in the Conflicts option.
Before	Unit ordering. Unit starts before the units listed.
After	Unit ordering. Unit waits until the units listed start.
OnFailure	Units to be run if the unit fails.
SourcePath	File the configuration was generated from, such as the mount unit files generated from **/etc/fstab**.
[Install]	
WantedBy	Sets up the unit's symbolic link in listed unit's **.wants** subdirectory. When the listed unit is activated, so is the unit. This is not a strict requirement.
RequiredBY	Sets up the unit's symbolic link in listed unit's **.requires** subdirectory. When the listed unit is activated, so is the unit. This is a strong requirement.
Alias	Additional names the unit is installed under. The aliases are implemented as symbolic links to the unit file.
Also	Additional units to install with this unit.

Table 12-2: systemd Unit and Install section options (common to all units, systemd.unit)

The Requires option sets up a dependency between units. This is a strong dependency. If one fails, so does the other. In the following Requires option from the **graphical.target** unit file, the graphical target can only be started if the multi-user and rescue targets are activated.

```
After=multi-user.target rescue.service rescue.target display-manager.service
```

The Wants option sets up a weaker dependency, requiring activation, but not triggering failure should it occur. This is the case with the graphical target and the display manager service.

```
Wants=display-manager.service
```

Several condition options are available such as ConditionACPower which, if true, checks to see if a system is using AC power. In the following example, ConditionPathExists checks for the existence of a file with runtime options for the DHCP server in the **/etc/default** directory.

```
ConditionPathExists=/etc/default/isc-dhcp-server
```

Some unit files are automatically generated by systemd, allowing you to use older configuration methods. For example, the unit file used to manage the mounting of your file systems is generated from the configuration information in the **/etc/fstab** file. The SourcePath option specifies the configuration file used to generate the unit file. The SourcePath option for the **boot.mount** unit file is shown here.

```
SourcePath=/etc/fstab
```

The Install section provides installation information for the unit. The WantedBy and RequiredBy options specify units that this unit wants or requires. For service units managing servers like Vsftpd and the DCHP servers, the install section has a WantedBy option for the **multi-user.target**. This has the effect of running the server at runlevels 2, 3, 4, and 5. When the multi-user target becomes activated so does that unit.

```
WantedBy=multi-user.target
```

The WantedBy option is implemented by setting up a link to the unit in a wants subdirectory for the wanted by unit. For the **multi-user.target** unit, a subdirectory called **multi-user.target.wants** has symbolic links to all the units that want it, such as **vsftpd.service** for the vsfptd FTP service. These wants symbolic links are set up in the **/etc/systemd/system** directory, which can be changed as you enable and disable a service. Disabling a service removes the link. RequiredBy is a much stronger dependency.

The Alias option lists other unit names that could reference this unit. In the **ssh.service** file you will find an Alias option for **sshd.service**.

```
Alias=sshd.service
```

The Also option lists other units that should be activated when this unit is started. The CUPS service has an Also option to start the CUPS socket and path.

```
Also=cups.socket cups.path
```

Different types of units have their own options. Service, socket, target, and path units all have options appropriate for their tasks.

special targets

A target file groups units for services, mounts, sockets, and devices. **systemd** has a set of special target files designed for specific purposes (see Table 12-3). Some are used for on-demand services such as bluetooth and printer. When a Bluetooth device is connected the bluetooth target becomes active. When you connect a printer, the printer target is activated which, in turn, activates the CUPS print server. The sound target is activated when the system starts and runs all sound-related units. See the **special.target** Man page for more details.

There are several special target files that are designed to fulfill the function of runlevels in System V (see Table 12-4). These include the rescue, multi-user, and graphical targets. On boot,

systemd activates the default target, which is a link to a special target, such as **multi-user.target** and **graphical.target**.

You can override the default target with a **systemd.unit** kernel command line option for GRUB. On the GRUB startup menu, you could edit the kernel boot line and add the following option to boot to the command line instead of the desktop.

```
systemd.unit=multi-user.target
```

The following will start up the rescue target.

```
systemd.unit=rescue.target
```

The following will start up the graphical target.

```
systemd.unit=graphical.target
```

Special units	Description
`basic.target`	Units to be run at early boot
`bluetooth.target`	Starts when a Bluetooth device becomes active
`printer.target`	Starts printer service when a printer is attached.
`sound.target`	Starts when sound device is detected, usually at boot.
`display-manager.service`	Link to display service such as LightDM or KDM.
`ctrl-alt-del.target`	Activated when the user presses Ctrl-Alt-Del keys, this is a link to the reboot.target which reboots the system.
`system-update.target`	Implements an offline system update. After downloading, the updates are performed when your system reboots, at which time it detects the presence of the target.

Table 12-3: special units

Special RunlevelTargets	Description
`default.target`	References special target to be activated on boot
`rescue.target`	Starts up base system and rescue shell
`emergency.target`	Starts base system, with option to start full system
`multi-user.target`	Starts up command line interface, multi-user and non-graphical (similar to runlevel 3)
`graphical.target`	Start graphical interface (desktop) (similar to runlevel 5)

Table 12-4: special runlevel targets (boot)

You could also simply add a 3 as in previous releases, as runlevel links also reference the special targets in **systemd**. The 3 would reference the runlevel 3 target, which links to the multi-user target. A copy of the **multi-user.target** file follows. The multi-user target requires the basic target which loads the basic system (Requires). It conflicts with the rescue target (Conflicts), and it is run after the basic target. It can be isolated allowing you to switch special targets (AllowIsolate).

multi-user.target

```
[Unit]
Description=Multi-User System
Documentation=man:systemd.special(7)
Requires=basic.target
Conflicts=rescue.service rescue.target
After=basic.target rescue.service rescue.target
AllowIsolate=yes
```

The **graphical.target** depends on the **multi-user.target**. A copy of the **graphical.target** unit file follows. It requires that the **multi-user.target** be activated (Requires). Anything run for the multi-user target, including servers, is also run for the graphical target, the desktop. The desktop target is run after the **multi-user.target** (After). It is not run for the **rescue.target** (Conflicts). It also wants the display-manager service to run (GDM or KDM) (Wants). You can isolate it to switch to another target (AllowIsolate).

graphical.target

```
[Unit]
Description=Graphical Interface
Documentation=man:systemd.special(7)
Requires=multi-user.target
Wants=display-manager.service
Conflicts=rescue.service rescue.target
After=multi-user.target rescue.service rescue.target display-manager.service
AllowIsolate=yes
```

Modifying unit files: /etc/systemd/system

systemd uses unit files to manage devices, mounts, and services. These are located in the **/lib/systemd/system** directory and are considered system files that you should not modify. You can modify a unit file either by specifying features that override those in the original, or by creating a separate copy that you can edit, which takes precedence over the original. In each case it is best to create the modifications using the **systemctl** command with the **edit** option.

To simply override or add entries to the unit file, you can create an associated drop in directory that contains configuration files with entries. Such a directory has the same name as the unit file with a **.d** extension. It contains configuration files with the extension **.conf**. To create a drop in directory and its configuration file, you simple edit the unit file with the **systemctl edit** command.

```
sudo systemctl edit vsftpd.service
```

This opens your default line editor and lets you add in the new entries. When you save, if the drop in directory does not exist, it is created. This creates an **override.conf** file in the **/etc/systemd/system/vsftpd.service.d** directory.

Should you want to make more extensive changes, you can create a copy of the original unit file in the **/etc/systemd/system** directory. Unit files in this directory take precedence over those in the **/lib/systemd/system** directory. You can then modify the unit file version in **/etc/systemd/system**. You would create this copy using the **systemctl edit --full** command.

```
sudo systemctl edit --full vsftpd.service
```

This opens your default line editor display the copy of the unit file, now in your **/etc/systemd/system** directory, and lets you modify or add entries.

Alternatively, you could copy a unit file to the **/etc/systemd/system** directory directly, and then edit it with a text editor. Use the **cp** command to copy the file. The following command copies the Samba service unit file.

```
sudo cp /lib/systemd/system/smbd.service   /etc/systemd/system/smbd.service
```

Execution Environment Options

The unit files of type service, sockets, mount, and swap share the same options for the execution environment of the unit (see Table 12-5). These are found in the unit section for that type such as **[Service]** for service units or **[Socket]** for socket unit. With these options, you can set features such as the working directory (WorkingDirectory), the file mode creation mask (UMask), and the system logging level (SysLogLevel). Nice sets the default scheduling priority level. User specifies the user id for the processes the unit runs.

```
User=mysql
```

Exec options	Description
WorkingDirectory	Sets the working directory for an application.
RootDirectory	Root directory for an application
User, Group	The application's user and group ids.
Nice	Sets priority for an application
CPUSchedulingPriority	CPU Scheduling priority for the applications.
UMask	File mode creation mask, default is 022.
Environment	Set environment variables for an application.
StandardOutput	Direct standard output a connection such as log, console, or null.
SysLogLevel	System logging level such as warn, alert, info, or debug.
DeviceAllow, DeviceDeny	Control applications access to a device.
ControlGroup	Assign application to a control group.

Table 12-5: systemd exec options (Service, Socket, Mount, Swap) (systemd.exec)

service unit files

A service unit file is used to run applications and commands such as the Samba (smbd) and Web (apache2) servers. They have a **[Service]** section with options specified in the **systemd.service** Man page. See Table 12-6 for a listing of several common service options. A service unit file has the extension **.service** and the prefix is the name of the server program, such as **isc-dhcp-server.service** for the DHCP server and **vsftpd.service** for the Very Secure FTP server. Table 12-7 lists several popular servers.

A copy of the Vsftpd service unit file, **vsftpd.service**, follows. The Vsftpd FTP service is started after the network has started. The server program to run is specified, **/usr/sbin/vsftpd** (ExecStart). The service is installed by the **multi-user.target** (WantedBy) when the system starts up.

vsftpd.service

```
[Unit]
Description=vsftpd FTP server
After=network.target

[Service]
Type=simple
ExecStart=/usr/sbin/vsftpd /etc/vsftpd.conf
ExecReload=/bin/kill -HUP $MAINPID
ExecStartPre=-/bin/mkdir -p /var/run/vsftpd/empty

[Install]
WantedBy=multi-user.target
```

Service options	Description
`ExecStart`	Commands to execute when service starts, such as running an application or server.
`Type`	Startup type such as simple (the default), forking, dbus, notify, or idle
`ExecStartPre,` `ExecStartPost`	Commands executed before and after the ExecStart command.
`TimeStartSec`	Time to wait before starting the ExecStart command.
`Restart`	Restart when the ExecStart command end.
`PermissionsStartOnly`	Boolean value, If true the permission based options are applied, such as User.
`RootDirectoryStartOnly`	Boolean value, if true, the RootDirectory option applies only to the ExecStart option.

Table 12-6: systemd service options [Service] (systemd.service)

The **named.service** file is even simpler, incorporating runtime options into the program command. It is run after the network service and is started by the **multi-user.target**. It also has an alias, which lets you manage the service either as **named** or as **bind9**.

named.service

```
[Unit]
Description=BIND Domain Name Server
Documentation=man:named(8)
After=network.target
Wants=nss-lookup.target
Before=nss-lookup.target
[Service]
Type=forking
```

```
EnvironmentFile=/etc/default/named
ExecStart=/usr/sbin/named -f $OPTIONS
ExecReload=/usr/sbin/rndc reload
ExecStop=/usr/sbin/rndc stop
Restart=on-failure
[Install]
WantedBy=multi-user.target
Alias=bind9.service
```

Service unit files	Description
apache2	Apache Web server
bind9	Bind 9 DNS server
cups	The CUPS printer daemon
isc-dhcp-server	Dynamic Host Configuration Protocol daemon
mysql	MySQL database server
network	Operations to start up or shut down your network connections.
nis	The NIS server
nfs-server	Network Filesystem
postfix	Postfix mail server
sendmail	The Sendmail MTA daemon
smbd	Samba for Windows hosts
squid3	Squid proxy-cache server
ssh	Secure Shell daemon
systemd-journald	System logging daemon
vsftpd	Very Secure FTP server
ufw	Controls the UFW firewall

Table 12-7: Collection of Service unit files

System V Scripts and generated systemd service files: /etc/init.d and /run/systemd/generator.late

Some services are not yet configured natively for use by systemd. They are installed without a systemd service file. Instead, a SysV script is installed in the **/etc/init.d** directory. The **systemd-sysv-generator** tool automatically reads this script and generates a corresponding systemd unit file in the **/var/run/systemd/generator.late** directory, which, in turn, will use the script to manage the service.

On Demand and Standalone Services (socket)

The On Demand activation of services, formerly implemented by inetd, is the default in systemd. Should you want a standalone service, you can specify that it is wanted by a special target so that it will be started up at boot time, instead of when it is first activated. In the Install section of a service unit file, a WantedBy option specifying the multi-user target will start the service at boot, making it a standalone service. In the following, the service is wanted by the **multi-user.target**. To put it another way, the service starts at runlevels 2, 3, 4, and 5. Note that the graphical target (5) is dependent on (Requires) the multi-user target (2, 3, and 4), so by specifying the multi-user target, the service is also started with the graphical target.

```
[Install]
WantedBy=multi-user.target
```

The Bluetooth service only wants the **bluetooth.target** which is only activated if a Bluetooth device is present. It is not started at boot.

```
[Install]
WantedBy=bluetooth.target
```

Use the basic target, should you want the service started at all runlevels.

```
[Install]
WantedBy=basic.target
```

To emulate an on-demand server service, as inetd used to do, you would use a **.socket** file to compliment a **.service** file. This is the case with CUPS, which has a cups service file and corresponding cups socket file (CUPS is not installed by default on the Server edition). The WantedBy option for **sockets.target** ties the socket to the special target **sockets.target**, which makes the unit socket-activated.

The Socket section lists options for the socket, usually what socket to listen on (ListenStream). The **systemd.socket** Man page lists socket options. Table 12-8 lists common options.

Socket options	Description
ListenStream	Address to listen on for a stream. The address can be a port number, path name for a socket device, or an IPv4 or IPv6 address with a port number.
Accept	If true, service instance is set up for each connection; if false, only one service instance is set up for all connections
MaxConnections	Maximum number of connections for a service
Service	Service unit to run when socket is active. Default is a service name that is the same as the socket name.

Table 12-8: systemd socket file options [Socket] (systemd.socket)

cups.socket

```
[Unit]
Description=CUPS Scheduler
PartOf=cups.service

[Socket]
ListenStream= /run/cups/cups.sock

[Install]
WantedBy=sockets.target
```

cups.service

```
[Unit]
Description=CUPS Scheduler
Documentation=man:cupsd(8)
After=network.target nss-user-lookup.target nslcd.service
Requires=cups.socket

[Service]
ExecStart=/usr/sbin/cupsd -l
Type=notify
Restart=on-failure

[Install]
Also=cups.socket cups.path
WantedBy=printer.target multi-user.target
```

Path units

        systemd uses path units to monitor a path. Sometimes a service unit has a corresponding path unit to monitor directories, as is the case with **cups.path** and **cups.service**. Options for the Path section are listed in Table 12-9 and on the **systemd.path** Man page. The **cups.path** unit file is shown here. The PathExists option checks if the printer spool files exist.

cups.path

```
[Unit]
Description=CUPS Scheduler
PartOf=cups.service

[Path]
PathExists=/var/cache/cups/org.cups.cupsd

[Install]
WantedBy=multi-user.target
```

path options	Description
`PathExists`	Activates if a file exists
`PathExistsGlob`	Activates if there exists a file matching a pattern, such as any file in a specified directory.
`PathModified`	Activates if a file has been modified

Table 12-9: path option (systemd.path)

Template unit files

        There is a special type of unit file called a template file, which allow for the generation of several unit files at runtime using one template file. Templates are used for services that generate instances of a service such as a getty terminal, an OpenVPN connection, and an rsync connection.

A template filename ends with an **@** sign. If a corresponding unit file is not found for a service, **systemd** will check to see if there is a template file that can be applied to it. **systemd** matches the service name with the template name. It then generates an instance unit file for that particular service.

For example, a terminal uses the getty service (get TTY). As you do not know how many terminals you may use, they are generated automatically using the **getty@.service** unit file.

In the configuration file, the **%I** specifier is used to substitute for the service name. Given the service name **getty@tty3**, the **%I** specifier substitutes for **tty3**.

```
ExecStart=-/sbin/agetty -o '-p -- \\u' --noclear %I $TERM
```

The **getty@.service** template file is shown here.

getty@.service

```
[Unit]
Description=Getty on %I
Documentation=man:agetty(8) man:systemd-getty-generator(8)
Documentation=http://0pointer.de/blog/projects/serial-console.html
After=systemd-user-sessions.service plymouth-quit-wait.service getty-pre.target
After=rc-local.service

# If additional gettys are spawned during boot then we should make
# sure that this is synchronized before getty.target, even though
# getty.target didn't actually pull it in.
Before=getty.target
IgnoreOnIsolate=yes

# On systems without virtual consoles, don't start any getty. Note
# that serial gettys are covered by serial-getty@.service, not this
# unit.
ConditionPathExists=/dev/tty0

[Service]
# the VT is cleared by TTYVTDisallocate
ExecStart=-/sbin/agetty --noclear %I $TERM
Type=idle
Restart=always
RestartSec=0
UtmpIdentifier=%I
TTYPath=/dev/%I
TTYReset=yes
TTYVHangup=yes
TTYVTDisallocate=yes
KillMode=process
IgnoreSIGPIPE=no
SendSIGHUP=yes

# Unset locale for the console getty since the console has problems
# displaying some internationalized messages.
Environment=LANG= LANGUAGE= LC_CTYPE= LC_NUMERIC= LC_TIME= LC_COLLATE=
LC_MONETARY= LC_MESSAGES= LC_PAPER= LC_NAME= LC_ADDRESS= LC_TELEPHONE=
```

```
LC_MEASUREMENT= LC_IDENTIFICATION=

[Install]
WantedBy=getty.target
DefaultInstance=tty1
```

Runlevels and Special Targets

Under the old System V, a Linux system could run in different levels, called **runlevels**, depending on the capabilities you want to give it. Under System V, Linux had several runlevels, numbered from 0 to 6. When you power up your system, you enter the default runlevel. Runlevels 0, 1, and 6 are special runlevels that perform specific functions. Runlevel 0 was the power-down state. Runlevel 6 was the reboot state (it shuts down the system and reboots). Runlevel 1 was the single-user state, which allowed access only to the superuser and does not run any network services.

systemd uses special targets instead of runlevels to create the same effect as runlevels, grouping services to run for specified targets. Runlevels are no longer implemented. There are two major special targets: multi-user and graphical. The multi-user target is similar to runlevel 3, providing you with a command line login. The graphical target is similar to runlevel 5, providing you with a graphical login and interface.

You set the default target (runlevel) by linking a target's **systemd** service file to the **systemd** default target file. This operation replaces the way inittab was used to specify a default runlevel in previous releases. The following makes the graphical interface the default (runlevel 5).

```
ln -s /lib/systemd/system/graphical.target  /etc/systemd/system/default.target
```

systemd does provide compatibility support for runlevels. Runlevel compatibility is implemented using symbolic links in **/lib/system/systemd** directory to **systemd** targets. The **runlevel0.target** link references the systemd **poweroff.target**. Runlevel 2, 3, and 4 targets all link to the same **multi-user.target** (command line interface). The **runlevel6.target** links to the **reboot.target** and **runlevel5.target** links to **graphical.target** (desktop interface). The runlevels and their targets are listed in Table 12-10.

System Runlevel links	systemd targets
runlevel0	poweroff.target
runlevel1	rescue.target
runlevel2	multi-user.target
runlevel3	multi-user.target
runlevel4	multi-user.target.
runlevel5	graphical.target.
runlevel6	reboot.target

Table 12-10: System Runlevels (States)

You can still use the **runlevel** command to see what state you are currently running in. It lists the previous state followed by the current one. If you have not changed states, the previous state will be listed as N, indicating no previous state. This is the case for the state you boot up in. In the next example, the system is running in state 3, with no previous state change.

```
# runlevel
N 3
```

Changing runlevels can be helpful if you have problems at a particular runlevel. For example, if your video card is not installed properly, then any attempt to start up in runlevel 5 (**graphical.target**) will likely fail, as this level immediately starts your graphical interface. Instead, you could use the command line interface, runlevel 3 (**multi-user.target**), to fix your video card installation.

No matter what runlevel you start in, you can change from one runlevel to another with the **telinit** command. If your default runlevel is 3, you power up in runlevel 3, but you can change to, say, runlevel 5 with **telinit 5**. The command **telinit 0** shuts down your system. In the next example, the **telinit** command changes to runlevel 1, the administrative state.

```
telinit 1
```

Before **systemd** was implemented, you could also use **init** to change runlevels. With **systemd**, both **telinit** and **init** are now **systemd** emulation versions of the original Unix commands. The **telinit** command is always used to change runlevels. If you use **init** with a runlevel number, it now merely invokes **telinit** to make the change.

Alternatively, you can use the **systemctl** command directly to change runlevels (targets). The **systemctl** command with the **isolate** option and the name of the target file changes to that target (runlevel). This is what the **telinit** command actually does. The following command changes to the multi-user target.

```
sudo systemctl isolate multi-user.target
```

You could also use the runlevel link instead.

```
sudo systemctl isolate runlevel3.target
```

systemd and automatically mounting file systems: /etc/fstab

The **systemd** unit files with the extension **.mount** can be used to mount file systems automatically. Normally systemd will read the **/etc/fstab** file for mount information. If a mount unit file exists in the **/etc/systemd** directory, it takes precedence, but **/etc/fstab** takes precedence over any unit mount files in the **/lib/systemd** directory. The **/etc/fstab** file is used for mount configuration information. Most of the options for a mount unit file correspond to those of the **/etc/fstab** file, specifying the device path name, the mount point, file system type, and mount options (see Table 12-11). The entries in the **/etc/fstab** file are converted to mount unit files at boot, which are then used by systemd to perform the actual mount operations. These mount unit files are created by the systemd-fstab-generator and can be found in the **/run/systemd/generator** directory.

The following fstab file entries have corresponding mount files created in the **/run/systemd/generator** directory: **boot.mount** for the boot file system (**boot-efi.mount** for an EUFI boot system), **home.mount** for the home file system, and **-.mount** for the root file system. For the swap file system, a swap file is generated.

mount options	Description
`What`	Path of the device
`Where`	Directory of the mount point.
`Type`	File system type
`Options`	Mount options
`DirectoryMode`	Permissions for created file system mount directories
`TimeoutSec`	Time to wait for a mount operation to finish
automount options	Description
`Where`	Mount point for the file system. If it does not exist, it will be created.
`DirectoryMode`	Permissions for any directories created.

Table 12-11: systemd mount and automount file options [Mount] [Automount]

```
UUID=1059a-4a86-4072-982e-000717229b9f / ext4   errors=remount-ro   0 1
UUID-=5537-AF41 /boot/efi    vfat    umask=0077   0 1
UUID=147b-4a86-4072-982e-000717229b6g /home ext4   default   0 1
/swapfile  none    swap    sw   0 0
```

For this example, the **-.mount** file used for the root file system will have the following mount options. The root directory is represented in the mount filename as a dash, **-**, instead of a slash, **/**. The mount options are listed in a **[Mount]** section.

```
[Mount]
Where=/
What=/dev/disk/by-uuid/1059a-4a86-4072-982e-000717229b9f
Type=ext4
Options=errors=remount-ro
```

The **home.mount** file references partition for the home file system and mounts it to the **/home** directory.

```
[Mount]
Where=/home
What=/dev/disk/by-uuid/147b-4a86-4072-982e-000717229b6g
Type=ext4
FsckPassNo=2
```

The **boot.mount** file mounts the ext4 file system that holds the kernel in the **/boot** directory.

```
[Mount]
What=/dev/disk/by-uuid/e759aa59-4a86-4072-982e-000717229b4a
Where=/boot
Type=ext4
FsckPassNo=2
```

On EFI boot systems, the **boot-efi.mount** file mounts the vfat EFI file system that holds the boot information.

```
[Mount]
Where=/boot/efi
```

```
What=/dev/disk/by-uuid/5537-AF41
Type=vfat
Options=umask=0077
```

All the unit files will designate the **/etc/fstab** file as the SourcePath, the file from which the configuration was generated.

```
SourcePath=/etc/fstab
```

All are mounted before any local file systems.

```
Before=local-fs.target
```

Local and remote file systems are distinguished by Wants options in their unit files for **local-fs.target** or **remote-fs.target**.

A mount unit file has to be named for the mount point it references. The path name slashes are replaced by dashes in the unit name. For example, the **proc-fs-nfsd.mount** file references the mount point **/proc/fs/nfsd**. The root path name, /, becomes a dash, **-**.

For file systems to be automatically mounted when accessed you can use the automount unit type. An automount unit must have a corresponding mount unit of the same name.

The **systemd-fsck@service** file provides a file system check with **fsck**, using the disk name as an argument.

```
RequiresOverridable=system-fsck@dev-disk-by\x2duuid-5537\x2dAF41.service
After=system-fsck@dev-disk-by\x2duuid-5537\x2dAF41.service
```

systemd slice and scope units

The slice and scope units are designed to group units to easily control their processes and resources. The scope units are generated by systemd to manage a process and its subprocesses. An example of a scope unit is a user session scope that groups the processes for a user session together. A slice is used to manage resources for processes, such as the machine slice for virtual machines, the system slice for system services, and the user slice for user sessions.

System V: /etc/init.d

The SysVinit support for services is no longer implemented. There are no **rc.d** scripts for starting services. **systemd** manages all services directly. Check the README file in the **/etc/init.d** directory. For a very few system tasks, you may find System V scripts in the **/etc/init.d** directory. **systemd** will read these scripts as configuration information for a service, generating a corresponding unit configuration file for it. The unit file, in turn, may use the **init.d** script to start, stop, and restart the service. Should there be a unit file already in existence, that unit file is used, and the System V script is ignored.

A few servers use unit files generated from System V scripts in the **/etc/init.d** directory, such as NIS. The unit files are generated by systemd-sysv-generator and located in the **/var/run/systemd/generator.late** directory.

An **rc-local.service** unit file in the **/lib/systemd/system** directory will run a **/etc/rc.local** file, if present. This is to maintain compatibility with older System V configuration.

Shutdown and Poweroff

You can use the **shutdown** and **poweroff** commands to power down the system. The **shutdown** command provides more options. Keep in mind that the **shutdown** command used is the **systemd** version, which will use **systemctl** to actually shut down the system.

You can also shut down your system immediately using the **poweroff** command with the **sudo** command. You may be prompted to enter your password.

```
sudo poweroff
```

To perform a reboot, you can use the **reboot** command.

```
sudo reboot
```

The **shutdown** command has a time argument that gives users on the system a warning before you power down. You can specify an exact time to shut down, or a period of minutes from the current time. The exact time is specified by *hh:mm* for the hour and minutes. The period of time is indicated by a + and the number of minutes.

The **shutdown** command takes several options with which you can specify how you want your system shut down. The **-h** option, which stands for halt, simply shuts down the system, whereas the **-r** option shuts down the system and then reboots it. In the next example, the system is shut down after ten minutes.

```
shutdown -h +10
```

To shut down the system immediately, you can use **+0** or the word **now**. The shutdown options are listed in Table 12-12. The following example shuts down the system immediately and then reboots.

```
shutdown -r now
```

With the **shutdown** command, you can include a warning message to be sent to all users currently logged in, giving them time to finish what they are doing before you shut them down.

```
shutdown -h +5 "System needs a rest"
```

If you do not specify either the **-h** or the **-r** options, the **shutdown** command shuts down the multi-user mode and shifts you to an administrative single-user mode. In effect, your system state changes from 3 (multi-user state) to 1 (administrative single-user state). Only the root user is active, allowing the root user to perform any necessary system administrative operations with which other users might interfere.

The shutdown process works through systemd using the **systemctl** command. The poweroff, halt, and reboot commands invoke systemd service files activated through corresponding target files. The **systemctl** command, in turn, uses the **/lib/systemd/system-shutdown** program to perform the actual shut down operation. In the **/lib/systemd/system** directory, the **systemd-poweroff.halt** file shows the **systemctl poweroff** command. The man page for the shutdown service is **systemd-halt-service**. Always use the **poweroff**, **reboot**, and **halt** commands to shut down, not the **systemctl** command. The corresponding systemd target and service files for these commands ensure that the shutdown process proceeds safely.

systemd-poweroff.service

```
#  This file is part of systemd.
#
#  systemd is free software; you can redistribute it and/or modify it
#  under the terms of the GNU Lesser General Public License as published by
#  the Free Software Foundation; either version 2.1 of the License, or
#  (at your option) any later version.

[Unit]
Description=System Power Off

Documentation=man:systemd-poweroff.service(8)
DefaultDependencies=no
Requires=shutdown.target umount.target final.target
After=shutdown.target umount.target final.target

SuccessAction=poweroff-force
```

Note: The halt command merely halts the system, it does not turn it off.

Command	Description
`shutdown` `[-rkhncft]` *time* [*warning*]	Shuts the system down after the specified time period, issuing warnings to users; you can specify a warning message of your own after the time argument; if neither `-h` nor `-r` is specified to shut down the system, the system sets to the administrative mode, runlevel state 1.
Argument	
Time	Has two possible formats: it can be an absolute time in the format *hh:mm*, with *hh* as the hour (one or two digits) and *mm* as the minute (in two digits); it can also be in the format *+m*, with *m* as the number of minutes to wait; the word `now` is an alias for +0.
Option	
`-t` *sec*	Tells `init` to wait *sec* seconds between sending processes the warning and the kill signals, before changing to another runlevel.
`-k`	Doesn't actually shut down; only sends the warning messages to everybody.
`-r`	Reboots after shutdown, runlevel state 6.
`-h`	Halts after shutdown, runlevel state 0.
`-n`	Doesn't call `init` to do the shutdown; you do it yourself.
`-f`	Skips file system checking (fsck) on reboot.
`-c`	Cancels an already running shutdown; no time argument.

Table 12-12: System Shutdown Options

Managing Services

You can select certain services to run. Most services are servers like a Web server or FTP server. Other services provide security, such as SSH or Kerberos. You can decide which services to use with the **systemctl** command.

Enabling services: starting a service automatically at boot

Services such as the Apache Web server, Samba server, and the FTP server are handled by the **systemd** daemon. You can manage services using the **systemctl** command. The older **service** command is simply a front end to the **systemctl** command.

To have a service start up at boot, you need to first enable it using the **systemctl** tool as the root user. Use the **enable** command to enable the service. The following command enables the **vsftpd** server and the Samba server (**smbd**). The **systemctl** command uses the service's service configuration file located in the **/lib/systemd/system** or the **/etc/systemd/system** directory.

```
sudo systemctl enable vsftpd.service
sudo systemctl enable smbd
```

Managing services manually: systemctl

Use the **start**, **stop**, and **restart** commands with **systemctl** to manually start, stop, and restart a service. The **enable** command only starts up a service automatically. You could choose to start it manually using the **start** command. You can stop and restart a service any time using the **stop** and **restart** commands. The **condrestart** command only starts the server if it is already stopped. Use the **status** command to check the current status of service.

```
sudo systemctl start vsftpd
sudo systemctl restart vsftpd
sudo systemctl condrestart vsftpd
sudo systemctl stop vsftpd
sudo systemctl status vsftpd
```

The service Command

The older **service** command is now simply a front end for the **systemctl** command which performs the actual operation using **systemd**. The **service** command cannot enable or disable services. It only performs management operations such as start, stop, restart, and status. With the **service** command, you enter the service name with the **stop** argument to stop it, the **start** argument to start it, and the **restart** argument to restart it. The **service** command is run from a Terminal window. You will have to use the **sudo** command. The following will start the **vsftpd** FTP service.

```
sudo service vsftpd start
```

The **systemd** version of the **service** command actually invokes the **systemctl** command to run the service's systemd **.service** unit file in **/lib/systemd/system**. If a service is not enabled, **systemd** will enable it. You can perform the same operations as the **service** command, using the **systemctl** command. The following is the equivalent of the previous command.

```
sudo systemctl start vsftpd
```

Cockpit

The Cockpit management console (provided by Red Hat) provides a Web interface for managing both system administration and internet servers on your system, as well as servers on your network (**https://cockpit-project.org**). The Web interface works best on a desktop system. You can use it to manage your system resources, including services, storage, and networking. The package name is **cockpit**.

```
sudo apt install cockpit
```

You can access Cockpit from Administration | Cockpit. This will open cockpit with your default browser. You can also access cockpit using a Web browser and accessing port 9090 on your local system (**localhost:9090**). The cockpit page initially prompts you for your username and password. The top menu on the left side shows a listing of the systems on your network. Your current system is already chosen. Links on the left side show administration categories such as System, services, networking, and storage. Click on the Services link to list your services, showing whether they are the enabled or disabled, including the network services such as Samba, the Apache Web server, and the vsftpd FTP server (see Figure 12-1). The "Limited access" button at the top with a lock icon prevents you from making changes. To manage the services as an administrator, click on this button to open a "Switch to administrative access" dialog that prompts your for your password. Click the Authenticate button. Then click on the Services tab to list enabled and disabled services. Clicking on a service opens a page where you can manage the service. The current status is shown. Clicking on an vertical alliteration button to the right of the service name displays a menu for actions you may want to take, such as stopping or restarting a service. To disable a service click its enable/disable button to the right of the service name. If disabled, its status on the services list will show disabled.

Figure 12-1: Services: cockpit

Cockpit dynamically updates with **systemctl**. Should you make changes in a terminal window using **systemctl**, the changes are immediately shown on Cockpit.

/etc/default

The **/etc/default** directory holds scripts for setting runtime options when a service starts up. For example, the **/etc/default/apache2** script sets cache cleaning options. The **/etc/default/ufw** scripts sets firewall default policies. You can edit these scripts and change the values assigned to options, changing the behavior of a service.

Network Time Protocol: Chrony

For servers to run correctly, they need to always have the correct time. Internet time servers worldwide provide the time in the form of the Universal Time Coordinated (UTC). Local time is then calculated using the local system's local time zone. The time is obtained from Internet time servers from an Internet connection. You have the option of using a local hardware clock instead, though this may be much less accurate.

Normally, the time on a host machine is kept in a Time of Year chip (TOY) that maintains the time when the machine is off. Its time is used when the machine is rebooted. A host using the Network Time Protocol then adjusts the time, using the time obtained from an Internet time server. If there is a discrepancy of more than 1000 seconds (about 15 minutes), the system administrator is required to manually set the time. Time servers in the public network are organized in stratum levels, the highest being 1. Time servers from a lower stratum obtain the time from those in the next higher level.

The time is synchronized for your host by the **systemd-timesyncd** daemon. You can manage and set the time on your host with the **timedatectl** command. However, if you want to set up a time server on your local network, you can use Chrony.

For servers on your local network, you may want to set up your own time server, ensuring that all your servers are using a synchronized time. If all your servers are running on a single host system that is directly connected to the Internet and accessing an Internet time server, you will not need to set up a separate time server.

The Chrony time server is used, replacing the older NTP time server. You can find documentation for Chrony at:

```
https://chrony.tuxfamily.org
```

There is a package on the Ubuntu repository for the Chrony server. You can install it with Software Manager, the **apt** command, or the Synaptic Package Manager.

```
sudo apt install chrony
```

There are man pages for the **chronyd**, **chrony.conf**, and **chronyc**. The command line interface for the **chronyd** server is **chronyc**.

```
chronyc
```

The Chrony server

The Chrony server name is **chronyd** and is managed by the **/lib/systemd/system/chrony.service** script.

chrony.service

```
 [Unit]
Description=chrony, an NTP client/server
Documentation=man:chronyd(8) man:chronyc(1) man:chrony.conf(5)
Conflicts=openntpd.service ntp.service ntpsec.service
Wants=time-sync.target
Before=time-sync.target
After=network.target

 [Service]
```

```
Type=forking
PIDFile=/run/chrony/chronyd.pid
EnvironmentFile=-/etc/default/chrony
ExecStart=/usr/lib/systemd/scripts/chronyd-starter.sh $DAEMON_OPTS

CapabilityBoundingSet=~CAP_AUDIT_CONTROL CAP_AUDIT_READ CAP_AUDIT_WRITE
CapabilityBoundingSet=~CAP_BLOCK_SUSPEND CAP_KILL CAP_LEASE CAP_LINUX_IMMUTABLE
CapabilityBoundingSet=~CAP_MAC_ADMIN CAP_MAC_OVERRIDE CAP_MKNOD CAP_SYS_ADMIN
CapabilityBoundingSet=~CAP_SYS_BOOT CAP_SYS_CHROOT CAP_SYS_MODULE CAP_SYS_PACCT
CapabilityBoundingSet=~CAP_SYS_PTRACE CAP_SYS_RAWIO CAP_SYS_TTY_CONFIG CAP_WAKE_ALARM
DeviceAllow=char-pps rw
DeviceAllow=char-ptp rw
DeviceAllow=char-rtc rw
DevicePolicy=closed
LockPersonality=yes
MemoryDenyWriteExecute=yes
NoNewPrivileges=yes
PrivateTmp=yes
ProcSubset=pid
ProtectControlGroups=yes
ProtectHome=yes
ProtectHostname=yes
ProtectKernelLogs=yes
ProtectKernelModules=yes
ProtectKernelTunables=yes
ProtectProc=invisible
ProtectSystem=strict
ReadWritePaths=/run /var/lib/chrony -/var/log
RestrictAddressFamilies=AF_INET AF_INET6 AF_UNIX
RestrictNamespaces=yes
RestrictSUIDSGID=yes
SystemCallArchitectures=native
SystemCallFilter=~@cpu-emulation @debug @module @mount @obsolete @raw-io @reboot @swap

# Adjust restrictions for /usr/sbin/sendmail (mailonchange directive)
NoNewPrivileges=no
ReadWritePaths=-/var/spool
RestrictAddressFamilies=AF_NETLINK

[Install]
Alias=chronyd.service
WantedBy=multi-user.target
```

Use the **start**, **stop**, and **restart** options with the **systemctl** command to manage the server.

```
sudo systemctl start chronyd
```

Your host systems can then be configured to use Chrony and access your Chrony time server.

The chrony.conf configuration file

The Chrony server configuration file is **/etc/chrony/chrony.conf**. This file lists the Internet time servers that your own time server used to determine the time. Check the **chrony.conf** Man page for a complete listing of the Chrony server configuration directives.

In the **chrony.conf** file, the server directive specifies the Internet time server's Internet address that your Chrony server uses to access the time. There is a default entry for the pool of Ubuntu time servers, but you can add more server entries for other time servers. You would use the **server** directive for a specific time server.

```
pool ntp.ubuntu.com
```

The default **/etc/chrony/chrony.conf** file is shown here.

```
# Welcome to the chrony configuration file. See chrony.conf(5) for more
# information about usuable directives.

# This will use (up to):
# - 4 sources from ntp.ubuntu.com which some are ipv6 enabled
# - 2 sources from 2.ubuntu.pool.ntp.org which is ipv6 enabled as well
# - 1 source from [01].ubuntu.pool.ntp.org each (ipv4 only atm)
# This means by default, up to 6 dual-stack and up to 2 additional IPv4-only
# sources will be used.
# At the same time it retains some protection against one of the entries being
# down (compare to just using one of the lines). See (LP: #1754358) for the discussion.
# About using servers from the NTP Pool Project in general see (LP: #104525).
# Approved by Ubuntu Technical Board on 2011-02-08.
# See http://www.pool.ntp.org/join.html for more information.
pool ntp.ubuntu.com        iburst maxsources 4
pool 0.ubuntu.pool.ntp.org iburst maxsources 1
pool 1.ubuntu.pool.ntp.org iburst maxsources 1
pool 2.ubuntu.pool.ntp.org iburst maxsources 2

# Use time sources from DHCP.
sourcedir /run/chrony-dhcp

# Use NTP sources found in /etc/chrony/sources.d.
sourcedir /etc/chrony/sources.d

# This directive specify the location of the file containing ID/key pairs for
# NTP authentication.
keyfile /etc/chrony/chrony.keys

# This directive specify the file into which chronyd will store the rate
# information.
driftfile /var/lib/chrony/chrony.drift

# Uncomment the following line to turn logging on.
#log tracking measurements statistics

# Save NTS keys and cookies.
ntsdumpdir /var/lib/chrony

# Log files location.
logdir /var/log/chrony

# Stop bad estimates upsetting machine clock.
maxupdateskew 100.0

# This directive enables kernel synchronisation (every 11 minutes) of the
# real-time clock. Note that it cannot be used along with the 'rtcfile' directive.
rtcsync

# Step the system clock instead of slewing it if the adjustment is larger than
# one second, but only in the first three clock updates.
```

```
makestep 1 3
# Get TAI-UTC offset and leap seconds from the system tz database.
# This directive must be commented out when using time sources serving
# leap-smeared time.
leapsectz right/UTC
```

The **allow** directive permits access by hosts on a local network to your time server, and the **deny** directive denies access. Those hosts can then use your time server. The deny directive denies access to specified hosts.

You can use the **cmdallow** command to allow client hosts to see your time server monitoring information. A host can then run the **cronyc** command line interface to run monitoring command. The **cmddeny** will deny access.

You can also run the time server in broadcast mode where the time is broadcast to your network clients. Use the **broadcast** directive and your network's broadcast address.

```
broadcast 192.168.123.255
```

cronyc

The **cronyc** command line interface lets you monitor your **chronyd** server, generating status reports, as well as letting you change the **chronyd** configuration as it is running. You start the cronyc interface with the **cronyc** command. This places you in an interactive shell with the **chrony>** prompt where you can enter **cronyc** commands. To leave the shell enter the **quit** command.

For security purposes, only monitoring commands can be used by normal users or from users on other hosts. The activity command will check for how many NTP sources are online, and **sourcestats** will list performance information for NTP sources.

```
$chronyc
chronyc>
```

Should you want to enter configuration commands you have to start **chronyc** as the root user. Use the **sudo** command. Keep in mind that the changes are not permanent. The **chrony.conf** file is not affected.

```
sudo chronyc
```

To set the time manually you would enter the **chronyc** shell as the root user, and use the **settime** command to specify the time. You may first have to run the **manual** command to enable the **settime** command.

```
$ sudo chronyc
chronyc> manual on
chronyc> settime Apr 7, 2018 18:24:09
chronyc> quit
```

AppArmor security

Linux Mint installs AppArmor as its default security system. AppArmor (Application Armor) is designed as an alternative to SELinux (Security-Enhanced Linux, **http://selinuxproject.org/page/Main_Page**). It is much less complicated but makes use of the same kernel support provided for SELinux. AppArmor is a simple method for implementing mandatory access controls (MAC) for specified Linux applications. It is used primarily for servers like Samba, the CUPS print servers, and the time server. In this respect, it is much more limited in scope than SELinux, which tries to cover every object. Instead of labeling each object, which SELinux does, AppArmor identifies an object by its path name. The object does not have to be touched. Originally developed by Immunix and later supported for a time by Novell (OpenSUSE), AppArmor is available under the GNU Public License. You can find out more about AppArmor at **https://gitlab.com/apparmor/apparmor/-/wikis/Documentation**.

AppArmor works by setting up a profile for supported applications. Essentially, this is a security policy similar to SELinux policies. A profile defines what an application can access and use on the system. Linux Mint will install the **apparmor** package. Also available are the **apparmor-profiles**, **apparmor-utils**, and **apparmor-doc** packages.

AppArmor is implemented with systemd, using the **/lib/systemd/system/apparmor.service** script. You can use the **systemctl** command to start, stop, and restart AppArmor.

```
sudo systemctl start apparmor
```

AppArmor utilities

The **apparmor-utils** packages install several AppArmor tools, including **aa-enforce**, which enables AppArmor and **aa-complain**, which instructs AppArmor to just issue warning messages (see Table 12-13). The **aa-unconfined** tool will list applications that have no AppArmor profiles. The **aa-audit** tool will turn on AppArmor message logging for an application (uses enforce mode).

The **apparmor_status** tool will display current profile information. The **--complaining** options lists only those in complain mode, and **--enforced** for those in enforcing mode.

```
sudo apparmor_status
```

Utility	Description
apparmor_status	Status information about AppArmor policies
aa-audit *applications*	Enable logging for AppArmor messages for specified applications
aa-complain	Set AppArmor to complain mode
aa-enforce	Set AppArmor to enforce mode
aa-autodep *application*	Generate a basic profile for new applications
aa-logprof	Analyzes AppArmor complain messages for a profile and suggests profile modifications
aa-genprof *application*	Generate profile for an application
aa-unconfined	Lists applications not controlled by AppArmor (no profiles)

Table 12-13: AppArmor Utilities

The **aa-logprof** tool will analyze AppArmor logs to determine if any changes are needed in any of the application profiles. Suggested changes will be presented, and the user can allow (**A**) or deny them (**D**). In complain mode, allow is the default, and in enforce mode, deny is the default.

You can also make your own changes with the new (**N**) option. Should you want the change applied to all files and directories in a suggested path, you can select the glob option (**G**), essentially replacing the last directory or file in a path with the * global file matching symbol.

The **aa-autodep** tool will generate a basic AppArmor profile for a new or unconfined application. If you want a more effective profile, you can use **aa-genprof** to analyze the application's use and generate profile controls accordingly.

The **aa-genprof** tool will update or generate a detailed profile for a specified application. **aa-genprof** will first set the profile to complain mode. You then start up the application and use it, generating complain mode log messages on that use. Then, **vgenprof** prompts you to either scan the complain messages to further refine the profile (**S**), or to finish (**F**). When scanned, different violations are detected, and the user is prompted to allow or deny recommended controls. You can then repeat the scan operation until you feel the profile is acceptable. Select finish (**F**) to finalize the profile and quit.

AppArmor configuration

AppArmor configuration is located in the **/etc/apparmor** directory. Configurations for different profiles are located in the **/etc/apparmor.d** directory. Loaded profile configuration files have the name of their path, using periods instead of slashes to separate directory names. The profile file for the **smbd** (Samba) application is **usr.sbin.smbd**. For CUPS (**cupsd**) it is **usr.sbin.cupsd**. Additional profiles like the Samba and Apache profiles are installed with the **apparmor-profiles** package (not installed by default).

```
sudo apt-get install apparmor-profiles
```

Configuration rules for AppArmor profiles consist of a path and permissions allowable on that path. A detailed explanation of AppArmor rules and permissions can be found in the **apparmor.d** Man page, including a profile example. A path ending in a * matching symbol will select all the files in that directory. The ** symbol selects all files and subdirectories. All file matching operations are supported (* [] ?). Permissions include **r** (read), **w** (write), **x** (execute), and **l** (link). The **u** permission allows unconstrained access. The following entry allows all the files and subdirectories in the **/var/log/samba/cores/smbd** directory to be written to.

```
/var/log/samba/cores/smbd/** rw,
```

The **/etc/apparmor.d/abstractions** directory has files with profile rules that are common to different profiles. Rules from these files are read into actual profiles using the **include** directive. There are abstractions for applications like audio, samba, and video. Some abstractions will include yet other more general abstractions, like those for the X server (**X**) or GNOME (**gnome**). For example, the profile for the Samba **smbd** server, **usr.sbin.smbd**, will have an include directive for the **samba** abstraction. This abstraction holds rules common to both the **smbd** and **nmbd** servers, both used by the Samba service. The <> used in an **include** directive indicates the **/etc/apparmor.d** directory. A list of abstraction files can be found in the **apparmor.d** Man page. The **include** directive begins with a # character.

```
#include <abstractions/samba>
```

In some cases, a profile may need access to some files in a directory that it normally should not have access to. In this case, it may need to use a sub-profile to allow access. In effect, the application changes hats, taking on permissions it does not have in the original profile.

The **armor-profiles** package will activate several commonly used profiles, setting up profile files for them in the **/etc/apparmor.d** directory, like those for samba (**usr.sbin.nmbd** and **usr.sbin.smbd**), the Dovecot mail pop and imap server (**usr.sbin.dovecot**), and Avahi (**usr.sbin.avahi-daemon**).

The package also will provide profile default files for numerous applications in the **/usr/share/doc/apparmor-profiles/extras** directory, such as the vsftpd FTP server (**usr.sbin.vsftpd**), the ClamAV virus scanner (**usr.bin.freshclam**), and the Squid proxy server (**usr.sbin.squid**). Some service applications are located in the **/usr/lib** directory, and will have a **usr.lib** prefix such as those for the Postfix server, which uses several profiles, beginning with **usr.lib.postfix**. To use these extra profiles, copy them to the **/etc/apparmor.d** directory. The following example copies the profile for the vsftpd FTP server.

```
sudo cp /usr/share/doc/apparmor-profiles/extras/usr.sbin.vsftpd  /etc/apparmor.d
```

Remote Administration

For remote administration, you can use OpenSSH and Puppet. OpenSSH lets you remotely control and transfer files securely over your network. Puppet lets you manage remote configuration of services.

Puppet

Puppet allows you to configure remote systems automatically, even though they may be running different Linux distributions with varying configuration files. Instead of configuring each system on a network manually, you can use Puppet to configure them automatically. Puppet abstracts administration tasks as resources in a resource abstraction layer (RAL). You then specify basic values or operations for a particular resource using a Puppet configuration language. Administration types include services, files, users, and groups. For example, you could use puppet to perform an update for a service (server) on systems using different package managers such as APT or Synaptic.

Puppet configuration can become very complex. Once set up, though, it fully automates configuration changes across all your networked systems. For detailed documentation and guides see the following.

```
https://puppet.com/docs/
```

Puppet configuration is located in the **/etc/puppet** directory. Puppet operations on services are specified in modules programmed in the **init.pp** file located in a **manifests** directory. In the Ubuntu example for Apache (Ubuntu Server Guide, Puppet), the apache module is created in the **init.pp** file in:

```
/etc/puppet/modules/apache2/manifests/init.pp
```

On Linux Mint and Ubuntu, clients use the puppet client (**puppet** package) and the server uses the puppetmaster daemon (**puppet-master** package). On puppet clients, use the **sytemctl** command to manually start and stop the **puppet** service. For the server, enable the **puppetmaster** service.

On the firewall add access for the Puppet port, 8140.

For the client, the puppet runtime configuration is set in the **/etc/default/puppet** file. Here you set the daemon to start by setting the **START** variable to yes

If your network is running a DNS server, you can set up a CNAME puppet entry for the puppet server. The puppet clients can then use the CNAME to locate the puppet server.

```
puppet   IN   CNAME   turtle.mytrek.com
```

You could also add a host entry for the puppet server in each client's **/etc/host** file.

On the server, the puppetmaster configuration in **/etc/default/puppetmaster** file lets you set port entries and the log service. Default entries are commented out. Remove the comment character, #, to enable.

When you first set up a client server puppet connection, the client and server have to sign the client's SSL certificate. First, run puppet on the client. On the server run the **puppet cert --list** command to see the clients certificate request. Then use **puppet cert --sign** to sign the certificate.

The Secure Shell: OpenSSH

Although a firewall can protect a network from attempts to break into it from the outside, the problem of securing legitimate communications to the network from outside sources still exists. A particular problem is one of users who want to connect to your network remotely. Such connections could be monitored, and information such as passwords and user IDs used when the user logs in to your network could be copied and used later to break in. One solution is to use SSH for remote logins and other kinds of remote connections such as FTP transfers. SSH encrypts any communications between the remote user and a system on your network.

The SSH protocol has become an official Internet Engineering Task Force (IETF) standard. A free and open source version is developed and maintained by the OpenSSH project, currently supported by the OpenBSD project. OpenSSH is the version supplied with most Linux distributions, including Linux Mint. You can find out more about OpenSSH at **https://www.openssh.com/**, where you can download the most recent version, though Linux Mint and Ubuntu will provide current versions from its repository. Traditionally there were two versions of SSH, the older SSH1 and its replacement SSH2. In the current release of OpenSSH, SSH1 is disabled by default. The OpenSSH server only supports SSH2. Should you need SSH1 tools for accessing an old SSH1 only server, you can install the **openssh-client-ssh1** package.

SSH secures connections by both authenticating users and encrypting their transmissions. The authentication process is handled with public key encryption. Once authenticated, transmissions are encrypted by a cipher agreed upon by the SSH server and client for use in a particular session. SSH supports multiple ciphers. Authentication is applied to both hosts and users. SSH first authenticates a particular host, verifying that it is a valid SSH host that can be securely communicated with. Then the user is authenticated, verifying that the user is who they say they are.

Encryption

The public key encryption used in SSH authentication makes use of two keys: a public key and a private key. The public key is used to encrypt data, while the private key decrypts it. Each host or user has its own public and private keys. The public key is distributed to other hosts, who can then use it to encrypt authenticated data that only the host's private key can decrypt. For example, when a host sends data to a user on another system, the host encrypts the authentication data with a public key, which it previously received from that user. The data can be decrypted only by the user's corresponding private key. The public key can safely be sent in the open from one host to another, allowing it to be installed safely on different hosts. You can think of the process as taking place between a client and a server. When the client sends data to the server, it first encrypts the data using the server's public key. The server can then decrypt the data using its own private key.

It is recommended that SSH transmissions be authenticated with public-private keys controlled by passphrases. Unlike PGP, SSH uses public-key encryption for the authentication process only. Once authenticated, participants agree on a common cipher to use to encrypt transmissions. Authentication will verify the identity of the participants. Each user who intends to use SSH to access a remote account first needs to create the public and private keys along with a passphrase to use for the authentication process. A user then sends their public key to the remote account they want to access and installs the public key on that account. When the user attempts to access the remote account, that account can then use the user's public key to authenticate that the user is who they claim to be. The process assumes that the remote account has set up its own SSH private and public key. For the user to access the remote account, they will have to know the remote account's SSH passphrase. SSH is often used in situations where a user has two or more accounts located on different systems and wants to be able to securely access them from each other. In that case, the user already has access to each account and can install SSH on each, giving each its own private and public keys along with their passphrases.

Authentication

For authentication in SSH, a user creates both public and private keys. For this, you use the **ssh-keygen** command. The user's public key then has to be distributed to those users that the original user wants access to. Often this is an account a user has on another host. A passphrase further protects access. The original user will need to know the other user's passphrase to access it.

When a remote user tries to log in to an account, that account is checked to see if it has the remote user's public key. That public key is then used to encrypt a challenge (usually a random number) that can be decrypted only by the remote user's private key. When the remote user receives the encrypted challenge, that user decrypts the challenge with its private key. The remote user will first encrypt a session identifier using its private key, signing it. The encrypted session identifier is then decrypted by the account using the remote user's public key. The session identifier has been previously set up by SSH for that session.

SSH authentication is first carried out with the host, and then with users. Each host has its own host keys, public and private keys used for authentication. Once the host is authenticated, the user is queried. Each user has their own public and private keys. Users on an SSH server who want to receive connections from remote users will have to keep a list of those remote user's public keys. Similarly, an SSH host will maintain a list of public keys for other SSH hosts.

SSH Packages, Tools, and Server

SSH is implemented on Linux systems with OpenSSH. The full set of OpenSSH packages includes the OpenSSH meta-package (ssh), the OpenSSH server (openssh-server), and the OpenSSH client (openssh-clients). These packages also require OpenSSL (openssl), which installs the cryptographic libraries that SSH uses.

The SSH tools are listed in Table 12-14. They include several client programs such as **scp**, **ssh**, as well as the **ssh** server. The **ssh** server (**sshd**) provides secure connections to anyone from the outside using the **ssh** client to connect. Several configuration utilities are also included, such as **ssh-add**, which adds valid hosts to the authentication agent, and **ssh-keygen**, which generates the keys used for encryption.

You can start, stop, and restart the server manually with the **systemctl** commands.

```
sudo systemctl restart sshd
```

Application	Description
ssh	SSH client
sshd	SSH server (daemon)
sftp	SSH FTP client, Secure File Transfer Program. Version 2 only. Use ? to list sftp commands(SFTP protocol)
sftp-server	SSH FTP server. Version 2 only (SFTP protocol)
scp	SSH copy command client
ssh-keygen	Utility for generating keys. -h for help
ssh-keyscan	Tool to automatically gather public host keys to generate ssh_known_hosts files
ssh-add	Adds RSD and DSA identities to the authentication agent
ssh-agent	SSH authentication agent that holds private keys for public key authentication (RSA, DSA)
ssh-askpass	X Window System utility for querying passwords, invoked by ssh-add (openssh-askpass)
ssh-askpass-gnome	GNOME utility for querying passwords, invoked by ssh-add
ssh-signer	Signs host-based authentication packets. Version 2 only. Must be suid root (performed by installation)
slogin	Remote login (version 1)

Table 12-14: SSH Tools

You have to configure your firewall to allow access to the **ssh** service. The service is set up to operate using the TCP protocol on port 22, tcp/22. If you are managing your IPTables or nftables firewall directly, you could manage directly by adding the following IPtables and nftables rules. This accepts input on port 22 for TCP/IP protocol packages.

iptables rule:

```
iptables -A INPUT -p tcp --dport 22 -j ACCEPT
```

nftables rule:

```
nft add rule ip filter INPUT tcp dport 22 counter accept
```

SSH Setup

Using SSH involves creating your own public and private keys and then distributing your public key to other users you want to access. These can be different users or simply user accounts of your own that you have on remote systems. Often people remotely log in from a local client to an account on a remote server, perhaps from a home computer to a company computer. Your home computer would be your client account, and the account on your company computer would be your server account. On your client account, you need to generate your public and private keys and then place a copy of your public key in the server account. Once the account on your server has a copy of your client user's public key, you can access the server account from your client account. You will be also prompted for the server account's passphrase. You will have to know this to access that account. Figure 12-1 illustrates the SSH setup that allows a user **george** to access the account **cecelia**.

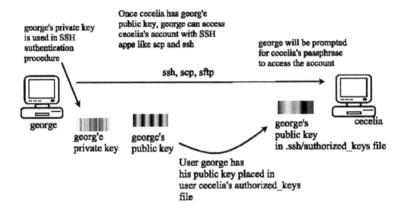

Figure 12-2: SSH setup and access

To allow you to use SSH to access other accounts:

You must create public and private keys on your account along with a passphrase. You will need to use this passphrase to access your account from another account.

You must distribute your public key to other accounts you want to access, placing them in the **.ssh/authorized_keys** file.

Other accounts also have to set up public and private keys along with a passphrase.

You must know the other account's passphrase to access it.

Creating SSH Keys with ssh-keygen

You create your public and private keys using the **ssh-keygen** command. You need to specify the kind of encryption you want to use. You can use either DSA or RSA encryption. Specify the type using the **-t** option and the encryption name in lowercase (**rsa**, **dsa**, **ecdsa**, and **ed25519**). In the following example, the user creates a key with the RSA encryption.

```
ssh-keygen -t rsa
```

The **ssh-keygen** command prompts you for a passphrase, which it will use as a kind of password to protect your private key. The passphrase should be several words long. You are also prompted to enter a filename for the keys. If you do not enter one, SSH will use its defaults. The public key will be given the extension **.pub**. The **ssh-keygen** command generates the public key and places it in your public key file, such as **.ssh/id_dsa.pub** or **.ssh/id_rsa.pub**, depending on the type of key you specified. It places the private key in the corresponding private key file, such as **.ssh/id_dsa** or **.ssh/id_rsa**.

File	Description
$HOME/.ssh/known_hosts	Records host keys for all hosts the user has logged into (that are not in **/etc/ssh/ssh_known_hosts**).
$HOME/.ssh/random_seed	Seeds the random number generator.
$HOME/.ssh/id_rsa	Contains the RSA authentication identity of the user.
$HOME/.ssh/id_dsa	Contains the DSA authentication identity of the user.
$HOME/.ssh/id_rsa.pub	Contains the RSA public key for authentication. The contents of this file should be added to **$HOME/.ssh/authorized_keys** on all machines where you want to log in using RSA authentication.
$HOME/.ssh/id_dsa.pub	Contains the DSA public key for authentication.
$HOME/.ssh/config	the per-user configuration file.
$HOME/.ssh/authorized_keys	Lists the RSA or DSA keys that can be used for logging in as this user.
/etc/ssh/ssh_known_hosts	Contains the system-wide list of known host keys.
/etc/ssh/ssh_config	Contains the system-wide configuration file. This file provides defaults for those values not specified in the user's configuration file.
/etc/ssh/sshd_config	Contains the SSH server configuration file.
/etc/ssh/sshrc	Contains the system default. Commands in this file are executed by ssh when the user logs in just before the user's shell (or command) is started.
$HOME/.ssh/rc	Contains commands executed by ssh when the user logs in just before the user's shell (or command) is started.

Table 12-15: SSH Configuration Files

If you need to change your passphrase, you can do so with the **ssh-keygen** command and the **-p** option. Each user will have their own SSH configuration directory, called **.ssh**, located in their own home directory. The public and private keys, as well as SSH configuration files, are placed here. If you build from the source code, the **make install** operation will automatically run **ssh-keygen**. Table 12-15 lists the SSH configuration files.

Authorized Keys

A public key is used to authenticate a user and its host. You use the public key on a remote system to allow that user access. The public key is placed in the remote user account's

.ssh/authorized_keys file. Recall that the public key is held in the **.ssh/id_dsa.pub** file. If a user wants to log in remotely from a local account to an account on a remote system, they would first place their public key in the **.ssh/authorized_keys** file in the account on the remote system they want to access. If the user **larisa** on **turtle.mytrek.com** wants to access the **aleina** account on **rabbit.mytrek.com**, **larisa**'s public key from **/home/larisa/.ssh/id_dsa.pub** first must be placed in **aleina**'s **authorized_keys** file, **/home/aleina/.ssh/authorized_keys**. User **larisa** can send the key or have it copied over. A simple **cat** operation can append a key to the authorized key file. In the next example, the user adds the public key for **aleina** in the **larisa.pub** file to the authorized key file. The **larisa.pub** file is a copy of the **/home/larisa/.ssh/id_dsa.pub** file that the user received earlier.

```
cat larisa.pub >>  .ssh/authorized_keys
```

Note: You can also use seahorse to create and manage SSH keys.

Note: The .ssh/identity filename is used in SSH version 1; it may be installed by default on
      older distribution versions. SSH version 2 uses a different filename, .ssh/id_dsa or
      .ssh/id_rsa, depending on whether RSA or DSA authentication is used.

Loading Keys

If you regularly make connections to a variety of remote hosts, you can use the **ssh-agent** command to place private keys in memory where they can be accessed quickly to decrypt received transmissions. The **ssh-agent** command is intended for use at the beginning of a login session. For GNOME, you can use the **openssh-askpass-gnome** utility, invoked by **ssh-add**, which allows you to enter a password when you log in to GNOME. GNOME will automatically supply that password whenever you use an SSH client.

Although the **ssh-agent** command enables you to use private keys in memory, you also must specifically load your private keys into memory using the **ssh-add** command. **ssh-add** with no arguments loads your private key from your private key file, such as. **.ssh/id_rsa**. You are prompted for your passphrase for this private key. To remove the key from memory, use **ssh-add** with the **-d** option. If you have several private keys, you can load them all into memory. **ssh-add** with the **-l** option lists those currently loaded.

SSH Clients

SSH was originally designed to replace remote access operations, such as **rlogin**, **rcp**, and Telnet, which perform no encryption and introduce security risks. You can also use SSH to encode X server sessions as well as FTP transmissions (**sftp**). Corresponding SSH clients replace these applications. With **slogin** or **ssh**, you can log in from a remote host to execute commands and run applications, much as you can with **rlogin** and **rsh**. With **scp**, you can copy files between the remote host and a network host, just as with **rcp**. With **sftp**, you can transfer FTP files secured by encryption.

ssh

With **ssh**, you can remotely log in from a local client to a remote system on your network operating as the SSH server. The term local client here refers to one outside the network, such as your home computer, and the term remote refers to a host system on the network to which you are connecting. In effect, you connect from your local system to the remote network host. It is designed to replace **rlogin**, which performs remote logins, and **rsh**, which executes remote commands. With **ssh**, you can log in from a local site to a remote host on your network and then send commands to be executed on that host. The **ssh** command is also capable of supporting X Window System connections. This feature is automatically enabled if you make an ssh connection from an X Window System environment, such as GNOME. A connection is set up for you between the local X server and the remote X server. The remote host sets up a dummy X server and sends any X Window System data through it to your local system to be processed by your own local X server.

The ssh login operation function is much like the **rlogin** command. You enter the **ssh** command with the address of the remote host, followed by a **-l** option and the login name (username) of the remote account you are logging in to. The following example logs in to the **aleina** user account on the **rabbit.mytrek.com** host.

```
ssh rabbit.mytrek.com -l aleina
```

You can also use the username in an address format with **ssh**, as in:

```
ssh aleina@rabbit.mytrek.com
```

The following listing shows how the user **george** accesses the **cecelia** account on **turtle.mytrek.com**.

```
[george@turtle george]$ ssh turtle.mytrek.com -l cecelia
cecelia@turtle.mytrek.com's password:
[cecelia@turtle cecelia]$
```

A variety of options is available to enable you to configure your connection. Most have corresponding configuration options that can be set in the configuration file. For example, with the **-c** option, you can designate which encryption method you want to use, for instance, **idea**, **des**, **blowfish**, or **arcfour**. With the **-i** option, you can select a particular private key to use. The **-c** option enables you to have transmissions compressed at specified levels (see the **ssh** Man page for a complete list of options).

scp

You use **scp** to copy files from one host to another on a network. Designed to replace **rcp**, **scp** uses **ssh** to transfer data and employs the same authentication and encryption methods. If authentication requires it, **scp** requests a password or passphrase. The **scp** program operates much like **rcp**. Directories and files on remote hosts are specified using the username and the host address before the filename or directory. The username specifies the remote user account that **scp** is accessing, and the host is the remote system where that account is located. You separate the user from the host address with an **@**, and you separate the host address from the file or directory name with a colon. The following example copies the file **party** from a user's current directory to the user **aleina**'s **birthday** directory, located on the **rabbit.mytrek.com** host.

```
scp party aleina@rabbit.mytrek.com:/birthday/party
```

Of particular interest is the **-r** option (recursive) option, which enables you to copy whole directories. See the **scp** Man page for a complete list of options. In the next example, the user copies the entire **reports** directory to the user **justin**'s **projects** directory.

```
scp -r reports justin@rabbit.mytrek.com:/projects
```

In the next example, the user **george** copies the **mydoc1** file from the user **cecelia**'s home directory.

```
[george@turtle george]$ scp cecelia@turtle.mytrek.com:mydoc1   .
cecelia@turtle.mytrek.com's password:
mydoc1     0% |                              |    0 --:--
ETA
mydoc1   100% |*****************************|   17 00:00
[george@turtle george]$
```

sftp and sftp-server

With **sftp**, you can transfer FTP files secured by encryption. The **sftp** program uses the same commands as **ftp**. This client operates much like **ftp**, with many of the same commands.

```
sftp download.ubuntu.com
```

To use the **sftp** to connect to an FTP server, that server needs to be operating the **sftp-server** application. The SSH server invokes **sftp-server** to provide encrypted FTP transmissions to those using the **sftp** client. The sftp server and client use the SSH File Transfer Protocol (SFTP) to perform FTP operations securely.

Port Forwarding (Tunneling)

If for some reason, you can connect to a secure host only by going through an insecure host, SSH provides a feature called port forwarding. With port forwarding, you can secure the insecure segment of your connection. This involves simply specifying the port at which the insecure host is to connect to the secure one. This sets up a direct connection between the local host and the remote host, through the intermediary insecure host. Encrypted data is passed through directly. This process is referred to as tunneling, creating a secure tunnel of encrypted data through connected servers.

You can set up port forwarding to a port on the remote system or to one on your local system. To forward a port on the remote system to a port on your local system, use **ssh** with the **-R** option, followed by an argument holding the local port, the remote host address, and the remote port to be forwarded, each separated by a colon. This works by allocating a socket to listen to the port on the remote side. Whenever a connection is made to this port, the connection is forwarded over the secure channel, and a connection is made to a remote port from the local machine. In the following example, port 22 on the local system is connected to port 23 on the **rabbit.mytrek.com** remote system.

```
ssh -R 22:rabbit.mytrek.com:23
```

To forward a port on your local system to a port on a remote system, use the **-L** option, followed by an argument holding the local port, the remote host address, and the remote port to be forwarded, each two arguments separated by a colon. A socket is allocated to listen to the port on the local side. Whenever a connection is made to this port, the connection is forwarded over the secure channel and a connection is made to the remote port on the remote machine. In the following example, port 22 on the local system is connected to port 23 on the **rabbit.mytrek.com** remote system.

```
ssh -L 22:rabbit.mytrek.com:23
```

You can use the LocalForward and RemoteForward options in your **.ssh/ssh_config** file to set up port forwarding for particular hosts or to specify a default for all hosts you connect to.

SSH Configuration

The SSH configuration file for each user is in their **.ssh/ssh_config** file. The **/etc/ssh/ssh_config** file is used to set site-wide defaults, with possible additional configuration files in the the **/etc/ssh/ssh_config.d** directory that are read by the **/etc/ssh/ssh_config** file. In the configuration file, you can set various options, as listed in the **ssh_config** Man document. The configuration file is designed to specify options for different remote hosts to which you might connect. It is organized into segments, where each segment begins with the keyword **HOST**, followed by the IP address of the host. The following lines hold the options you have set for that host. A segment ends at the next **HOST** entry. Of particular interest are the **User** and **Ciphers** options. Use the **User** option to specify the names of users on the remote system who are allowed access. With the **Ciphers** option, you can select which encryption method to use for a particular host (the **Cipher** option is an SSH1 option, which is no longer supported):

```
Host turtle.mytrek.com
    User larisa
    Compression no
    Ciphers aes128-ctr
```

Most standard options, including ciphers, are already listed as commented entries. Remove the # to activate.

```
#   Ciphers aes128-ctr,aes192-ctr,aes256-ctr,aes128-cbc,3des-cbc
```

To specify global options that apply to any host you connect to, create a **HOST** entry with the asterisk as its host, **HOST ***. This entry must be placed at the end of the configuration file because an option is changed only the first time it is set. Any subsequent entries for an option are ignored. Because a host matches on both its own entry and the global one, its specific entry should come before the global entry. The asterisk (*) and the question mark (?) are both wildcard matching operators that enable you to specify a group of hosts with the same suffix or prefix.

```
Host *
   PasswordAuthentication yes
   ConnectTimeout 0
   Ciphers aes128-ctr
```

You use the **/etc/ssh/sshd_config** file to configure an SSH server, with possible additional configuration files in the the **/etc/ssh/sshd_config.d** directory that are read by the **/etc/ssh/sshd_config** file. Here you will find server options like the port to use, password requirement, and PAM usage. Once configured, you can check the validation of your configuration file with the **sshd** command and the **-T** option.

```
sudo sshd -T
```

13. Print Services

Printer Services: CUPS

Printer Devices and Configuration

Configuring Printers on the Desktop (system-config-printer)

CUPS Configuration files

CUPS Command Line Print Clients

CUPS Command Line Administrative Tools

Print services configure and make available printers on your local system, as well as on your network. Printers are managed as network resources by print servers. As a network resource, several hosts on a network could access the same printer. Printing sites and resources are listed in Table 13-1.

Check the Linux Mint manual for information on printers, such as disabling driverless printing (automated configuration) and proprietary drivers. For HP drivers you can install the **hplp-gui** package which provides a graphical interface for managing your HP driver.

```
https:/linuxmint-user-guide.readthedocs.io/en/latest/printers.html
```

CUPS

The Common Unix Printing System (CUPS) provides printing services, developed by Apple as an open source project, and is freely available under the GNU Public License. CUPS is the primary print server for most Linux distributions, including Linux Mint. The CUPS site at **https://www.cups.org/** provides detailed documentation on installing and managing printers. CUPS uses the Internet Printing Protocol (IPP), which provides a printing standard for the Internet (**https://pwg.org/ipp/**). The IPP protocol provides support for networking, PostScript, and web interfaces. The older line printer (LPD) printing systems only supported line printers. CUPS functions as network server, using a configuration format similar to the Apache web server. The networking supports lets users access printers remotely. GNOME provides integrated support for CUPS, allowing GNOME-based applications to directly access CUPS printers.

Resource	Description
https://cups.org	Common Unix Printing System
http://pwg.org/ipp	Internet Printing Protocol
http://lprng.sourceforge.net/	LPRng print server (Universe repository)

Table 13-1: Print Resources

Once you have installed your printers and configured your print server, you can print and manage your print queue using print clients. A variety of print configuration tools is available for the CUPS server such as Settings | Printers, system-config-printer, the CUPS configuration tool, and various line printing tools such as **lpq** and **lpc**, described in detail later in this chapter. Check the Ubuntu Server Guide | Services | Service - CUPS for basic configuration.

```
https://ubuntu.com/server/docs/service-cups
```

CUPS is managed by systemd using an on demand socket implementation with **cups.service**, **cups.socket**, **cups.path**, and **cups-browsed** files. In addition, a special **printer.target** unit detects when a printer is connected to your system. The **cups.service** file runs the CUPS server, **/usr/sbin/cupsd** (ExecStart). It is run when the **printer.target** is activated, which happens when a user connects a printer (WantedBy). The **cups.socket** unit file has CUPS listen for request at the CUPS socket, **/var/run/cups/cups.sock** (ListenStream). In effect, CUPS runs like the old inetd daemons, activated only when requested. The **cups.path** unit sets up CUPS print directories at **/var/cache/cups** (PathExists) when the system starts up (WantedBy=multi-user.target). The **cups-browsed.service** file supports access remote printers on your network.

cups.service

```
[Unit]
Description=CUPS Scheduler
Documentation=man:cupsd(8)
After=network.target nss-user-lookup.target nslcd.service
Requires=cups.socket

[Service]
ExecStart=/usr/sbin/cupsd -l
Type=notify
Restart=on-failure

[Install]
Also=cups.socket cups.path
WantedBy=printer.target multi-user.target
```

cups.socket

```
[Unit]
Description=CUPS Scheduler
PartOf=cups.service

[Socket]
ListenStream=/var/run/cups/cups.sock

[Install]
WantedBy=sockets.target
```

cups.path

```
[Unit]
Description=CUPS Scheduler
PartOf=cups.service

[Path]
PathExists=/var/cache/cups/org.cups.cupsd

[Install]
WantedBy=multi-user.target
```

cups-browsed.service

```
[Unit]
Description=Make remote CUPS printers available locally
Requires=cups.service
After=cups.service avahi-daemon.service network-online.target
Wants=avahi-daemon.service network-online.target

[Service]
ExecStart=/usr/sbin/cups-browsed

[Install]
WantedBy=multi-user.target
```

Note: Line Printer, Next Generation (LPRng) was the traditional print server for Linux and UNIX systems, but it has since been dropped from many Linux distributions. You can find out more about LPRng at http://lprng.sourceforge.net/.

Driverless Printing

Most newer printer models support driverless printing. Instead of installing a driver, the printer supports a driverless driver. You can print to any of these printers without first downloading and installing a driver for them. The printers are automatically detected through DNS Service Discovery (DNS-SD). The CUPS Web configuration interface, system-config-printer, GNOME printers, and lpadmin already support driverless printing.

CUPS uses the **driverless** utility to detect available driverless printers and to generate PPD configuration files for them. The drivers may not be as complete in features as their official drivers, but will print. Currently printers compatible with IPP Anywhere and Apple Raster supported printers can make use of driverless drivers, usually newer printers. GNOME Printer, system-config-printer, and the CUP Web interface all use the driverless tool to detect and configure driverless printers. See the man page for **driverless** for more information.

Conflicts may occur with the cups-browsed daemon, which was an earlier effort to implement a version of driverless printing, and is still useful for printers that do not support driverless printing. You may have to set option in the **/etc/cups/cups-browsed.conf** file to support driverless printing. You need to set the OnlyUnsupportedByCUPS and CreateIPPPrinterQueues options.

If an automatically detected and configured driverless printer fails to work correctly, you can remove the **ipp-usb** and **airscan** packages, and then install a driver manually. You may have to do this for proprietary drivers you have to download from printer vendor sites.

Printer Devices and Configuration

Before you can use any printer, you first have to install it on a Linux system on your network. A local printer is installed directly on your own system. This involves creating an entry for the printer in a printer configuration file that defines the kind of printer it is, along with other features such as the device file and spool directory it uses. On CUPS, the printer configuration file is **/etc/cups/printers.conf**. Installing a printer is fairly simple. Linux attempts to detect and configure printers automatically. If it cannot, then you determine which device file to use for the printer and the configuration entries for it.

Tip: If you cannot find the drivers for your printer, you may be able to download them from OpenPrinting database at http://www.openprinting.org/drivers. The site maintains an extensive listing of drivers.

Printer Device Files

Linux dynamically creates the device names for printers that are installed. USB-connected printers will be treated as a removable device that can easily be attached to other connections and still be recognized. For older printers connected to a particular port, dedicated device files will be generated. As an example, for parallel printers, the device names will be **lp0**, **lp1**, **lp2**, and so on. The number used in these names corresponds to a parallel port on your PC; **lp0** references the LPT1 parallel port and **lp1** references the LPT2 parallel port. Serial printers will use serial ports, referenced by the device files like **ttyS0**, **ttyS1**, **ttyS2**, and so on.

Printer URI (Universal Resource Identifier)

Printers can be local or remote. Both are referenced using Universal Resource Identifiers (URI). URIs support both network protocols used to communicate with remote printers, and device connections used to reference local printers.

Remote printers are referenced by the protocol used to communicate with it, like **ipp** for the Internet Printing Protocol used for UNIX network printers, **smb** for the Samba protocol used for Windows network printers, and **lpd** for the older LPRng Unix servers. Their URIs are similar to a Web URL, indicating the network address of the system the printer is connected to.

```
ipp://mytsuff.com/printers/queue1
smb://guest@lizard/myhp
```

For attached local printers, especially older ones, the URI will use the device connection and the device name. The **usb:** prefix is used for USB printers, **parallel:** for older printers connected to a parallel port, **serial:** for printers connected to a serial port, and **scsi:** for SCSI connected printers.

In the CUPS **/etc/cups/printers.conf** file the DeviceURI entry will reference the URI for a printer. For USB printers, the URI uses **usb:**.

```
DeviceURI usb://Canon/S330
```

Spool Directories

When your system prints a file, it makes use of special directories called spool directories. A print job is a file to be printed. When you send a file to a printer, a copy of it is made and placed in a spool directory set up for that printer. The location of the spool directory is obtained from the printer's entry in its configuration file. On Linux, the spool directory is located at **/var/spool/cups** under a directory with the name of the printer. For example, the spool directory for the **myepson** printer would be located at **/var/spool/cups/myepson**. The spool directory contains several files for managing print jobs. Some files use the name of the printer as their extension. For example, the **myepson** printer has the files **control.myepson**, which provides printer queue control, and **active.myepson** for the active print job, as well as **log.myepson,** which is the log file.

CUPS start and restart

You can start, stop, and restart CUPS using the **systemctl** command and the **cups** script. When you make changes or install printers, be sure to restart CUPS to have your changes take effect. You can use the following command:

```
sudo systemctl restart cups
```

The CUPS server is configured to start up when your system boots. The **/etc/default/cups** script holds startup options for the cups server, such as the LOAD_LP_MODULE option to load the parallel printer driver module.

Installing Printers

Several tools are available for installing CUPS printers. The easiest method is to use the **system-config-printer** tool on a desktop system. You can also use the CUPS Web browser-based configuration tools, included with the CUPS software (will work with **lynx** command line browser). Or you can just edit the CUPS printer configuration files directly.

Configuring Printers on the Desktop with system-config-printer (System Settings Printers)

Linux Mint attempts to detect and configure printers automatically. For removable printers, like a USB printer, the printer is detected and configured as soon as you connect your printer. It is configured by System Settings Printers (system-config-printer) and an icon for it appears in the System Settings Printers dialog. If the driver is not available, the printer is not configured and there is no printer icon for it. You will have to manually add and configure the printer.

system-config-printer

To change your configuration or to add a remote printer, you can use the printer configuration tool, system-config-printer, which is accessible from the System Settings dialog as Printers. This utility enables you to select the appropriate driver for your printer, as well as set print options such as paper size and print resolutions. You can configure a printer connected directly to your local computer, or a printer on a remote system on your network. You can start system-config-printer by choosing Printers in the Applications dash, System filter.

Figure 13-1: system-config-printer tool

The Printing configuration window displays icons for installed printers (see Figure 13-1). The menu bar has menus for Server configuration and selection, Printer features like its properties and the print queue, printer classes, and viewing discovered printers. A toolbar has buttons for adding new printers manually and refreshing print configuration. A Filter search box lets you display only printers matching a search pattern. Click on the x icon in the search box to clear the pattern. Clicking on the Looking glass icon in the File search box will display a pop-up menu that will let you search by Name, Description, Location, and Manufacturer/Model. You can save searches as a search group.

To see the printer settings such as printer and job options, access controls, and policies, double-click on the printer icon or right-click and select Properties. The Printer Properties window opens up with six tabs: Settings, Policies, Access Control, Printer Options, Job Options, and Ink/Toner Levels (see Figure 13-2).

Figure 13-2: Printer properties window

The Printing configuration window's Printer menu lets you rename the printer, enable or disable it, and make it a shared printer. Select the printer icon and then click the Printer menu (see Figure 13-3). You can also display the Printer menu by right-clicking on a printer icon. The Delete entry will remove a printer configuration. Use the Set As Default entry to make the printer a system-wide or your personal default printer. The properties entry opens the printer properties window for that printer. You can also access the print queue for the selected printer. If the printer is already a default, the Set As Default entry is shaded out.

Figure 13-3: Printer configuration window Printer menu

When print jobs are waiting in the print queue, a printer icon will appear on the top panel. Clicking on this icon opens the Document Print Status window listing the pending print jobs. You can also open this window from the system-config-printer's Printer menu, View Print Queue item (Printer | View Print Queue). On the Document Print Status window, you can change a job's queue position as well as stop or delete a job (see Figure 13-4). From the job menu, you can cancel, hold (stop), release (restart), or reprint a print job. Reprint is only available if you have set the preserve jobs option in the printer settings Advanced dialog. You can also authenticate a job. From the View menu, you can choose to display just-printed jobs and refresh the queue.

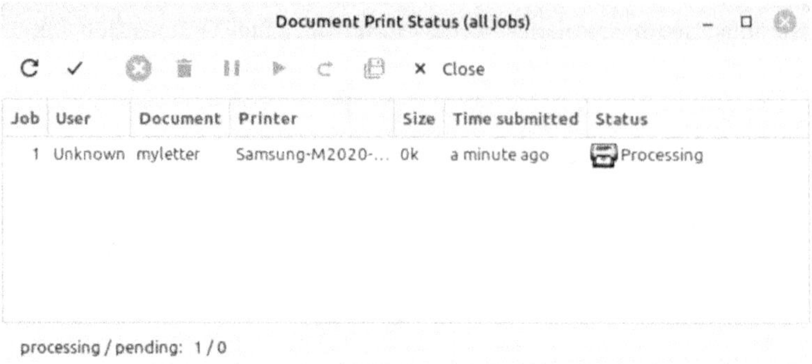

Figure 13-4: Printer queue

To check the server settings, select Settings from the Server menu. This opens a new window showing the CUPS printer server settings (see Figure 13-5). The Advanced expand button displays job history and browser server options. If you want to allow reprinting, then select the "Preserve job files (allow reprinting)" option.

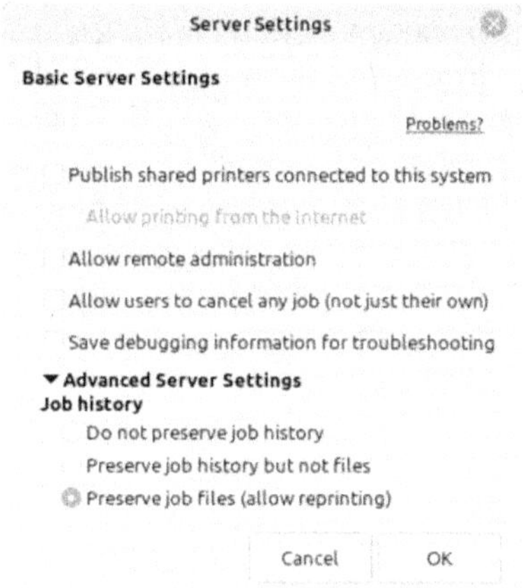

Figure 13-5: Server Settings

To select a particular CUPS server, select the Connect entry in the Server menu. This opens a "Connect to CUPS Server" window with a drop down menu listing all current CUPS servers from which to choose (see Figure 13-6).

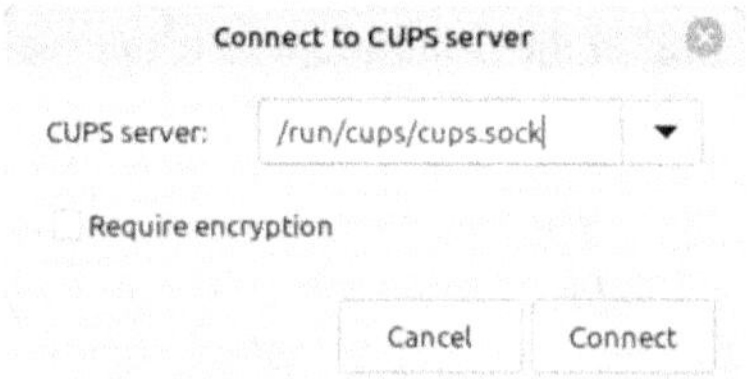

Figure 13-6: Selecting a CUPS server

Editing Printer Configuration

To edit an installed printer, double-click its icon in the Printer configuration window, or right-click and select the Properties entry. This opens a Printer Properties window for that printer. A sidebar lists configuration tabs. Click on one to display that tab. There are configuration tabs for Settings, Policies, Access Control, Printer Options, Job Options, and Ink/Toner Levels (see Figure 13-7).

Once you have made changes, you can click Apply to save your changes and restart the printer daemon. You can test your printer using the Tests and Maintenance tasks on the Settings tab. The Print Test Page prints a page, whereas the Print Self-Test Page also checks the printer hardware such as ink-jet heads.

On the Settings tab, you can change configuration settings like the driver and the printer name, and run test pages (see Figure 13-2). Should you need to change the selected driver, click on the Change button next to the Make and Model entry to open printer model and driver windows like those described in the "Add new printer manually" section. There you can specify the model and driver you want to use, even loading your own driver. Should you have to change the device URI (location and protocol), you can click the Change button to the right of the Device URI entry to open a "Change Device URI" dialog.

The Policies tab lets you enable and disable the printer, determine if it is to be shared, and whether to let it accept jobs or not (you also can enable or share the printer from the Printer menu). You can also specify an error policy, which specifies whether to retry or abort the print job, or stop the printer should an error occur. You can choose to print banners at the start or end indicating the level of security for a document, like confidential and secret.

The Access Control tab lets you deny access to certain users.

The Printer Options tab is where you set particular printing features like paper size and type, print quality, and the input tray to use (see Figure 13-7).

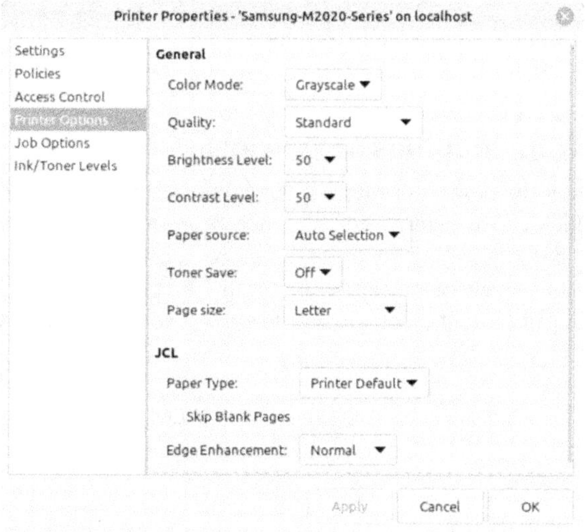

Figure 13-7: Printer Options

On the Job Options tab, you can select default printing features (see Figure 13-8) such as the number of copies, orientation, and single or double-sided printing. Options are arranged into three categories: Common Options, Image Options, and Text Options. Only the more common options are displayed. Each category has an expand button that will display all the options for that category. Double sided, output order, and media are all expanded options in the Common Options category.

The Ink/Toner Levels tab will display Ink or Toner levels for supported printers, along with status messages.

Figure 13-8: Jobs Options

Default System-wide and Personal Printers

To make a printer the default printer, either right-click on the printer icon and select "Set As Default", or single click on the printer icon and then from the Printer configuration window's Printer menu select the "Set As Default" entry (see Figure 13-3). A Set Default Printer dialog open with options for setting the system-wide default or setting the personal default (see Figure 13-9). The system-wide default printer is the default for the system served by your CUPS server.

Figure 13-9: Set Default Printer

The system-wide default printer will have a green check mark emblem on its printer icon in the Printing configuration window.

Should you wish to use a different printer yourself (user-specific) as your default printer, you can designate it as your personal default. To make a printer your personal default, select the entry "Set as my personal default printer" in the Set Default Printer dialog. A personal emblem, a yellow star, will appear on the printer's icon in the Printer configuration window. In Figure 13-10, the Samsung M2020 printer is the system-wide default, whereas the HP-DeskJet printer is the personal default.

Figure 13-10: System-wide and personal default printers

Adding New Printers Manually

Printers are detected automatically, though, in the case of older printers and network printers, you may need to add the printer manually. In this case, click the Add button and select Printer. A New Printer window opens, displaying a series of dialog boxes where you select the connection, model, drivers, and printer name with location.

On the Select Device dialog, select the appropriate printer connection information. Connected local printer brands will already be listed by name, such as Canon, and a Connection list appears at the lower right of the dialog showing the connection. For remote printers you will specify the type of network connection, like "Windows printers via Samba" for printers connected to a Windows system, "AppSocket/HP Direct" for HP printers connected directly to your network, and the "Internet Printing Protocol (ipp)" for printers on Linux and Unix systems on your network. These connections are displayed under the Network Printer heading. Click the expansion arrow to display them.

For most connected printers, your connection is usually determined by udev, which now manages all devices. A USB printer will simply be described as a USB printer, using the usb URI designation (see Figure 13-11). For an older local printer, you may have to choose the port the printer is connected to, such as LPT1 for the first parallel port used for older parallel printers, or Serial Port #1 for a printer connected to the first serial port. To add a USB printer manually, you would select the "Enter URI" Entry and enter the URI consisting of the prefix **usb://** and the name you want to give to the printer, like **usb://myhp**.

A search is conducted for the appropriate driver, including downloadable drivers. If the driver is found, the Choose Driver screen is displayed with the appropriate driver manufacturer already selected for you. You need only click the forward button. On the next screen, also labeled

Choose Driver, the printer model and driver files are listed and the appropriate one is already selected for you. Just click the Forward button. The Describe Printer screen is then displayed where you can enter the Printer Name, Description, and Location. These are ways you can personally identify a printer. Then click Apply.

Figure 13-11: Selecting a new printer connection: connected and unconnected

If the printer driver is not detected or is detected incorrectly, on the Choose Driver screen you have the options to choose the driver from the printer database, from a PPD driver file, or from a search of the OpenPrinting online repository. The selection display will change according to which option you choose.

Note: Some drivers are installed directly from the printer's company website, such as some of the Samsung drivers. These you may have to install directly, using a shell script run in a terminal window. Once installed, the printer is automatically detected and configured when you connect it. The drivers will also appear on the system-config-printer's Choose Driver local database listing dialog.

The database option lists possible manufacturers. Use your mouse to select the one you want (see Figure 3-12). The search option displays a search box for make and model. Enter both the make (printer manufacturer) and part of the model name (See figure 3-13). The search results will be available in the Printer model drop down menu. Select the one you want. Then click Forward.

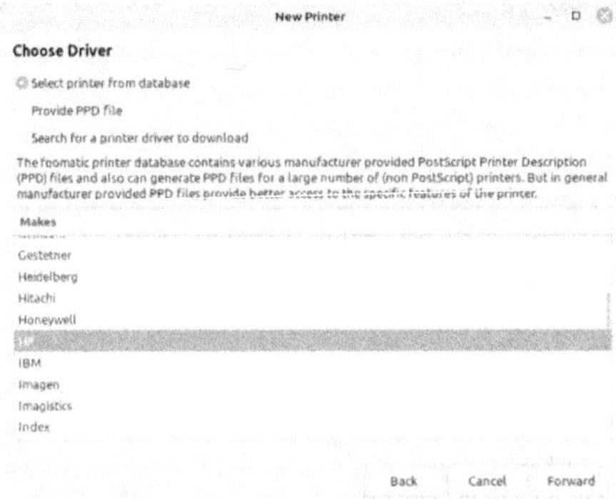

Figure 13-12: Printer manufacturer for new printers

Figure 13-13: Searching for a printer driver from the OpenPrinting repository

The PPD file option displays a file location button that opens a Select file dialog you can use to locate the PPD file on your system.

If you are selecting a printer from the database, on the next screen you select that manufacturer's model along with its driver (see Figure 13-14). For some older printer, though the driver can be located on the online repository, you will still choose it from the local database (the drivers are the same). The selected drivers for your printer will be listed. If there are added options for your printer, the Installable Options screen lists them allowing you to check the ones you want.

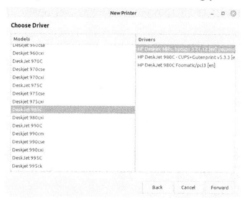

Figure 13-14: Printer Model and driver for new printers using local database

You can then enter your printer name and location (see Figure 13-15). These will be entered for you using the printer model and your system's hostname. You can change the printer name to anything you want. When ready, click Apply. You will be prompted to print a test page. An icon for your printer will be displayed in the Printing configuration window. You are now ready to print.

Figure 13-15: Printer Name and Location for new printers

CUPS Web Browser-based configuration tool

The CUPS configuration Web interface is a web-based tool that can also manage printers and print jobs. A Web page is displayed with tabs for managing jobs and printers and performing administrative tasks. You can access the CUPS configuration tool using the **localhost** address and specifying port **631**. Enter the following URL into your Web browser:

```
http://localhost:631
```

Entering the **localhost:631** URL in your Web browser opens the Home screen for the CUPS Web interface. There are tabs for various sections, as well as links for specialized tasks like adding printers or obtaining help (see Figure 13-16). Tabs include Administration, Classes, Help, Jobs, and Printers. You can manage and add printers on the Administration tab. The Printers tab will list installed printers with buttons for accessing their print queues, printer options, and job options, among others. The Jobs tab lists your print jobs and lets you manage them.

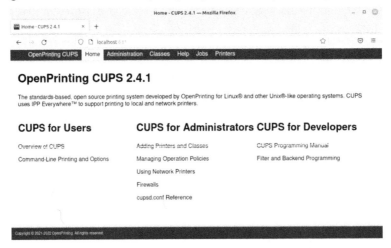

Figure 13-16: CUPS Web-based Configuration Tool: Home tab

When you try to make any changes for the first time during the session, you will first be asked to enter a\username with administrative access (your username) and password (your user password), just as you would for the **sudo** command.

The Administration tab displays segments for Printers, Classes, Jobs, and the Server (see Figure 13-17). The server section is where you allow printer sharing. Buttons allow you to view logs and change settings.

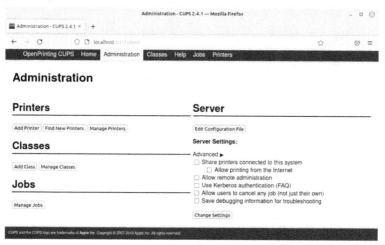

Figure 13-17: CUPS Web-based Configuration Tool: Administration tab

With the CUPS configuration tool, local printers are automatically detected and configured. You can install a printer manually on CUPS through a series of Web pages, each of which requests different information. To install a printer, click the Add Printer button either on the Home page or the Administration page. You must first specify the protocol. On the next screen, you enter a URI to use for the printer. For a local printer, this is the protocol and the hostname. A page is displayed where you enter the printer name and location (see Figure 13-18).

Figure 13-18: Adding a new printer: CUP Web Interface

A Sharing checkbox lets you choose to share the printer. The location is the host to which the printer is connected. The procedure is similar to **system-config-printer**. Subsequent pages will prompt you to enter the make and model of the printer, which you select from available listings. You can also load a PPD driver file instead if you have one. Click the Add Printer button when read. On the following page, you then set default options for your printer, like paper size and type, color, print quality, and resolution.

To manage a printer, click the Printers tab or the Manage Printers button in the Administration page. The Printers page will list your installed printers (see Figure 13-19). Clicking a printer link opens a page for managing your jobs and performing administrative tasks (see Figure 13-20). From the Maintenance drop down menu lets you perform printer and job tasks like pausing the printer, printing a test page, and canceling all jobs. The Administration menu lets you modify the printer, delete it, and set default options. Choosing the Administration menu's Set Default Options entry displays a page can configure how your printer prints (see Figure 13-21). Links at the top of the page display pages for setting certain options like general options, output control, banners, and extra features such as printer direction, ink type, color density, and drop size. The general options are listed first, where you can set basic features like the resolution and paper size.

Figure 13-19: CUPS Web-based Configuration Tool: Printers tab

Figure 13-20: CUPS Web-based Configuration Tool: Managing Printers

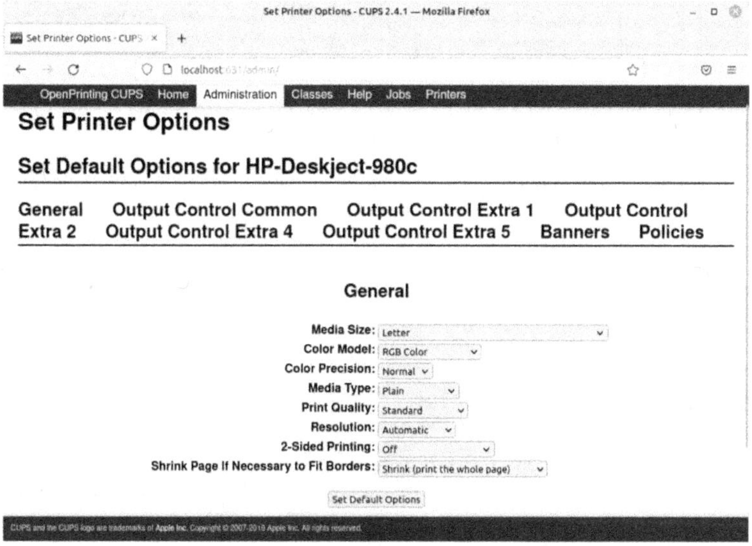

Figure 13-21: CUPS Web-based Configuration Tool: Printer Options

Note: You can perform all administrative tasks from the command line using the lpadmin command. See the CUPS documentation for more details.

Configuring Remote Printers on CUPS

As previously noted, most newer printers support driverless printing allowing you automatic access to remote printers. The driverless configurations are generated by CUPS. Should the driverless configuration be inadequate or absent, as is the case for older printers, you would have to install the driver using the CUPS Web-based configuration tool or system-config-printer. To manually install a remote printer that is attached to a Windows system or another Linux system running CUPS, you specify its location by using special URL protocols. For another CUPS printer on a remote host, the protocol used is **ipp**, for Internet Printing Protocol, whereas for a Windows printer, it would be **smb**. Older UNIX or Linux systems using LPRng would use the **lpd** protocol.

Configuring Remote Printers with system-config-printer

You can use system-config-printer to set up a remote printer on Linux, UNIX, or Windows networks. When you add a new printer or edit one, the New Printer dialog will list possible remote connection types under the Network entry. When you select a remote connection entry, a pane will be displayed to the right where you can enter configuration information.

To find most connected printers on your network automatically, click the Find Network Printer entry. Enter the hostname of the system the remote printer is connected to, then click the Find button. The host is searched and the detected printers are displayed as entries under the Network Printer heading. Because of the changes from SMB1 to SMB3 in Samba, the Find operation does not work for Windows printers.

Figure 13-22: Finding a network printer

To configure a specific type of printer, choose from the available entries. For a remote Linux or UNIX printer, select either Internet Printing Protocol (ipp), which is used for newer systems, or LPD/LPR Host or Printer, which is used for older systems. For an Apple or HP jet direct printer on your network, select the AppSocket/HP jetDirect entry.

For Windows, the **smbclient** package must be installed, which was done when you installed Linux Mint.

A "Windows printer via Samba" printer is one located on a Windows network (see Figure 13-24). You need to specify the Windows server (hostname or IP address), the name of the share, the name of the printer's workgroup if needed, and the username and password. The format of the printer SMB URL is shown on the SMP Printer pane. The share is the hostname and printer name in the **smb** URI format *//workgroup/hostname/printername.* The workgroup is the windows network workgroup that the printer belongs to. On small networks, there is usually only one. The hostname is the computer where the printer is located. The username and password can be for the printer resource itself, or for access by a particular user. The pane will display a box at the top where you can enter the share host and printer name as an **smb** URI.

Because of the changes from SMB1 to SMB3, the Browse operation accessed by the Browse button does not work. Because of this, you have to enter the exact name of the printer, including special characters such as spaces and parenthesis (see Figure 13-23). These special characters are referenced with a preceding percent sign, **%**, followed by the ASCII hexadecimal value for the character. A space is referenced as **%20**, an open parenthesis as **%28**, and a close parenthesis as **%29**. In these examples, the Windows name of the Samsung M2020 printer is:

```
Samsung M2020 Series (USB001)
```

This would be:

```
Samsung%20M2020%20Series%20%28USB001%29
```

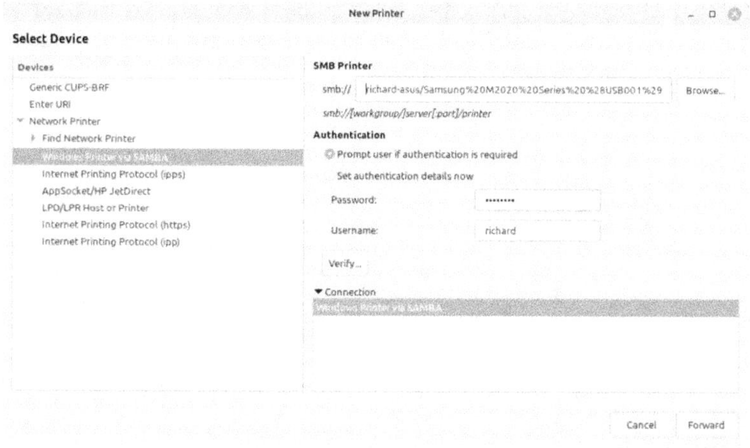

Figure 13-23: Selecting a Windows printer with full name and authentication

Be sure to also include your host name. If you have multiple workgroups on your network, include the workgroup name also. The full entry for the previous example, with the host 'richard-asus" would be:

```
richard-asus/Samsung%20M2020%20Series%20%28USB001%29
```

With the workgroup name "workgroup" it would be:

```
workgroup/richard-asus/Samsung%20M2020%20Series%20%28USB001%29
```

You also can enter in any needed Samba authentication, if required, like username or password. Check "Authentication required" to allow you to enter the Samba Username and Password. The Connections section to the lower right will list "Windows Printer via Samba" as the connection. With the current version of Samba, if you do not enter it now though, it will prompt you for a user name and password when you try to use the printer. This may not work. To be sure of access you should enter the user and password on this dialog now.

You then continue with install screens for the printer model, driver, and name. Once installed, you can then access the printer properties just as you would any printer (see Figure 13-24).

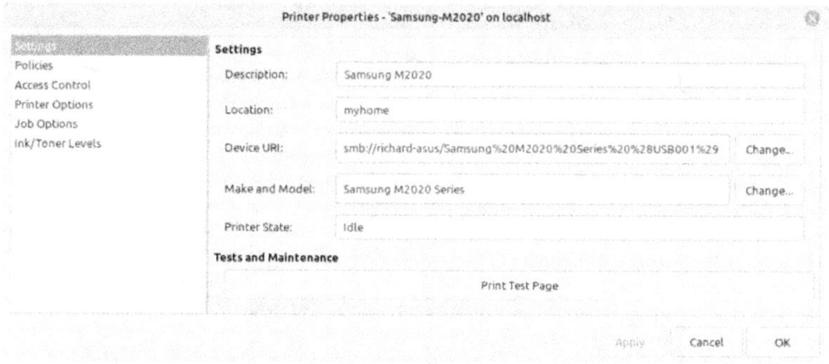

Figure 13-24: Remote Windows printer Settings

The configured remote printer is then listed in the system-config-printer window, along with other printers (see Figure 13-25). When you choose to print from an application, the remote printer will be listed along with your local printers.

Figure 13-25: Remote Windows Printers

Shared Windows printers on any of the computers connected to your local network are automatically accessible once configured. Supporting Samba libraries are already installed and will let you access directly any of shared Windows printers.

Should you want to share a printer on your Linux Mint computer with users on other computers, you need to install the Samba server (Samba package) and have the Server Message Block services enabled using the **smbd** and **nmbd** daemons. You can use the **systemctl** command to restart, stop, and start the services.

```
sudo systemctl restart smbd
sudo systemctl restart nmbd
```

Configuring Remote Printers with the CUPS Web-based Browser

To use the CUPS Web-based browser configuration tool to install a remote printer, specify the remote printer network protocol on the initial Add Printer page. You can choose from Windows, Internet Printing Protocol (other UNIX or Linux systems), Apple and HP JetDirect connected printers, and the older LPD line printers (see Figure 13-26). If a network printer is connected currently, it may be listed in the Discovered Network Printers list.

Figure 13-26: CUPS Web-based Configuration Tool: Network Printers

Because of the changes from SMB1 to SMB3, the Browse operation accessed by the Discovery capability does not work. Because of this, you have to enter the exact name of the printer, including special characters such as spaces and parenthesis (see Figure 13-27). These special characters are referenced with a preceding percent sign, %, followed by the ASCII hexadecimal value for the character. A space is referenced as %20, an open parenthesis as %28, and a close parenthesis as %29. In these examples, the Windows name of the Samsung M2020 printer is:

```
Samsung M2020 Series (USB001)
```

This would be:

```
Samsung%20M2020%20Series%20%28USB001%29
```

For authentication through Samba for a Windows printer, you also have to add the username and password in the URL for the printer. The format is the username following the **smb** protocol, then a colon followed by the password, and then the **@** sign followed by the host name, and then a slash and the printer name (see Figure 13-27).

```
smb://user-name:password@hostname/printer-name
```

Figure 13-27: CUPS Web-based Configuration Tool - Windows Remote Printer

The full entry for the previous example with a username "richard" and password "mypassword" at the host "richard-asus" would be:

```
smb://richard:mypassword@richard-asus/Samsung%20M2020%20Series%20%28USB001%29
```

You are then asked to enter the make, followed by the model. On the final screen you enter the name, description, and location (see Figure 13-28).

Figure 13-28: CUPS Web-based Configuration Tool - Remote Printer Name and Location

Configuring remote printers manually

In the **printers.conf** file, for a remote printer, instead of listing the device, the DeviceURI entry, will have an Internet address, along with its protocol. For example, a remote printer on a CUPS server (**ipp**) would be indicated as shown here (a Windows printer would use the **smb** protocol):

```
DeviceURI ipp://mytsuff.com/printers/queue1
```

When you install the Windows printer on CUPS, you specify its location using the URL protocol **smb**. The username of the user allowed to log in to the printer is entered before the hostname and separated from the hostname by an @ sign. On most configurations, this is the **guest** user. The location entry for a Windows printer called **myhp** attached to a Windows host named **lizard** is shown next. It's Samba share reference would be **//lizard/myhp**.

```
DeviceURI smb://guest@lizard/myhp
```

To enable CUPS on Samba, you also have to set the printing option in the **/etc/samba/smb.conf** file to **cups**, as shown here.

```
printing = cups
printcap name = cups
```

Also for Samba, be sure to include the username and password for authentication, as well as the full name of the printer, including special characters such as spaces (%20).

```
DeviceURI smb://richard:mypa@richard-asus/Samsung%20M2020%20Series%20%28USB001%29
```

CUPS Printer Classes

CUPS lets you select a group of printers to print a job, instead of selecting just one. If one printer is busy or down, another printer can be selected automatically to print the job. Such groupings of printers are called classes. Once you have installed your printers, you can group them into different classes. For example, you may want to group all inkjet printers into one class and laser printers to another, or you may want to group printers connected to one specific printer server in their own class.

On the Linux Mint desktop, you can use system-config-printer to set up classes for printers. The Class entry in the Server | New menu lets you create a printer class. You can access the New menu from the Server menu or from the Add button. This feature lets you select a group of printers to print a job, instead of selecting just one. That way, if one printer is busy or down, another printer can be selected automatically to perform the job. Installed printers can be assigned to different classes. When you click the Class entry in the New menu, a New Class window opens. Here you can enter the name for the class, any comments, and the location (your hostname is entered by default). The next screen lists available printers on the right side (Other printers) and the printers you assigned to the class on the left side (Printers in this class). Use the arrow button to add or remove printers to the class. Click Apply when finished. Tabs for a selected class are much the same as for a printer, with a Members tab instead of a Printer Options tab. In the Members tab, you can change which printers belong to the class. You can also select a printer or set of printers and choose "Create class" from the Printer menu, automatically adding them to the new class.

You can also create classes on the CUPS Web Configuration tool. Select the Administration tab, and click the Add Class button. On the Add Class page, you enter the name of the class, its location and then select the printers to add to the class from the Members list. The class will then show up on the Classes tab, showing its members and status.

CUPS Configuration files

The configuration files for the CUPS server are located in the **/etc/cups** directory (see Table 13-2). The **classes.conf** and **printers.conf** files can be managed by desktop applications such as GNOME Printer and the CUPS Web Configuration tool. Others, such as **cupsd.conf**, you have to edit with a text editor.

Filename	Description
classes.conf	Contains configurations for different local printer classes
client.conf	Lists specific options for specified clients
cupsd.conf	Configures the CUPS server, **cupsd**
printers.conf	Contains printer configurations for available local printers
cups-files.conf	File and directories used by CUPS
cups-browsed.conf	Access to remote and local printers
subscriptions.conf	Subscription controls for printer and print job information

Table 13-2: CUPS Configuration Files

cupsd.conf

The configuration file for the CUPS server is **/etc/cups/cupsd.conf**. To configure the CUPS server, use a text editor to edit the configuration entries in this file. When the CUPS software package was installed, it installed a detailed commented version of the **cupsd.conf** file. Most options are listed, though many are commented out, with a # symbol at the beginning of their entries. The CUPS server is configured using directives, similar in syntax to that used by the configuration for the Apache web server. Just as with Apache, directives can can be organized into blocks.

For a detailed explanation of **cupsd.conf** directives check the CUPS documentation for **cupsd.conf**. You can also reference this documentation from the Online Help page | References link on the CUPS browser-based administration tool, **http://localhost:631**.

```
https://www.cups.org/documentation.html
```

The **cupsd.conf** file begins with log settings.

```
LogLevel warn
```

On Linux Mint, CUPS logging is disabled.

```
MaxLogSize 0
```

The Listen directives set the machine and socket on which to receive connections. These are set by default to the local machine, localhost port 631. If you are using a dedicated network interface for connecting to a local network, you would add the network card's IP address, allowing access from machines on your network.

```
# Only listen for connections from the local machine.
Listen localhost:631
Listen /run/cups/cups.sock
```

Browsing directives allow your local printers to be detected on your network, enabling them to be shared. For shared printing, the Browsing directive is set to on (it is set to Off by default). A BrowseOrder of **allow,deny** will deny all browse transmissions, then first check the BrowseAllow directives for exceptions. A reverse order (**deny,allow**) does the opposite, accepting all browse transmissions, and first checks for those denied by BrowseDeny directives. The default **cupsd.conf** file has a BrowseOrder **allow,deny** directive followed by a BrowseAllow directive, which is set to **all**. To limit this to a particular network, use the IP address of the network instead of **all**. The BrowseLocalProtocols lists the network protocols to use for advertising the printers on a local network. The BrowseAddress directive will make your local printers available as shared printers on the specified network. It is set to **@LOCAL** to allow access on your local network. You can add other BrowseAddress directives to allow access by other networks.

```
# Show shared printers on the local network.
Browsing On
BrowseOrder allow,deny
BrowseAllow all
BrowseLocalProtocols dnssd
BrowseAddress @LOCAL
```

CUPS supports both Basic and Digest forms of authentication, specified in the **AuthType** directive. Basic authentication requires a user and password. For example, to use the web interface, you are prompted to enter the root user and the root user password. Digest authentication makes use of user and password information kept in the CUPS **/etc/cups/passwd.md5** file, using MD5 versions of a user and password for authentication. In addition, CUPS also supports a BasicDigest and Negotiate authentication. BasicDigest will use the CUPS md5 password file for basic authentication. Negotiate will use Kerberos authentication. The default authentication type is set, using the DefaultAuthType directive, set to Basic.

```
# Default authentication type, when authentication is required...
DefaultAuthType Basic
```

The Web interface setting is set to yes.

```
WebInterface Yes
```

Location Directives

Certain directives allow you to place access controls on specific locations. These can be printers or resources, such as the administrative tool or the spool directories. Location controls are implemented with the **Location** directive. There are several Location directives that control access. The first controls access to the server root directory, /. The Order allow, deny entry activates restrictions on access by remote systems. If there are no following Allow or Deny entries then the default is to deny all. There is an implied Allow localhost with the "Order allow, deny" directive, always giving access to the local machine. In effect, access here is denied to all systems, allowing access only by the local system.

```
# Restrict access to the server...
<Location />
  Order allow,deny
</Location>
```

Another **Location** directive is used to restrict administrative access, the **/admin** resource. The **Order allow,deny** directive denies access to all systems, except for the local machine.

```
# Restrict access to the admin pages...
<Location /admin>
  Order allow,deny
</Location>
```

Allow from and **Deny from** directives can permit or deny access from specific hosts and networks. If you wanted to just allow access to a particular machine, you would use an **Allow from** directive with the machine's IP address. CUPS also uses **@LOCAL** to indicate your local network, and **IF**(*name*) for a particular network interface (*name* is the device name of the interface) used to access a network. Should you want to allow administrative access by all other systems on your local network, you can add the **Allow from @LOCAL**. If you add an **Allow** directive, you also have to explicitly add the **Allow localhost** to ensure access by your local machine.

```
# Restrict access to the admin pages...
<Location /admin>
  Allow from localhost
  Allow from @LOCAL
  Order allow,deny
</Location>
```

The following entry would allow access from a particular machine.

```
 Allow From 192.168.0.5
```

The next location directive restricts access to the CUPS configuration files, **/admin/conf**. The **AuthType default** directive refers to the default set by DefaultAuthType. The **Require user** directive references the **SystemGroup** directive, **@SYSTEM** (defined in the **cups-files.conf** file). Only users from that group are allowed access.

```
# Restrict access to configuration files...
<Location /admin/conf>
  AuthType Default
  Require user @SYSTEM
  Order allow,deny
</Location>
```

Default Operation Policy: Limit Directives

A default operation policy is then defined for access to basic administration, printer, print job, and owner operations. The default operation policy section begins with the **<Policy default>** directive. Limit directives are used to implement the directives for each kind of operation. Job operations covers tasks like sending a document, restarting a job, suspending a job, and restarting a job. Administrative tasks include modifying a printer configuration, deleting a printer, managing printer classes, and setting the default printer. Printer operations govern tasks like pausing a printer, enabling or disabling a printer, and shutting down a printer. The owner operations consist of just canceling a job and authenticating access to a job.

See the CUPS documentation on managing operations policies for more details.

```
https://www.cups.org/documentation.php/doc-1.6/policies.html
```

On all the default **Limit** directives, access is allowed only by the local machine (localhost), **Order allow,deny**.

The policy section begins with access controls for user and job information. The default for **JobPrivateAccess** limits access to owner, system, and access control lists. **JobPrivateValues** specifies values made private, such as the job name, originating host, and originating user. **SubscriptionPrivateAccess** and **SubscriptionPrivateValues** specify access for subscription attributes such notifications of printer events like job completed or job stopped.

Limit directives are set up to create and print jobs.

```
<Limit Create-Job Print-Job Print-URI Validate-Job>
  Order deny,allow
</Limit>
```

Both the administrative and printer **Limit** directives are set to the **AuthType default** and limited to access by administrative users, **Require user @SYSTEM**. The administrative directive is shown here.

```
# All administration operations require an administrator to authenticate...
<Limit CUPS-Add-Modify-Printer CUPS-Delete-Printer CUPS-Add-Modify-Class CUPS-
Delete-Class CUPS-Set-Default CUPS-Get-Devices>
  AuthType Default
  Require user @SYSTEM
  Order deny,allow
</Limit>
```

Both the job related and owner Limit directives require either owner or administrative authentication, **Require user @OWNER @SYSTEM**. The **Owner Limit** directive is shown here.

```
# Only the owner or an administrator can cancel or authenticate a job...
<Limit Cancel-Job CUPS-Authenticate-Job>
  Require user @OWNER @SYSTEM
  Order deny,allow
</Limit>
```

For all other tasks, **<Limit All>**, access is restricted to the local machine (localhost).

```
<Limit All>
 Order deny,allow
</Limit>
```

The **AuthClass** directive can be used within a **Limit** directive to specify the printer class allowed access. The **System** class includes the root, sys, and system users.

An authenticated set of policy directives follows the default policy, with similar entries and an added **AuthType** entry in the Limit directive to create and print jobs.

```
<Limit Create-Job Print-Job Print-URI Validate-Job>
  AuthType Default
  Order deny,allow
</Limit>
```

cupsctl

You can use the **cupsctl** command to modify your **cupsd.conf** file, rather than editing the file directly. Check the **cupsctl** Man page for details. The **cupsctl** command with no options will display current settings.

```
cupsctl
```

The changes you can make with this command are limited to turning off remote administration or disabling shared printing. The major options you can set are:

remote-admin   Enable or disable remote administration

remote-any   Enable or disable remote printing

user-cancel-any   Enable or disable users to cancel the print jobs of others

share-printers   Enable or disable sharing of local printers with other systems

printers.conf

Configured information for a printer will be stored in the **/etc/cups/printers.conf** file. You can examine this file directly, even making changes. Here is an example of a printer configuration entry. The **DeviceURI** entry specifies the device used, in this case, a USB printer. It is currently idle, with no jobs.

```
# Printer configuration file for CUPS
# Written by cupsd
<Printer mycannon>
Info Cannon s330
Location richard-server
MakeModel Canon S330
DeviceURI usb://Canon/S330
```

```
State Idle
StateTime 1166554036
Accepting Yes
Shared Yes
ColorManaged Yes
JobSheets none none
QuotaPeriod 0
PageLimit 0
KLimit 0
OpPolicy default
ErrorPolicy retry-job
</Printer>
```

subscriptions.conf

Configured information for printer and job information is located in the **/etc/cups/subscriptions.conf** file. Those receiving the information are specified by the **SubscriptionPrivateAccess** and **SubscriptionPrivateValues** directives in the policy section of the **cupd.conf** file. The **Events** directive specifies notifications of events to be sent, events such as job-completed, printer-stopped, and server-started. The **Owner** directive lists the users for this subscription. **LeaseDuration** is the time the subscription remains valid (0 value is the life of the print job or forever). **Interval** is the time between notifications. **Recipient** is the recipient URI for the notification. In the following example it is dbus:// (your desktop). The **subscriptions.conf** file is managed by **cupsd** directly and is not to be edited.

A sample **subscriptions.conf** file is shown here:

```
# Subscription configuration file for CUPS v2.3.1
NextSubscriptionId 16
<Subscription 15>
Events printer-state-changed printer-restarted printer-shutdown printer-stopped
printer-added printer-deleted job-state-changed job-created job-completed job-
stopped
Owner richard
Recipient dbus://
LeaseDuration 3600
Interval 0
ExpirationTime 1569258630
NextEventId 1
</Subscription>
```

cups-files.conf

The files and directories that CUPS uses to manage print jobs can be configured in the **/etc/cups/cups-files.conf** file. The **ErrorLog** directive specifies the CUPS error log file.

```
ErrorLog  /var/log/cups/error_log
```

The SystemGroup directive defines the users referenced by **@SYSTEM** in **cupsd.conf**.

```
SystemGroup lpadmin
```

cups-browsed.conf

The **cups-browsed.conf** file configures the **cups-browsed** daemon, used for browsing remote and local printers. With driverless printing this is managed by CUPS directly. The **cups-browsed** daemon is used for those printers not yet covered by CUPS driverless printing.

The BrowseRemoteProtocols defines the protocols to use.

```
BrowseRemoteProtocols  dnssd cups
```

The BrowseAllow directive can be used to restrict browsing to specified servers or networks.

```
BrowseAllow 192.168.1.0/24
```

The CreateIPPPrinterQueues directive allows the detection of non-CUPS IPP printers.

CUPS Command Line Print Clients

On the desktop, you can use the print clients such as GNOME printer and the CUPS Printer Configuration tool to manage your print jobs. For the shell command line, you can use several command line print commands instead. These include the **lpr**, **lpc**, **lpq**, and **lprm** commands. These commands let you print documents, display the print queue, and delete print jobs. For network connections, CUPS provides the -**E** encryption option, which allows you to encrypt print jobs. The command line print commands are listed in Table 13-3.

Printer Management	Description
GNOME Print Manager	GNOME print queue management tool (CUPS)
CUPS Configuration Tool	Prints, manages, and configures CUPS
lpr *options file-list*	Prints a file, copies the file to the printer's spool directory, and places it on the print queue to be printed in turn. -P *printer* prints the file on the specified printer
lpq *options*	Displays the print jobs in the print queue. -P *printer* prints the queue for the specified printer -1 prints a detailed listing
lpstat *options*	Displays printer status
lprm *options printjob-id* or *printer*	Removes a print job from the print queue. You identify a particular print job by its number as listed by lpq. -P *printer* removes all print jobs for the specified printer
lpc	Manages your printers. At the lpc> prompt, you can enter commands to check the status of your printers and take other actions

Table 13-3: CUPS Print Clients

lpr

The **lpr** command stands for line print and submits a print job to the print queue. Its argument is the name of the file to be printed. With the -**P** option you can select a particular printer.

Otherwise the default printer is used. In the following example, the file **myletter** is printed, and then prints the file **report** to the printer with the name **myprinter**.

```
$ lpr myletter
```

In this example, the file **myreport** is printed on the **myprinter** printer.

```
$ lpr -P myprinter myreport
```

lpc

With the **lpc** command you can enable or disable a printer, reorder print queues, and reload configuration files. When you enter the command **lpc** on the command line, an **lpc>** prompt is displayed. You can then enter **lpc** commands to manage your printers and reorder print jobs. The **status** command with the name of the printer displays a printer's status, displaying information such as the readiness of the printer and the number of print jobs in its queue. To stop or start printing use the **stop** and **start** commands. The **lpc** command shows the printers configured for your CUPS print server.

```
$ lpc
lpc> status myprinter
myprinter:
 printer is on device 'usb' speed -1
 queuing is enabled
 printing is enabled
 1 entry in spool area
```

lpq and lpstat

Use the **lpq** command to list the print jobs in the print queue. To see the jobs for a particular printer use the **-P** option with the printer name. To list the jobs for a specific user, enter the username. Use the **-l** option to display detailed information for each job. To display information for a specific job, use that job's ID number. The **lpstat** command lets you check the status of a printer.

```
$ lpq
myprinter is ready and printing
Rank    Owner  Jobs  File(s)        Total Size
active  chris   1    report         1024
```

lprm

You can remove a print job from the printer queue with the **lprm** command, deleting the job before it could be printed. **lprm** uses many of the same options as **lpq**. To remove a job, use **lprm** with the job number. You can use **lpq** to list the job number. Use the **-P** option with a printer name to remove all jobs for that printer. If no options are specified for **lprm** then the current print job printing is removed. The next command removes the first print job in the print queue.

```
lprm 1
```

CUPS Command Line Administrative Tools

CUPS command-line administrative tools includes such commands as **lpadmin**, **lpoptions**, **lpinfo**, **cupsenable**, **cupsdisable**, **cupsaccept**, and **cupsreject** (**cups-client** package).

You can use the **cupsenable** and **cupsdisable** commands start and stop print queues, and use the **cupsaccept** and **cupsreject** commands start and stop print jobs. With the **lpinfo** command you can display printer information. The **lpoptions** allows you to set print options. With the **lpadmin** command you can perform administrative tasks such as adding printers and changing configurations. CUPS administrative tools are listed in Table 13-4.

Note: The command line clients have the same name, and much the same syntax, as the older LPR and LPRng command line clients used in Unix and older Linux systems.

Administration Tool	Description
lpadmin	CUPS printer configuration
lpoptions	Sets printing options
cupsenable	Activates a printer
cupsdisable	Stops a printer
accept	Allows a printer to accept new jobs
reject	Prevents a printer from accepting print jobs
lpinfo	Lists CUPS devices available

Table 13-4: CUPS Administrative Tools

lpadmin

The **lpadmin** command lets you choose the default printer and to configure options for a printer. Use the **-d** option to select a printer as the default. In the next example, **myprinter** is chosen as the default printer.

```
lpadmin -d myprinter
```

To set options for a printer, first use the **-p** option to select a printer. The next example sets printer description information (**-D** option) for the **myprinter** printer.

```
lpadmin -p myprinter  -D  Epson550
```

Some of the options allow you to set per-user quotas for print jobs. The **job-k-limit** option limits the size of a job allowed per user, **job-page-limit** determines the page limit for a job, and **job-quota-period** restrict the number of jobs using a specified time period. The next command sets a page limit of 100 for each user.

```
lpadmin -p myprinter  -o job-page-limit=100
```

You can control access by users with the **-u** option and an **allow** or **deny** list. Use an allow list for users permitted access. The allow list has an **allow:** label followed by a list of users. To deny access use a **deny:** list. In the following command, access is granted to **cora** but denied to **orrin** and **harlow**.

```
lpadmin -p myprinter -u allow:cora  deny:orrin,harlow
```

To simply deny or allow access to all users or none, use the terms **all** or **none** to permit or deny access to all or no users. You can create exceptions by having both an allow and deny list where one uses the **all** or **none** list. The next command allows access to all users except **dylan**.

```
lpadmin -p myprinter  -u allow:all   deny:dylan
```

lpoptions

With the **lpoptions** command, you can set print formatting options a defaults, such as the color or page format. Use the **-l** option to see a list of possible option for a printer. The **-p** option selects a printer, and the **-d** option sets the default printer. The following command lists the current options for the myprinter printer.

```
lpoptions -p myprinter -l
```

To assign a value to an option, you would use the **-o** option with the option name and value, **-o** *option=value.* You can can use the **-r** option to remove a printer option. In the next example, the **sides** option is assigned the value **two-sided** to enable printing on both sides of a paper.

```
lpoptions -p myprinter -o sides=two-sided
```

You could later use the **-r** option to remove that option.

```
lpoptions -p myprinter -r sides
```

To see a list of available options, check the standard printing options in the CUPS Software Manual at **https://www.cups.org/**.

cupsenable and cupsdisable

The **cupsenable** command starts a printer, and the **cupsdisable** command stops it. With the **-c** option, you can cancel all jobs on the printer's queue, and the **-r** option broadcasts a message explaining the shutdown. This command disables the printer named **myepson.**

```
cupsdisable myepson
```

cupsaccept and cupsreject

With the **cupsaccept** and **cupsreject** commands you can control access to a printer's printer queue. You can use the **cupsreject** command to stop a printer accepting jobs. The **cupsaccept** command allows print jobs. The following command prevents the **myepson** printer from accepting print jobs.

```
cupsreject myepson
```

lpinfo

The **lpinfo** command displays information about the CUPS devices and drivers that are available on your system. The **-v** options show information about devices and the **-m** option for drivers.

```
lpinfo -m
```

14. Network File Systems and Network Information System: NFS and NIS

Network File Systems: NFS and /etc/exports

NFS Configuration: /etc/exports

Controlling Accessing to NFS Servers

Mounting NFS File Systems: NFS Clients

Network Information Service: NIS

Name Service Switch: nsswitch.conf

Linux provides several tools for accessing files on remote systems connected to a network. The Network File System (NFS) enables you to connect to and directly access resources such as files or devices that reside on another machine. The new version, NFS4, provides greater security, with access allowed by your firewall. The Network Information Service (NIS) maintains configuration files for all systems on a network.

Network File Systems: NFS and /etc/exports

With NFS you can mount a file system located on a remote computer and access it as it were local file system on your system. In this way, different hosts on a network could access the same file system. The NFS website is **http://nfs.sourceforge.net**. Check the Ubuntu Server Guide | Services | Service - NFS for basic configuration and management.

```
https://ubuntu.com/server/docs/service-nfs
```

To set up the NFS service for your system, install the **nfs-kernel-server**, **nfs-common**, and **rpcbind** packages (selecting just the **nfs-kernel-server** will select the others automatically).

```
sudo apt install nfs-kernel-server
```

NFS Daemons

NFS uses Remote Procedure Calls (RPC) to provide remote access to file systems on a TCP/IP network. A host system makes some of its file systems available to other hosts on the network by exporting those file systems. The export operations are configured with entries in the **/etc/exports** file. The exports are implemented by several daemons such as **rpc.mountd**, **rpc.nfsd**, and **rpc.gssd**, which support access by remote hosts. You can control to the NFS server with entries in the **/etc/hosts.allow** and **/etc/hosts.deny** files. The NFS server daemons provided in the **nfs-kernel-server** package are listed here. You can configure options in the **/etc/default/nfs-kernel-server** file.

rpc.nfsd   Receives NFS requests from remote systems and translates them into requests for the local system.

rpc.mountd   Performs requested mount and unmount operations.

Additional NFS support daemons are provided by the **nfs-common** package. You can configure options in the **/etc/default/nfs-common** file.

rpc.svcgssd   Performs security for rpc operations (rpcsec_gss protocol).

rpc.gssd   Client support for the rpcsec_gss protocol for gss-api security in NFSv4.

rpc.idmapd   Maps user and group IDs to names.

rpc.statd   Provides locking services when a remote host reboots.

rpc.blkmapd   Provides device discovery and mapping.

The **rpcbind** server converts remote procedure calls program number to appropriate port numbers.

The **rpc.statd**, **rpc.idmapd**, and **rpc.gssd** daemons can be accessed using the **systemctl** command.

```
sudo systemctl restart statd
sudo systemctl restart idmapd
sudo systemctl restart gssd
```

zThe NFS daemons are managed by **systemd** using several service unit files located in **/lib/systemd/system**. The NFS daemons and their **systemd** unit files are listed in Table 14-1.

The **nfs-server.service** file is shown here. Runtime configuration information is read from **/etc/default/nfs-kernel-server** (EnvironmentFile).

nfs-server.service

```
[Unit]
Description=NFS server and services
DefaultDependencies=no
Requires=network.target proc-fs-nfsd.mount
Requires=nfs-mountd.service
Wants=rpcbind.socket network-online.target
Wants=rpc-statd.service nfs-idmapd.service
Wants=rpc-statd-notify.service
Wants=nfsdcld.service

After=network-online.target local-fs.target
After=proc-fs-nfsd.mount rpcbind.socket nfs-mountd.service
After=nfs-idmapd.service rpc-statd.service
After=nfsdcld.service
Before=rpc-statd-notify.service

# GSS services dependencies and ordering
Wants=auth-rpcgss-module.service
After=rpc-gssd.service gssproxy.service rpc-svcgssd.service

[Service]
Type=oneshot
RemainAfterExit=yes
ExecStartPre=-/usr/sbin/exportfs -r
ExecStart=/usr/sbin/rpc.nfsd
ExecStop=/usr/sbin/rpc.nfsd 0
ExecStopPost=/usr/sbin/exportfs -au
ExecStopPost=/usr/sbin/exportfs -f

ExecReload=-/usr/sbin/exportfs -r

[Install]

WantedBy=multi-user.target
```

Use the **systemctl** command to start, stop, and restart the NFS server manually.

```
sudo systemctl start nfs-kernel-server
```

The corresponding **systemd** unit files for the **nfsd**, **mountd**, **idmapd**, **statd**, and **svcgssd** daemons, will run these daemons (**nfs-** and **rpc-** prefixes).

To see if NFS is actually running, you can use the **rpcinfo** command with the **-p** option. You should see entries for **mountd** and **nfs**. If not, NFS is not running.

The **rpc.statd**, **rpc.idmapd**, and **rpc.gssd** daemons can be accessed using the **systemctl** command.

```
sudo systemctl restart statd
sudo systemctl restart idmapd
sudo systemctl restart gssd
```

Options for the **nfs-kenel-server** are now located in the **/etc/nfs.conf** file. To see what options are specified use the **nfsconf** command with the **--dump** option. Results are listed according to sections. Each server has a section. In the current Linux Mint install, there are only two options active.

```
nfsconf --dump
[general]
pipefs-directory = /run/rpc_pipefs

[mound]
  manage-fids - y
```

The **/etc/nfs.conf** file arranges options into different sections for the different NFS servers, such as gssd, nfsd, and statd. Most options are commented out. To activate an option remove the preceding comment character, #. A safer way to activate an option is to use the **nfsconf** command with the **--set** option.

```
nfsconf --file /etc/nfsconf --set statd debug 1
nfsconf --file /etc/nfsconf --set nfsd gracetime 80
```

See the man page for **nfs.conf** and **nfsconf** for more details.

```
man nfs.conf
man nfsconf
```

Options were previously specified in the configuration files locate in the **/etc/default** folder (**nfs-kernel-server** and **nfs-common**). Though these are still present, they are ignored. Should you modify these files, the conversion script **/usr/share/nfs-common/nfsconvert.py** will generate a compatible configuration file as **/etc/nfs/conf.d/local.conf**. This may not work. If not, you will have to set options directly in the **/etc/nfs.conf** file.

The following is a listing of the **/etc/nfs.conf** file. Section are encased in brackets.

/etc/nfs.conf

```
#
# This is a general configuration for the
# NFS daemons and tools
#
[general]
pipefs-directory=/run/rpc_pipefs
#
[exports]
# rootdir=/export
#
[exportfs]
# debug=0
#
[gssd]
```

```
# verbosity=0
# rpc-verbosity=0
# use-memcache=0
# use-machine-creds=1
# use-gss-proxy=0
# avoid-dns=1
# limit-to-legacy-enctypes=0
# context-timeout=0
# rpc-timeout=5
# keytab-file=/etc/krb5.keytab
# cred-cache-directory=
# preferred-realm=
#
[lockd]
# port=0
# udp-port=0
#
[mountd]
# debug=0
manage-gids=y
# descriptors=0
# port=0
# threads=1
# reverse-lookup=n
# state-directory-path=/var/lib/nfs
# ha-callout=
#
[nfsdcld]
# debug=0
# storagedir=/var/lib/nfs/nfsdcld
#
[nfsdcltrack]
# debug=0
# storagedir=/var/lib/nfs/nfsdcltrack
#
[nfsd]
# debug=0
# threads=8
# host=
# port=0
# grace-time=90
# lease-time=90
# udp=n
# tcp=y
# vers2=n
# vers3=y
# vers4=y
# vers4.0=y
# vers4.1=y
# vers4.2=y
# rdma=n
# rdma-port=20049
#
```

```
[statd]
# debug=0
# port=0
# outgoing-port=0
# name=
# state-directory-path=/var/lib/nfs/statd
# ha-callout=
# no-notify=0
#
[sm-notify]
# debug=0
# force=0
# retry-time=900
# outgoing-port=
# outgoing-addr=
# lift-grace=y
#
[svcgssd]
# principal=
```

NFS Configuration: /etc/exports

Exported file systems are listed in the **/etc/exports**. An entry consists of the pathname of the folder where the file system is located on the host system, followed by the list of hosts that can access it and any control access options. The options for each host are placed within parentheses in a comma-separated list. The options may be different for certain hosts. Some may have read-only access and others read and write access. If you want to specify options that can be applied to all hosts, you use an asterisk (*****) in place of a host name, followed by the options lists. A list of options is provided in Table 14-1. The syntax of an export entry in the **/etc/exports** file follows.

folder-pathname   host-designation(options)

NFS Host Entries

The same folder can have several host entries, each with different access options.

folder-pathname   host(options) host(options)   host(options)

There are various ways to designate a host. For those hosts located within your domain, you just have to specify the hostname. Hosts in other domains require a fully qualified domain name. Instead of a hostname, you can use the host's IP address. To reference multiple hosts at once, such as those in a certain domain, you can use the asterisk, *****, followed by the domain name. For example, ***.mytrek.com** references all the hosts in the **mytrek.com** domain. Should you want to use IP addresses instead of domain names, you would use the IP network addresses. The network address uses a netmask to reference a range of IP addresses. Alternatively, you could use an NIS netgroup name for a designated group of hosts. NIS netgroup names are preceded by an **@** sign.

```
folder     host(options)
folder     *(options)
folder     *.domain(options)
folder     192.168.1.0/255.255.255.0(options)
folder     @netgroup(options)
```

General Option	Description
secure	Requires that requests originate on secure ports, those less than 1024 This is on by default
insecure	Turns off the secure option
ro	Allows only read-only access. This is the default
rw	Allows read/write access
sync	Performs all writes when requested. This is the default
async	Performs all writes when the server is ready
no_wdelay	Performs writes immediately, not checking to see if they are related
wdelay	Checks to see if writes are related, and if so, waits to perform them together. Can degrade performance. This is the default.
hide	Automatically hides an exported directory that is the subdirectory of another exported directory
subtree_check	Checks parent directories in a file system to validate an exported subdirectory. This is the default.
no_subtree_check	Does not check parent directories in a file system to validate an exported subdirectory
insecure_locks	Does not require authentication of locking requests. Used for older NFS versions
User ID Mapping	**Description**
all_squash	Maps all UIDs and GIDs to the anonymous user. Useful for NFS-exported public FTP directories, news spool directories, and so forth
no_all_squash	The opposite option to all_squash. This is the default setting.
root_squash	Maps requests from remote root user to the anonymous UID/GID. This is the default.
no_root_squash	Turns off root squashing. Allows the root user to access as the remote root
anonuid	Sets explicitly the UID and GID of the anonymous account used for all_squash and root_squash options. The defaults are nobody and nogroup

Table 14-1: The /etc/exports Options

NFS Options

Several NFS options in **/etc/exports** let you control access to exported folders. The **ro** option provides read-only access, and the **rw** option specifies read/write access, allowing changes. Write tasks can be performed at once (the **sync** option), or when the server decides (the **async** option). For better efficiency, by default, related write requests are written at the same time (**wdelay**). This can cause a delay which can degrade performance. Should you wish, you can use the **no_wdelay** option to have writes executed immediately instead. If a folder you have exported, is actually a subfolder of another exported folder, then that subfolder is not accessible unless it is mounted. This feature is implemented with the **hide** option, the default. The subfolder is, in a sense, hidden until it is explicitly mounted. The **no_hide** option will override this feature, allow a folder to be accessed if its parent is mounted, even though the folder is exported and has not been mounted.

The **subtree_check** option check the validity of the parent folders of an exported folder. Though this check works with read-only file systems, problems can occur with read/write file systems, where filenames and folder may be changed at any time. The **no_subtree_check** option lets you override this check.

NFS User-Level Access

Several NFS options and features apply to user-level access. As a matter of security, the NFS server treats an NFS client's root user as an anonymous user, a procedure known as squashing the user. This squashing will not allow the client to appear as the NFS server's root user. The **no_root_squash** option lets you override this squashing, allowing a particular client's root user to have root-level control over the NFS server.

Squashing can also be applied to all users. The **all_squash** option treats all NFS users as anonymous users, restricting them to the anonymous group. This will prevent a client user from attempting to appear as a user on the NFS server.

A user can only mount and access folders on the NFS server if that user has a corresponding account on the NFS server with the same user ID. If the user IDs are different, they are considered to be two different users. Instead of maintaining two accounts, it is possible to use a NIS server to maintain your user IDs just in one location.

NFSv4

NFS version 4 is the latest version of the NFS protocol with enhanced features, such as better security, speed, and reliability. Only a few of the commands, though, are different. When you mount an NFSv4 file system, you have to use the **nfs4** file type, not **nfs**.

```
mount -t nfs4  rabbit.mytrek.com:/  /home/dylan/projects
```

You can also use the **fsid=0** option to reference the root export location. The following entry would let you mount a file system to the **/home/richlp** folder without having to specify it in the mount operation.

```
/home/richlp          *(fsid=0,ro,sync)
```

NFSv4 also supports the RPCSEC_GSS (Remote Procedure Call Security, Generic Security Services) security mechanism which provides for private/public keys, encryption, and authentication with support for Kerberos. Kerberos comes in two flavors: **krb5i** which validates the integrity of the data, and **krb5p** which encrypts all requests but involves a performance hit. Samples for using the GSS and Kerberos security are listed as comments in the **/etc/exports** file. Instead of specifying a remote location, the rpcsec_gss protocol (**gss**) is used with **krb5i** security, **gss/krb5i**. The directory mounted in the sample is the **/srv/nfs4/homes** directory.

```
# /srv/nfs4/homes  gss/krb5i(rw,sync,no_subtree_check)
```

NFS File and Directory Security with NFS4 Access Lists

NFS4 allows you to set up access control lists (ACL) for folders and files. Use the NFS4 ACL tools to manage these lists (**nfs4-acl-tools** package). The NFS4 file system ACL tools include **nfs4_getfacl**, **nfs4_setfacl**, and **nfs4_editfacl**. Check the Man page for each for detailed options and examples. **nfs4_getfacl** will list the access controls for a specified file or directory. **nfs4_setfacl** will create access controls for a directory or file, and **nfs4_editfacl** will let you change them. **nfs4_editfacl** simply invokes **nfs_setfacl** with the -e option. When editing access controls, you are placed in an editor where you can make your changes. For setting access controls, you can read from a file, the standard input, or list the control entries on the command line.

The format for ACL entries is described on the **nfs4_acl** Man page. The first element in an ACL entry is the entry type such as an accept or deny entry (**A** or **D**). The entry type is followed by an ACL flag to denote group or inheritance capability. After the flag is the principal to which the ACL is applied. This is usually the URL of a user that is to be permitted or denied access. You could also specify groups, but you would have to include the **g** group flag. There are special URLs (OWNER@, GROUP@, and EVERYONE@) that correspond to the owner, group, and other access used for standard permissions. After the principal there follows the list of access options, such as **r** for read or **w** for write. The read, write, and execute permissions are **r,w,x**. The following example provides full access to the owner but gives only read and execute access to the user **mark@mypics.com**. Group write and execute access is denied.

```
A::OWNER@:rwadtTnNcCy
A::mark@mypics.com:rxtncy
D:g:GROUP@:waxtc
```

ACL permissions can be further refined by attributes. There are attribute reads (**t,n**) and attribute writes (**T,N**), as well as ACL read (**c**) and write (**C**) access. The **y** option enables NFS read and write synchronization. The **d** option lets you to delete files and folders, and the the **D** option allows deleting of subfolders. With the **a** option you can append data and create subfolders. The **rtncy** options are the read options and **wadDTNC** are the write options, whereas **x** is the execute option. The **y** option is required for synchronized access. The **C** option allows a user to change the access controls. The lowercase **c** lets users display the access controls.

NFS /etc/exports Example

The following example of the **/etc/exports** file shows samples of file system exports. In the first entry, all hosts have read-only access to the file system mounted at the **/srv/pub** folder. The **/srv** folder is normally used for the folders maintained by different servers. The **all_squash** option treats users as anonymous. The next entry provides read and write access to the **lizard.mytrek.com** host for the file system mounted at the **/home/mypics** folder. The following entry lets the **rabbit.mytrek.com** host to have read-only access to the NFS server's DVD-ROM. With the last entry users have secure access to the **/home/richlp** folder.

/etc/exports

```
/srv/pub          *(ro,insecure,all_squash,sync)
/home/mypics      lizard.mytrek.com(rw,sync)
/media/dvdrom     rabbit.mytrek.com(ro,sync)
/home/richlp      *(secure,sync)
```

The default **/etc/options** file shows examples for using NFSv2, NFSv3, and NFSv4 formats.

/etc/exports

```
# /etc/exports: the access control list for filesystems which may be exported
#               to NFS clients.  See exports(5).
#
# Example for NFSv2 and NFSv3:
# /srv/homes     hostname1(rw,sync,no_subtree_check)  hostname2(ro,sync,no_subtree_check)
#
# Example for NFSv4:
# /srv/nfs4         gss/krb5i(rw,sync,fsid=0,crossmnt,no_subtree_check)
# /srv/nfs4/homes   gss/krb5i(rw,sync,no_subtree_check)
#
```

Applying Changes

Whenever the NFS server is started, the file systems listed in the **/etc/exports** file are exported. The export process involves reading the entries in the **/etc/exports** file and and creating corresponding entries in the **/var/lib/nfs/xtab** file. NFS reads the **/var/lib/nfs/xtab** file uses it to perform the actual exports. In this sense, the **xtab** file holds the list of active exports.

Should you add entries to the **/etc/exports** file, and then want to export them without rebooting your system, you would use the **exportfs** command with the **-a** option. The added entries are exported. Adding the **-v** option displays messages showing the tasks NFS is performing.

```
exportfs -a -v
```

Should you edit the **/etc/exports** file, making changes to the entries, you can use the **-r** option to re-export those entries. The **-r** option will re-sync the **/var/lib/nfs/xtab** file with the **/etc/exports** entries, removing any missing exports in the **/etc/exports** file and re-exporting those with different options. In effect, you are applying any changes you made to the **/etc/exports** file.

```
exportfs -r -v
```

If you both add entries and also change current ones, you can combine the added and re-export options (**-r** and **-a**) to export the added entries and re-export edited ones, as well as removing deleted entries.

```
exportfs -r -a -v
```

Manually Exporting File Systems

Instead of using entries in the **/etc/exports** file, you can use the **exportfs** command on a shell command line to export file systems. The exported filesystems are added to the **/var/lib/nfs/xtab** file. When using the **exportfs** command, use the **-o** option to specify permissions. After the options, enter the host and file system to export. Be sure to separate the host and file system names with a colon. For example, to export the **/home/myprojects** directory to **golf.mytrek.com** with the permissions **ro** and **insecure**, you use the following:

```
exportfs -o rw,insecure golf.mytrek.com:/home/myprojects
```

You can also use **exportfs** with the **-u** option to un-export an exported filesystem. This operation removes the exported filesystem's entry from the **/var/lib/nfs/xtab** file. The next example performs an un-export operation on the **/home/foodstuff** folder.

```
exportfs -u lizard.mytrek.com:/home/foodstuff
```

Controlling Accessing to NFS Servers

You can control access on your local network to the NFS server using the **hosts.allow** and **hosts.deny** files. You can also use firewall rules to control access from external hosts, those outside your local network.

/etc/hosts.allow and /etc/hosts.deny

The **/etc/hosts.allow** and **/etc/hosts.deny** files are used to restrict access to services provided by your server to hosts on your network or on the Internet (if accessible). For example, you can use the **hosts.allow** file to permit access by certain hosts to your FTP server. Entries in the **hosts.deny** file explicitly denies access to certain hosts. For NFS, you can provide the same kind of security by controlling access to specific NFS daemons.

rpcbind Service

The rpcbind service informs hosts where the NFS services are located on your system. The name used to reference rpcbind is **rpcbind**, as shown in the previous example. The rpcbind configuration file is **/etc/default/rpcbind**. Here you can set options for the rpcbind service.

By denying access to it, a remote host cannot locate NFS. To secure NFS, you would deny access to all hosts and then make exceptions for those you want to allow. In the **hosts.deny** file, the following entry will deny access to all hosts. The rpcbind service is referenced with the name **rpcbind**. ALL is a special term referencing all hosts.

```
rpcbind:ALL
```

For those hosts you want to allow access to NFS, you would place their names in the **hosts.allow** file. Each entry would have the term rpcbind followed by a colon, and then a list of IP addresses of allowed hosts, separated by commas. The addresses can be single addresses or a range of addresses specified with a netmask. The next example permits access only by the hosts in the local network, 192.168.0.0 (indicated using a range), and to the single host 10.0.0.43.

```
rpcbind: 192.168.0.0/255.255.255.0, 10.0.0.43
```

Keep in mind, though, that **rpcbind** is also used by other services such as NIS. Should you close all access to the rpcbind in **hosts.deny**, you will have to allow access to NIS services, such as ypbind and ypderser, in **hosts.allow**. Also, should you want to allow access to remote commands you like **ruptime** and **rusers**, you will have to add entries for them.

You should also add the same controls for the other NFS services, such as **mountd** and **statd**, as shown here for the **hosts.deny** file.

```
mountd:ALL
statd:ALL
```

Corresponding entries for them in the **hosts.allow** file, allows access to certain hosts.

```
mountd:  192.168.0.0/255.255.255.0, 10.0.0.43
statd:   192.168.0.0/255.255.255.0, 10.0.0.43
```

Netfilter Rules

With Netfilter, you can control access to NFS services from hosts outside your local network, usually Internet access. The **rpcbind** service uses port 111, and **nfsd** uses 2049. Should you want to deny access to NFS from networks outside your local network, you can set up Netfilter rules to deny that access. In the next examples, access is denied to ports 111 and 2049 for transmissions on the eth1 network device. Internet packets attempting access on port 111 or 2049 are rejected. In these examples, the eth1 device connects to outside networks.

iptables rule:

```
iptables -A INPUT -p tcp -i eth1 --dport 111 -j DENY
iptables -A INPUT -p tcp -i eth1 --dport 2049 -j DENY
```

nftables rule:

```
nft add rule ip filter INPUT iifname "eth1" tcp dport 111 counter jump DENY
nft add rule ip filter INPUT iifname "eth1" tcp dport 2049 counter jump DENY
```

For NFS to work on your local network, you will have to allow packet fragments with the **-f** option. With **eth0** as the device used for the local network, the next example enables packet fragments locally.

iptables rule:

```
iptables -A INPUT -p tcp -i eth0 -f -j ACCEPT
```

nftables rule:

```
nft add rule ip filter INPUT iifname "eth0" ip frag-off & 0x1fff != 0 ip protocol tcp counter accept
```

Mounting NFS File Systems: NFS Clients

Hosts can mount and access folders that NFS has made available. The hosts, of course, have to be functioning as NFS clients. NFS client capability is built in to the Linux kernel. Any Linux host can can mount a remote NFS folder with a mount operation.

Mounting NFS Automatically: /etc/fstab

NFS folders can be mounted by an entry in the **/etc/fstab** file, as well as by a **mount** command. In effect, an entry for the NFS mount operation in the **/etc/fstab** file will mount the NFS file systems automatically at startup. The mount type for an NFS entry in the **/etc/fstab** file is **nfs**. To reference an NFS file system in a mount operation, you need to provide both the folder name and the hostname of the remote host where it is located. The folder and hostname are separated by a colon. For example, **rabbit.trek.com:/home/project** references a file system mounted at **/home/project** on the **rabbit.trek.com** host. The mount operation also requires the pathname of the folder where it is to be mounted on your system. The format for an NFS entry in the **/etc/fstab** file is shown below. The file type for NFS versions 1 through 3 is **nfs**, whereas for NFS version 4 it is **nfs4**.

```
host:remote-directory   local-directory     nfs   options   0   0
```

An NFS mount operation, can also include NFS mount options, such as the size of datagrams for reading and writing (**rsize** and **wsize**), and the wait time for responses from remote host (**timeo**). There are also options to let you perform a hard or soft mount (**hard** and **soft**). If a file system is to be hard mounted, should the remote host fail to respond, your system will repeatedly try to make contact. A hard mount is the default. If a file system is to be soft-mounted, then, if the remote host fails to respond, repeated attempts will stop after a specified time limit and an error message displayed. To avoid using system resources for continually failing hard-mount attempts, it may be preferable to use soft mount instead, which will stop such attempts. You can find a list of NFS mount options in the **mount** Man page (see Table 14-2).

In the following NFS mount example, the remote system is **rabbit.mytrek.com**, and the file system to be mounted is **/home/projects**. It will be mounted on the local system as the **/home/dylan/projects** folder, which must already exist on the local system. The filesystem type is **nfs** for NFS, and the **timeo** option sets up a wait time of 20 tenths of a second (two seconds) for a response. The **soft** options indicates that this is a soft mount.

```
rabbit.mytrek.com:/home/projects /home/dylan/myprojects  nfs  soft,intr,timeo=20
```

Option	Description
`rsize=`*n*	The number of bytes NFS uses when reading files from an NFS server. The default is 1,024 bytes. A size of 8,192 can greatly improve performance.
`wsize=`*n*	The number of bytes NFS uses when writing files to an NFS server. The default is 1,024 bytes. A size of 8,192 can greatly improve performance.
`timeo=`*n*	The value in tenths of a second before sending the first retransmission after a timeout. The default value is seven-tenths of a second.
`retry=`*n*	The number of minutes to retry an NFS mount operation before giving up. The default is 10,000 minutes (one week).
`retrans=`*n*	The number of retransmissions or minor timeouts for an NFS mount operation before a major timeout (default is 3). At that time, the connection is canceled or a "server not responding" message is displayed.
`soft`	Mount system using soft mount.
`hard`	Mount system using hard mount. This is the default.
`intr`	Allows NFS to interrupt the file operation and return to the calling program. The default is not to allow file operations to be interrupted.
`bg`	If the first mount attempt times out, continues trying the mount in the background. The default is to fail without backgrounding.
`tcp`	Mounts the NFS file system using the TCP protocol, instead of the default UDP protocol.

Table 14-2: NFS Mount Options

Mounting NFS Manually: mount

With the **mount** command and the **-t nfs** option you can mount an NFS file system manually. Use **-t nfs4** option for an NFSv4 file system. The next command mounts the previous example manually.

```
mount -t nfs -o soft,intr,timeo=20  rabbit.mytrek.com:/home/projects  /home/dylan/myprojects
```

Use the **umount** command to unmount an NFS folder. The mountpoint can be either a local folder or one on a remote host as shown the in the next example.

```
umount /home/dylan/projects
umount  rabbit.mytrek.com:/home/projects
```

Mounting NFS on Demand: autofs

NFS file systems can be mounted automatically with the automount service, autofs (**autofs** package). With the autofs service active, a file system is mounted when it is accessed. For example, a directory change command (**cd**) to a folder configured to autofs mounting, will mount that remote folder.

The autofs configuration uses a master file to reference map files, which designate the file systems to be automatically mounted. The autofs master file is **/etc/auto.master** file. In the master file you will find a list of the full pathnames of folders to be mounted and their corresponding map files. A map file holds a key (the folder's name), mount options, and the file systems that can be mounted (its host and pathname). The configuration file for autofs is **/etc/autofs.conf**. Here you can define options such as the master map file and the default timeout.

```
master_map_name = /etc/auto.master
```

The **/misc** folder is already configured as the pathname for automatically mounted file systems. You can then add file systems in the **/etc/auto.master** file, including their corresponding map files. In the **/etc/auto.master** file, you will find an entry for the **/misc** directory, showing **auto.misc** as its map file.

```
/misc    /etc/auto.misc
```

A map file entry in the the master file can also have options for mounting the folder, such as the **timeout** option, which set up a waiting period of inactivity before performing an automatic unmount.

A map file holds the key, mount options, and the full pathname and host of the file system to be mounted. The key is the folder name of the folder on the local system where the file system is mounted. For example, to mount the **/home/projects** folder on the **rabbit.mytrek.com** host to the **/auto/projects** folder, use the following entry. The **/etc/auto.misc** holds samples of map file entries.

```
projects  soft,intr,timeo=20   rabbit.mytrek.com:/home/projects
```

To mount to a folder other that **/misc**, you place an entry for it in the master file. The next entry mounts to the **/myprojects** folder using the **auto.myprojects** map file.

```
/myprojects   auto.myprojects   --timeout 60
```

The **/etc/auto.myprojects** map file would then have entries for NFS files system mounts, as shown here.

```
dylan    soft,intr,rw   rabbit.mytrek.com:/home/projects
newgame  soft,intr,ro   lizard.mytrek.com:/home/supergame
```

Network Information Service: NIS

For a network that provide NFS services, file systems and devices can be shared by client systems on that network. Each system would have to have configuration files for a shared device or file system. Any configuration changes for the device or file system would mean updating the corresponding configuration file located on each system. To avoid this complication, NFS provides Network Information System (NIS) service. The NIS service maintains the configuration files for shared file systems and devices for the network. Should there be any changes to the devices and file systems, you would only have to update the NIS configuration files for those devices and file systems. You can also use the NIS service to maintain administrative information for users such as user IDs and and passwords. For a password change, you would only have to update the NIS password file.

The NIS service is configured for use by the **/etc/nsswitch** configuration file. Here are some standard entries:

```
passwd:          compat
shadow:          compat
networks:        files
protocols:       db files
```

Note: NIS+ is a more advanced form of NIS that provides support for encryption and authentication. However, it is more difficult to administer.

NIS was developed by Sun Microsystems and was originally known as Sun's Yellow Pages (YP). NIS files are kept on an NIS server (NIS servers are still sometimes referred to as YP servers). Individual systems on a network use NIS clients to make requests from the NIS server. The NIS server maintains its information on special database files called maps. Linux versions exist for both NIS clients and servers. Linux NIS clients easily connect to any network using NIS.

Note: Instead of NIS, many networks now use LDAP to manage user information and authentication.

The NIS package is part of the Universe repository and can be installed as **nis**, which will also install the **yp-tools** package. NIS client programs and tools are ypbind (the NIS client daemon), ypwhich, ypcat, yppoll, ypmatch, yppasswd, and ypset. Each has its own Man page with details of its use. The NIS server programs and tools are ypserv (the NIS server), ypinit, yppasswdd, yppush, ypxfr, and netgroup. Each has its own Man page. When you install the NIS server (**nis** package) you will be prompted to enter an NIS domain, listing your hostname as the default.

The NIS server is managed by **systemd** using the **ypserv.service** , **ypbind.service**, **yppasswdd.service**, and **ypxfrd.service** unit files in the **/lib/systemd/system** directory.

/etc/nsswitch.conf: Name Service Switch

Different functions in the standard C Library must be configured to operate on your Linux system. Previously, database-like services, such as password support and name services like NIS or DNS, directly accessed these functions, using a fixed search order. This configuration is carried out by a scheme called the Name Service Switch (NSS), which is based on the method of the same name used by Sun Microsystems Solaris 2 OS. The database sources and their lookup order are listed in the **/etc/nsswitch.conf** file.

File	Description
ethers	Ethernet numbers
group	Groups of users
hosts	Hostnames and numbers
netgroup	Network-wide list of hosts and users, used for access rules; C libraries before glibc 2.1 only support netgroups over NIS
network	Network names and numbers
passwd	User passwords
protocols	Network protocols
publickey	Public and secret keys for SecureRPC used by NFS and NIS+
rpc	Remote procedure call names and numbers
services	Network services
shadow	Shadow user passwords

Table 14-3: NSS-Supported databases

Service	Description
files	Checks corresponding **/etc** file for the configuration (for example, **/etc/hosts** for hosts); this service is valid for all files
db	Checks corresponding **/var/db** databases for the configuration; valid for all files except **netgroup**
compat	Provides **nis** and **files** services, with compatibility support for + and - entries. Valid only for **passwd**, **group**, and **shadow** files
dns	Checks the DNS service; valid only for **hosts** file
nis	Checks the NIS service; valid for all files
nisplus	NIS version 3
hesiod	Uses Hesiod for lookup
myhostname	Obtain the local configuration for a host name using the **gethostname** operation

Table 14-4: NSS Configuration Services

The **/etc/nsswitch.conf** file holds entries for the different configuration files that can be controlled by NSS. The system configuration files that NSS supports are listed in Table 14-3. An entry consists of two fields: the service and the configuration specification. The service consists of the configuration file followed by a colon. The second field is the configuration specification for that file, which holds instructions on how the lookup procedure will work. The configuration specification can contain service specifications and action items. Service specifications are the services to search. Currently, valid service specifications are nis, nis-plus, files, db, dns, systemd, and compat (see Table 14-4). Not all are valid for each configuration file. For example, the dns service is valid only for the **hosts** file, whereas nis is valid for all files. The following example will first check the local **/etc/password** file and then systemd.

```
passwd:   files systemd
```

For more refined access to passwd, group, and shadow sources, you can use the + and - symbols in file entries to determine if the entry can be accessed by the nsswitch service. The **compat** service provides a compatible mode that will check for such entries. With no such entries, the nis service will be used for all entries. The **compat** service can only be applied to the passwd, group, and shadow databases. This provides the equivalent of the files and nis services.

If your passwd, group, and shadow files already have + and - entries, and you need to have the file entries take precedence over the nis service, you can specify the files database before the compat entry.

```
passwd:   files compat
```

An action item specifies the action to take for a specific service. An action item is placed within brackets after a service. A configuration specification can list several services, each with its own action item. In the following example, the entry for the **hosts** file has a configuration specification that says to check the **/etc/hosts** files and **mdns4_minimal** service and, if not found, to check the DNS server (**dns**) and then, if still not resolved, obtain the local configuration (**myhostname**) for the host name such as **localhost**.

```
hosts: files mdns4_minimal [NOTFOUND=return] dns myhostname
```

An action item consists of a status and an action. The status holds a possible result of a service lookup, and the action is the action to take if the status is true. Currently, the possible status values are SUCCESS, NOTFOUND, UNAVAIL, and TRYAGAIN (service temporarily unavailable). The possible actions are **return** and **continue**: **return** stops the lookup process for the configuration file, whereas **continue** continues on to the next listed service. In the preceding example, if the record is not found in NIS, the lookup process ends.

Shown here is a copy of the **/etc/nsswitch.conf** file, which lists commonly used entries. Comments and commented-out entries begin with a # sign:

/etc/nsswitch.conf

```
# /etc/nsswitch.conf
#
# Example configuration of GNU Name Service Switch functionality.
# If you have the `glibc-doc-reference' and `info' packages installed, try:
# `info libc "Name Service Switch"' for information about this file.

passwd:        compat  systemd
group:         compat  systemd
shadow:        compat
gshadow:       files

hosts:         files mdns4_minimal [NOTFOUND=return] dns myhostname
networks:      files

protocols:     db files
services:      db files
```

```
ethers:        db files
rpc:           db files

netgroup:      nis
```

15. Samba

Samba Applications

User Level Security

The Samba smb.conf Configuration File

Testing the Samba Configuration

Domain Logons

Accessing Samba Services with Clients

The Linux Samba server, lets your Windows clients on a Microsoft Windows network to access shared files and printers on your Linux system, and, in turn, also allows Linux systems to access shared files and printers on Windows systems. It allows you to connect to Windows systems over a Windows network. In effect, Samba allows a Linux system to operate as if it were a Windows server, using the same protocols as used in a Windows network.

UNIX and Linux systems use the TCP/IP protocol for networking, whereas Microsoft Windows networking uses the Server Message Block (SMB) protocol. The SMB protocol makes use of a network interface called Network Basic Input Output System (NetBIOS) that allows Windows systems to share resources, such as printers and folders. SMB was originally designed for small networks. For large networks, Microsoft developed the Common Internet File System (CIFS), which still uses SMB and NetBIOS for Windows networking.

The Samba server and client was created by Andrew Tridgell in an effort to connection a Linux system to a Windows PC. They allow UNIX and Linux systems to connect to a Windows network seamlessly. UNIX/Linux systems can share resources on Windows systems, and Windows systems can share resources on Unix/Linux systems. In a sense, Samba is a professional-level, open source, and free version of CIFS. With Samba you can mount shared Windows folders directly to your Linux system, using the Linux **cifs** file system.

Samba software is organized into several packages (see Table 15-1). By selecting the samba server package, necessary supporting packages such as **smbclient** and **samba-common** will be automatically selected. Samba software packages can be installed using **apt**, the Synaptic Package Manager, or Software Manager.

Package name	Description
samba	The Samba server
samba-common	Samba configuration files and support tools
smbclient	Samba clients for accessing Windows shares
nemo-share	Nemo file manager extension to share a folder
caja-share	Caja file manager extension to share a folder

Table 15-1: Samba packages on Linux Mint

You can obtain extensive documentation from the Samba Web and FTP sites at **https://www.samba.org/**. Examples are provided on your system in the **/usr/share/doc/samba/examples** directory. Check the Ubuntu Server Guide | Services | Samba for basic configuration and management.

```
https://ubuntu.com/server/docs/samba-introduction
```

Samba Applications

The Samba server provides four services: file and printer services, authentication and authorization, name resolution, and service announcement. Two server daemons (**smbd** and **nmbd**) and several utility programs are installed by the Samba software package (see Table 15-2). The SMB daemon, **smbd**, provides the file and printer services, along with the authentication and authorization for those services. This allows users on the network to share folders and printers. Access to these services is controlled by user passwords. When users try to access a shared folder, they are prompted for the password. A different password is provided for each user, and Samba maintains a separate Samba password file.

The **nmbd** server provides Name resolution and service announcements. Name resolution resolves IP addresses with NetBIOS names. Service announcements makes known the available services on a network, enabling browsing.

Application	Description
nemo-share	File sharing extension for the Nemo file manager
caja-share	File sharing extension for the Caja file manager
smbd	Samba server daemon that provides file and printer services to SMB clients
nmbd	Samba daemon that provides NetBIOS name resolution and service browser support
winbind	Uses authentication services provided by Windows domain
mount.cifs	Mounts Samba share directories on Linux clients (used by the `mount` command with the `-t cifs` option)
smbpasswd	Changes SMB-encrypted passwords on Samba servers
pdbedit	Edit the Samba users database file. This is a Secure Accounts Manager (SAM) database.
tdbbackup	Backup the Samba .tdb database files.
smbcontrol	Send the Samba servers administrative messages, like shutdown or close-share.
smbstatus	Displays the current status of the SMB network connections
testparm	Tests the Samba configuration file, **smb.conf**
nmblookup	Maps the NetBIOS name of a Windows PC to its IP address
/etc/default/samba	Samba startup options

Table 15-2: Samba Server Applications

Basic Samba configuration support is already implemented by **nautilus-share**, letting you use your file manager to browse Samba shares. For a more complex configuration, you can edit the **/etc/samba/smb.conf** file directly. Configuration files are kept in the **/etc/samba** directory.

You can also install the **winbind** package which runs the **winbind** daemon. This daemon allows Samba servers to use authentication services provided by a Windows domain. With **winbind**, a Samba server can make use of a Windows domain authentication service to authenticate users, instead of using its own set of users.

The Samba package also includes support tools such as **smbstatus**, which displays the current status of the SMB server and who is using it, and **pdbedit**, which is used to edit the SMB password database. Additional packages provide support tools, like **smbclient** which lets a Linux system access Samba services (command line only). The **mount.cifs** and **umount.cifs** commands let Linux systems mount and unmount Samba shared folders. They are invoked by the **mount** command with the **-t cifs** option. You use **testparm** to test your Samba configuration. **smbtar** is a shell script that backs up SMB/CIFS-shared resources directly to a Unix tape drive. The **nmblookup** command will map the NetBIOS name of a Windows PC to its IP address. With the **smbcontrol** command you can send administrative messages to the Samba servers (smbd, nmbd, and winbindd) such as to close shares, reload the configuration, or shutdown the server.

Starting up and accessing Samba

Once installed, Samba is normally configured to start up automatically. You can edit **/etc/samba/smb.conf** file directly to make changes. If you make changes, you must restart the Samba server for them to take effect. To restart Samba with your new configuration, use the **systemctl** command. The start, stop, and restart options will start, stop, and restart the server. Run the following command from the command line or a terminal window to restart Samba.

```
sudo systemctl restart smbd
sudo systemctl restart nmbd
```

The Samba server consists of two daemons: **smbd** and **nmbd**. You may have to first enable them with the **systemctl** command, and then start them using the **systemctl** command. At the prompt (on the desktop open a terminal window), use the **sudo** command for administrative access followed by a **systemctl** command for the **smbd** server with the **enable** command to enable the server. Do the same for the **nmbd** server. Then use **systemctl** command with the **start** command to start them. Once enabled, the server should start automatically whenever your system starts up.

```
sudo systemctl enable nmbd
sudo systemctl enable smbd
sudo systemctl start nmbd
sudo systemctl start smbd
```

Samba is managed by **systemd** using the **smbd.service** and **nmbd.service** unit files in **/lib/systemd/system** directory. The **smbd.service** file is shown here. Samba is started after networking (After). It is dependent on the **multi-user.target** (WantedBy). The service is started using the **smbd** script in the **/usr/sbin** directory (ExecStart).

smbd.service

```
[Unit]
Description=Samba SMB Daemon
Documentation=man:smbd(8) man:samba(7) man:smb.conf(5)
Wants=network-online.target
After=network.target network-online.target nmbd.service winbind.service

[Service]
Type=notify
NotifyAccess=all
PIDFile=/var/run/samba/smbd.pid
LimitNOFILE=16384
EnvironmentFile=-/etc/default/samba
ExecStartPre=/usr/share/samba/update-apparmor-samba-profile
ExecStart=/usr/sbin/smbd --foreground --no-process-group $SMBDOPTIONS
ExecReload=/bin/kill -HUP $MAINPID
LimitCORE=infinity
```

```
[Install]
WantedBy=multi-user.target
```

The NMB daemon is started after networking (After). It starts the **nmbd** server using the **/usr/sbin/nmbd** script.

nmbd.service

```
[Unit]
Description=Samba NMB Daemon
Documentation=man:nmbd(8) man:samba(7) man:smb.conf(5)
After=network-online.target
Wants= network.target network-online.target

[Service]
Type=notify
NotifyAccess=all
PIDFile=/var/run/samba/nmbd.pid
EnvironmentFile=-/etc/default/samba
ExecStart=/usr/sbin/nmbd --foreground --no-process-group $NMBDOPTIONS
ExecReload=/bin/kill -HUP $MAINPID
LimitCORE=infinity

[Install]
WantedBy=multi-user.target
```

Firewall access

The UFW firewall used on Linux Mint and Ubuntu prevents browsing Samba and Windows shares from your Linux desktop. To work around this restriction, you need to make sure your firewall treats Samba as a trusted service. To allow firewall access to the Samba ports you should enable access using a firewall configuration tool like **ufw**. The Samba ports are 139/TCP, 137/UDP, 138/UDP, and 445/TCP. In addition, the multicastService Discovery service (mdns) uses port 5353/UDP.

Figure 15-1: Gufw Samba Firewall Access

If you are working from a desktop interface, you can use the Gufw tool to set the Samba ports for the UFW firewall. You will have to add the ports as simple rules (see Chapter 10) (see Figure 15-1) .

On the command line interface, using the UFW default firewall, you would use the following **ufw** commands. The UFW firewall maintains its IPtables files in **/etc/ufw**.

```
ufw allow 139/tcp
ufw allow 137:138/udp
ufw allow 445/tcp
ufw allow 5353/udp
```

If you are using FirewallD with firewall-config instead (Administration | Firewall), be sure to select the the **samba**, **samba-client**, and **mdns** entries on the Zone's Service tab (Permanent configuration) (see Figure 15-2) .

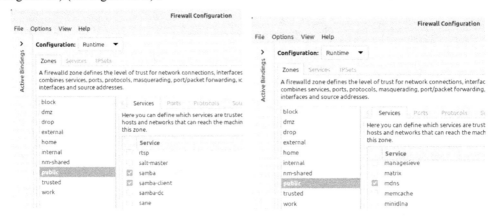

Figure 15-2: FirewallD Samba Firewall Access (samba, samb-client, mdns)

If you are managing your IPtables or nftables firewall directly, you could manage access by adding the following IPtables and nftables rules. This accepts input on ports 137, 138, and 139 for TCP/IP protocol packages.

iptables rules:

```
iptables -A INPUT -p tcp --dport 139 -j ACCEPT
iptables -A INPUT -p udp --dport 137:138 -j ACCEPT
iptables -A INPUT -p tcp --dport 445 -j ACCEPT
iptables -A INPUT -p udp --dport 5353 -j ACCEPT
```

nftables rules:

```
nft add rule ip filter INPUT tcp dport 139 counter accept
nft add rule ip filter INPUT udp dport 137-138 counter accept
nft add rule ip filter INPUT tcp dport 445 counter accept
nft add rule ip filter INPUT udp dport 5353 counter accept
```

User-Level Security

Security for Samba is based on usernames and passwords, known as user level security. Users on a remote client log in to the Samba server with Samba passwords. The need for Samba passwords came about to accommodate Windows password encryption and login requirements, which are different from that used for Linux. To manage such passwords, Samba has to maintain a separate Windows-compatible password database. It cannot use the Linux password database. For logins, Windows also uses additional information such as the user log in location.

For a user to login to a Samba share from a Windows system, the user has to already have a corresponding user account on that Samba server. That user account must also have a Samba password. In effect, the account has two password, the Linux user account password for accessing the account on Linux, and a Samba password used to access Samba shares from remote systems. In this way, a Linux user also become a Samba user.

Often, the Samba user account is not the same name as that of the Window account attempting to log in. To deal with this situation, a Windows username can be associated with a corresponding Samba user name. The name may or may not be the same. The mapping of windows users to Samba (Linux) users is stored in the **/etc/samba/smbusers** file. The following maps the Windows user **rpetersen** to the Samba (Linux) user **richard**.

```
richard = rpetersen
```

When a Windows user in Windows tries to access a Samba share, the user will be prompted to login. With the previous example, the Windows user would then enter **rpetersen** as the username and the Samba password that was set up for **richard**.

User-level security is managed by a password **tdb** (trivial data base) back-end database. A **tdb** database file stores Samba passwords with Windows extended information. By default, the **tdbsam** back-end database is used. The **tdbsam** database is designed for small networks. For systems using LDAP to manage users, you can use the LDAP-enabled back-end, **ldbsam**, which is designed for larger networks.

For standalone Samba servers, user level security and the tdbsam database is the default. So they are not specified in the the **smb.conf** configuration file. You can explicitly configure them with the **security** and **passdb backend** options.

```
security = user
passdb backend = tdbsam
```

You can use the **username map** option to designate the file used to associate Windows and Linux users. A Windows user can use a Windows username to login as the associated user. The username map file is usually **/etc/samba/smbusers**.

```
username map = /etc/samba/smbusers
```

For an LDAP Samba database, **ldbsam**, you use LDAP Samba tools to manage users (the **smbldap-tools** package). These tools have the prefix smbldap. The tools include those for adding, modifying, and deleting users and groups (**smbldap-useradd**, **smbldap-userdelete**, and **smbldap-groupmod**). The **sbmldap-passwd** command manages Samba passwords with LDAP. The **smbldap-userinfo** command displays user information. LDAP Samba tools are configured in the **/etc/smbldap-tools/smbldap.conf** file.

The Samba server has a password Pluggable Authentication Module (PAM) module, **pam_smbpass.so**, which provides PAM authentication for Samba passwords. This will allow Windows hosts to work on a PAM-controlled network. The module is configured in your PAM **samba** file. The following entries in the PAM **samba** file require PAM authentication and passwords for the Samba server.

```
auth required pam_smbpass.so nodelay
password required pam_smbpass.so nodelay
```

For PAM to work with Samba, enable PAM in the **smb.conf** file.

```
obey pam restrictions = yes
```

Note: The **smbpasswd** file previously used is still available, but it is included only for backward compatibility.

Samba Passwords: smbpasswd

Each user attempting to access a Samba server will need a Samba server user name and password. Such user-level security requires that this username and Samba password be stored in the Samba password database, which is maintained separately by the Samba server. To add or change a user Samba password, use the **smbpasswd** command with the username.

```
$ sudo smbpasswd dylan
New SMB Password: new-password
Repeat New SMB Password: new-password
```

Any user can use the **smbpasswd** command to change their password, as shown here. If you have no Samba password, just press ENTER.

```
$ sudo smbpasswd
Old SMB password: old-password
New SMB Password: new-password
Repeat New SMB Password: new-password
```

If you want to give a user access without having to use a password, you would use **smbpasswd** with the **-n** option. In addition, the **smb.conf** file will need to have the **null passwords** option set to yes.

If you are using the older smb passwords file (not the tdbasm database), you should configure Samba to use encrypted passwords. Set the **encrypt passwords** option to **yes** and specify the SMB password file. You can also use the **mksmbpasswd** script to create a smbpasswd file from the users in your **/etc/passwd** file. Pipe the contents of the passwd file to mksmbpasswd and then use redirection (>) to create the file.

Managing Samba Users: smbpasswd and pdbedit

You can use the **smbpasswd** command or the **pdbedit** tool to manage Samba user passwords. For the **smbpasswd** command, the **-a** option will add a user and the **-x** option will remove one. Use the **-e** and **-d** options to enable or disable users.

```
sudo smbpasswd -a aleina
```

The **smbpasswd** command can save Samba passwords to either the older smbpasswd file or the newer tdbsam backend database file. Linux Mint currently uses the tdbasm backend database. The **pdbedit** command was designed to work with this database. Normally would use the **pdbedit** command, instead of **smbpasswd** to manage your Samba users. To add a user with **pdbedit** you would use the **-a** option and to remove a user you use the **-x** option. You can also change passwords and set the user's home folder, as well as import or export the user entries to or from other back-end databases.

```
sudo pdbedit -a dylan
```

Unlike **smbpasswd**, with the **pdbedit** command you can display more information about users. The **-L** option displays users from the back-end database. Add the **-v** option for detailed information. For a particular user, add the username, as shown here.

```
sudo pdbedit -Lv richard
```

You can even display domain policies (the **-P** option) such as minimum password lengths or retries.

```
sudo pdbedit -P
```

If you want to import and export database entries, use the **-i** and **-e** options. The following will import entries from the old **smbpasswd** file to the new **tdbsam** back-end database.

```
sudo pdbedit -i smbpasswd -e tdbsam
```

Note: If your system is using an LDAP-enabled Samba database, use the smbldap tools to manage users and groups.

The Samba smb.conf Configuration File

Samba configuration is held in the **smb.conf** file located in the **/etc/samba** directory. It holds the configuration for the various shared resources, as well as global options that apply to all resources.

You use the **testparm** command in a terminal window to check the syntax of any changes you have made to the **/etc/samba/smb.conf** file.

```
testparm
```

The **/etc/samba/smb.conf** file is organized into two basic parts: one for global options and the other for shared services. Shared services, also known as shares, can either be file space services (used by clients as an extension of their native file systems) or printable services (used by clients to access print services on the host running the server). The file space service is a directory to which clients are given access. Clients can use the space in it as an extension of their local file system. A printable service provides access by clients to print services, such as printers managed by the Samba server.

The **/etc/samba/smb.conf** file contains default settings used for Linux Mint. You can edit the file to customize the configuration. Comment lines are preceded with a # sign. Entries that are disabled are preceded by a semicolon, ;. To enable such an entry, remove its initial semi-colon symbol. For a complete listing of the Samba configuration parameters, check the Man page for **smb.conf**.

The **smb.conf** file is organized into two main groups with the labels (comments) Global Settings and Share Definitions. The Global Settings section has several subsections:

Browsing/Identification, Networking, Debugging/Accounting, Authentication, Domains, Printing, and Misc. The global options are set first, followed by each shared resource's configuration.

Samba is configured according to resources such as shared folders and printers. Each resource in the **smb.conf** file is defined in its own section. A section is the basic element of the **smb.conf** file. A section holds its service name, enclosed in brackets, followed by options applied to the resource. For example, a section for a shared folder holds options that reference the folder and define the access rights for users. Global options are placed in a special section named **global**. There are also special sections, called **printers** and **homes**, which provide default options for user folders and for all shared printers. After these special sections, you can enter services for specific folders and printers on your server.

The format of a section always begins with a section label, the name of the shared resource encased in brackets. Other than the special sections, the section label can be any name you choose. Following the section label, on separate lines, different parameters (options) for this service are entered. Most of the parameters define the access rights for the service. For example, you may want a shared folder to be browseable, but read-only, and use a certain printer. Parameters are entered in the format *parameters name = value*. You can place comments in a section by placing a semicolon at the beginning of the comment line.

A simple example of a section configuration follows. The section label is encased in brackets and followed by two parameter entries. The **path** parameter references the shared folder. The **writeable** parameter specifies whether the user has write access to this folder.

```
[mysection]
 path = /home/chris
 writeable = true
```

A printer service has the same format but requires certain other parameters. The path parameter specifies the location of the printer spool folder. The **read-only** and **printable** parameters are set to **true**, indicating the service is read-only and printable. The **public** parameter lets anyone access the service.

```
[myprinter]
 path = /var/spool/samba
 read only = true
 printable = true
 public = true
```

The **writeable** option is an alias for the inverse of the **read only** option. The **writeable = yes** entry is the same as **read only = no** entry. The **read only = no**, **writeable = yes**, and **write ok = yes** options all provide write access to the user.

Variable Substitutions

For string values assigned to parameters, you can incorporate substitution operators. This provides greater flexibility in designating values that may be context-dependent, like usernames. For example, suppose a service needs to use a separate directory for each user who logs in. The path for such directories could be specified using the **%u** variable that substitutes in the name of the current user. The string **path = /tmp/%u** would become **path = /tmp/justin** for the **justin** user and **/tmp/dylan** for the **dylan** user. Table 15-3 lists several of the more common substitution variables.

Tip: The writeable option is an alias for the inverse of the read only option. The **writeable = yes** entry is the same as **read only = no** entry.

Global Settings

The Global Settings section provides configuration for the Samba server, as well as specifying defaults that may be used in the home and folder sections. In this section, you will find entries for the workgroup name, password configuration, browsing, and log files. The Global section begins with the **[global]** label.

Variable	Description
%S	Name of the current service
%P	Root directory of the current service
%u	Username of the current service
%H	Home directory of the user
%h	Internet hostname on which Samba is running
%m	NetBIOS name of the client machine
%L	NetBIOS name of the server
%M	Internet name of the client machine
%I	IP address of the client machine

Table 15-3: Samba Substitution Variables

Browsing/Identification

The Workgroup entry specifies the workgroup name you want to give to your network. The default Workgroup entry in the **smb.conf** file is shown here:

```
[global]

# Change this to the workgroup/NT-domain name your Samba server will part of
 workgroup = WORKGROUP
```

The workgroup name has to be the same for each Windows client that the Samba server supports. On many Windows networks, this is defaulted to WORKGROUP. This is also the default name specified in the **smb.conf** file. If you want to use another name, you have to change the **workgroup** entry in the **smb.conf** file. The **workgroup** entry in the **smb.conf** file and the workgroup name on each Windows client has to be the same. In this example the workgroup name is **mygroup**.

```
workgroup = mygroup
```

The server string entry holds the descriptive name you want displayed for the server on the client systems. On Windows systems, this is the name displayed on the Samba server icon. The default is Samba Server, but you can change this to any name you want.

```
# server string is the equivalent of the NT Description field
   server string = %h server (Samba, Ubuntu)
```

Note: You can also configure Samba to be a Primary Domain Controller (PDC) for Windows NT networks. As a PDC, Samba sets up the Windows domain that other systems will use, instead of participating in an already established workgroup.

Networking

This subsection has interface directives for assigning a network interface device to a particular network to use for your server. The entries are commented out by default. The commented default entry is shown here for localhost on the first Ethernet device. Be sure to replace eth0 with the actual name of your network device (predicable name), such as enp7s0. You can use **ifconfig** to find the name.

```
;    interfaces = 127.0.0.0/8 eth0
```

If the system your Samba server runs on is not protected by a firewall, or the firewall is running on the same system, you should also enable the following.

```
;    bind interfaces only = yes
```

Debugging/Accounting

This section has directives for setting up logging for the Samba server. The log file directive is configured with the **%m** substitution symbol so that a separate log file is set up for each machine that connects to the server.

```
log file = /var/log/samba/log.%m
```

The maximum size of a log file is set to 1000 lines.

```
max log size = 1000
```

To have Samba log to the Samba log file, set **logging** to **file**. Add syslog01 to log also through syslog.

```
# We want Samba to only log to /var/log/samba/log.{smbd,nmbd}.
# Append syslog@1 if you want important messages to be sent to syslog too.
logging = file
```

The panic action directive notifies the administrator in case of a crash.

```
panic action = /usr/share/samba/panic-action %d
```

Authentication

The server role for the Samba server can be standalone, a member server, or a domain controller (primary, backup, or active directory). Usually the server is a standalone server. The server role determines the security. For standalone server the security is user, which requires a password logon.

```
server role = standalone server
```

Windows clients use encrypted passwords for the login process. Passwords are encrypted by default and managed by the password database.

You can use the security option to specify the security: **user** (user password), **domain** (Windows domain), or **ads (**Kerberos) security. The **auto** setting is the default, which derives the security from the server role. If the server role is **standalone server**, then the security is **user** and is not specified in the **smb.conf** file. In the **smb.conf** file, as the **server role** is set to **standalone server**, the security is set to the user-level (**user**) and the password database file uses **tdbsam**.

Support for Pluggable Authentication Modules (PAM) security is then turned on.

```
obey pam restrictions = yes
```

When Samba passwords are changed, they need to be synced with UNIX passwords. The **unix password sync** directive turns on syncing, and the **passwd program** and **passwd chat** directives use the **passwd** command and specified prompts to change the password.

```
unix password sync = yes

passwd program = /usr/bin/passwd %u
passwd chat = *Enter\snew\s*\spassword:* %n\n *Retype\snew\s*\spassword:* %n\n
*password\supdated\successfully* .
```

PAM is also used for password changes by Samba clients.

```
pam password change = yes
```

As a security measure, you can restrict access to SMB services to certain specified local networks. On the host's network, type the network addresses of the local networks for which you want to permit access. To deny access to everyone in a network except a few particular hosts, you can use the EXCEPT option after the network address with the IP addresses of those hosts. The localhost (127) is always automatically included. The next example allows access to two local networks.

```
hosts allow = 192.168.1. 192.168.2.
```

The map to guest directive is set to bad user. This will allow any unknown users to login as guests. Samba users that fail to login though will not be allowed access, even as guests.

```
map to guest = bad user
```

Domains

The Domains subsection configures your Samba server as a Microsoft Public Domain Controller (PDC). All of these directives are commented out by default. See the section later in this chapter on Public Domain Controller on how to set up your Samba server as a PDC on a Microsoft network.

Misc

The Misc subsection has entries used to customize your server. Most are commented out, except for the **usershare** directive that allows users to create public shares. An **include** directive lets you set up configuration files for particular machines in the **/home/samba/etc** directory, that are then read when the machine connects.

```
;   include = /home/samba/etc/smb.conf.%m
```

There are also entries for those using the Winbind server, specifying the user and group id ranges, and the shell to use.

```
# Some defaults for winbind (make sure you're not using the ranges
# for something else.)
```

```
;    idmap config * :              backend = tdb
;    idmap config * :              range   = 3000-7999
;    idmap config YOURDOMAINHERE : backend = tdb
;    idmap config YOURDOMAINHERE : range   = 100000-999999
;    template shell = /bin/bash
```

The **usershare** directives allow non-root users to share folders. A commented entry for user max shares can be used to limit the number of shares a user can set up.

```
;        usershare max shares = 100
```

The **user allow guests** directive permits users to create public shares, allowing guests to access the shares.

```
# Allow users who've been granted usershare privileges to create
# public shares, not just authenticated ones
usershare allow guests = yes
```

You can use a guest user login to make resources available to anyone without requiring a password. A guest user login would handle any users who log in without a specific account. Samba is usually set up to use the **nobody** user as the guest user. Alternatively, you can set up and designate a specific user to use as the guest user. You can designate the guest user with the **guest ok** and **guest account** entries in the **smb.conf** file. Be sure to add the guest user to the password file.

```
guest ok = yes
guest account = nobody
```

In addition, this section provides several performance tweaks, such as setting socket options for Linux systems.

Share Definitions

The Share Definitions part will hold sections for the definition of commonly used shares, as well as any shares you have set up yourself, like shared folders or printers. There are several special sections such ae the homes, netlogon, printers, and profiles sections that are used for special purposes. Users can be referenced in the share definitions either by their user names or by groups. A group is indicated the a preceding @ character. Certain groups reference administrative users such as **@lpadmin**, **@syslog**, and **@adm**.

Homes Section

The **homes** section applies to the home folders of users on the system. It sets the default controls for accessing a user home folder by remote users. Setting the **browseable** option to **no** prevents a remote user from listing the files in a file browser. Read access to files by remote users is determined by the **read only** option. The **create mask** and **directory mask** options set default permissions for new files and folders created in the home folder by remote users. Normally these permissions are set to 0700, which allows owner read/write/execute permission. The **valid users** option uses the **%S** macro to map to the current service. You can add the **writeable** directive to allow write access.

```
writeable = yes
```

The **homes** entries are commented out in the **smb.conf** configuration file, disabling access to user home directories by default. To enable access to home directories, remove the semi-colon comment in front of each entry in the **homes** section.

If you are setting up a PDC and chose to save user profiles in the user home directories, then the **homes** section and its entries have to be un-commented.

```
[homes]
 comment = Home Directories
 browseable = no
 read only = yes
 create mask = 0700
 directory mask = 0700
 valid users = %S
```

The printers and print$ Sections

The printers section specifies the default controls for accessing printers. These are used for printers for which no specific sections exist. Setting **browseable** to **no** simply hides the Printers section from the client, not the printers. The **path** option lists the location of the spool folder that Samba will use for printer files. The **printable** option must be set to yes to allow any printing. Otherwise, printing is disabled. To allow guest users to print, set the **guest ok** option to **yes**. The Printers section is shown here.

```
[printers]
 comment = All Printers
 browseable = no
 path = /var/spool/samba
 printable = yes
 guest ok = no
 read only = yes
 create mask = 0700
```

The **print$** section, shown next, specifies where a Windows client can find a print driver on your Samba server. The printer drivers are located in the **/var/lib/samba/printers** directory and are read-only. The browseable, read-only, and guest directives are commented out. They can be enabled to allow browsing of the drivers. The **write list** directive would allow you to remotely administer the Windows print drivers. **lpadmin** is the name of your administrator group.

```
# Windows clients look for this share name as a source of downloadable
# printer drivers
[print$]
  comment = Printer Drivers
  path = /var/lib/samba/printers
  browseable = yes
  read only = yes
  guest ok = no
;  write list = root, @lpadmin
```

Shares

The sections for shared resources, such as folders on your system, are placed after the Homes and Printers sections. A sections for a shared folder, begins with a label for that share. It is followed by options for its pathname and permissions, each on a separate line. The **path** = *option* entry holds the full pathname for the folder. In the **comment** = *option* entry you can describe the share. Permission options let you make the folder writeable, public, or read-only. The **valid users** option lets you control access to shares by certain user. For any options not entered, the the defaults in the Global, Homes, and Printers sections are used.

The following example, the **myprojects** share defines the **/myprojects** folder as a shared resource that is open to any user with guest access.

```
[myprojects]
    comment = Great Project Ideas
    path = /myprojects
    read only = no
    guest ok = yes
```

Use the **valid users** option to limit access to certain users. To then shut off access to all other users, the **guest ok** option is set to **no**.

```
[mynewmusic]
 comment =  New Music
 path = /home/specialprojects
 valid users = mark, richard
 guest ok = no
 read only = no
```

In the following example, the Documents folder is accessible and writeable to the george and richard users.

```
[Documents]
path = /home/richard/Documents
writeable = yes
browseable = yes
valid users = george, richard
```

If you want to allow public access to a folder, set the **guest ok** entry to **yes**, with no valid users entry.

```
[newdocs]
 comment =  New Documents
 path = /home/newdocs
 guest ok = yes
 read only = no
```

The users listed in a **valid users** option gives each user control of the files they create. You can further manage control of their files by using the **create mask** option to specify file permissions. In this example, the permissions are set to 765, which provides read/write/execute access to owners, read/write access to members of the group, and only read/execute access to all others (the default is 744, read-only for the group and other permission).

```
[myshare]
 comment = Writer's projects
 path = /usr/local/drafts
 valid users = Justin, chris, dylan
 guest ok = no
```

```
read only = no
create mask = 0765
```

You can further refine control with the **read list** and **write list** options. The **read list** option provides read only access to the listed users, whereas the **write list** option provides both read and write access.

```
[myshare]
 comment = Writer's projects
 path = /usr/local/drafts
 read list = Justin, chris
 write list dylan
 guest ok = no
 read only = no
 create mask = 0765
```

Printer shares

Access to specific printers is defined in the Printers section of the **smb.conf** file. For a printer, you need to include the Printer and Printable entries, as well as specify the type of Printing server used. With the Printer entry, you name the printer, and by setting the **printable** entry to yes, you allow it to print. You can control access to specific users with the **valid users** entry and by setting the **public** entry to no. For public access, set the **public** entry to yes. For the CUPS server, set the **printing** option to **cups**.

The following example sets up a printer accessible to guest users, which lets the printer to be used by any user on the network. The **read only** option is set to **no** to allow users write-access to the printer's spool directory, located in **/var/spool/samba**. The printer should already be installed. The printer in this example was installed as **myhp**. You use the CUPS administrative tool to set up printers for the CUPS server. The Printing option can be inherited from the Printers share.

```
[myhp]
    path = /var/spool/samba
    read only = no
    guest ok = yes
    printable = yes
    printer = myhp
    oplocks = no
    share modes = no
    printing = cups
```

Should you want, you can also restrict printer use to certain users, denying it to public access, just as you can shares. The the next example, the printer is accessible only by the users **larisa** and **aleina**. You could add other users if you want.

```
[larisalaser]
    path = /var/spool/samba
    read only = no
    valid users = larisa aleina
    guest ok = no
    printable = yes
    printing = cups
    printer = larisalaser
```

```
oplocks = no
share modes = no
```

Testing the Samba Configuration

If you have modified the **smb.conf** file, you should test it to check for errors. Use the **testparm** command to see if the entries are correct. **testparm** checks the syntax and validity of Samba entries. By default, **testparm** checks the **/etc/samba/smb.conf** configuration file. If you want to use different configuration file, you can enter it as an argument to **testparm**.

Samba Public Domain Controller: Samba PDC

Samba can also operate as a Public Domain Controller (PDC). The domain controller will be registered and advertised on the network as the domain controller. The PDC provides a much more centralized way to control access to Samba shares. It provides the netlogon service and a NETLOGON share. The PDC will set up machine trust accounts for each Windows and Samba client. Though you can do this manually, Samba will do it for you automatically. Keep in mind that Samba cannot emulate a Microsoft Active PDC, but can emulate a Windows NT4 PDC.

For basic configuration check the Ubuntu Server Guide | Services | Samba - Domain Controller.

```
https://ubuntu.com/server/docs/samba-domain-controller
```

Microsoft Domain Security

As noted in the Samba documentation, the primary benefit of Microsoft domain security is single-sign-on (SSO). In effect, logging into your user account also logs you into access to your entire network's shared resources. Instead of having to be separately authenticated any time you try to access a shared network resource, you are already authenticated. Authentication is managed using Security IDs (SID) that consists of a network ID (NID) and a relative ID (RID). The RID references your personal account. A separate RID is assigned to every account, even those for groups or system services. The SID is used to set up access control lists (ACL) the different shared resources on your network, allowing a resource to automatically identify you.

Essential Samba PDC configuration options

To configure your PDC, edit the **Domains** section in the **smb.conf** file. Here you will find entries for configuring your Samba PDC options. You will need to add the **domain logons** and **domain master** entries.

The essential PDC options are shown here.

```
workgroup = myworkgroup
domain logons = yes
domain master = yes
security = user
```

If the netbios name is different from the hostname on which the server is run, you can add a **netbios name** option to specify it.

```
netbios name = myserver
```

Basic configuration

Like most Samba configurations, the PDC requires a Samba back-end. The **tdbsam** is already configured for you. The security level should be **user**. This is normally the default and is already set. The **smb.conf** entry is shown here.

```
passdb backend = tdbsam
```

The PDC must also be designated the domain master. This is set to auto by default. For a PDC, set it to yes, and for a BDC (backup domain controller) set it to no.

```
domain master = yes
```

The PDC has browser functionality, with which it locates systems and shares on your network. These features are not present in the **smb.conf** file, but you can add them if needed. The **local master** option is used only if you already have another PDC that you want to operate as the local master. You could have several domain controllers operating on your network. Your Microsoft network holds an election to choose which should be the master. The **os level** sets the precedence for this PDC. It should be higher than 32 to gain preference over other domain controllers on your network, ensuring this PDC's election as the primary master controller. The **preferred master** option starts the browser election on startup.

```
;       local master = no
os level = 33
preferred master = yes
```

Domain Logon configuration

Samba PDC uses the domain logons service whereby a user can log on to the network. The domain logon service is called the netlogon service by Microsoft. The samba share it uses is also called netlogon. To configure the domain logon service, you set the **domain logons** option to yes, or set the **server role** option to "primary classic domain controller" or to "backup domain controller."

```
domain logons = yes
```

The logon path, specified by the **logon path** optin references the profile used for a user. The **%N** will be the server name, and the **%U** references the username. Profiles can be set up either in a separate **profiles** share or in the user home directories. The following would reference user profiles in the **profiles** share. You would also have to define the **profiles** share by un-commenting the profiles share entries in the **smb.conf** file.

```
logon path = \\%N\profiles\%U
```

If the profile is stored in the user's home directory instead of the profiles share, you would uncomment the following entry instead. You will also have to allow access to user home directories, un-commenting the homes share entries.

```
logon path = \\%N\%U\profile
```

The **logon drive** and **logon home** options specify the location of the user's home directory. The logon drive is set as the H: drive. The **%N** evaluates to the server name and **%U** to the user.

```
logon drive = H:
logon home = \\%N\%U
```

The login script can be one set by the system or by users.

```
logon script = logon.cmd
```

You can then enable **user add** operations for adding users, groups, and machines to the PDC. The **add machine** option allows Samba to automatically add trusted machine accounts for Windows systems when they first join the PDC controlled network.

```
add user script = /usr/sbin/adduser --quiet --disabled-password --gecos "" %u
add machine script  = /usr/sbin/useradd -g machines -c "%u machine account" -d
/var/lib/samba -s /bin/false %u
add group script = /usr/sbin/addgroup --force-badname %g
```

You then need to set up a netlogon share in the **smb.conf** file. This share holds the **netlogon** scripts, in this case, the **/var/lib/samba/netlogon** directory, which should not be writable, but should be accessible by all users (Guest OK). In the share definitions section of the **smb.conf** file, you will find the **[netlogon]** section commented. Remove the semi-colon comments from the entry, as shown here.

```
# Un-comment the following and create the netlogon directory for Domain Logon
# (you need to configure Samba to act as a domain controller too.)
[netlogon]
comment = Network Logon Service
path = /home/samba/netlogon
guest ok = yes
read only = yes
```

If you choose to use a profiles share to store user profiles in, then you should enable the **profiles** share. Un-comment the following to define a **profiles** share. The entries are located just after the **netlogon** shares.

```
[profiles]
comment = Users profiles
path = /home/samba/profiles
guest ok = no
browseable = no
create mask = 0600
directory mask = 0700
```

The **profile** share is where user netlogon profiles are stored. If instead, you are using the user's home directories to store their profiles, you will not need to define and use a **profiles** share. If you choose to store user profiles in the user home directories, you would uncomment the **homes** share entries instead.

Samba Active Directory Domain Controller

With Samba version 4 you can run Samba as an Active Directory Domain Controller, instead of as a classic domain controller. You will also have to run a DNS server and Kerberos authentication server. You will have to select and configure a server to operate as the domain controller. It must have a static IP address. To allow the Active Directory software to be more easily updated, it is advised that the domain controller should not also function as a file server. See the Samba documentation for detailed instructions on how to set up a server as an Active Directory Domain Controller.

```
https://wiki.samba.org/index.php/Setting_up_Samba_as_an_Active_Directory_Domain_C
ontroller
```

Be sure to remove any previous installation of Samba, including **winbindd**. Do a restart to ensure that all Samba processes have ended, or manually detect and stop them. Also, if you previously installed Samba, remove any Samba configuration files, including Samba databases. On Ubuntu, the Samba configuration files are located at **/etc/samba**. If you previously installed Kerberos, remove the Kerberos configuration file **/etc/krb5.conf**.

Take care in choosing a hostname for the server running the Active Directory Domain Controller. See the Samba documentation on selecting an appropriate hostname.

```
https://wiki.samba.org/index.php/Active_Directory_Naming_FAQ
```

In order to coordinate with the DNS server, disable any support for automatically updating the **/etc/resolvconf** file. This means disabling the **resolved** daemon. In the **/etc/hosts** file, be sure that the domain controller server name is correctly resolved to the static IP address you are using for it.

You then use the **samba-tool** command to provision the Active Directory, configuring it by setting up databases, an administration account, DNS entries, and configuration files.

The **samba-tool** command has an interactive and non-interactive mode. The interactive mode prompts for options such as the domain name you are using for the Active Directory Domain Controller, and the static IP address you are using for it. Use the **--interactive** option to use the interactive mode. You may want to include several options with the **samba-tool** command. The **--rfc2307** option will provide NIS support, which is difficult to add later should you need it. If your server has several network interfaces, you should specify the one to use, as in eth0 in this example.

```
-option="interfaces=lo eth0" --option="bind interfaces only=yes"
```

To see a listing of the **samba-tool** options for provisioning use the following command.

```
samba-tool domain provision --help
```

The command to perform an interactive provisioning follows. Be sure to add any other options you may need.

```
samba-tool domain provision --use-rfc2307 --interactive
```

In the non-interactive mode you would have to list all the options and their values with the **samba-tool** command.

Once the provisioning is finished, be sure the **/etc/resolv.conf** file has entries to search your Active Directory server's domain and that there is an entry specifying your DNS nameserver's IP address. Also, to configure Kerberos for the Active Directory, copy the version of the **krb5.conf** file generated by the provisioning in the **/var/lib/samba/private** directory to the /etc directory. In the **/etc/samba/smb.conf** file the **server role** option must be set to "active directory domain controller."

```
server role = active directory domain controller
```

The service name for the Samba Active Directory Domain Controller is **samba-ac-dc**. You can manage it with the **systemctl** command.

```
sudo systemctl enable samba-ac-dc
sudo systemctl start samba-ac-dc
```

Accessing Samba Services with Clients

Any client systems connected to the SMB network can access the shared services provided by the Samba server. You can use the **smbclient** command to access a shared folder and then run commands to to manage the files there. If you want to mount a shared folder to a local folder on your system, providing direct access, you can use the the **mount** command with the **-t cifs** option. Be sure that firewall access for Samba is enabled.

Accessing Windows Samba Shares from the Desktop

On the desktop, you can use a file manager like Nemo to access your Samba shares. Currently, both Linux and Windows are in the process of transitioning from the older SMBv1 protocol (Secure Message Block) to the more secure SMBv3 protocol. As a result, network browsing through the Linux file manager does not currently work. You can access Windows shares directly using the Nemo file manager's location textbox. Enter in the **smb://** protocol (Avahi) and the name of the shared folder or that of the remote Windows system you want to access. After being prompted to enter your Samba password, the particular shared folder or the shared folders on that host will be displayed.

smbclient

You can use **smbclient** to access SMB-shared services and folders on the Samba server or on a Windows system. It works much like FTP and but has different protocols, the SMB protocols. **smbclient** has many of the same commands as FTP, for example, **mget** to transfer a file or **del** to delete a file. **smbclient** also provides options to query and connect to a remote system. For a complete list of options and commands, check the **smbclient** Man page. **smbclient** has as its argument a server name and the service you want to access. The server name is preceded by a double slash, and the service is preceded by a single slash. The service is any shared resource, such as a folder or a printer. The server name is its NetBIOS name, which may or may not be the same as its IP name. For example, to specify the **myreports** shared directory on the server named **turtle.mytrek.com**, use **//turtle.mytrek.com/myreports**. Should you have to specify a pathname, keep in mind that, though Windows uses backward slashes for its path names, Unix/Linux systems use forward slashes.

```
//server-name/service
```

If the service is password protected, you will have to provide the password. Enter the password as an argument following the service name. If no password is provided, and it is required for the service, you will be prompted to enter it.

The **smbclient** command provides several options for accessing shares. The **-I** option references a system by its IP address. To specify a login name you use **-U**. Should a password be needed, attach **%** with the password. The **-L** option displays a list of the services provided on a server, such as shared folders or printers. The following command will list the shares available on the host **turtle.mytrek.com**:

```
smbclient -L turtle.mytrek.com
```

In order to access a particular folder on a remote system, you enter the folder name and any options you want. Be sure to use forward slashes for Windows path names. Upon connecting to the server, an SMB prompt is displayed. You can then enter **smbclient** commands such as **get** and **put** to transfer files. Use the **quit** and **exit** commands to quit and end the connection. The **recurse** command lets you to turn on recursion to copy whole subfolders at a time. With the UNIX file-matching operators, you can reference multiple files. The file-matching operators are *****, **[]**, and **?**. The default mask is *****, which matches everything. The following example uses **mget** to copy all files with a **.c** suffix, as in **myprog.c**:

```
smb> mget *.c
```

In the following example, **smbclient** accesses the folder **myreports** on the **turtle.mytrek.com** system, using the **dylan** login name and the **-I** option, the IP address of the server.

```
smbclient //turtle.mytrek.com/myreports -I 192.168.0.1 -U dylan
```

Normally you just use the server name to reference the server, as shown here. You do not need to specify the IP address.

```
smbclient //turtle.mytrek.com/myreports -U dylan
```

Should you want to access a user's home folder on the Samba server, you would use the **homes** service. In the next example, the user accesses the home folder of the **aleina** account on the Samba server. As the password is not provided, the user will be prompted for it.

```
smbclient //turtle.mytrek.com/homes -U aleina
```

smbclient also lets you access Windows shared resources. Enter the computer name of the Windows client and the shared folder on that client you want access to. In the next example, the user accesses the **windata** folder on the Windows client named **mycomp**. If the folder allows access to anyone, you just press ENTER at the password prompt.

```
smbclient //mycomp/windata
```

mount.cifs: mount -t cifs

You can mount a shared folder onto your local system by using the **mount** command and the **-t cifs** option. The **cifs** option will run the **mount.cifs** command, which, in turn, invokes the **smbclient** command to perform the mount. The **mount.cifs** command requires the names of the Samba server, shared folder, and the local folder where the shared folder is to be mounted. The following example mounts the **mybooks** folder to the **/mnt/mybks** folder on the local system.

```
mount -t cifs //turtle.mytrek.com/mybooks /mnt/mybks -U dylan
```

If you want to unmount a folder, you run the **umount** command with the **-t cifs** option and the folder name. The **umount** command will invoke the **umount.cifs** command which performs the unmount.

```
umount -t cifs  /mnt/mybks
```

Should you want to mount the home folder of a user, specify the **homes** service and the user's login name. The following example mounts the home folder of the user **aleina** to the **/home/harlow/aleinastuff** folder on the local system.

```
mount -t cifs //turtle.mytrek.com/homes /home/harlow/aleinastuff -U aleina
```

It is also possible to mount shared folders on Windows clients. Use two forward slashes to precede the name of the Windows computer and the Windows folder. If the folder name contains spaces, enclose it in single quotes. In the following example, the user mounts the **mydocs** folder on **mywin** as the **/mywindocs** folder. For a folder with access to anyone, just press ENTER at the password prompt without entering a password.

```
$ mount -t cifs //mywin/mydocs /mywindocs
Password:
$ ls /mydocs
mynewdoc.doc myreport.txt
```

When you are finished with that shared folder, you can use the **umount** command and the **-t cifs** option to unmount it as you would a Linux folder.

```
umount -t cifs /mywindocs
```

Should you want to control user access to the folder, you can specify a username and password as options when you mount it, as shown here.

```
mount -t cifs -o username=harlow passwd=mypass //mywin/mydocs /mywindocs
```

If you want the folder mounted automatically whenever you start up the system, you can create an entry for the mount operation in the **/etc/fstab** file. Use the **cifs** file type in the entry:

```
//mywin/mydocs   /mywindocs   cifs   defaults   0  0
```

Table Listing

Table 1-1: Linux Mint Editions 30

Table 1-2: Linux Mint resources and help 32

Table 1-3: Ubuntu help and documentation 34

Table 3-1: Window and File Manager Keyboard shortcuts 74

Table 4-1: Linux Software Package File Extensions 140

Table 4-2: apt and apt-get commands 141

Table 4-3: snap commands 148

Table 5-1: X-App Applications 159

Table 5-2: LibreOffice Applications 160

Table 5-3: Calligra Applications 161

Table 5-4: Office Applications for GNOME 161

Table 5-5: PostScript, PDF, and DVI viewers 163

Table 5-6: Ebook Readers 163

Table 5-7: Desktop Editors 164

Table 5-8: Database Management Systems for Linux 165

Table 5-9: Linux Mail Clients 166

Table 5-10: Linux Newsreaders 167

Table 5-11: Graphics Tools for Linux 170

Table 5-12: Music players, editors, and rippers 171

Table 5-13: Video and DVD Projects and Applications 174

Table 5-14: CD/DVD Burners 177

Table 5-15: Web browsers 178

Table 5-16: Java Packages and Java Web Applications 180

Table 5-17: Linux FTP Clients 181

Table 5-18: Instant Messenger, Talk, and VoIP Clients 183

Table 6-1: Cinnamon Keyboard Shortcuts 195

Table 6-2: File Manager View Menu 224

Table 6-3: File Manager File Menu 225

Table 6-4: File Manager Edit Menu 226

Table 6-5: File Manager Pop-up Menu 227

Table 6-6: File Manager Go Menu 228

Table 6-7: The File Manager Sidebar Pop-Up Menu 229

Table 6-8: The File and Folder Pop-Up Menu 232

Table 6-9: Desktop System Settings 240

Table 7-1: The Desktop Menu 265

Table 7-2: File Manager Go Menu 280

Table 7-3: File Manager File Menu 281

Table 7-4: File Manager View Menu 285

Table 7-5: File Manager Edit Menu 286

Table 7-6: File Manager Pop-up Menu 286

Table 7-7: The File Manager Side Pane Pop-Up Menu 287

Table 7-8: The File and Folder Pop-Up Menu 289

Table 7-9: The MATE Preferences 295

Table 8-1: Linux Mint System Tools 310

Table 8-2: Sensor packages and applications 317

Table 8-3: Sound device and interface tools 321

Table 8-4: PulseAudio commands (command-line) 325

Table 9-1: Linux Mint Administration Tools 340

Table 9-2: Backup Resources 383

Table 10-1: Linux Mint Network Configuration Tools 400

Table 10-2: The nmcli objects 420

Table 10-3: Variables for wvdial 424

Table 10-4: Service ports 434

Table 10-5: UFW firewall operations 439

Table 10-6: Network Interface Device Naming 448

Table 11-1: Shell Invocation Command Names 454

Table 11-2: Shell Configuration Files.. 455

Table 11-3: BASH Shell Special Features 458

Table 11-4: Shell Variables, Set by the Shell 459

Table 11-5: System Environment Variables Used by the Shell..................................462

Table 12-1: systemd unit types and man pages 480

Table 12-2: systemd Unit and Install section options (common to all units, systemd.unit) 482

Table 12-3: special units..484

Table 12-4: special runlevel targets (boot) 484

Table 12-5: systemd exec options (Service, Socket, Mount, Swap) (systemd.exec) 486

Table 12-6: systemd service options [Service] (systemd.service)...........................487

Table 12-7: Collection of Service unit files..488

Table 12-8: systemd socket file options [Socket] (systemd.socket)........................489

Table 12-9: path option (systemd.path) 490

Table 12-10: System Runlevels (States)...492

Table 12-11: systemd mount and automount file options [Mount] [Automount]...........494

Table 12-12: System Shutdown Options 497

Table 12-13: AppArmor Utilities..504

Table 12-14: SSH Tools 509

Table 12-15: SSH Configuration Files 511

Table 13-1: Print Resources...518

Table 13-2: CUPS Configuration Files..539

Table 13-3: CUPS Print Clients..545

Table 13-4: CUPS Administrative Tools..547

Table 14-1: The /etc/exports Options..555

Table 14-2: NFS Mount Options 561

Table 14-3: NSS-Supported databases...564

Table 14-4: NSS Configuration Services...564

Table 15-1: Samba packages on Linux Mint 568

Table 15-2: Samba Server Applications..569

Table 15-3: Samba Substitution Variables..577

Figure Listing

Figure 1-1: Linux Mint 21 Cinnamon Desktop 29

Figure 1-2: Linux Mint 21 Cinnamon Live DVD 30

Figure 1-3: Linux Mint Welcome dialog 32

Figure 1-4: Welcome dialog - Documentation 33

Figure 2-1: Upgrade Tool (mintupgrade) 39

Figure 2-2: Upgrade Tool Preferences Requirements 39

Figure 2-3: Upgrade Tool Preferences Orphan Packages 40

Figure 2-4: Upgrade Tool tests 40

Figure 2-5: Upgrade Tool upgrade 41

Figure 2-6: Upgrade Tool download and update 41

Figure 2-7: Upgrade Tool upgrade completion 41

Figure 2-8: Live DVD/USB (Desktop) with Install icon. 45

Figure 2-9: Keyboard Layout 46

Figure 2-10: Install Third-Party Software 46

Figure 2-11: No detected operating systems 48

Figure 2-12: LVM install option 48

Figure 2-13: LVM selection 49

Figure 2-14: LVM with encryption 49

Figure 2-15: Security key for encrypted system 50

Figure 2-16: Security key login 50

Figure 2-17: Something Else (manual partitioning) 53

Figure 2-18: Manually partitioning a new hard drive 54

Figure 2-19: Create a new partition table on a blank hard drive 54

Figure 2-20: Select free space on a blank hard drive 54

Figure 2-21: Create a new boot partition 55

Figure 2-22: Create a new root partition 55

Figure 2-23: Manual partitions 56

Figure 2-24: Where Are You, Time zone 57

Figure 2-25: Who are you? 58

Figure 2-26: Install progress slide show 59

Figure 2-27: Reboot or Continue Testing 59

Figure 2-28: Grub advanced options menu with recovery kernels 60

Figure 2-29: Recovery options 60

Figure 2-30: Boot Repair 61

Figure 3-1: Linux Mint GRUB menu 64

Figure 3-2: Editing a GRUB menu item 65

Figure 3-3: GRUB2 Linux Mint Theme 66

Figure 3-4: LightDM Login Screen with user list 67

Figure 3-5: LightDM Login Screen with Shut Down options 67

Figure 3-6: LightDM Login screen with desktop choices 68

Figure 3-7: Login Window Preferences 69

Figure 3-8: Login Window with no hostname or keyboard layout 70

Figure 3-9: Lock Screen and Screensaver 70

Figure 3-10: Shut Down and Restart dialog 71

Figure 3-11: Log Out dialog 71

Figure 3-12: Linux Mint Cinnamon desktop 73

Figure 3-13: Linux Mint Cinnamon menu 74

Figure 3-14: Nemo File manager 75

Figure 3-15: Linux Mint MATE desktop 76

Figure 3-16: Linux Mint Menu (MATE) 76

Figure 3-17: Caja File manager 77

Figure 3-18: Xfce desktop 78

Figure 3-19: Xfce Whisker menu 79

Figure 3-20: Xfce Settings Manager 80

Figure 3-21: Welcome Screen - First Steps 81

Figure 3-22: Computer folders 82

Figure 3-23: Accessing removeable drives on the desktop 83

Figure 3-24: Disk Writer, writing ISO image to USB drive. 85

Figure 3-25: Network Manager panel system tray connections icons................................. 86

Figure 3-26: Network Manager connections menu 87

Figure 3-27: Network Manager connections menu: wired and wireless............................. 87

Figure 3-28: Network Manager wireless authentication... 88

Figure 3-29: System Settings Networking wireless connections (Cinnamon) 89

Figure 3-30: System Settings Networking wireless History (Cinnamon) 89

Figure 3-31: System Settings Networking wireless information (Cinnamon).................... 90

Figure 3-32: Proxy settings (System Settings Networking) (Cinnamon)........................... 90

Figure 3-33: Connect to a Hidden Wireless Network... 91

Figure 3-34: Warpinator UFW Firewall Automatic Configuration 92

Figure 3-35: Warpinator FirewallD Configuration with warpinator service...................... 92

Figure 3-36: Warpinator Host List.. 93

Figure 3-37: Warpinator - selecting files to send 93

Figure 3-38: Warpinator - File Transfer... 94

Figure 3-39: Warpinator - Completed Transfer 94

Figure 3-40: Warpinator - Received Transfer Approval 94

Figure 3-41: Warpinator - Received Transfer.. 95

Figure 3-42: Warpinator Preferences.. 96

Figure 3-43: Desktop Printer applet menu with print jobs... 96

Figure 3-44: Hardware Drivers: Driver Manager 97

Figure 3-45: Displays... 98

Figure 3-46: Color Management dialog 99

Figure 3-47: Color Management dialog 100

Figure 3-48: Online Accounts.. 101

Figure 3-49: System Reports - System reports 102

Figure 3-50: System Reports - Crash reports 102

Figure 3-51: System Reports - System information... 103

Figure 3-52: Terminal Window... 105

Figure 3-53: Terminal Window without menubar.. 105

Figure 3-54: Terminal Window Find dialog 105

Figure 3-55: Terminal Window with tabs... 106

Figure 3-56: Terminal Window Profile configuration 107

Figure 4-1: Software Sources Linux Mint Official Repositories. 115

Figure 4-2: Software Sources Mirrors 115

Figure 4-3: Software Sources Additional Repositories.. 116

Figure 4-4: Software Sources PPA 116

Figure 4-5: Software Sources Authentication Keys.. 117

Figure 4-6: Update Welcome 118

Figure 4-7: Update Manager update icon and package information dialog 118

Figure 4-8: Update Manager with selected packages.. 119

Figure 4-9: Update download and install 119

Figure 4-10: Update Manager Preferences - Options.. 120

Figure 4-11: Update Manager - Linux Kernel dialog.. 121

Figure 4-12: Timeshift - snapshots... 122

Figure 4-13: Snapshot wizard... 123

Figure 4-14: Snapshot wizard - Location... 123

Figure 4-15: Snapshot wizard - Level... 124

Figure 4-16: Timeshift Settings - Users tab.. 124

Figure 4-17: Timeshift Settings - Filters tab 125

Figure 4-18: Software Manager... 126

Figure 4-19: Software Manager sub-categories.. 126

Figure 4-20: Software Manager search... 127

Figure 4-21: Software Manager application 128

Figure 4-22: Software Manager Installing application 129

Figure 4-23: Software Manager Currently working on packages.................................. 129

Figure 4-24: Software Manager Installing multiple applications 130

Figure 4-25: Software Manager - Flatpak Package List 131

Figure 4-26: Software Manager - Flatpak Package.. 131

Figure 4-27: Synaptic Package Manager: Quick search 133

Figure 4-28: Synaptic Package Manager: Sections 134

Figure 4-29: Synaptic Package Manager: Status 134

Figure 4-30: GDebi Package Installer 136

Figure 4-31: Listing of popular available snaps: find..147

Figure 4-32: Listing of installed snaps: list 149

Figure 4-33: Snap Store on menu..153

Figure 4-34: Snap Store on Linux Mint...154

Figure 4-35: Snap Store categories..154

Figure 4-36: Snap Store software page 155

Figure 4-37: Snap Store (snapcraft.io) snap package channels..155

Figure 4-38: Snap Store package permissions...156

Figure 4-39: Snap Store installed packages 156

Figure 5-1: Thingy X-App Document Manager (Library)..162

Figure 5-2: Xreader X-App Document Viewer 162

Figure 5-3: Xed X-App editor...164

Figure 5-4: Xviewer X-App Image Viewer 168

Figure 5-5: Pix X-App Image Viewer, Organizer, and Editor 169

Figure 5-6: Linux Mint mint-meta-codecs install..171

Figure 5-7: Celluloid Video Player 173

Figure 5-8: Hypnotix (IPTV Player)...175

Figure 5-9: Web Apps..178

Figure 5-10: Web Apps, adding...179

Figure 5-11: Web Apps, on menu, desktop, and panel 179

Figure 5-12: GNOME FTP access Connect to Server dialog 182

Figure 5-13: GNOME FTP access with Connect to Server and the file manager 183

Figure 6-1: Cinnamon desktop..188

Figure 6-2: Cinnamon desktop with Cinnamon Menu and Nemo file manager................189

Figure 6-3: Desktop menu and Current Monitor Layout window (Customize)..............190

Figure 6-4: Desktop Settings...190

Figure 6-5: Desklets Manage tab..191

Figure 6-6: Desklets Download and Settings tabs...192

Figure 6-7: System Settings Hot Corners 193

Figure 6-8: System Settings Keyboard, Keyboard Shortcuts..194

Figure 6-9: Cinnamon menu 195

Figure 6-10: Cinnamon menu search 196

Figure 6-11: Cinnamon menu favorites.. 196

Figure 6-12: Cinnamon menu.. 197

Figure 6-13: Cinnamon Linux Mint menu menu configuration 198

Figure 6-14: Cinnamon Main Menu editor.. 199

Figure 6-15: Windows Settings: Titlebar tab 200

Figure 6-16: Windows Settings: Behavior tab 200

Figure 6-17: Windows Settings: Alt-tab tab... 201

Figure 6-18: Window Tiling and Edge Flip 201

Figure 6-19: Window List button menus 202

Figure 6-20: Window List Preferences menu.. 203

Figure 6-21: Grouped Window List configuration - General and Panel tabs...................... 203

Figure 6-22: Window List Button Labels - None, Application, Title 204

Figure 6-23: Window List Button Thumbnails 204

Figure 6-24: Grouped Window List Configuration - Thumbnails tab 205

Figure 6-25: Windows QuickList menu... 206

Figure 6-26: Scale: zoomed windows to switch windows (Hot corners, Show all windows)
.... 206

Figure 6-27: Window switching with Alt-Tab (Icons and Thumbnails)............................... 207

Figure 6-28: Window switching with Alt-Tab (Coverflow 3D) 208

Figure 6-29: System Settings Effects 208

Figure 6-30: Workspace Switcher applet.. 209

Figure 6-31: Hot Corner with Expo enabled 210

Figure 6-32: Expo workspace configuration (square grid).................................... 210

Figure 6-33: Expo workspace configuration (no grid) 211

Figure 6-34: System Settings Workspaces 211

Figure 6-35: The Linux Mint panel with menu, grouped window list, and applets, at the
bottom of Linux Mint desktop.. 212

Figure 6-36:XApp Status Applet system tray with mouse wheel support and
XAppStatusicon icons... 212

Figure 6-37: The panel pop-up menu (right-click on middle) and panel applet menu 213

Figure 6-38: The panel menu Troubleshoot submenu... 213

Figure 6-39: The Linux Mint panel in edit mode..214

Figure 6-40: The panel settings dialog...214

Figure 6-41: The Applets Dialog Manage tab..215

Figure 6-42: The Applets dialog "Available applets (online)" tab........................216

Figure 6-43: Traditional Layout panel..217

Figure 6-44: Traditional Layout Panel Launchers applets and menus..................218

Figure 6-45: Traditional Layout User applet...218

Figure 6-46: Traditional Layout switches..218

Figure 6-47: Nemo file manager home folders..219

Figure 6-48: File manager with sidebar..220

Figure 6-49: File manager sidebar with bookmarks menu.....................................221

Figure 6-50: File manager sidebar Places menus, expanded and unexpanded......221

Figure 6-51: File manager sidebar Treeview menus, expanded and unexpanded...222

Figure 6-52: File manager window with tabs...222

Figure 6-53: File manager File, View, and Edit menus..223

Figure 6-54: Favorites...227

Figure 6-55: File manager navigation...228

Figure 6-56: Expanded and unexpanded paths and location.................................229

Figure 6-57: Nemo File Manager Search..230

Figure 6-58: Bulky bulk rename..231

Figure 6-59: File properties on Nemo..233

Figure 6-60: Choose an Icon for a file, folder, or application...............................234

Figure 6-61: Nemo File Manager Preferences...235

Figure 6-62: Nemo Plugins and Extensions...236

Figure 6-63: System Settings dialog (Appearance and Preferences)....................237

Figure 6-64: System Settings dialog (Hardware and Administration)...................237

Figure 6-65: Backgrounds: Images tab...241

Figure 6-66: Backgrounds: Settings tab..241

Figure 6-67: Font Selection...242

Figure 6-68: Themes - Applications...243

Figure 6-69: Themes - Desktops..244

Figure 6-70: Themes (Online Themes) 244

Figure 6-71: Themes (Settings tab) 245

Figure 6-72: Preferred Applications 246

Figure 6-73: Preferred Applications: Removable media 247

Figure 6-74: Calendar applet 247

Figure 6-75: Date & Time settings, network time 248

Figure 6-76: Calendar applet 249

Figure 6-77: Screensaver Settings tab 249

Figure 6-78: Screensaver - Customize tab 250

Figure 6-79: Languages 251

Figure 6-80: Input Method 251

Figure 6-81: Accessibility 252

Figure 6-82: Startup Applications Preferences 252

Figure 6-83: Extension Manage tab 253

Figure 6-84: Extensions Download tab 253

Figure 6-85: Notifications 254

Figure 6-86: Privacy 254

Figure 6-87: General 255

Figure 6-88: System Info 255

Figure 6-89: System Settings, Mouse and Touchpad 256

Figure 6-90: GNOME Power Manager menu and applet configuration 257

Figure 6-91: GNOME Power Manager 257

Figure 6-92: GNOME Power Manager: Brightness tab 258

Figure 6-93: Keyboard Typing 258

Figure 6-94: Keyboard: Layouts tab 259

Figure 6-95: Keyboard Layout Options 259

Figure 7-1: MATE desktop and panel 262

Figure 7-2: MATE with Linux Mint menu and Caja file manager 263

Figure 7-3: MATE Desktop Settings 264

Figure 7-4: MATE window 266

Figure 7-5: Switching Windows with thumbnails 266

Figure 7-6: Window List applet...267

Figure 7-7: Window List Preferences 267

Figure 7-8: Workspace switcher, one row and two rows 268

Figure 7-9: Switching workspaces, Ctrl-Alt-*arrow*..................................268

Figure 7-10: Workspace Switcher Preferences 268

Figure 7-11: Linux Mint Menu for MATE..269

Figure 7-12: Linux Mint Menu search 270

Figure 7-13: Linux Mint Menu Applications pop-up menu. 270

Figure 7-14: Linux Mint Menu Favorites 271

Figure 7-15: Linux Mint Menu Preferences dialog.....................................271

Figure 7-16: Linux Mint Menu with Recent Documents option - General tab.................272

Figure 7-17: MATE Panel..273

Figure 7-18: MATE Panel pop-up menu 273

Figure 7-19: MATE Panel Properties..274

Figure 7-20: MATE Panel "Add to Panel" dialog for panel applets 276

Figure 7-21: Caja file manager home folders..278

Figure 7-22: Caja file manager with sidebar 279

Figure 7-23: Caja navigation buttons: back, forward, parent, home, computer..............279

Figure 7-24: Caja locations: unexpanded, expanded, and location path 280

Figure 7-25: File manager side pane menu and views 281

Figure 7-26: File manager side pane with bookmarks menu......................282

Figure 7-27: File manager window with tabs..283

Figure 7-28: File manager File, Edit, and View menus 284

Figure 7-29: File manager File | Open with submenu for folders and files 287

Figure 7-30: File properties on Caja..290

Figure 7-31: GNOME Control Center..293

Figure 7-32: Mouse and Keyboard Preferences 296

Figure 7-33: About Me: Preferences | About Me 297

Figure 7-34: Selecting GNOME themes..297

Figure 7-35: Choosing a desktop background, System | Preferences | Appearance 299

Figure 7-36: Fonts...299

Figure 7-37: MATE Power Manager 301

Figure 7-38: Preferred Applications tool 302

Figure 7-39: File Management Preferences for Media 303

Figure 7-40: Screensaver Preferences 304

Figure 7-41: Assistive Technologies Preferences and Accessibility Preferred Applications 304

Figure 7-42: Popup Notifications 305

Figure 8-1: GNOME System Monitor: Resources 311

Figure 8-2: GNOME System Monitor: Processes 312

Figure 8-3: Glances System Monitor 313

Figure 8-4: Logs 315

Figure 8-5: Disk Usage Analyzer 315

Figure 8-6: Disk Usage Analyzer: Scan dialog 316

Figure 8-7: The ClamTK tool for ClamAV virus protection. 316

Figure 8-8: Disk Utility 318

Figure 8-9: Disk Utility, hard drive 319

Figure 8-10: Disk Utility, Volumes 319

Figure 8-11: Disk Utility: Hard Disk hardware SMART data 320

Figure 8-12: Sound Menu 322

Figure 8-13: Sound Menu, right click, mute options 322

Figure 8-14: Sound: Sounds 323

Figure 8-15: Sound: Input 323

Figure 8-16: Sound: Output 324

Figure 8-17: Sound: Applications 324

Figure 8-18: Sound: Settings 325

Figure 8-19: PulseAudio Volume Control, Playback 326

Figure 8-20: PulseAudio Volume Control, Output Devices 327

Figure 8-21: dconf editor 328

Figure 8-22: Seahorse Passwords and Keys (version 3.3) 329

Figure 8-23: Seahorse Keyring key Properties dialog 329

Figure 8-24: Choose Encryption key type 330

Figure 8-25: Create Encryption key 330

Figure 8-26: Passphrase for encryption key...330

Figure 8-27: My Personal Keys...331

Figure 8-28: GnuPGP key dialog: Owner tab..331

Figure 8-29: GnuPGP key dialog: Details tab 332

Figure 8-30: Seahorse Preferences - Keyservers..332

Figure 8-31: Seahorse Add Key Server 333

Figure 8-32: Seahorse Preferences with added Ubuntu key server......................333

Figure 8-33: Searching for keys 334

Figure 8-34: Importing keys...334

Figure 8-35: Key information 334

Figure 8-36: Imported keys..335

Figure 8-37: Imported key Trust tab for an unsigned key...335

Figure 8-38: Signing a key 335

Figure 8-39: Signed key 336

Figure 8-40: Trusted keys 336

Figure 8-41: Seahorse Preferences..337

Figure 9-1: Nemo File Manager with Elevated Privileges (as root).....................346

Figure 9-2: Prompt to open file manager as root (administrative access) 346

Figure 9-3: Editing System Files from the file manager opened as root 347

Figure 9-4: pkexec prompt for secure access 347

Figure 9-5: Invoking Xed with the pkexec command 349

Figure 9-6: Users and Groups (Cinnamon) 350

Figure 9-7: Users and Groups: new users...350

Figure 9-8: Users and Groups: inactive user...351

Figure 9-9: Users and Groups: password dialog 351

Figure 9-10: Users and Groups: Groups tab 352

Figure 9-11: Users and Groups: add a group...352

Figure 9-12: Users and Groups: Users group dialog 352

Figure 9-13: Users and Groups (MATE) 353

Figure 9-14: User Settings: Change User Password dialog 354

Figure 9-15: User Settings: Change User Account Type 354

Figure 9-16: Users and Groups: Change User Privileges 355

Figure 9-17: Users and Groups: Create New User.. 356

Figure 9-18: Users and Groups: new user password 356

Figure 9-19: Users and Groups: Groups settings... 357

Figure 9-20: Group Properties: Group Users panel 357

Figure 9-21: Access permission on user's home folder 360

Figure 9-22: Accessing shared folders using multicast DNS discovery (Avahi) 362

Figure 9-23: Permission to access a remote shared Linux folder... 362

Figure 9-24: Accessing and mounting a shared Linux folders using Avahi........................ 362

Figure 9-25: Gufw and FirewallD configuration for multicast DNS discovery (Avahi), mdns
service 363

Figure 9-26: Network authorization 364

Figure 9-27: Connect to Server... 365

Figure 9-28: Mount remote Windows shares 365

Figure 9-29: Window remote host... 365

Figure 9-30: Folder Sharing prompt to install Samba 366

Figure 9-31: Folder Sharing Options 367

Figure 9-32: Folder Share panel 367

Figure 9-33: Folder Sharing permissions prompt 368

Figure 9-34: Samba Firewall Configuration, Gufw (UFW) and firewall-config (FirewallD)
.... 369

Figure 9-35: Accessing Linux Shared Folders from Windows.. 369

Figure 9-36: File Permissions 370

Figure 9-37: Folder Permissions 371

Figure 9-38: Bluetooth Settings (System Settings).. 373

Figure 9-39: Bluetooth Adapters 373

Figure 9-40: Bluetooth Plugins... 374

Figure 9-41: Bluetooth Local Services... 374

Figure 9-42: Bluetooth Device menu 375

Figure 9-43: Bluetooth Devices 376

Figure 9-44: Bluetooth Sound... 376

Figure 9-45: Bluetooth Setup Device Wizard: phone... 377

Figure 9-46: Bluetooth applet menu 377

Figure 9-47: Editing the /etc/default/grub file 381

Figure 9-48: Backup Tool 383

Figure 9-49: Backup Tool backup 383

Figure 9-50: Deja Dup settings - overview 384

Figure 9-51: Deja Dup Preferences... 384

Figure 9-52; Deja Dup settings - storage for Windows share and Local folder 385

Figure 9-53: Deja Dup settings - backup times... 385

Figure 9-54: Deja Dup settings - Folders to save and ignore....................... 386

Figure 9-55: Deja Dup backup: encryption 386

Figure 9-56: Deja Dup backup: encryption 387

Figure 9-57: Deja Dup Restore.. 387

Figure 9-58: Deja Dup restore locations.. 387

Figure 10-1: Network Manager wired, wireless, and disconnect icons. 403

Figure 10-2: Network Manager applet menu 403

Figure 10-3: Network (System Settings) Wi-Fi Tab and History..................... 404

Figure 10-4: Network wireless configuration: Security tab 404

Figure 10-5: Network wireless configuration: Identity tab............................. 405

Figure 10-6: Network wireless configuration: IP tabs, manual...................... 405

Figure 10-7: Network wired tab 406

Figure 10-8: Network wired configuration dialog 406

Figure 10-9: Network wired configuration, Security.. 407

Figure 10-10: Network wired configuration, Identity...................................... 407

Figure 10-11: Network wired configuration, IPv4 407

Figure 10-12: VPN Selection... 408

Figure 10-13: VPN configuration.. 408

Figure 10-14: Network Connections... 409

Figure 10-15: Choosing a connection type for a new network connection....... 409

Figure 10-16: New connection types.. 410

Figure 10-17: General tab 410

Figure 10-18: DHCP Wired Configuration 411

Figure 10-19: Manual IPv4 Wired Configuration...412

Figure 10-20: Manual IPv6 Wired Configuration...412

Figure 10-21: 802.1 Security Configuration 413

Figure 10-22: Wi-Fi configuration 413

Figure 10-23: Wi-Fi Security: WEP and WPA 414

Figure 10-24: DSL manual configuration 414

Figure 10-25: Mobile Broadband Wizard 415

Figure 10-26: Mobile Broadband Provider Listings..415

Figure 10-27: Mobile Broadband configuration...415

Figure 10-28: PPP Configuration...416

Figure 10-29: VPN connection types..417

Figure 10-30: VPN configuration (openvpn)...417

Figure 10-31: VPN configuration (pptp) 418

Figure 10-32: WireGuard configuration 419

Figure 10-33: Gufw...435

Figure 10-34: Gufw Preconfigured rules 435

Figure 10-35: Gufw Simple rules 436

Figure 10-36: Gufw Advanced rules...437

Figure 10-37: Gufw edit a rule 437

Figure 10-38: Gufw create a rule for an active port 438

Figure 10-39: firewall-config: Runtime Configuration..441

Figure 10-40: firewall-config: Permanent Configuration..442

Figure 10-41: Default Zone 442

Figure 10-42: Base Zone Settings 443

Figure 10-43: Service Settings 443

Figure 10-44: Service Protocols and Ports 444

Figure 10-45: Port Forwarding 444

Figure 10-46: ICMP Filters 445

Figure 10-47: Gnome network tool 447

Figure 12-1: Services: cockpit...499

Figure 12-2: SSH setup and access...510

Figure 13-1: system-config-printer tool...522

Figure 13-2: Printer properties window 523

Figure 13-3: Printer configuration window Printer menu.....................................523

Figure 13-4: Printer queue...524

Figure 13-5: Server Settings..524

Figure 13-6: Selecting a CUPS server...524

Figure 13-7: Printer Options 525

Figure 13-8: Jobs Options..526

Figure 13-9: Set Default Printer 526

Figure 13-10: System-wide and personal default printers....................................527

Figure 13-11: Selecting a new printer connection: connected and unconnected...........528

Figure 13-12: Printer manufacturer for new printers..528

Figure 13-13: Searching for a printer driver from the OpenPrinting repository.............529

Figure 13-14: Printer Model and driver for new printers using local database.............529

Figure 13-15: Printer Name and Location for new printers....................................530

Figure 13-16: CUPS Web-based Configuration Tool: Home tab 530

Figure 13-17: CUPS Web-based Configuration Tool: Administration tab..............531

Figure 13-18: Adding a new printer: CUP Web Interface 531

Figure 13-19: CUPS Web-based Configuration Tool: Printers tab.........................532

Figure 13-20: CUPS Web-based Configuration Tool: Managing Printers...............532

Figure 13-21: CUPS Web-based Configuration Tool: Printer Options....................533

Figure 13-22: Finding a network printer...534

Figure 13-23: Selecting a Windows printer with full name and authentication..............535

Figure 13-24: Remote Windows printer Settings 535

Figure 13-25: Remote Windows Printers...536

Figure 13-26: CUPS Web-based Configuration Tool: Network Printers.................536

Figure 13-27: CUPS Web-based Configuration Tool - Windows Remote Printer 537

Figure 13-28: CUPS Web-based Configuration Tool - Remote Printer Name and Location
....538

Figure 15-1: Gufw Samba Firewall Access 571

Figure 15-2: FirewallD Samba Firewall Access (samba, samb-client, mdns).....................572

Index

.bash_logout, 473
.bashrc, 469
.local
   Avahi, 363
.mount, 493
.path, 490
.profile, 465, 466
.service, 486
.socket, 488
.target, 483, 492
.wine, 137
/dev/mapper, 395
/etc/apparmor, 505
/etc/apparmor.d, 505
/etc/apt/sources.list, 113
/etc/bash.bashrc, 471
/etc/default, 499
/etc/fstab, 493
/etc/hostname, 349
/etc/nsswitch.conf, 563
/etc/profile, 468
/etc/profile.d, 468
/etc/ssh/ssh_confi, 515
/etc/systemd/system, 481, 485
/lib/systemd/system, 478, 481
/media, 359

A

aa-genprof, 505
Active Directory Domain Controller, 586
Administration
   Cockpit, 499
   Disk Usage Analyzer, 315
   GDebi Package Installer, 136
   glances, 313
   GNOME System Monitor, 310
   Linux Mint Administrative Tools, 340
   Linux Mint System Tools, 309
   Logs, 314
   MATE Control Center, 292

new printers, 527
pkexec, 347
PolicyKit, 341
Puppet, 506
root user, 345
services, 358, 478
Snap Store, 153
Software Manager, 125
su, 345
sudo, 343
Synaptic Package Manager, 133
systemctl, 498
systemd, 358, 478
Tools
   Blueman device manager, 372
   Gufw, 434
   Linux kernels, 121
   Services, 358
   System Monitor, 310
   system-config-printer, 522
   terminal window, 104
   Timeshift, 122
   Update Manager, 117
   virus protection, 316
  Upgrade Tool, 38
Administrative Tools, 340
Advanced Linux Sound Architecture, 321
Advanced Package Tool, 110
Aliases, 456
alien, 144
ALSA
  alsamixer, 321
  amixer, 321
alsamixer, 321
Amanda, 389
AMD
  DKMS, 378
amixer, 321
AppArmor, 503
  /etc/apparmor.d, 505
  aa-genprof, 505

apparmor_status, 504
apparmor_status, 504
Appearance, 240, 297
  System Settings, 240
applets, 215, 277
  network, 86
  sound menu, 322
  time & date menu, 247
Applications
  administration, 340
  burners, 177
  databases, 164
  defaults, 231, 289
    Cinnamon, 245
  document manager, 162
  document viewers, 162
  ebook readers, 163
  editors, 163
  email, 166
  FTP, 180
  GDebi Package Installer, 136
  GStreamer, 170
  Internet, 177
  mail, 166
  messenger, 183
  multimedia, 170
  music, 172
  networks, 400
  newsreaders, 167
  Office, 159
  removable media, 246
  Snap Store, 153
  Software Manager, 125
  Synaptic Package Manager, 133
  TV, 176
  video, 172
  VoIP, 183
  web browsers, 177
  X-Apps, 159
apt, 140
  install, 141
APT, 110, 145
  apt, 140
  apt-get, 140
apt cache tools, 142
apt-cache, 143
apt-get, 140

install, 141
update, 142
upgrade, 142
Archive Manager, 84
auth_admin_keep, 342
Authentication
  root user, 345
  su, 345
  sudo, 343
Avahi, 359
  FirewallD, 362
  mDNS, 361
  mdns.allow, 363
  mdns4, 363
  Samba, 364
  shared file systems, 361, 364

B

backgrounds
  Cinnamon, 240
  MATE, 298
Backports
  repository, 112, 113
backup, 382
  Amanda, 389
  Backup Tool, 383
  BackupPC, 389
  Deja Dup, 382, 384
    restore, 386
  duplicity, 382, 384
  rsync, 388
  shapshots, 122
  tar, 388
  Timeshift, 122
BackupPC, 389
bad
  Gstreamer, 172
base
  Gstreamer, 172
bash.bashrc, 471
bash_completion, 469
BASH_ENV, 463
bash_logout, 473
bashrc, 469
battery, 301
BitTorrent, 180

Transmission, 180
Blueman device manager, 372
Bluetooth, 372
  Blueman, 372
  sound, 376
bookmarks, 219, 278
boot
  fstab mount units, 493
  graphical.target, 485
  runlevels, 492
  special targets, 492
Boot Repair, 61
Bootloader
  Boot Repair, 61
  configuration, 379
  edit, 65
  GRUB, 64, 379
  GRUB_DEFAULT, 380
  grub-install, 62
  Linux Mint theme, 65
  Plymouth, 65, 320
  re-install, 61
  update-grub, 382
Brasero, 177
brightness
  System Settings, 249, 304
Bulky, 230

C

Caja, 77, 278
  bookmarks, 278
  desktop settings, 278
  displaying files and folders, 283
  File Manager search, 288
  file properties, 290
  folder properties, 291
  media, 303
  navigation, 284
  preferences, 291
  side pane, 282
  tabs, 283
  xdg-user-dirs, 278
calendar, 247
calendar menu, 247
Calibre
  E-book reader, 163

Calligra Suite, 161
CD Burners and Rippers, 177
CD burning, 84
CD/DVD disc images
  Archive Manager, 84
Celluliod, 172, 173
channels
  Snap, 149
Chrony, 500
chrony.conf, 501
cifs, 589
Cinnamon, 73, 188
  Appearance, 240
  applets, 215
  application defaults, 245
  backgrounds, 240
  calendar, 247
  date, 247
  dconf, 327
  desklets, 190
  desktop icons, 190
  documentation, 103
  expo, 192
  Expo, 209
  Expo applet, 209
  favorites, 196
  File Manager, 75
  FTP, 220
  grouped window list, 202
  input method, 251
  keyboard, 258
  keyboard shortcuts, 193
  languages, 250
  layouts, 81
  menu
    Cinnamon, 195
  menu (edit), 199
  modern layout, 212
  Nemo, 219
  notifications, 254
  panel, 212
  privacy, 254
  removable media, 246
  Startup Applications, 252
  switching windows, 206
  system info, 255
  system tray, 212

themes, 242
tiles, 205
time, 247
traditional layout, 217
universal access, 251
Users and Groups, 349
Web Apps, 178
windows, 199
windows quicklist menu, 205
workspace switcher applet, 209
XApp Status Applet, 212
XAppStatusicon, 212
Cinnamon Power Manager, 256
cinnamon-settings-users, 349
ClamAV
virus protection, 316
clocks
GNOME Clocks, 164
Cockpit
services, 499
codecs, 117
Matroska, 176
MPEG-4, 176
Xvid, 176
color profiles, 99
command line, 107
terminal window, 104
command line interface, 71
commands, 107
Common Unix Printing System (CUPS), 518
Common User Directory Structure, 219, 278
compression
LZMA, 388
Computer folder, 82
configuration, 539
dconf editor, 327
networks, 402
system-config-printer, 522
configuration files
editing, 378
configuring users, 349, 353
confinement
Snap, 150
Connect to Server
FTP, 182
connections
hidden wireless, 91

networks, 86
options, 88
wired, 86
wireless, 87
Control Center
MATE, 292
cron, 314
CUPS, 518
configuration, 539
cups-browsed.conf, 545
cupsctl, 543
cupsd.conf, 539
cups-files.conf, 544
lpadmin, 546
print clients, 545
printers.conf, 543
subscription.conf, 544
system-config-printer, 522
cupsaccept, 548
cups-browsed.conf, 545
cupsctl, 543
cupsd.conf, 538, 539
cupsdisable, 548
cupsenable, 548
cups-files.conf, 544
cupsreject, 548

D

Database Management Systems, 164
database servers
MySQL, 164
PostgreSQL, 164
Databases
LibreOffice, 165
MySQL, 165
PostgreSQL, 165
SQL Databases, 165
date
timedatectl, 249
dconf editor, 327
DEB, 139
Debian alternatives system, 320
default applications
MATE, 303
System Settings
Cinnamon, 245

default.plymouth, 320
Deja Dup, 382, 384
  restore, 386
desklets, 190
Desktop
  Appearance, 240
  backgrounds
    Cinnamon, 240
    MATE, 298
  Cinnamon, 73, 188
  dconf, 327
  default applications, 231, 289
  desklets, 190
  desktop settings
    MATE, 264
  displaying files and folders, 223, 283
  expo, 192
  Expo, 209
  Expo applet, 209
  favorites, 196, 225, 269
  file manager, 75, 77
  file properties, 233, 290
  fonts
    MATE, 299
  FTP, 220
  icon chooser, 233
  icons
    Cinnamon, 190
    MATE, 264
  keyboard
    Cinnamon, 258
  keyboard shortcuts, 193
  layouts
    Cinnamon, 81
  Linux Mint Administrative Tools, 340
  Linx Mint menu
    MATE, 269
  MATE, 76, 262
  menu, 199
    Cinnamon, 195
    MATE, 269
  modern layout
    Cinnamon, 212
  Nemo, 219
  notifications
    Cinnamon, 254
  online accounts (GNOME), 101

  panel
    Cinnamon, 212
    MATE, 272
  Power Manager
    Cinnamon, 256
    MATE, 300
  privacy
    Cinnamon, 254
  Removable media, 83
  shut down, 71
  spices, 188
  startup applications
    Cinnamon, 252
  switching windows
    Cinnamon, 206
  system tray, 212
  themes
    Cinnamon, 242
    MATE, 297
  tiles, 205
  traditional layout
    Cinnamon, 217
  Web Apps, 178
  window list, 267
  windows, 199, 266
  workspace switcher applet, 209, 268
  workspaces
    MATE, 268
  XFce, 78
devices
  Bluetooth, 372
  Computer folder, 82
  Udisks, 318
disk crashes
  System Reports, 101
Disk Usage Analyzer, 315
Disk Utility, 318
  burning ISO, 84
display
  AMD, 98
  configuration, 96
  Displays, 96
  HiDPI settins, 99
  Nvidia, 97
  Nvidia Optimus, 98
  System Settings, 98
  vendor drivers, 97

display manager
LightDM, 66
DivX, 176
Xvid, 176
dkms, 378
DKMS, 377
dkms command, 377
document manager
Thingy (Library), 162
Document Viewers, 162
Okular, 162
Xreader, 162
documentation
GNOME, 103
info pages, 104
Linux Mint User Guide, 103
Man pages, 103
domain controller
active directory, 586
Domain Controller
active directory, 586
download, 180
dpkg, 140, 142, 144
alien, 144
dpkg-query, 143
Dragon Player, 174
drawers, 277
Drawing, 169
DSL, 414
dual-booting, 42
duplicity, 382, 384
DVB
Kaffeine, 176
DVD
burning, 84
Brasero, 85
Disk Image Writer, 84
K3b, 177
Linux Mint, 29
DVD burning, 84
DVI
Okular, 162
Dynamic IP Address, 401
Dynamic Kernel Module Support, 377

E

E-book reader
Calibre, 163
Foliate, 163
ecryptfs, 100
edit
GRUB, 65
editions
Linux Mint, 28
Editors, 157, 163
Xed, 163
Email, 166
Encryption
ecryptfs, 100
importing public keys, 333
installation, 49
recovery key, 50
keyrings, 329
Port Forwarding, 514
private encrypted directory, 100
Seahorse, 328
sharing keys, 336
SSH, 507
ssh-keygen, 510
Engrampa, 388
Environment Variables, 458
Expo, 192, 209
Expo applet, 209
export, 458
exports, 554

F

favorites
Cinnamon, 196
MATE, 269
File Manager, 229, 288
bookmarks, 219, 278
Bulky, 230
Caja, 278
Caja preferences, 291
Computer folder, 82
default applications
MATE, 303
desktop icons, 219

desktop settings, 278
displaying files and folders, 223
   Caja, 283
Favorites folder, 225
navigation
   Caja, 284
   Nemo, 227
Nemo, 219
preferences
   Nemo, 234
rename, 230
side pane
   Caja, 282
sidebar, 220
tabs, 222, 283
thumbnails, 223
user home folder permissions, 360
user shared folders, 361
xdg-user-dirs, 219, 278
file permission
   GNOME, 370
File Roller, 388
file systems, 359, 493
  encryption, 49
  fstab, 371
  Linux, 359
  LVM, 389
  NTFS, 359
  Windows, 359
  ZFS, 389, 396
File Systems
  encryption
    recovery key, 50
files
  default applications, 231, 289
  display, 223, 283
  favorites, 225
  properties, 233, 290
  Warpinator, 91
  XAppIconChooser, 233
Firefox
  FTP, 181
Firewall, 433
  Avahi, 362
  firewall-config, 440, 441
  FirewallD, 440
  Gufw, 434

iptables-nft, 433
masquerading, 444
nftables, 433
ports, 433
Ports, 444
Samba, 571, 572
ufw, 434, 438
Warpinator, 91
firewall-config, 440, 441
FirewallD, 440
  Avahi, 362
  mdns, 362
  nftables, 433
  Samba, 368, 572
  Warpinator, 92
folders
  display, 223, 283
  favorites, 225
  properties, 234, 291
    Caja, 291
  user shared folders, 361
Foliate
  E-book reader, 163
fonts
  MATE, 299
fstab, 371, 493, 560
FTP, 181
  Cinnamon, 220
  Connect to Server, 182
  Linux Mint desktop, 220, 283
  Nemo, 182
  sftp, 514
  SSH, 182
FTP Clients, 180

G

GDebi Package Installer, 136
GIMP, 168
Glances, 313
GNOME
  Clocks, 164
  dconf, 327
  display configuration, 96
  display manager (LightDM), 66
  documentation, 103
  DVD/CD burner, 84

file permission, 370
folder properties, 234, 291
Foliate, 163
groups, 351, 357
Gufw, 434
logs, 314
Panel Objects, 275
Photos, 168
shared folders, 364, 588
GNOME Control Center, 292
GNOME movie player, 173
GNOME office applications, 161
GNOME System Monitor, 310
Processes, 311
gnome-nettool, 446
GNU General Public License, 35
good
Gstreamer, 172
GPG keys
Passwords and Keys, 330
Grand Unified Bootloader, 379
graphical.target, 485
Graphics
default applications
MATE, 303
Drawing, 169
GIMP, 168
Inkscape, 169
Pix, 168
Xviewer, 168
Grouped Window List, 202
groups
managing, 351, 357
Users and Groups
GNOME, 351, 357
GRUB, 64, 379
Boot Repair, 61
configuration, 379
editing, 65
grub-install, 62
grub-set-default, 381
History (ZFS), 397
Linux Mint theme, 65
re-installing the boot loader, 61
update-grub, 382
GRUB 2, 379
GRUB_DEFAULT, 380

grub2-theme-mint, 65
grub-install, 62
grub-set-default, 381
GStreamer, 170
bad, 172
base, 172
good, 172
Plug-ins, 171
ugly, 172
Gufw, 434

H

hard drives
SMART information, 320
hardware sensors, 317
HDTV, 176
Kaffeine, 176
Help
info pages, 104
Man pages, 103
help.ubuntu.com, 34
hidden wireless networks, 91
High Dots per Inch, 99
HOME, 461
hostname, 349
hostnamectl, 349
hosts.allow, 559
Hypnotix, 174

I

icons
Cinnamon, 190
MATE, 264
XappIconChooser, 233
XappStatusicon, 212
import
repository, 112
importing public keys, 333
info, 104
info pages, 104
inittab, 478
Inkscape, 169
input method
System Settings
Cinnamon, 251

install, 141
Installation
 computer name, 58
 encryption, 49
 help, 38
 Linux Mint, 38
 Live DVD/USB, 44
 LVM, 49
 overview, 38
 partitions, 47
 Prepare disk space, 47
 recovery key, 50
 reuse existing Linux partitions, 56
 specify partitions manually (advanced), 53
 upgrade from 20.3, 38
 user, 58
interfaces
 Snap, 150
iptables
 nftables, 433
iptables-nft, 433
IPTV
 Hypnotix, 174
IPv6, 411

J

Java, 180
 OpenJDK, 180
Java Runtime Environment, 180
JRE, 180

K

K3b, 177
Kaffeine, 173, 174, 176
KDE, 28, 73
 Kaffeine, 173
keyboard, 45
 Cinnamon, 258
 MATE, 293
 System Settings
  Cinnamon, 258
keyboard layout
 localectl, 259
keyboard shortcuts, 193
keyrings, 329

Passwords and Keys, 329
keys
 ssh-keygen, 510
keyservers
 Passwords and Keys, 332
kill, 312
Kubuntu, 28, 73

L

languages
 Input Method, 251
 System Settings
  Cinnamon, 250
laptop, 85
 brightness, 249
 Network Manager, 85
 power management, 85
 wireless networks, 85
Layouts, 81
 modern, 212
 traditional, 217
libdvdcss, 117
LibreOffice, 160
 Thingy, 162
LibreOffice Base, 165
libxvidcore, 176
LightDM Display Manager, 66
 configuration, 68
Linux, 35
 Man pages, 103
Linux kernels
 managment, 121
Linux Mint
 Administrative Tools, 340
 Cinnamon, 73, 188
 display configuration, 96
 Displays, 96
 editions, 28
 folder properties, 234, 291
 FTP, 283
 GDebi Package Installer, 136
 Installation, 38
 installation help, 38
 Introduction, 27
 KDE, 28, 73
 laptop, 85

LightDM, 68
Live DVD/USB, 29
Live USB, 31
login window, 68
LTS, 28
MATE, 76, 262
menu
   MATE, 269
recovery, 60
releases, 28
snapshots, 122
software packages, 31
spices, 188
Spices, 188
Synaptic Package Manager, 133
Timeshift, 122
update, 117
upgrade, 38
Users, 349
Users and Groups
   MATE, 353
Linux Mint official-pakcages-
   repositories.list, 113
Linux Mint repositories, 111, 112
Linux Mint Software manager, 125
lm-sensors, 318
localectl
   keyboard layout, 259
   location, 259
location
   localectl, 259
lock
   System Settings, 249, 304
Logical Volume Manager, 389
login
   LightDM display manager, 66
   logind, 64
login window
   preferences, 68
logind, 64
logs
   GNOME Logs, 314
lpadmin, 546
lpc, 545
lpinfo, 548
lpoptions, 546, 548
lpq, 545

lpr, 545
lprm, 545
LVM, 389
   /dev/mapper, 395
   commands, 390
   device names, 395
   encryption, 49
      recovery key, 50
   groups, 391
   installation, 49
   Logical Volumes, 392
   physical volume, 391
   snapshots, 395
   vgcreate, 391
lynx, 522
LZMA, 388

M

Mail, 166
Mail applications, 166
main
   repository, 112
man, 103
Man pages, 103
MariaDB, 166
masquerading, 444
MATE, 76, 262
   adding panel objects, 276
   Appearance, 297
   Applets, 277
   backgrounds, 298
   Caja, 77, 278
   Celluloid, 172, 173
   desktop icons, 264
   desktop settings, 264
   drawers, 277
   favorites, 269
   fonts, 299
   keyboard, 293
   menu, 269
   menu (edit), 271
   panel, 272
   panel objects, 275
   popup notifications, 305
   preferences, 293
   Preferred Applications, 301

themes, 297
universal access, 304
users and groups, 353
window list, 267
windows, 266
workspace switcher applet, 268
workspaces, 268
MATE Power Manager, 300
Matroska, 176
mdns
    Avahi, 361
    FirewallD, 362
    mdns4, 363
    Samba, 361
    user home folder permissions, 360
mdns.allow, 363
menu
    Cinnamon, 195
    edit, 199
    grouped window list, 202
    Linux Mint menu, 269
    MATE, 269
    panel
      MATE, 277
    preferences
      MATE, 271
    windows quicklist menu, 205
Microsoft Domain Security, 584
mintBackup, 383
mintinstall, 125
mint-meta-codecs, 117
mintupgrade, 38
    Upgrade Tool, 38
mkv
    Matroska, 176
Mobile Broadband, 414
Monitoring
    glances, 313
mount
    cifs, 589
MP3, 172
MPEG-4, 176
    Matroska, 176
MPlayer, 173, 174
MPV, 173
multicast DNS discovery, 361, 364
    FirewallD, 362

mdns.allow, 363
    Samba, 364
Multimedia, 170
    applications, 172
    CD Burners and Rippers, 177
    Celluloid, 172, 173
    codecs, 117, 170
    default applications
      MATE, 303
    DVD, 173
    GStreamer, 170
    HDTV, 176
    Hypnotix, 174
    Kaffeine, 173, 176
    Matroska, 176
    mint-meta-codecs, 117
    MPEG-4, 176
    MPlayer, 173
    mpv, 173
    Photos, 168
    PiTiVi Video editor, 174
    Shotcut Video editor, 174
    Sound, 321, 323
    Totem, 173
    TV Players, 174
    VideoLAN, 173
    vlc, 173
    Xvid, 176
multiverse
    repository, 112
Music Applications, 172
MySQL, 164, 165
MythTV, 176

N

Name Service Switch, 563
Nemo, 75, 219
    bookmarks, 219
    Connect to Server, 182
    desktop icons, 219
    File Manager rename, 230
    File Manager search, 229
    file properties, 233
    FTP, 182
    icons (XappIconChooser), 233
    navigation, 227

preferences, 234
xdg-user-dirs, 219
NetBIOS, 568
Netplan, 429
 configuration, 425
 networkctl, 425, 432
 NetworkManager, 432
 systemd-networkd, 425
 Wi-Fi, 431
Nettool, 446
Network Configuration, 399
Network Connections
 Wireguard, 418
Network File System (NFS), 550
Network Information, 401
Network Information Service, 563
Network Information System (NIS), 563
Network Object Model Environment, 262
Network Time Protocol, 500
 Chrony, 500
 chrony.conf, 501
 TOY, 500
 Universal Time Coordinated, 500
 UTC, 500
networkctl, 425, 432
Networking
 link files, 451
 Netplan, 425, 429
 networkctl, 425, 432
 NetworkManager, 432
 nmcli, 419
 predictable network device names, 447
 renaming device names, 450
 renaming network device names, 450, 451
 Samba user shared folders, 361
 systemd-networkd, 426, 451
 udev, 450
 user home folder permissions, 360
 user shared folders, 360
 Wi-Fi, 431
 Zeroconf, 359
NetworkManager, 86, 402
 connections, 86
 device names, 447
 DSL, 414
 hidden wireless, 91
 IPv6, 411

laptop, 85
 manual configuration, 404
 Mobile Broadband, 414
 Network (System Settings), 88
 network menu, 86
 networkctl, 425, 432
 network-manager, 432
 nmcli, 419
 PPP, 416
 udev, 450
 VPN, 416
 wired configuration, 410, 411
 wired connection, 86
 wireless configuration, 413
 wireless connections, 87
 wireless security, 413
NetworkManager Command Line Interface
 (**nmcli**), 419
Networks
 Avahi, 359, 361, 364
 configuration, 402
 connections, 86
 device names, 447
 firewall, 440
 Glances, 313
 hidden wireless networks, 91
 manual configuration, 404, 408
 Mobile Broadband, 414
 multicast DNS discovery, 361, 364
 Nettool, 446
 Network (System Settings), 88
 network connections, 86
 networkctl, 425, 432
 NetworkManager, 86, 402
 nework menu, 86
 nmcli, 419
 PPP, 416
 proxies, 90
 renaming device names, 450, 451
 renaming network device names, 450
 Samba, 361
 shared file systems, 361, 364
 shared folders, 366
 SSID, 91
 System Settings, 88
 systemd link files, 451
 udev, 450

user home folders permissions, 360
Warpinator, 91
wired configuration, 410, 411
wired connections, 86
Wireguard, 418
wireless configuration, 413
wireless connections, 87
Zero Configuration Networking, 359
NeworkManager
   systemd-networkd, 432
newsreaders
   NNTPSERVER, 167
   par2, 168
NFS, 368, 550
   /etc/exports, 554
   fstab, 560
   hosts.allow, 559
   nfs4, 556
   NIS, 563
   options, 555
   rpcbind, 559
nfs4, 556
nfs4_getfacl, 557
nftables, 433
   iptables-nft, 433
NIS, 563
   Name Service Switch, 563
nmbd, 368, 536
nmcli, 419
NNTPSERVER, 167, 465
notifications
   Cinnamon, 254
   System Settings
      Cinnamon, 254
NTFS, 359
Nvidia
   DKMS, 378
   nvidia-settings, 97
   Optimus, 98

O

Office Suites, 159
   Calligra, 161
   GNOME office applications, 161
   LibreOffice, 160
   OpenOffice, 160

Okular, 162
online accounts
   GNOME, 101
Online Accounts, 101
Open Source, 34
OpenJDK, 180
openjdk-11-jre, 180
OpenOffice, 160
OpenSSH, 507
OpenVPN, 417
OpenZFS, 396

P

Package Management Software, 111
packages
   software, 31, 158
packages.mint.com, 139
Panel
   adding objects
      MATE, 276
   Cinnamon, 212
   drawers
      MATE, 277
   layouts, 81
   MATE, 272
   menus, 277
   modern layout, 212
   panel objects
      MATE, 275
   printer applet, 96
   system tray, 212
   traditional layout, 217
   Web Apps, 178
   XApp Status Applet, 212
   XAppStatusicon, 212
par2, 168
Partitions, 47
   blank hard drive, 53
   new partitions, 53
   reusing, 56
passwd, 358
Passwords, 358
   keyrings, 329
Passwords and Keys
   GPG keys, 330
   importing keys, 333

keyrings, 329
keyservers, 332
Seahorse, 328
sharing keys, 336
PATH, 461
pdbedit, 574
PDC, 584
logon configuration, 585
PDF
Okular, 162
Thingy, 162
Xreader, 162
permissions
files (GNOME), 370
user home folders, 360
Photos
GNOME Photos, 168
Pix, 168
Shotwell, 168
Photoshop, 137
physical volume, 391
PiTiVi Video editor, 174
Pix, 168
pkexec, 347
policy file, 347
Xed, 347
Plymouth, 65, 320
default.plymouth, 320
update-alternatives, 320
PolicyKit, 341
auth_admin_keep, 342
pkexec, 347
PolicyKit-1, 341
polkit-1, 342
popup notifications
System Settings
MATE, 305
Port Forwarding, 514
Ports
firewall, 433, 444
PostgreSQL, 164, 165
Power Manager
GNOME Power Manager
Cinnamon, 256
laptop, 85, 257, 301
MATE Power Manager
MATE, 300

poweroff, 496
PPP, 416, 423
predictable network device names, 447, 450, 451
link files, 451
systemd-networkd, 451
udev, 450
Preferences
file manager
Caja, 291
Nemo, 234
Linux Mint menu
MATE, 271
MATE, 293
Control Center, 292
monitors, 96
Software Sources, 116
sound, 321, 323
windows, 199
Preferred Applications
MATE, 301
presentation
LibreOffice Impress, 160
print jobs
Printer applet, 96
system-config-printer, 523
Print server
configuration, 539
CUPS, 518
cupsd.conf, 538, 539
lpadmin, 546
remote printer, 538
system-config-printer, 522, 533
Print services, 518
Printers
default personal printer, 526
default system printer, 526
editing printers, 525
job options, 526
new printers, 527
options, 525
print queue, 523
Printer applet, 96
remote printer, 533
Samba, 534, 583
system-config-printer, 522
Windows, 534

printers.conf, 543
privacy
    Cinnamon, 254
    System Settings
        Cinnamon, 254
private encrypted directory, 100
processes, 311
    Gnome System Monitor, 311
    kill, 312
    ps, 312
profile, 465, 468
Prompt, 464
properties
    files, 233, 290
    folders, 234, 291
        Caja, 291
    XAppIconChooser, 233
proprietary graphics drivers, 378
Proxy
    Network (System Settings), 90
ps, 312
Psensor, 317
Public Domain Controller, 584
public keys
    importing, 333
PulseAudio, 321, 325
    PulseAudio Configuration, 327
    PulseAudio Volume Control, 326
    PulseAudio Volume Meter, 327
    Sound, 321, 323
PulseAudio Volume Control, 326
Puppet, 506
puppetmaster, 506

R

Recovery, 60
recovery key, 50
re-install bootloader, 61
remote printer, 538
removable media, 83
    System Settings, 246
rename
    File Manager search
        Nemo, 230
reports
    system information, 103

system reports, 101
System Reports, 101
repositories, 111, 112, 113
    /etc/apt/sources.list, 113
    Backports, 112, 113
    import, 112
    main, 112
    multiverse, 112
    official-package-repositories.list, 113
    restricted, 112
    Security updates, 113
    sources.list, 114
    universe, 112
    Updates, 113
    upstream, 112
restricted
    repository, 112
revisions
    Snap, 151
risk levels
    Snap, 150
root user, 345
    su, 345
rpcbind, 559
rsync, 388
runlevels, 492
    /etc/init.d, 495

S

Samba, 368, 534, 568
    active directory domain controller, 586
    Active Directory Domain Controller, 586
    Avahi, 364
    cifs, 589
    clients, 588
    firewall, 571, 572
    FirewallD, 368, 572
    GNOME, 364, 588
    Microsoft Domain Security, 584
    multicast DNS discovery, 364
    nmbd, 368
    pdbedit, 574
    PDC, 584
    printers, 534
    Printers, 583
    Public Domain Controller, 584

shares, 582
smb.conf, 575
smbclient, 588
smbd, 368
smbpasswd, 569
UFW, 368, 572
user level security, 573
winbind, 569
Windows, 369
scanner, 163
schedule tasks
   cron, 314
   systemd timers, 314
scope unit files, 495
scp, 513
Screensaver, 249
Seahorse, 328
   importing keys, 333
   keyrings, 329
   Passwords and Keys, 328
   sharing keys, 336
search
   File Manager search
      Caja, 288
      Nemo, 229
   software, 136
Secure Shell, 507
Security
   AppArmor, 503
   OpenSSH, 507
   pkexec, 347
   PolicyKit, 341
   virus protection, 316
Security updates
   repository, 113
sensors, 317
   Disk Utility, 318
   lm-sensors, 318
   Psensor, 317
Server Message Block (SMB), 568
service, 498
Services, 358, 477, 498
   /etc/systemd/system, 481
   /lib/systemd/system, 478, 481
   Cockpit, 499
   execution environment options, 486
   graphical target, 485

   management, 499
   managing, 498
   mount units, 493
   path units, 490
   runlevels, 492
   service, 498
   service units, 486
   Snap, 153
   socket units, 488
   systemctl, 358, 498
   systemd, 358, 478
   target units, 483, 492
   template units, 490
   unit files, 479
sessions
   Startup Applications
      Cinnamon, 252
sftp, 514
shared file systems, 361, 364
   Avahi, 361, 364
   FirewallD, 362, 368
   mdns.allow, 363
   multicast DNS discovery, 361, 364
   UFW, 368
   Windows, 369
shared folders, 366
   GNOME, 364, 588
   NFS, 368
   Samba, 364, 588
Shared resources
   NFS, 550
   NIS, 563
   Samba, 568
shares, 582
Shell
   .bashrc, 469
   .profile, 466
   Aliases, 456
   bash.bashrc, 471
   bash_logout, 473
   Environment Variables, 458
   HOME, 461
   PATH, 461
   profile, 465, 468
Shell Configuration, 453
Shell Configuration Files, 455
Shell Initialization, 454

Shell Prompt, 464
Shell Variables, 459
Shotcut Video editor, 174
Shut down, 71
shutdown, 496
side pane, 282
sidebar, 220
slice unit files, 495
SMART, 318, 320
smb.conf, 575
smbclient, 588
smbd, 368, 536
snap, 147
Snap, 145
   channels, 149
   confinement, 150
   interfaces, 150
   revisions, 151
   risk levels, 150
   services, 153
   snap command, 147
   Snap Store, 153
   tracks, 150
Snap Store, 153
Snapshots
   LVM, 395
   Timeshift, 122
   ZFS, 397
snap-store, 153
Social networking, 183
software
   /etc/apt/sources.list.d/official-package-
      repositories.list, 113
   alien, 144
   apt, 140
   APT, 110, 145
   apt-cache, 143
   apt-get, 140
   confinement, 150
   DEB, 139
   dpkg, 144
   GDebi Package Installer, 136
   install
      Software Manager, 128
   Linux Mint, 31
   Linux Mint Software manager, 125
   mintinstall, 125

open source, 34
packages, 31, 158
remove
   Software Manager, 128
   Synaptic Package Manager, 135
search, 136
Snap, 145
Snap Store, 153
Software Manager, 125
Software Sources, 116
Synaptic Package Manager, 133
Ubuntu, 31
Upgrade Tool, 38
Software Manager, 125
software package types, 139
Software Sources, 116
sound
   alsamixer, 321
   amixer, 321
   preferences, 321
   PulseAudio, 321, 325
   PulseAudio Configuration, 327
   PulseAudio Volume Control, 326
   PulseAudio Volume Meter, 327
   Sound, 321, 323
   sound interfaces, 325
   sound menu, 322
   SPDIF, 324
   volume control, 322
Sound, 321, 323
Sound Preferences
   PulseAudio, 321
Source code, 138
sources.list, 114
SPDIF, 324
Spices, 188
spreadsheet
   LibreOffice Calc, 160
SQL Databases, 165
ssh, 512
SSH
   authentication, 508
   configuration, 515
   FTP, 182
   OpenSSH, 507
   Port Forwarding, 514
   scp, 513

Secure Shell, 507
sftp, 514
ssh, 512
ssh/ssh_config, 515
ssh-agent, 512
ssh-keygen, 510
ssh-agent, 512
ssh-keygen, 510
SSID, 91
Startup Applications, 252
startup-animation
  Plymouth, 65, 320
Static IP address, 401
su, 345
subscription.conf, 544
Subshells, 458
sudo, 343
  configuration, 343
Synaptic Package Manager, 133
system administration, 340
  MATE Control Center, 292
System Environment Variables, 462
system info
  System Settings
    Cinnamon, 255
system information
  System Reports, 103
System Reports, 101
System Settings
  Appearance, 240
  brightness, 249, 304
  color, 99
  default applications, 245
  displays, 98
  General, 99
  Hi-DPI, 99
  Input Method, 251
  keyboard, 258
  languages, 250, 251
  lock, 249, 304
  network, 88
  notifications, 254
  online accounts, 101
  popup notifications, 305
  privacy, 254
  removable media, 246
  screen, 249, 304

Sound, 323
  system info, 255
  System Reports, 101
  universal access, 251, 304
  Users and Groups, 349
System Tools, 309
  Disk Usage Analyzer, 315
  Disk Utility, 318
  GNOME System Monitor, 310
  Logs, 314
system tray, 212
System V, 495
system-config-printer, 522, 533
  Printer applet, 96
systemctl, 358
systemd, 358, 478
  /etc/systemd/system, 481
  /lib/systemd/system, 478, 481
  execution enironment options, 486
  file systems, 493
  graphical target, 485
  logind, 64
  mount units, 493
  Netplan, 425
  path units, 490
  runlevels, 492
  scope units, 495
  service units, 486
  slice units, 495
  socket units, 488
  special targets, 492
  systemd timers, 314
  systemd-networkd, 426
  target units, 483
  template units, 490
  unit files, 479
  Wi-Fi, 431
systemd timers, 314
systemd-networkd, 426
  configuration, 429
  Netplan, 425
  networkctl, 425, 432
  NetworkManager, 432
  renaming device names, 451
  Wi-Fi, 431

T

tabs
    File Manager
        Caja, 283
        Nemo, 222
tar, 388
targets
    graphical, 485
temperature
    Disk Utility, 318
template unit files, 490
terminal window, 104
themes
    Cinnamon, 242
    Grub Linux Mint theme, 65
    MATE, 297
    sound, 323
Thingy, 162
tiles
    Cinnamon, 205
time
    Cinnamon, 247
    GNOME Clocks, 164
    timedatectl, 249
timedatectl, 249
    time and date, 249
timer
    GNOME Clocks, 164
Timeshift, 122
Totem, 173, 174
    totem plugins, 174
tracks
    Snap, 150
transfers
    Warpinator, 91
Transmission, 180
TV Players, 174
    Hypnotix, 174
    Kaffeine, 176
    MythTV, 176
    tvtime, 176

U

Ubuntu, 33
    help, 34
    repository, 112
    software, 31
udev
    predictable network device names, 447,
        450
Udisks, 318
    SMART, 320
ufw, 434, 438
    commands, 438
    Gufw, 434
    Samba, 368, 572
    Warpinator, 91
ugly
    Gstreamer, 172
unexpanded panels
    movable and fixed, 275
units
    execution environment, 486
    fstab, 493
    mount units, 493
    paths, 490
    runlevels, 492
    scope, 495
    service, 486
    slice, 495
    sockets, 488
    special targets, 492
    targets, 483
    templates, 490
    unit files, 479
universal access
    System Settings
        Cinnamon, 251
        MATE, 304
Universal Time Coordinated, 500
universe
    repository, 112
update, 142
    automatic, 120
    Linux kernels, 121
    software, 117
Update Manager, 117

Linux kernels, 121
Preferences, 120
update-alternatives, 320
update-grub, 382
updates
repository, 113
upgrade, 142
from 20.3, 38
Upgrade Tool, 38
Upgrade Tool, 38
upstream
repository, 112
USB
burning
Brasero, 85
Disk Image Writer, 84
Linux Mint, 29, 31
Usenet News, 167
user level security
Samba, 573
useradd, 357
Users, 353
cinnamon-settings-users, 349
groups, 351, 357
installation, 58
managing users, 349, 353
new users, 355
Passwords, 358
root user, 345
su, 345
System Settings, 349
Users and Groups
Cinnamon, 349
MATE, 353
users-admin, 353
Users and Groups
Cinnamon, 349
users-admin, 353
UTC, 500

V

vendor display drivers, 97
AMD, 98
Nvidia Optimus, 98
vgcreate, 391
video

Shotcut Video editor, 174
Video
Celluloid, 172, 173
default applications
MATE, 303
Kaffeine, 173
MPEG-4, 176
MPlayer, 173
mpv, 173
PiTiVi Video editor, 174
Totem (GNOME movie player), 173
VideoLAN, 173
vlc, 173
VideoLAN, 173, 174
Virtual Private Networks
OpenVPN, 416
PPTP, 416
Wireguard, 418
virus protection, 316
vlc, 173
volume control, 322
VPN, 416

W

Warpinator, 91
firewall, 91
FirewallD, 92
Preferences, 95
UFW, 91
Web Apps, 178
Web Browser, 177
Web Apps, 178
Wi-Fi
Netplan, 431
winbind, 569
window list, 267
windows, 199, 266
configuration, 199
grouped window list, 202
preferences, 199
switching, 206
tiles, 205
Windows compatibility layer, 137
windows quicklist menu, 205
Windows
file systems, 359

printers (Samba), 534
Samba, 369, 568
shared file systems, 369
Windows compatibility layer
Wine, 137
Wine, 137
wired
configuration, 410, 411
Network (System Settings), 88
network connections, 86
nmcli, 422
Wireguard, 418
Network Connections, 418
wireless
laptop, 85
network connections, 87
nmcli, 423
wireless configuration, 413
wireless security, 413
Workspaces
Expo, 209
MATE, 268
workspace switcher applet, 209, 268
wvdial, 423

X

X Window System
Displays, 96
RandR, 96
vendor drivers, 97
XApp Status Applet system tray, 212
XappIconChooser

file and folders, 233
menu, 197
X-Apps, 159
Pix, 168
Thingy, 162
XApp Status Applet, 159, 212
XappIconChooser, 159
XAppStatusicon, 212
Xed, 163
Xreader, 162
Xviewer, 168
Xed, 163
pkexec, 347
XFce, 78
Xreader, 162
Xvid, 176
Xviewer, 168

Z

Zero Configuration Networking, 359
Zeroconf, 359
Avahi, 359
mDNS, 359
zfs, 397
ZFS, 396
History, 397
snapshots, 397
zfs, 397
zfsutil-linux, 396
zsysctl, 397
zsysctl, 397